PAUL MARTIN LESTER
CALIFORNIA STATE UNIVERSITY, FULLERTON

VISUAL COMMUNICATION

IMAGES WITH MESSAGES

THIRD EDITION

THOMSON

WADSWORTH

Australia • Canada • Mexico • Singapore • Spain • United Kingdom • United States

THOMSON

WADSWORTH

PUBLISHER: Holly J. Allen
ASSISTANT EDITOR: Nicole George
EDITORIAL ASSISTANT: Mele Alusa
MARKETING MANAGER: Kimberly Russell
MARKETING ASSISTANT: Neena Chandra
ADVERTISING PROJECT MANAGER: Shemika Britt
PROJECT MANAGER, EDITORIAL PRODUCTION:
  Cathy Linberg
PRINT/MEDIA BUYER: Tandra Jorgensen
PERMISSIONS EDITOR: Robert Kauser
PRODUCTION SERVICE: Buuji, Inc.
TEXT DESIGNER: Books by Design, Inc.
PHOTO RESEARCHER: Terri Wright

COPY EDITOR: Adrienne Armstrong
COVER DESIGNER: Joan Greenfield
COVER IMAGES: (CLOCKWISE FROM LIGHTBULB)
  PhotoDisc; man on the moon, NASA/Hulton
  Archive/Getty Images; Muybridge horses,
  George Eastman House/Edweard Muybridge/
  Hulton Archive/Getty Images; eye, PhotoDisc;
  Florence Griffith Joyner, photographer: ©
  Duomo/CORBIS, image: ™/© 2002 Final
  Kick Marketing under license authorized by
  CMG Worldwide, Inc., www.cmgww.com
COMPOSITOR: Buuji, Inc.
PRINTER: Phoenix Color Corporation

For Tom and Jody who gave me my eyes, for J. B. Colson who taught me how to use them, and for Allison and Denison who fill them with memorable visual messages.

For more information about our products, contact us at:
Thomson Learning Academic Resource Center
1-800-423-0563
For permission to use material from this text, contact us by:
Phone: 1-800-730-2214 **Fax:** 1-800-730-2215
Web: http://www.thomsonrights.com

Wadsworth/Thomson Learning
10 Davis Drive
Belmont, CA 94002-3098
USA

Thomson Learning
60 Albert Street, #15-01
Albert Complex
Singapore 189969

Australia
Nelson Thomson Learning
102 Dodds Street
South Melbourne, Victoria 3205
Australia

Canada
Nelson Thomson Learning
1120 Birchmount Road
Toronto, Ontario M1K 5G4
Canada

Europe/Middle East/Africa
Thomson Learning
Berkshire House
168-173 High Holborn
London WC1V 7AA
United Kingdom

Library of Congress Control Number: 2002102245

ISBN: 0-534-56244-2

CONTENTS

Where did the idea come from that words communicate better than pictures? Since they were first invented to communicate complex thoughts, words and pictures have been locked in a struggle for dominance, with words being the clear-cut leader. With the widespread use of Gutenberg's printing press, words became more important than pictures to convey complex thought. Images were relegated to an occasional medical diagram, a "pretty" border decoration, or a sensational eye-catching view. Reading and writing became curriculum requirements, but visual literacy wasn't considered a necessary component of an individual's education.

However, the invention of television and the computer—and the recent spread of desktop publishing and the World Wide Web—dramatically changed the role of visual messages in communication. Nowhere on Earth can a person avoid being confronted with some sort of visual message. In addition, new knowledge about the nature and uses of light, the physiology of the brain, and the technological gadgets that people invent to present information all demand that we become more visually literate.

The third edition of *Visual Communication: Images with Messages* explores several questions:

- What are your personal responses toward a particular visual presentation?

- How can you relate what you see with the history of the medium of presentation?

- What do you know about the technology that makes possible the presentation of the information displayed?

- Are you aware of the ethical responsibility that producers of visual messages have in creating images that are compelling and yet do not stereotype individuals?

- How do cultural influences determine the type of messages displayed and diverse interpretations of them?

This book also explores the simple idea that visual messages that are *remembered* have the greatest power to inform, educate, and persuade an individual and a culture—and why some images are remembered but most are forgotten.

But an emphasis on visual messages does *not* mean that words are considered less important than images. The most powerful, meaningful, and culturally important messages are those that combine words and pictures equally and respectfully.

The first step toward understanding visual communication is to educate yourself about the many ways that information is produced and consumed in a modern, media-rich society.

Typographic, graphic, informational, cartoon, still, moving, television, and computer images are analyzed within a framework of personal, historical, technical, ethical, cultural, and critical perspectives in order to complete this first step.

This book also is a direct result of the new age in communications initiated and promoted by computer technology, which makes production, presentation, and viewing of visual messages easier; and links the various types of visual materials, those who produce the images, and those who are affected by what they see in numbers unequaled in the history of mass communications.

Computers allow professional and amateur writers and designers to produce graphic, informational, photographic, motion picture, and television images in graphic designs with ease.

For hundreds of years technology has kept writers and visual artists separate and unequal. Before Johannes Gutenberg's invention of the commercially successful printing press, less than 30 percent of the people could read. Seventy years after his invention, 80 percent of the entire population of Europe could read. Seventy years after Louis Daguerre's introduction of the first practical photographic process, almost everyone had a Kodak camera and looked at pictures in their local newspapers. And yet, educators never developed a visual grammar for photographs in the same way that a verbal grammar was developed for words after Gutenberg. People are taught to read words but are never taught to read pictures.

■ WE LIVE IN A VISUALLY INTENSIVE SOCIETY

Bombarded daily with a steady, unrelenting stream of visual stimulation from all manner of media, we seek to understand pictures, but we are taught to understand only words. We see mediated images more than we read words. Some experts warn that if the trend continues, civilization will regress to illiteracy and lawlessness. More optimistic researchers predict that technological advances will merge words and pictures in new ways to create innovative educational possibilities.

In this new technological age, a person cannot afford to know only how to write or to know only how to make an image. Today, someone interested in advertising, graphic design, journalism, motion pictures, photocommunications, public relations, television, or visual perception must know how to use and analyze the words and pictures presented in all those ways. The artificial walls between the various media imposed by tradition and older technology are beginning to crumble. This book can help you breach those walls and enter the brave new (visual) world on the other side.

■ FEATURES OF THE BOOK

Visual Communication: Images with Messages, third edition, contains the following features:

- Section 1 presents the latest scientific and medical information available about light, the eye, and the brain.

- Section 2 features theoretical approaches to visual perception.

- Section 3 addresses ethical issues related to persuasive images and stereotyping.

- Section 4 begins with a detailed procedure for analyzing any type of visual message. A specific example of this type of analysis is found in this section. The chapters in this section concentrate on the media by which we see visual messages: typography, graphic design, informational graphics, cartoons, photography, motion pictures, television and video, computers, and the World Wide Web. Each chapter in Section 4 is introduced with a detailed analysis of a significant example from the medium being discussed, followed by a general discussion of the medium from personal, historical, technical, ethical, cultural, and critical perspectives. Each chapter ends with a brief predictions section.

- More than 350 black and white and color graphics and photographs from still and moving image sources give life to the text's historical references and contemporary ideas. In addition to the illustrations, many examples are described in such a way as to evoke visual messages in the mind of the reader.

- The book exhibits the best that can be achieved in graphic design when words and pictures are treated with equal importance and respect.

- An informal writing style explains detailed information in a thorough, yet easily understandable, way.

- A cutline for each illustration identifies the image and often describes it in terms that are used in the text.

- A glossary contains nearly 150 key words that are introduced in the text.

- A detailed bibliography presents sources of additional information.

- A World Wide Web site includes online lecture notes with links for each lecture, predictions from students about the future of visual communication, a fictionalized story of how virtual-reality technology may change the way visual communication courses are taught, and suggestions for teaching a visual communication course.

■ FEATURES NEW TO THIS EDITION

Much of the writing of this third edition was influenced by the tragic events of September 11, 2001 when commercial airlines were hijacked and purposefully crashed into the twin towers of the World Trade Center in New York City, the Pentagon in Washington DC, and a field outside Pittsburgh, Pennsylvania. Almost every chapter reflects aspects of the media coverage related to the events of that day and beyond, in the hope that the media's role in a tragedy of this magnitude is critically examined and made more relevant.

Specifically, some of the additions are:

- Many of the quotations by philosophers and scientists at the start of each chapter have been updated and replaced.

- Each chapter begins with specific learning goals for that chapter and ends with discussion topics and exercise additions. In addition, every chapter contains Info-Trac® College Edition Assignments for further study on specific topics.

- A section added to the chapter on light explains such aspects as "glow in the dark" objects and chemicals used to detect blood at crime scenes by police personnel.

- A discussion of color deficiencies in humans and other animals and the latest in research about the connection between memory and the hippocampus have been added to the chapter on the eye, the retina, and the brain.

- The section on the sociological aspects of color has been expanded in the chapter on the four visual cues.

- In the chapter on visual communication theories, a study on the reason for the confusion over the use of "butterfly" ballots during the 2000 presidential election is featured.

- The most recent advertising campaigns of the Benetton clothing company and sensational news event coverage are explained and analyzed in the chapter on visual persuasion.

- The latest information concerning the Jerry Lewis Muscular Dystrophy Telethon and the use of sports mascots and their negative effects have been added to the chapter on pictorial stereotypes.

- An expanded procedure for analyzing visual messages is introduced and demonstrated in the beginning of Section 4.

- Many of the most important facts related to each media of presentation in chapters 8 through 16 have been updated and expanded. For example, chapter 16 begins with the rise of Steve Case, America Online, and the World Wide Web. In addition, there is a critical discussion on the effect of media mergers on content and consumer choice with an expanded section on ethical issues related to the Web.

- Chapter 17 concludes with a discussion on the importance of remembering famous visual messages related to such events as the space shuttle explosion, the Oklahoma City bombing, and the 9-11 aerial attacks.

■ *ORGANIZATION OF THE BOOK*

The seventeen chapters are divided into four sections that discuss technical and sociological issues relevant to advertising, computers, graphic design, journalism, motion pictures, photocommunications, public relations, and television media presentations.

■ *Section 1: How We See*

This section of the book calls for more sophisticated visual perception techniques on the part of viewers in order to get the most from visual messages. The chapters in this section explain the physics and physiology of how light enters the eye and forms images in the brain. Knowing about these physical and mental processes will help the student understand why some pictures are memorable and others are not.

Chapter 1: To Sense. To Select. To Perceive.

This chapter features the philosophy of the writer Aldous Huxley, who wrote "the more you know, the more you see," and how that phrase relates to the study, appreciation, and production of visual messages.

Chapter 2: Light

This chapter explores the history, physics, and sociological characteristics of light. Light is the natural starting point for a visual communication textbook because images receive life through this form of electromagnetic energy. Consequently, having an understanding of the nature of light—how it shapes the objects we see and how it can direct our attention—is vital for image analysis and creation.

Chapter 3: The Eye, the Retina, and the Brain

The parts of the eye and brain responsible for sight are discussed. The physiology of these vital body parts is used as a model for many of the machines that help make the world more visible. An understanding of the basic components of the eye and brain can lead to insights regarding the images that cameras and computers produce.

■ *Section 2: Why We See*

Seeing is not simply a function of having enough light in a room. This section explores how the brain processes the individual graphic elements that make up a pictorial scene. The many theories of how the mind puts the individual parts of an image together into logical patterns of thought are explained and discussed.

Chapter 4: What the Brain Sees: Color, Form, Depth, and Movement

Every image, whether still, moving, real, or imagined, can be broken down into its simple graphic components. Because of the way the brain functions, these graphic elements combine to make quick sense of what the eyes see. Being able to identify and use those basic graphic elements helps in the analysis and production of images.

Chapter 5: The Sensual and Perceptual Theories of Visual Communication

Psychologists have come up with several theories based on either sensual data received in the eye or perceptual information processed in the brain. The two types of approaches are discussed with an emphasis on how someone can use this information to make memorable images.

■ Section 3: The Ethics of What We See

Before a discussion of each medium's role in the production and distribution of images, an understanding of the ethical problems associated with images is necessary. Pictures often are used, knowingly or unknowingly, to mislead and distort.

Chapter 6: Visual Persuasion in Advertising, Public Relations, and Journalism

Probably the most common use of images is for advertising and public relations purposes. People expect pictures used in these contexts to be exaggerated visions of reality because their visual claims are intended to persuade and provoke. However, images used for editorial purposes also are designed to conform to preconceived perceptions.

Chapter 7: Images That Injure: Pictorial Stereotypes in the Media

This chapter contains a historical perspective and a current analysis of how under-represented groups are portrayed in the media. Understanding the effect that stereotyping has on society as a whole is important. Pictures may be used to communicate a society's desire to segregate various groups based on race, gender, age, physical condition, and many other characteristics. Being able to identify pictorial stereotyping is the first step toward securing equality and justice.

■ Section 4: The Media Through Which We See

This section includes a chapter on each medium of presentation. Each chapter is introduced with a description of a significant image or object presented by that medium. Subsequent analysis involves the personal, historical, technical, ethical, cultural, and critical perspectives described at the start of the section. These six perspectives promote a thorough understanding of the medium, the works produced by it, and its effects on the culture.

Chapter 8: Typography

The chapter introduces the student to the life and work of Johannes Gutenberg, who invented the first commercially successful printing press, on which the Gutenberg Bible was printed.

Chapter 9: Graphic Design

The graphic designs of Saul Bass, particularly the movie title sequence for *The Man with the Golden Arm*, are featured.

Chapter 10: Informational Graphics

George Rorick's design of the *USA Today* full-page weather map is a striking example of an informational graphic that directly influenced many other newspaper publishers.

Chapter 11: Cartoons

The work of Matt Groening, originator of "The Simpsons" in both comic strip and animated television productions, begins the discussion in this chapter.

Chapter 12: Photography

A discussion of Dorothea Lange's famous portrait of a mother and her children, "The

Migrant Mother," begins the chapter that describes the major technological and stylistic innovations in still photography. Ethical issues involved in photojournalism also are part of the discussion.

Chapter 13: Motion Pictures

The close-up shot of Orson Welles saying the word "Rosebud" in his innovative motion picture *Citizen Kane* begins the discussion of the movie industry. Historical, ethical, and cultural considerations are emphasized.

Chapter 14: Television and Video

The videotape shot by amateur George Holliday that showed the beating and forceful arrest of Rodney King, which later helped spark civil unrest in Los Angeles and convict some of the officers involved, introduces the power of televised images.

Chapter 15: Computers

Computer technology allows the creation of unusual computer-generated forms that include a friendly sea creature in *The Abyss,* a terrifying monster in *Terminator 2: Judgment Day,* and animated stunt doubles in *Titanic.* The full impact of computer technology on communication is discussed.

Chapter 16: World Wide Web

The phenomenal rise of the America Online bulletin board and its founder, Steve Case, into the largest media conglomerate in the world is featured. The social benefits and concerns of the newest and fastest growing medium of the World Wide Web are also discussed in this chapter.

Chapter 17: The More You Know, the More You See

The book's conclusion stresses that a thorough knowledge of visual communication not only will help in the production and analysis of mediated images but also will aid in the observation and interpretation of direct visual experiences. The link among all the information contained in the preceding chapters is discussed.

■ *Glossary*

About 100 terms that may be unfamiliar to the reader are defined briefly in this section. Each word in the glossary is first emphasized in the text by boldface type and explained there.

■ *Bibliography*

Most of the resource materials on which this book is based are listed so that the reader can obtain additional information about each subject presented in the text.

■ *ACKNOWLEDGMENTS*

In this section for the first edition I wrote that writing a book is like running a 26.2-mile marathon. In the second edition I wrote that writing it was like running a 10K race—a lot easier. But with innovations in visual technology and thinking as well as the tragic events of September 11, this edition was bumped up to a half marathon. Thanks to all who continue to teach me the value of friendship, love, and lifelong learning. You know who you are.

Paul Martin Lester
Fullerton, California

How We See

Visual communication relies both on eyes that function and on a brain that makes sense of all the sensory information received. An active, curious mind remembers and uses visual messages in thoughtful and innovative ways. Knowing about the world and the images that it conveys will help you analyze pictures. And if you can examine pictures critically, you have a good chance of producing high-quality images that others will remember.

General knowledge of the physics of light, how the eyes focus light, how the retinas collect light, and how the brain processes, sorts, and stores light is important because camera and computer construction is based on some of the same principles. A knowledge of the physics and physiology of light will enhance your use of the technologies of the future and the ability to decipher innovative visual messages. It is light that gives visual messages their life.

TO SENSE. TO SELECT.
TO PERCEIVE.

The greatest thing a

human soul ever does in

this world is to see

something ... To see

clearly is poetry,

prophecy, and religion,

all in one.

John Ruskin, 1819–1900

ARTIST, SCIENTIST, POET,

ENVIRONMENTALIST, AND

PHILOSOPHER

By the end of this chapter you should know:

- That visual analysis is vital for understanding the visually intensive world in which we live.

- That if you can learn to be more observant, you will see, learn, and remember more.

- That the work of Aldous Huxley teaches you that clear seeing is a lifelong process.

From the morning of September 11, 2001, radio, television, and print media sources along with their Web site counterparts all went to work to try to inform and explain the horrific personal carnage and destruction that was unleashed against thousands of innocent Americans. Reporters gathered as much information as quickly as possible during the confusing and unbelievable first hours after the attack. With the north tower of the World Trade Center already on fire from a previous direct hit from a commercial airliner, viewers on television saw live and unedited video footage of another airliner slam into the south tower and then witnessed the collapse of both 110-story structures. At least 3,000 people were killed.

Many stunned viewers watching live television reports commented that they thought the pictures seemed more appropriate for a Hollywood movie than actual events (Figure 1.1).

In fact, it was those striking, unforgettable visual messages that made this story so compelling and memorable. President George W. Bush acknowledged the power of visual communication in his speech to the country the first evening of the tragedy: "The *pictures* of airplanes flying into buildings, fires burning, huge structures collapsing, have filled us with disbelief, terrible sadness, and a quiet, unyielding anger."

It's easy to understand why we remember **visual messages** in the media that have been

Figure 1.1

With the north World Trade Center tower already on fire from an earlier commercial airliner direct hit, a fiery blast from a second airliner rocks the south tower.

Peter C. Brandt, Getty Images

replayed several times on countless news reports for such an important national story. But what about all of the everyday images that are the totality of our lives? Consider all the visual messages that are a part of your life—a cracked bat given to you by a professional baseball player; your fingers on the handlebars during your first bicycle ride; the smile from your favorite teacher during your high school graduation; red blood dripping from a cut on your leg; the sight of a small stream during a quiet walk in the country; a passionate look from a lover. These pictures are all a part of your repertoire of memories. Images weave themselves into your memory system, sometimes lying dormant for years. You remember and communicate these mental images because they are highly meaningful visual messages (Figure 1.2).

But think of all the personal visual messages you have experienced but may have forgotten—the billboard advertisements on the outfield wall during the baseball game;

where you ended up on your first bicycle ride; the faces of your fellow graduates sitting next to you as you waited for your diploma; the face of the doctor who treated your cut leg; all the colors of the plants as you walked along the trail; the pictures on the wall of your lover's bedroom. Actually, the proportion of remembered to forgotten images is quite small. Why are a chosen few easily recalled whereas a vast array of ambiguous memories is lost?

To answer that question you must know how the brain works. The brain processes three types of visual messages: mental—those that you experience from inside your mind such as thoughts, dreams, and fantasies; direct—those that you see without **media** intervention; and **mediated**—those that you see through some type of **print** or **screen** (movie, television, or computer) **medium.** What you experience and what you remember are products of a mind that actively thinks, with images and words, the mental, direct, and/or mediated visual messages you imagine or experience in your life. One reason dreams are so often forgotten, for example, is that the mental images are not translated into words, but if you immediately tell a friend or write down a dream, you have a better chance of remembering it. You will not remember much through visual messages alone. Memory happens when you think about pictures using words and images. That's why a textbook about **visual communication** takes so many words!

For an image to be consciously remembered, it must also make such a strong impression that you want to recall it again and again. Through repetitive mental viewing and thinking about it with thoughts in your mind over time, the image becomes permanent and your brain stores the visual memory. These pictures become a part of your visual message bank. When you see new images, you make new associations and comparisons with previously stored mental pictures. The content of the new and old images constantly bounces back and forth in your mind so that you learn from the images. Otherwise, you will forget them, as you do most words and pictures that stream across you as you journey through your life. At the end of the science fiction movie classic *Blade Runner,* the character played by Rutger Hauer recounts memories from his life to Harrison Ford. Hauer sums up the fragility of memory best when he confesses that, "All those moments will be lost in time like tears in the rain."

Many famous and often reproduced images throughout the book have visual messages that are so strong that millions of people who have seen them have memorized them. No doubt, you have seen some of them too. And when you see them again, you will learn something more because you make new connections in your brain. These images are strong and compelling. They have helped shape Western culture and how most of us feel about ourselves. Although separate and individual in their intent, content, and medium, all are linked by the inescapable elements common to all visual messages: They are objects that get their life from light. That life comes not only from the light of day but also from the light of revelation, the light of understanding, and the light of education.

■ *THE VISUAL PROCESS*

Aldous Huxley, author of the novel *Brave New World* and forty-six other books of philosophical and futuristic vision, detailed his efforts to teach himself how to see more clearly in his 1942 work *The Art of Seeing* (Figure 1.3). From the age of sixteen, Huxley suffered from a degenerative eye condition known as *keratitis punctata,* an inflamma-

Paul Martin Lester

Figure 1.2

As with your own memory, a family snapshot often contains visual messages that you will always remember, but also elements that you have forgotten.

tion of the cornea. One eye was merely capable of light perception, and the other could only view an eye chart's largest letter from 10 feet away. Today, the condition is rare and attributed most likely to bacterial or viral infection. It can be treated easily with medications. In his book Huxley described the physical exercises he used to overcome his disability without the aid of glasses. However, his main idea is that seeing clearly is mostly the result of thinking clearly. Huxley summed up his method for achieving clear vision with the formula: "Sensing plus selecting plus perceiving equals seeing."

The first stage of clear vision is to **sense.** To sense simply means letting enough light enter your eyes so that you can see objects immediately around you. Sensing also depends on how well the many parts of the eye work. Obviously, a damaged or improperly functioning eye will hamper sensing. Think of sensing as a camera without film; that is, there is no mental processing of the image during this phase of visual perception.

Huxley's next stage is to **select** a particular element from a field of vision. To select is to isolate and look at a specific part of a scene

Figure 1.3

Blind in one eye and nearly blind in the other, Huxley was forced to wear glasses with thick lenses. Nevertheless, the low camera perspective, dramatic lighting effect, and his eye contact with the viewer reveal a strong personality behind the glasses.

Figure 1.4

Aldous Huxley's method for clear seeing makes a strong visual message. The words arranged in a circle and separated with dots stand out because of the familiar shapes (see Chapter 4).

within the enormous frame of possibilities that sensing offers. That isolation is the result of the combination of the light gathering and focusing properties of the eye with the higher-level functions of the brain. In other words, selecting is a conscious, intellectual act. When you select you engage more fully the objects in the scene than when you merely look. Selecting starts the process of classification of objects as harmful, helpful, known, unfamiliar, meaningful, or confusing. To select is to isolate an object within the area where the sharpest vision takes place in the eye: the fovea centralis region in the retina of your eyes (see Chapter 3). By selecting individual objects within a scene, you are doing what the eye's physiology is made to do—to focus your mental activities on a single, small object that is isolated from all others.

The last stage in Huxley's visual theory is to **perceive;** that is, you must try to make sense of what you select. If your mind has any chance of storing visual information for long-term retrieval and to increase your knowledge base, you must actively consider the meaning of what you see.

To process an image mentally on a higher level of cognition than simply sensing and selecting means that you must concentrate on the subjects within a field of view with the intent of finding meaning and not simply as an act of observation. This process demands much sharper mental activity. Previous experience with specific visual messages is a key in seeing clearly. Huxley wrote that "the more you know, the more you see." A former baseball player watches and sees a game much more attentively than someone who attends one for the first time. The newcomer probably will miss signals from a manager, scoreboard details, the curve of the ball's flight as it speeds from pitcher to batter, and many other details observed by the former player. Although you can certainly isolate a particular visual element with little mental processing when it is a new or a surprising occurrence, analyzing a visual message ensures that you will find meaning for the picture. If the image becomes meaningful, it is likely to become a part of your long-term memory.

■ VISUAL COMMUNICATION'S CIRCLE DANCE

The more you know, the more you sense. The more you sense, the more you select. The more you select, the more you perceive. The more you perceive, the more you remember. The more you remember, the more you learn. The more you learn, the more you know. For clear seeing, this circle repeats itself on and on (Figure 1.4).

The greatest aid to clear seeing isn't eyes that function with or without glasses or a telescope that brings into sharp focus the craters of the moon. The process of sensing, selecting, and perceiving takes a curious, questioning, and knowledgeable mind. The goal of a visual communicator isn't simply to have an image published or broadcast. The goal of a visual communicator is to produce powerful pictures so that the viewer will remember their content. Images have no use if the viewer's mind doesn't use them. As

future image consumers and producers, you will want to see images that you remember and make images that others remember.

The goal of this book is to give you a method for analyzing visual messages regardless of the medium of presentation. Without systematically analyzing an image, you may see a televised picture and not notice the individual elements within the frame. You might not consider its content as it relates to the story and to your life. Without considering the image, you will not gain any understanding or personal insights. The picture will simply be another in a long line of forgotten images. Analyzing visual messages makes you take a long, careful look at the pictures you see—a highly satisfying intellectual act. Those images become a part of your general knowledge of the world. You discover how images are linked in ways that you never thought of before. You also become a more interesting, curious person.

DISCUSSION AND EXERCISE IDEAS

- Show any abstract art piece and lead a general discussion about its meaning. What is the mood of the artist? How is the mood conveyed through technique? What symbols do you see in the drawing? What do you think it means?

- Spend about 15 minutes talking about your most memorable direct and mediated images. Lead a discussion about the power visual messages have on your life and why these messages were remembered when most are forgotten.

- Cut out or copy advertising images from magazines and write a brief description of your reaction to each image. Do you think the picture is good or bad? Why did the image attract you?

- Write a brief paper describing how the phrase "the more you know, the more you see" is true in your life.

INFOTRAC® COLLEGE EDITION ASSIGNMENTS

- With "Subject guide" checked, type "World Trade Center and Pentagon Attacks, 2001" in the search area. Click "See also" within "Subdivisions." Click "View" within the subdivision, "chronology." Read David Whitman's article "Day of infamy: A timeline of terror." Get three sheets of paper. On the front side of the papers, write every factual event you remember concerning the September 11 attacks. On the reverse side of the sheets, write everything you felt when you learned of the attacks and afterward. Fold up the papers and seal them in an envelope with the current date. Put the envelope in a safe place—with other important papers perhaps. Years from now open the envelope and read what you wrote. This assignment comes from Communications Professor Dr. Coral Ohl, California State University, Fullerton.

- With "Subject guide" checked, type "Aldous Huxley" in the search area. Click "View" in "Periodical references." Find the article "The Future Brought to Book." Write a short paper that details your opinion about one of the predictions made in Huxley's book, *Brave New World,* as reported in the article.

 Go to the Web site for this book at www.wadsworth.com/product/0534562442 to find more Web links on this subject.

LIGHT

By the end of this chapter you should know:

- That humans have always been awed and curious about the nature of light.

- Some of the scientific findings about light.

- Some of the ways light is used commercially.

- How light conveys mood and meaning.

Throughout human history, people have been fascinated by light. Civilizations prayed at and celebrated the start of each new sunrise and invented gods that ruled the sun. Religious leaders equate light with life and begin the Bible with its creation (Figure 2.1). When the light from fire was discovered probably by accident through a lightning strike, most were awed by its power.

Literary references and colloquial expressions about light and vision abound because of the importance placed on seeing. When we want to learn the truth, we say, "Bring light on the subject." After a revelation of some truth we have "seen the light." If we are concerned that we are not getting the full story, we complain, "Don't keep me in the dark." Professor of Journalism at the University of Texas, Austin, and documentary photographer J. B. Colson sums up this sentiment with, "May the light be bright for all you do."

To know the physics and physiology of how light enters the eye and forms images in the brain is important because much of how we see is a matter of how much we know and want to observe about the world. The connection between a lit subject, the eyes, and the brain has as much to do with the physical nature of the link as it does with our psychological response. In addition, it is vital to understand the nature of light so you will better observe how light is used to convey meaning and mood in visual messages.

Light is a natural starting point for a visual communication book because images receive life from this form of electromagnetic energy. But visible light is simply a chemical reaction that occurs in our brains. Without the stimulus created from a photon on photoreceptors in the back of the eye, light would not be visible. Consequently, having an understanding of the nature of light—how it shapes the objects we see and how it can direct our attention—is vital for image analysis and creation. Knowing both the physical and mental processes involved with light creation will help you understand why some images are memorable and some are not. Such knowledge will help to make you a successful producer of visual messages (Figure 2.2).

■ *WHERE DOES LIGHT COME FROM?*

The study of the nature of light excited the minds of some of the greatest scientists who have ever lived. One of the first questions that scientists addressed was: Where does light originate? Two Greeks shaped the early answer to the question. The philosopher Empedocles and the mathematician Euclid believed that light rays began in each person's eyes and traveled outward, illuminating all the objects in the world. In a poetic description, Empedocles said that the eyes were "like a lantern" that gave light to all that could be seen.

Abu Ali Hasan Ibn al-Hayitham, or simply Alhazen to his English friends, wrote seven books on optic sometime around C.E.

1000. He was one of the first scientists to understand that light originates in the sun, fire, and other lit objects and does not emit from human eyes. Alhazen based his argument largely on commonsense observations. He simply thought it impossible for light to emit from the eyes and instantly illuminate objects at great distances.

■ *WHAT IS THE SPEED OF LIGHT?*

Another intriguing question to be answered by scientists curious about the nature of light was its speed. They knew that light must travel rapidly, but pinpointing the exact speed was difficult. The actual speed of light traveling in a vacuum measured by modern, sophisticated equipment is 186,282.3959 miles per second or just under 700 million miles per hour.

Consistent with his theory concerning the origination of light, Euclid supposed that it must travel at an extremely high speed because when you close and then open your eyes, the world is illuminated instantly. Lucky for science, he concentrated on mathematics.

Courtesy Autodesk, Inc.

Figure 2.1
The use of lighting in this computer-generated image helps create a sense of depth in this view of a chapel. The lighting effect also communicates religious meaning.

Figure 2.2
See color section following page 132.

Alhazen knew that the speed of light is not infinite but that it must be great. He also discovered that the speed slows when light moves through water. The astronomer from Pisa, Italy, Galileo Galilei in the late sixteenth century concluded after a series of crude experiments that light travels at least ten times faster than sound. (In reality, the speed of sound in air is about 740 miles per hour making the speed of light almost a million times faster, which is of course why you see a lightning bolt before you hear any thunder and why Galileo should have stuck with astronomy.)

In 1926 Albert Michelson, the first American to win a **Nobel Prize** for science, developed an accurate measuring tool. He set up rapidly rotating mirrors at a known distance from each other and reflected a beam of light from one to the other. Using a much more exact timing device than those available to previous scientists, he measured the speed of light to within 2.5 miles per second of the actual velocity.

■ *PARTICLES OR WAVES?*

A third mystery of light was whether it is composed of individual particles or is actually a series of waves similar to the effect of ripples on water. The founder of the modestly named Pythagorean School, the Greek philosopher Pythagoras, around 520 B.C.E. introduced his "particle" theory of light in which he assumed that the eyes were constantly bombarded with tiny light particles. A couple of centuries later, Aristotle, the philosopher and official tutor of Alexander the Great, concluded that light traveled in a kind of wave. Sir Isaac Newton was an early proponent of the particle theory. Besides his famous work on gravity, he produced the first scientific work on light—*Opticks,* published in 1704. He reasoned that, because

light travels in a straight line, it must be composed of individual particles; waves would not behave in such a manner. Newton called the light particles *corpuscles* and his idea the corpuscular theory.

In 1803 Thomas Young, an English physician, physicist, and Egyptologist (he made important contributions that helped decipher the Rosetta Stone; see Chapter 8), reasoned that light must be composed of waves similar to those in water. You can see this effect by standing in shallow water on a sunny day. Looking down at your feet you will see waves of light colliding with each other, creating interference patterns on the bottom. Many scientists supported Young's explanation because it fit scientific observation. However, Newton's view remained dominant.

Finally in 1900 Max Planck theorized that both the particle and the wave theories describe light energy. Planck, a German theoretical physicist known for his work in the study of thermodynamics, discovered that energy actually is a discrete package he called *quanta.* These individual packets later were called *photons.* When photons behaved independently, they acted like Newton's light particles. But when they combined to form packets of energy, they became energy waves. Planck was awarded the Nobel Prize in Physics for this work in 1918.

■ *ELECTROMAGNETIC ENERGY*

There were more mysteries to solve about light. In 1800 Sir William Herschel, a music teacher and astronomer, discovered with a thermometer that the light spectrum contained more than what could be seen. He discovered infrared radiation by projecting the colors of the visual spectrum through a prism onto a sheet of white paper. Curious to find out whether each color had its own temperature, he moved a thermometer from one color to the next. Each color did possess a separate temperature, but more intriguing was that when he moved the thermometer past the red color, beyond the visible spectrum, he found a different temperature. He concluded correctly that light must have components that humans cannot see. Consequently, other researchers started to experiment with his finding and made their own startling discoveries.

One of the greatest scientific discoveries pertaining to light came from Scottish scientist James Clerk Maxwell. He also is a key figure in the history of photography—he invented the first color film process in 1861 (described in Chapter 12). In that same year, he made his most important finding. Maxwell proposed that the forces of magnetism and electricity actually were one and the same, for the first time unifying two separate forces into a single theory. He called this new combination of energy forces electromagnetism. Through experimentation with magnets and electricity, Maxwell showed that a magnetic field in a vacuum travels at about the same speed as light. From this observation, he concluded that light is simply another form of an electromagnetic wave. His conclusion explained Herschel's discovery of energy waves past the visible light spectrum and led to other electromagnetic energy discoveries.

In 1888 German physicist Heinrich Hertz discovered another form of electromagnetic energy that could travel over long distances. Originally called Hertzian waves, they now are known as radio waves. By 1895 the Italian physicist and inventor Guglielmo Marconi was using the newly discovered waves to send radio transmissions over a mile. In 1901 he sent a radio broadcast across the Atlantic Ocean. Scientists now know that many different waves constitute the full electromagnetic spectrum. In 1895 Wilhelm Röntgen, a German physicist, discovered electromagnetic energy outside the range of light that humans could see. These fields were later called X rays. Gamma rays are 10 million times smaller than the visible light wavelengths, whereas AM radio waves can be several miles in length. Hertz also discovered ultraviolet waves, but he died before he had a chance to realize the importance of his finding. In 1905 Albert Einstein, the German physicist, educator, and pacifist, explained the photoelectric effect caused by ultraviolet radiation (Figure 2.3). Einstein won a Nobel Prize in 1921 for his discoveries concerning light.

■ THE CURIOUS NATURE OF LIGHT

Scientists, artists, communicators, and entrepreneurs have learned to manipulate the unique properties of light for a variety of purposes and products. Some molecules become, in scientific terms, excited, or go to a high-energy state, when light photons fall on them. Other compounds glow when light is taken away. The general term for this process is called *luminescence*. There are many different types of luminescence. Electroluminescence, produced by electric discharges that you can see, sometimes happens when you take off a sweater or when adhesive surfaces are separated in the dark. *Bioluminescence* is the light produced by fireflies, glowworms, sea creatures, and some fungi. In the summer of 2001, some Alaskan fishermen were concerned when they noticed salmon glowing in the dark. This phenomenon is not because of exposure to radiation but comes from bioluminescent bacteria living on the scales of fish.

If a chemical compound is bombarded with a radiant form of energy such as ultraviolet radiation or X rays and quits glowing

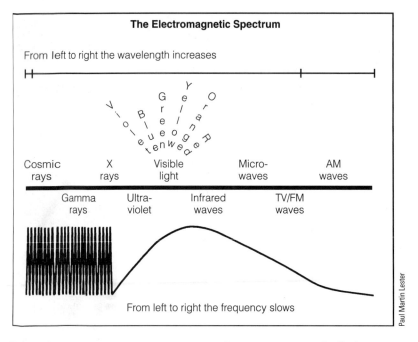

The Electromagnetic Spectrum

From left to right the wavelength increases

Cosmic rays X rays Visible light Micro-waves AM waves

Gamma rays Ultra-violet Infrared waves TV/FM waves

From left to right the frequency slows

Paul Martin Lester

Figure 2.3

Electromagnetic spectrum charts in most textbooks are crowded with numerical information that is quickly forgotten. Only the essential elements are presented here—the placement of the various forms of energy and the connection between wavelength and frequency.

as soon as the energy is turned off, the type of luminescence is called *fluorescence*. Fluorescence is, of course, the principle behind fluorescent lights. If the material still glows after the energy has been removed, the type of light is called *phosphorescence*.

"Glow-in-the-dark" watches, light sticks, circles, gels, and so on exhibit *chemilumines-cence*. When light shines on these substances, their excited state causes us to see light, for a period of time. You might have noticed that some motion picture or television detective drama police personnel when

trying to find bloodstains spray a liquid around a crime scene. The most common chemical used by the police is called luminol, a chemiluminescence that reacts to the iron in blood. When light in a room is turned off, luminol will cause blood to glow an eerie blue color. Luminol is extremely sensitive as it can detect bloodstains that have been diluted up to 10,000 times—a handy trait especially if a murderer worked to clean any blood from the scene of a crime. However, in real-life detective work, luminol is used as a last resort because it can react to other metal compounds and give false reactions, it can destroy any DNA information within the blood, and because it is water-based, it can smear the sample so that it becomes useless as evidence. Most detectives simply use a high-intensity light instead of luminol to search for any traces of blood.

■ WHY STUDY LIGHT?

By spending time thinking about the qualities that make up light and how people have thought about it since before recorded history, you have a much better chance of noticing how light is used by visual communicators to convey mood and meaning (Figure 2.4). Color will be explored in detail in Chapter 4.

DISCUSSION AND EXERCISE IDEAS

- Think of all the references to light in songs, literature, and the media.

- Explain in a short paper all of the moods and meanings possible because of the way light is used in a still photograph or moving image.

- Start a collection of pictures from magazines or video from motion pictures or on television in which the photographer or director used light in creative, yet meaningful ways.

ℹ INFOTRAC COLLEGE EDITION ASSIGNMENTS

- With "Subject guide" checked, type "light" in the search area. Note all of the different ways the word is used. What does that say about the importance of light in human history, development, and societies?

- With "Keywords" checked, type "James Clerk Maxwell" in the search area. Read Davin Sang's article for *Catalyst* magazine. What were the early events in Maxwell's life that you think influenced him to become such a famous scientist?

Go to the Web site for this book at www.wadsworth.com/product/0534562442 to find more Web links on this subject.

Paul Martin Lester

Figure 2.4

The way light falls on a subject often conveys a mood the photographer wants expressed. Soft window lighting enhances the gentle personality of singer and actress Andrea Marcovicci.

THE EYE, THE RETINA, AND THE BRAIN

My eyes make pictures

when they are shut.

Samuel Taylor Coleridge,

1772 – 1834

POET, AUTHOR, SCIENTIST,

AND LITERARY CRITIC

By the end of this chapter you should know:

- The major components of the eye, retina, and brain and their functions.
- The importance in having someone with a color deficiency view your Web site designs.
- How eye contact in a visual message directs meaning and mood.

Study your eyes in a mirror for a moment. What do you see? You see ancient, prehistoric eyes. In fact, the configuration of two eyes set in the front of the head, protected by a heavy layer of surrounding bone, and sending their dual images to a brain that fuses the double view into a single, coherent picture is at least 50 million years old.

Over countless generations, modern humans eventually emerged from tree-dwelling animals (Figure 3.1). Our Ice Age ancestors had the same brain size, shape, and functions as the reader of this line of text. Although minuscule in comparison to evolutionary time changes, the 50,000-year-old life span of the contemporary human nevertheless has adapted to the requirements of its modern age. Such complex and unanticipated evolutionary skills as driving a car or piloting an airplane are possible only because of the way the eye and brain function together to control the rest of the body.

■ WINDOWS TO THE SOUL

When lovers engage in long, passionate kisses, they often close their eyelids to shut out distracting visual messages the eyes give them. They want to concentrate their sensory receptors on the lover's soft sighs, the aroma of hair and skin, the taste of the mouth, and the feel of caresses. As Leonardo da Vinci once wrote, "The sense which is

14

Uncensored Situations, 1966, The Dick Sutphen Studio, Inc.

Figure 3.1

Moving from the ground to trees where it was a bit safer had the added benefit of improving eyesight after thousands of generations.

Figure 3.2

See color section following page 132.

nearest to the organ of perception functions most quickly, and this is the eye, the chief, the leader of all other senses" (Figure 3.2).

More than 70 percent of all the sensory receptors in the human body are in the eyes. Hearing, smelling, tasting, and touching all take a backseat. Given such an important sense, the eyes should never be subjected to unnecessary harm. In an American Academy of Pediatrics report it was estimated that seventy children in 1999 became permanently blind because of a fireworks-related injury. In another publication the Academy found that being struck by a pitched ball while playing baseball is the leading cause of sports-related eye injuries in children.

■ *A CAMERA IS LIKE AN EYE*

The eye is an instrument that collects light and focuses it to the rear surface of the eyeball. Since the invention of the camera, the eye has been compared to its simple mechanism for focusing and capturing "light drawings" on film. This analogy isn't surprising because knowledge of the physical workings of the eye helped in the camera's development. The essential parts of the still or motion picture photographic process are housed within a protective box or carrying case; the eye is protected by an outgrowth of the skull. A visual artist often uses a drop of solution to clean the glass elements of the lens from dust and smudges; the eye has a built-in lens-cleaning system with its salty tears. The shutter regulates the amount of time film is exposed to light; the eyelids open and shut so that vision is possible. The aperture is an opening that lets light enter the camera; the pupil performs the same function in the eye. In still and motion picture photography, as with the eye, the lens focuses the outside image to a point at the back of the dark chamber. In photography, a sheet of thin, light-sensitive emulsion records the picture, as photoreceptors in the back of the eye process the light rays. Photographers process and print their images in a darkroom or on a computer; humans process their images within the **visual cortex** region of the brain.

■ *PHYSIOLOGY OF THE EYE*

The eye is a complex system of various body parts acting in unison to achieve sight. Opening the eyes exposes the central nervous system directly. Nowhere else in the human body can such a condition be created. Consequently, many protective measures are built into the eye system.

Hairy eyebrows act as sunshades and grit catchers. Eyelashes filter dust and other foreign matter. Each eyelash is rooted in nerve cells so sensitive that the tiniest piece of dust will cause the eyelids to close immediately. The eyelids also will close reflexively to protect the nerve system from a threatening movement, an object that comes too close to the eyes, a blinding flash of light, or a sudden loud noise. When the eyelids are shut, the soft part of the eyes is waterproof and airtight. Each eye sits in an orbit surrounded by seven of the skull's bones as a plate of armor to further protect it. The orbit or socket contains fatty tissue behind the eye that helps to cushion the eye when hit. With a normal field of vision you can comfortably see 160 degrees horizontally and 135 degrees vertically. The eyebrows and nose obstruct part of the vertical view.

Humans normally blink about once every five seconds or about 17,280 blinks a day. Blinking washes the eyes with soothing, slightly salty tears—perhaps our link to the time when we were amphibious animals swimming in the salty seas of prehistoric Earth. All animals that live in the air produce tears to clear and moisten their eyes. Humans are the only animals who cry.

The first layer of the eyeball itself is a tough, protective membrane called the sclera. About 80 percent of the eyeball is composed of this white-colored tissue (Figure 3.3).

The cornea is a tough, transparent window that bulges slightly in front of the center of the eye. The cornea consists of four transparent layers that reduce the speed of light by about 25 percent and bend the light toward the center of the eye to aid in focusing. The cornea accomplishes about 70 percent of focusing, and the lens achieves the rest. The cornea's transparency is ensured by protein and water with no blood vessels. This peculiarity of construction makes the cornea slow to heal, but it also means that the cornea survives the body's death longer than any other organ. Consequently, it is an excellent candidate for transplanting in another person having a faulty cornea.

The **iris,** named for the Greek word for rainbow, gives the eye its color. The iris is a muscle that changes the size of the black hole in the center of the eye, the pupil. The circular muscles in the iris change the size of the pupil from about 2 to 8 mm. (A millimeter is roughly twice the width of the tip of a pencil.) The unique pattern of these fibers in each person may make them useful for purposes of identification, similar to fingerprints.

The amount of light in a scene causes the iris to enlarge or contract the opening. Research shows that emotional responses or special interests do the same thing. Observant jewelry sales personnel will notice if a particular ring or necklace causes a customer's irises to contract or enlarge the pupil's opening. Such a response would indicate an interest in that piece of jewelry. Appropriately, the word *iris* is the name of the Greek goddess who was a messenger for the Olympian gods. Drugs also can affect the size of the opening. Heroin and other opiates enlarge the eye's portal, whereas amphetamines constrict it. The color of the iris is a result of how much melanin is present. The function of the color is to protect the eyes further from the effects of harsh sunlight. Generally, human irises have more melanin and appear darker in people who live near the equator, where the sun is brightest. Those living in northern regions have lighter colored eyes, or less melanin in their irises.

If a person has a genetic deficiency and cannot produce melanin, albinism is a result. A person with albinism has pale skin, light hair, and pinkish eyes, and has trouble seeing in bright light. In America during the nineteenth century, the condition was considered so odd that many with albinism could only find employment in circuses with sideshows. The photographer Mathew Brady (see Chapter 12) and others made pictures of those with albinism and sold them as postcards, exploiting their physical appearance. However, many Native American and South Pacific tribes revered such individuals as divine, believing that they were messengers from the gods. Unfortunately, **prejudices** still remain against people without color. The 1995 motion picture *Powder* tells of the **discrimination** and physical abuse a boy with albinism, yet with magical powers, experiences in a small town. Fortunately, organizations such as The National Organization for Albinism and Hypopigmentation (www.albinism.org/) are working to educate the public about the condition and provide information for those with albinism.

The pupil is simply the dark opening in the center of the iris. The word has an interesting history, as it comes from the Latin *pupilla*, meaning "a little doll." Romans gave the opening that name after noticing their doll-like reflections in the eyes of others. An

old Hebrew expression for the pupil, *eshonayin*, refers to the "little man of the eye."

Behind the iris is the slightly yellow, rubbery lens. Its function is to receive the light rays bent slightly by the cornea and further focus them to a tiny spot of acute visual sharpness at the back of the eye. About the size of an aspirin tablet, the lens has no blood vessels and is composed of about 2,200 fine layers that look like stacked plywood when greatly magnified. As a person ages, the lens becomes hard and loses some of its power to focus. A four-year-old child can easily focus on an object four inches away. Without the aid of glasses, an aging adult must hold a newspaper about sixteen inches away from the eyes in order to focus the words.

Between the cornea and the lens is a space that contains the white, nourishing fluid known as the aqueous humor. As new fluid is produced, the old liquid is drained. If the drainage mechanism is blocked, pressure can build up behind the iris. The result is one of the most common causes of blindness—glaucoma. More than 2 million

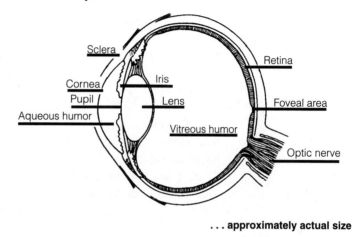

Parts of the eye . . .

. . . **approximately actual size**

Modified after James Kalat, *Biological Psychology*, 4th ed., Wadsworth Publishing Company, 1992

Figure 3.3

The gestalt law of continuation is at work in this infographic (see Chapter 5). The gray boxes at the top and bottom link the headlines and shift the viewer's attention to the center. As with the shape of the eye, the viewer is purposefully led around a circle pattern. Note the slight indentation of the fovea area. The dent means that this spot, where vision is most acute, contains no cells in front of the rods and cones.

people over the age of thirty-five have glaucoma. If left untreated, nerve fibers in the optic nerve degenerate, causing blindness.

A clear, jellylike substance that fills the main cavity, called the **vitreous humor,** maintains the eyeball's shape and pressure so that the eyes keep their round shape. If ever punctured, the eyes would deflate like a flat basketball. The vitreous humor is matched optically with the slightly yellow color of the lens. This color matching ensures that light rays will not change their intended course from the cornea, through the lens, through the vitreous humor, and to the back of the eye. Normally the fluid chamber is clear, but red corpuscles and other small particles, called *floaters* or *flying gnats,* break off over time and float within the jellylike fluid. You can see these harmless tiny dots or filaments, but never in focus, by looking at any light-colored surface or area.

■ *THE RETINA*

About the size and thickness of a first-class postage stamp, pink in color and as fragile as wet tissue paper, the retina is a net (the Latin word *rete* means "net") of approximately 125 million photoreceptors that lines about 85 percent of the back of the eyeball. This net contains about 7 million cells responsible for color vision and 118 million receptors used for nighttime viewing. The huge difference in the number of day-sensitive and night-sensitive cells is a reminder that humans were once nocturnal, night-loving creatures.

■ *Light Path to the Retina*

Before light arrives in the retina's net of photoreceptors, it must pass through the cornea, the aqueous humor, the iris, the lens, the vitreous humor, and small blood vessels in the eye. Just before any light reaches the retina, it must pass through several layers of nerve cells that lie on top of the retina. These cells form the first link between the retina and the brain. Fortunately, they are nearly transparent and little clarity is lost to their complex structures as light passes through them.

As with a camera's lens, the image on the retina is inverted. The brain corrects this upside-down vision. Behind the retina is a dark layer called the choroid, which gets its color from melanin, the same material that causes skin color and color in the iris. The choroid acts like a blotter and soaks up excess light. Without this choroid layer, as in people with albinism, light not absorbed by the photoreceptors in the retina would bounce around the eye diluting the colors and dimming the image from the outside world.

■ *Regions of the Retina*

The retina has two major fields: peripheral and fovea. Imagine holding in front of your face a ten-by-ten-inch pane of frosted glass with a clear, polished spot in the center of about one-half inch in diameter. This setup would represent the two regions of the retina. As you look through the panel you will notice immediately that the center clear portion is used for focusing on objects and seeing colors, and the outside portion can detect sudden movements reasonably well.

The outside edge of the eye is the **peripheral field.** An evolutionary holdover that protects the body from possibly harmful actions, it is the least developed field. The peripheral field does not see colors well, cannot see objects with much clarity, but is sensitive to slight movements by other people or objects and is most useful under darkened conditions. Patients with degenerative peripheral vision slowly lose the capacity to see in dim light, colors, and objects at their sides.

Within each eye, 85 percent of the total photoreceptors, or approximately 100 million, are located along the peripheral region. But the impulses received by these neurons lining the back of the eye are funneled into a single channel to the brain. Consequently, peripheral vision isn't as acute as fovea vision, which has many more direct impulse-to-brain connections. However, most of the photoreceptors in the peripheral area of the retina are sensitive to low levels of light. This area of the retina allows humans to function reasonably well in a darkened room.

The **fovea field** is responsible for the most acutely focused detail in the eye. Under normal lighting conditions, it brings objects into the sharpest focus possible so that the brain can concentrate and analyze the visual image. The fovea field, however, represents only about a 1 degree angle of coverage. Consequently, the object under scrutiny by the fovea field is about the size of the letter "e" on this printed page. You must consciously move your eyes directly off an object in low light in order to see it because the fovea field doesn't function well when there is little light.

The fovea field is divided into two parts: the **macula lutea** and the fovea centralis. The macula lutea is a tiny yellow pit in the center of each retina. The yellow color protects this sensitive area from the sun's harmful ultraviolet rays. The area is recessed because the many other neuroconnector cells that link the photoreceptors with the brain are missing from this region, giving as clear a path to this sensitive light-gathering and light-focusing area as possible. Within that tiny area is the even smaller fovea centralis. Most of the color-sensitive photoreceptors are located in this area. Each light-sensitive neuron is about 0.00004 inch wide. About 30,000 of them can fit on the head of a pin. Because cells in the fovea region are not use-ful in low light, seeing an object clearly in dimmed light often requires a conscious effort to move the eye away from the center of the object. Next time you are in a darkened room, look closely at the phosphorescent minute hand of your watch. The tiny greenish bar will disappear if you try to look at it directly. But steady your concentration on a nearby area of the watch's face and you will be able to see the time. The cells sensitive to dim light in the macula lutea region of the retina allow tiny objects to be visible in the dark. However, acute focus is the goal of the eye's physiology, so this system works best in bright sunshine.

The peripheral and fovea portions of the retina work in tandem. The outside edge of the retina alerts the body that something has moved and is worth your attention. Moving the head will bring the object directly into line for focusing by the fovea region. The brain is constantly telling muscles to move the eyes in order to concentrate on objects observed by the sensual data received from the peripheral area. The brain is always looking for change. Thus a flashing light will attract more attention from the sensors in the brain than a steady beam.

Because acute vision is centered in the fovea, the mind automatically moves the eyes so that an interesting visual target is always in the center. These tiny, automatic eye movements, called *saccades* (French for "jerk" or "jolt"), keep the eyes moving and the image fresh on the retina. Because the image quickly fades from the face of the retina, without these movements visual perception would be severely restricted. One of the basic principles of graphic design is to exploit this phenomenon. Layouts are considered well designed when they move a viewer dynamically from one element to another. An eye that is in constant motion is an eye that will have the best chance to find

Figure 3.4

Most of the retina is a complicated mass containing six types of cells. Although four kinds of nerve cells initially are in the way of an image's path to the rods and cones, they eventually relay light from the photoreceptors to the optic nerve. Note that the names of the cells in the infographic are set in italic type and are carefully aligned with each other to improve their appearance (see Chapter 8).

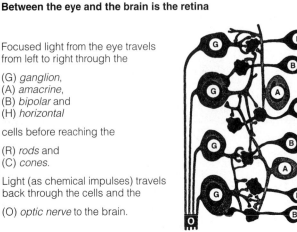
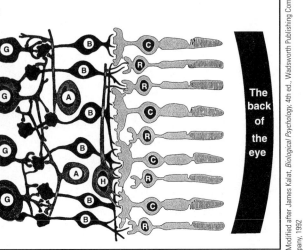

Between the eye and the brain is the retina

Focused light from the eye travels from left to right through the

(G) *ganglion,*
(A) *amacrine,*
(B) *bipolar* and
(H) *horizontal*

cells before reaching the

(R) *rods* and
(C) *cones.*

Light (as chemical impulses) travels back through the cells and the

(O) *optic nerve* to the brain.

The back of the eye

Modified after James Kalat, *Biological Psychology,* 4th ed., Wadsworth Publishing Company, 1992

meaning within a complicated graphic design (see Chapter 5).

■ *Photoreceptors: Rods and Cones*

The retina contains two types of photoreceptors: rods and cones. They get their names from their shapes: Rods are long and slender; cones are shaped like upside-down funnels. The approximately 118 million rods are primarily responsible for night vision, and the 7 million cones allow us to see colors.

The brain cannot process electrical impulses from outside sources. The rods and cones convert the electrical energy of light to chemical energy that the brain can use. Light energy stimulates the photoreceptors to produce chemical energy that is passed from one cell to the next so that the visual message eventually enters the brain (Figure 3.4).

The Rods

If you were able to see a rod under a microscope, it would appear to be colored purple. Termed *visual purple,* this reddish-purple pigment inside each rod is chemically bleached by strong light. The bleaching

process inactivates the rods, making them insensitive to light. Without chemical bleaching of the rods, we wouldn't be able to see during the day. Think of the last time you went to a matinee movie and were nearly blinded by the bright, late-afternoon sunshine as you left the theater. However, as the rods were bleached, you could begin to see well in the bright light. If you had to reenter the theater because you had left your sweater on the seat, you would have to wait a few minutes until your irises expanded before you could see. Expansion of the irises allows as much light as possible to enter your eyes and the visual purple to become unbleached and sensitive to light again. From the outside to the center of the retina, rods become less numerous. The outside edges of the retina are composed entirely of rods. This region is responsible for most of the eyes' peripheral vision. Objects at the far edges of peripheral vision appear gray because there are no cones to see colors.

Rods also are sensitive to slight movements by outside objects. Exposure to light immediately starts the bleaching process. The excess energy from that process excites a fellow rod, causing it to be bleached while the original rod immediately becomes unbleached. This excitatory and inhibitory process of the rods allows the brain to distinguish edges easily so that it can detect slight changes in movement (Figure 3.5). For example, fluorescent light tubes flicker, and the outer region of the retina can sometimes spot this effect. Because of the bleaching and unbleaching phenomenon, rods also are useful in distinguishing form, depth, and texture.

The Cones

Although relatively small in number, cones in the retina allow us to see color, fine details, light intensity changes, and quick movements. They become most active during the day when there is the most light.

Three different types of cones represent sensitivity to short and long visible light wavelengths (see Chapter 2). The cones themselves are colorless. Light from a broad source such as the sun appears white because it stimulates the short and long wavelengths in the cones equally. With unequal stimulation, that is, more stimulation from one color than another color, the brain receives a combination of cone impulses, allowing the color to be perceived. By using this process, the brain can easily distinguish some 200 colors.

■ COLOR DEFICIENCIES

Because many animals have only two kinds of photosensitive cones in their retinas, their color vision is limited. Octopuses and squid can only see blue. Spiders can see ultraviolet and green. Squirrels can only see blue and yellow. Dogs can tell the difference between the colors yellow and blue, but cannot distinguish between green and red. And as a general rule, animals that are mostly active at night, such as bats and owls, do not have highly developed color vision.

Paul Martin Lester

Color deficiency in humans is almost always a malfunction of the cones in the retina as a result of hereditary conditions or, in rare cases, disease. Cone cells devoted to a certain wavelength may be functioning abnormally or may be totally absent. About 99 percent of those with a color deficient condition report that they cannot tell the difference between the colors green and red. In the United States, about 8 percent of males and only 1 percent of females experience some form of color deficiency. The Ishihara Test, developed by Dr. Shinobu Ishihara, Professor Emeritus of the University of Tokyo, is a series of plates with numbers composed of colored dots that can detect the extent of a person's color deficiency (Figure 3.6).

Although there is no cure, most with a color deficiency live normal and full lives, quite able to compensate for their condition. At a **Web site** created to explain the condition (www.toledo-bend.com/colorblind/aboutCB.html), the author lists a number of challenges that are faced—being confused when told to use specific colored markers as

Figure 3.5

As you move your head from side to side, try to count the black dots. The optical illusion is not caused by graphic elements within the picture itself. The faint and fleeting black dots replace the white ones only within the mind of the viewer. The illusion is a result of the rods in your retinas going through the excitatory and inhibitory process.

Figure 3.6

See color section following page 132.

a child, wearing "unusual" color combinations of clothes, not knowing when a steak is cooked, and not being able to tell if a friend is sunburned. Visual communicators sensitive to those with a color deficiency should be aware of the color choices used for making weather and other types of maps and the color of text and backgrounds for printed materials and Web sites. Especially if you are using colors to convey meaning, let someone with a color deficiency view your work to make sure that it is clearly understood.

■ *The Optic Nerve*

Whether from rods or cones, the light energy responsible for allowing us to see objects and lights eventually finds its way through a series of neuron connections to the optic nerve. This thick rope of nerve cells on the nasal side of each eye in the back of the eyeball enters the brain through a connection known as the blind spot.

Ironically, without the blind spot, humans could not see. About a million nerve ropes form the optic nerve. One indication of how much more acute human vision is than the other senses is the number of connections eyes have to the brain. The ears, for example, have only 30,000 links to the brain. With no photoreceptors where the optic nerve enters the back of the eyeball, vision is arrested in that one, tiny region.

Such a small area of absent vision has no effect on the quality of eyesight. In fact, covering one eye has little effect over a scene that is viewed. Objects within our field of vision appear just as bright and in focus with one or two eyes open. However, the use of only one eye results in a loss of up to 30 degrees in horizontal vision and, more important, severely limits depth perception. Two eyes, slightly separated, give humans the illusion of depth perception. Shapes, forms, and textures gain added dimension. For the protec-

tion of a species that moves so frequently in a complicated, object-filled environment, such a feature is vital for its survival.

Depth perception is not only a result of having two eyes but also of a separation of each eye's image within the brain. The optic nerves from each eye intersect behind the eyeballs at a place called the optic chiasma (Figure 3.7). Sir Isaac Newton discovered this crossing of the nerves. In this area, which is named for the Greek term for "two crossed lines," the two separate strands of nerve fibers join and then split again. Half of each eye's set of optic nerves continues to travel to the half of the brain corresponding to that eye. Half of the left eye's nerve cells, for example, end up at the left hemisphere of the brain. The other half of the optic nerve crosses over to the opposite hemisphere. This physiology allows for an even distribution of the visual message throughout the brain, which may aid in quicker recognition of objects. Splitting of the optic nerve also helps maintain partial sight if there is damage to the optic nerve connection with the brain after the split. If a severe injury causes the nerve bunch on one side of the head to be severed after the center cross, blindness will occur in only one-half of each eye. Total blindness in one eye can thus be avoided by this configuration of nerve fibers.

■ *THE BRAIN*

The next step in the path from light to eye to retina to optic nerve is the connection with the brain. Without the image processing capabilities of the brain, pictures would simply be variations in light and dark regions without meaningful associations.

There are about 100 billion nerve cells or neurons in a brain. But a single neuron can be linked with up to 10,000 other neurons making up to one quadrillion neural connections, called synapses. One quadrillion is represented by a one followed by fifteen zeros. If you started right now to count by ones to one quadrillion, it would take you 32 million years. Thoughts and actions are communicated from one cell to another throughout these links in the brain. Repetition and practice strengthen them. Stronger links lead to quicker recognition and associations of objects and ideas. The brain, then, is a huge and sophisticated **communication** network. It is the most wondrous and mysterious organic entity that is, despite sophisticated measurement and viewing devices, largely not understood by scientists.

The optic nerves eventually make a connection to the part of the brain known as the thalamus. All impulses that arise from the sensory systems (except the sense of smell) pass through the golfball-size group of cells of the thalamus. The thalamus is one of the oldest parts of the brain in evolutionary terms and is part of the limbic system, or reptilian brain, which is responsible for basic survival functions. The thalamus suppresses sensual information that the conscious mind doesn't need to know about. When you are watching a television program, for example, you do not need to be aware of the tension within your muscle system or the temperature of your body. But when there is a need for such information, as in the case of a fire, the thalamus springs to action to warn the brain of the smell of smoke or the heat from the flames. Visual data, however, are not subject to this censorship. The thalamus simply receives the optic nerve's impulses and transfers them directly to the part of the brain known as the visual cortex located in the back of the brain.

The main body of the brain, the cerebrum, is divided into four lobes horizontally and two halves vertically. The frontal lobe of the cerebrum is responsible for long-term planning, judgments and decision making,

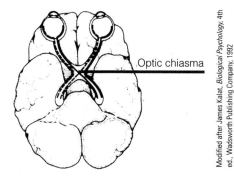

Optic chiasma

Modified after James Kalat, *Biological Psychology*, 4th ed., Wadsworth Publishing Company, 1992

Figure 3.7
Sir Isaac Newton discovered the curious crossing structure of the optic nerve cells. Note that if one side behind the chiasma is severed because of an accident, sight from both eyes will still be maintained.

certain types of goal-oriented behavior, and some aspects of emotional behavior. Damage to the frontal lobe may result in the inability to plan complex actions. The parietal lobe compares input data from the senses in order to report on spatial orientations. Damage to this lobe may result in difficulty in telling the difference between objects. The temporal lobe is responsible primarily for hearing, perception, and memory. Finally, the **occipital lobe,** or visual cortex, interprets visual impulses and transmits information about them to other areas in the brain (*occipital* is Latin for "toward the back"). One of the reasons you "see" a bright light when you are hit in the back of the head is because of the light receptors in that part of the brain.

■ *The Cortex*

If you form an image of a brain in your mind that you saw in the movie *Hannibal*, you unfortunately remember seeing the wrinkled, gray cortex of actor Ray Liotta. However, the cortex (*cortex* is Latin for the "bark of a tree") is only a thin layer that forms the outer edge of the cerebrum. Nevertheless, if it were stretched out, it would be four feet by five feet in size. The cortex represents about half the volume of the brain. The wrinkles efficiently fit the maximum amount of cortex material into the compressed space inside the protective skull. The

Modified after James Kalat, *Biological Psychology*, 4th ed. Wadsworth Publishing Company, 1992

Figure 3.8

The significant fact of this diagram for a visual communication textbook is that the visual cortex, where sensory information from the eyes is processed, is in the back of the brain.

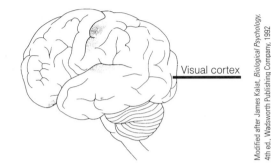

Visual cortex

cortex is only one-eighth of an inch thick and contains about 200 million cells. Within the complicated structure of the cortex, most learning takes place. Nerve impulses in the cortex travel about seven miles an hour. An image can travel from the retina through the thalamus and to the cortex in only one-tenth of a second. Even so, sleight-of-hand magicians can make objects seemingly disappear in that length of time.

There are six layers of neurons that make up the cortex. The fourth layer, with its pyramid-shaped neurons concentrated in the back of the visual cortex, is responsible primarily for processing visual messages. The visual cortex maintains the one-to-one photoreceptor-to-neuron arrangement. The visual cortex creates a kind of topological copy of the image on its wrinkled surface through the use of specialized cells without a loss of resolution (Figure 3.8).

However, where perception takes place in the brain is still a mystery. A visual message in the cortex is not an exact copy of the image seen in the real world. The visual cortex divides it into several different parts. Cells in the visual cortex are highly specialized: Some are responsible only for color recognition, others locate edges, and still others look for lines. The basic perception elements of size, distance, shape, color, location, and subject-to-background relationships have their links to individual cells in the cortex. Thus, the brain divides visual

messages into the basic graphic design building blocks that artists use to create their pictures. The visual cortex is a wholly natural link between the inner workings of the mind and the way humans produce and analyze visual messages, but it is not the center where those parts are finally put together and where meaning is established.

■ *The Hippocampus*

The visual cortex can process some visual information and determine whether a visual message must evoke a response. But it does not store the pictures. Near the thalamus is a small part of the brain called the hippocampus, Greek for "sea horse," which its shape resembles (Figure 3.9). The **hippocampus** is a memory storage area where short-term memories are thought to be processed into long-term ones. New images are compared with old pictures already stored in the mind. It is the seat for all sensory memory. It is the place where powerful visual messages, images with meaning, are stored. When needed by the higher brain functions, the brain somehow retrieves images from the hippocampus.

An object illuminated by enough light causes its image to travel through the eyes, activates photoreceptors in the retina, moves through the optic nerve to the thalamus, and gets sent to the visual cortex. If the image is memorable, that is, if it is filled with meaningful content for the viewer, it finds a home in the hippocampus. There the image rests until recalled by higher brain functions an hour, a year, or even decades later.

It was once thought by scientists that we are born with all of the brain cells we will ever have, and that as we live our lives those cells gradually die, never to be replaced. But through research, that notion is being challenged. For example, Dr. Eleanor Maguire and a team of British researchers compared brain scans of sixteen London cab drivers with those of fifty men of similar age. They found that for the London "cabbies," who must memorize an incredibly complex system of roads for the city of London, the hippocampus actually grew larger as their knowledge of the city expanded through experience. This research has profound implications not only for those with brain diseases such as Alzheimer's, but also for those wanting to improve their mental abilities. A conclusion that can be made is that the more you use your brain, the more it will be useful to you.

When a child grows, connections between neurons are strengthened by a gradual buildup of layers of myelin, a fatty substance. This process is called myelinization. Memory is a direct result of the myelinization process. The hippocampus, as it turns out, is slow to myelinize. That's why we're unable to form memories before the age of three or four. The hippocampus is also the place where Alzheimer's disease, a debilitating condition in which patients gradually lose their capacity for short- or long-term memory, first appears.

■ WHY STUDY THE EYE, THE RETINA, AND THE BRAIN?

The answer to that question is really quite simple. Remember Aldous Huxley's charge of "the more you know, the more you see." Taking time to learn the parts of the eyes and how light travels through these remarkable organs to the retina and into the brain will help you notice how the eyes are used to convey a mood or specific idea in a visual message. The next

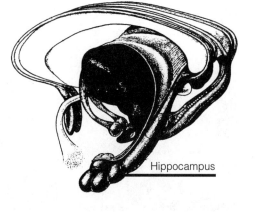

Modified after James Kalat, *Biological Psychology*, 4th ed., Wadsworth Publishing Company, 1992

Figure 3.9

Left: Wrapped around the thalamus is the curved structure of the hippocampus where visual messages are stored. Right: The familiar shape of the sea horse could easily be used as an icon for this book because this tiny creature gave the hippocampus its name.

time you flip through the pages of a popular news or entertainment magazine, study the eyes of persons portrayed in editorial and advertising images. If a person's eyes stare right into your eyes, you might think that she is confident, proud, and comfortable with having her picture taken. On the other hand, if the eyes are looking off in another direction or are covered, you might think that that person is shy, not confident, or doesn't want her picture taken. Visual communicators—whether for news organizations or advertising agencies—know that the eyes communicate messages that a curious and knowledgeable mind will notice (Figure 3.10).

But just as looking at a road map can show you only how to arrive at a specific destination and not the wonders you discover along the journey itself, knowing the route light takes doesn't explain fully how humans recognize and respond to specific visual messages. Visual perception and visual theory will further refine your knowledge of how images become permanent fixtures within our personal image banks.

Figure 3.10

The eyes are the windows to the soul, or at least sometimes an indication of a person's inner thoughts. Learning how the eyes work helps you notice eyes in visual messages. Left: Two persons not maintaining eye contact with a photographer's lens might mean that they are uncomfortable with being pictured or with each other. Right: Looking right into the camera's lens usually reveals a confident personality.

DISCUSSION AND EXERCISE IDEAS

- Present a slide show of portraits in which the eyes of the subjects are looking into and away from the camera lens. Discuss the use of eye direction as a way of getting attention.

- Cut out or copy a printed image (or describe a video image) of a person in which the eyes are the focus of the picture. In a brief paper, discuss why you think the photographer had the subject look into or away from the camera's lens.

INFOTRAC COLLEGE EDITION ASSIGNMENTS

- With "Subject guide" checked, type "hippocampus" in the search area. Click "View" for the "Periodical references." Read the article "Aging, Memory, and the Brain." Can you think of any activities that might keep your brain young and healthy, as you grow older?

- With "Subject guide" checked, type "color" in the search area. Within the "Color Blindness" section, click "View" in "Periodical references." Read the article "Yellow Skies, Blue Trees? (living with color blindness)" by Joe Rogers. What graphic design choices—whether for print or screen media—can you make that might help those with color deficiencies to better see and understand your work?

Go to the Web site for this book at www.wadsworth.com/product/0534562442 to find more Web links on this subject.

WHY WE SEE

It is the brain—not the eyes—that understands visual messages. Therefore, to consider how the mind processes the visual information it receives from the eyes is vital.

The brain processes images as four basic visual perception cues (color, form, depth, and movement). Knowing how the brain divides and sorts visual messages will help you create images that take advantage of that fact. Theories further refine our understanding of why some pictures are remembered but most are forgotten. Knowing how we see helps explain why we see.

What the Brain Sees: Color, Form, Depth, and Movement

A mind that works primarily with meanings must have organs that supply it primarily with forms.

Suzanne Langer,

1895–1985

PHILOSOPHER

AND EDUCATOR

By the end of this chapter you should know:

- How it was discovered that brain cells "see."
- The various attributes and social meanings of the four visual cues.
- How graphic designers exploit the four visual cues in order to attract attention.

In 1962, David Hubel and Torsten Wiesel of the Johns Hopkins University in Baltimore reported on their experiments with a cat's brain. Their work provided clues to how the mind sees images provided by the eyes, and the two scientists received a Nobel Prize in 1981 for it.

The scientists attached a microelectrode, as small as an individual brain cell, to a nerve in the visual cortex of an anesthetized cat (Figure 4.1). They attached the microelectrode to both an amplifier and an oscilloscope. The amplifier converted electrical energy to a "put-put" sound, and the oscilloscope converted signals to a blip on a screen. With the cat's eyes open and focused toward a screen, the scientists flashed simple straight and slanted light patterns. Thus Hubel and Wiesel could see and hear immediately the effect of any nerve cell stimulation by the patterns of light. After they flashed the light on the screen several times and adjusted their equipment, the scientists recorded what they had thought was possible: the stimulated activity of a single brain cell responsible for vision. They discovered that a single cell within the visual cortex was activated when the line of light was vertical and moved from the left to the right. When that same upright line was moved up and down while connected to the same nerve cell, there was no response.

Figure 4.1

David Hubel and Torsten Wiesel shared a Nobel Prize for attaching a tiny electrode to a cat's visual cortex and identifying the types of visual cortex cells responsible for sight.

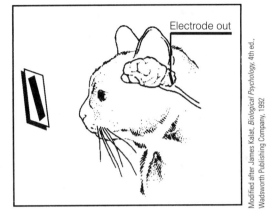

Electrode out

Modified after James Kalat, *Biological Psychology*, 4th ed., Wadsworth Publishing Company, 1992

The visual cortex actually is composed of several thin layers of nerve tissue. By this tedious and perhaps ethically disturbing method of placing microelectrodes in various cells within each layer, Hubel and Wiesel found that some cells responded to a spot of light, the edges of objects, certain angles of lines, specific movements, and specific colors and that some responded to the space between lines rather than the lines themselves. In short, each brain cell in the cortex almost reacts in a one-to-one relationship with the type of visual stimulation it receives. From all this information, the brain constructs a *map* of the retinal image.

The brain, through its vast array of specialized cells, most quickly and easily responds to four major attributes of all viewed objects: color, form, depth, and movement. These four visual cues are the major concerns of any visual communicator when designing a picture to be remembered by a viewer.

■ COLOR

Various philosophers, scientists, and physicians throughout recorded history have attempted to explain the nature of color. Aristotle thought that light and color were different names for the same visual phenom-

enon. Technically, he would have been correct had he stopped at that point. But being a man of letters, he continued writing, recording that he thought that all the colors were simply mixtures of black and white.

Much later, Leonardo da Vinci, with no laboratory experimentation to back his claim proposed a more accurate theory of the nature of color. Based on his observations of the natural world, he thought that six primary colors—white, black, red, yellow, green, and blue—existed. He came to the conclusion simply by reasoning that the six colors were wholly independent and unique. Da Vinci believed that, by mixing these six colors in varying degrees, all the other colors capable of being seen by a normal human eye could be created.

His interest in and theories on the mixing of colors came directly from his experience as one of the great masters of painting. Although all the colors desired by painters can be made by mixing those six color pigments together in varying degrees, this property of paints doesn't explain how light is mixed.

Thomas Young was the first to link color and the human eye. In 1801 he suggested that the eye must be composed of three different light-sensitive materials so that humans could perceive color. Unaware of Young's work in the field, Hermann von Helmholtz, a German physiologist and physicist, further refined Young's ideas.

Helmholtz was the first scientist to measure the speed of the nerve impulses within the nervous system. He also invented the ophthalmoscope—a device used by doctors to examine the eye. The Young-Helmholtz theory, also known as the three-component theory or the trichromatic theory, became the dominant color theory to explain how the eye physically sees color.

Young and Helmholtz maintained that there are three different kinds of photoreceptors in the eye with each one specifically sensitive to a particular color. Color perception, they reasoned, is a result of mixing red, green, and blue once the photoreceptors are stimulated.

■ *Additive and Subtractive Color*

Every color we see can be made with three basic, primary colors—red, green, and blue. Some students get confused because they are taught that the primary colors are red (or more accurately, magenta), yellow, and blue (or more accurately, cyan). But those colors are the primaries used for paint pigments and printing presses—not light. When light of different color frequencies is mixed, the color becomes whiter. This method of color mixing is called additive color. For example, equal amounts of red, green, and blue light will produce white light. The additive mixing of colors is the basis for color we see from our eyes and in photography, television and computer monitors, and stage lighting.

Secondary colors in light are formed when any two primary colors are mixed together. When mixed equally, red and blue light will produce magenta, red and green will make yellow, and blue and green will create cyan light (Figure 4.2).

Complementary colors are any two colors that when mixed together provide "white light." For example, magenta and green, yellow and blue, and cyan and red will all produce white light when mixed together equally.

When paints are mixed together the colors in the paint absorb every color except the wavelength that we see reflected back. Mixing more and more paint colors results in a gradually darker color because more light frequencies get absorbed until there are none left to reflect. This method of color mixing is called subtractive color because the light frequencies get subtracted from the initial mixture. Equal amounts of magenta, yellow, and cyan paint will produce black paint. Subtractive color is used in offset printing in which four colors are used to create color photographs and illustrations on paper—magenta, yellow, cyan, and black (for added definition).

The difference between additive and subtractive color mixing is the reason why visual communicators should use caution when working with images and graphic designs seen on a computer that later will be printed. Sometimes the comparisons are not favorable. That's because a computer screen can exhibit about 16 million different colors, but a printing press can only handle up to 6,000 colors. In addition, the light under which a printed piece is viewed (fluorescent, incandescent, or natural light) and the quality of the paper stock used for printing make a difference between what you see on a computer screen and what you see on paper.

■ *The Principle of Color Constancy*

The Young-Helmholtz theory explained much about how colored light works, but not every factor involved with experiencing color. For example, color constancy is a phenomenon of human color perception by which colors viewed under different **brightness** conditions retain their hue. During the day a red jacket will appear red either outside or inside a house. But if you are outside at night and look into a room lit by an incandescent bulb, a red jacket worn by someone inside the room will appear to be yellow. When you are inside the room, the light from the bulb appears to be white and the jacket is red again. The mind tries to keep a color constant in order to avoid confusing sensual stimulations. In the 1950s, Edwin Land, the inventor of instant photography (discussed in Chapter 12), was not satisfied with the popular view of how the

Figure 4.2

See color section following page 132.

eye perceives color. His experiments concluded that there are no specific retinal photoreceptors for the colors red, green, and blue, as thought by Young and Helmholtz. Rather, the photoreceptors take in short and long visible light wavelengths from an entire scene. Color vision and the phenomenon of color constancy are a result of the mixing of wavelengths.

■ *Three Ways of Discussing Color*

Three different methods are used to describe color: objective, comparative, and subjective. The objective method for describing colors depends on known standards of measurement; the comparative and subjective methods rely on the evaluation of the person who sees the color. Color is a highly subjective and powerful means of communicating ideas. James Maxwell, the Scotsman who invented color photography in 1861 (see Chapter 12), once wrote that the "science of color must be regarded essentially as a mental science." Consequently, no two individuals see a color in exactly the same way.

Objective Method

The **objective method** for describing colors rests on the assumption that the perception of color is simply the result of various light wavelengths stimulating the cones along the back of the eyes' retinas (discussed in Chapter 3). A color can be accurately measured by the location of its wavelength on the electromagnetic spectrum. The length of an energy wave is measured in parts per millimeter. The wavelength of the visible light spectrum is only about 0.0003 millimeter, or 300 nanometers, wide. That's about one one-hundredth of an inch. The entire electromagnetic spectrum sensitive to the photoreceptors in the eyes therefore is only from 400 to 700 nanometers on the visible light portion of the electromagnetic

spectrum. Blue shows up on the visible spectrum at about 430 nanometers, green has a wavelength that starts at about 530 nanometers, and red has a wavelength beginning at 560 nanometers (Figure 4.3).

A color's temperature can also be measured. As first demonstrated by Sir William Herschel (see Chapter 2), each color has a unique temperature that distinguishes it from every other color. The temperature of colors is measured in Kelvin (K). Absolute zero on the Kelvin scale, the lowest temperature that is physically possible, is approximately 273 degrees below zero on the Celsius scale. The color red, for example, is about 1,000°K, and a deep blue color is approximately 60,000°K. Sunlight at noon, depending on the time of year, is between 4,900° and 5,800°K. The Kelvin scale is derived from the heat required to change the color of a black metal radiator. As the temperature increases, colors reveal themselves. The next time you look at logs burning in a fireplace, note the various colors produced. Yellow and red colors are cooler on the temperature scale than green or blue colors.

A highly energetic color—one with a high wavelength frequency—does not indicate how quickly the eye will notice the color. Violet, with its high frequency, is considered to be the most active color, whereas red, with a low frequency, is the least active color. Yet, for the human eye, violet is the least noticeable color, and red is the most noticeable color. Because of its long wavelength and quick recognition by the eye, red is used for signal lights, stop signs, and other warning or attention-getting purposes. The reason that the eye notices red more easily is not because there are more red-sensitive cones in the retina. The reason is that the cornea is colored yellow to protect the eye from harmful ultraviolet rays. Yellow absorbs the shorter wavelengths of blue and green and lets the longer wavelength of red pass through to the retina. Older adults often have trouble seeing blue and green objects because corneas tend to turn more yellow as they age. The more yellow the cornea, the less likely blue and green colors will be seen.

Color has three characteristics: **chroma, value,** and brightness. Chroma, or hue, refers to the name of the color. Scientifically speaking, it is the difference in wavelengths between individual colors. Value, or saturation, is the amount of color concentration. Strong concentrations of a color have a high value, and weak dilutions of a color have a low value. Brightness is the amount of light emitted from a colored object. Subtle changes in a color's chroma, value, and brightness can yield literally millions of colors. However, the human eye cannot detect the minute differences.

Comparative Method

The second technique for describing colors is the **comparative method.** As with a dictionary definition, the color red, for example, would be compared to the color of blood. The color blue might be compared to that of the sky on a clear, sunny day. For the comparative method to be of use, the color that another color is compared to must be accepted universally as a standard. However, a physiologist might be momentarily confused by the comparison because blood inside the body that has not been exposed to oxygen is blue in color. Furthermore, one person's conception of the color red isn't always someone else's. Blood red is dark, but the red on an American flag is much lighter.

Subjective Method

The third technique for describing color is the **subjective method.** A person's mental state or association with a colored object strongly affects the emotional response of the message. In their drawings, children tend

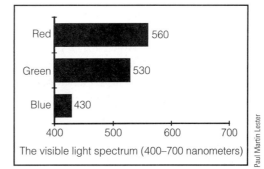

The visible light spectrum (400–700 nanometers)

Paul Martin Lester

Paul Martin Lester

Figure 4.3

This graphic shows that red has a longer wavelength than the other colors. The thickness of the horizontal columns has no meaning other than to attract attention.

Figure 4.4

See color section following page 132.

to prefer abstract colors to shapes and lines. Girls generally use more intense colors than boys do in their early pictures. Educational psychologists consider such use of color to indicate enjoyment of social interactions and possession of higher reasoning abilities.

Painters have known for years that the warm colors—reds and yellows—appear closer than cool colors—blues and greens. The terms *warm* and *cool* are psychological distinctions and are not related to the actual temperature of the color. (Recall that blue is one of the hottest colors available.) Lighter colors tend to be viewed as soft and cheerful, and darker colors have a harsh or moody emotional quality about them. A room painted a light color will appear larger than the same room painted a dark color. Colors that are tinted tend to recede, whereas shaded colors advance toward the viewer, making the room look smaller (Figure 4.4).

Because people associate colors with objects and events, this visual attribute is highly subjective and emotional.

Physically, most people can distinguish between 150 and 200 of the millions of possible colors but can't name 150 colors. However, artists, house painters, and interior decorators who work with colors every day may know hundreds of names for colors.

By the way, many animals can see a variety of colors; some can see more colors than humans. Beetles, bees, wasps, ants, crabs, frogs, toads, some salamanders, flies, snakes, turtles, birds that are active during the day, and most mammals can see color. However, birds that are active at night, rats, hamsters, and rabbits are color deficient. Some animals compensate for their lack of color vision by being able to see ultraviolet light.

■ *Sociological Uses of Color*

We tend to associate a pleasant or bad experience with the colors of the objects that constitute the event. Blood red might remind someone of an accident. Green might recall a pleasant walk in the grass. Yellow might be the color of a balloon bought at a circus. Imagine any color of your choosing. Do you relate it to a specific object? Most people never associate color with a formless blob, but with a definite object. For that reason, memory of a color affects the perception of it.

According to a Web site that is a guide to the floral industry (www.barbarasfloral expressions.com/), the colors of flowers are associated with their corresponding meaning:

Red:	Love/Respect
Yellow:	Joy/Friendship
Coral:	Desire
Peach:	Modesty
Lavender:	Enchantment
White:	Innocence/Secrecy
Dark Pink:	Thankfulness
Orange:	Fascination
Pale Pink:	Grace/Joy

Of course, whether you understand the meaning being expressed through a flower's color is largely dependent on your experiences and associations with color meaning. Throughout recorded history various colors have been associated with magical spells, medical cures, and personality revelations. A general love for color is considered to be a sign of an enthusiastic person. An indifference to color is a trait of an introspective personality.

In ancient Egypt, women so loved color that they used green powder topped with the glitter obtained by crushing beetles for eye shadow, black paint as lipstick, red rouge for their cheeks, blue paint to outline the veins of their breasts, gold paint to coat their nipples, and a reddish brown dye called henna to stain their fingers and feet. But Egyptian women did not use color merely to brighten their complexions. Color had social meaning. Red fingernails signaled that the woman considered herself to be a member of the highest social class. Unfortunately, many of the paints and powders used as makeup contained toxic metals that slowly killed their wearers.

The color purple often is associated with dignity or sadness. Many artistic people say that they prefer purple to the other colors. Egyptians wore a purple necklace to thwart adversity.

Baby boys are dressed in blue because the color is associated with the color of the sky—where the gods lived. The color supposedly gives boys power and protects them from evil spirits. Some adults wear blue for the same reason—to ward off the evil eye. Parents once draped blue and violet stones around children's necks because they associated the colors with virtue and faith. The parents hoped that the gods would protect their children and at the same time make them obedient.

Green is a favorite color of those who are outgoing and have large appetites. An emerald green connotes versatility and ingenuity, whereas a grayish green signifies deceitful behavior. Green stones worn around the neck were thought to promote fertility. Green also is believed to have a calming effect. Many backstage waiting rooms in theaters are called "greenrooms" because of the color of their painted walls.

Jaundice has long been considered a condition that can be cured through exposure to sunlight. For many years, however, people mistakenly thought that the sun's yellow color was the curative agent. Consequently, to combat jaundice in Germany, patients ate yellow turnips and wore gold coins and saffron clothing. Russian physicians had their wealthy patients wear necklaces made of gold beads. In England, victims of the disease were forced to eat yellow spiders rolled in butter.

Red-colored objects supposedly relieved many medical ailments. In Ireland and Russia red flannel clothing was believed to be a remedy for scarlet fever. Red woolen blankets were applied to a sprained ankle in Scotland, to a sore throat in Ireland, and to prevent fever in Macedonia. To prevent smallpox, the physician to Edward II demanded that the king's entire room be painted red. To prevent the scars caused by the disease, red light was used in Denmark. Red stones were often used to treat any disease. Some people still believe that an injury such as a black eye should be covered immediately with a blood red, raw steak. The Japanese thought that the color red overcame nightmares. The Chinese tied a red ribbon to a child's hair to promote long life. Parents dress baby girls in pink because a European legend claimed that girls were born inside little pink flowers. Many people believe that a room that is painted pink will calm children, whether girls or boys.

Cultural heritage, training, and personal experiences give colors special meanings not shared by everyone. An average person sees the color red as red. An anthropologist sees red as a power **symbol** for an ancient civilization. A psychologist sees red as a clue to a patient's personality. An artist sees red as one of a hundred different red-hued solutions to a painting's composition. Again, the more you know, the more you see. The eye sees the color—all colors—but the brain interprets its meaning.

Because color—more than any other visual attribute—has the capacity to affect the emotions of the viewer, a message may be forever remembered or forever lost, depending on how it is utilized. For that reason, pay particular attention to the use of colors in graphic design (discussed in Chapter 9). Color easily draws attention to itself. Used the right way, color can emphasize an important part of a message; if used casually or too often, color can be a serious distraction (Figure 4.5).

■ FORM

Another common attribute of images that the brain responds to is the recognition of form. Form defines the outside edges and the internal parts of an object and has three parts: dots, lines, and shapes.

■ Dots

The dot is the simplest form that can be written. A dot anywhere within a framed space demands immediate attention (Figure 4.6). Moved to the center, the dot becomes the hub of a wheel. If off to one side in a frame, the dot creates tension as the layout appears out of balance. Two dots within a framed space also create tension as the viewer is forced to divide attention between the two objects. Two dots within a field of view also can imply a measurement between two points in space. When three or more dots appear in an image, the viewer naturally tries to connect them with an imaginary

Figure 4.5

See color section following page 132.

Paul Martin Lester

Figure 4.6

The silhouette of a child standing alone on a small hill is all the more noticeable because of the dot that shapes his head.

form the back of the retinas in the eyes. The rod and cone dots enable you to see the dot at the end of this sentence.

■ *Lines*

When dots of the same size are drawn so closely together that there is no space between them, the result is a line. The word *line* is used in many different contexts because it is such an important concept. Lines, whether straight, curved, or in combination, have an energy that comes from the sequence of individual dots. Hence lines almost always evoke an emotion in the viewer (Figure 4.8).

According to anthropologist Evelyn Hatcher, straight lines convey a message of stiffness and rigidity. Straight lines can be horizontal, vertical, or diagonal. Horizontal lines, especially when low in the frame, remind viewers of a horizon with plenty of room to grow. If the horizontal line is high in the frame, the viewer feels confined, as the layout seems heavy. In a layout, vertical lines bring the eye of the viewer to a halt. The eye attempts to travel around the space created by the line. Diagonal lines have a strong, stimulating effect in a field of view. The most restful diagonal line is one that extends from the top right to the lower left corner of a frame. It is a perfect compromise between horizontal and vertical forces. Any other diagonal line strongly moves the eye of the viewer in the line's direction. Several diagonal lines within a composition create a nervous dynamic energy.

Curved lines convey a mood of playfulness, suppleness, and movement. Curves have a gracefulness about them that softens the content of their active message.

If lines are thick and dark, their message is strong and confident. If thin and light with a clear separation between them, their mood is delicate, perhaps a bit timid.

line. It may be a straight or curved line or take the basic shape of a square, triangle, or circle. Hundreds of small dots grouped together can form complex pictures. Georges Seurat and other pointillist artists in the nineteenth century used a technique called **pointillism** in which they peppered their paintings with small colored dots that combined in the viewer's mind to form an image when viewed from about eight feet away (Figure 4.7).

Dots also figure prominently in the halftone process that allows the printing of photographs. A picture is photographed through a screen with hundreds of small holes. The result is an image that is actually a collection of dots in the pointillist tradition.

A television screen is a collection of phosphor-filled red, green, and blue dots that glow to fluorescence when shot with electrons from a cathode-ray tube. Again, the mind combines these small dots into a coherent picture. The principle of the color television set has its roots in the dots that

Grouped lines form blank spaces that the eyes naturally want to inspect. When drawn or as part of an object, they also combine to simulate the sensation of touch. The lines that form the surface of an object may be part of an illustration or part of the natural lighting where the object is located. A rough surface has several small curved lines that make up its bumpy exterior. A smooth surface has few lines that mark its coating. Texture stimulates the visual sense by the image itself and the tactile sense through memory. For example, previous experience with the sharp points of the needles of a cactus transfers to a picture of the plant.

■ Shapes

The third type of form, shapes, is the combination of dots and lines into patterns that occur throughout nature and in graphic design. Shapes are figures that sit on the plane of the visual field without depth and define the outside edges of objects. They can be as simple as a beach ball and as complex as the side of a person's face. A shape that is quickly recognized is clearly separated from the background of the image.

The three basic shapes are parallelograms, circles, and triangles. From these three shapes, variations that compose all known or imagined forms can be created. Polygon is the name of the form created by a combination of shapes. As with all visual attributes, a particular culture assigns meaning to each shape.

The Parallelogram

The parallelogram is a four-sided figure with opposite sides that are parallel and equal in length. The two major types of parallelograms are squares and rectangles. "Be there or be square" is often a challenge given by those organizing a party. In Western culture, a *square* is defined as an unsophisti-

cated or dull person. Similarly, a square shape, with its formally balanced, symmetrical orientation, is the most dull and conventional shape. But strength also comes from its plain appearance. A square is considered sturdy and straightforward. In language, the equivalents are a *square deal* or a *square shooter*. The implication from the phrases is that the business transaction or person so described may not be flamboyant but that you can trust that person to be fair.

Rectangles are the slightly more sophisticated cousins of squares. Of all the geometric figures, rectangles are the most common and are the favored shape of the frame for mediated images. Still and motion picture photographers learn to see scenes through the rectangular format of film's horizontal 35-mm viewfinder. Because a television's screen is close to a square shape, videographers most often place subjects in the center of the screen. As discussed in Chapter 14, the advent of high-definition television technology changed the shape of television screens

Figure 4.7

The nineteenth-century French pointillist Georges Seurat constructed his paintings by using a series of dots and only twelve separate colors, never mixing one color with another. The tedious, mathematically based painting technique found few advocates because the style lacked spontaneity. Nevertheless, his paintings accurately reflect how the photoreceptors in the retina and in color monitors divide images into a series of dots. Seurat, Georges-Pierre. Port-en-Bessin: Entrance to the Harbor, *(1888). Oil on Canvas. The Museum of Modern Art, New York. Lillie P. Bliss Collection.*

Figure 4.8

Two schoolgirls in New Orleans riding a streetcar provide the illusion of a mirror image when the bar in the center acts as a dividing line.

Paul Martin Lester

to the wide-screen rectangular form used in movie theaters. Composition in motion picture and still photography formats often takes advantage of the horizontal sides that a rectangle naturally creates. In a rectangular frame, the chief object of focus does not have to be in the center for the piece to appear balanced. White or blank space offsets the object in the frame to create a unified composition. With a square format, an object close to one side of the frame creates an unbalanced appearance.

The Circle

The first shapes primitive humans probably took notice of were the bright, circular forms in the sky—the sun and the moon. Consequently, circles have always been asso-

Figure 4.9

Because the sun, the moon, and faces have circular shapes, this form is one of the most noticeable of all. Photographers often use it to add interest.

Paul Martin Lester

ciated with the endless rhythmic patterns of time, symbolizing eternity without clear beginnings or endings. A popular country song, "May the Circle Be Unbroken," implies that a circle of friends and family members will always maintain their closeness—even after death.

A graphic designer must use circles carefully. They immediately draw the viewer's eye in their direction and thus can overpower an image's main message (Figure 4.9).

The Triangle

Triangles are the most dynamic and active of shapes. As energetic objects, they convey direction, but they can burden a design with the tension they can create.

The two types of triangles—equilateral and isosceles—have vastly different moods. All three sides of an equilateral triangle are the same length. Its shape conveys a serene mood because of symmetrical balance. Think of the silent stone pyramids of Egypt. They calmly watch the passing of each millennium and tourist with an instamatic camera. Seen from a distance, they are an abrupt change in the naturally sloping sand-dune-filled horizon. Seen up close, their power obviously comes from their stable bases. The triangle juggles its two parts—the base and the apex—to create a dynamic energy. From its base comes stability, but from its peak comes tension (Figure 4.10).

In contrast, the isosceles triangle draws its power not from its base but from its sharp point. Think of the Washington Monument in Washington, D.C. When the point is vertical and used in architecture, the shape is called a steeple and symbolizes a religious person's hoped-for destination. But pointed in any direction, isosceles triangles challenge the eye to follow. When using the isosceles shape, a visual communicator must be sure to give the viewer a message to see at the end of its point.

■ *Depth*

If humans had only one eye and confined their visual messages to drawings on the walls of caves, there would be no need for more complex illustrations that could be made from dots, lines, and shapes. But because we have two eyes set slightly apart, we naturally see in three rather than two dimensions. Consequently, we expect our pictures to have the illusion of depth even though they are actually presented on a flat surface.

Depth is related to volume because when a basic shape has volume, it exhibits the illusion of weight and mass. There are five volumetric forms: cube, cylinder, sphere, pyramid, and cone. A cube is composed of six squares. A cylinder is a rectangle with two circular shapes on each end. A sphere is two circles cut in half and joined at the middle. A pyramid is four triangles. A cone is a circular shape and a triangle combined. When each form is rotated in space, its volume becomes obvious and the illusion of three dimensions is achieved. Each form transmits symbolic messages similar to those of their flat counterparts.

In 1838, one year before photography was introduced to the public, Sir Charles Wheatstone presented a paper to the Royal Society in London detailing his views on **binocular vision.** He had concluded that two eyes seeing slightly different views actually create the illusion of depth. The images are projected onto each two-dimensional retinal screen, and the two retinal views travel to the brain, which interprets the difference between them as depth.

He later used his studies in depth perception to invent the stereoscope. An early example of the modern Viewmaster, the stereoscope presents a two-dimensional view of two slightly different photographs mounted

Paul Martin Lester

Figure 4.10

A triangular shape is implied in this photograph of dune buggy riders on Sand Mountain, Nevada.

side by side on a cardboard backing. When each eye views them simultaneously, the brain merges the images into one, three-dimensional image. The difference between looking at an ordinary photograph and an image through a stereoscope is striking. Stereoscopically enhanced views were enormously popular as educational and entertainment sources from about 1860 until 1890. Before the invention of the halftone method for printing pictures in publications, stereocards viewed through stereoscopes were the main source of pictorial news.

■ *The Eight Depth Cues*

Subsequently, researchers have identified eight possible factors, used singly or in combination, that give viewers a sense of depth: space, size, color, lighting, textural gradients, interposition, time, and **perspective.**

Courtesy Autodesk, Inc.

Figure 4.11

In this computer-generated image, note how light creates the illusion of depth.

known size in order to determine its size. Archaeologists take pictures of **artifacts** found at historical sites with a ruler in the scene so that viewers will know how large the recovered object is. Tourists often are disappointed when they travel to Mount Rushmore in South Dakota because, with no frame of reference, the presidential faces carved in the rock do not convey a sense of their enormous size. Educational psychologist Jean Piaget found that, if much attention were given to an object, its size would be overestimated. A small, refined figure often attracts attention within a visual frame because the viewer must concentrate on it. Scale and attention are related to depth perception because there is no illusion of depth if objects are viewed as the same size.

Space

Space is the frame in which an image is located. With a natural scene, the space depends on how close you are to the subject. Standing in an open field gives the feeling of a large amount of space and enhances the feeling of depth. If an object is close to the eyes, depth perception is limited.

Size

Size can help in the illusion of depth perception if the viewer is aware of the object's actual size. An airliner seen from a distance is a small size on the viewer's retina. If someone has no idea of what the flying object is, she would conclude that it is quite small. But because we are familiar with the actual size of the aircraft, we simply know that it is far away and not as small as a robin. Size, consequently, is closely related to our ability to determine an object's distance. Distance is related to space and helps in our perception of depth.

Size also is related to **scale** and mental attention. Without knowing an object's size, we have to view it next to an object of

Color

As indicated at the start of this chapter, an object's color can communicate depth. Warm-colored objects appear closer than cool-colored objects. High-contrast pictures with great differences between light and dark tones seem closer than objects colored with more neutral tones (Figure 4.11).

Lighting

Differences in light intensities can communicate depth. A television studio technician will position a light above and behind a news announcer. Called a "hair light," the brightness level is slightly higher than the lights in front in order to separate the person from the background. The prevalence of shadows also indicates an object's volume and gives the viewer another depth cue. The light's brightness and position create shadows that the viewer notices (Figure 4.12).

Textural Gradients

The ripple effect seen in a still pond suddenly disturbed by a rock or ridges from the wind against a sand dune are called textural gradients. The ridges appear closer together as the viewer moves away.

Interposition

Interposition is the placement of one object in front of another to give the illusion of depth. Similar objects positioned side by side without lighting from behind and simple line drawings do not communicate three-dimensional depth. A near object is in the foreground, whereas a far object is in the background. Determining the difference between foreground and background objects is an important depth cue.

Time

Time and space are intricately related concepts that find expression in visual messages. In one sense, time as a depth cue refers to the first element a viewer sees in a frame. That picture will be in the foreground of the viewer's mind, with other images seen later in the background. But time as a cultural communication is more complicated. According to Evelyn Hatcher, cultures that think about time differently present depth cues differently.

A culture that places more importance on past events will place close objects on the same level as distant objects. Murals in Belfast, Northern Ireland, for example, often display this type of perspective (Figure 4.13). The creators of these often emotional messages relive the past as a way of continuing the feud between Catholics and Protestants in the present. Cultures that are more interested in capturing and controlling the present moment often exhibit a normal field of view. The prevalence of the camera, with its emphasis on linear perspective, indicates how cultures try to control time. Edward Hall's book *The Dance of Life* eloquently explores the ways that cultures experience and manipulate time. Finally, cultures that emphasize long-term planning and the

Uncensored Situations, 1966, The Dick Sutphen Studio, Inc.

importance of future events often exhibit images without any recognizable depth perceptual dimensions. For example, traditional Japanese and Chinese works of art often have no noticeable depth cues.

Perspective

Probably the most complex depth perception cue is perspective. A person's cultural heritage has more bearing on the interpretation of perspective attributes than any other factor. The concept of perception as used in Western art is relatively new compared with the entire history of art. In Europe, during the Renaissance, from about the fourteenth

Figure 4.12

Three prisoners hang grotesquely from the spar of an American flagship in the nineteenth-century engraving. The use of dramatic, silhouette lighting amplifies the horror of this image.

Figure 4.13

Cultures that tend never to forget past events, such as Northern Ireland, where many people still discuss seventeenth-century battles, produce murals that often have few depth cues.

Paul Martin Lester

to the sixteenth centuries, visual communicators usually were artists and scientists. Probably the most famous artist/scientist during this era was Leonardo da Vinci. His paintings reflect an early attention to duplicating on a two-dimensional surface the illusion of depth as viewed in the real world. One of Leonardo's most famous works, *The Last Supper,* uses perspective to express the social importance of the Christ figure (Figure 4.14).

Leonardo da Vinci is credited with inventing the "Leonardo box" to aid perspective renderings, although Filippo Brunelleschi or Leone Battista Alberti probably developed the technique. It involved tracing a scene on a sheet of paper (later on glass) with the artist's eye remaining in the same position. Using this method, the artist could be sure that the lines drawn accurately mimicked an actual scene (Figure 4.15). Communications scholar Kevin Barnhurst notes that the device "created a version of things seen by a Cyclops, whose eye remains

immobile, recording uniformly the details before it as it peers from a box."

The "box" most commonly used by artists of the day to draw accurate landscapes was the camera obscura. Recall that a small hole in a box projects an upside-down view of the outside scene if lighting conditions are favorable. Artists inside a large camera obscura simply traced the image on a thin sheet of paper. Much later, light-sensitive material replaced paper and became the basis for modern photography. Photography, more than any other invention, spurred artists to render scenes in their proper perspective.

In her book *Visual Metaphors: A Methodological Study in Visual Communication,* Evelyn Hatcher identifies three major forms of perspective: illusionary, geometrical, and conceptual. The visual artist's own style heavily influences geometrical and conceptual perspective. For both, the placement of the objects within an image's frame is important.

Figure 4.14

The Last Supper *by Leonardo da Vinci is a classic example of the use of linear perspective to emphasize the main subject of a visual message. All of the diagonal lines in the painting converge on the face of the Christ figure at the vanishing point.*

Illusionary Perspective An illusionary perspective can be achieved through size, color, lighting, interposition, and linear perspective. When you stand on a railroad track and look down the ties, the steel rails seem to converge into a single area, or vanishing point, in the distance. This trait of parallel lines when seen at a distance is called linear perspective. This aspect of illusionary perspective that provides the illusion of three-dimensional depth on a painting or in a photograph is what artists were trying to duplicate with the aid of the Leonardo box and camera obscura (Figure 4.16).

Geometrical Perspective In geometrical perspective, the artist shows near figures in the lower portion of the picture, and objects farther away higher in the frame on a vertical line above the near object. This type of perspective is common among traditional Japanese and Mayan artwork. Children often exhibit this type of perspective in their drawings.

Conceptual Perspective Conceptual perspective is a compositional trait that relies on a more symbolic definition of depth perception than the other types of perspective. It can be divided into two types: multiview and social. With the multiview perspective, a viewer can see many different sides of an object at the same time. The picture is often an X-ray, or transparent, view of the object. Near objects overlap far objects only by the outside edges or lines that make up their shapes. Pablo Picasso liked to use this type of perspective (Figure 4.17).

In social perspective, the most important person in a group picture, a government or corporate leader, is larger in size than other, less important people (Figure 4.18). A viewer often assumes power relationships because of social perspective. In a picture of a couple, the man's dominance over the woman often is signified by the man being nearer and

larger in the frame with his hand resting on or arm wrapped around the woman's shoulder. Over the past three decades, the feminist movement has made advertisers and others more sensitive to nonverbal, negative **stereotypes** such as these.

It is difficult for a mediated image to accurately duplicate the depth cues seen in an actual view because the mind cannot forget that the picture is a contrivance presented on a flat screen or sheet of paper. However, technological advances may change this major difference between real and mediated images in the future. The brain can be fooled if the environment where the image is viewed can be controlled. For example, viewers wear helmets in virtual reality systems to eliminate all outside visual cues. In this case, the system challenges the normal depth perceptual cues that identify a picture as different from reality. Psychologists should be prepared for the implications of a viewer's being unable to distinguish between direct and mediated images as with virtual reality technology.

As with all marks that artists make and all images that machines record, complicated

Figure 4.15

This 1525 woodcut by Albrecht Dürer demonstrates a drawing table called a Leonardo box (named after Leonardo, but probably invented by Filippo Brunelleschi or Leone Battista Alberti). The perspective tool uses a frame to achieve an accurate linear perspective of an object.

Modified after Ben Bova, *The Beauty of Light*, John Wiley & Sons, 1988. Reprinted by permission of John Wiley & Sons, Inc.

Figure 4.16

The "ponzo" or railroad track illusion occurs when horizontal lines of equal length appear to be different sizes. As in Leonardo's The Last Supper, *photographers also utilize linear perspective and its vanishing point to create a more dynamic composition.*

Figure 4.17

The early works of Pablo Picasso often are clear examples of the multiview form of perspective. Picasso, Pablo. Violin and Grapes. *Céret and Sorgues (spring-summer, 1912). Oil on Canvas. The Museum of Modern Art, New York. Mrs. David M. Levy Bequest.*

meanings are overtly or covertly communicated. An image that shows a ball's volume may be the simple picture that it appears to be, or it may reveal a hidden world of cultural communications (Figure 4.19).

■ MOVEMENT

Color, form, and depth join movement to constitute the principal qualities of images that make the cells in the visual cortex respond quickly to a stimulus. Recognizing movement is one of the most important traits in the survival of an animal. Knowing whether an object or other animal is moving closer avoids potentially harmful encounters. There are four types of movement: real, apparent, graphic, and implied.

■ *Real Movement*

Real movement is motion not connected with a picture presented in the media. It is actual movement either by a viewer or by

some other person or object. Because real movement does not involve mediated images, we don't emphasize it in this book.

■ *Apparent Movement*

Apparent, or illusionary, movement is a type of motion in which a stationary object appears to move. The most common example of this type of movement is motion picture films. People in a film appear to move when a movie is projected onto a screen. In reality, the filmed characters aren't moving at all. Motion pictures and televised images are simply a series of still images spliced together on a long strip of film or videotape. Movement is perceived in the brain through a phenomenon called *persistence of vision*. In 1824 Peter Mark Roget, who later became famous for his popular *Thesaurus*, proposed this phenomenon, which he thought resulted from the time required for an image to fade from the cells of the retina. Scientists now know that persistence of vision also is a result of the time needed for the brain to receive and analyze the picture. Consequently, a character in a film appears to move because of a blurring between individual frames as they pass through a projection device at a speed of at least twenty-four frames a second.

■ *Graphic Movement*

Graphic movement can be the motion of the eyes as they scan a field of view or the way a graphic designer positions elements so that the eyes move throughout a layout. One of the first psychologists to study a viewer's eye movements over an image was Julian Hochberg. His *constructivism theory* of visual communication states that viewers see successive parts of a picture over time with eyes that scan a scene. The mind then puts these scanned parts of a picture together to form a whole image (see Chapter 5).

Visual communicators often position the graphic elements in a design to take advantage of the eyes' movement over a picture. A viewer will scan an image based on previous experiences and current interests, seeing certain parts of the picture and ignoring others. Scanning is a subjective—not a random—choice. A viewer often scans pictures with a left-to-right, top-to-bottom preference (in cultures where reading and writing follow the same rules). However, if the viewer spots an area of particular interest in an image, reading rules do not apply (Figure 4.20). A visual communicator can direct a viewer's eye in a preconceived direction in a limited way. The eye will usually follow a line, a slow curve, or a horizontal shape before it follows other graphic elements. Of course, colors, sizes of individual pieces, and placement of elements against a frame's white space also are crucial (Figure 4.21). Chapter 9 contains a complete discussion of graphic elements at work in layout and design.

■ *Implied Movement*

Implied movement is a motion that a viewer perceives in a still, single image without any movement of object, image, or eye. Some graphic designs purposely stimulate the eyes with implied motion in order to attract attention (Figure 4.22). Optical or "op" art has been used in advertisements and in posters to achieve frenetic, pulsating results. Visual vibration is the term used for the images. Through high-contrast line placement or the use of complementary colors, moiré (wavy) patterns seem to move as if powered by an unseen light source.

Courtesy of Apple Computer, Inc.

■ *BRAIN CELLS NOTICE THE DIFFERENCE*

David Hubel, Torsten Wiesel, and the many scientists that built on their work through experiments with rats, monkeys, and people with brain injuries demonstrated that the brain cells in the visual cortex respond primarily to color, form, depth, and movement. For thousands of years visual communicators have used the four visual cues in their work, whether it appears on cave walls or on computer screens. An important lesson for image producers who want to make memorable messages is to understand that brain cells are complex "difference detectors." They are stimulated more by the relative difference between visual elements than by the intensity of each element.

Consequently, a gaudy, colorful presentation may lose much of its impact if all its graphic elements have the same intensity. But differences between the colors, lines, and shapes detected by brain cells are only part of the reason that some messages are noticed and others are not. The content of a visual message also plays a vital role, which we discuss next.

Figure 4.18

The low camera angle and position of the models emphasize that the man in front is the boss—an example of social perspective. Not surprisingly, he is the one holding the personal digital assistant.

Figure 4.19

The dog causes problems for the lady of the house in this nineteenth-century woodcut. But with the flat perspective of the illustration, the dishes might have fallen without the pet.

Uncensored Situations, 1966, The Dick Sutphen Studio, Inc.

Paul Martin Lester

Courtesy Autodesk, Inc.

Figure 4.20 (left)

The photograph of a woman pondering her next step on a sidewalk in downtown San Francisco presents two lines of motion. Although the line of people and the two boys move to the right, the woman's gaze directs the viewer's eyes to the left. This crossing of lines contributes to a feeling of tension.

Figure 4.21 (right)

Screen image presentations often use text animation to gain the viewer's attention. In this computer-generated picture, motion is supplied by the mind.

Figure 4.22

In this promotional still for the Back to the Future *motion simulation ride at Universal Studios, the use of motion lines creates an illusion of excitement and visual stimulation.*

DISCUSSION AND EXERCISE IDEAS

- Lead a general discussion about the ethics of using animals as the subject of medical and scientific research.

- Cut out or copy a printed image (or describe a video image) that contains a graphic design that exploits one of the four visual cues more than the others.

- Write a paper explaining all of the societal uses you can think of for a particular color.

INFOTRAC COLLEGE EDITION ASSIGNMENTS

- As you read in this chapter, David Hubel and Torsten Wiesel experimented with live cats to learn how brain cells in the visual cortex coordinate to provide us with the visual cues of color, form, depth, and movement. With "Subject guide" checked, type "Animal Experimentation" in the search area. Click "View" in "Periodical references." Read "Animal Research" by Sarah Rose A. Miller. What do you think are the positive and negative aspects of animal experimentation?

- With "Subject guide" checked, type "Color Therapeutic Use" in the search area and read the article by Nan Kathryn Fuchs concerned with color therapy. Do you think there is anything to this kind of treatment? Why or why not?

© 1993 Universal Studios, Florida

COMMUNICATION CAFE

Go to the Web site for this book at www.wadsworth.com/product/0534562442 to find more Web links on this subject.

The Sensual and Perceptual Theories of Visual Communication

There can be no words

without images.

Aristotle, 384–322 B.C.E.

PHILOSOPHER, SCIENTIST,

AND EDUCATOR

By the end of this chapter you should know:

- The difference between visual sensation and visual perception.
- The various components and uses for gestalt, constructivism, semiotics, and cognitive theories of visual communication.
- Why the perceptual theories offer a higher understanding of visual messages than the sensual theories.

Psychologists, philosophers, and practitioners have devised several approaches that help explain the way we see and process images. Knowing the four visual attributes the brain responds to—color, form, depth, and movement—is only part of the story for the visual communicator. The four theories we discuss in this chapter can be divided into two fundamental groups: sensual and perceptual. Those who advocate the sensual theories (gestalt and constructivism) maintain that direct or mediated images are composed of light objects that attract or repel us. The perceptual theories (semiotics and cognitive) are concerned mainly with the meaning that humans associate with the images they see.

To understand any of these approaches to visual communication, you must first know the difference between visual sensation and visual perception. A visual sensation simply is a stimulus from the outside world that activates nerve cells within your sense organs. Wood burning in a fireplace activates the cells in your ears because you can hear the logs cracking and hissing; in your nose because you can smell the rich aroma of the wood; in your hands and face because you can feel the warmth of the fire; and in your eyes as you watch the hypnotizing glow of the yellow flames. Sensations are lower order, physical responses to stimuli and alone convey no meaning. Nerve cells in your ears, nose, hands, and eyes do not have the capacity to make intelligent thoughts. They are simply conveyors of information to the brain.

When stimuli reach the brain, it can make sense of all the sensual input. Conclusions based on those data are almost instantaneous. Your brain interprets the noises, smells, temperatures, and sights as a fire in a fireplace. Visual perception is the conclusion that is made by combining all of the information gathered by your sensual organs. Sensations are the raw data. Visual perception is the meaning concluded after visual sensual stimuli are received.

■ SENSUAL THEORIES OF VISUAL COMMUNICATION

■ Gestalt

The gestalt theory of visual perception emerged from a simple observation. German psychologist Max Wertheimer received his inspiration during a train trip in the summer of 1910. Wertheimer happened to look out the window as the train moved through the sunny German countryside. He suddenly realized that he could see the outside scene even though the opaque wall of the train and the window frame partially blocked his view. He left the train in Frankfurt, went to a toy store, and bought a popular children's toy of the day—a stroboscope or flipbook. The flipbook is a simple form of cartoon animation. On the first page of the book, a drawing, say, of a cartoon character in a running position is displayed on the left-hand side of the page. On each subsequent page, the drawing of the figure is to the right of the previous drawing until the last page shows the character at the right-hand side of the page. To see the effect of the character running from the left to the right side, the viewer simply flips the pages rapidly. Wertheimer's observations during the train trip and using the flipbook led to a famous laboratory experiment at the University of Frankfurt.

Wertheimer concluded that the eye merely takes in all the visual stimuli and that the brain arranges the sensations into a coherent image. Without a brain that links individual sensual elements, the phenomenon of movement would not take place. His ideas led to the famous statement:

The whole is different from the sum of its parts.

In other words, perception is a result of a combination of sensations and not of individual sensual elements.

The word *gestalt* comes from the German noun that means form or shape. Gestalt psychologists further refined the initial work by Wertheimer to conclude that visual perception was a result of organizing sensual elements or forms into various groups. Discrete elements within a scene are combined and understood by the brain through a series of four fundamental principles of grouping that are often called laws: similarity, proximity, continuation, and common fate.

Similarity states that, given a choice by the brain, you will select the simplest and most stable form to concentrate on. This principle stresses the importance of basic shapes in the form of squares, circles, and triangles (Figure 5.1).

Proximity states that the brain more closely associates objects close to each other than it does two objects that are far apart. Two friends standing close and holding hands will be viewed as being more closely related than a third person standing twenty yards from the couple (Figure 5.2).

Paul Martin Lester

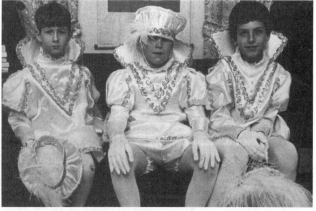

Paul Martin Lester

Continuation rests on the principle, again assumed by gestalt psychologists, that the brain does not prefer sudden or unusual changes in the movement of a line. In other words, the brain seeks as much as possible a smooth continuation of a line (Figure 5.3). The *line* can be a line in the traditional sense of the word, as in a drawing, or several objects placed together that form a line. Objects viewed as belonging to a continuous line will be mentally separated from other objects that are not a part of that line. Continuation also refers to objects that are partially blocked by a foreground object (Figure 5.4).

Another principle of gestalt psychology is common fate. A viewer mentally groups five arrows or five raised hands pointing to the sky because they all point in the same direction. An arrow or a hand pointed in the opposite direction will create tension, because the viewer will not see it as part of the upwardly directed whole (Figure 5.5).

One of the first uses of the gestalt principles was to explain the phenomenon of reversible figure and ground spatial patterns (in painting and photography, called negative and positive space). For figure and ground patterns the crucial question was: How do we know what is in the foreground and what belongs in the background of an

image? This question is related directly to the important need of the brain to label objects as near or far in order to judge their relative importance or danger.

In 1915, Edgar Rubin, a Danish gestalt psychologist, experimented with figure and ground patterns by drawing an object that could be interpreted as either a face or vase (Figure 5.6). Sensually, both the face and the vase images are stimulating photoreceptors in the retina. However, the brain cannot see both images at once—you must make a conscious decision whether to see a face or a vase in the drawing.

Rubin also outlined the principle of camouflage in which there is little or no separation between the foreground and the background (Figure 5.7). Understanding and manipulating this trait of visual perception led directly to military applications of merging the colors of uniforms and equipment with those of surrounding backgrounds in order to hide them. This principle also influenced the work of artists M. C. Escher and Paul Klee, both of whom were influenced by the writings and findings of several gestalt psychologists.

Gestalt and Visual Communication

The strength of the gestalt theory of visual perception is its attention to the

Figure 5.1 (left)

Similarity. Six tourists who rest on a bench at Versailles outside Paris come from a similar cultural group and are linked together in our minds. Because the woman to the right reads a book and is from a different generation, she looks as if she does not belong, or is dissimilar.

Figure 5.2 (right)

Proximity. Three boys dressed in similar Mardi Gras costumes, but with dissimilar personalities, wait to be photographed with the queen of a ball in New Orleans. One of the reasons the brain links the boys as a single unit is because they are sitting so close together.

Paul Martin Lester

Figure 5.3

*Continuation. A billboard for a Target department store in Adelaide, Australia demonstrates continuation as you continue the circles that make up the store's **logo** in your mind. This image also demonstrates that non-American advertisers can get away with more than American marketers.*

individual forms that make up a picture's content. Any analysis of an image should start by concentrating on those forms that naturally appear in any picture. Recall that color, form, depth, and movement all are basic characteristics of an image that the brain notices. Gestalt teaches a visual communicator to combine those basic elements into a meaningful whole. The approach also teaches the graphic artist to focus attention on certain elements by playing against the gestalt principles. For example, a company's logo (or trademark) will be noticed in an advertisement if it has a dissimilar shape, size, or location in relation to the other elements in the layout.

The work of gestalt theorists clearly shows that the brain is a powerful organ that classifies visual material in discrete groups. What we see when looking at a picture is modified by what we have seen in the past and what we want to see (Figure 5.8).

Constructivism

The gestalt approach had been criticized for describing perceptions rather than giving explanations of how these perceptions actually give meaning to an image. Consequently, several gestalt psychologists attempted to develop theories that helped explain the importance of the viewer's own mental state during active viewing.

In 1970, Julian Hochberg, a professor of psychology at Columbia University, found that the eyes of observers are constantly in motion as they scan an image. These quick focal fixations all combine within the viewer's short-term memory to help build a mental picture of a scene. The viewer constructs the scene with short-lived eye fixations that the mind combines into a whole picture. For Hochberg, the gestalt approach described a viewer as being too passive. In contrast, constructivism emphasizes the viewer's eye movements in an active state of perception.

Hochberg had his subjects use eye-tracking machines in his visual perception experiments. These devices can chart the way a viewer looks at an image. Because the fovea region of the eye is a tiny area, the eye constantly moves in order to maintain focus (Chapter 3). Eye-tracking machines simply made obvious the eyes' frenetic journey across a direct or mediated image.

Dr. Mario Garcia and Dr. Pegie Stark of the Poynter Institute in St. Petersburg, Florida, used an Eye-Trac testing machine to record on videotape the eye movements of participants as they read different versions of a newspaper. The researchers found that the content, size, and placement of photos on a newspaper page are more important than whether the image is printed in color.

Communications researcher Sheree Josephson of Weber State University, Utah, uses an eye-tracking device to record the eye movements of those viewing Web sites in order to gain insights into human physiology, psychology, and graphic design. In one study she had students make presidential choices with the controversial "butterfly" ballots of Palm Beach County, Florida, that were used during the 2000 presidential election. It was estimated that Vice President Al Gore may have lost at least 13,000 votes because of the confusing design. Josephson's analysis of eye-tracking results indicated that the ballot design did cause confusion (Figure 5.9).

Impossible objects are a good example of how constructivists analyze visual works (Figure 5.10). When first viewed, the drawing looks like an object with three horizontal poles. But when the mind attempts to assemble all the parts, it concludes that such an object would be difficult to reproduce in the real world.

Although vital in helping to explain the reason for the eyes' constant travels across an image, constructivism actually is only a minor clarification of the gestalt approach. The reason is that the link between the numerous eye fixations and past experiences locked within a person's memory in helping to explain a picture is never made clear.

■ *PERCEPTUAL THEORIES OF VISUAL COMMUNICATION*

The semiotics and cognitive approaches to visual perception may be considered content-driven or perceptual theories. Although recognizing that vision cannot happen without light illuminating, structuring, and sometimes creating perceptions, these three approaches stress that humans are unique in the animal kingdom because they assign complex meaning to the objects that they see.

■ *Semiotics*

The flag that is raised high above a football stadium and is watched reverently during the singing of the national anthem by those in the stands and on the field is a **sign**. The right hand placed over the approximate location of the heart during the singing of the anthem is a sign. The words printed in the program about the football players on the field are signs. The close-up photographs of players crouched and awaiting the snap of the ball during the game are signs. The officials' striped uniforms and their hand signals indicating penalties are signs. The illuminated numbers on the scoreboard are signs. Even the cleat marks in the sod after a running back's score are signs. The "high-five" slap with a friend after a team's touchdown is a sign. The simple silhouette drawing of a man above the men's room door is a sign. The green traffic light as you make your way home from the game is a sign (Figure 5.11).

Courtesy of the Medina County Gazette

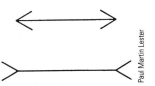

Paul Martin Lester

Figure 5.4

One of the most well known optical illusions is called the Muller-Lyer illusion. Two lines of equal length appear to be different lengths because of the addition of outward and inward arrows. The gestalt principle of continuation may help explain the effect. The brain naturally extends the length of the second line because the outward arrows continue the horizontal direction.

Figure 5.5 (left)

Common fate. Besides their similar shapes, the two cola bottles are linked graphically by their upward direction.

Figure 5.6 (below)

As you concentrate on the white area of a variation of the popular Peter and Paul Goblet *illusion, the cup becomes the foreground figure. Stare at the black shapes and the faces will appear.*

Paul Martin Lester

Figure 5.7

Edgar Rubin used the gestalt principles to draw conclusions about how foregrounds and backgrounds are identified— leading to camouflage clothing. In this photograph, the symmetrical shape, the curved form, the familiar subject, and the vertical orientation help identify the model and not the shadow as the foreground (or positive) shape.

Figure 5.8

The gestalt approach maintains that the "whole is different from the sum of its parts." This advertising photograph, which uses a montage effect to create excitement in the viewer's mind about the motorcycle, demonstrates that philosophy. A single image would be difficult for a viewer to interpret, but taken as a whole, the meaning is clear.

Sarah Wue

Kevin Keithley

A sign is simply anything that stands for something else. After reading the preceding list of signs you might well ask: What is *not* a sign? That is a good question because almost any action, object, or image will mean something to someone somewhere. Any physical representation, from a gesture to an orange jacket, is a sign if it has meaning beyond the object itself. Consequently, the meaning behind any sign must be learned. In other words, for something to be a sign, the viewer must understand its meaning. If you do not understand the meaning behind the orange color of a jacket, it isn't a sign for you.

Semiotics (called semiology in Europe) is the study or science of signs. Actually, it is the culmination of Aldous Huxley's anthem: The more you know, the more you see. Thus, images will be much more interesting and memorable if signs that are understood by many are used in a picture. The study of semiotics is vital because signs permeate every message. The academic study of semiotics attempts to identify and explain the signs used by every society in the world.

Although semiotics has gained popularity only recently, it is an old concept. In 397 C.E., Augustine, the Roman philosopher and linguist, first proposed the study of signs. He recognized that universally understood enti-

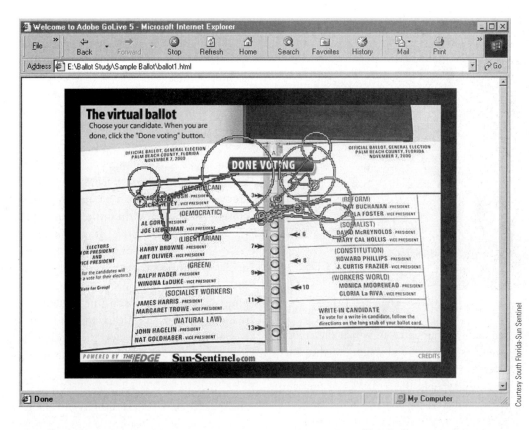

Figure 5.9

Using eye-tracking technology to study the eyes' path over Palm Beach County's "butterfly" ballot, researcher Sheree Josephson was able to determine by the location and size of circles (indicating the time of eye fixations) and lines (representing the eyes' path) that this subject "who was told to vote for Gore fixated frequently on the punch holes, indicating some level of confusion."

ties afforded communication on many nonverbal levels. For Augustine, signs were the link between nature and culture. The word *semiotics* comes from the language of his country: *Semeion* is the Greek word for sign.

Contemporary semiotics emerged through the work of two linguistic theorists just before World War I. Swiss linguist Ferdinand de Saussure developed a general theory of signs that was taken from notes by his students while he was a professor at the University of Geneva. At about the same time, American philosopher Charles Sanders Peirce published his own ideas about the effect of signs on society. These two philosophers inspired others to concentrate in this field of study. The Americans Arthur Asa Berger, Charles Morris, and Thomas Sebeok, the Italian Umberto Eco, the Frenchman Roland Barthes, and many others have contributed greatly to the study of semiotics.

Acceptance of Semiotics

Peirce and de Saussure weren't particularly interested in the visual aspects of signs. They were traditional linguists who studied the way words are used to communicate meaning through narrative structures. However, over the years semiotics has evolved into a theory of perception that involves the use of images in unexpected ways. For example, Sebeok identified some of the topics that semiotics researchers have studied. Besides the obvious subject of visual signs and symbols used in graphic design, they include the semiotics of the theater, where performance elements are analyzed; the

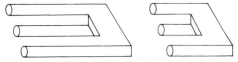

Modified after Carolyn Bloomer, *Principles of Visual Perception.* Design Press, 1990

Figure 5.10

Because the eyes do not have to scan a smaller image as much as a larger one, determining that the illustration at the right is an impossible object is easy. This conclusion is a result of Julian Hochberg's eye-fixation research.

AP/Wide World Photos

Figure 5.11

Examples of symbolic signs are easily spotted during a football game. Students from the University of Oklahoma support their team by painting their faces red and white.

semiotics of puppetry, in which the colors, costumes, gestures, and staging of the characters are studied; the semiotics of television and commercials; the semiotics of tourism; the semiotics of the signs used in Boy Scout uniforms and rituals; the semiotics of notational systems used in dance, music, logic, mathematics, and chemistry; and urban semiotics, in which cities are seen as social symbols. The field has become so popular that journals, international conferences, and academic departments at universities now are devoted to semiotics.

Three Types of Signs

Peirce's contribution to semiotics was in the formulation of three different types of signs: iconic, indexical, and symbolic. All signs must be learned, but the speed of comprehension of each type of sign varies.

Thinking about iconic, indexical, and symbolic signs is a way to really look and study a visual message in a much more thorough and critical way. Once this process is done, you soon realize that even the simplest image has complex cultural meaning. However, it is important to realize that the three

categories of signs—iconic, indexical, and symbolic—are not mutually exclusive. The written and visual examples given in this section are meant to focus your attention on one particular type of sign. Realize that any picture often has all three types represented at the same time.

Iconic Signs Iconic signs, or icons, from the Greek word *eikon*, which means image, are the easiest to interpret because they most closely resemble the thing they represent. Icons can be the simple drawings above restroom doors that communicate the gender allowed inside, the trashcan and "Recycle Bin" images on the desktops of many computers that mean to discard unwanted files, many street signs that clearly indicate a dangerous road condition, and the most common of all—photographs and motion pictures (Figure 5.12).

Indexical Signs Indexical signs have a logical, commonsense connection to the thing or idea they represent rather than a direct resemblance to the object (Figure 5.13). Consequently, their interpretation takes a little longer than that of icons. We learn indexical signs through everyday life experiences (Figure 5.14). Peirce used a sundial as an illustration of indexical signs. Other indexical signs can be a footprint on the beach or on the surface of the moon, smoke spewing out of a high smokestack or automobile exhaust pipe, and even the finding of fever in a sick patient. Footprints stand for the person who impressed them. Smoke represents the pollution generated by the furnace or engine. Fever indicates that the patient has an infection (Figure 5.15).

Symbolic Signs The third type of sign is the most abstract. Symbols have no logical or representational connection between them and the thing they represent. Symbols, more than the other types of signs, have to be taught (Figure 5.16). For that reason, social and cultural considerations influence them greatly. Words, numbers, colors, gestures, flags, costumes, most company logos, music, and religious images all are considered symbols (Figure 5.17). Because symbols often have deep roots in the culture of a particular group, with their meanings being passed from one generation to the next, symbolic signs usually evoke a stronger emotional response from viewers than do iconic or indexical signs (Figure 5.18).

Images—A Collection of Signs

Roland Barthes described the *chain of associations* or signs that make up a picture's narrative. In verbal language the narrative is linear. One word follows the next in a specific rule-based order. In that regard, verbal communication is considered discursive. Pictures, on the other hand, are presentational. Signs within an image are presented in various ways, many times depending on the style of the image-maker. Although the chain of signs is more tightly controlled with text than with images, one exception might be poetry, in which the order of the words can have nonlinear, presentation qualities. In fact, the Greek poet Simonides in about 500 B.C.E. wrote that paintings were "silent poetry and poetry painting that speaks."

The common term for Barthes's chain of associations is **codes.** Through its history and customs, a society develops a complex system of codes. Individual signs are thus combined to communicate complicated ideas in the form of these codes. Asa Berger suggests four types of codes: **metonymic,** analogical, displaced, and condensed.

A metonymic code is a collection of signs that cause the viewer to make associations or assumptions. A photograph in an advertisement that shows the signs of a living room

Arthur Rothstein, the Library of Congress

with expensive paintings on the walls, real wood paneling, richly upholstered furniture, subdued lighting, and a fire glowing under a mantle would communicate metonymically the prospect of romance or comfort for upper-class residents.

An analogical code is a group of signs that cause the viewer to make mental comparisons. Yellow writing paper might remind the author of the yellow peel of a lemon because of its similar color.

Displaced codes are those that transfer meaning from one set of signs to another. In the movie *Dr. Strangelove* (directed by Stanley Kubrick), rifles, missiles, airplanes, and other phallic shapes were photographed purposely to communicate the idea of sexual tension among certain military characters (Figure 5.19). Images of penises are not acceptable pictures for most members of society and so are displaced by other symbolism. Liquor, lipstick, and cigarette advertisers also commonly use phallic imagery in the form of their products' shapes in the hope that potential customers will link the use of their products with possible sexual conquest.

Figure 5.12

The image is an iconic sign because it represents what was in front of a camera's lens, but the cracked earth and bleached skull are indexical signs that mean the land has been without water for some time. The long shadow also is an indexical sign showing how low the sun is to the horizon. Furthermore, a cow's skull symbolizes the dire weather conditions experienced by many farmers during severe droughts in U.S. history.

Figure 5.13

This nineteenth-century line drawing presents good examples of an indexical sign. There are two possible sources for the smoke—a steam engine on the horse-drawn fire engine and a fire inside the house. But is there a blaze on the fire engine, and is the man at the window simply smoking a (rather large) cigar? Experience helps us decipher indexical signs. But as with all images, there are other signs to analyze. The photographic quality of the image makes it an iconic sign while the buildings, clothing, and horses are symbolic signs of an earlier age.

Uncensored Situations, 1966. The Dick Sutphen Studio, Inc.

Finally, condensed codes are several signs that combine to form a new, composite sign. Televised music videos and the advertisements inspired by them have unique and often unexpected meanings. The signs of musicians, dancers, music, quick editing techniques, graphics, colors, multiple images, and the like all form a complex message. Within the culture the message is intended for, the condensed code has relevant meaning. But for those outside that culture, the images often are confusing, random, and without purpose. The way individuals combine signs and form their own meaningful messages often cannot be controlled by the creators of the signs. This type of code is the most promising for a new mode of communication and is where most research in semiotics needs to take place.

Symbols often evoke strong emotional responses among viewers. The burning of a country's national flag as a protest gesture is a powerful symbol of defiance and anger. It isn't simply an act to create heat through the burning of a piece of fabric. Semiotics teaches the importance of symbolism in the act of visual perception and communication. A viewer who knows the meaning behind the signs used in a complex picture will gain insights from it, making the image more memorable. The danger of using complex signs as a part of an image is that they may be misunderstood, ignored, or interpreted in the wrong way. Nevertheless, the challenge for visual communicators, expressed in the study of semiotics, is that, when used correctly, signs can offer modes of communication previously unknown.

■ *Cognitive*

According to the cognitive approach, a viewer does not simply witness a light-structured object as in the gestalt theory, but actively arrives at a conclusion about the perception through mental operations.

Carolyn Bloomer identifies several mental activities that can affect visual perception: memory, projection, expectation, selectivity, **habituation, salience, dissonance,** culture, and words.

Memory

Arguably the most important mental activity involved in accurate visual perception, memory is our link with all the images we have ever seen. People have long used pictures as memory aids, or **mnemonics,** to help themselves recall certain events or long verbal passages. Simonides invented the first mnemonic system. While giving a performance of one of his lyrical poems at the home of a friend in about 500 B.C.E., he was called out of the room. Suddenly, the ceiling of the room he had just exited collapsed and killed several of the guests. Later, anxious relatives of the victims asked him the fate of their loved ones. Simonides was able to recall those who had been crushed by the stone roof by mentally re-creating the seating arrangement for those around the dinner table. This tragic experience led him to experiment with this form of mental exercise. He found that he could memorize long passages of his writings by dividing them into sections and mentally placing them within various rooms of an imagined house.

Modern-day mnemonic experts use absurd pictures to help people recall names, complex words, and important facts. For example, an image of a young girl sipping a soda through a thirty-foot straw might be a mnemonic for the state of Mississippi. Although many researchers do not actively study mnemonic systems, medical students regularly use them in trying to remember the many complicated medical terms they encounter in their studies.

Projection

Creative individuals see recognizable forms in the cornflakes floating in a bowl of milk in the morning. Others make sense out of cloud, tree, and rock formations or find comfort in the messages learned from **tarot cards,** astrological signs, and the I-Ching (Figure 5.20). One reason that psychologists use the common Rorschach inkblot test is that individuals often reveal personality traits by deriving meaning from the oddly formed shapes. A person's mental state of mind is thus "projected" onto an inanimate object or generalized statement. One person will walk past a tree trunk without the slightest hesitation. Another person will spend hours marveling at the humanlike face formed by the curves and shadows in the wood. The difference between the two individuals may be in the mental processes that affect what they see.

Expectation

When you walk into a living room, you may expect to see a couch, pictures on the wall, and perhaps a television set. If you have a strong mental picture of what should constitute a living room setting, you may fail to notice the typewriter that sits on a nearby card table. Having preconceived expectations about how a scene should appear often leads to false or missed visual perceptions (Figure 5.21).

Selectivity

Most of what people see within a complicated visual experience is not part of conscious processing. For example, rarely do people think about their own breathing unless consciously made aware of the process. Most of visual perception is an unconscious, automatic act by which large numbers of images enter and leave the mind without being processed. The mind focuses only on significant details within a scene. If you are trying to locate a friend sitting in the packed bleachers during a baseball game, all the other unknown faces in the crowd will have little significance. When you see your friend, your mind suddenly locks on that known appearance as if with the help of a spotlight in a darkened room.

Habituation

To protect itself from overstimulation and unnecessary pictures, as with selectivity, the mind tends to ignore visual stimuli that are a part of a person's everyday, habitual activities. When you walk or drive to school or work the same way every day, your brain doesn't really notice the sights along your route. People like to travel to new areas because the images experienced in an unfamiliar place often are striking and interesting. However, overstimulation, particularly if a culture is much different from the one left, can result in a phenomenon called culture shock. A person may grow irritable and tired if presented with too many visual sensations for the brain to filter.

Paul Martin Lester

Figure 5.14

A restaurant's napkin contains many signs. The lines emitting from the chicken pot pie illustration do not represent strings for a marionette (as my daughter when she was four years old assumed), but steam rising from the freshly baked entrèe—indexical signs indicating a hot, fresh meal. However, the steam is represented by vertical wavy lines, which we learn are symbols for freshness and heat. In addition, the picture of the pot pie itself is iconic while the words and typography used on the napkin are symbolic signs.

Figure 5.15 (top left)

This billboard advertisement displays a clear example of an indexical sign—a footprint in the sand is a sign that a human has walked on the beach.

Figure 5.16 (top right)

In Belfast, Northern Ireland, the UDA is the Ulster Defense Association, an ultraconservative paramilitary organization. The sans serif typeface urges the Irish hunger strikers in 1981 to starve themselves in the prison wing known as "H-Block." The cross used for the "I" in "DIE" is an ironic religious symbol when it is associated with this violent message.

Figure 5.17 (bottom left)

Clasped hands symbolize prayer or contemplation in many cultures. The unusually tight cropping of the top of the image emphasizes the importance of the gesture by a doctor who treats young patients who have been paralyzed by gunshots.

Figure 5.18 (bottom right)

A black cloth over the head of a person symbolizes death in many cultures. In reality, this man is avoiding the sun on the boardwalk of Atlantic City.

Generally, we are ambivalent about visual stimulation. On the one hand, we enjoy new experiences. On the other hand, we do not enjoy too many of them. One way to prevent your mind from thinking habitually is to search constantly for new ways to think about familiar objects or events. Practicing creative thought readies your mind to think actively about new images when you see them.

Salience

A stimulus will be noticed more if it has meaning for the individual. If you recently met someone you like whose favorite food is from India, whenever you smell curry or hear other people talking about the country, you will be reminded of that person. A person who is hungry will notice the smells of cooking food emanating from an open window. A trained biologist will see more in a slide under a microscope than the average

person will; both individuals see all there is to see under the microscope, but what the biologist sees is consciously processed in the mind. Shapes and colors have more meaning for an artist.

Dissonance

Trying to read with a television or stereo loudly playing in the same room is difficult because the mind really can concentrate on only one activity or the other. A book is set aside the moment a television program or the lyrics of a song become interesting. As with Rubin's face or vase drawing, concentration is limited to one activity at a time. Television programs that combine written and spoken words, multiple images, and music run the risk of creating visual messages that the viewer cannot understand because of all the competing formats.

A classic example of dissonance comes from the cable network CNN, which introduced in August 2001 its new version of the 1982 staple, "Headline News." Television critics across the country voiced their negative opinion about the new format because of all the competing bits of information—an anchorperson talking on camera or as a voice-over, still and/or moving images, graphics with headlines, stock details, weather reports, and advertising logos, all within the confines of the television screen (Figure 5.22). However, many viewers have praised what has been called a "newer, hipper look."

In addition, if a room is too warm or too cold, if someone is speaking to you, or if there is a personal matter that you cannot stop thinking about, you will find it difficult to concentrate on a visual message.

Culture

As a manifestation of the way people act, talk, dress, eat, drink, behave socially, and practice their religious beliefs, cultural influences have a tremendous impact on visual perception. Religious icons, state and country flags, T-shirt designs, and hairstyles all have individual and cultural meanings. If you are aware of the signs that are a part of a particular culture (such as those presented in the section on semiotics) you also will comprehend some of the underlying reasons behind their use. Culture isn't simply the concept of a country's borders or the idea of high-class or upper-class "culture." Culture spans ethnicity, economic situation, place of work, gender, age, sexual orientation, physical disability, geographic location, and many other aspects of a person's life. Culture also determines the importance of the signs that affect people who live in that culture.

Words

Although we see with our eyes, for the most part our conscious thoughts are

© 2002 The Museum of Modern Art

Figure 5.19

Stanley Kubrick's Dr. Strangelove, Or How I Learned to Stop Worrying and Love the Bomb *is a classic study of the displaced code. The missile that actor Slim Pickens rides to his doom at the end of the movie is the ultimate phallic symbol. In this publicity still, Pickens poses on the nuclear warhead prop.*

Figure 5.20

Tarot cards are an example of the mental activity known as projection. They are one of the many symbol systems that people use to help them discover traits about their personalities or look into the future. After the illustrated cards are shuffled, a reader familiar with their symbolism explains their meaning.

Shirley Chan

Figure 5.21

Expectation is a mental condition that leads to poor visual perception. A casual viewer would most likely overlook a photograph of boys mugging for the camera. However, the viewer's attention is drawn to the image when these Belfast boys proudly display their hidden knives. Suddenly, the viewer is shocked out of an expected scene.

Paul Martin Lester

framed as words. Consequently, words, like memory skills and culture, profoundly affect our understanding and subsequent long-term recall of a direct or mediated image. One of the strongest forms of communication is when words and images are combined in equal proportions.

■ *Clear Seeing Is a Human Activity*

Semiotics and cognitive approaches to visual communication state that the human mind is an infinitely complex living organism that science may never fully understand. But meaningful connections between what people see and how they use those images arise when mental processing is viewed as a human rather than a mechanical process.

DISCUSSION AND EXERCISE IDEAS

- Show a small, cropped portion of an image and lead a discussion about it. Now reveal the entire image and talk about the differences in meaning and content between the two views.

- Select any photograph and isolate all of the iconic, indexical, and symbolic signs you can find.

- Pick an advertising image out of a magazine and discuss the ad's content in terms of semiotics codes.

- Bring to class a copy of a visual symbol that has special significance for you. Share your picture in small groups and then with the entire class.

- Think of all the ways you might be distracted from seeing anything clearly.

INFOTRAC COLLEGE EDITION ASSIGNMENTS

- With "Subject guide" checked, type "Gestalt Principles" in the search area and read of the experiment using gestalt principles to improve memory by David S. Wallace, et al. Try to replicate the experiment with other students in your class or come up with your own ideas of using gestalt principles to improve a person's memory.

- With "Subject guide" checked, type "Dr. Strangelove" in the search area and read the review of Margot A. Henriksen's book *Dr. Strangelove's America: Society and Culture in the Atomic Age* by Michael McGuckin. Go to your local video store and rent the movie. Make a note of all the examples of displaced codes in the form of phallic symbols in the film. Keeping in mind Henriksen's critique, what do you think the use of such code says about American society in the 1960s?

Go to the Web site for this book at www.wadsworth.com/product/0534562442 to find more Web links on this subject.

Figure 5.22

With no point of visual impact, a typical highway scene becomes a study of dissonance as cars, street signs and advertising billboards compete for a viewer's attention.

AP/Wide World Photos

THE ETHICS OF WHAT WE SEE

Visual messages are a powerful form of communication because they stimulate both intellectual and emotional responses—they make us think as well as feel. Consequently, images can be used to persuade and to perpetuate ideas that words alone cannot. When controlled by economic interests and corporate considerations, pictures can be powerful tools to persuade people to buy a particular product or think a specific way. Any viewer or producer of visual messages must be aware of the ways that pictures are used to convince others of a certain point of view.

A creator of images also has an ethical and moral responsibility to ensure, for example, that a picture is a fair, accurate, and complete representation of someone from another culture. Too often, however, that knowledge is gained after an image causes harm. Fortunately, sensitivity and knowledge about other cultures can give you an understanding of the correct use of pictures.

VISUAL PERSUASION IN ADVERTISING, PUBLIC RELATIONS, AND JOURNALISM

By the end of this chapter you should know:

- The uses and abuses of shock advertising.
- How the Benetton clothing company uses the media for additional advertising.
- The difference between persuasion and propaganda.
- How visual persuasion is used in advertising, public relations, and journalism.

A newborn baby lying alone with umbilical cord still attached, two horses mating, a priest kissing a nun romantically on the lips, an AIDS victim on his deathbed, sensitive portraits of death row inmates—the connection between these striking images is not readily apparent. Nevertheless, there is one. The pictures have all been used as advertisements to sell colorful, large-weave sweaters for the Benetton clothing chain. They have also generated an enormous amount of controversy in newspapers, magazines, and television news reports throughout the world (Figure 6.1).

As the old saying goes, "Any publicity is good publicity." For even though most of the news articles and televised reports about the advertising campaigns were negative, business boomed. Luciano Benetton, 66, sells about 100 million sweaters, shirts, and other articles of clothing through some 7,000 outlets in 120 countries. Total sales in 2001 were more than $4 billion.

But the strategy of using shocking images to generate editorial condemnation backfired when the company went too far and executives of a large U.S. retail chain decided to remove Benetton sweaters from

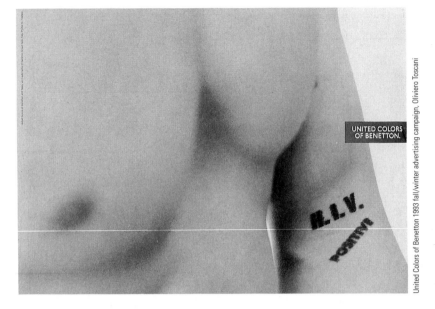

UNITED COLORS
OF BENETTON.

Figure 6.1

*An AIDS reference in this
studio photograph using a
male model provoked protests
from various Jewish groups
upset over the use of a tattoo
that resembled a Holocaust
victim's markings.*

their shelves. Benetton apologized and
promptly terminated the employment of
Oliviero Toscani, who had been the creative
director for the advertising campaigns for
the past eighteen years.

■ *SHOCK ADVERTISING*

Because of photography's ability to arouse
interest, pictures are sometimes used to
shock potential customers. A young Brooke
Shields probably began the manifestation of
"soft porn" advertisements when she posed
in tight-fitting Calvin Klein jeans in 1980
and cooed, "Nothing comes between me and
my Calvins." Although a risky marketing
strategy, commercial interests recognized the
impact of images to shock viewers, and then
obtained free publicity because of the controversial ad campaigns, which generated
sales.

In fact, Calvin Klein has consistently used
shock advertising as a way of generating
enormous controversy and publicity. A
$6 million campaign was withdrawn in 1996

after a public outcry over the teenage boys
and girls featured in sexually provocative
poses photographed by Stephen Meisel, who
took pictures of Madonna for her 1992 book
Sex.

Shock advertising can make a little-
known company a media standout. For
example, Diesel, an Italian jeans manufacturer, was criticized for its campaign featuring guns pointed at the viewer along with
the copy, "How to teach your children to
love and care." The communications director for Benetton, North America, Peter Fressola, defended the Diesel advertisements,
saying, "Jeans are about sex and danger. And
the people who are offended by these ads are
probably not Diesel customers anyway."
Nevertheless, the ads were quickly with-
drawn from many magazines—but sales of
the jeans doubled because of the controversy they inspired. Shockingly violent or
sexual images used in ads are the culmination of corporate cynicism in which almost
any sensational still or moving image is justified if it gets the attention of potential customers. In 1999 an advertisement for a Sony
PlayStation game was banned in many
countries because it featured a body in a
mortuary.

But not all shock advertising is used for
commercial reasons. Barnardo's, a London-
based charity that works with more than
50,000 children and their families in more
than 300 projects across Great Britain, is
known for its striking and controversial
campaigns. In 2000, an ad showed a baby
about to inject heroin (Figure 6.2). Their latest campaign features five death and suicide
scenes. One poster shows the legs of a fictional victim lying on the bloody floor of a
grimy parking garage (Figure 6.3). The copy
reads: "From the age of three, Jane was
neglected and a large part of her died. Her
hope and self-esteem died. Her future died.
19 years later, after being lured into prostitu-

tion, she was beaten so badly by her Pimp she died for real. What a waste." One newspaper group rejected the ads as too shocking. Nevertheless, donations grew by 5 percent, while surveys showed public awareness of the charity had doubled. Andrew Nebel, director of marketing and communications at Barnardo's, said, "Our new adverts reflect the harsh reality of the work we do. We live in a crowded media world and, as a charity, we have little money to spend. We have to make sure it works." If Benetton were a charitable organization, criticism of their advertising campaigns would probably be much more muted.

■ ADVERTISEMENTS AND SOCIAL ISSUES

Benetton's target audience has always been young (18- to 24-year-olds), perhaps more socially conscious clothing buyers than other age groups. Beginning in 1989, Benetton used photographs in catalogs, store posters, and billboards to promote the company's ideal of multicultural harmony. In all the advertising pictures, the only copy on the page was that of the Benetton logo. Images of a black woman breast-feeding an Anglo baby, a black child resting on several white teddy bears, a close-up of black and white hands cuffed together, and a black and a white child sitting side by side on matching toilets symbolically emphasized racial harmony and equivalence. But a close analysis of a typical example from this campaign—a white man kissing a black woman—reveals a *white* version of racial harmony that is demeaning (Figure 6.4). Dr. Bette Kauffman, a professor at the University of Louisiana at Monroe, writes, "The black woman's face is completely confined, contained, imprisoned by the white man's hands and forceful kiss. Indeed, for his hand to cover her forehead

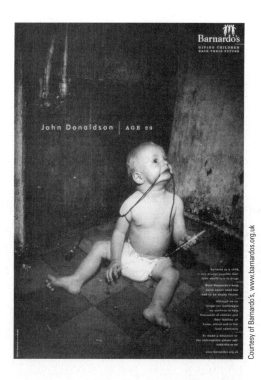

Courtesy of Barnardo's, www.barnardos.org.uk

Figure 6.2

"John Donaldson Age 23." With harsh lighting and tilted frame amid a stark and dingy backdrop, the baby shocks a viewer and potential donor to the charity by its striking reality. The child is a model.

Figure 6.3

See color section following page 132.

like that, he has to have her entire head trapped in his left arm. This would be a problematic image if the woman were white! The goofy 'smile' on her face does nothing to combat the impression that she had no say in this matter."

In 1991, the advertising campaign switched to more overtly political images. One ad showed a picture of several rows of crosses in a cemetery. The ad was banned in Italy, France, Britain, and Germany. Arab countries refused to print a picture of black, white, and Asian children sticking their tongues out at the camera. Members of the Catholic Church were outraged that a picture of a priest and nun kissing on the lips was used in an advertisement (Figure 6.5). During this era, though, no picture received as much attention as that of a child photographed fresh from the womb of her mother, covered in blood and with the umbilical cord still attached. This shockingly realistic image was printed large on billboards, but banned in Italy and Britain.

United Colors of Benetton 1991 spring/summer advertising campaign, Oliviero Toscani

UNITED COLORS OF BENETTON.

Figure 6.4

Benetton has long maintained that its advertising campaigns attract attention and promote racial harmony. But the image was criticized as it reveals a demeaning, "white" view of how people from different races should interact.

Never one to rest on previous publicity-seeking achievements, creative director Toscani embarked on other Benetton campaigns that used previously published news photographs. The long list of disturbing images without context or explanation included a woman sobbing over the bloody body of a Mafia victim (published only in Italy), a mercenary soldier holding high the thigh bone of a human, the image of Albanian refugees escaping on an Italian ship, a red-eyed duck coated with oil after a recent spill, a Zulu woman with albinism who appeared embarrassed next to two brown-skinned women who appear to shun her, an Indian couple wading through flood waters, South American children working as laborers, a man sprawled on the ground while being forced to submit to a radio interview by men on top of him, and the picture that has been called "the most shocking photo used in an ad," David Kirby surrounded by family members shortly before his death due to AIDS (Figure 6.6).

Taken by Ohio University student Therese Frare, the image was published in *Life* magazine. Benetton executives first saw the picture after it had won the Budapest

Award and second place in the general news category for the prestigious World Press Photo contest. Frare had been photographing in the Pater Noster House in Columbus, a hospice-approach home, where Kirby received treatment. Kirby allowed her to take pictures of him that were to accompany a story for a school project. Their relationship eventually led to the moving, deathbed image that caused little reaction as an editorial picture in *Life*. Kirby's parents, Bill and Kay, gave permission to Benetton to use the image in its ad campaign because they thought it would raise AIDS awareness around the world. Benetton executives donated $50,000 to the Pater Noster House to furnish and renovate the facilities.

David Kirby was from Stafford, Ohio, a small town of only ninety-four residents. Lured by the prospects of a better life, he traveled west after high school and eventually ended up in California. He soon lost touch with his family. But after contracting AIDS, Kirby telephoned his parents and asked if he could return home. He wanted to die with family members around him. They immediately welcomed him back. His return to the town, however, caused panic among many residents uneducated about the disease. The emergency workers who took him to the hospital later burned everything in the ambulance that Kirby had touched. Schoolchildren screamed in horror about an "AIDS monster" living near them. But Kirby didn't shrink from the cruel characterizations. He often went door to door to educate neighbors about him and AIDS. As an AIDS activist, he did much to calm the fears of Stafford's residents.

When the disease progressed to its inevitable conclusion, Kirby (then thirty-two) was at the hospice-approach home with his family. At the moment of his death, Frare took the picture of Kirby surrounded by his father, sister Susan, and niece Sarah openly weeping over the loss of their loved one. His mother was in the next room crying. The picture is a riveting moment in which a family faced with unspeakable tragedy is united by their grief. Barb Cordle, who is the volunteer director at the Pater Noster House and who helped care for Kirby, said that "the picture in the ad has done more to soften people's hearts on the AIDS issue than any other I have ever seen. You can't look at that picture and hate a person with AIDS. You just can't."

But others, particularly AIDS activists, cannot look at the picture and not feel horror, anger, and outrage over the image being used in an advertisement. They cite the use of the picture as another example of a large corporation exploiting a personal tragedy to sell a product. They wonder why a phone number for AIDS information could not be included in the ad if an 800 number was printed so that customers could obtain the company's new catalog. Critics ask whether using such an emotionally powerful image for commercial purposes without any written copy in the advertisement to explain the meaning of the picture is ever morally acceptable.

The picture generated much discussion about shock advertising on television talk shows and in newspaper and magazine articles. Unfortunately, the controversy over the image has swirled around its use in the advertisement. Such a narrow discussion ignores the fact that Frare's image is a brilliant example of **decisive moment** photojournalism. Because of all the media attention, more than 1 billion people around the world probably have seen the Kirby family scene. But interest in the controversy doesn't necessarily mean that more people have become educated about AIDS around the world.

Fressola of Benetton asserts that the reason for the ad campaign is to make people

United Colors of Benetton 1991 spring/summer advertising campaign, Oliviero Toscani

think, to get them to talk about serious issues, and to promote worldwide multiculturalism. Toscani also wants to expand the way advertisements are used. He believes that ads can be used to inform and spark commentary about serious issues. "Advertising can be used to say something that is real about things that exist," says Toscani. Both Fressola and Toscani admit that they also want to create advertising that breaks traditional banal presentations in order to focus more attention on the company (Figure 6.7). Without doubt the campaign has been a tremendous success. Estimated worldwide sales jumped 10 percent, or by more than $100 million, from 1991 to 1992 during the controversy.

Figure 6.5

Two models employed by Benetton wear the clothing of a priest and nun who kiss for the camera in this studio image. Many Catholics were upset by the image because it seemed to mock their religious beliefs.

Figure 6.6

See color section following page 132.

■ END OF AN ERA FOR BENETTON?

But it was a recent campaign that caused Benetton to rethink the philosophy behind shock advertising.

In January 2000 Benetton initiated a $20 million campaign in an issue of *Talk* magazine. It contained a ninety-six-page booklet

Figure 6.7

In another effort to communicate important social issues, not be quite so "shocking," and to no doubt sell more clothing, in 2001, in collaboration with the United Nations' "International Year of Volunteers," Benetton began a new press and billboard campaign. Typical of the graphic look and content of the ads is a portrait of Tajidin Agah, an Afghan working in a Pakistani refugee camp.

entitled "We, on Death Row." With the bright green Benetton logo interspersed on several pages, photographer Oliviero Toscani posed twenty-six death row inmates from across the United States like models. However, none wore Benetton clothing (Figure 6.7). They simply answered questions about their favorite foods, activities, their mothers, and fear of execution. Benetton expressed hope that the campaign, which included billboards and pages in other national magazines, would draw attention to the issue of executions in America. But many were outraged, including the families of those killed by the inmates. Benetton was accused of glamorizing the murderers while ignoring their crimes.

One couple who was outraged decided to fight back. Donata and Emery Nelson saw the image of Victor Dewayne Taylor on a billboard. Taylor kidnapped, sodomized, and murdered their teenage son along with his friend. The Nelsons started a petition and began picketing branches of the Sears department store that had recently begun selling Benetton clothing. Donata Nelson explained, "I know they have strange ads for Benetton, but how low can they go? They've

sunk about as low as the men on death row." Sears executives canceled the multimillion-dollar deal with Benetton and quit selling its clothing in about 800 outlets. In addition, the attorney general of Missouri, Jay Nixon, filed a lawsuit against the company alleging that Benetton misrepresented its intent when gaining access to four murderers within a Missouri prison.

Faced with an enormous blitz of unfavorable publicity and a trial, Benetton paid $50,000 to a fund for victims of crimes in Missouri. Benetton also sent letters to the families of victims of the Missouri inmates in which the company expressed its regret for any renewed pain the campaign may have caused them. The case never went to trial. Nevertheless, defending the campaign, Benetton said, "We wanted to attack the policy of the death penalty. We knew that a debate could emerge from our advertising but nevertheless we wanted to test and see what type of debate would emerge. A debate, as with our previous AIDS pictures, emerged." And after eighteen years of a controversial, yet creative partnership, Oliviero Toscani and Benetton parted ways. Toscani is now, perhaps not surprisingly, a contributing photographer for *Talk* magazine.

The lesson from the Benetton case is that perhaps a company can go too far in seeking publicity for itself—maybe too much bad publicity is not a good thing after all.

■ *THE FINE LINE BETWEEN PERSUASION AND PROPAGANDA*

Regardless of how you assign motives to actions, the Benetton campaigns that use editorial pictures in advertisements that generate enormous publicity highlight an important feature of **mass communication:** The fields of advertising, public relations, and journalism always have been closely related. Each one uses persuasive techniques in varying degrees to support existing **opinions,** change **attitudes,** and cause actions by those who view their output. The overt blurring between corporate and editorial interests is one of the most pressing concerns of media critics today.

Through everyday experiences, a person acquires a certain set of **beliefs** and attitudes about other people, places, objects, and issues. Perhaps as a youth you were punished by a high school principal and thus dislike all persons in authority. Maybe you have heard that Mexico City has high pollution levels, so you never want to visit it. Perhaps your father doesn't like to eat broccoli and so neither do you. Maybe someone you admire opposes capital punishment, influencing you to adopt that same attitude. A belief is the information that people have about another person or a place, object, or issue that forms or changes their attitudes. Attitudes are general and long-lasting positive or negative feelings about people, places, objects, or issues. If information is limited or its source isn't trusted, a belief can become an enduring attitude that can lead to stereotypical generalizations (discussed in Chapter 7).

The goal of education is to teach an individual how to seek factual information and base reasoned conclusions on those data. Persuasion uses factual information and emotional appeals to change a person's mind and to promote a desired behavior. In contrast, propaganda uses one-sided and often nonfactual information or opinions that appear to be facts, along with emotional appeals, to change a person's mind and promote a desired behavior.

Most information, whether factual or not, is communicated through the mass media. More and more, that information relies on the emotional appeal inherent in visual presentations. In *Public Opinion,* Walter Lippmann stressed the need for images to change a person's attitude. "Pictures have always been the surest way of conveying an idea," wrote Lippmann, "and next in order, words that call up pictures in memory." Recognizable symbols used in visual presentations will become long-lasting memories with the power to change attitudes if viewers have a chance to actively think about the content of the image and relate it to their own situation. "Unless that happens," added Lippmann, the picture "will interest only a few for a little while. It will belong to the sights seen but not felt, to the sensations that beat on our sense organs, and are not acknowledged."

All human communication—whether advertising layouts, lectures from parents and professors, closing arguments by lawyers in a trial, or campaign speeches—uses persuasion and propaganda in an attempt to mold or change a listener's or viewer's attitude. Communications educator James Carey says that "communication is fundamentally and essentially a matter of persuasion, attitude change, behavior modification, and socialization through the transmission of information."

■ *The Role of Persuasion*

In the fourth century B.C.E., Aristotle was the first to write about the art of persuasion. He defined it as communication designed to influence listeners' choices. According to Aristotle, persuasion has three components: **ethos, logos,** and **pathos.** Ethos refers to a source's **credibility.** Logos refers to the logical arguments used to persuade an individual. Pathos refers to emotional appeals used in the persuasive argument. Aristotle believed that, if a speaker is believable or imbued with authority, uses factual arguments in a reasoned presentation, and gains an audience's attention through emotional means, persuasion is possible.

Persuasion is a socially accepted way of attempting to change individuals' attitudes. In a pluralistic, democratic society, the government most commonly attempts to persuade the public through an independent press. When the president introduces a new budget, the government mobilizes its huge public relations bureaucracy to "sell" the plan to Congress and the American people. The president and the administration use the print and broadcast media to present their ideas. Such a system naturally leads to tension between the government and the media, as both groups compete for the public's attention, but ultimately it is the best check of a government's truthfulness.

■ *The Role of Propaganda*

The word *propaganda* started out as a neutral term, without negative connotation. It simply meant a way to spread an idea to a large population. In the seventeenth century, the Roman Catholic Church set up the *Congregation for Propagating the Faith* as an effort to bring more members into the church. Subsequently, its use by governments intent on conveying their version of the truth to friends and enemies alike has given the term a pejorative connotation that can't be ignored. Whereas persuasion is the gentle art of convincing someone that your position is correct through factual information, propaganda is thought of as the duping of an unsuspecting public through misleading or false information.

Various authors have contributed to the negative connotation that the word now bears. The British author and poet, F. M. Cornford, defined it as "that branch of the art of lying which consists in very nearly deceiving your friends without quite deceiving your enemies." Terence Qualter, the author of *Advertising and Democracy in the Mass Age,* wrote that propaganda is "the

deliberate attempt by the few to influence the attitudes and behavior of the many by the manipulation of symbolic communication." The word has long been associated with the thought-control techniques used by totalitarian regimes, but critics have expanded the definition to include many of the persuasion techniques utilized by all governments and large corporations to persuade an unsuspecting public. Nicholas Pronay, a professor at the Institute of Communications Studies at the University of Leeds, said that propaganda is "what practical people are paid to do, in practical ways, to achieve practical objectives; that is, to make people do something they would not otherwise have done."

Media personnel do not like to use the word because it is closely related to their jobs as persuasive communicators. Sociologist Harold Lasswell said that "both advertising and publicity fall within the field of propaganda." Media critic John Merrill enlarged the definition to include journalism, saying that "three-fourths of all media content . . . contains propaganda for some cause, idea, institution, party or person." In the end, the best definition may be that propaganda is the use of spoken, written, pictorial, or musical representations to influence thought and action through debatable techniques. In many ways, the difference between persuasion and propaganda is simply the social definition of the words.

■ *VISUAL PERSUASION IN ADVERTISING*

Media critic and educator Everette Dennis defines advertising as "any form of nonpersonal presentation and promotion of ideas, goods, and services by an identified sponsor." The advertising industry in the United States employs about 200,000 people and generates more than $100 billion in annual billings. According to Dennis, advertising benefits society because it funds most of the media, provides consumer information in the form of public service announcements, and stimulates the economy (Figure 6.8).

There are two major types of advertising: commercial and noncommercial. In newspapers and magazines, commercial advertising appears most frequently as either classified or display advertisements. In classified ads, readers actively search a separate section of the publication for goods and services desired. Display advertising uses graphic elements to attract attention to the content of the ads and the products or services offered. Classified advertising usually lacks the persuasive appeal of display advertising. In television, cable channels that show inexpensively produced slides for companies are the classified ad equivalent. All other television advertising is display in nature.

Noncommercial advertising includes government notices and information and public service announcements (PSAs). The Advertising Council, a national association concerned with ethical advertising practices, usually arranges to produce these messages. PSAs include short advertisements that might urge safe sexual practices and racial harmony. The Barnardo's campaigns fall in this category.

■ *Advertising Controversial Tactics*

The purpose of an advertisement is to attract attention, arouse interest, stimulate desire, create an opinion, and move the viewer to a specific action (to buy the product). Visual messages are essential components of advertisements. Well-crafted images with their inherent emotional qualities can produce all the motivational changes desired of customers by advertisers when carefully combined with well-chosen words.

Paul Martin Lester

But the story of the advertising profession is largely one in which motives for messages are questioned, criticized, and sometimes regulated.

In 1912, Congress passed the Newspaper Publicity Law that required all printed matter published for the purpose of making money to be identified as an "Advertisement" somewhere in the ad because of concern that unsophisticated readers might not know the difference between a news story and an advertisement. Beginning in the 1920s, ads featured photographs because newspapers were using photographs. When combined with testimonials, realistic scenes, and layout styles that mimicked news pages, ads could be produced to fool readers.

The trend toward masking advertisements as entertainment or informational programs continues unabated. **Infomercials,** which resemble talk-show programs, are long-form advertisements that pitch hair care products, new inventions, and diet plans, have attractive hosts, and pay enthusiastic audience members to clap loudly. In print, the equivalent is called **advertorials.** A Benetton campaign that was designed to resemble a news story is an excellent example.

Figure 6.8

As with the Benetton image of David Kirby, the advertising photograph for the Kenar clothing company is meant to alert the public about AIDS. But what is the connection between supermodel Linda Evangelista, seven older women wearing black dresses, an empty wooden chair, and the AIDS issue? The striking image attracts attention, but says nothing about AIDS to most people walking along Times Square in New York City.

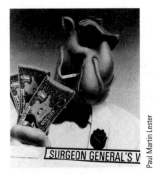

Figure 6.9

Although denied by R. J. Reynolds Tobacco Company officials, the cartoon character Joe Camel has been criticized for enticing young people to smoke by making the habit look fun and sophisticated.

In the 1920s, critical opinions of advertising's motives emerged. Critics voiced concern that advertisements were directed to those with money, excluding the poor, ethnic minorities, and other disenfranchised groups. Advertising seemed to be a mirror that reflected the shortcomings of a society in which class differences are highlighted and showcased. For example, women used as models during this period were tall and slender. Such physical attributes became associated with class and activity: Angular-shaped women were "on the move" and rejected women's traditional roles. The conflict between the reality of women's body shapes (in 1928, only 17 percent of all American women were thin and over five feet three inches tall) and the shape seen in the advertisements continues to the present. Through rigorous exercise and potentially dangerous diet programs, many women force themselves to be slender like the models in advertisements.

In 1952, the National Association of Broadcasters (NAB), urged by the concerns voiced by the Federal Communications Commission (FCC), which regulates broadcasting, established guidelines for television programming and advertisements. Ad content had to be truthful, in good taste, and fair. However, advertisements in publications and on television during the 1950s perpetuated the illusion that America was filled with confident and successful Anglo men with supportive and desirable women at their sides ready to do their bidding.

By the 1970s, the trade journal *Advertising Age* was beginning to receive letters to the editor complaining about the sexist attitudes portrayed in advertisements. Consumer complaints about commercial advertising also brought an end to cigarette advertising on television, although it still is permitted in print advertisements. Complaints also ended

the career of "Joe Camel," the brightly colored, sunglasses-wearing cartoon camel spokesperson for Camel cigarettes. In 1991, R. J. Reynolds Tobacco Company was publicly charged in the *Journal of the American Medical Association* with targeting children through its Joe Camel cartoon campaign. Critics claimed that the cartoon illustrations appealed to children, who were attracted by the brightly colored drawings. A survey at the time of one group of schoolchildren showed that Joe Camel, because of the aggressive advertising campaign, was recognized more often than Mickey Mouse (Figure 6.9). A lawsuit was filed against the tobacco company for using the cartoon image to attract children to smoking. In 1997 Reynolds settled the lawsuit and terminated the advertising campaign.

Product Placements

Subliminal or hidden advertising is the practice of showing images so quickly on a screen that the conscious mind doesn't notice them, yet the unconscious mind, it is hoped, does. It is thought that even if not noticed, these messages can influence people. It became a popular source for concern because of Vance Packard's 1957 book *The Hidden Persuaders* and gained new ground in the 1970s with Wilson Key's book, *Media Sexploitation*. Movie theater owners were accused of using subliminal messages to sell soda and popcorn while liquor company executives were said to have hidden the word "sex" and naked women in ice cubes to sell their products. Subliminal advertising has been largely discredited and it has never been proved that it works.

However, that doesn't stop some advertising art directors from trying. Most recently, the FCC investigated complaints from two Democratic senators about a political advertisement that was produced by the Republican National Committee during the 2000 presidential campaign. In the commercial Vice President Al Gore is criticized for his proposal to add a prescription drug benefit to Medicare. When the word *bureaucrats* flashes across the screen, the word *rats* appears in large type for one-thirtieth of a second (Figure 6.10). After communicating with 179 television stations that broadcast the advertisement, the FCC decided that no penalty was warranted because 162 stations said they were not aware of the hidden message. Although there are no laws against using subliminal advertising techniques, television stations and advertisers can be fined for doing so. Then presidential candidate George W. Bush said that the use of subliminal messages in advertising is "not acceptable."

Products in motion pictures and on television are supposed to be noticed. Although they take up much of a producer's time, lucrative placement deals can offset some production costs. The producers of *E.T.: The Extra-Terrestrial* initially offered the makers of M&Ms the chance to be the main character's favorite candy, but Hershey officials declined the offer. Sales of Reese's Pieces candies increased by 65 percent after moviegoers watched E.T. follow the candy trail. Seagram's, the parent company for Mumm's champagne, paid $50,000 for Cher to drink that brand in the movie *Moonstruck.* General Motors paid to have Tom Cruise drive Chevrolet Luminas in *Days of Thunder* (Figure 6.11). Disney offered a sliding scale to advertisers for their little-seen film *Mr. Destiny.* Simply showing the product on the screen cost $20,000. But if a main character actually used the product, a $60,000 fee was demanded and received.

The Miller Brewing Co. is particularly adept at product placements. Out of the top 100 box office hits of 2000, 45 of the movies included characters drinking beer. Miller products, according to a spokesperson, were in 24 of those movies. In the 2001 movie *Pearl Harbor,* the main characters are all drinking Miller High Life before the Japanese attack. But other products were featured in the film as well. When nurses were scrambling to find containers to store donated blood, Coca-Cola bottles were used.

One reason product placements are becoming more popular on television

Figure 6.10

Although the practice of slipping a hidden message within moving film is discredited as an advertising gimmick, a Republican National Committee ad attacking Al Gore's prescription drug program for seniors used the technique to link governmental bureaucrats with rats. The political ad was widely criticized. (Left) A frame shows the ad without the hidden message. (Right) The hidden message is seen when the ad is stopped.

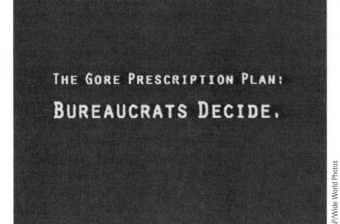

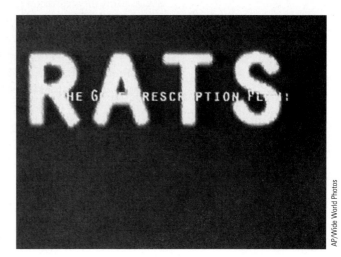

AP/Wide World Photos

AP/Wide World Photos

Figure 6.11

General Motors paid the producers of the movie Days of Thunder *thousands of dollars to have the Chevrolet name and Lumina automobile prominently displayed in the film.*

Getty Images/Hulton Archive

programs is the nature of new technology. Digital video recorders (DVRs) such as those made by TiVo allow viewers to avoid traditional commercials. As more and more consumers use the device, advertisers have to find clever ways to plug their products. Producers for reality television game shows such as "Survivor," "Big Brother," and "Temptation Island" have "product integration" deals with companies to show off their products. For example, contestants on "Survivor" were rewarded products from Reebok and Target.

Digital imaging technology is being used to place products into old television shows. Princeton Video Image Inc., the company that created the imaginary first down line for televised football games, now produces "virtual ads" for marketers. Besides being able to place ads only the television audience can see behind goal posts, home plate, and on NASCAR racetracks, the technology can be used to put products in scenes. Imagine a

rerun of "Cheers" in which the characters drink Miller beer.

Clever Web site marketers are using a variety of methods to get their advertising message noticed. In a variation of the advertorial, display or banner advertisements on many Web sites are often masked as editorial content. When an unsuspecting user clicks on words or pictures, a link is made to a traditional commercial pitch. And taking a lesson from many pornographic Web sites where they were first introduced, "pop up" and "pop under" windows automatically advertise products and services when a user visits a Web site (see Chapter 16). Pop up windows appear over the intended information while pop under windows are placed under the Web site. You see them after you think you have closed down your browser. Although sometimes highly annoying, these types of windows are sometimes effective in attracting customers because it is difficult to ignore the message.

Possibilities are endless when entertainment and advertising are combined through sophisticated technology.

With all these advertising techniques, critics argue that the public eventually won't be able to tell the difference between advertising, news, and entertainment. Because advertising largely supports the media, traditional media outlets offer little criticism of this trend.

Media critic Daniel Boorstin asserts that "it is considered appropriate to attempt to persuade." If people are too easily persuaded to buy products they do not really need, education levels should be higher to make consumers more wary of advertising claims. Australian educator Gunther Kress asserts that advertising simply mirrors the society in which it operates. "Every culture," he writes, "has the kind of advertising it deserves." A strong educational system produces individuals who are culturally literate and skeptical of the claims made by advertisers. The mass media should carry advertisements that give potential customers the information they require to make intelligent choices without resorting to tricks that blur the line between advertisements and news stories. However, the blurring of the two simply may be a commentary on the way a capitalist society operates in order to survive in a visually saturated and economically insecure time. For Kress, "If we are happy with society, we are happy with the ads. If we want to change the ads, we must bring about wider social changes." But where else can wider social changes get support than in the mass media—a media controlled by the advertisements that support it? There lie the media's conflict of interest and the reason that social change seldom occurs quickly.

■ VISUAL PERSUASION IN PUBLIC RELATIONS

Opinion makers, whether in government or business, long ago learned that what is reported in a news story sometimes isn't as important as how it is presented. Public relations specialists try to influence news reporters in the hope that favorable coverage will result. Public relations people also attempt to influence public opinion positively about a particular product, company, or issue.

The public relations industry helps gain the public's support for issues and services identified as important by corporate executives. As part of that process, public relations executives help journalists identify important stories by giving them tips, making the reporters secondary news sources. Media ethicist John Merrill asserts that 50 percent of all the stories presented in the media—whether print or broadcast—probably are generated initially by a public relations per-

son. Unfortunately, the public relations industry has some unethical members who concentrate on deception, emphasize the way a story appears rather than its substance, and create news events that end up being low-cost or free advertisements for their clients.

As part of a corporation's structure, management uses public relations to explain a situation or product. In time of a company crisis, management mobilizes its public relations forces to give information to the public. Those who use the media almost always recognize commercial advertising as a direct attempt at persuasion. However, public relations personnel use the journalistic practices of the press release and the press conference subtly to sway public opinion to a preconceived point of view.

Public relations has its beginning in the public opinion campaign initiated by President Wilson during World War I to convince the American public of the necessity of joining Britain and France in their fight against Germany.

Because of the censorship restrictions imposed by the British and German governments, reporting was so neutral that a 1914 poll of American newspaper readers indicated that two-thirds of them had no sympathy for either side. Consequently, by the time the United States entered the war in 1917, many Americans were reluctant to take up arms against the Germans. Recognizing that drastic action was necessary, eight days after Congress declared war, President Wilson set up a Committee on Public Information (CPI) headed by a former journalist, George Creel. Creel promised Wilson "a plain publicity proposition, a vast enterprise in salesmanship, the world's greatest adventure in advertising." From $5 million of a $100 million national defense fund, the CPI made movies and posters and organized 75,000 speakers. Called "Four-Minute Men," these hired hands traveled around the country, making short speeches to whip up support for the war effort. Their talks often contained inflammatory and false information about rumored atrocities committed by the Germans. The efforts were successful as American citizens learned to hate the Germans and enlisted in the military in great numbers. Because of the massive outpouring of public opinion, journalists of the day simply were not permitted to write anything critical about the nation's propaganda campaign.

Considered the founder of the public relations profession, Edward L. Bernays worked for the CPI. After the war, he applied the techniques utilized so successfully to sway public opinion to the promotion of products, a company's image, the platform of a political candidate, and fund-raising drives. At a time when experts agreed that the mass media could influence large numbers of people, public relations was born to take advantage of that phenomenon. By the 1920s, the concept of a press agent responsible for a company's image began to emerge, and politicians and corporate heads began to hire individuals to control their public image.

Another early public relations practitioner, Ivy Lee, was a former newspaper reporter. Rich individuals hired Lee to help change the public's perception about them in the hope that historical records would be kind to them or that sales of their company's products would increase. For example, oil tycoon John D. Rockefeller had a much-deserved reputation as someone who regularly resorted to unfair business practices and was cruel to his employees. Automobile maker Henry Ford had a similar problem with the public because of anti-Semitic articles he wrote early in his career. Through press releases and public statements, Lee successfully turned public opinion around for the two corporate giants so

that they were perceived as loving and generous individuals.

In 1922, Walter Lippmann published the book *Public Opinion,* in which he tried to put a positive social face on public relations. He cautioned the industry to maintain high ethical standards because the temptation is great to exploit a strategic position in the company's favor. At the same time, Lippmann recognized that the person responsible for a company's publicity "is censor and propagandist, responsible only to his employers, and to the whole truth responsible only as it accords with the employer's conception of his own interests." In other words, reporters are to know only the company's truth, not all the truth about a particular product, situation, or issue.

Because of the economic boom in the United States after World War II, the number of people working in public relations grew tremendously. Manufacturers, financial institutions, religious groups, government agencies, and communications firms all employed press agents.

■ Advertising and Public Relations

By the 1970s, advertising agencies realized that public relations firms were competing with them for corporate funds to promote campaigns to an external audience. Advertisers purchased space and time in the media for promotion, whereas public relations people worked to obtain them free. Nevertheless, companies had to pay advertising or public relations executives for the campaigns, so large, international ad agencies began buying public relations firms. Advertising agencies now own six of the ten largest public relations firms. However, the public relations and advertising components of communications companies often maintain separate client lists and do not work together much. Part of the reason is that companies would rather work with specialized small agencies that can communicate and act more quickly.

Politics and Public Relations

During the 1970s, the use of public relations in politics also grew. Almost every government agency now has a public affairs or public information office to handle publicity. During the Watergate scandal, President Nixon's advisers convinced him to make speeches denouncing the media's efforts to associate him with the illegal acts by governmental officials. They hoped that his criticism would reduce the credibility of the press and that readers and advertisers would pressure the media to back off the story.

During the most recent American presidential campaign, public relations specialists were criticized for conducting political campaigns that rely more on visually appealing "photo opportunities" and scare-tactic commercials than on substantive issues.

Another type of public relations practitioner is the lobbyist. A lobbyist is paid by corporations and other special interest groups to influence lawmakers' decisions on legislation that directly affects their operations or members. For example, the Edison Electric Institute employed lobbyists to persuade members of Congress to vote against a proposed energy tax that would affect their 150 million utility customers. Wright Andrews, Jr., partner of a Washington lobbying firm, said, "lobbying is an honorable profession. We are primarily advocates and communicators on behalf of people."

Journalism and Public Relations

By 2000, more than 1,500 firms employed some 95,000 practicing public relations spe-

cialists. Fully one-third of all companies retain a public relations consultant. Most newspaper editors like to use well-written and interesting news items from public relations personnel. Editors often can fill the newspaper with stories that readers are concerned about and at the same time please corporate clients and potential advertisers with the free publicity. An additional benefit is that such articles don't hurt the paid, commercial advertising that is vital to the publication's continued existence.

One of the main jobs of public relations professionals is to get free, favorable publicity about a product, situation, or issue. Although directly influencing the tone of a news article is seldom possible, a public relations person can provide favorable story angles and information that a reporter might not have time to obtain otherwise.

Public relations people like to use newspapers because the information has a chance of being read, reread, and absorbed. Producing news releases for newspapers is relatively inexpensive, and the number of outlets is large. Currently, more than 1,600 daily and 7,500 weekly newspapers are published in the United States. That's a lot of space that must be filled with something.

Many events are staged to attract media attention. From a journalist's point of view, these types of assignments are most dreaded because they offer little in the way of real communication to viewers about a celebrity's personality. Tightly controlled cliché events such as a politician's victory speech at a podium or a sports winner holding a trophy above the head are contrived moments that offer little to readers and viewers. In an ideal world, political handlers should not have a say over any journalistic image. Unfortunately, in a time in which image is more important than content, behind the scene and candid moments are difficult to impossible for a photojournalist to capture.

Nevertheless, media events, photo ops, or pseudoevents are staples of today's journalism. They require the public relations specialist to be creative and see beyond the pictorial cliché. News editors will not be happy and probably will reject a traditional check-handling, ribbon-cutting, or groundbreaking ceremony. As a publicist, the key to getting a picture published is the uniqueness of the visual message. If it contains unusual, dramatic, or emotional pictorial elements, an editor will be more inclined to use the story.

Public relations people who work with television broadcasters also apply these criteria. The average American family watches the television screen about seven hours a day. With 101 million U.S. households having at least one television set, any message on television is almost guaranteed a large audience. However, because there are fewer television stations (about 1,400) than newspapers, public relations personnel must be particularly well attuned to the needs of television program directors to get their messages aired. The advantage of television over other communications sources is that the persuasive impact of visual communication can be exploited easily. Television is a medium that relies on the content of its visual message; without compelling video, a viewer quickly loses interest in the program. More and more viewers have a wide range of choices of programs to watch and can change channels quickly and repeatedly.

In the mid-1970s, some 92 percent of prime-time television viewers watched one of the top three networks: ABC, CBS, or NBC. With the advent of cable broadcasting, the proportion shrank to 60 percent with expectations that it will drop even further. Cable television offers public relations personnel excellent opportunities because of its specialized audiences, the need to fill large amounts of airtime with some type of programming, and relatively inexpensive advertising rates. Whether for the networks or for cable stations, visual techniques used by a public relations specialist can influence programming.

Guest Appearances

Producers are anxious to have provocative guests as interviewees or panelists. Because of the visual impact of television, the medium emphasizes personality over substance in most cases. Consequently, public relations specialists coach their clients when they are about to be interviewed, say, on a talk show. They tell their clients to dress conservatively, not to wear reflective jewelry or white shirts (or blouses), to maintain eye contact at all times, to use strong and purposeful hand gestures, and not to cross their legs. Such attention to detail is important because manners often are more important than matters on television.

Video News Releases

Although expensive to produce (between $10,000 and $30,000), video news releases (VNRs) provide pictures and interviews that a television station doesn't have access to or time to get. If a VNR provides information on a timely, important subject, a program director is likely to use it on a newscast. Public relations textbooks advise students that the key to designing a VNR is to present the material as if it were an actual news story produced by the station—not as an aggressive sales pitch. That way, viewers will believe that a member of the station's staff, not some outside corporate source, generated the program, increasing its credibility. Few VNRs, except in smaller markets, run without some type of editing by the station. Nevertheless, public relations personnel pride themselves in getting their client noticed favorably regardless of the content or the time slot in which the VNR airs.

Expanded News Releases

Also known as infomercials, long-form programs on a particular subject are becoming quite popular. Thinly disguised as news or talk shows, expanded news releases vary from blatant advertisements for a particular product to religious programming that relies heavily on viewer donations to corporate-sponsored programs that may feature a non-profit organization or even a foreign locale in a travel format. Although company executives spend about $400 million a year for infomercials, the return is estimated to be between $750 and $900 million annually.

Cable outlets are more highly pressured to come up with programming than are networks and so are more likely to run shows at a modest advertising rate. Celebrities such as Cher and Vanna White help sell hair products and teeth whiteners for a percentage of the profits. Susan Powter, creator of a diet program called "Stop the Insanity," became a celebrity because of her infomercial. Typically, audiences for these programs are tourists lured into a studio by their curiosity and the offer of free orange juice and bagels. Inside, the production staff carefully coaches them to react with laughing, chuckling, or clapping to the claims made by the professional actors.

■ Criticism and the Industry's Response

The public relations profession is criticized because it sometimes hides its commercial intent from unsuspecting readers and viewers. A newspaper reader cannot determine whether a persuasive public relations person originally suggested a news story to a reporter. For example, political public relations specialists use visual persuasive techniques to put the politician's positive *spin* on a story. "Spin doctors," as these specialists are called, have a mission to convince the average citizen that a politician should be trusted or forgiven. More often than not, because of the time constraints, budget cutbacks, and the history of commercialism of the mass media, their accounts are published or aired with little criticism or cross-checking of facts.

A controversial method that some public relations specialists for large corporations use was recently in the news. Politicians are expected to ask for funding from most anyone who can give it. The naïve assumption is that such corporate gift giving does not influence a politician's thinking on a particular issue. Most would agree that these donations are a part of political life in America. However, when the largest energy trader in the world, Houston-based Enron, filed for bankruptcy in 2001, its stock crashed from a high of $82 to a few pennies, and 4,500 workers were laid off with most losing all of their pension benefits, several congressional committees were established to investigate this extraordinary collapse. One of the outgrowths of all the media attention on Enron and its executives was the discovery that over several years, the corporation was paying numerous journalists for services such as writing speeches and sitting on advisory boards.

A journalist receiving large fees for giving speeches is not new. In the mid-1990s, ABC correspondent Sam Donaldson, for example, received $30,000 from an insurance group. Enron used its money in an apparent attempt to influence opinions, but most of the funds were doled out to conservative columnists who were all for Enron's business dealings—until the bottom dropped out, of course. *Wall Street Journal* columnist and a former presidential speechwriter Peggy Noonan received between $25,000 and $50,000 for speechwriting help. Lawrence

Kudlow of CNBC and the *National Review* got $50,000 for some consulting and research work. The big winner was the conservative editor of the *Weekly Standard*, William Kristol, who received $100,000 from an Enron advisory board for eight days' worth of work that spanned over two years. Media critic and *Washington Post* columnist Howard Kurtz wrote, "Many of these commentators wax indignant when politicians of all stripes appear to be doing the bidding of those who fill their campaign coffers. For media people to line up at the same corporate trough is just asking for trouble." To be fair, it must be hard for working journalists to turn down such large amounts of money from public relations personnel of large corporations wanting to influence coverage any way possible.

Fortunately, the public relations industry is filled with many bright, articulate, and caring individuals who work hard to overcome the historical stereotypes of the publicity hounds who spent their time gladhanding at cocktail parties or hacks churning out press releases dictated by management. Concern about negative perceptions of the industry led to the formation, in 1948, of the Public Relations Society of America (PRSA), with student chapters around the world. The society established a code of ethics, accredits public relations professionals and academic programs, promotes scholarly research in the field, and showcases successful public relations activities. Consequently, the public relations profession gets better publicity.

■ VISUAL PERSUASION IN JOURNALISM

The communications industry is first and foremost a corporate enterprise that obtains its income largely from advertisers who purchase space or time, not from readers or viewers. The often hidden mission of a mass media institution is to supply advertisers with educated and upscale consumers—those with extra money to spend. As Walter Lippmann said in 1922, "The newspaper that goes into the homes of the prosperous has more to offer to the advertisers . . . it may go into the homes of the poor, but an ad agent will not rate that highly. Ad agents buy space in publications where there is a chance for the product to be bought by a reader." What was true in the third decade of this century is still true today, and what was true for newspapers is equally true for television.

■ *Corporate Influence in Newsrooms*

Advertiser pressure to influence editorial stories can be pervasive and persuasive. The University of Wisconsin conducted a survey of 250 editors of daily newspapers on the subject of advertiser pressure in 1991. It reported that 93 percent of the editors had received calls from advertisers threatening to cancel expensive display ads because of the content of a news story. Of those advertisers, 89 percent followed up on their threat. One auto dealer, for example, canceled $9,000 worth of ads after the news department labeled a car "funny looking." Small newspapers with their tighter budgets are more susceptible to advertising pressures than are large-circulation newspapers. Editors get calls not only from outside advertisers but from internal personnel as well. Fifty-five percent of the editors reported that they had received calls from their own advertising departments to modify a story's content to please an advertiser.

A research study performed for the American Council on Science and Health looked at 13 different women's magazines over a five-month period in 1996. Many full-page advertisements for cigarettes were found within the pages of the magazines. However, there were no editorial stories in any of the magazines concerning the dangers of smoking. Although journalists seldom like to admit it, there is evidence of correlation between advertisers and editorial choices.

■ *IMPACT OF ADVERTISING*

Advertisers have always viewed newspapers as a powerful medium for selling their products. In 1890, expenditures for advertising in all daily U.S. newspapers were $300 million. By 1998, they had jumped to $43.9 billion. Subscription and individual sales were slowly diminishing in importance as sales of advertising increased. Publishers realized that newspapers should serve advertisers and not the public.

In the 1920s, advertisers began to be concerned about the tabloids' excessive sensationalism. They generally believed that only the lowest members of society—without much buying power—were attracted by such stories. Consequently, publishers started moving away from sensational reporting to follow the lead of the *New York Times*. They hoped that wealthier individuals would read the papers and make the publications more attractive to advertisers.

In the 1940s, advertising occupied about 55 percent of the space in newspapers. Today it represents 68 percent and is growing. Increased advertising means less news story and editorial space. And that remaining space is even more precious when public relations driven information is considered.

The national newspaper *USA Today* was introduced in 1982 to great fanfare. Part of the media's attention to the newspaper was its large, colorful weather map that filled a whole page (see Chapter 10). Its color repro-

duction generally was ahead of its time technically and influenced many newspapers around the country to use color. But the color photographs and graphic elements weren't necessarily intended to be a journalistic achievement. Color was used to show advertisers how beautiful their ads could look in newspapers. Modular design techniques, colorful photographs, and short, easily readable stories were aimed at attracting readers by showing them how much newspapers could resemble television programs. Pictures were used to create an upscale look so that advertisers would see that the publication was, according to media critic Fred Ritchin, "a good environment for advertising." When editorial photographs become advertisements for the publication in order to attract advertisers, stage-managing, reenactment, and subject and electronic touch-up manipulations become acceptable (see Chapter 12).

Feature stories and special sections on fashion, food, lifestyles, and other topics fill newspapers and televised reports. These *soft news* stories are designed to attract consumers who can afford to buy the products advertised. Accompanying this trend is the rise in celebrity journalism, in which every move a famous star makes is documented with images. Entertainment and gossip news, particularly promoted if a report includes details about the personal problems of a celebrity, has exploded. Consequently, public relations personnel for celebrities are particularly concerned with their clients' images and limit journalists' access to them.

Television program directors are pressured to put dramatic moments at the end of an editorial segment so that the viewer will be watching when the commercial appears. Long, complicated stories don't work well on television because a viewer might change channels. Similarly, images should be dramatic and emotional to rivet the viewer to the content of the program (to get ready to watch the ads). The local station will promote docudramas that re-create sensational events (often murder cases) with the promise of "seeing the real" people involved in the tragedy during the local newscast.

To keep ratings high, dramatic "live" shots at news scenes, long police car chases videotaped from a pursuing helicopter, "reality-based" crime shows in which journalists participate in (and some say glorify) intrusive actions by members of the police force, and crime reenactments are becoming the norm rather than the exception. Shows such as "A Current Affair," "Inside Edition," and "Hard Copy," with their double entendre sexual titles, regularly feature the type of stories once the province of supermarket tabloids. As economic pressures become greater and advertising dollars become scarcer, the tabloid journalism mentality—the idea that anything can be aired as long as there is video—becomes a part of mainstream journalism practice (see Chapter 14) (Figure 6.12).

In a 1993 speech to broadcasters, CBS journalist and anchor Dan Rather criticized all networks for their sensational, corporate-driven news philosophy. "Too often for too long," Rather admitted, "we have answered to the worst, not the best within ourselves and within our audiences."

Rather's criticism of the news industry obviously had little effect a year later because in June 1994 one of the biggest and most sensational news stories broke. For the thirty-two months that followed, readers, listeners, and viewers were inundated almost every day with stories about the participants, facts and rumors concerning the case, and analyses from anchors and paid pundits. The murders of Nicole Brown Simpson, the ex-wife of the famous football player, O. J. Simpson, and her friend Ron Goldman produced a media firestorm unprecedented in the history of American news coverage. Images broadcast during the news coverage included the site of the murders, O. J.'s slow-speed chase in his white Bronco, his criminal trial and acquittal, and his civil trial and subsequent guilty verdict on February 4, 1997. And although many criticized the news coverage, others couldn't get enough of the soap opera story.

Former President Bill Clinton's relationship with a young White House intern, Monica Lewinsky, and its aftermath was a story of huge national interest, yet the media were criticized for its sensational coverage. In January 1998, the "Drudge Report," an online gossip and news column run by fedora donned Matt Drudge, reported rumors of an affair. Two days later, several news organizations reported the story and the scandal began. Newspaper, television, and World Wide Web journalists circulated almost daily reports. Such events as the progress of Independent Counsel Ken Starr's investigation, the impeachment of the president, and his subsequent acquittal in February 1999 were eagerly reported. Although personally tragic and historic at the same time, many thought the coverage could have been less strident.

Figure 6.12

Print and television journalists often are criticized for traveling in packs when covering the news. Here, New York City television reporters follow a witness after his appearance in a highly publicized trial.

Paul Martin Lester

Nine months later, the media were at it again. From November 25, 1999, when Elián González was snatched from certain death off the coast of Florida until July 6, 2000, when his father was named a national hero in Cuba, the *Miami Herald* ran more than 600 stories that detailed Elián and the custody fight between estranged family members. The national news media were equally enthralled with the melodrama. After all the legal avenues had been exhausted, the family still refused to hand over the boy. Early Saturday morning on April 22, 2000, armed U.S. Immigration and Naturalization Service (INS) agents rushed into the Miami house and forcibly removed Elián so that he could be reunited with his father. Photojournalist Alan Diaz, inside the house during the raid, won a Pulitzer Prize for his image of a rifle-toting INS agent about to take Elián. Newspapers around the world printed images and stories on their Easter Sunday front pages.

But sometimes we need totally saturated, 24-7 coverage because the stories demand such attention. The assassination of President John F. Kennedy in 1963, the *Challenger* space shuttle explosion in 1986, and the latest tragedy to grip the nation—aerial attacks upon New York City, Washington, D.C., and other locations in 2001—are examples of stories that are sensational, yet unite us all out of concern and interest (see Chapter 1).

The major television networks all agreed to suspend their competitive nature and share all footage they gathered at the various scenes of destruction and chaos. National Public Radio (NPR) News and other radio and television stations broadcast continuous news reports. Several newspaper editors quickly printed special or "extra" editions. **Internet** traffic on the World Wide Web slowed as information was sought online. In an ironic response to the fear that new media might replace the old, the **search engine** Google suggested that those who

wanted more information should simply listen to the radio or watch television. And although the news reports were sometimes repetitive and incomplete, the earnest efforts of all those involved in reporting the stories outweighed much of the criticism that might be contemplated.

Nevertheless, some aspects of the visual coverage were criticized. Several news media outlets were accused of sensational coverage while others complained of privacy rights violations when harrowing images captured with still and video cameras were printed and broadcast that showed desperate souls gathered around open windows frantically trying to gain the attention of rescue workers far below on the ground. Some media outlets also presented persons in midair after jumping to their deaths (see Chapter 12).

The challenge of media presentation and analysis is to know when coverage is proper and necessary and when it is gratuitous and shameful. Sometimes it is much too easy to tell the former from the latter.

On April 30, 2001, Chandra Levy, a Washington, D.C., intern romantically linked to California Representative Gary Condit, was missing and was feared dead. Over several weeks, ABC's "World News Tonight" aired fourteen minutes and NBC's "NBC Nightly News" aired sixty minutes about the case. CNN covered the story exhaustively with hourly updates on most days. CBS only ran one, two-minute story.

Ironically, Rather and CBS News were under a critical spotlight for *not* covering the Levy case. Some industry critics complained that the story had to be covered and so couldn't understand CBS's refusal to air reports. In defense, Rather responded, "What we were seeing, what we were hearing, wasn't always solid. Often, it was rumor or gossip. We chose not to report that until we had something that we thought was

Figure 6.13

See color section following page 132.

important to the story. Without passing judgment on anybody else, I've tried to stand for what I believe in—decent, responsible journalism."

Is Rather's defense a feeble blockade against the rushing tide of increased media sensationalism or a prescient rebirth of journalism ethics and values? Time will tell. But about a year after Levy's disappearance, her body was found, causing a new wave of media interest. In the face of stiff competition and other economic considerations, journalists seldom consider how corporate concerns contrive to sensationalize the content of their words and pictures.

■ *BACK TO DAVID KIRBY*

Look at the Benetton advertisement of David Kirby on his deathbed surrounded by family members one more time. The original cutline in *Life* magazine reads, "THE END. After a three-year struggle against AIDS and its social stigma, David Kirby could fight no longer. As his father, sister and niece stood by in anguish, the 32-year-old founder and leader of the Stafford, Ohio, AIDS foundation felt his life slipping away. David whispered, 'I'm ready,' took a labored breath, then succumbed."

The cutline for the Benetton ad reads, "United Colors of Benetton."

The words in the journalism context of *Life* magazine are meant to stir the reader's emotions, to educate the reader about a family's courage and love for each other, and perhaps to persuade the reader to do something tangible about the AIDS crisis. The words in the advertising context for Benetton are meant to sell sweaters.

Before assigning nothing but positive motives to the editors of *Life* magazine, take a look at what else is on the page with the Kirby family (Figure 6.13). Therese Frare's black and white image is on a double-page spread inside a black border framed by a thin, white rule. The cutline is at the lower left of the picture. The text is printed in white and set inside a black box. But stuck between the two pages—attached between the image of Kirby and his father on the left page and his sister and niece on the right page—is a cheery, white insert printed with colorful holiday graphics and photographs. It is a promotion to get the reader to subscribe to the magazine. "Give the gift that shows you care . . ." the copy reads, "all year long. Give LIFE." When you turn the little card over it reads, next to the crying face of David Kirby's father, "With LIFE your holiday shopping's a snap." Except, of course, if you are dead. Advertising and journalism merge in a shockingly ironic and insensitive way.

DISCUSSION AND EXERCISE IDEAS

- Discuss the appropriateness of making people aware of AIDS, the death penalty, or any other social issue through advertising.

- Lead a general discussion about the ways images are used for advertising, public relations, and journalism.

- Think of examples of when you think journalists have gone too far when covering a story. How else should a story be covered?

- Cut out or copy a printed image (or describe a video image) from an advertising, public relations, or journalism context. Explain the hidden message that the viewers are being led to accept.

InfoTrac College Edition Assignments

- With "Subject guide" checked, type "Benetton ad" in the search area. Click "View" for the "Periodical references." At the end of the article, "Ads for Life," Brian J. Taylor writes, "So is the campaign a 'sick' and 'cynical' marketing ploy that glamorizes murderers, or, as Benetton claims, simply an 'innovative mode of corporate communication'? Or both? Neither?" Can you answer his questions?

- With "Subject guide" checked, type "Sensationalism in Journalism" in the search area. Click "View" for the "Periodical references." Read the article "When you need to know, but don't need to see" by Deni Elliott and Paul Martin Lester. If Osama bin Laden is captured, brought back to this country, tried, convicted, and sentenced to die, do you think his execution should be televised? Why or why not?

Go to the Web site for this book at www.wadsworth.com/product/0534562442 to find more Web links on this subject.

IMAGES THAT INJURE: PICTORIAL STEREOTYPES IN THE MEDIA

Whether right or

wrong . . . imagination

is shaped by the pictures

seen. . . . Consequently,

they can lead to

stereotypes that are

hard to shake.

Walter Lippmann,

1889–1974

WRITER, EDITOR, AND

POLITICAL COMMENTATOR

By the end of this chapter you should know:

- How telethons sometimes use stereotypical portrayals in order to inspire donations.
- How media messages sometimes communicate prejudicial thinking.
- How specific cultural groups are stereotyped through pictorial representations.
- Some examples of media messages that do not stereotype.

For many, Labor Day marks the end of the summer season. It is a U.S. holiday that recognizes the transition between lazy days full of relaxation and the start of a new season of productivity for students and workers alike. As that last picnic, last stroll along a trail, or last dive into a pool begin to fade into pleasant memories, about 750 million viewers worldwide settle into comfortable chairs, turn on their television sets, and watch some or all of the 23-hour Jerry Lewis Muscular Dystrophy Association (MDA) telethon, the annual fund-raising program that has become a staple of the medium (Figure 7.1). The only other televised pro-

gram that gets more viewers is the NFL's Super Bowl.

Jerry Lewis, seventy-six, has been the emcee for the show since 1966. With his professional charm and slick-backed black hair, he introduces each performance, from comedians to singers, with the same level of enthusiasm, despite the many hours he has been awake.

Entertaining acts are interspersed with filmed spots about MD research and people afflicted with the disease. We see scientists in white lab coats mixing chemicals in test tubes, doctors talking passionately into the camera of the need for more money to further their research, and children in wheelchairs being pushed to their next physical therapy session. Parents and other family members of these children talk with tears in their eyes about the shock of learning of their child's illness.

Filmed segments or cutaways to a local station's activities usually end with emotional monologues from Lewis. A child in a wheelchair being rolled to the front of the small stage by an adult almost always accompanies these tearful eulogies. After an introduction, the child nervously recites a brief message (Figure 7.2). Lewis, with tears welling in his eyes, delivers an emotional appeal for money. At the end of his performance, a spokesperson for a large corporation walks on stage, introduces a slickly produced video about the company's fight against MD, and delivers a check in true public relations fashion to Lewis. Lewis hoots with joy and announces that the check has a number "followed by lots of zeros." The lights flash, the audience applauds, and the camera zooms in to reveal the dancing numbers of the electronic tote board high above the stage as it registers a new total.

Muscular dystrophy is a name for several inherited diseases that affect the muscles attached to the skeleton. The most common and serious form of MD is called Duchenne, named for the French neurologist Guillaume Duchenne, who first described the condition in 1868. Duchenne MD affects only boys. The first sign of the disease appears at about age four when a child begins to have trouble walking. By age ten, the child can no longer walk. As the disease progresses, all the muscles eventually are affected, almost always causing death by age thirty. Without doubt, Duchenne MD is tragic, but the disease is rare. It results in only 30 cases per 100,000 male births. Although the gene responsible for causing the disease has been identified, as yet there is no cure.

Paul Martin Lester

The more than forty other kinds of neuromuscular diseases do not receive as much emotional publicity because they are much less severe than Duchenne MD. These less life-threatening forms of MD can affect both males and females. Despite numbness in the face and extremities, MD patients aided by physical therapy can lead long, productive lives, some with and some without the use of wheelchairs. Nevertheless, the public's stereotypical perception, promoted by the telethon, is that MD victims cannot walk and always die prematurely.

Figure 7.1

Jerry Lewis is doing all right. Before the start of his 1993 MDA telethon, he steps out of his luxury Rolls-Royce automobile in front of a Las Vegas casino.

Figure 7.2

As 1993 poster child Lance Fallon looks offstage, Jerry Lewis makes an emotional pitch for viewers to contribute to the MDA while every five seconds a new message appears at the bottom of the screen. However, home viewers contribute only a small percentage of the overall total. Corporate sponsors have already committed most of the money during the telethon in exchange for promotional spots.

Paul Martin Lester

The Muscular Dystrophy Association has been criticized because much of the money raised by the telethon goes to support other fund-raising events while MDA executives receive salaries as high as $300,000 a year. But to MDA's credit, it meets the Council of Better Business Bureaus (BBB) standards for a charitable organization. The BBB requires that at least 50 percent of all income be spent on programs related to the organization's purpose, at least 50 percent of all public contributions be spent on the organization's purpose, and fund-raising costs cannot exceed 35 percent of related contributions. MDA gives money to further research and to sponsor worldwide scientific conferences. The organization also provides some funds for equipment and services to patients.

■ CURIOUS OPENING ACT

But the show almost always starts with an ironic twist. It is a fund-raiser that exists to help those who do not have full muscle function, or have other mobility challenges.

With seeming insensitivity, previous telethons have begun with the most energetic activity that can possibly be performed by someone with two healthy legs: several men and women high-kicking and tap dancing, a troupe of frenetic stomping dancers that smash garbage can lids, or an Irish-music inspired clog dance group. Imagine that you are watching the performance while sitting in a wheelchair and you might start to understand why the telethon is criticized every year for insensitivity toward those whom it supposedly supports.

The 2001 telethon was unfortunately no exception. Shown over 200 U.S. television stations, the thirty-sixth annual, twenty-three-hour fund-raising event once again presented an opening act that featured activities that a person using a wheelchair could not perform. Dancers from the Broadway musical *Contact,* a new "dance play" directed by Tony-award-winning choreographer for Mel Brooks's *The Producers,* Susan Stroman, danced energetically and effortlessly across the small television studio stage. New York theater critics have criticized the musical for its stereotypical view of women. One critic wrote that Stroman has "created a work of theatre that consistently demeans, debases, and denigrates women. *Contact* is vulgar, crass, ugly; what it says about the interaction between the sexes is disgusting." This oddly curious opening act managed to offend those who use wheelchairs and women as well (Figure 7.3).

■ PITY CAMPAIGN CRITICIZED

It is the "pity approach" to fund-raising that most irks those who use wheelchairs to navigate through their daily lives. In 1994, former telethon poster children calling themselves "Jerry's Orphans" started to publicly object to the pity campaign by calling it a "pity-thon." Although he later apologized for his remarks

Figure 7.3

The 2001 MDA telethon began with an ironic opening sequence. For a fund-raiser that purportedly helps many who must use wheelchairs to get around, it curiously chose to start the program with an energetic, high-kicking act from the "dance play" musical, Contact. *The musical has also been severely criticized for its stereotypical portrayals of women.*

Courtesy of Jim Gordon

after a public outcry, Jerry Lewis made clear the connection between making money and exploiting pity. He also showed his contempt for those who criticize this tactic during an interview on the show "CBS Sunday Morning." On May 20, 2000, Lewis told correspondent Martha Teichner, "I'm telling about a child in trouble. If it's pity, we'll get some money. I'm giving you facts. Pity. You don't want to be pitied for being a cripple in a wheelchair? Stay in your house."

CBS News was criticized when a week before the 2001 fund-raiser it rebroadcast the interview without the offensive words contained in the last two sentences. A spokesperson for CBS explained that in light of Lewis's apology and his statement, "I admire people with disabilities," the tape was edited "out of fairness to him."

However, Harriet Johnson, a lawyer from South Carolina with a neuromuscular disease, said that CBS should have aired the example of "shocking bigotry" because many might believe that Jerry Lewis never used the derogatory term *cripple* for those who use a wheelchair.

The Jerry Lewis/MDA telethon is a chance for physically normal viewers to be entertained, to feel sorry for "Jerry's Kids" who are afflicted with the disease, and perhaps to contribute money in the hope of finding a cure.

But for other individuals, the Labor Day telecast is a source of dread and embarrassment. For those who use wheelchairs, the telecast is an annual reminder of how mainstream media communicate stereotypical attitudes, even for a good cause. Those in wheelchairs aren't seen as active, independent, and normal people. They are viewed as helpless and fragile individuals to be pitied—and who can exist only if the viewer picks up the telephone and pledges a donation. You can find more information on this and other issues by contacting the National Center on Disability and Journalism at www.ncdj.org.

■ *REINFORCING STEREOTYPES WITH IMAGES*

Whether an individual is identified because of gender, age, cultural heritage, economic status, sexual orientation, or physical disability, the visual message generally communicated about that person often is misleading and false (Figure 7.4). Because pictures affect a viewer emotionally more than words alone do, pictorial stereotypes often become misinformed perceptions that have the weight of established facts. These pictures can remain in a person's mind throughout a lifetime.

When pictorial stereotypes are repeated enough times, they become part of a society's culture. Recall that *culture* describes a set of learned and mutually accepted rules that define all forms of communication for a group of people during a particular time period. People form attitudes about others, both within and outside their own culture, through direct experiences, interactions with family members and friends, educational institutions, and the media. Culture tells us what we should do to get along within a particular society as well as what our actions mean to others (Figure 7.5).

Communication is easier when people share the same cultural meanings (speak the same language or use the same visual symbolism). To be successful, communication (from the Latin word for commonness) requires mutual understanding of the symbols used. By definition, different cultures attribute different meanings to similar actions. Consequently, members of one culture often are easy to identify and have trouble communicating with members of another culture. In a multicultural society, members of other cultures often are stigmatized because of their inability to articulate the symbols of the **dominant culture**.

One of the chief functions of the brain is to categorize visual information into basic

Figure 7.4

Stereotypical images can be seen in the strangest places. Men's heads are neatly arranged but women's figures are haphazardly placed in a mannequin supply warehouse.

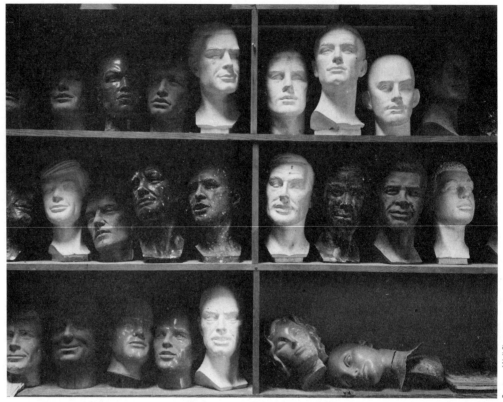

Courtesy of Neil Chapman

Figure 7.5

The girl posing for the photographer in a southern California neighborhood is representative of her age and social group. By holding a toy submachine gun she also becomes an icon for the fear that many people have of living in that area.

Paul Martin Lester

units that can be easily and quickly analyzed. Selectivity is the process by which the mind decides which objects are important, insignificant, helpful, or harmful.

Unfortunately, this trait of the brain also leads to instant categorization of people. Noticing a person's gender, age, ethnic background, and the like is perfectly natural. But preconceived attitudes or opinions that may or may not be true about that person are learned through enculturation.

■ MEDIA COVERAGE AND PREJUDICIAL THINKING

Stereotypical media coverage manifests itself as a sin of either admission or omission. Media coverage of individuals in a specific cultural group usually presents them as special cases to be pitied for their terrible living situations, admired for bettering themselves, or, most often, reviled for their violent criminal actions. The stories of hardworking, decent members of various cultural groups often are ignored. Accounts of their lives simply are not considered to be "news."

Part of the problem with the media's portrayals of minority groups is that few practicing journalists are from diverse cultural groups. Only 5.8 percent of all media personnel identify themselves as a member of another culture. Sixty-one percent of the daily newspapers in the United States do not have any diverse staff members, and 92 percent have no diverse group members in management positions. In addition, media schools have few if any culturally diverse professors or students. Sensitivity to the stereotyping of ethnic and other groups isn't a high priority when newsrooms all exhibit the same skin color.

Throughout the world an estimated 17,000 distinct cultural groups almost never receive media attention within their societies. In Latin America, for example, 600 separate tribes live in lowland regions alone. In the United States, some 20 million people belong to so-called "fringe" religious groups; 75 million U.S. citizens classify themselves as belonging to more than 120 separate ethnic cultures. But the faces that most often appear in still photographs and moving images are white. The 2000 U.S. census identified this country's four most numerous ethnic groups: German, Irish, English, and African. Those same four groups also headed the 1790 census. But there are strong indications that the number of Latinos may overtake the number of African Americans within the next fifty years.

The dominant cultural groups—those with the most power and influence in the social structure, including the media—are the ones that control which images get seen. It is always to the advantage of the dominant groups to stereotype other groups in order to secure their dominance.

■ SPECIFIC EXAMPLES OF STEREOTYPING

Every form of prejudice is based on the assumption that members of one group are better than members of another because of false opinions about physical, intellectual, and social characteristics. Throughout history, the dominant groups in societies have discriminated against various ethnic and other groups. Some groups have managed to overcome discrimination and become a part of the dominant societal force. Most others have not been so successful.

Almost any group you can think of has been the target of prejudice and discrimination at some time—children, the elderly, religious and political conservatives and liberals, the homeless, the disabled, students, professionals, the unemployed, the poor and the rich, foreigners, Asian Americans, Latinos, city or country dwellers, people with southern accents, people with Brooklyn accents, and on and on until every person can find his or her own category.

African Americans, women, homosexuals, and Native Americans are good examples of groups that have long been discriminated against. Pictorial stereotypes presented in the media of all these cultural groups shape the public's perception of them.

■ African-American Stereotypes

African-American history is directly tied to past government-sanctioned enslavement. Since the early days of the slave trade, pictorial stereotypes have been used to maintain the dominant culture's power over them. Consequently, African Americans have faced tremendous difficulty in overcoming

Figure 7.6

A seventeenth-century diagram of a slave ship shows how African kidnap victims were packed for their transatlantic journey. But its impersonal draftsmanship cannot possibly detail the horrors during such a voyage.

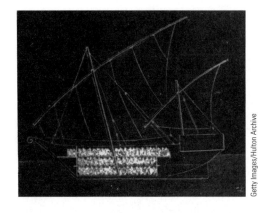

Getty Images/Hulton Archive

stereotypes, despite legal, economic, and social reforms.

Racism is the belief that one race is better than another because of the genes in a person's chromosomes. When European explorers came into contact with Africans in the sixteenth century, many concluded that Africans must not have the Europeans' mental processing abilities because African societies lacked the technological advances common in Europe. Later, evolutionary theory became a scientific justification for racism, with western Europeans thought to be on a higher evolutionary plane than other races.

Those with economic interests in the slave trade used all these rationalizations. Thinking of Africans simply as animals only a few steps up from apes and gorillas, or ordained because of a curse uttered during a hangover to become eternal slaves, excused their severe treatment during capture, transport to the New World, and enslavement (Figure 7.6).

Unlike other ethnic groups that immigrated voluntarily and retained their own cultures, African Americans were not allowed to re-create their own African cultures in the slave colonies. The master–slave mentality also made assimilation extremely difficult after the Thirteenth Amendment outlawed slavery following the Civil War (Figure 7.7).

However, discrimination was rampant in the North. Few in the North had had any contact with African Americans. Up until 1860, there were more than 500,000 free African Americans living in the South. They had been born of free mothers, had paid for their own freedom, or had been set free by their owners. In the South these freed slaves had occupations as diverse as architects and hotel clerks. But in the North, discrimination in jobs, housing, and education was much more common and institutionalized, making the assimilation of African Americans into the dominant culture particularly difficult.

Recent studies of African-American pictorial coverage in print and broadcast media have noted the pictorial legacy of discrimination based on stereotyping. Although more African Americans are seen in the media, the most common pictures of African Americans still relate to crime, sports, and entertainment. Having African-American entertainment and sports heroes is important for children, but the message being sent to these children is that they can "make it" in society only if they excel in those fields.

Figure 7.7

With a bust of Caesar overhead—a symbol of power—a nineteenth-century plantation owner is shocked from his reading when a nurse midwife presents an African-American baby freshly delivered by his wife. Such images played on the fears that many had at the time about the consequences of different races mixing socially.

Uncensored Situations, 1966, The Dick Sutphen Studio, Inc.

Motion pictures and television have come a long way in eliminating many of the most blatant stereotypical portrayals of African Americans ("Amos and Andy" is no longer a program choice). Despite a few exceptions, African-American representations in movies and music videos present a stereotypical pattern that concentrates on sexual and violent acts. Many critics are concerned that television's situation comedies also continue false impressions about African Americans (Figure 7.8).

One place to find numerous programs and commercials that feature African-American actors is on the cable network Black Entertainment Television (BET). Dramatic presentations, situation comedies, sports shows, discussions of social problems, and advertisements help create a balance in the media for that cultural group. Unfortunately, the number of viewers is limited because not every cable company carries the network.

Despite the efforts of BET executives and others, for the most part, the media themselves rarely challenge media-created stereotypes. Thus distorted, oversimplified images as a part of news or entertainment coverage by the print, broadcast, and screen media constantly reinforce the prejudicial thinking that perpetuates social discrimination (Figure 7.9).

■ Female Stereotypes

Males in almost every culture in the world and throughout the history of social interaction have thought that they are the dominant and more important gender. Such patterns of thought have led to prejudice and pervasive discrimination against women (Figure 7.10). At birth, girls are treated more gently than boys. Girls are taught to stay home and attend to household duties. Boys are encouraged to be

Getty Images/Hulton Archive

Figure 7.8

During the taping of his television show Bill Cosby is surrounded by symbolism of a wealthy lifestyle—original artwork on the walls of the character's two-story house, well-made furniture, and magazines on a coffee table. Some critics complained that "The Bill Cosby Show" was not characteristic of a typical African-American family because the sitcom was intended to attract a predominantly Anglo audience.

adventurous and active. Women are expected to find fulfillment in marriage and motherhood. Men are expected to find fulfillment in their careers. Women are valued for their appeal as sexual objects. Men are valued for their intelligence, strength, and energy.

Cultural norms are learned behaviors and are based on several interrelated factors. A study of 156 separate societies worldwide revealed that cultures that had high incidences of rape competed for limited natural resources, tended to engage in wars, tolerated high levels of violent crime, and supported the male (macho) image of toughness (Figure 7.11).

During the Industrial Revolution in the nineteenth century, many poor women were allowed to work in the factories for the first time because of labor shortages. Despite this advance in social thinking, women were still not allowed to vote, own property, testify in court, make a legal contract, spend their wages without getting permission from their

Figure 7.9

Yard ornaments in front of houses in Garland, North Carolina (left), and Chicago (right) are offensive to many because they symbolize a time when racists thought that African Americans were useful only as servants or had an intelligence level only slightly higher than monkeys.

Paul Martin Lester

husbands, or even retain guardianship over their children. **Abolitionist** activism on behalf of freedom for slaves in the South led many also to consider freedom for women in the North. Eventually, Wyoming became the first state to give women the right to vote. In 1920, the Nineteenth Amendment, which gave women national voting rights, was ratified.

Although voting reform was an important step, efforts to reform other discriminatory practices were unsuccessful. Texan columnist Molly Ivins notes that women's

rights were especially slow in coming in Texas, for example. "Until June 26, 1918," she writes, "the Texas Constitution mandated that all Texans had the right to vote except 'idiots, imbeciles, aliens, the insane and women.'" Women weren't allowed to serve on juries until 1954.

During World War II women again were needed in the factories, this time to produce armaments, to replace the men serving in the armed forces (Figure 7.12). When the war ended, many women succumbed to tremendous social pressure to take care of

Figure 7.10

Making generalizations about a cultural group is always problematic, but pictorial stereotypes may be found in the most innocent of situations. Whether in McClellanville, South Carolina (left), or Elko, Nevada (right), boys often play rougher than girls—but not always.

Paul Martin Lester

their returning men, have babies, and let the male "breadwinners" have the jobs they needed in order to support their families. The result was "the baby boom," named for the large number of children born during the late 1940s and the 1950s.

Despite social progress for women in the 1960s and beyond, media stereotypes of women in news, entertainment, and advertising contexts constantly remind viewers of society's male-dominated view (Figure 7.13). Women often are portrayed as sex objects designed only for a man's pleasure, as wives whose chief duty is to serve their husbands, and as mothers who often must rear children without a husband's help. Women are portrayed as being less intelligent than men, being dependent on men for support, and thus being inferior. Obviously, such stereotypes do not portray men and women equally (Figure 7.14). Early television situation comedies such as "I Love Lucy," "The Adventures of Ozzie and Harriet," "Father Knows Best," "The Donna Reed Show," and "Leave It to Beaver" reinforced the view that the women should stay home

Uncensored Situations, 1966, The Dick Sutphen Studio, Inc.

and take care of the house and children (Figure 7.15).

Sexism in Advertising

Nowhere is the unequal status of men and women as obvious as in advertising. Images in magazine advertisements and in television commercials show women as sexual objects to attract the attention of potential customers to the product (Figure 7.16). Hair-care, clothing, and makeup advertisements regularly give women the impression

Getty Images/Hulton Archive

Getty Images/Hulton Archive

Figure 7.11

Many women are forced by religious and/or social customs to cover their faces while in public, as this nineteenth-century woodcut demonstrates.

Figure 7.12 (left)

With so many young men in the armed forces during World War II, women became assembly-line workers. "Rosie the Riveter" poses in front of a ship's riveted steel hull holding the tool of her trade. Although her hairstyle and clothes connote a no-nonsense working philosophy, her smile and makeup, along with the halo effect of the lighting behind her, play to her feminine characteristics.

Figure 7.13 (right)

Vincent Price plays the evil lead character in the forgettable Dr. Goldfoot and the Bikini Machine *while surrounded by actresses who have little purpose in the movie other than to be sex objects for men.*

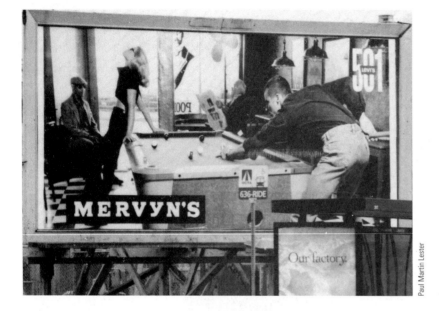

Paul Martin Lester

Figure 7.14

This billboard for Mervyn's department stores in southern California and Levi's jeans presents at least two stereotypes: that old men are content to fritter away the day in a pool hall and that a young woman likes to pose seductively. Look closely: Is she posing for a blind African-American man? Carefully composed advertising images are rich in semiotic meanings.

that they are inferior if they do not measure up to the impossible beauty standards demonstrated by high-priced models. Research on television commercials reveals that men are used as voice-overs when an authority figure is desired, women are portrayed mainly in a family setting in which men are benefited, women often are noticeably younger than their male counterparts, and fewer girls and women are used in advertisements than boys and men. American researchers Deni Elliott and Allison Lester found that advertisements during the summer of 2000 in twelve popular magazines showed that men and boys in ads are almost always portrayed as engaging in energetic activities and interacting with other men or boys in the images. Women and girls, however, are much more often simply looking into the camera and not actively participating in any significant activity.

Although never the only cause for gender discrimination, print, television, and movie images that show bikini-clad models holding phallic-shaped beer bottles reinforce the idea that women are mentally inferior to men and good only for sexual pleasure (Figures 7.17

and 7.18). Such objectification of women can lead to degradation, intimidation, stalking, assault, rape, and murder (Figure 7.19).

■ *Gay and Lesbian Stereotypes*

If someone advocates that the disabled, Native Americans, African Americans, women, or others being discriminated against should be forced to suffer the physical and emotional scars of such acts, most people would roundly condemn that individual as a crackpot. That is, prejudice and discrimination generally are opposed on legal and moral grounds. However, the approximately 25 million gay and lesbian members of our society belong to one of the few groups that can be discriminated against legally. Yet, gays and lesbians are the most diverse of any group. In fact, data from the 2000 federal census showed that same-sex couples head nearly 600,000 homes in the United States, or one gay or lesbian couple in nearly every county in America.

Homosexuals cannot be isolated by race, gender, economic situation, social position, region of the country, religious belief, political orientation, or any other physical attribute. Fears about AIDS increased discrimination against homosexuals. Again, the media reinforce negative stereotypes that perpetuate prejudice, causing many gays and lesbians to remain extremely hesitant to admit to their sexual preference in fear of further employment, housing, and social backlash.

With the AIDS crisis, media portrayals of homosexuals are much more common. But the homosexual in the story line is cast as either a victim or a villain, with little concern about an objective presentation. Independent and well-financed videos produced and distributed by conservative religious organizations that operate their own cable networks play on the fear of AIDS. Such programs include "The Gay Agenda" and "Gay

Rights/Special Rights." For example, in "Gay Rights," an AIDS patient talks of having fifty sexual partners in one night, hardly representative of homosexuals as a group. Pro gay rights commercials—one featuring a gay soldier who was killed in Vietnam with the ending message of "End Discrimination"—are seldom seen, as the major networks refuse to air most political advertisements.

Overcoming ingrained stereotypes takes many years for a culture to achieve. That process could be speeded if the images of culturally diverse groups, including gays and lesbians, show ordinary people who have ordinary needs, fears, and hopes and lead ordinary lives (Figure 7.20).

■ *Native American Stereotypes*

Portrayed as bloodthirsty savages, alcoholic indigents, romantic princesses, and silent but wise sidekicks, Native Americans have long been a staple of paperback, movie, and television stereotypes. But the practice of stereotyping Native Americans probably goes as far back as the seventeenth century. In *Publick Occurrences Both Domestick and Foreign*, the first English-language newspaper in America, there were two stories concerning Native Americans: one praised "their industry and communal spirit in staving off starvation" and the other accused them of "kidnapping white children, presumably to ravage or eat them." It seems the dominant culture has always wanted to portray Native Americans both ways—as noble savages and as feared adversaries—in order to pigeonhole their culture and justify the treatment of native peoples throughout American history.

There is always debate, it seems, whether Hollywood and other portrayals honor or marginalize native peoples. For example, in 1995 Disney released an animated movie about a Powhatan woman named *Pocahon-*

Getty Images/Hulton Archive

Kurt Renfro

Figure 7.15 (above)
In this publicity still of Donna Reed and Carl Betz for the 1950s program "The Donna Reed Show," a woman's place is clearly in the home. The husband can only hover while the housewife calmly solves the problem.

Figure 7.16 (left)
Student photographers often mimic the sexist poses they see in advertising photography. The woman's provocative stance serves no other purpose than to objectify her.

tas. In defending the romantic princess stereotype in the movie, Roy Disney wrote that the film is "responsible, accurate, and respectful." However, Chief Roy Crazy Horse said, "It is unfortunate that this sad story, which Euro-Americans should find embarrassing, Disney makes 'entertainment' and perpetuates a dishonest and self-serving

Figure 7.17

In this advertisement for Cointreau liqueur, the shape and position of the models' fingers and the bottle itself are meant to link drinking the alcoholic beverage with sexual conquest.

Figure 7.18

Although at first glance the man appears to be holding the woman's breasts in the Seagram's billboard, she is actually touching herself. Media critic Irving Goffman has written that such a gesture by women connotes subservience to men. The metonymic code of dress style, jewelry, and background details communicates an upscale environment. Ironically, the JVC advertisement displays the words that Seagram executives hope male buyers of their gin will believe, "Hold everything."

Figure 7.19

This all too obvious example of sexism advertises an automobile parts supply facility in southern California. Perhaps more offensive than the actual image is the fact that it was allowed to remain displayed next to a major freeway for several years. It was recently removed.

Courtesy of Neil Chapman

Paul Martin Lester

myth at the expense of the Powhatan Nation."

But no debate is as fierce as the one currently raging outside huge professional sports arenas and small-town grass fields. Groups such as the National Indian Education Association, the National Congress of American Indians, the American Civil Liberties Union, the U.S. Commission on Civil Rights, and others have condemned the use of native symbols as sports mascots. Nevertheless, the use of native mascots is still popular. In California alone, 187 public schools use Native American

mascots. Alumni of schools and universities and fans of professional teams throughout the United States use the same defense, "Indian people should be proud that there are people that want to represent them and follow in their footsteps and conduct themselves with dignity and honor."

But names like the Washington Redskins, which is a racial slur on par with "nigger" or "jewboy," cartoon images like the toothy grin of Chief Wahoo, the Cincinnati Reds' mascot, and the "tomahawk chop" employed by fans of the Atlanta Braves are not honoring native peoples and are denounced by experts who offer a variety of reasons for ending such depictions (Figure 7.21). Native advocates say that these stereotypes desecrate religious symbols. Psychologists testify that they damage children by making them feel inferior. Lawyers claim that having such mascots exposes schools to racial harassment lawsuits. Another argument against the use of mascots is what is called "collateral use." Fans from opposing teams often use racial slurs and obscene cartoon depictions based on the mascot (Figure 7.22).

Lucy Ganje, Associate Professor of Communications with the University of North Dakota, writes, "Native children have the right to grow up believing they're more than mascots for products and sports teams. They have the right to attend a football game without standing next to someone yelling, 'Scalp the Indians!'"

Sensitivity to the mascot issue seems to be gaining ground. According to a New York State Education Department survey, more than 600 educational institutions have changed from their native mascots in recent years. The Redskins of St. John's University in New York became the Red Storm in 1991 while Ohio's Miami University in 1997 changed their mascot from the Redskins to the Redhawks. The NCAA, the organization responsible for supervising most college athletic programs around the country, is currently investigating the use of sports mascots. Education about the true meaning of honoring someone from another culture has an effect.

San Francisco Chronicle columnist Jon Carroll perhaps summed up the issue best when he wrote, "Whenever a significant number of people identified with a subsection of the human species objects to a name, then the name gets changed."

Courtesy of Laurie Williams

When our days become dreary with low hovering clouds of despair, and when our nights become darker than a thousand midnights, let us remember that there is a creative force in this universe, working to pull down the gigantic mountains of evil, a power that is able to make a way out of no way and transform dark yesterdays into bright tomorrows. Let us realize the arc of the moral universe is long but it bends toward justice.

■ *WHERE DO WE GO FROM HERE?*

Martin Luther King, Jr., wrote those words as the title of his last book and also the title of a speech he gave to the Tenth Anniversary Convention of the Southern Christian Leadership Conference in Atlanta on August 16, 1967, eight months before he was assassinated. In the speech he said:

Lucy Ganje

Figure 7.20

Two women publicly proclaim their love for each other by gestures and signs during an International Women's Conference in Houston, Texas. Images of homosexuals can depict sweet, personal, and universal moments just as with everyone else.

Figure 7.21

See color section following page 132.

Figure 7.22

The University of North Dakota has the "Fighting Sioux" as its mascot, despite protests from students, faculty, and others. An example of "collateral use" is this T-shirt worn by fans of North Dakota State University, a football rival.

Figure 7.23

This billboard for PruCare of California presents a positive example of racial harmony.

PruCare® of Californi

In his book *A Theory of Justice,* John Rawls writes of the "veil of ignorance." He asserts that members of all cultural groups must retreat to an "original position" in which cultural rules and social differences disappear. When all barriers between individuals are lifted, everyone is freed to experience what it is like to be in the "other person's shoes." At that point, Rawls believes, everyone in a society will have equal status and access to the goods and services produced by that society. The need is to build spiritual bridges between people that are not based on superficial, stereotypical, and visible symbols.

The only place where people regularly and over a long time see members from other cultural groups is in the pages of newspapers and magazines, on television, in the movies, and on computer screens. But when most of those media images are misleading, viewers aren't challenged to examine the bases of their prejudices and do something about them. To change people's minds about diversity may require far-reaching changes in the entire society.

Advertising executives occasionally get it right simply by including a person who happens to be a member of a little-seen cultural group in an everyday situation. The California Milk Board was praised for its commercial that showed an Asian-American teacher drinking milk. Kellogg's Corn Flakes used a deaf teenage girl to describe the taste of the cereal. American Express featured an African-American couple in the same symphony orchestra box as an Anglo couple to help sell its gold card (Figures 7.23 and 7.24).

Another hopeful sign of cultural togetherness might be results of a 2001 Nielsen Media Research study that showed African American and Anglo viewers are more likely to watch the same television programs than was noted five years ago. The findings showed that the twenty most popular shows watched by Anglo audiences were also the top twenty shows watched by African American audiences. Programs on the list of favorites included "Survivor," "ER," "Law & Order," and "The Practice." Because of criticism from various groups, television producers in the last five years have made a greater effort to include more multiethnic casts.

But there are also signs of little progress being made in race relations. For example, the United Nations in 2001 sponsored the World Conference Against Racism in Durban, South Africa, which was noted for its acrimonious and inconclusive debates among members of delegations from around the world. In fact, the United States and Israel delegations left the conference because of disputes over the wording of a final document. Wade Henderson, executive director of the U.S.-based Leadership Conference on Civil Rights, said, "The majority of countries were reluctant to focus attention on their own practices and many took a very cynical posture to the conference. They had a willingness to accuse others of transgression without a willingness to admit to transgression within their own borders."

Also in 2001, Melody Twilley, a personable junior at the University of Alabama with a 3.87 grade point average and who sings in the campus choir, wanted to join a sorority. The only trouble was, Twilley is African American. All fifteen sororities have never had an African-American member. She was turned down. Conversely, no African-American man has ever been accepted into any of the school's twenty-one Anglo fraternities. Incidentally, there are a few African-American sororities and fraternities that have Anglo members. In a perfect example of Rawls's veil of ignorance philosophy, Twilley asked, "What if I started a new sorority next year where everybody would have to wear pillowcases over their heads during rush? It may look funny. And maybe the other houses wouldn't like it. But you would get picked not by how you looked, but by who you are."

Dennis Shulman, Ph.D. Psychoanalyst and Professor Fordham University

Vivian Yacu, Staff System Designer Port Authority of New York/New Jersey

Erik Weihenmayer, English Teacher and Wrestling Coach Phoenix Country Day School (AZ)

Don Wardlow, Sportscaster New Britain Red Sox

Lou Calesso, Computer Systems Analyst AT&T Bell Labs

Celeste Lopes, Asst. District Attorney Brooklyn, NY

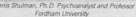

NOT ALL BLIND PEOPLE SELL PENCILS.

Courtesy of the American Foundation for the Blind

Another indication as to how far American society is from the equality of treatment for those from diverse cultures is the social hysteria that followed the World Trade Center and Pentagon attacks in 2001. Mosques were firebombed while individuals

Figure 7.24

This American Foundation for the Blind advertisement counters the stereotype of those who cannot see as helpless and dependent on others.

Figure 7.25

On the crowded steps in front of the Dallas City Hall during a civil rights demonstration, an African-American man stares dully at the photographer (left). If this portrait is the only image of the man, the viewer receives a misleading and stereotypical impression. Fortunately, the photographer made two more exposures (below left and right): one of the man studying an object from around his neck and the other showing him proudly displaying his religious symbol. An image captures but one of infinitely many moments—some images are more truthful about subjects than others.

of Arab descent were vocally abused and physically attacked. At least six people of Arab descent were murdered. In addition, five months after the attacks on September 11, Arab Americans filed 260 claims of workplace discrimination with the federal government, an increase of 168 percent over the same time period the previous year. Equally alarming is a CNN/Gallup poll that asked Americans if they would support a policy requiring all individuals of Middle Eastern heritage to wear some form of identification indicating they had been checked by security. Half of those polled would support such a policy.

Increased economic and political power for disenfranchised groups is the best way to combat prejudice. Unequal power, ownership, privilege, and respect are at the core of communication problems between cultural groups.

When the media regularly celebrate cultural diversity with words and images instead of concentrating on conflict and stereotypes, the goal of ending prejudice, racism, and discrimination will come a little closer (Figure 7.25).

DISCUSSION AND EXERCISE IDEAS

- Lead a general discussion about the concept of culture and how it can refer to much more than a person's racial or ethnic background.

- Break into small groups and discuss when you thought you were being discriminated against. Open the stories up to the entire class. Look for solutions or positive responses to such behavior.

- Lead a general discussion concerning the possible changes the producers of the MDA telethon might make if they were aware of the impact of media stereotypes on those who use wheelchairs.

- Cut out or copy a printed image (or describe a video image) that is an example of negative stereotyping and one that is a positive portrayal.

INFOTRAC COLLEGE EDITION ASSIGNMENTS

- With "Subject guide" checked, type "The Misfit and Muscular Dystrophy" in the search area. Read the thoughtful article by Beth Haller. A cartoon reproduced in the article shows Jerry Lewis during a telethon giving a patronizing pat on the head of a young and upset girl in a wheelchair. Note Haller's references to spatial relationships, camera angles and other visual devices that denote a kind of parent-child affiliation between Lewis and those the telethon is purporting to help. Do you think these visual cues increase the stereotypes that the average viewer of the telethon has about people who use wheelchairs? Why or why not?

- With "Subject guide" checked, type "Stereotype in Mass Media" in the search area. Click "View" for the "Periodical references." Read the research article " 'Fixing' Stereotypes in News Photos: A Synergistic Approach with the Los Angeles Times" by Shelly Rodgers and Esther Thorson. Try to replicate the study using your local newspaper or a newspaper of your choice. Did you find differences between your findings and the authors' results? What conclusions can you make about stereotyping in the media after working on your study?

Go to the Web site for this book at www.wadsworth.com/product/0534562442 to find more Web links on this subject.

THE MEDIA
THROUGH WHICH WE SEE

Critics throughout the history of literature have used many methods to analyze works created by others. For example, David Lodge in his book *Small World* lists fourteen different analytical perspectives: allegorical, archetypal, biographical, Christian, ethical, existentialist, Freudian, historical, Jungian, Marxist, mythical, phenomenological, rhetorical, and structural.

To fully appreciate visual communication, you must be able to use some sort of critical method to analyze pictures. In the remaining chapters of this book, we emphasize six perspectives for analyzing images.

1. *Personal:* a gut reaction to the work based on subjective opinions.

2. *Historical:* a determination of the importance of the work based on the medium's time line.

3. *Technical:* the relationship between light, the recording medium used to produce the work, and the presentation of the work.

4. *Ethical:* the moral and ethical responsibilities that the producer, the subject, and the viewer of the work have.

Figure S4.1

See color section following page 132.

5. *Cultural:* an analysis of the symbols used in the work that conveys meaning within a particular society at a particular time.

6. *Critical:* the issues that transcend a particular image and shape a reasoned personal reaction.

By studying any image—whether still or moving—from personal, historical, technical, ethical, cultural, and critical perspectives, you become intellectually involved with the picture. Using the six perspectives will encourage you to base conclusions about images on rational rather than emotional responses. You will find that any and *all* images have something to tell you because every picture created has some meaning to communicate. The producer of the image took the time to frame and make the picture for a reason. The message that the artist wants to communicate may simply be a literal summary, the hope that the viewer will appreciate the image's aesthetic beauty, or an underlying political agenda. Just because you cannot initially see any purpose for the image is no reason to discard it. Many large lessons are lost because of a failure to study small, captured moments. An image, regardless of its medium of presentation, is forgotten if it isn't analyzed. A forgotten image simply becomes another in a long stream of meaningless pictures that seem to flood every aspect of communication. Meaningless pictures entertain a viewer only for a brief moment and do not have the capacity to educate. But an analyzed image can affect a viewer for a lifetime.

Image analysis teaches two important lessons about the creation of memorable pictures:

1. A producer of messages must know the culture of the intended audience.

2. The symbols used in the image must be understood by that culture.

■ *PROCEDURE FOR ANALYZING A VISUAL MESSAGE*

Before using any of the six perspectives, you should first look at all the major graphic and content elements within the frame of the picture (Figure S4.1). In the text below, one possible interpretation of each question is printed in italics. Remember: Your interpretation of the image, or anyone else's, may be quite different. Even though a photograph is used for this analysis demonstration, the techniques described below can be used with *any* form of visual message.

1. Make an inventory-like list of all the objects—animal, vegetable, and mineral—in the picture.

   Building, people, sidewalk, trees, leaves, grass, chain, pole, eagle sculpture, steps, African-American boy, T-shirt, shorts, tennis shoes, orange juice carton.

2. Actively notice the picture's composition. What elements are in the center and what elements are toward the edges? Note the use of shadows and lighting effects.

   The eagle sculpture is a bit off-center and to the right. The boy is to the right. In the upper left corner are other people, a tree, and a building. Sun is shining in the background. The boy is shaded. A bit of sidewalk to the right is partly sunny.

3. Study the visual cues of color, form, depth, and movement within the image. Note how the various visual cues interact and conflict. How are colors used? How are shapes and lines utilized within the frame of the image? How is the illusion of depth achieved? Are your eyes actively moving around the frame?

   The color of the boy's skin, his blue T-shirt, and blue striped shorts contrast with the cream-colored sculpture. There is some red typography on his shoes ("Jesse" as in Jesse

Owens, the African-American track star from the 1936 German Olympics?). The orange logo on the opened carton identifies the contents as orange juice. The round shapes of the bird and those of the boy complement one another. People in the background all seem to be moving to the right of the frame as well. The large bird and the smaller boy are in the foreground with the trees, grass, and people in the background. A chain-link fence attached to a pole is on the same level as the sculpture and the boy and further divides the foreground from the background. The eagle is looking off to the right of the frame although its wings are spread open and toward the photographer. The boy sits to the right of the frame as well and seems to be looking at something that is to his left. Consequently, the viewer's eyes are directed to the center and then to the right of the frame.

4. Where do you think the picture was made? What do you think is the image's purpose? Is it news, art, a personal snapshot, or some other type of image?

The picture was made in a park—possibly in Central Park in New York City. Perhaps the point of the picture is to simply show the contrast between the sculpture and the boy. The picture could be a family snapshot or a magazine feature picture.

Now you are ready to analyze the image in terms of the six perspectives.

Personal Perspective

Upon first viewing any image, everyone draws a quick, gut-level conclusion about the picture based entirely on a personal response. Words and phrases such as "good," "bad," "I like it," or "I don't like it" indicate that a person initially analyzes an image on a superficial, cursory level. Personal perspectives are important because

they reveal much about the person making the comments. However, such opinions have limited use simply because they are personal. These comments cannot be generalized beyond the individual, nor do they reveal much in the way of how a culture would view the image. A memorable image always sparks strong personal reactions, either negative or positive, and also reveals much about the culture from which it was made. A viewer who rests a conclusion about an image on personal perspective denies the chance of perceiving the image in a more meaningful way.

However, the personal perspective has been expanded in an important way by the recent work of Rick Williams at the University of Oregon.

Omniphasism

Rick Williams, a philosopher, photographer, and educator at the University of Oregon, developed a theory of visual communication he calls *omniphasism*. It's a theory that attempts to combine the rational and intuitive aspects of the mind into a balanced whole. Scientific, economic, educational, and cultural systems have traditionally favored the rational, quantitative mind while neglecting the insights that occur from intuitive, qualitative input. Rather than favor one over the other, omniphasism (which literally means "all in balance") celebrates the equal mixing of both ways of experiencing the world in everything from problem solving to visual communication analysis.

If you don't consider your own personal response to an image, you sacrifice much of the qualitative and aesthetic meaning that can be learned from the picture. When omniphasism is employed, the rational and intuitive components and responses to visual messages get equal treatment.

Williams uses eight steps for analyzing a visual message using his omniphasism technique called a "Personal Impact Assessment." He explains, "Part of the idea of going from primary words to associative words to significant words is to move away from a literal interpretation of the photo to a symbolic understanding of it." The eight steps are:

Take Time with the Image Does the content of the image stimulate your imagination or alienate you? What is the story the picture is trying to tell?

I feel attracted to the image somewhat. However, it seems like an isolated moment that rests more on composition than content. The story in the image seems simple enough—a boy decides to rest next to a large statue of an eagle.

List Primary Words On a separate sheet of paper, write single words that describe the visual cues, objects, and feelings you get when looking at the image.

eagle sculpture, boy, park, rest

List Associative Words Write any words that come to mind after thinking about each primary word.

eagle sculpture: American symbol, strong, vigilant, protecting

boy: African American, comfortable, observant

park: Peaceful, haven, green, lush

rest: Time off, getting away from it all, respite

Select the Most Significant Associative Words For each primary/associative word group quickly choose a single associative word that you feel is the most important, interesting, and/or significant.

Protecting, comfortable, haven, getting away from it all

Put the Primary and Significant Associative Words into Pairs Combine the primary words with the most significant associative words.

eagle sculpture: protecting

boy: comfortable

park: haven

rest: getting away from it all

Relate the Primary and Significant Associative Word Pairs to Yourself To the right of each primary and significant associative word, write what each word symbolizes or represents to you.

eagle sculpture/protecting: America uses its strength to protect its citizens.

boy/comfortable: Children are young and vulnerable and need to feel safe.

park/haven: A public space can be a refuge from troubles of the day.

rest/getting away from it all: Taking time to relax is important.

Review Your Inner Symbolism Look over these symbolic words and phrases and see if they reveal any inner conflicts, emotions, values, or feelings that you have about the image.

Certainly the events of 9/11 come to mind. There is a need to get away from the relentless media coverage of the initial attacks, the conflict in Afghanistan, and the anthrax scares and find a restful spot in a park away from other people. And perhaps to be reminded of the strengths and freedoms that America possesses.

Write a Story Write a story that details any personal insights you learned by completing this exercise.

Perhaps I long for the time when I was a child and could innocently play in a peaceful park knowing without knowing that I was protected by the strength of America.

After you have studied the image in terms of its composition, content, and personal perspective using the omniphasic approach, you are ready to analyze the visual message, concentrating upon the subsequent five perspectives.

Historical Perspective

Each medium of presentation—from typography to the World Wide Web—has a unique history of circumstances that were set in motion and fostered by individuals interested in promoting the medium. For typography, the history of writing dates from the dawn of recorded history. For the World Wide Web, the historical developments are relatively recent. Knowledge of a medium's history allows you to understand current trends in terms of their roots in techniques and philosophies of the past. Creative visual message production always comes from an awareness of what has come before, so present applications also will influence future uses.

Ask yourself: When do you think the image was made? Is there a specific style that the image imitates?

I would assume that the image was taken recently. The style of the photograph reminds me of "street photographers" from the 1960s and beyond—a sort of relaxed, feature, nonmoment moment.

Technical Perspective

You must know something about how each medium of presentation works. A thorough critique of any visual presentation requires knowledge of how the producer generated the images that you see. With an understanding of the techniques involved in producing an image, you are in a better position to know when production values are high or low, when great or little care has been taken, or when much or little money was spent to make the images.

Ask yourself: How was the image produced? What techniques were employed? Is the image of good quality?

The picture was probably taken with a 35-mm SLR camera using standard color film and with a wide-angle lens. The photographer was probably fairly technically competent because the picture was taken seemingly without the boy knowing it. Although the image seems a little overexposed, the main part of the image is exposed correctly. It is in sharp focus. Overall, the quality of the image is good.

Ethical Perspective

Six principle ethical philosophies can and should be used to analyze a picture. They are the categorical imperative, utilitarianism, hedonism, the golden mean, the golden rule, and the veil of ignorance. These are the principle theories that have survived from 2,500 years of Western moral philosophy. They are familiar to all who have grown up in the United States or other European-influenced cultures. Aspects of these theories are evident in our public policies, laws, and social conventions.

Categorical Imperative

Immanuel Kant, born in the East Prussian city of Königsberg, established the concept of the categorical imperative in the eighteenth century. *Categorical* means unconditional, without any question of extenuating circumstances, without any exceptions. Right is right and must be done even under the most extreme conditions. Consistency is the key to the categorical imperative philosophy. Once a rule is established for a proposed action or idea, behavior or opinions must be consistently and always applied in accordance with it. For example, if a photojournalist's rule is to take pictures regardless if she thinks her newspaper will print them or not, then this decision becomes a categorical imperative. She takes the pictures because it is her duty to do so.

Utilitarianism

British philosophers Jeremy Bentham and John Stuart Mill developed the philosophy of utilitarianism, which is the belief in "the greatest good for the greatest number of people." In utilitarianism, various consequences of an act are imagined, and the outcome that helps the most people is the best choice under the circumstances. However, Mill specified that each individual's moral and legal rights must be met before applying the utilitarian calculus. Although an act might not be beneficial to a few individuals, it might result in helping many. Newspaper editors frequently use and misuse utilitarianism to justify the printing of disturbing accident scenes in their newspapers. Although the picture may upset a few readers because of its gruesome content, it may persuade many others to drive more carefully. That action is acceptable under the utilitarianism philosophy because people do not have a moral right not to be offended on occasion.

Hedonism

From the Greek word for pleasure, hedonism is closely related to the philosophies of nihilism and narcissism. A student of Socrates, Aristippus (who died in Athens in 366 B.C.E.) founded this ethical philosophy on the basis of pleasure. Aristippus believed that people should "act to maximize pleasure now and not worry about the future." However, Aristippus referred to pleasures of the mind—intellectual pleasures—not physical sensations. He believed that people should

fill their time with intellectual pursuits and use restraint and good judgment in their personal relationships. His phrase sums up the hedonistic philosophy: I possess; I am not possessed. Unfortunately, modern usage of the philosophy ignores his original intent. Phrases such as "eat, drink, and be merry, for tomorrow we die," "live for today," and "don't worry, be happy" currently express the hedonistic philosophy. In other words, if an opinion or action is based purely on a personal motivation—money, fame, relationships, and the like—the modern interpretation of hedonistic philosophy is at work. The classical interpretation of hedonism is at work when a photography editor considers only the aesthetic pleasure that a picture will bring.

Golden Mean

Aristotle's golden mean refers to finding a middle ground or a compromise between two extreme points of view or actions. Formulated in about the fourth century B.C.E., this philosophy of taking the middle way doesn't involve a precisely mathematical average but is an action that approximately fits that situation at that time. Compromise and negotiation are actions aimed at finding a link between the opposing viewpoints of two competing interests. When faced with the choice of printing or broadcasting a gruesome picture or not, the golden mean thinker will look for some less gruesome alternative.

Golden Rule

The golden rule teaches people to "love your neighbor as yourself." From Judeo-Christian tradition, this philosophy holds that an individual should be as humane as possible and never harm others by insensitive actions. A television producer who decides not to air close-up footage of family members mourning the loss of a loved one at a funeral because seeing themselves on television might compound their grief is invoking the golden rule.

⌐ Veil of Ignorance

The phrase "put the shoe on the other foot" is a popular adaptation of the veil of ignorance philosophy. Articulated by John Rawls in 1971, it considers all people equal. No one class of people is entitled to advantages over any other. Imagining oneself without knowing the advantages or positions that one brings to a situation results in an attitude of respect for all involved. This philosophy may be one answer to prejudice and discrimination.

Dr. Deni Elliott, director of the Practical Ethics Center at the University of Montana, professor of philosophy, and gourmet chef, advises that you should look at pictures through an ethical perspective by asking yourself the following questions:

1. Does the taking and displaying of the picture fit the social responsibility of the professional involved?

   It seems so, yes, because it is the responsibility of a professional documentary photographer to record human nature wherever it is exhibited.

2. Has anyone's rights been violated in the taking and displaying of the picture?

   There may be a problem with the boy's privacy. Shouldn't the boy reasonably expect to be able to be in a park without a photographer taking his picture? Where are his parents or guardians? Would they object to the picture being taken? What is the boy's name? Did he sign a release form for the photographer to use the image?

3. Does the display of the image meet the needs of the viewers?

   Yes. The image is clearly and fairly reproduced in this book.

4. Is the picture aesthetically appealing?

Yes. It is a pleasant image to look at.

5. Does the picture choice reflect moderation?

   Yes. There might have been other moments in the boy's life that were photographed that might show him doing something embarrassing, but the photographer chose not to show them.

6. Does the professional choice reflect empathy for the subject's experience?

   That's hard to tell other than the assumption in number 5.

7. Could a professional justify the choice if she didn't know which of the parties (subject, shooter, or viewer) she would turn out to be?

   If this were a picture of the photographer's son, for example, I can't imagine there would be much objection to it.

8. Does the visual message cause unjustified harm? (see Figure S4.2)

   No one seems to be harmed by this image.

 ### Cultural Perspective

The process for finding a cultural perspective is similar to the one found in the Williams method above. But here is your chance to redefine your analysis given the influence from the historical, technical, and ethical perspectives. Cultural analysis of a picture involves identifying the symbols used in the image and determining their meaning for the society as a whole. Symbolism may be analyzed through the picture's use of heroes and villains, by the form of its narrative structure, by the style of the artwork, by the use of words that accompany the image, and by the attitudes about the subjects and the culture communicated by the visual artist. Cultural perspective is closely related to the semiotics approach.

Ask yourself: What is the story and the symbolism involved with the elements in the visual message? What do they say about current cultural values?

The symbol of America—the bald eagle—is strong and vigilant, but at the same time slightly cold and distracted. A young boy stops to rest in a park at the foot of the large eagle perhaps unaware of the sculpture's symbolism because he is distracted as well. Should children be taught to notice important cultural symbols found in everyday life? Otherwise, will deeper understanding of the freedoms taken for granted be lost?

Critical Perspective

The final step in analyzing a picture is to apply a critical perspective. That requires an attempt to transcend a particular image and draw general conclusions about the medium, the culture from which it is produced, and the viewer. A critical perspective allows the viewer to use the information learned about a medium, its practitioner, and the image produced to make more general comments about the society that accepts or rejects the images. As such, a critical perspective redefines a person's initial personal perspective in terms of universal conclusions about human nature.

Ask yourself: What do I think of this image now that I've spent so much time looking at and studying it?

When I first saw the image, I didn't think much of it. It simply shows a boy resting at the feet of a large eagle statue in a park, seemingly unaware of its existence. But upon closer inspection and reflection, the image can mean that the strengths of a

country will shade and protect its citizens and visitors even when those persons are unaware or unappreciative of that charge.

■ APPLYING ANALYTICAL PERSPECTIVES

Your ultimate goal with regard to any analysis of a picture is to understand your own reaction to the image. David Lodge wrote, "analysis is ego-driven. The main thing is that it always reveals the person making the analysis—not really the piece itself." Through this analytical process, you review, refine, and renew your personal reaction to the image. Analysis of an image is therefore a cyclic event in which you move from an initial, emotional, and subjective personal reaction to a rational, objective, and thoughtful personal response. Being critical is a highly satisfying intellectual exercise. The nine chapters on typography, graphic design, informational graphics, cartoons, photography, motion pictures, television and video, computers, and the World Wide Web analyze images produced by each medium of presentation within the analytical framework described. Although analysis is time-consuming at first, practice reduces the amount of time required. Because most visual messages are shown with little or no verbal information, you are once again left with the old adage, "The more you know, the more you see." It is up to you, and only you, to find meaning in and use for any image. If you take the time to study images carefully, you will become a much more interesting and knowledgeable person. You will also be more likely to produce images that have more meaning for more people.

San Jose Mercury News, George Wedding

Figure S4.2

Andy Carr, eleven, lies in the back of an ash-filled pickup truck, a victim of the Mt. St. Helens 1980 explosion. The image invokes all six ethical philosophies just discussed. Editors for the San Jose Mercury News *published the photograph on the front page, because it was a strong news picture and the editor thought he had a duty to print it (categorical imperative). It also communicated the tragic result of not heeding official warnings to evacuate from the area (utilitarianism). Many upset readers, however, were sure that the image ran in order to sensationalize the event (hedonism). Some readers thought that the picture should have run smaller and on an inside page (golden mean). Readers also were concerned that the published image deepened the family's grief (golden rule) or were so upset that they imagined their own family member in a similar situation (veil of ignorance).*

TYPOGRAPHY

Typography is to writing as soundtracks are to movies.

Jonathan Hoefler, 1970–

TYPEFACE DESIGNER

By the end of this chapter you should know:

- The importance of Johannes Gutenberg's printing process for the development of mass communications.
- The six typeface families and how each one expresses a particular mood.
- The opposing arguments for readable versus artistic typographical displays.
- Future considerations for various uses of typography.

The Lilly Library on the campus of Indiana University in Bloomington has a copy of Johannes Gutenberg's 42-line Bible—one of the first books ever printed with a successful commercial printing process. There is no clearer indication of the religious roots of books and the power of the printed word.

Also in the lobby of the Lilly Library is a replica of a seventeenth-century wooden press similar to the one Gutenberg used to produce the pages (Figure 8.1). But just like viewing a camera obscura, an antique motion picture camera, a small-screen, black and white television set, or one of the first room-sized computers, we are not so much in awe of the machine as we are of the product that it creates. Although we may admire the technique required to produce the sturdy printing press, our attention is immediately drawn to the colorful, 500-year-old book that is kept in a protective display case. The Lilly Library has a paper copy of the first volume with only fourteen pages missing. While studying the open pages of the book, our silence shows respect not only for the content of the material presented but also because the work represents the end of the Dark Ages and the beginning of a revolution in communication.

The Lilly Library, Indiana University; used by permission

Figure 8.1

What Gutenberg's press might have looked like is demonstrated in the lobby of the Lilly Library on the campus of Indiana University in Bloomington. The two bell-shaped structures sitting on the press at the left were used to ink the metal type.

Gutenberg's Bible is impressive not only as a symbol for the dawn of modern civilization but as a work of art (Figure 8.2). In medieval Europe, religious **scribes** living in monasteries spent their entire lives copying the words and illustrations of previously copied books for abbey libraries. They copied by hand, using calligraphy, which means *beautiful writing.* They hoped that their efforts would please their God.

Gutenberg fashioned metal type to mimic the hand-drawn writing of scribes. His goal was to show that a mechanical printing process could produce work as beautiful as that of a monk. German scribes most commonly used a **typeface** called **textur.** It is a square, compact typographical style with little space between individual letters to get as many words on a page as possible. Because of Gutenberg's artistry, his printed version of textur was almost indistinguishable from the hand-drawn letters.

Each page of text for the Bible is set in two completely justified columns with a wide **alley** between them. At the beginning of each chapter, a large, hand-drawn, and colorfully decorated letter introduces the text. Gutenberg allowed blank spaces in the copy to accommodate this artwork. The red, blue, and gold hand-drawn illustrations show characters from biblical stories. Large margins around the text often are illustrated with elaborate vines, flowers, colorful birds, and other decorative drawings (Figure 8.3).

The justified columns set in the middle of each page give the work a formal balance that corresponds with its religious importance. Printed in Latin, the lines of type could be easily justified because the written Latin of the day contained many ligature characters that allowed for hyphenation or the abbreviation of words with as many as six letters. The tiny ligature symbols appear above the letters at the end of each line of text.

Although the first nine pages have only 40 lines and the tenth page 41, the work is called a 42-line Bible because all the other 1,282 pages have 42 lines of type in each column. The change in the number of lines probably was an efficiency measure to save paper.

The book is printed in two volumes that together weigh more than fifty pounds. Each volume measures 11 by 16 inches, and each page contains approximately 2,500 letters. With the press that Gutenberg invented, printing a page took about three minutes. Approximately 300 copies of the same page could be printed in a 15-hour day. Even with six assistants working for him, two years were required just to set the type for the entire book and two more years to print it. Gutenberg printed approximately 180 copies—about 140 on paper and perhaps as many as 40 on high-quality and enormously expensive parchment (vellum) made from more than 5,000 carefully prepared calfskins.

Today, only 48 copies of the work are known to exist—36 on paper and 12 on vellum. Fourteen copies of the book are in the United States. The Library of Congress has one of only three "perfect" copies, or complete versions of the book printed on vellum. The other two "perfect" copies are located in the British Library in London and the Bibliothèque Nationale in France. The first Gutenberg Bible to come to this country was sold at an auction in 1847 for $2,600. Today it is housed in the New York City Public Library and is worth millions of dollars. But Gutenberg never made a guilder from his Bible or the innovative press on which it was produced.

Gutenberg's Bible was introduced to the world in 1456. At the time, Gutenberg was about 55 years old. Leonardo da Vinci was 3 years old, Christopher Columbus would not make his first voyage across the Atlantic until 37 years later, and William Shakespeare would not write his first sonnet for another 100 years. Unlike those and other famous people of his and subsequent times, there is little official record of his achievement. No known book contains a printer's mark with his name on it to indicate that the work was his. In fact, the famous Bible contains the logo of two other printers who won his books and his equipment in a financial judgment by a court. The court order even locked Gutenberg out of his own printing establishment.

Less than 50 years later, print shops had sprung up throughout Europe. The basic design and practice of his press remained virtually unchanged for the next 350 years, but Gutenberg never received any royalties from his invention. As an indication of his lack of fame during his own lifetime, no portrait painter ever thought to capture his profile on canvas. If it hadn't been for the kindness of an archbishop, he would have died penniless (or guilderless). His death,

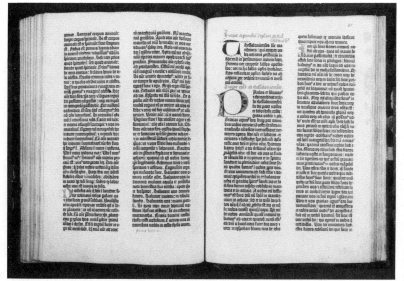

Figure 8.2

The 42-line Gutenberg Bible is an excellent example of typography and graphic design. The text is set in a blackletter typeface family and uses tight kerning. However, there is enough leading to include the ligature characters necessary to abbreviate and hyphenate the Latin text in order to have justified columns. The balanced composition of the columns with ample white space connotes the visual messages of formality, seriousness, and reverence.

Figure 8.3

See color section following page 132.

like his birth, went largely unnoticed, and his place of burial has been long forgotten. But the name Johannes Gutenberg has become a symbol for a communication medium that married typography—the printing of words—to pages to form a book. His innovation revolutionized education, scientific exploration, artistic expression, business dealings, and society itself. However, like so many other great inventors, he led a troubled life.

■ THE CURIOUS HISTORY OF JOHANNES GUTENBERG

Johannes Gensfleisch zum Gutenberg is believed to be the third son of wealthy parents, Friele and Else Gensfleisch. Some have speculated that his birth was illegitimate, because no official record of his birth exists. He was born sometime between 1387 and 1400 in Mainz, Germany. Although unusual for someone of his social standing, but explained by the fact that his uncle was the master of the mint at Mainz, early in his career he apprenticed as a goldsmith. He learned metalworking, engraving skills, and the arts of mirror making and decorating objects with precious stones. Sometime during this early period, he dropped the unflattering family name of Gensfleisch (or *goose-flesh* in German) and took the name of the town of his mother's birth, Burg Gutenberg.

At the time, the aristocracy and trade guild members were locked in a bitter struggle known as the "guild rebellion." The trade unionists wanted a greater say in their political future. Gutenberg's upbringing and outgoing personality earned him a leadership role in the dispute, but he and his father were forced to leave Mainz in 1428 because they feared for their safety. The two settled in Strasbourg, then a German city, about 100 miles southwest of Mainz, leaving his mother behind to manage the family's home.

In only fifteen years while living in Strasbourg, he made a name for himself as a metalworker and a gem cutter. He invented improved methods for polishing precious stones and manufacturing mirrors. He made handheld mirrors that religious pilgrims could use to hold above the crowds within a cathedral in order to get a better view of religious relics. Court records suggest that he also was working on a "secret art," which most likely was an early version of his printing press.

But his personal troubles kept interfering with his work. He became known as a quick-tempered litigant and borrower of large sums of money. In 1434 he embarrassed city officials when he had a municipal officer of Mainz, who was visiting Strasbourg, jailed under an old law that allowed such an action if money was owed between private citizens from two different towns. In 1437, a respectable woman, Ennelin zu der Iserin Thure, sued him for breach of contract when he changed his mind about marrying her. At his trial, he so berated one of her witnesses that the man later sued Gutenberg for libel. The experience must have soured him on marriage, for he remained a bachelor his whole life.

The next year he needed money to continue his printing experiments, so he agreed to a five-year contract to teach two partners his secret printing method. When one of his associates died, his former partner's sons sued for the advance their father had given to Gutenberg. Court documents reveal that he won the case. An important part of the official court document, an inventory of his workshop, showed that it included a press, various examples of type, and a "mysterious instrument" that was probably a device for casting type molds in metal. For historians, this record is crucial in establishing the fact that Gutenberg was indeed a printer because there is little other evidence.

During that time he also borrowed a large sum of money from the Church of St. Thomas in Strasbourg, which he failed to repay. The church elders took the drastic and unsuccessful step of suing Gutenberg for the money. Either because of embarrassment over his personal and business dealings in Strasbourg or because the political climate had calmed in his hometown, he returned to Mainz in 1443, where he lived the rest of his life.

Knowing that he had an invention that could drastically change the method of written communication and yet not have the funds to produce a working model must have been exceedingly frustrating. By this time, his family's fortune had greatly diminished, so he could not expect any help from his parents. The funds required to support his experiments were enormous, and trying to secure enough money to continue his work caused most of the troubles in his life.

Although the popular assumption is that Gutenberg invented printing, that isn't the case. His genius was in combining what was known at the time with some of his own ideas about the following:

1. A type mold acceptable for printing
2. A suitable metal alloy
3. Ink manufacture
4. Paper and parchment use
5. Bookmaking
6. A press to make mechanical printing commercially possible

Gutenberg wasn't the first to use movable type as a substitute for writing by hand. In 1908 an Italian archaeologist found a clay **tablet** on a Greek island that indicated the use of movable type to print characters as early as 1500 B.C.E. However, Pi-Sheng probably invented movable type in China with characters made from hardened clay and wooden blocks in the ninth century. A famous work of the period, the *Diamond Sutra,* was a roll of paper sixteen feet long printed with writing from wooden blocks. Marco Polo reported the Chinese use of printed money in about 1300. The Koreans developed separately cast bronze and copper type characters and they were widely used in China and Japan. The first known book printed with movable metal type—almost 80 years before Gutenberg's Bible—was titled *Jikji,* produced in a Buddhist temple in Korea in 1377. However, Gutenberg and everyone else in Europe probably were unaware of the extent of printing developments in Asia because of the limited communications of the time.

Gutenberg was well aware of the method of relief printing from wooden blocks used in the Netherlands, France, Italy, and his own country to produce popular holy images, playing cards, and advertising handbills. But wood wasn't acceptable for a mechanical printing process because it tended to warp easily. He may have learned of experiments by Propius Walkfoghel of France, who was supposedly working on

"alphabets of steel" in about 1444, but with no known result.

Gutenberg most likely used his skills as a metalworker to invent a metal alloy that was soft enough to cast as an individual letter and hard enough to withstand several thousand impressions on sheets of paper, and that would not shrink when it cooled in a type mold. For the press to be successful, every letter had to maintain a consistent height and width. Through hundreds of experiments, Gutenberg developed a mixture of lead, tin, and antimony that satisfied his strict requirements.

Fortunately, printing inks and paper were common printing tools by that time and easier to adapt. The Egyptians and Chinese had used writing ink as early as 2600 B.C.E. By the eleventh century, inkmaking in China was a treasured art in which earth colors were mixed with soot and animal fat and used to produce colorful documents. European relief block printers made their own inks from secret formulas probably learned from painters of the day. However, inks used for wood blocks that would soak into the grains weren't appropriate for printing with metal type from which they'd simply run off. The ink formula that worked for Gutenberg was one developed by the Dutch artist Jan Van Eyck twenty years earlier. His ink formula called for the boiling of linseed oil and lampblack or soot that produced a thick, tacky ball that could be smeared on the metal type.

Another piece of the printing puzzle was the use of paper. Although the Egyptians had long used papyrus, a crude paper made from reeds that grew along the banks of the Nile River, as a **substrate** for their writing, the eunuch Ts'ai Lun for the emperor's court in 105 C.E. probably invented paper in China.

Paper as a medium for writing gradually made its way to the West. When Arab warriors defeated the Persians at the battle of Samarkand, they brought the craft of paper-making as far west as Spain. By Gutenberg's time, paper mills were well established in Germany, Spain, France, and Italy.

Although it was vastly more expensive, Gutenberg preferred the use of parchment as a printing substrate. Vellum is the name for the highest-quality parchment made from the skins of young or stillborn calves. The Old French word *velin* means "calf" and is the basis for the English word *veal.* Vellum is a long-lasting substance that can be printed on both sides. Because it doesn't soak up printing inks and because inks are better preserved on its surface, it was used for the most colorful illustrations.

The modern concept of books in which individual pages are sewn together and bound by front and back covers also was quite well known to Gutenberg. Every abbey library contained a collection of handwritten books. For example, the abbey library at Canterbury housed more than 2,000 books. The most common type of book was religious in content: Bibles, collections of psalms, and other religious work; most were written in Latin. By 1450, some 30 to 40 percent of the population in many areas of Europe could read. However, writing, like art, was considered a craft and only a few practiced it.

Printing also requires a press. The machine had to be sturdy enough to withstand the weight of the platen and the type itself. Presses at the time were used to produce wine, cheese, and bailing paper. Gutenberg's tax records show that he had a wine cellar in Strasbourg that contained 420 gallons. Not surprisingly, his printing press was a modification of wine presses in use at that time: It was simply a large screw that lowered a weight onto a sheet of paper or parchment against a plate of inked type. This basic design remained the same until the invention of steam-powered presses about 350 years later.

But the last pieces to the printing puzzle—the ones that Gutenberg never found and that eventually caused his downfall—were the coins needed to pay for all his experimentation during the twenty years required to perfect his printing press. All his experiments with metal alloys, type molds, paper, and inks and the rent for his workspace, wages for his assistants, and room and board for himself required money that he simply did not have. Consequently, he was forced to borrow from others.

In 1450, Gutenberg borrowed 800 guilders at 6 percent interest from a wealthy Mainz merchant, Johannes Fust. Gutenberg used his printing equipment as collateral. Soon afterward, he borrowed another 800 guilders from Fust. In 1455 with the work nearly completed on the Bibles that could easily pay off any debt owed, Fust grew impatient or greedy and brought suit against Gutenberg for 2,026 guilders covering the loans and interest payments owed. Gutenberg claimed in court that their agreement was for Fust to supply 300 guilders a year for supplies and that they would split the profits. The court didn't believe Gutenberg, gave Fust the presses and all of the work in progress, and locked Gutenberg out of his own print shop.

Fust immediately formed a partnership with one of Gutenberg's assistants, Peter Schöffer. Their printing establishment lasted as a family business for the next 100 years, as Schöffer married Fust's daughter. Instead of using Gutenberg's printer's mark, the two designed their own logo and imprinted the Bibles with it (Figure 8.4). Fust traveled to several European capitals selling the books.

After losing the court case to Fust, Gutenberg quickly fell into bankruptcy, unable to pay even the interest on previous loans. Miraculously, a Mainz doctor offered him financial support to open another print shop in 1460 (Figure 8.5). Perhaps feeling sorry for Gutenberg in his economic plight and as a tribute for his great contribution to communication, Archbishop Adolf of Mainz gave him the rank of nobleman with an annual pension that allowed him to live the last years of his life in relative comfort. He is believed to have died on February 3, 1468, and was buried somewhere in the cemetery of the Franciscan church in Mainz. No marker was erected to identify his grave.

For several years after Gutenberg's death, movable metal type printing was centered in Mainz. But because several German factions were at war, many people—printers included—left their homes for safer countries. Consequently, print shops opened in France and Italy and quickly spread throughout Europe. By 1500, there were 1,120 print shops in 260 towns in 17 European countries. More than 10 million copies of 40,000 different works had been printed by that year. As books became plentiful and inexpensive, literacy and educational opportunities quickly grew as societies moved from oral presentations to reading as the primary method of teaching. As people became better educated, democratic ideas spread. Secularism challenged traditional ideas about religious attitudes. Business opportunities and cities expanded as printing sped the recording of transactions. More than any other single invention the printing press signaled an end to the Dark Ages that followed the collapse of the Roman Empire and the beginning of the Renaissance.

The Gutenberg Bible not only showed the world the potential of the print medium, it also signaled the start of typography—the reproduction of words through a mechanical process. Typography, as exemplified in Gutenberg's work, gave printed words an equal artistic footing as hand-lettered words. A few years after Gutenberg's achievement,

Modified after Hendrik van Loon, *Observations of the Mystery of Print*, Book Manufacturers' Institute Inc., 1937

Figure 8.4

Early publications often contained the marks or logos of printers who created the documents. These marks became as recognizable to knowledgeable readers and collectors as the names of the printers themselves. At the top right is the famous logo of the printers Fust and Schöffer—the only printer's mark in Gutenberg's Bible.

typographic artists—specialists in the creation and use of various typographical styles—combined the craft of sculpture with the art of graphic design to produce lettering that was both practical and beautiful.

Typography, of course, has its roots in writing. The story of writing is the gradual acceptance of the idea, over thousands of years, that words and images are separate and different. Writing and reading without knowledge of design reinforces the notion

Modified after Jeremy Hornsby, *The Story of Inventions*, Crescent Books, 1977

Figure 8.5

Although we don't know exactly what Johannes Gutenberg or his printing press looked like, this early woodcut portrays the inventor of the press as one of the first copy editors in the history of printing.

that words are more important than pictures in formulating messages. Typography reminds us that words are graphic elements with pictorial qualities as important as any illustration.

■ ANALYSIS OF THE GUTENBERG BIBLE

Gutenberg's work should be praised for at least three technical achievements: its typeface, its longevity, and its design. Gutenberg magnificently mimicked the textur typographical style of the abbey scribes. The book's longevity is another credit to his craft because few books in human history have lasted as long. Finally, the design, probably Peter Schöffer's work, is a pleasing combination of text and graphic elements arranged to connote power, prestige, and artistic beauty—a perfect fit for the content of the work.

Production of the Gutenberg Bible marks the start of commercially viable printing, but it also is a commentary on ethical business practices. Both Fust and Gutenberg were tarred by their business dealings with each other. Fust should have been more patient and allowed Gutenberg to finish his work instead of locking him out of his own print shop and trying to take credit for printing the book. Gutenberg should have been more careful about handling other people's money in the operation of his printing business.

The commercial printing press demonstrated how much people of the day yearned for reading matter beyond the simple printed playing cards or religious works available to them. When more and more people learned to read, writers supplied them with words. For example, humanist writers supported by the Pope believed that turning to the Greek and Roman philoso-

phers for answers could solve all ethical dilemmas. The humanist movement became the dominant philosophy during the Renaissance, but was later denounced by the Catholic Church when the humanist writers questioned the content of the Bible. "Since the advent of movable type," writes Elizabeth Eisenstein, "an enhanced capacity to store and retrieve, preserve and transmit has kept pace with an enhanced capacity to create and destroy, to innovate or outmode." Printing not only increased the need for more printing but also increased the need for more critical thinking. Stated another way by media critic Marshall McLuhan, "Print created national uniformity and government centralism, but also individualism and opposition to government as such."

However, two researchers have recently put into question Gutenberg's printing innovation. Paul Needham, the Scheide Librarian at Princeton University, and physicist Blaise Aguera y Arcas analyzed extreme close-ups of individual printed letters using high-resolution digital images. For example, Needham studied one letter of the alphabet as it was printed on one page. He reported that the letters lacked the degree of consistency one would expect from a printing process in which the same letter mold was used throughout. He concluded that Gutenberg might have actually had to produce separate molds for the same letter—a painstaking and inefficient process that would not be revolutionary. There is speculation that perhaps topographical designer and printer Nicolaus Jenson was the real inventor of the movable metal type printing press. As master of the mint for the French government, Jenson was sent to Mainz in 1458 to learn Gutenberg's printing technique. He subsequently moved to Venice, Italy, where he opened a printing workshop producing about 150 books using his self-designed and elegant typefaces.

Nevertheless, Gutenberg will always be credited for inventing the first commercially viable printing press. When analyzing his legacy, his book and his life should never be separated from historical accounts about printing. He was a person with all too human frailties. Despite the events in his life, or because of them, he accomplished what he set out to do. Perhaps in the end he dedicated so many years of his life to producing a Bible as an act of contrition for his relationships with other people. We will never actually know his motives because, ironically, the inventor of commercialized printing left no printed record of his own life (Figure 8.6).

■ TYPOGRAPHY AND THE SIX PERSPECTIVES

Because words are so important in communicative messages, the way those words are presented form a vital link between what the words mean and how the words are seen.

Personal Perspective

Most people do not think of typography when they read, but it determines every aspect of the way printed words are presented. Look at the way the words are placed on this page. A typographical designer for this book has made attribute selections that:

1. Determined the style of the typeface that best reflects the content of the verbal message

2. Made decisions about the various sizes for headlines, subheads, **captions, cutlines,** and the body of the text

3. Decided the color for the words (black) and the **fonts** used (italics, boldface, reverse, and so on)

4. Determined the length and width of the text blocks, the style of justification (left, right, centered, or fully justified), and the white space between individual letters (kerning), lines of type (leading), and columns of type (alleys)

The average reader seldom notices such decisions—they simply make the text easy to read. But not being aware of the many typographical choices available to a designer is like watching a motion picture only because of its plot—much that is there is missed.

Historical Perspective

Although the art of typography officially began with the first edition of Gutenberg's Bible, typography is linked directly to the history of writing. The placement of symbolic messages on a medium of presentation is a practice about 20,000 years old. The linking of writing and typography involved four developmental stages:

1. Painting
2. Writing
3. Hot type production
4. Cold type production

Painting

Graphic designer and researcher Georges Jean in his book *Writing: The Story of Alphabets and Scripts* wrote that "writing cannot be said to exist unless a symbol system is agreed upon." Beginning about 20,000 years ago, humans began to preserve their observations and thoughts by drawing pictures on the walls of caves, on mountains, on desert plateaus, and on the bones of slaughtered animals. Petroglyphs (rock drawings) and other illustrations were a realization by early humans that spoken communications were ephemeral—they could not be made permanent.

Modified after Otto Fuhrmann, *The 500th Anniversary of the Invention of Printing*, Philip C. Duschnes, 1937

Figure 8.6

This woodcut faithfully recreates the statue erected in the town of Mainz, Germany, that honors the memory of Johannes Gutenberg. Note that his left hand holds his Bible close to his heart and that his right hand holds type molds.

Drawings of human figures and symbols for the sun and moon abound, but overwhelmingly the main subjects were the animals that were hunted in the part of the world where the drawings were found (Figure 8.7). In the Lascaux caves in southern France, for example, early artists mixed charcoal or colors from the soil with animal fat or their own saliva. They spread these paints with their fingers or crude reed brushes to produce paintings of animals with remarkable clarity and artistry. These drawings represent the first known attempts to create a written language.

The drawings represent two kinds of visual messages: **pictographs** and ideographs. Pictographs are pictures that stand for objects, plants, or animals. Ideographs are images that represent abstract ideas. Modern humans can easily understand ancient pictographs, but the ideographs created by early humans remain a mystery (Fig-

ure 8.8). Hence one of the problems with early iconic communication is that the images used in this form of written communication were not standardized, making translation difficult or even impossible. Another problem was that producing the images required a skilled artist—everyday cave dwellers could throw spears at animals, but they could not easily paint animal images on a wall.

Writing

The Sumerians Like the animals they hunted, for thousands of years early humans were wanderers who constantly searched for food, shelter, and water in small tribes of individuals with similar interests. But in about 8000 B.C.E. in what is now Iraq, thousands of these nomads started to congregate in the fertile valley between the Tigris and Euphrates rivers. For more than 7,000 years these Sumerians lived in Mesopotamia or

Figure 8.7

You may find it hard to believe that the words you are presently reading evolved from cave paintings on walls in prehistoric times, but they did. Cave wall space is limited in the Lascaux region of southern France.

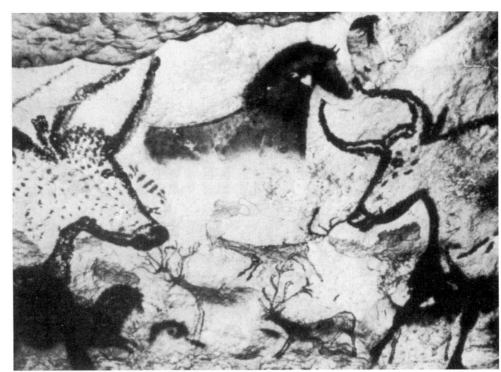

"the land between the rivers." They planted crops, domesticated animals, initiated the Bronze Age when they mixed copper with tin for stronger tools and weapons, invented the wheel, created a complex system of religious and social discipline, buried their dead in organized services, and invented the first system of writing.

At the temple in Uruk in about 3500 B.C.E., scribes wrote on clay tablets for the first time in history. This monumental step in human development took the form of crude pictographic text arranged in columns from right to left. The words described the agricultural lives of the people and reported the number of cattle and sacks of grain that people possessed.

Specially educated scribes used a sharp-edged **stylus** to make impressions in damp clay tablets that they later dried by the sun or in kilns. In about 2800 B.C.E., the scribes started to turn the pictures over on their sides to ease in their production. Three hundred years later, the scribes replaced their pointed sticks with triangular-tipped styluses that they pushed into rather than dragged through the clay. This innovation, along with more abstract representations of objects and ideas, meant that those with less artistic skill than earlier pictographic scribes could produce Sumerian writing. Nevertheless, this writing style called *cuneiform* (Latin for "wedge-shaped") required strict schooling from childhood on, because there were hundreds of characters to learn (Figure 8.9).

The Egyptians Stretching more than 4,000 miles, the Nile is the longest river in the world. Along its banks a civilization as innovative as that of the Sumerians emerged. About 3500 B.C.E., the Egyptian and Sumerian cultures peacefully overlapped. Sometime in 3100 B.C.E., Sumerian ideas about writing reached the Egyptians. But the Egyptian writing system that evolved was

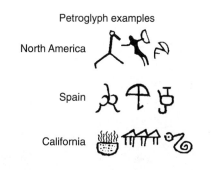

Petroglyph examples

North America

Spain

California

Modified after Duncan Davies, *The Telling Image*, Clarendon Press, 1990

Figure 8.8

Throughout the world, writing systems were invented to describe and explain personal observations and thoughts. Many of the symbols have little literal meaning for us today.

different from that of the Sumerians in two important ways:

1. Unlike the Sumerians who eventually replaced their pictographic system with abstract symbols, the Egyptians never lost the illustrative quality to their writing.

2. Instead of using clay tablets as a substrate for their writing, the Egyptians used papyrus reeds that grew plentifully along the Nile.

Hieroglyphs remained the chief written language of the Egyptians until the Romans conquered the area in 390 C.E. The name is derived from the Greek words *hieros* for "holy" and *gluphein* for "to engrave." This "writing of the gods" reveals that Egyptian culture was much more sensitive to the pictorial qualities of writing than the Sumerian culture. Egyptian hieroglyphics not only told the story of their culture, but also did so in a poetic, beautifully visual way (Figure 8.10).

From an initial symbol set of 700, hieroglyphs eventually expanded to more than 5,000 characters. Hieroglyphic writing actually was more complicated than the Sumerian system because it was a combination of pictographs, ideographs, and determinatives—symbols that indicated whether a character should be read as a picture or as a sound. Scribes were so highly respected for their mastery of the language and their artistic talents that they were one of the few groups that were exempt from taxation. The script was difficult to translate because it

Figure 8.9

Examples of cuneiform writing, like this one, can be found at the Louvre Museum in Paris.

Figure 8.10

As with the petroglyphs in caves throughout the world, the meaning of hieroglyphic writing would have been impossible to decipher had it not been for the discovery of the Rosetta Stone. Oval outlines mark the names of important political and religious figures in this Egyptian reproduction. The rough background texture comes from the papyrus paper used as a writing substrate.

Paul Martin Lester

In the collection of Paul Martin Lester

could be read from right to left, from left to right, from top to bottom, or from bottom to top, depending on the scribe who produced it. By 1500 B.C.E., hieroglyphic writing divided into two forms: hieratic and **demotic scripts.** The hieratic form is the most familiar style of writing and was used for official business and religious documents. The demotic script was more popular for everyday types of writing because it was less illustrative and its characters were highly abstract and symbolic.

For hundreds of years, the meaning of Egyptian hieroglyphs remained a mystery for researchers. But in 1799, during Napoleon's expedition to Egypt, the Rosetta Stone was found near the port city of Rashid. Written in 196 B.C.E., the stone contained the same information in Greek, hieroglyphic, and demotic versions. It had been written to honor the arrival of 12-year-old Ptolemy V to Egypt. In 1808 Jean-François Champollion in Paris was able to translate most of the Rosetta Stone. The stone is now on exhibit in the British

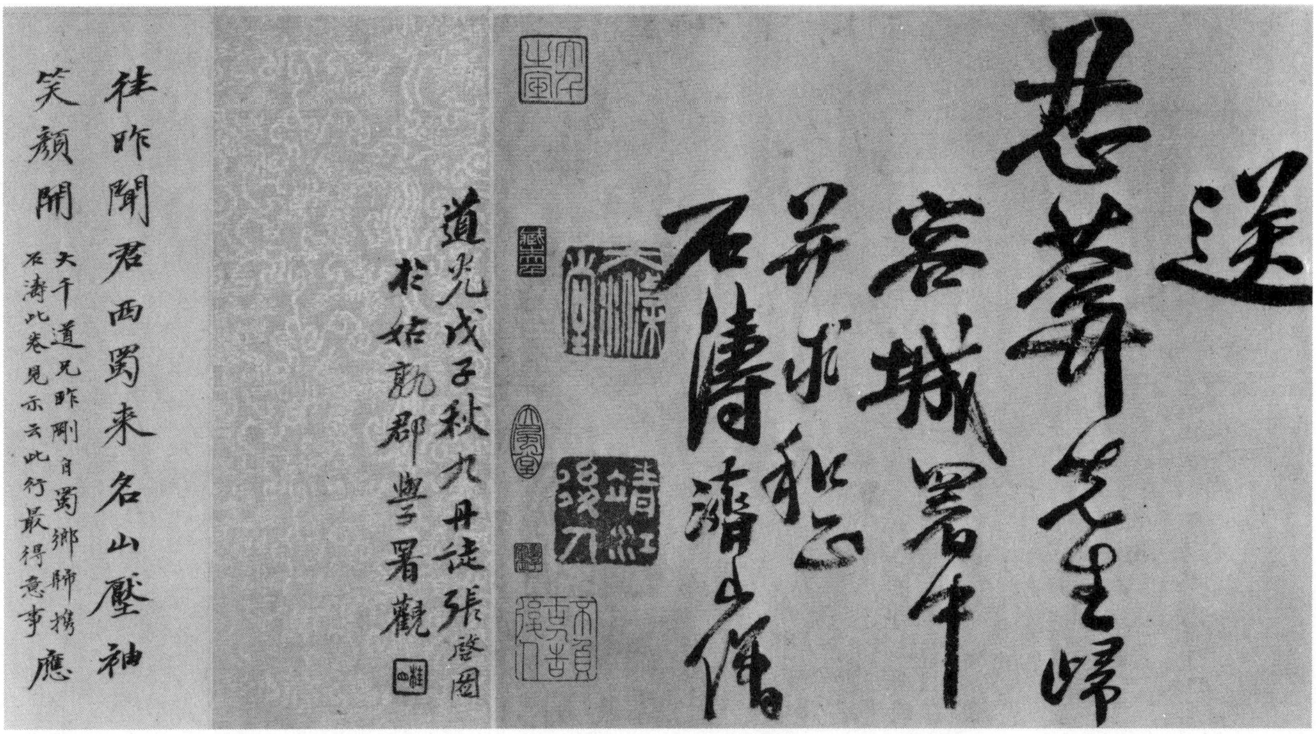

Keith McLeod Fund; gift of Mrs. Charles Amos Cummings, Museum of Fine Arts, Boston

Figure 8.11

"Mountain and River Landscape," from the early Ching dynasty (1630 to about 1707). Note how the three separate panels contrast with the thickly drawn black letters of Chinese calligraphy and the fine lines of the wood block seals.

Museum in London. By 1822, Champollion could translate any hieroglyphic text. Just before his death at age 42, he published a dictionary to enable Egyptologists to learn about the ancient culture.

What experts found were documents written mostly for religious purposes. But there were also business accounts, laws, and marriage contracts. During the thirteenth century B.C.E., the most popular form of religious writing was the *Books of the Dead.* These beautifully illustrated funerary scripts charted the progress of great leaders and ordinary citizens after their deaths.

The Chinese In 1800 B.C.E., Tsang Chieh, after noticing the footprints left behind by a bird, supposedly invented calligraphy. Chinese calligraphy is the most complicated form of communication known (Figure 8.11). It was never reduced to abstract symbols, as were many of the other systems; it remained a written language comprising more than 44,000 individual symbols for centuries. As in other cultures, scribes who knew the language were highly respected for their intelligence and wisdom. They also possessed much political power, because they controlled the information that became recorded for history.

Chinese pictographs, known as logograms, are symbols that represent an entire word, just as the symbol "%" stands for the word *percent.* The main reason for the complexity of Chinese writing was that none of the symbols represent the sounds the Chinese make while speaking; the spoken and written languages are completely different. By royal decree in 210 B.C.E., the Chinese writing system was simplified to about 1,000 basic characters that are still in use today.

Such a writing system made use of the language in mechanical presses difficult. Devising metal typefaces, as Gutenberg had done, for every Chinese character simply was too costly and time-consuming. Chinese printers would spend all their time finding and sorting symbols. Consequently, the Chinese developed a pictorial calligraphic style that is praised as an art form throughout the world.

The Phoenicians Between Egypt to the west and Sumeria to the southeast, the great society of merchants known as Phoenicia prospered along the Mediterranean Sea in the area now known as Lebanon, Syria, and Israel. By about 2000 B.C.E., the Phoenicians possessed some of the fastest sailing ships known and traded goods throughout the world. They learned the Egyptian and Sumerian writing systems in order to trade with them successfully, but cultural pride led them to develop their own system.

The Phoenician culture is forever linked to one of the greatest advances in the history of communication: the alphabet (Figure 8.12). Derived from the first two words of the Greek alphabet, *alpha* and *beta*, an alphabet is a collection of symbols in a specified order that represent the sounds of spoken language. The genius of an alphabet was that it reduced to a handful the number of characters needed to write a language. The Egyptians used about 5,000 symbols, the Phoenicians only 22. Found in the limestone of a **sarcophagus** in the Phoenician city-state of Byblos, the 22 abstract symbols represent the final phase in the transition from pictorial to purely symbolic characters.

A compact, easily learned alphabet ended the political power of well-educated scribes, because anyone could learn the writing system. It also meant that more individuals could produce writings that a large audience would read (Figure 8.13).

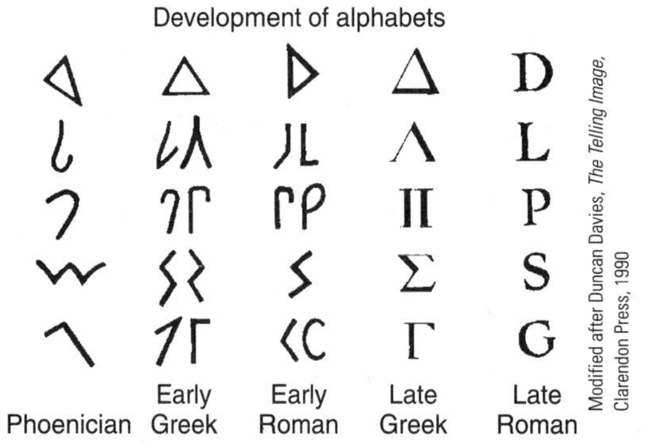

The Greeks Because the Greeks obtained their papyrus from the Phoenician capital of Byblos, they gave their papyrus writing paper the same name. The English word *bible* is from the Greek phrase that means "a papyrus book." The Greeks also learned the Phoenician alphabet sometime between 1000 and 700 B.C.E. The Phoenicians had little use for vowel sounds, but the Greeks did and they changed five consonants to the vowels a, e, i, o, and u and added two other vowel sounds for a total of 24 characters.

The Greeks not only advanced world civilization with their writings about philosophy, science, and government with the alphabet they used, but they also advanced the art of typography by combining their ideas about the beauty and **symmetry** of nature with the letters they used in writing. Greek letters mimicked the natural forms around them: the letter "M" was based on a perfect square, "A" was inspired by the shape of an isosceles triangle, and the letter "O" was based on a nearly perfect circle. The Greek letters were set on an imaginary horizontal baseline to achieve a sense of order by

Figure 8.12

Development of the alphabet. From the almost haphazard strokes of the Phoenician letters, the Western alphabet gradually became standardized and symmetrical.

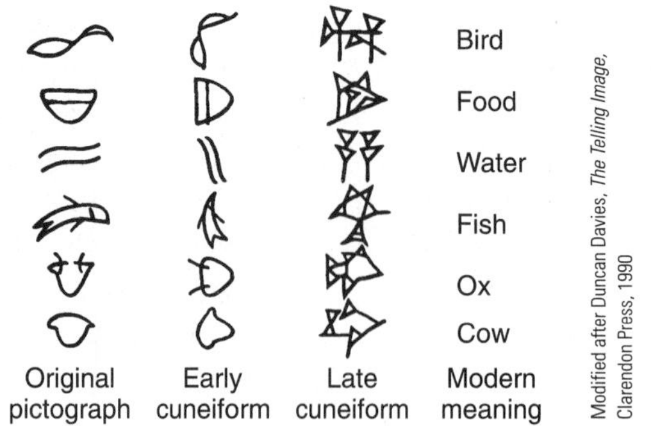

Figure 8.13

A system of letters gradually replaced the native innocence of pictographic communication. An advantage was that more people could learn to read and write. However, the word fish *and the picture of a fish conjure two completely different emotional responses from a viewer. With the invention of cuneiform, words and pictures became forever separated in the minds of literate people.*

Development of alphabets

Phoenician | Early Greek | Early Roman | Late Greek | Late Roman

Modified after Duncan Davies, *The Telling Image*, Clarendon Press, 1990

Original pictograph | Early cuneiform | Late cuneiform | Modern meaning

Bird
Food
Water
Fish
Ox
Cow

Modified after Duncan Davies, *The Telling Image*, Clarendon Press, 1990 their alignment. The individual strokes of the letters were uniform in weight, unlike calligraphy and other forms of writing. They also introduced uppercase and lowercase letters; capitals were reserved for writing on stone, whereas lowercase letters were used on papyrus.

The Greek sense of natural beauty and order brought an artistic style to the symbolic letters. But they also were the first to recognize that alphabetic letters possessed informational as well as **aesthetic qualities** (Figure 8.14).

The Romans Roman society was one of the largest and most influential in the history of Western civilization. From a sleepy little village in 750 B.C.E. on the Tiber River in what now is central Italy in a region known as Latium, these "Latins" built and ruled an empire that stretched from England on the north to Egypt on the south and from Spain on the west to Mesopotamia on the east by the first century C.E. As with all the peoples they conquered, when they overwhelmed the Greeks, the Romans absorbed much of Greek culture, including its alphabet.

The Romans made many adjustments to the Greek writing system. Late in the tenth century C.E. the Latin letter "W," a variation of the common letter "V," was added. Finally in the fourteenth century, some 400 years after Latin had died as a spoken language, the 26th letter, "J," was added to complete the alphabet.

As the Greeks had done, the Romans used uppercase letters (usually painted red) on buildings and lowercase characters when writing on papyrus rolls or wax tablets (Figure 8.15).

Hot Type Production

As indicated earlier, Gutenberg combined several different operational steps—ink, type production, paper, and a press—to develop

Keith McLeod Fund; gift of Mrs. Charles Amos Cummings, Museum of Fine Arts, Boston

the first commercially successful printing method. Printers commonly used his basic procedure without any major changes for the next 350 years (Figure 8.16). One of the great early printers was the Venetian Aldus

Paul Martin Lester

Figure 8.14

"Votive Stele [a vow—as indicated by the upraised hands on a stone pillar] with Four Figures in Relief." This Hellenistic marble from the fifth century B.C.E. *uses letters with serif embellishments. The piece clearly reflects the culture's appreciation for the natural beauty of common shapes—triangles, squares, and circles.*

Figure 8.15

For writing on stone, Romans used all capital letters as in this example found at the Louvre Museum in Paris.

Figure 8.16 (left)

This woodcut portrays a typical print shop during the first century after the invention of the commercial printing press. Typesetters in the background set the printing plates with metal type molds. Meanwhile, the man in the front right inks a plate of type with two ball-like pads. After he lowers the platen, the other man removes the printed work from the press.

Figure 8.17 (right)

One of the first printed books with woodcut illustrations is Francesco Colonna's The Hypnerotomachia Poliphili *(The Dream of Poliphilus). The Aldine Press produced the 1499 edition in the print shop of the Venetian Aldus Manutius. Notice that in only a few years after Gutenberg's Bible, the highly readable roman type family replaces the difficult blackletter typeface.*

Manutius. His Aldine Press published high-quality works by Greek and Roman philosophers and illustrated works of fiction. In 1498 he finished a five-volume set of Aristotle's works. He also published *The Dream of Poliphilus,* a curious tale about a young man searching for his lover. The book is noted for its sexually explicit illustrations (Figure 8.17). His type designer, Francesco Griffo, helped develop the first **font** for the title page of Virgil's *Opera.* Early italic was not designed to emphasize a certain phrase as it is today but to make more money for Aldus. The slanted italic script allowed pages to be filled with more characters, thus using less paper. *Opera* was also innovative because it was the first pocket book, measuring only 3¾ by 6 inches.

Evidence of Gutenberg's legacy is found throughout the world. In the sixteenth century, the first newspapers in the world were printed in the Netherlands and in Germany. In 1704, the *Boston News-Letter* became the first single-sheet American newspaper (Figure 8.18). Benjamin Franklin returned to Philadelphia with a press after a trip to England in 1726 and published the *Pennsylvania Gazette* and the famous *Poor Richard's Almanac.* When the French Revolution erupted in 1789, a call for the freedom of the press was answered with the establishment of more than 300 newspapers in France the next year.

The principal invention of the Industrial Revolution (1760 to 1840) was James Watt's steam engine, invented in 1769. Johannes Gutenberg's quaint wooden press became a historical relic in 1814 when the German Frederich Koenig used the steam engine to power a printing press in London that could print 1,110 sheets a day. Police had to guard the press from printers who feared the loss of their jobs and were angry about this technological development. In 1828, Augustus Applegath and Edward Cowper invented a four-cylinder press that could handle 4,000 sheets a day for *The Times* of London. Later

Figure 2.2

In Las Vegas, colored flashing lights are used to attract gamblers and photographers.

Figure 3.2 (middle left)

Window to the soul: The eye not only absorbs light but also reflects it.

Figure 3.6 (middle right)

The Ishihara Test for color deficiency involves several colored circles with numbers. With this example, a person with normal color vision will see the number 5 while those with a red/green deficiency will see the number 2.

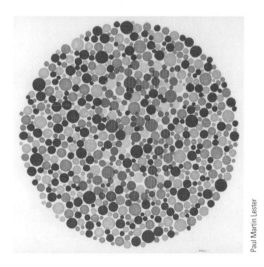

Figure 4.2 (bottom left)

This arrangement of primary and secondary colors is a demonstration of Max Wertheimer's gestalt approach to visual perception (see Chapter 5). The illusion of the solid white triangle linking the primary colors is caused not by the triangle itself but by all the other elements in the diagram. Cover the primary color circles and the white triangle vanishes.

Figure 4.4 (bottom right)

Three-dimensional depth is the result when a darker blue color is used in the background.

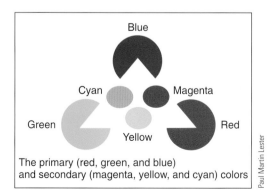

The primary (red, green, and blue) and secondary (magenta, yellow, and cyan) colors

Figure 4.5

In this publicity still for the 1991 movie, Terminator 2, *actor Arnold Schwarzenegger fights off the T-1000 chrome entity (see Chapter 15). Because of the symbolism attached to the color red, the warning light and its reflection add tension to the scene.*

Figure 6.3

"Jane Kent. Died: Age 3 years." Like so much trash, the body of Jane Kent is cruelly discarded and photographed in a straight-on official way much like a police photographer's style. The eerie blue-green glow from a halogen light, the graffiti-inspired "MEAN" on a back window, and the text with a line through add to a viewer's discomfort. The copy at the bottom reads, "NEXT time you read a story like Jane's in this newspaper (and you will) you'll say, 'this must never happen again.'"

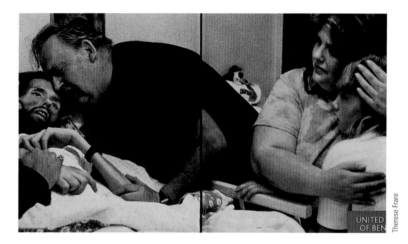

Figure 6.6 (top)

David Kirby, thirty-two, is on his deathbed surrounded by grieving family members. Therese Frare's photograph is an unforgettable emotional moment. But the green logo of Benetton makes it clear that the image is intended not only to make people care but to remind viewers to buy clothing.

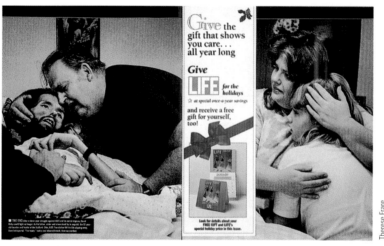

Figure 6.13 (middle)

David Kirby's private family tragedy was published originally in a November 1990 issue of Life *magazine. The black and white tones give a documentary look to the photograph but contrast starkly with the brightly colored holiday advertisement insert.*

Figure 7.21 (bottom left)

In 1948, Walter Goldbach, seventeen, designed the Cleveland Indians' logo. Dr. Robert Bane, who teaches multicultural education at John Carroll University, said, "The feather on Chief Wahoo's head is a sacred symbol. The hooknose and the grinning buckteeth are caricatures. And no Native Americans have red skin. Also, cartoons are demeaning."

Figure S4.1 (bottom right)

This photograph is used in the analysis described at the beginning of Section 4.

Figure 8.3

Gutenberg made white space gaps in the layout so that artists could include enlarged letters and other decorative features on the pages. Note how the red ink color demands your attention while enlivening the tedious blackletter text.

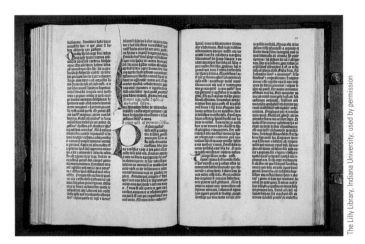

Figure 9.13

Above: The cover of Wired *magazine, a publication devoted to innovations in communication technologies, is an example of words used as pictures to attract attention. Top right: The magazine's table of contents can be a confusing array of illustrations, colors, and text attributes for the uniniti-ated. Nevertheless, the care-fully planned graphic ele-ments are meant to convey a modern, energetic style.*

Right: Text and graphics are merged into a single visual message in this two-page Wired *spread. The orange headline color coincides with the dominant color in the manipulated photograph.*

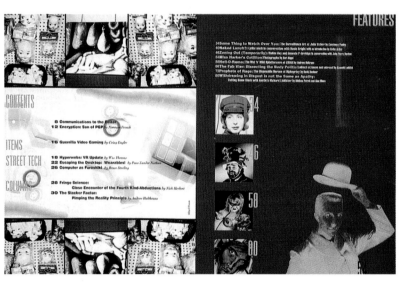

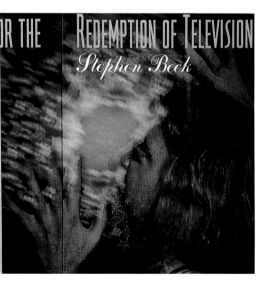

The Boston News-Letter.

Published by Authority.

From Monday May 1. to Monday May 8. 1704.

Courtesy of Vis-Com, Inc.

Modified after M. Thomas Inge. Comics as Culture, University Press of Mississippi. 1990

set back their deadlines to allow printing of more up-to-date news in each edition. For the consumer, efficient presses made newspapers and other publications much more affordable. The faster presses were the namesake of the "penny presses." But as Rolf Rehe notes in his book *Typography: How to Make It Most Legible,* they also were responsible for the unattractive, old-style, and vertical look common to early newspapers. Because cylinder presses ran faster, type had a tendency to fly off the rollers unless it was secured with vertical rules or wedges.

High-speed presses wouldn't have been of much advantage if printers still sorted and set the many typeface styles by hand as in Gutenberg's day. A skilled person could set 1,500 letters per hour by hand. But in 1886 a thirty-two-year-old inventor named Ottmar Mergenthaler from Baltimore introduced the Linotype automated typesetting machine, which could set *9,000 letters an hour.* It cast a whole line of type in lead from letters typed on a keyboard. When an entire story had been set, the type could be fitted onto a form for printing with other stories. After printing, the lead was simply melted and used again— the origination of the term *hot type.* The

Figure 8.18 (left)

The first American news-paper with a regular circulation. With its two columns of aligned type introduced by an enlarged letter, it is similar in style to Gutenberg's Bible.

Figure 8.19 (right)

The Hoe press was used primarily to publish Sunday newspapers that used color. The symmetrical composition of this woodcut helps organize the complicated structure of the steam-driven press.

improvements increased that output to *8,000 sheets per hour!* The American Richard Hoe introduced the rotary press in 1847 (Figure 8.19). With the invention of **lithography** and the halftone photoengraving screen (see Chapter 9), color illustrations and photographs could be printed during the same pressrun as the copy. By the late 1880s, most high-circulation newspapers used the web perfecting press with coated papers that allowed high-quality, fast-paced printing on both sides of a long roll of paper. The advent of stereotyped plates further sped the printing process, as several duplicate pages could be printed on different presses at the same time.

Faster presses drastically reduced the cost of each page. Newspaper publishers added more pages, increasing the amount of advertising space available—and profit. They also next year, Tolbert Lanston introduced the Monotype machine, which could set individual letters. Corrections were much easier than with the Linotype machine because a mistake did not require that a whole line be reset. In 1928, Walter Morey introduced the Teletypesetter, which used perforated tape similar to that used for years for printing stock market prices. When attached to a Linotype machine, the Teletypesetter automatically produced the copy in lead slugs. Noisy and huge Linotype machines were still common in newspapers until the 1960s when they were replaced by cold type technology.

Printing with traditional materials and methods is still an honored craft that a few individuals around the world practice. For example, Andrew Hoyem of San Francisco produces high-quality, limited edition books that he sells for as much as $1,000 each. Three hundred copies of Frank Dobie's adventure about the Southwest, *Coronado's Children,* printed on handmade Italian paper with initial letters printed in 22-karat gold, were sold for $700 each at Neiman Marcus department stores.

Cold Type Production

In a print shop the space needed to store all the lead slugs that represented not only every typeface, but also every size and attribute variation of that font, was enormous. Print shops therefore usually specialized in certain kinds of typeface styles. Inspired by the relatively new invention of photography, phototypesetting, or *cold type,* was a method for creating typeface letters without the need for metal. The transition from metal hot type methods to photographic and later digital cold type procedures produced a radical change in typeface design. Fonts could be made cheaply, quickly, and with nearly the same quality as with metal. More important, designers could create and manipulate type placement easily once the physical limitations of metal type were eliminated.

Cold type is produced in two ways: typesetting without a computer (phototypesetting, photocomposition, and photo-optic or filmsetting) and digital typesetting using a computer. Phototypesetting works on the principle of photography. Depending on the system, typefaces may be stored on punched tape, film, disks, grids, or drums. The typesetter uses a typewriter keyboard to select individual letters. When the machine turns to the appropriate letter, a strong beam of light shines through the letter, exposing a sheet of photographic paper. A fixed focal or zoom lens built into the device controls the size of the typeface. When developed, the positive printed letters are cut, pasted up (keylined) on a layout, sent to a printer where an engraving of the page is made, and then printed.

Digital typesetting is similar to phototypesetting except that an operator uses a computer to generate letters. The computer creates a series of dots that represent characters stored in its memory. The words created are projected onto a video monitor where the operator can view and edit them. When the operator is satisfied with the text, a helium-neon laser can output to photosensitive paper, toner-based printers, positive or negative film, or a printer's engraving plate directly (a process known as stereotyping). Recent advances in digital technology have merged typesetting and publishing into a single operation—desktop publishing.

Initially, only governments and large corporations could afford digital typesetting and the elaborate equipment necessary for the printing operation. But in 1984, the Apple Computer Company introduced its Macintosh computer with on-screen layout capabilities for the production of words and graphics on the same, inexpensive system (see Chapter 15). Desktop publishing was born. The quality of digital output is measured in dots per inch (dpi). An average laser printer will produce 300 dpi printouts. However, professionals use expensive laser printers with resolutions of 2,540 dpi or higher.

Digital typesetting has been a boon to typographical designers. On many professional systems, 30,000 characters can be sent to a printer in less than a minute. With type and graphics in digital form, satellite connections make it possible for the *Wall Street Journal* and *USA Today* to transmit pages to printing plants throughout the United States for the next day's editions. With old phototypesetting systems, typeface sizes were limited from 6 to 72 points in large 6-point jumps. With digital technology, type sizes typically range from 4 to 127 points and can be varied by less than a point. In addition, without the placement restrictions of metal type, designers can condense, expand, and position type in unusual configurations. One of the early masters at type manipulation was Herb Lubalin, who cofounded the International Typeface Corporation in 1970. His designs show a creative merging of form and content and have inspired many other typographical designers.

Digital designs also make typeface creation much easier. Typographical artists use computer software to invent their own styles. Roger Black, one of the most successful new typographical designers, has created the typefaces used in such diverse magazines as *Rolling Stone, Newsweek,* and *Esquire.*

 Technical Perspective

In order to analyze the use of typefaces in print or screen communications, you must be aware of the various choices available to the typographer. A designer who uses words in a piece must make choices about various typeface styles in relation to overall size, color, fonts, text block size, justification, and white space.

Typeface Families

Typography is a big business. It is estimated that computer companies, typesetters, printers, publishers, advertising agencies, and writers spend more than $300 million a year to purchase type. Johannes Gutenberg had an easy time selecting the typeface style for his Bible because there was only one—textur. Since Gutenberg's day, at least 40,000 different typeface styles have been invented, with more than 176,000 attribute variations.

About 3,000 typefaces are commonly used today. If a previously published style doesn't fit the requirements of a piece, an artist simply uses a computer program to create a specialized typeface that does. During the past ten years, more than 1,000 typefaces have been invented with computer technology. So many choices required that a method be devised to group typefaces into categories or families. The resulting six basic typeface families are blackletter, roman, script, miscellaneous, square serif, and sans serif. Think of each typeface family as separate colors, each with their own mood and purpose, depending on the culture in which they are used.

Blackletter Sometimes called gothic, old style, renaissance, or medieval, the blackletter typeface family is highly ornate and decorative. Individual strokes that make up the letters are thick and have sharply diagonal lines. Many of the strokes in capital letters are connected with thinner supporting lines. The ends of the letters usually have small stylized strokes that were early predecessors of the serif. Because it happened to be the style that scribes in monasteries used for their handwritten works, Gutenberg fashioned his metal type characters accordingly.

Consequently, the family is associated with traditional, conservative, and religious content. Blackletter's use in body copy is limited because of its low level of **legibility.** However, for large headlines the use of this typeface connotes classical values and historical importance (Figure 8.20). The most common use of the blackletter family of type is for the names of newspapers and on diplomas and certificates. Designers may change typeface families in a paper to give it a modern appearance, but the nameplate remains blackletter to symbolize traditional values and stability. As text in printed books, blackletter had a relatively brief life. Within twenty years of its use by Gutenberg, most printers had abandoned it for the roman family style.

Roman In a tribute to the Roman civilization that gave the world a modern, 26-letter alphabet, French designers named a major typeface family in its honor. The roman typeface family is the most commonly used of all the typeface families. It is used almost exclusively for body copy in books, magazines, and newspapers because it is familiar to readers and exceedingly legible and the gently curved serifs create lines that are easy to read.

Development of the style of roman used today took approximately 300 years from the time the roman typeface was introduced in 1465. During that period, three forms were introduced: old style, transitional, and modern.

1. *Old style:* Two Venetian printers, Nicolaus Jenson and Aldus Manutius, working separately realized that the blackletter type was fine for Bibles, but they had other works in mind that needed to be read more easily. The two shaved the metal of the blackletter characters so that the strokes were not quite as thick or ornate. The public and other printers immediately favored this design change (Figure 8.21). In 1475, William Caxton of Great Britain printed the first book in English, a translation from the French of *Recuyell of the Histories of Troy.* One hundred years later, one of the greatest typeface designers, Claude Garamond, who established the first type foundry, developed a roman typeface in which the lowercase letters were considered more beautiful than the uppercase letters. That led to printing the titles of books in uppercase and lowercase letters for the first time. In the United States in 1722, William Caslon applied a different design philosophy to old style roman typeface. In an early example of the gestalt approach, he wanted his type to have beauty when all the letters were printed together. The appearance of individual letters wasn't as important to Caslon as the total effect. The Declaration of Independence and the Constitution were printed with Caslon's typeface.

Figure 8.20

The editors of Boston.com, the Web site that posts the electronic version of The Boston Globe, *try to maintain the link with a paper version by using a blackletter typeface for the name.*

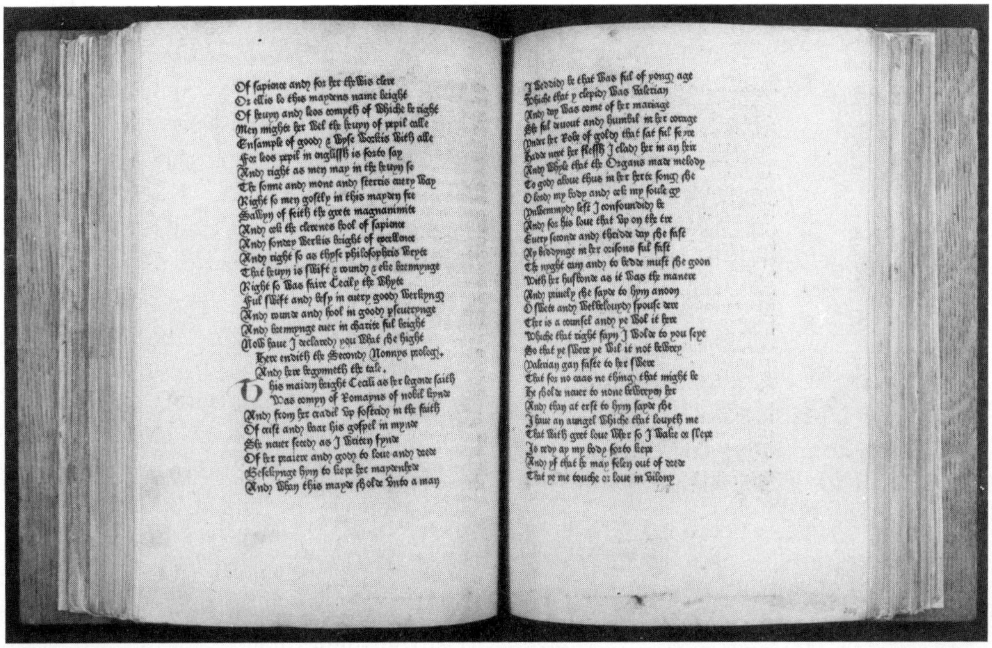

The Lilly Library, Indiana University

Figure 8.21

These two pages represent the old style roman typeface family from a first edition of Chaucer's Canterbury Tales *printed in England by William Caxton in 1477. Because the English language does not contain the ligature characters of Latin, the text is set in ragged right instead of justified columns. This technique conveys a more informal design to the work than Gutenberg's product.*

2. *Transitional:* The typeface of John Baskerville of England in the eighteenth century best exemplifies the transitional period for the roman typefaces. Baskerville transformed Caslon's type by making the letters more vertical. He also allowed a bit more contrast between the thin and thick strokes and gave the type flatter, less ornate serifs.

3. *Modern:* One of the most prolific early typeface designers was the Italian Giambattista Bodoni. He produced more than 100 different alphabet collections. In 1768, his roman typeface became the standard style for the family, which is still used. With Bodoni's type, the roman typeface style lost its early link to blackletter and became a distinctive family. Its letter strokes changed from thick lines with little contrast to thinner strokes with a noticeable difference in width (Figure 8.22).

Script Cursive writing is defined as letters that are linked. In 1557, Robert Granjon of France introduced the first typeface designed to mimic the handwriting of ordi-

nary people. High-priced scribes usually used the blackletter style, but Granjon developed the delicately graceful script style in which the letters, whether uppercase or lowercase, were joined by elongated and connecting serifs. Ironically, the script typeface family, which originally was intended to look like ordinary handwriting, is now used almost exclusively for documents and publications that want to promote a high-quality,

Courtesy of the *Daily Titan*

Figure 8.22

After fires devastated parts of southern California, the Daily Titan, *student newspaper of California State University, Fullerton, printed a special edition. The all-capital, roman typeface headline is a perfect choice for the front page. It is as if the letters themselves are "rising from the ashes" as much as the spirit of the people.*

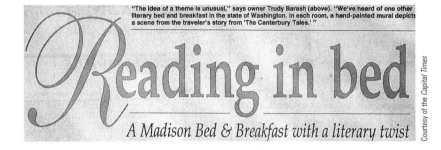

Figure 8.23

The script typeface family "R" reinforced by an italic roman subhead lends an air of sophistication to a story on a bed and breakfast.

Figure 8.24

Many nineteenth-century advertisements used typography to attract a reader's attention. In this typical example, five of the six typeface families are represented: sans serif (The Health Jolting Chair), roman (COPYRIGHT), blackletter (The most important Health . . .), script (A Practical Household . . .), and square serif (PERFECT). By today's standards such a mixing of typefaces might be called a "typographic car wreck" or considered modern when used in a "garbage font" publication.

high-class appearance. Wedding invitations and licenses, for example, commonly are printed in script because the fine letters, perhaps more than any other family's style, give the piece an air of handmade attention to detail (Figure 8.23).

Miscellaneous Sometimes referred to as novelty or display type, the members of the miscellaneous typeface family, as the name suggests, cannot easily be sorted into the other families. Miscellaneous type first began appearing for advertising purposes during the Industrial Revolution. As more people made more money because of the efficiency of new machines, they demanded

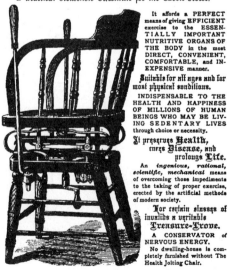

more products. Printing came to be thought of as not simply for disseminating information and news through books, magazines, and newspapers, but also as a way to attract potential customers through advertising (Figure 8.24).

The miscellaneous family's unique feature is that its style purposely draws attention to itself. For example, creative typographers even designed typefaces with letters formed by collections of flowers or contorted human figures. During the Industrial Revolution, designers also created several specialty type effects. In 1803, Robert Thorne made the lines of Bodoni's modern roman type much thicker and produced a type attribute he named "fat face." Today the popular style is called *boldface*. Other specialty attributes such as reverse, light, condensed, expanded, and three-dimensional type were used in advertisements on printed pages, tin cans, and billboards—often in graphically unpleasant, but certainly eye-catching, combinations (Figure 8.25). The Industrial Revolution also spurred the final two typeface families.

Square Serif In 1815, probably inspired by the architecture and other sights reported after Napoleon's conquest of Egypt, Vincent Figgins designed a typeface similar to the modern roman but with right angle curves jutting from the letter strokes. Sometimes called 3-D, slab-serif, or Egyptian, the square serif typeface family is intended, as is the miscellaneous family, to draw attention to itself and the product it is helping to advertise. Square serif is the least used typeface family today because of its bricklike appearance, which gives it an unpleasant rigid look. Curiously, in American culture this typeface family is associated with the Wild West because it was used commonly on storefronts in pioneer towns in the Western movies made in Hollywood.

Sans Serif In 1832, the great-great-grandson of William Caslon, William Caslon IV, designed the last type family. The sans serif typeface family was immediately controversial. The French word *sans* means "without." Caslon simply took existing letters and trimmed off all their serifs. The result was a type style that Caslon named "block type." Typographical critics of the day immediately voiced their objections to the type family as being too simple and without style.

Despite the early criticism, sans serif typefaces have enjoyed several periods of popularity. Printers in the 1880s liked the new style. Many felt that the streamlined, clean-looking letter strokes fit the new, fast-paced machine age. The architectural and graphic design style of art deco in the 1920s revived interest in the type. In the 1970s, newspaper publishers asked designers to modernize their front pages. Many turned to the sans serif family for headlines and photo cutlines to offset the roman type of the body copy (Figure 8.26). Screen media presentations again have demonstrated the importance of the sans serif style. Roman type, with its delicate serifs, often is hard to read on a screen unless it is quite large. Consequently, sans serif typefaces are used most often in motion picture titles and credits, in identification cutlines for television news programs, and for menu and text announcements on a computer screen. Without serifs, the type style connotes a no-nonsense, practical approach to lettering in which a viewer isn't distracted by the addition of serifs. For that reason, street signs and warning labels most often are printed in the sans serif style (Figure 8.27).

Typeface Attributes

Whether for print or screen presentations, a typographical designer must make choices about six major type attributes: size, color, font, text block size, justification, and

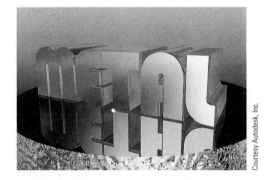

Courtesy Autodesk, Inc.

white space. We discuss the graphic design considerations of text placement and style consistency in Chapter 9.

1. *Size:* Type is measured in points. A single point is 0.0138 inch. For printed text blocks, the best type sizes are between 9 and 12 points. Display type is considered to be anything larger than 14 points. **Banner** newspaper headlines for some significant event may be 72 points or larger (Figure 8.28). Screen presentations require a type size twice that of printed body copy. Size also is related to uppercase and lowercase letters because uppercase letters take

Figure 8.25

Although this typeface generated by a computer program has roots in the sans serif family, it is considered an example of a miscellaneous typeface because its metallic appearance matches its verbal message.

Figure 8.26

In order to connote a modern appearance, the nameplate for this online version of the newspaper is taken from the sans serif typeface family. Further proof of a forward-thinking approach to typographical design is the use of illustrations, text, and white space on the layout. Newspaper front pages usually are tightly packed word and picture displays with little room for white space.

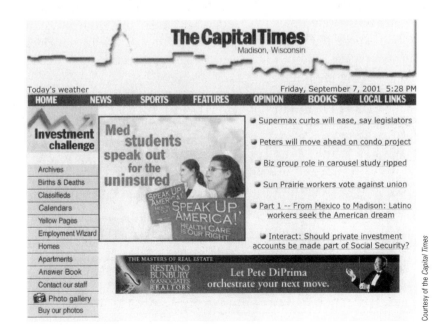

Courtesy of the *Capital Times*

Figure 8.27

The sans serif typeface family is used to communicate a serious message. This warning sign appears at the site of the Little Big Horn Battlefield National Monument in central Montana.

Paul Martin Lester

Figure 8.28

The streamlined and bold headline across the entire width of the page, with illustrations and text in separate modules, gives a modern look to this early twentieth-century newspaper.

Modified after Howard Finberg and Bruce Itule, *Visual Editing*, Wadsworth Publishing Company, 1990

up more space than lowercase letters. As a general rule, reading text that contains both capitals and small letters is much easier. However, uppercase letters work well with any short line of text.

2. *Color:* Actually two colors are implied—the color of the type and the color of the background. Research on type consistently shows that the most legible combination of colors for long blocks of copy is black type against a white background. Any other combination is hard to read and becomes tiring. For eye-catching headlines, designers occasionally use white type against a black background (called reverse type), colored type against a white background, or white type against a colored background. A long copy block set in reverse type is difficult to read. For

cutlines set inside pictures (not recommended), motion picture subtitles, or identifying text for televised images, a designer must take care that the color of the type does not match the color of the image because the words will be hard to read. Graphic artists for motion picture previews often make movie credits white and the title of the movie, the most significant part of the copy block, another color. Television graphic artists often place white text on top of a colored box or banner to identify a person speaking in the frame.

3. *Font:* Typically, a font refers to all of the letters and symbols that are possible with an individual typeface. For many typographical designers, font also means the attributes of plain text, **boldface,** *italic,* <u>underline</u>, ⓞⓤⓣⓛⓘⓝⓔ, and any other attention-grabbing graphic devices available (Figure 8.29). Most designers, whether for print or screen mediums, use such fonts conservatively. Plain text with boldface headlines and italic fonts for book titles should be enough font choices for most designs.

4. *Text block size:* Two factors are involved with the text block size: line width and column length, both of which are measured in picas (a pica contains 12 points). For the best reading width, lines should be no longer than 24 picas or contain no more than 12 words. Two columns are more readable than one wide column (Figure 8.30).

5. *Justification:* Text may be set with aligned imaginary left and/or right or centered margins. Left justified text is the most common style, with the right side of the text not justified (also called ragged right). Such a justification connotes an informal, modern, and highly readable style. Right justified or ragged left and centered type are seldom used for long passages of type

because a viewer has trouble determining when the next line starts. Completely justified type, as used by Gutenberg, has a rigid, organized appearance.

6. *White space:* Areas not filled with text or graphics, regardless of the color of the paper or the frame, are called white space. Space between individual letters is called kerning. A modern, informal appearance can be achieved if the kerning is made an obvious design factor. When kerning is too little or too much, however, the copy may be difficult to read. Leading (pronounced "ledding") is the word used to describe the white space between horizontal lines of type. Boldface, or any heavy typeface style, may require additional leading for readability. The space between two columns of type is called the alley and the space between the pages of a book or magazine is called the gutter.

Ethical Perspective

Typographical designers usually invent and use typefaces that combine utilitarianism with the golden rule. In other words, a design is both useful and adds beauty to our lives. But if typefaces are made to draw attention to them or to satisfy a designer's personal needs, hedonism is at work.

Graphic artist Milton Glaser, responsible for the design of *New York* magazine and the "I♥NY" logo, among others, warns that "there's a tremendous amount of garbage being produced under the heading of new and innovative typographical forms." Despite the danger of typefaces being designed solely for the amusement of a particular graphic artist, others predict that the prevalent use of typographical computer programs will produce ways of thinking about the use of type never before imagined.

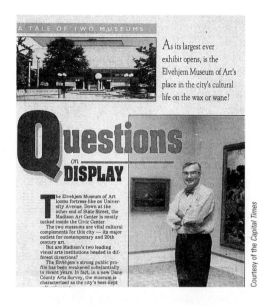

Courtesy of the Capital Times

An extreme example of personalized typeface styles is the trend in typography called "garbage fonts." People create typefaces with names such as "degenerate," "international disgrace," and "futile" from bits and pieces of established fonts by using desktop publishing technology. In print and screen presentations, the use of type in a cacophony of mixed colors, styles, and sizes

Courtesy of Vis-Com, Inc.

Figure 8.29

A drop shadow box behind the capital "Q" gives a three-dimensional illusion to the layout, helping to attract attention to the display. Note that the typeface family for the story (roman) is different from that for the photograph's cutline (bold sans serif). A typographical designer often will use such a subtle technique to separate the two text messages.

Figure 8.30

The New York Times *was created in response to the sensational illustrations and stories in many publications of the day. As indicated by the conservative nature of the layout, this publication was meant for those who wanted to read long, in-depth stories.*

Why Wired?

Content

Figure 8.31

As with the quick editing cuts of an MTV-style music video, Wired, *a magazine produced for those interested in new communication technologies, features typographical displays that break many accepted rules. The magazine's table of contents, for example, uses illustrations, alignment differences, and leading variations.*

is not unlike other expressions inspired by Dada art. Magazines aimed at young urban audiences, such as the defunct *Beach Culture* or the current *Ray Gun, Wired,* and *Mondo 2000,* as well as MTV-like videos and commercials, present the latest fads (Figure 8.31). Other people will learn how to read these typographical arrangements, or the fad will simply continue to be a part of an urban youth subculture. After trying to read articles produced by "garbage font" designers, you probably would yearn for the simple lines and classical use of white space of the typography in the *New Yorker* magazine. But Jonathan Hoefler, who invents typefaces for *Sports Illustrated* and other magazines, likes "unusual fonts that challenge typographical assumptions. After all, design is about breaking the rules. Rule-breakers become rulers." Acceptable typography styles often are a matter of what the dominant culture deems acceptable. Typography critic Kevin Barnhurst in his book *Seeing the Newspaper* writes that "from the earliest manuscripts and books to the twentieth-century typographic movements, people have pushed for expression while society pulled them toward uniformity and clarity." The world is certainly large enough to support both

dynamic, cacophonous displays and quiet, traditional typographical presentations.

Another serious problem for typographical designers is protecting their creative output. Creating unauthorized versions of other designers' typestyles is unethical and in some countries illegal. *FontChameleon,* produced by the Ares Software Corporation, can make "billions" of variations of a master typeface from an outline of the typestyle. Strict copyright laws in Germany and the United Kingdom make such manipulations of a typeface designer's work illegal. But in the United States, where copyright laws for typefaces are less restrictive, the product could find a ready market despite the unethical nature of the practice.

Cultural Perspective

Because typography gives the artist's style to a text, it is linked, as is any art form, to a particular culture at a particular time. The history of typography may be divided into five major typographical eras: pre-Gutenberg, Gutenberg, industrial, artistic, and digital (Figure 8.32).

1. *Pre-Gutenberg (before 1456):* For the most part, typography wasn't thought of as a design element separate from illustrations. Words and images were linked as equal partners in communication. Egyptian hieroglyphics, Greek and Roman letterforms, and the illustrative works of religious scribes during medieval times are particularly good examples of early texts that were functional and attractive at the same time. Combining form and function also was a goal of the cultures that produced such works.

2. *Gutenberg (1456–1760):* This is the "golden age" of typographical design when the word became the chief means of communication. Printers such as Aldus

Paul Martin Lester

Paul Martin Lester

Figure 8.32

Somewhere in the deserts of Arizona (left) and Texas (right) are two typographical designers with different opinions about the proper typeface for attracting the attention of tourists.

and type designers such as Garamond knew that words were worthy of the best presentations possible. The rise in literacy and the need for books of all types produced a tremendous explosion in the number of publishing houses. Unfortunately, pictures were reserved for illustrative decorations around text blocks or for medical and other scientific textbooks.

3. *Industrial (1761–1890):* This period is known as the "dark ages" of typographical design. Machine mentality ruled style, and efficiency in design rather than the appearance of a typeface was praised. For example, designers criticized the sans serif family for its unattractive appearance, but printers praised it. Printers were tired of replacing letters in the roman family style because their serifs broke off easily. The increase in all kinds of printed advertising called for typefaces that customers noticed. Elaborately shaped typefaces, often used in combination with

several others and sprinkled around the images of products in an advertisement, gave the appearance of a "typographical car wreck." But the style was popular in an era of fast-paced efficiency.

4. *Artistic (1891–1983):* A problem for typography during the Industrial Revolution was that the most respected art movement of the time, Impressionism, rarely was expressed in poster form. Henri de Toulouse-Lautrec was the exception: He painted posters for theatrical openings. Typography as a respected art form was first expressed with the art nouveau decorative style. Later, several modern art styles in the twentieth century (Dada, de Stijl, Bauhaus, art deco, pop art, and postmodern) were linked with specific cultures and expressed specific messages related to political content, architecture, product design, and art in general. These art movements used typography as an integral part of their

graphic design. Because of that link, we discuss them in connection with graphic design in Chapter 9.

5. *Digital (1984–present):* The introduction of inexpensive Macintosh computers by Apple in 1984, combined with the networking capabilities of the World Wide Web ten years later, allowed typographical artists to more easily match their original design concepts with tools that were relatively inexpensive and easily mastered for a global audience. Consequently, designers have learned to create typefaces for print and screen media whether for a small circulation flyer or for a World Wide Web site that receives several million user hits a day (Chapter 16).

 Critical Perspective

When the history of typography is viewed as part of the larger history of writing, it becomes clear that words in the print or screen media are expressive, graphic elements with emotional qualities that transcend the actual meaning of the words themselves. Early scribes lost much of their political power when alphabets were invented. But they gained much of their status back when they developed calligraphic and illustrative skills that turned words into works of art. Today's scribes are the typographical designers who can use a computer to make sure that the words match the style of the illustrations and the content of the piece.

■ FUTURE DIRECTIONS FOR TYPOGRAPHY

As we show in the subsequent chapters, every medium of presentation—from typography to the World Wide Web—has been influenced by computer technology. All are becoming digital media. We discuss the implications of such a technical convergence in Chapter 15. When individuals are linked around the world via a home computer and telephone line, electronic mail will reveal a person's character not only by the services selected and the messages sent but also by the way those written messages appear. Many people complain that literacy is on a downward spiral, but computer technology probably will spark a rebirth in writing and reading just as Gutenberg's invention did fifty years later.

For example, an estimated 20,000 homemade magazines are produced in the United States alone every year in garages, dens, and bedrooms with pens, with typewriters, and on Web sites. With names like *Technology Works, Mudflap,* and *Tweak,* these specialty publications called *zines* (pronounced "zeens") identify fringe cultures, products, and lifestyles (Figure 8.33). The modern roots of these publications date to 1930s comic book and science fiction and Hollywood zines of the 1950s.

In addition, book publishing as it is currently known may dramatically change in the future. Jason Epstein, editorial director for Random House from 1958 to 1998, predicted that readers might be able to buy "a physical book printed on-demand, one copy at a time, by machines much like bank ATM

Figure 8.33

A miscellaneous typeface helps set the mood for Tweak, *an online zine located at www.tweak.com.*

Courtesy of *Tweak*

machines." These books would have the look and feel of traditional books with binding, a cover, and familiar typography on paper that could be purchased at convenience stores and coffee shops. Already, there are Web sites where an author can bypass all the steps in the editorial process and make a book available to readers as an electronic or a printed version. As this process becomes more popular, publishing companies will no longer be needed to print, store, or ship books.

DISCUSSION AND EXERCISE IDEAS

- Analyze a page from the Gutenberg Bible or any example of typography using the six perspectives.
- Describe your favorite use of typography.
- Find a particular typeface that reflects your personality or a city's reputation or character.
- Write a paper that discusses the ethical concerns with typography.
- Lead a discussion about the future of typography.

INFOTRAC COLLEGE EDITION ASSIGNMENTS

- With "Subject guide" checked, type "Johann Gutenberg" in the search area. Click the first "View" for the "Periodical references." Read the two articles "Gutenberg's millennium" and "Gutenberg's Invention Disputed." Do you think the whole history of printing needs to be rewritten if it is true that Gutenberg did not invent the movable type printing press? Is his legacy to communications in doubt? Why or why not?

- With "Subject guide" checked, type "Advertising Layout and Topography" in the search area. Click "View" for the "Periodical references." Scroll down and click on Steven Heller's brief article "Separated at Birth" concerning typographic clichés and appropriation in two beer advertisements. Look through a number of popular magazines and see if you can find examples of similar styles of typography and graphic design among different ads. Do you think appropriate is a sincere form of flattery or an indication of a lazy and uncreative designer?

Go to the Web site for this book at www.wadsworth.com/product/0534562442 to find more Web links on this subject.

GRAPHIC DESIGN

Design is thinking made

visual.

Saul Bass, 1920–1996

TITLE AND LOGO DESIGNER,

FILMMAKER, AND

STORYBOARD ARTIST

By the end of this chapter you should know:

- The importance of the work of Saul Bass to the development of graphic design as an art form.

- Some of the historical influences including art movements upon today's graphic designs.

- How to produce and analyze graphic designs that fit the needs of a particular audience.

- Some of the ethical concerns that influence the graphic designs that we see in everyday life.

Although you may not know it, your life is unavoidably connected to a Bronx-born graphic designer by the name of Saul Bass. You see his pictures in your kitchen, on your television screen, on charities' stationery letterheads, on grocery store shelves, in magazines and newspapers, in gas stations, in movie theaters, atop corporate buildings, and on airplanes. Bass has designed packages for everyday food products and corporate trademarks for Fortune 500 companies. He has designed gasoline stations for major oil companies. He has made an Oscar-winning film and has produced the titles and ending credits for numerous well-known motion pictures. Unlike many other designers, Saul Bass was equally at home with print and screen media presentations.

Born in 1920 to immigrant parents in New York, he earned an early reputation for spending all his free time drawing whatever he saw and reading whatever he could find. Bass trained at the Art Students' League and Brooklyn College. He worked as an apprentice in the art department of the New York office of Warner Brothers Studio. His job was to help create movie posters (or "one sheets") used to promote motion picture new releases.

Movie posters in the late 1930s and 1940s tried to show as much of the content of a movie as possible, considering the limited space. Large, miscellaneous typeface family lettering usually identified the movie's title. Close-up colorful paintings of the film's stars captured during an emotional moment usually were surrounded by smaller drawings of other scenes from the movie. These posters were important marketing pieces before the advent of television; they were used in newspaper advertisements and adorned the front of movie theaters to attract ticket buyers. Almost always they were graphically extravagant and appealed to the emotions.

One of the books that Bass read on his daily commute changed his life. It was *The Language of Vision* by Hungarian Bauhaus instructor Gyorgy Kepes. The Bauhaus art movement advocated focusing on essentials. For movie posters, the philosophy implied that instead of throwing in every possible significant scene in a movie, as in many previous and modern-day previews or trailers, a poster should feature a single idea or theme expressed in the film that would catch the imagination of potential customers. Bass decided to follow the Bauhaus design philosophy for movie posters and title sequences and in all the other graphic work he produced.

■ *BASS'S CONTRIBUTIONS TO GRAPHIC DESIGN*

The first movie poster Bass designed was for the Kirk Douglas film *Champion* in 1949. It was a startling, full-page demonstration of reductionism. Centered within a black page was a tiny image of Douglas and actress Marilyn Maxwell. Interestingly, the text above the embracing couple was a compromise to previous sensational displays. The copy read, "Fighting or loving he was the . . .

CHAMPION." But the total visual effect was anything but traditional. The small amount of text and the tiny picture of the stars surrounded by black supported the theme that the Douglas character was anything but a champion. The design shocked advertisers because it was a visually dramatic departure from previous movie posters. But it cemented Bass's idea that graphic design should reduce a subject's elements to one dominant idea.

Despite the success of the *Champion* advertising campaign, Bass generally was forced to make posters in the traditional form and quickly became frustrated. A year later, at the age of twenty-nine, he moved to Los Angeles. He soon landed a job working for Howard Hughes and his movie studio, RKO. But Bass again became frustrated when he realized that Hughes controlled every aspect of his company and allowed few ideas other than his own to be used. In 1952, he quit and formed his own design studio. His first employee, Elaine Makatura, later became his wife.

■ *Movies*

In 1954, Bass met famed film director Otto Preminger and designed a poster for his movie *Carmen Jones*. Preminger liked it so much that he used it as part of the title sequence for the movie. Until that time, the titles for motion pictures were, for the most part, one of the last decisions a director made about a movie. Title and credit graphics simply were not a high priority. When films were first introduced, movie titles, as in *The Birth of a Nation,* one of the first feature-length motion pictures, were little more than display posters with bad lettering. Titles rarely set the mood of a picture. Exceptions were epic dramas that showed a well-manicured hand turning the pages of a book that contained the title and credits. Titles almost always were typeset on neutral colored

Figure 9.1

The opening sequence for The Man with the Golden Arm *by Saul Bass conveys the desperation and confinement of drug addiction. As Bass explains, "The intent of this opening was to create a mood . . . spare, gaunt, with a driving intensity. The staccato movement of white bars against a black background creates a strident geometry that finally forms 'The Arm,' the symbol of the distorted, disjointed life of a drug addict."*

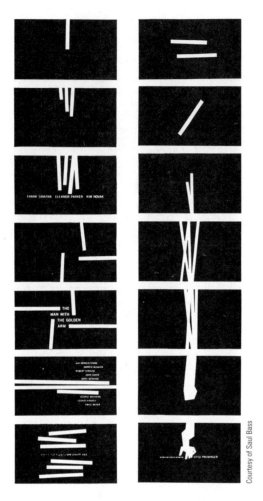

Courtesy of Saul Bass

backgrounds and never ran during the movie, as is common today. In 1955, Bass inspired the creative design of future movie titles with the opening sequence for the film *The Man with the Golden Arm*. Bass admits that he used the title sequence "to create a little atmosphere."

The mood that Bass established in the animated sequence perfectly matched the story line for the movie. In the film, Frank Sinatra plays a drug-addicted poker dealer. Backed by Elmer Bernstein's staccato jazz score, white bars with text moved across the screen in a tense, abstract dance, eventually forming a pictographic arm that became the symbol for the film. In 1959, Bass again used jazz music, this time by Duke Elling-

ton, to introduce another Preminger movie, *Anatomy of a Murder*. Both title sequences were inspired by the Bauhaus art movement, which forged new ways of thinking about music, animation, and graphic design (Figure 9.1).

Besides creating the title sequences, Bass also designed the advertising posters for the movies, using minimal pictographs that symbolically presented the essence of the plot. Theater owners were uncomfortable with the posters because they wanted traditional works with large, close-up images of the stars. But when Preminger threatened to pull the movie from theaters that didn't use the posters, the owners capitulated. The public had no objections to the new poster presentations and title sequences (Figure 9.2).

For the next thirty years, his firm (known today as Bass/Yager & Associates) made title sequences for many major motion pictures. At first, Bass was nervous about designing for the motion picture medium. He once admitted that "I . . . found myself confronted with a flickering, moving, elusive series of images that somehow had to add up to communication." But the success of his work, as noted by historian Estelle Jussim, demonstrates "the ingenuity of a brilliant graphic designer conquering the difficulties of a new medium." In 1960, Bass created the emotionally charged title sequence for the film *Exodus*, with raised arms holding a rifle in triumph. In a 1962 movie, *Walk on the Wild Side*, the opening sequence showed a catfight that was a metaphor for the street life of New Orleans portrayed in the motion picture. He also made the titles for the movies *The Seven Year Itch* (in which the "t" in "itch" scratches itself, 1955), *Around the World in 80 Days* (1956), *The Big Country* (1958), *Vertigo* (1958), *North by Northwest* (1959), *Psycho* (1960), *Ocean's Eleven* (1960), *It's a Mad, Mad, Mad, Mad World* (1963),

Bunny Lake Is Missing (1965), *Grand Prix* (1966), *That's Entertainment: Part 2* (1976), *Broadcast News* (1987), *War of the Roses* (in which the titles are supposedly in front of a red, satin sheet, which turns out to be Danny DeVito's handkerchief, 1989), Martin Scorsese's *Goodfellas* (1991), *Cape Fear* (1992), *The Age of Innocence* (1993), and his last, *Casino* (1995).

Scorsese said of Bass that he "fashioned title sequences into an art, creating in some cases, like *Vertigo,* a mini-film within a film. His graphic compositions in movement function as a prologue to the movie—setting the tone, providing the mood and foreshadowing the action."

For Bass, title sequences are the first chance to set a mood for the motion picture. Consequently, a film director should never lose that opportunity. "Titles can be sufficiently provocative and entertaining to induce the audience to sit down and look," he explained, "because something is really happening on screen." Bass inspired several generations of title designers including Pablo Ferro (*Dr. Strangelove*), Wayne Fitzgerald (*Bonnie and Clyde*), Friz Freleng (*The Pink Panther*), Stephen Frankfurt (*To Kill a Mockingbird*), Maurice Binder (*Dr. No*), Richard Greenberg (*The World According to Garp*), Juan Gatti (*Women on the Verge of a Nervous Breakdown*), and Kyle Cooper (*Seven*).

Because of his success with titles, Bass became interested in directing his own short films about the creative process. He won a Grand Award at the Venice Film Festival for *Searching Eye,* a Gold Hugo award at the Chicago Film Festival for *From Here to There,* and Oscar nominations for his films *The Solar Film* and *Notes on Popular Art.* In 1968 he won an Oscar in the short subjects category for his film about human creativity, *Why Man Creates.*

A little known fact is that Bass also is responsible for one of the most memorable

Courtesy of Saul Bass

Figure 9.2

Saul Bass was the first designer to create a visual message that was used in an advertisement and opening sequence for a movie—the poster for The Man with the Golden Arm.

visual messages in the history of motion pictures. After he created storyboards for the "shower murder scene" with Janet Leigh and Anthony Perkins in the movie *Psycho*, Alfred Hitchcock asked Bass to direct the scene (Figure 9.3).

■ *Packaging and Logos*

As much recognition as he has received for contributions to the movie industry, Bass is just as well known for his packaging and corporate trademark designs. He designed the visual elements seen on such diverse products as Wesson oils, Lawry's seasonings, Northern towels, Ohio Blue Tip matches, and Instant Quaker Oats. In 1970, he redesigned the logo for the Quaker Oats Company to give it a more modern look (Figure 9.4). In an ultimate design package, he and his firm designed the entire visual system, including architecture, for the BP America and Exxon worldwide networks of service stations.

Figure 9.3

After Saul Bass designed the storyboards for the memorable shower murder scene in Psycho, *Alfred Hitchcock asked him to direct the classic sequence.*

Getty Images/Hulton Archive

Before being acquired by Philip Morris, General Foods had Bass redesign its logo. The leaf pictograph within a thick black, open-ended line symbolizes wholesomeness, growth, strength, and dynamism (Figure 9.5). He has also designed logos for United Way, the YWCA, the Girl Scouts, Continental Airlines, United Airlines, Warner Communications, and Minolta (Figure 9.6). When U.S. District Judge Harold Green ordered AT&T to break up into regional telephone companies in 1983, he also demanded that the parent company change its "bell in a circle" logo (designed by Saul Bass in 1969). Bass came up with a blue globe encircled by white lines varying in width that connotes a worldwide network that cares about its customers (Figure 9.7).

Saul Bass was a master at distilling a visual message to its most essential part. He understood the importance of visual communication in gaining a viewer's attention and keeping the message in a person's long-term memory. Because of Bass, graphic designers and corporate executives have learned that the proper display of words and images is vital to the success of a presenta-

tion. Bass died in 1996, but his design studio continues to prosper.

Lou Dorfsman, the designer of the CBS "eye" logo, among others, said, "Saul Bass practiced his craft for more than 50 years, yet his work was always consistently new and provocative. His work remains relevant because it continues to touch people and because his ideas and imagery appeal as much to the emotions as they do to the intellect."

■ *ANALYSIS OF* THE MAN WITH THE GOLDEN ARM

The 1955 title sequence for *The Man with the Golden Arm* demonstrated that graphic design elements could match the content of the piece. Words and pictures, in other words, are employed to complement rather than conflict with each other. Bass not only influenced others but also established himself as an important contributor to **popular culture.** He single-handedly created a graphic design specialty—the movie title sequence designer.

The title sequence, however, now seems dated. It has a jazzy, beatnik, 1950s feel that is slightly old-fashioned. Nevertheless, it is a direct ancestor of the current hip-hop style. Like viewing the opening credits to the 1955 television show "I Love Lucy" with its orchestrated sound track, large script lettering, and schmaltzy valentine's heart, you know that you are watching something completely different from anything previously produced. In that sense, Bass's title sequence has a lasting, memorable effect.

The opening title sequence will always have a place in history because it showed directors, theater owners, the public, and other graphic designers the value of text and graphics in telling the story of the movie from the first second that light hits the screen in a darkened theater. If nothing else, it helped ensure that theatergoers were in their seats and quiet by the time the movie started. *The Man with the Golden Arm* as a title sequence and as a poster used for the marketing campaign made clear for many that graphic design, simply by the choice of elements and the way they are used, can convey meanings as complicated and emotional as those in the movie itself.

The title sequence for *The Man with the Golden Arm* is an example of the Bauhaus style brought to life in a moving picture. Instead of being randomly located in order to create tension in the Dada tradition, word and picture elements are purposely presented in the frame in a tightly controlled manner. Bass bridged the gap between print presentations used in movie posters and kinetic designs that are a part of the motion picture. He extended the life of the Bauhaus design movement by incorporating its philosophy of reductionism into a popular visual art form. But his title sequence would not have been possible without a strong and successful director advocating its use to overcome the objections of those with economic interests tied to a movie's advertising—the theater owners.

■ *GRAPHIC DESIGN AND THE SIX PERSPECTIVES*

Graphic design is the art and craft of bringing organized structure to a group of diverse elements, both verbal and visual. Graphic design usually is thought of with regard to the print medium, but because of the spread of design applications to all the media, its meaning has expanded to include the use of words, pictures, and even sounds in motion pictures, on television, and through computers.

Courtesy of Saul Bass

Figure 9.4

The Quaker graphic reminds the consumer of the company's link to its oats breakfast cereal product, but also conveys a modern, forward-looking message.

Figure 9.5

The round shape of the General Foods logo conveys wholesomeness.

Figure 9.6

The United Airlines logo uses long curved lines that simulate flight.

Figure 9.7

The AT&T logo with its pulsating horizontal lines within a circular shape connotes the worldwide communication network of the telephone company.

Personal Perspective

The next time you look at a print page or view a screen presentation, take the time to note the various graphic elements within your field of view. Most people are unaware of the many decisions a graphic designer makes in order to communicate the literal message of the design and also to convey the emotional quality or mood of the piece. Selecting and placing all the word and image elements of a presentation is the task of the graphic designer.

Historical Perspective

Designer W. A. Dwiggins first used the term *graphic design* in 1922. During his career Dwiggins worked on more than 300 book designs for the Alfred A. Knopf publishing company. Although the term may be relatively new, the practice is as old as recorded history. As with the history of typography, the history of graphic design may be divided into five eras: pre-Gutenberg, Gutenberg, industrial, artistic, and digital.

Pre-Gutenberg (before 1456)

The Egyptians were the first culture to produce illustrated manuscripts and wall decorations that combined their writing system with illustrations. The *Books of the Dead* (2300—1200 B.C.E.) are excellent examples of illustrated scrolls that were commonly used for both exalted and less-well-known members of Egyptian society (who could pay for the service). In the fifth century, the Greeks introduced the concept of symmetry based on their observations about the natural world. They identified certain basic shapes as pleasing to the eye. Later, Roman artists developed symmetric arrangements of letters and graphic ele-

ments, a practice that spread throughout the Roman Empire. After the collapse of Rome, clerics in monasteries managed to produce colorful, hand-drawn illustrated religious works within codices. They paid careful attention to the selection and placement of each graphic element on a page and to maintenance of a consistent style throughout the work.

Gutenberg (1456–1760)

With the invention of the commercial printing press, less time was needed for the actual production of lettering. Consequently, more care could be given to typography, illustrations, and graphic design. A publisher or art director for a book had assistants design pleasing typefaces, arrange the text in functional and aesthetically pleasing ways, draw elaborate cover, border, and whole-page illustrations, and put all these elements together in a unified format. In Germany, enlarged letters, colored borders, and wide alleys and margins were the common stylistic elements in books. In Italy and France, roman typefaces were commonly used to improve readability. Pages were illustrated with floral decorations or drawings related to the story. Leading for title pages and body copy was standardized in order to present a unified look.

Industrial (1761–1890)

Steam-powered printing presses, mechanical typesetting machines, and a great need for advertising materials promoted the idea that graphic design's sole purpose was to attract the attention of potential customers through advertising. An important invention—lithography—expanded the range of graphic design by making easier the use of images with words. Before that invention, pictures could be included with their verbal counterpart in print material only through hand-drawn illustrations or crudely fabricated drawings in wood or metal.

Aloys Senefelder of Munich in 1800 patented the lithographic process, which is a printing method based on the principle that oil and water don't mix. The word *lithography* means "writing on stone" (from the Greek *lithos* for "stone").

Beginning in 1813, Joseph Niépce of France substituted pewter plates for the Munich limestone used by Senefelder. Niépce would invent photography fourteen years later (see Chapter 12). Niépce and his son Isidore were independently wealthy inventors who made lithographs of popular religious personalities of the time. But as the two weren't artists, they had to pay others to create the drawings. The elder Niépce invented photography as a way of making drawings directly from nature without having to hire an artist. He used a pewter plate coated with a photosensitive emulsion to make a print of Cardinal Georges d'Ambroise, the minister to Louis XII, in 1826. The etching was the first photographic print made because it involved the use of sensitized plates inside a small camera obscura and a photochemical reaction to light.

In 1837, Godefroy Engelmann of France invented color lithography. Magazines soon began to exploit this new technology, combining words and images in a single press-run (Figure 9.8). In 1857, one of the first illustrated magazines, *Harper's Weekly,* employed the first "visual artist," Thomas Nast. He was famous for his sketches of Civil War battles that were published on the cover of the magazine. Nast also is known as the founder of American political cartooning as he drew the popular "Uncle Sam" and Republican Party "elephant" icons (see Chapter 11).

In 1868, Richard Hoe made improvements to his steam-powered press so that color lithographs could be easily and eco-nomically reproduced in great numbers. From 1860 to 1900, lithography was used to place images on paper and tin for art reproductions, political posters, all kinds of novelty items used as souvenirs, and for greeting and business cards. Printed, colored greeting cards became enormously popular gifts when the American printing firm of Currier and Ives in the middle of the nineteenth century distributed them. Nathaniel Currier and James Ives published more than 4,000 color drawings that pictured everyday and historic American events. These early postcards are valued collectors' items today. But until the invention of the halftone engraving process, printing high-quality photographs along with the text on a press was still impossible.

Artistic (1891–1983)

The artistic period is known for the widespread use of images because of the invention of the halftone screen for the printing of still photographs. It also is noted for the use of visual materials in motion pictures and television and on computer screens.

Although lithography is fine for black and white or color drawings, it cannot be used to make high-quality photographic reproductions. Hence lithography today is used mainly for high-priced color art prints. The halftone engraving process uses a screen to transform a photograph into a series of small dots. When a halftone plate is inked, dots close together produce dark tones and dots separated by blank spaces produce lighter tones in the picture.

An American, Stephen Horgan, introduced the first crudely reproduced photograph using a printing press. On March 4, 1880, "A Scene in Shantytown," photographed by Henry J. Newton, was printed in the New York *Daily Graphic.* It was not part of a story about a troubled area in the city but simply one of several printing

Figure 9.8

Before the use of the halftone printing process for photographs, engraving artists for newspapers and magazines often made images more dramatic through "artist license." The horror of the dead soldiers and horses after a Civil War battle originally seen in Harper's Weekly *is intensified because it is a combination of several photographs and eyewitness accounts.*

Courtesy of the University of Central Florida

innovations being demonstrated on the newspaper's presses under the general heading "Fourteen Variations of the Graphic Process." In short, one of the first published photographs was used as an advertisement for the newspaper.

The shantytown image was produced by lithography from a crude engraving plate based on the photograph (Figure 9.9). This method wasn't practical for rotary web presses that used curved printing plates, so Horgan adapted his invention for such a purpose in 1897. By then, other inventors had made their own improvements. In 1881, the first color photographs were reproduced in a Paris magazine, *L'Illustration,* but the process was much too complicated and costly for widespread use. Frederic Ives of Philadelphia introduced a halftone screen composed of horizontal and vertical lines printed on a sheet of film in 1885. When a photoengraved plate was used with such a screen, the result was a much higher quality image than Horgan

was able to reproduce. Two other Philadelphians, Max and Louis Levy, introduced a halftone plate in 1893 that reproduced high-quality printed images. Such advances in photoengraving and halftone techniques allowed the regular use of photographs in print media by World War I, which continues to this day.

Digital (1984–present)

A machine that changed the face and practice of graphic design whether for print or screen media—the computer—marks the digital era. The combination of the small, inexpensive, easy-to-use Macintosh computer (Chapter 15) and high-quality laser printers and networking innovations has led to a proliferation in the use and presentation of words and images. For example, because of the computer, methods for working with and presenting photographs have radically changed. Halftone screens can now be simulated with computer programs that sidestep the entire photoengraving process. Further-

George Eastman House

Figure 9.9

Henry Newton of the Daily Graphic *took this photograph of a "shantytown" village near the newspaper's office. Stephen Horgan used it to demonstrate his halftone printing process in 1880. Note the crude vertical lines of the halftone screen.*

more, with the global distribution possible with the World Wide Web (Chapter 16), still and moving pictures can be taken with digital cameras and uploaded to a Web server through a cellular telephone so that a worldwide audience can see the images minutes after they were taken.

The work of Saul Bass and others demonstrates the creative and effective combination of size and placement for motion picture, television, and computer screen applications. Movie titles and credits have to be large enough to be viewed from the back of a theater, yet arranged efficiently so that text doesn't take up too much time and space. Television news graphic artists have learned to organize complicated visual messages. They make bold presentations that combine the on-screen elements of announcer or reporter, moving video shot at a story scene, icons or logos, and textual information all within the small, television format. World Wide Web presentations for commercial, educational, and entertainment programs have introduced sound and user interactivity as design elements that graphic designers must incorporate into their work.

Technical Perspective

Attempting to identify "good" graphic design is always dangerous because, like beauty, it is often a highly subjective determination. What is considered good design changes over time and varies among cultures. Styles, as do fads, can capture immediate interest but become outdated just as quickly. But humans are rational and need to quantify all types of things, including what constitutes good graphic design. One method for determining good design is to be aware of the visual cues that the brain most readily responds to (Chapter 4) and the sensual and perceptual theories (Chapter 5). Without question, some designs are noticed more than others are, some designs are remembered longer than others are, and some arrangements of words and images soothe but others cause nervous tension.

Out of that mix of sensual and perceptual elements, most graphic design experts have come up with four suggestions that lead to the concept of good design: contrast, balance, rhythm, and unity. Because good graphic design can follow or challenge them, they are called suggestions, not rules or principles. The discussion of the four suggestions that follows is in accordance with mainstream graphic design thought. A designer should always have a clear reason for using each one in a presentation; the design should never be more important than the message it is supposed to communicate.

Contrast

Contrast refers to differences in color, size, symbolism, time, and sound in print or screen designs. A lot of contrast among elements signifies a busy and youthful design. Little contrast among elements usually indicates a no-nonsense and conservative approach. However, length of time is an exception. For screen media, little time between the showings of images indicates highly dynamic displays.

A good design will usually use colors that complement each other slightly rather than contrast with each other greatly. For example, a colored rule used to separate a headline from body copy should be close in hue to the dominant color in a photograph that accompanies the story. A design with colors that contrast with each other (for example, yellow and blue) will create tension in the viewer. Of course, if that kind of an emotional reaction is desired, such a design strategy is called for.

The size of the graphic elements should vary but be proportional to the overall frame of the design. Proportion, or scale, refers to the spatial relationship between design elements and the size of the page or frame. Sometimes a small element within a large frame has more visual impact than a large element that fills the frame.

Designer and educator Mario Garcia asserts that every design should have a "center of visual impact." A design should have one element that is emphasized, most often by its dominant size, more than the others should. That is the element the viewer notices first. For the most part, viewers prefer a design that presents the most important element in an obvious way because it minimizes the frustration that occurs when they must hunt for the significant elements.

White space is related to size because the scale of the elements determines how much white space is available. Spaces among the various elements keep the eye from becoming fatigued. The front pages of most daily newspapers have little white space because they are filled with stories and pictures. White space is sacrificed in order to fit as many important news stories as possible on the page. Inside each section the stories tend to be more feature-oriented and thus allow the designer more freedom in using layouts with white space separate from typographical white space (kerning and leading). As a general rule, white space should be present around the edges of a frame and not trapped in the center. A design with a lot of white space is considered modern or classy, whereas a crowded design with little white space is viewed as traditional and serious (Figure 9.10).

Designers of screen presentations also have to deal with decisions related to contrasting lengths of time and sounds. An element shown on the screen for a long time gains emphasis over one that flashes on the screen and quickly disappears. Transitions between various segments may be long with slow fades or quick editing cuts (see Chapter 13). A long, fading transition from one scene to another has a romantic, restful connotation; quick cuts signify action and energy.

When designers work with screen presentations, sound becomes an important consideration. Sound refers to all the audio

Doctor teaches lesson in black pride

Courtesy of the Capital Times

Courtesy of the Capital Times

aspects involved with a presentation—music, narration, dialogue, and sound effects. Sometimes television commercials are slightly louder than the program in order to gain the attention of potential customers. Robert Altman, director of *M·A·S·H* (1970), *The Player* (1992), and many other movies, is known for his use of sound to make smooth transitions between scenes. Graphic designers who use computers have a wide variety of sound options for their educa-tional and entertainment programs. Digital music and sound effects add drama, realism, and explanations to World Wide Web pre-sentations (see Chapter 16).

Balance

Balance refers to the placement of ele-ments within a design's frame (Figure 9.11). A design is considered balanced if it equal-izes the weight between the *x* (horizontal) and *y* (vertical) axes. A single design element

Figure 9.10

Although both layouts use well-executed photographs, the design on the left is much more unified. If there is too much space between graphic elements, as in the layout on the right, the images seem to be floating on the page rather than linked into a coherent whole.

Courtesy *The Florida Times-Union*. Photo © AP/Wide World Photos

Figure 9.11

This symmetrical top half of The Florida Times-Union newspaper in Jacksonville was typical of the graphic designs displayed the day after the aerial attacks on September 11. A balanced layout rivets the reader's attention to the center of the page where a hijacked 767-200 commercial airliner is about to strike the south tower of the World Trade Center.

set in a square, rectangle, or circle midway along both axes results in a perfectly symmetric design. The frame, like the human face, may be divided into two similar parts. A balanced design is most appropriate for formal and classy presentations in which a traditional or conservative approach is desired. Like the square from which it comes, a symmetric design is stable, but a bit dull. Asymmetric designs are less formal and create dynamic tension within the frame.

Rhythm

Rhythm refers to the way design elements are combined to control movement of the viewer's eye from one element to another (Figure 9.12). Sequencing and simplicity help determine a viewer's path through a piece. Sequencing is the positioning of individual elements so that a viewer naturally views one and then another element in the order desired by the designer. Placing material on separate pages naturally sequences

newspapers and magazines. Because motion pictures are a collection of moving, single frames, they are automatically sequenced as well. But within a single page or frame, elements also can be positioned to lead the viewer through the design. A large, banner headline attracts the reader's attention, and the placement of a photograph and the story close to the headline provides a sequence for the three elements. A sequence also can be initiated within an image. The direction of a person's eyes or hands in a picture will cause the viewer's gaze to move toward that part of the frame. A designer should be sure that it makes sense for a viewer to look in that direction (Chapter 4).

Simplicity is part of the rhythm of a design. A simple design—one that contains few elements—will attract little viewer eye movement. But a complex design with several units will create tension as the viewer's eye dances from one element to another.

Unity

Unity is a matter of related content as well as stylistic consistency. Elements within a design should all be similar in content, with words and pictorial elements fitting the same mood. For example, a bright color used as a background for a somber subject is not appropriate. Stylistic consistency refers to a design concept in which multiple pages or frames of a piece appear to be unified. Magazine designers take great care in organizing typographical and pictorial elements so those pages form a unified look (Figure 9.13). *Newsweek, Life, Interview,* and *Mondo 2000* all express different styles. However, within each magazine its pages maintain the magazine's individual approach to graphic design that fits the editor's purpose for the publication.

Contrast, balance, rhythm, and unity are guidelines for designers to either follow or challenge. But they are design considerations that can result in clear, noticeable, pleasing, and useful visual messages. Remember that good design is culturally dependent—what works in one context may be confusing or silly in another.

Ethical Perspective

A graphic designer must balance three conflicting approaches. Utilitarianism stresses "the greatest good for the greatest number." In the context of graphic design, it means that a design should be readable, legible, and useful. But hedonism can lead to designs that attract attention only for the purpose of satisfying commercial interests, shocking viewers, or expressing a personal statement. Between those two extremes is the golden rule approach, which advocates design decisions based on adding beauty to a person's life. To achieve Aristotle's golden mean philosophy, then, the designer must reach a difficult compromise by juggling the purpose of the piece, the need for it to be noticed, the idea that it should be pleasing to look at, and the need to create a unique style. Because innovation seldom comes from designers who follow the "middle way," being sensitive to conflicting ethical philosophies is one of the reasons that the field of graphic design is challenging and rewarding. As Saul Bass said, "Sometimes we design for our peers and not to solve communications problems." Communicating visual messages—not winning awards—should always be the graphic designer's ultimate goal.

Graphic designers and all other visual communicators also must be sensitive to other ethical considerations: the perpetuation of negative stereotypes, the promotion of products that are harmful to people, and the appropriation of previously presented graphic designs. Because the combination of text, graphic elements, and images forms a powerful communication link, a print or screen media message can easily persuade a viewer by its content. A graphic designer's choices can reinforce stereotypes in the media that can leave lasting impressions.

Milton Glaser, a graphic designer for almost five decades, decries the current trend toward commercialism in graphic design that is used solely for marketing purposes. Says Glaser, "Our whole view of culture is linked to money and success, and it is recognized that design is a potent instrument of sales. People have come to see that there is a strong link between how things look and how they can sell them."

Many products that are sold legally to consumers are harmful if used regularly and

Courtesy of Vis-Com, Inc.

Figure 9.12

Until the 1960s, newspaper front pages usually were eight, highly vertical columns of text with small photographs, as in this 1923 issue of The World. *Readers were expected to start at the top left and read down each column of text.*

Figure 9.13

See color section following page 132.

over a long period of time. Cigarettes, alcohol, and other drugs certainly fall in that category. The production or use of some products harms the environment. Every graphic designer must decide whether to work for a company that sells such products to consumers. There is a growing trend among graphic designers to pay attention to this issue when selecting clients. For example, Saul Bass and his associates made a conscious effort not to work for companies that make harmful products. Subtly referring to this issue was a typewritten message on a wall in Bass's office: "They need us more than we need them."

The concept of fair representation involves giving credit for a design when credit is due. Most graphic designers are not geniuses who are suddenly inspired to produce a completely new style of design. Most graphic design ideas are variations of previously created compositions. A graphic designer who reproduces wholesale someone else's work is acting unethically and courting legal problems. Designers should be inspired by other work, but not directly copy it.

Cultural Perspective

Steven Heller and Seymour Chwast in their book *Graphic Style* identify twelve graphic design trends of the past 150 years: Victorian, arts and crafts, art nouveau, early modern, expressionism, modern, art deco, Dadaism, heroic realism, late modern, pop art, and postmodern. In addition to these major approaches to art and design, artists from different countries, because of their different cultures, express unique variations of each major style. Each art movement not only changes the way words and images are used for print and screen media, but also has significantly influenced architecture and the design of furniture, clothing, and even household objects. Most of the trends in

graphic design initially began as styles for political and advertising posters that were nailed to walls in cities with large numbers of pedestrians. After a time, other designers and mainstream media outlets adopted the styles.

Seven of the principal art movements, or trends, of the last 100 years have had the most influence on graphic design. They may be divided into two main groups: free form and grid. Leading proponents of both groups have expressed not only aesthetic foundations for their art but political intent as well. Most design trends initially expressed the hope that the world could become more unified and peaceful if graphic design were a part of everyone's lives. The way to achieve that lofty goal marked the most striking difference between the two groups.

The free form artistic styles of art nouveau, Dadaism, art deco, pop art, and postmodern are noted for their free-flowing placement of text and other graphic elements within a design's frame. Their practitioners intended to turn established rules about the traditional placement of visual elements on a page on their head. In many of their graphic messages, designers communicated angry rebellion and frustration over political and social structures that allowed world wars and injustice to flourish. They hoped that, by calling attention to obvious hypocrisies of the society, people would act to change such conditions.

The grid artistic approach exemplified by the de Stijl and Bauhaus styles was less obvious in its political message. Nevertheless, their practitioners believed that technology when wedded with artistic sensibilities could bring world harmony through their graphic designs. The grid styles attempted to give objective, unemotional organization to graphic design. Designers developed a geometric approach based on horizontal and vertical lines and the basic shapes of squares, rectangles, and circles and combined the use of the colors red, yellow, and blue with black, gray, and white. They carefully placed each design element within a frame to ensure unity in the gestalt tradition—individual elements are not as important as the whole design.

Free form and grid approaches are not limited to print design. It is important to consider how these two approaches also apply to television and film visual messages. For example, the prevalent technique seen in such television series as "ER," "NYPD Blue," or "Survivor," in which the camera is constantly moving through a set or location as if it were a character itself and sometimes referred to as a "single camera" technique, is an example of the free form approach for moving images. Conversely, almost any **situation comedy** with characters in a tightly controlled and choreographed theater set ("Friends" or "Spin City") is an example of the grid approach, sometimes called a "multi-camera" style.

Free Form Approaches

Art Nouveau The coronation of Queen Victoria of England in 1837 gave the Victorian era its name. It heralded the rise of technology and the hope that it would improve social conditions. But the Victorian age was a bleak time for artistic sensibilities as commercial interests used words and pictures almost exclusively as advertising devices to attract the attention of potential customers. Modern graphic design was saved with the introduction of the art nouveau (or "new art") style around 1890. Art nouveau artists disliked the injection of crass commercialism into graphic design. Consequently, it was the first commercial art style intended to make products and their advertisements more beautiful.

Art nouveau was highly influenced by traditional Japanese art (Figure 9.14). Bor-

Photograph © The Museum of Modern Art/Licensed by SCALA/Art Resource, NY.

Figure 9.14

"Divan Japonais. 1893. Lithograph: 31⅝ × 23⅞." With their flowing graphic elements and matching typography, the posters of Henri de Toulouse-Lautrec are excellent examples of the art nouveau movement that propelled graphic design out of the "dark ages" of advertisements inspired by the Industrial Revolution.

ders were marked by stylized plantlike vines, and typography mimicked the flowing curves of the graphic elements. At first, critics severely criticized art nouveau, using such phrases as "linear hysteria," "strange decorative disease," and "stylistic free-for-all" to describe the art style. Eventually, however, it was accepted. Although much more popular in Europe, the movement was best demonstrated in the United States on the covers of *Harper's Monthly.* Artists in the mid-1890s, such as Will Bradley and Maxfield Parrish, produced graphic designs for advertisements that were so praised for their beauty that they soon became collectors' items. Parrish was known for his dreamy landscapes filled with golden nymphlike characters. Bradley started as an errand boy and apprentice to a printer in Chicago and went on to become art director for *The Chap-Book,* where he worked with other art nouveau artists such as Henri de Toulouse-Lautrec and Aubrey Beardsley. Bradley also created his own striking covers for the literary journal. He later became art director for

Collier's magazine, and in the 1920s he supervised all the graphic production for William Randolph Hearst's newspapers, magazines, and motion pictures.

The movement inspired other designers to link artistry with functionalism for the first time since Gutenberg's time. It was a revolutionary art movement because it rejected the Victorian traditions of commercial excesses and a machine mentality.

Dadaism In 1916 Europe was preoccupied with the horrors of World War I. Dadaism emerged as a critical examination of the social structures that allowed such an event to occur. It expressed artists' rage with political leaders by the use of absurd, asymmetric designs (Figure 9.15). Writings and graphics were intended to confuse, educate, and gain attention. One of the founders of the movement, Romanian-born poet Tristan Tzara, said simply that "dada means nothing." The name supposedly came out of a meeting of poets, painters, and graphic designers at the Cabaret Voltaire in Zurich, Switzerland, in 1916. The German refugee Hugo Ball sponsored the social gathering. Opening a French dictionary at random, one of the members quickly pointed to the word for a child's hobbyhorse: *dada.* Its practitioners viewed harmony and symmetry as stifling. For the Dadaists, graphic design elements reflected the way modern life actually was lived— quickly paced and tense. By such designs they communicated criticism of the many hypocrisies they perceived during and after the war. Politicians and wealthy individuals were particular targets of Dada publications.

Graphic designs consisted of typography of different sizes and styles randomly distributed on a page. At first glance, such designs are extremely difficult to read. However, Marshall McLuhan argued that Dadaism showed a way to escape the confines of the Western tradition of reading from left to right in tightly controlled rows as the only way to present verbal messages. He preferred the "words in liberty" demonstrated by Dada artists.

Dada designers also experimented with nontraditional ways of displaying images. Painter Marcel Duchamp, famous for his *Nude Descending the Staircase,* stretched the boundaries of acceptable fine art. Dada designers introduced **montage** techniques in which they cut out and arranged pieces of pictures on a page. In film, this photomontage innovation was best demonstrated by Sergei Eisenstein's classic 1925 film *Battleship Potemkin* (see Chapter 13). Later, the Nazis also used the photomontage technique effectively in their propaganda posters. Ironically, it was the Nazi Party that ended the Dada movement and forced its leaders to flee from Germany. Dadaism evolved into the **surreal** art movement and later influenced the pop art and postmodern styles.

Figure 9.15

"Die Kathedrale. 1920. Lithograph: 81⁄16 × 55⁄8." The anti-establishment energy of the Dada art movement is evident in this piece by Kurt Schwitters.

Art Deco Called "the last of the total styles," art deco united buildings, objects, fashions, typographical designs, and graphic designs by its stylish and distinctive look. Art deco (called *art moderne* in Europe) takes its name from a 1925 exhibition in Paris titled *Exposition Internationale des Arts Décoratifs et Industriels Modernes,* which covered both banks of the Seine River. Art deco began because designers concluded that middle-class consumers were put off by tense Dada designs. The public seemed to want a less threatening style that was not controversial but new in its approach. Hence art deco's purpose was largely commercial.

The distinctive art deco style with streamlined shapes and curved sans serif typographical lettering had a modern graphic look that appealed to both left-wing and fascist propaganda poster designers. Advertisers at first didn't like the style because the conservative nature of U.S. design at the time favored function over form. Critics viewed art deco as anti-utilitarian. Nevertheless, *Harper's Bazaar* signed one of the most famous art deco artists, Erté, to a ten-year contract to make erotically styled drawings for its covers (Figure 9.16). Today his posters are valuable collectors' items. As the public embraced the style, advertisers started using art deco designs. Use of the style spread to department stores, corporate headquarters, and even automated vending machines. The Chrysler Building in New York City is a classic example of art deco architecture, as are the multicolored hotels and apartment buildings on Miami Beach.

The stock market crash of 1929 signaled the beginning of the end of the architectural excesses of the art movement. The last major art deco exhibition was at the New York's World Fair of 1939–1940. The conservatism of World War II and its aftermath dealt the final blow to this decorative style that gave a

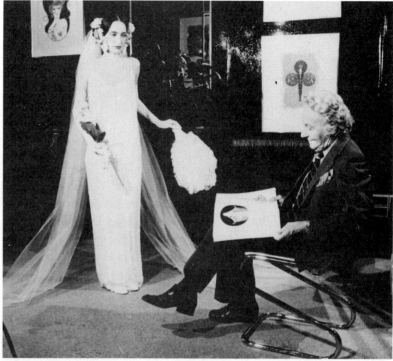

Paul Martin Lester

modern look to the free-flowing ornamentation of art nouveau.

Pop Art The pop art movement combined the organic vines of art nouveau designs and the rebellious philosophy of Dadaism. Pop art gets its name from a group of London artists and designers who met in the mid-1950s. *Pop,* short for "popular," was the label given to objects—from sensational movie posters to the tail fins of Detroit automobiles—that were viewed as unworthy of serious artistic attention and yet were a part of a society's popular culture. In the United States, pop art can be traced to the time when San Francisco was the capital of "beat" generation poets and writers such as Allen Ginsberg and Jack Kerouac. The style was connected with alternative lifestyles and rebellion against authority demonstrated by the "beatnik" culture. The poem *Howl* by Ginsberg, the novel *On the Road* by Kerouac, the peace sign designed by Gerald Holtom in

Figure 9.16

The French art deco master, Erté, poses with a model and examples of his graphic design work.

Figure 9.17

"Love Festival. 1967. Silkscreen: 29 ⅞ × 40." *The organic shapes of art nouveau inspired artists such as Michael English in the 1960s to create posters that combined text and images in dynamic ways.*

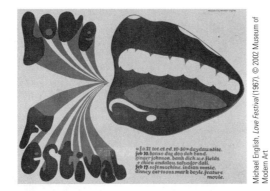

Figure 9.18

Andy Warhol, the undisputed master of the pop art movement, created this icon of Marilyn Monroe titled, "Untitled from Marilyn." At the Museum of Modern Art in New York City, the painting hangs on a wall where it can be viewed or ignored.

1956 as a nuclear disarmament symbol, and the photographs published in Robert Frank's *The Americans* (1956) were verbal and visual examples of artists questioning traditional cultural values.

In the 1960s, pop art combined grass-roots political movements concerned with civil rights and anti–Vietnam War opinions with the "hippie" culture, centered on the corner of Haight and Ashbury streets in San Francisco (Figure 9.17). Posters that adver-

tised rock concerts and political rallies displayed psychedelic art that tried to represent the visual sensations that people experienced after taking a hallucinogenic drug. Intensely contrasting colors in vinelike forms with hand-drawn lettering in the same style were visually arresting, but hard to read for a viewer not part of the culture. Consequently, the designs were a symbolized code that relayed factual information but also served to link those within the culture. Artist Peter Max brought pop art into the mainstream with his colorful posters, as did New York artist Andy Warhol, who used innovative printing techniques on common American icons (Campbell soup cans and Marilyn Monroe) to create strikingly visual works of art (Figure 9.18). By the early 1970s, pop art had reached its peak, but not before influencing everything from fast-food restaurants to comic books to supermarket product packaging.

Postmodern In the late 1970s, a new form of graphic design, initially called Neo-Dada and punk, emerged. Practitioners of the postmodern style placed typographical and other visual elements on pages in angry, rebellious, and random ways in the style of "ransom note" cutouts. Underground comic books were one of the first outlets for this art form (see Chapter 11). Postmodern artists were critical of the lavish spending habits of the wealthy, as were their Dada predecessors. Punk, as with many other art movements, quickly became absorbed into mainstream culture and renamed new wave and most recently hip-hop. Cartoonist Gary Panter decries the transition into respectability when he says: "Punk was an honest expression, while New Wave is a packaging term."

The new wave and hip-hop styles are highly influenced by the ease of typographical and visual manipulations made possible

by computer technology. New wave is connected with a youthful culture that views all new technology as exciting. The colorful cutout titles that Tiber Kalman and Alexander Isley made for the movie *Something Wild* (1986) are examples of new wave that have been critically praised.

Hip-hop started as a fashion, graphic design, and dance accompaniment to rap music. The quick editing of visual messages to the beat of pulsating rhythms is combined with pictographic images on walls, clothing, and within the pages of such magazines as *Vibe* and *Blaze.* Hip-hop music came of age in 1999 when singer Lauryn Hill won five Grammy Awards. The 1993 comedy *Who's the Man?* was designed to attract moviegoers sensitive to hip-hop culture. In addition, quick editing techniques are the hallmark of music videos, as shown on cable networks such as Music Television (MTV) and Video Hits 1 (VH1) and have influenced the way television commercials and programs are produced (see Chapter 14).

Grid Approaches

The idea of a grid came from careful observations of nature. The Greek philosopher Plato and the architect Vitruvius expressed a "dynamic symmetry" composed of natural shapes found in the world: the square, the triangle, and the circle. In architecture, typography, and graphic design, naturally occurring objects inspired designers. Even in the twentieth century, the circular shape of a common seashell, for example, led the architect Le Corbusier to develop a floor plan for a museum exhibition that combined the strength of square and rectangle shapes with the dynamic flowing character of a spiral (Figure 9.19).

De Stijl In the summer of 1917 several Dutch painters, including Theo van Does-

Figure 9.19

Natural forms found in nature inspired many of the letter and graphic design concepts invented by the Greeks.

Ole Skaug

burg and Piet Mondrian, perceived the use of the grid as a way to search for universal harmony in the wake of World War I. They believed that an unemotional use of lines, common shapes, and the colors of red, yellow, and blue would usher in a new utopian spirit of cooperation among the people of the world. Thus de Stijl, translated as *the style,* introduced contemporary graphic designers to the grid format through a journal of the same name. Today, editors commonly use a variation of the grid format for newspaper front pages to express a modern approach.

Mondrian composed abstract paintings of thick black horizontal and vertical lines that divided his canvases into basic shapes, which he filled in with colors (Figure 9.20). His artwork inspired graphic designers to use the same system with text and images. Stefan Lorant, an editor for London's *Lilliput* and *Picture Post* magazines in the 1930s, used the grid to showcase what he called "the third effect." Two photographs printed the same size and side-by-side created new meaning in the mind of the reader that each photograph alone could not achieve. To

Figure 9.20

"Textuel. 1928. Photolitho-graph: 24³⁄₁₆ × 16¹⁵⁄₁₆." The basic shapes, simple colors, and aligned text, as seen in this poster by Piet Mondrian of the de Stijl art movement, inspired the modular design style favored by newspaper layout artists.

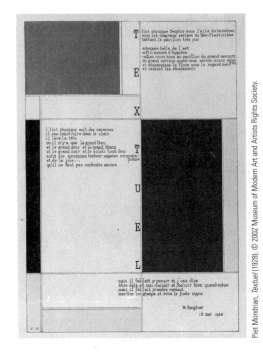

voice his criticism of the Nazi appeasement policy of the British government just before World War II, for example, Lorant ran a picture of Neville Chamberlain next to that of an ostrich. The third effect created by the two equal grid spaces produced a critical comment about Chamberlain's action. It was an opinion deeply felt by Lorant, who had recently fled from Germany because of Nazi Party abuses.

Architect and designer Le Corbusier made an important contribution for the use of the grid in architecture with his 1948 book *Modulor* and the design system of the same name. Le Corbusier was a pseudonym, taken from the name of a maternal relative, of Swiss-born Charles Édouard Jeanneret. He was known for his innovative designs of high-rise buildings surrounded by parks. By the 1960s modular design, named after Le Corbusier's book, became the dominant force in modernizing the front pages of newspapers around the world. In modular design, text and images for each story are placed within rectangular shapes called

modules. The "J" or reversed "J" shapes, sometimes called "dog legs," were abandoned as being old-fashioned. A newspaper redesigned modularly has more of a horizontal than vertical orientation.

Kevin Barnhurst in his monograph *News as Art* noted that the transition from vertical to horizontal modules began as early as the 1890s when banner headlines crossed over several columns. In the 1930s, newspapers started to change from centered headlines to a design style called *streamlining* in which headlines were justified to the left, the most common practice today. One of the first newspapers in the 1960s to be redesigned in the modular format was the New York *Herald Tribune*. Peter Palazzo gave the front page a more contemporary look by creating horizontal rather than vertical text and graphic modules. Will Hopkins, art director for *Look* in 1969 and later for *American Photographer,* did the same for magazine design.

Through his 1981 book *Contemporary Newspaper Design* and workshops at newspapers around the world, Mario Garcia spread the modular design approach. When the national newspaper *USA Today* was introduced in September 1982, its design was heavily influenced by the philosophy of Garcia and other modular advocates (Figure 9.21). Newspaper editors around the world ordered redesigns of their publications because modular design attracted new and younger readers with its horizontal orientation that many compared to television, improved readability with clear and simple story placement, and sped composing room production because the design elements were easier to formulate.

Bauhaus In 1919, architect Walter Gropius headed a design workshop and think tank in Weimar, Germany, called the *Das Staatliches Bauhaus.* Bauhaus comes from the German words *bauen* for "to build" and *haus* for "house." Although originally intended as an architectural school, Bauhaus design quickly embraced the de Stijl concept of creating harmony in the world through unifying art and technology. Although similar to de Stijl in its use of the grid, Bauhaus allowed more individual freedom.

Bauhaus design began with a set of formal ideas about the function and production of objects, but its different political purposes during its history influenced the work of its designers. Therefore, to refer to Bauhaus as one, unified style is misleading. Nevertheless, its product, industrial, and graphic designs are characterized by their emphasis on useful, simple, and clearly defined shapes. Designers favored squares and rectangles created with a T square and curves accurately drawn with a compass. They also preferred the sans serif typeface family because most of its letters could be drawn with right angles, making a good fit with the basic shapes used in their designs.

Gropius was purposely anti-academic, organizing the Bauhaus school as a Renaissance workshop. He preferred that his teachers are called masters, and students were apprentices who worked not in studios but in workshops. Gropius wanted to enhance the notion that the school graduated designers capable of making significant contributions to the real world. Three of the most famous masters at the school were abstract painter Paul Klee, designer and photographer Laszlo Moholy-Nagy, and his assistant, designer Gyorgy Kepes, who is the author of ten books, including *The Language of Vision* (1944), *The Vision Arts Today* (1960), *The Nature and Art of Motion* (1965), *Module, Perception, Symmetry, Rhythm* (1966), and *Sign, Image, Symbol* (1966).

Moholy-Nagy experimented with all types of art—still and moving images, painting, and graphic design (Figure 9.22). He was particularly interested in the poster as a

Figure 9.21

The front page of the fifth anniversary issue of USA Today *is organized with the same modular design concept used in all of its issues. The cover story is always in the middle of the page, a USA Snapshots infographic is always at the lower left, and political, sports, and entertainment mug shots are always presented in the same locations.*

medium for expression. He called the combination of type and images on a poster "the new visual literature." One of his photographic innovations was the "photogram" in which objects are placed on photosensitive paper and then exposed to light. Moholy-Nagy thought, as did many of the Bauhaus designers, that because of its truthful representations, photography could be a positive influence in the world. As with de Stijl, Bauhaus was a reaction to the horrors of World War I.

In 1932, the Nazi Party, disturbed by what it considered to be liberal ideas, closed the school. Many of the faculty fled to Switzerland and the United States. Gropius taught architecture at Harvard, and Moholy-Nagy started a New Bauhaus school in what is now part of the Illinois Institute of Technology in Chicago. The first Bauhaus art exhibition in the United States was at the Museum of Modern Art in 1938. For the first time, American designers were

Figure 9.22

"Z II. 1925. Oil on canvas: 37⅝ × 29⅝." Laszlo Moholy-Nagy was a photographer, painter, and teacher for the Bauhaus school. His use of basic forms and colors attempts to convey a sense of inner and outer vision.

introduced to and inspired by a style that, unlike Dadaism, presented clear messages without drawing attention to it.

Critical Perspective

What is considered good graphic design always depends on the cultural values of the audience. As with different generations that often do not appreciate the musical tastes of younger or older generations, design sensibilities are shaped by the values expressed by the producing and receiving cultures. The free form and grid approaches to graphic design clash because one set of styles is meant to draw attention to it, whereas the other maintains that the message is more important than the design.

A graphic design style, whether classified as free form or grid, will not last long unless a large number of designers take it up and use it in presentations that make sense to their audiences. Milton Glaser, however, is concerned about the prevalence of poorly designed Web sites. He observes, "There's a whole mess of very ugly things on the Web. And to some extent that's because technicians are doing the design." Graphic design education is a key in using computer technology to produce work that is functional and aesthetically pleasing at the same time. But because the dominant, product-oriented culture in the United States relies on television and other screen media for educational and entertainment purposes, marketing personnel, not artists or their fans, make many of the decisions that determine whether a graphic design style remains popular. As more and more people are educated about good design, computer technology, which allows everyone to produce works easily that are sensitive to graphic design issues, may take style decisions out of the hands of the commercial interests. If not, graphic design may revert to the **consumerism** of the Victorian period.

■ *FUTURE DIRECTIONS FOR GRAPHIC DESIGN*

In the near future, computer programs will make it possible for every individual to create his or her graphic design style for whatever purpose. Whether the style is free form, grid, or a totally new kind of graphic innovation, a person's selection and placement of pictorial elements within a frame will express the individual's personality. When the computer, television, and telephone are merged into the same machine (most likely to be called a **teleputer**), sophisticated home design studios will be linked to other workshops throughout the world. Information in the form of textual and visual materials will be obtainable from databases located everywhere on the planet. For example, letters to family members and friends will be sent electronically and will be elaborate, multimedia messages in which images, both still and moving, will be transmitted in a format that accommodates many types of typography and graphic design decisions.

Virtual-reality technology may further revolutionize interpersonal communications by creating "cyberspace" worlds in which the designer actually becomes a visual element within the frame (see Chapter 16). Marshall McLuhan once spoke of the *global village* as a metaphor for new technology that links the world's citizens into one giant community. Perhaps the utopian dreams of the early twentieth century free form and grid designers will be realized when communication equipment is combined with an aesthetic sensitivity to graphic design. As professionals, educators, students, and the public become more visually aware and literate, such dreams can become reality in this era of the World Wide Web.

DISCUSSION AND EXERCISE IDEAS

- Lead a discussion about the work of Saul Bass using the six perspectives.
- Describe your favorite use of graphic design.
- Design a logo that reflects your personality.
- Write a paper that discusses the ethical concerns with graphic design.
- Lead a discussion about the future of graphic design.

INFOTRAC COLLEGE EDITION ASSIGNMENTS

- With "Subject guide" checked, type "Motion Picture Posters" in the search area. Click "View" for the "Periodical references." Scroll down and click on "Screen Gems" about the Mexican film poster collection of Rogelio Agrasanchez, Jr. Why do you think the style of the typography, images, and design are so much different from American movie posters?

- With "Subject guide" checked, type "Virtual Reality" in the search area. Scroll down and click on any links that interest you and read the articles. Try to think of ways virtual-reality technology might be useful within educational settings. What about for journalism? How might news and feature stories be improved if they were communicated through virtual reality?

Go to the Web site for this book at www.wadsworth.com/product/0534562442 to find more Web links on this subject.

INFORMATIONAL GRAPHICS

By the end of this chapter you should know:

- The history of informational graphics for *USA Today.*
- How important informational graphics are in telling complex stories.
- The important historical precedents for today's informational graphics.
- The different types of informational graphics and how they are used.
- Some of the trends that lead to the future use of informational graphics.

When two hijacked commercial airliners slammed into the World Trade Center twin towers in New York City on September 11, 2001, the still photographs and video seen in print, television, and World Wide Web sources stunned viewers (see Chapter 1). And when the skyscrapers collapsed in heaps of bodies, concrete, steel, and dust, the visual messages were almost too incomprehensible to be believed or understood. Voice-over commentary from hurried reporters tried to explain what the eyes were communicating, but these pictures and words couldn't tell the whole story.

A third component from a **visual journalist's** toolbox was necessary-informational graphics.

Informational graphics (called info-graphics or news graphics) are visual displays that can be anything from a pleasing arrangement of facts and figures in a table to a complex, interactive diagram with accompanying text that helps explain a complex story's meaning. With headlines, text, photographs, video, and audio, informational graphics are included in media presentations in order to explain aspects to a story that words and traditional pictures and video alone could not explain fully.

The *USA Today* Web site at www.usatoday.com was no exception. Soon after the airliners crashed into the twin towers of the World Trade Center, researchers and graphic artists for the newspaper were at work completing several informational graphics that showed the airliners' flight paths, the location of the planes' hits upon the towers, and the reason for the collapse of the buildings, among other details of the story (Figure 10.1).

But it is no accident that the newspaper's Web site offered such advanced communication techniques. *USA Today* has been on the forefront and has inspired countless other media entities in the use of informational graphic design since the newspaper was introduced on Wednesday, September 15, 1982.

The Gannett newspaper chain headed by Allen Neuharth saw an unfilled niche in the newspaper market. The United States had no national, general interest daily publication. The closest competitors were the *Wall Street Journal*, exclusively a business-oriented newspaper, and weekly newsmagazines such as *Newsweek* and *Time.* Aimed initially at highly educated and wealthy business executives and travelers, *USA Today* provided national news along with short, local stories from every state in the country. To avoid circulation problems, initially the newspaper was sold almost exclusively at airport terminals and from busy downtown sidewalks in only a few cities.

From the start, the newspaper was created to attract the attention of the generations brought up on television. *USA Today* is a kind of printed version of the Cable News Network (CNN) channel. Its brief story treatment combined with multicolored graphic illustrations pays tribute to the printing industry's chief rival—television. Even the paper racks designed by Fred Gore resemble television sets.

But it was the *look* of the newspaper that attracted the most attention. George Cotliar, managing editor of the *Los Angeles Times,* admits that *USA Today's* "major contribution to journalism is, of course, its graphics. And it has helped bring a lot of newspapers into the twentieth century."

The most striking graphic feature in the newspaper is the infographic on the back page of the first section (Figure 10.2). The large weather map has received universal acclaim since its introduction. Media critic Peter Boyle called the map "the most imitated feature in American journalism." In a 1987 poll of newspaper editors, more than half had increased their weather coverage since the introduction of *USA Today* and 25 percent of them admitted that it was because of the popularity of the large, colorful weather map. Soon after its introduction, newspapers around America started printing their own version of the map—but in regional versions more suited for their readers (Figure 10.3).

■ WEATHER MAPS

The *USA Today* infographic would not be possible had it not been for many factors in weather mapmaking history. No other kind of map—printed or broadcast—enjoys such a favorable and persistent following or is so dependent on the telecommunications industry for delivery of its data.

■ Newspaper Use

The first printed weather map did not show high and low temperatures or warm and cold fronts. Drawn by Edmond Halley in

Figure 10.1

See color section following page 276.

Figure 10.2

See color section following page 276.

Figure 10.3

Although unable to afford the same type of colorful, full-page map as USA Today's, many small newspapers run regional weather information and a U.S. data map supplied by the Associated Press.

Figure 10.4

One of the first data maps, in which a map was combined with statistical data, was this 1686 infographic by Edmond Halley. Prevailing wind currents throughout the world are indicated by the direction of the tiny strokes.

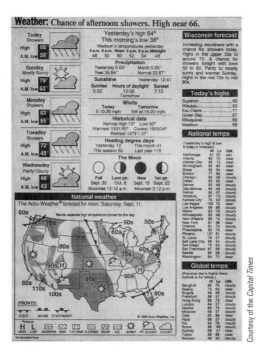

Courtesy of the Capital Times

1686, its symbols simply indicated wind directions over the oceans (Figure 10.4). Based on reported observations, his graphic was a crudely drawn map of part of the world, which showed the direction of trade winds and monsoons. As such, it was an early aid to mariners. Halley is best known for the comet that bears his name: In 1682, he accurately predicted that the comet would return in 1758.

More than 150 years would pass before weather maps would be used regularly. Introduction of the telegraph in 1848 allowed weather observations from around a country (and later the world) to be depicted on a map. The 1851 Great Exhibition in London's Crystal Palace was where people could not only see examples of the newly invented photography medium but also read daily weather reports imposed on a map of England for the first time.

On April 1, 1875, *The Times* of London printed the first daily weather map composed by a pioneer of statistical presentations, Francis Galton. But because of its larger landmass, getting weather reports for the entire United States was much more difficult. However, the U.S. Weather Service, formed in 1870 as a branch of the U.S. Army Signal Office, supplied weather information to the *New York Herald* and the *New York Daily Graphic*. As a onetime experiment in 1876, the *Herald* published America's first weather map. On May 9, 1879, the *Daily Graphic* first began regular publication of a weather map. Stephen Horgan, inventor of the halftone engraving screen, made the weather maps for the *Daily Graphic*.

By 1910, the newly formed U.S. Weather Bureau had been placed in the Department

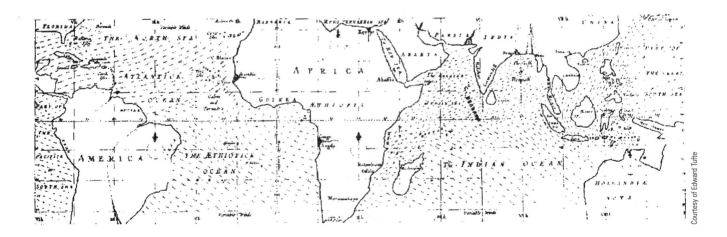

Courtesy of Edward Tufte

of Agriculture. The bureau supplied 65 newspapers with national and regional weather information via telegraph. Two years later the bureau provided service to 147 newspapers in 91 cities. But like many innovations, the weather map fad quickly diminished in popularity.

The conservative *New York Times* signaled the beginning of the weather map's comeback when it published its first map on August 4, 1934. The next year, the Associated Press (AP) Wirephoto network began transmitting weather maps electronically via telephone lines to its member newspapers across the country. Publishers liked the AP maps because they could use them in local newspapers almost without alteration.

In 1960, NASA launched the first geosynchronous weather satellite, TIROS-1, which sent back pictures of the United States from 22,000 miles in space. The National Weather Service provided the images to newspapers and television stations for use in their weather coverage (Figure 10.5).

■ *Television Weather Segments*

Before the 1970s, weather segments of local TV news programs were intended as light-hearted diversions from the other, more important news and sports segments. Sexy women with no other apparent qualifications than their appearance or people dressed up in clown suits and makeup read the weather reports in a comical way. Despite the fact that some stations still hire weather people to be stand-up comedians and announce 100-year-olds' birthdays (the talk show entertainer David Letterman began his television career explaining the weather for an Indianapolis station), the trend is toward more professionalism among weather personnel. Many now have degrees in meteorology and receive the "seal of approval" from the American Meteorological Society after finishing a training session for television meteorologists.

Before computer graphics, the TV weather announcer often used hand-drawn symbols on chalkboards and Plexiglas sheets. Magnetized strips that indicated weather fronts were stuck on large boards and sometimes would fall off. But viewer surveys revealed that 70 percent of the audience tuned in to news programs to learn about the next day's weather. Consequently, station managers began to invest in expensive computer graphic equipment to

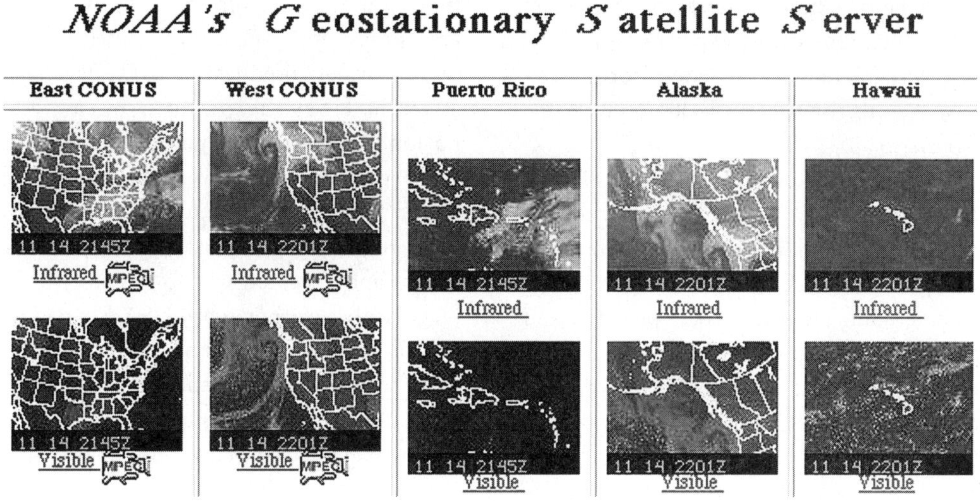

Figure 10.5

The National Oceanic and Atmospheric Administration (NOAA) allows World Wide Web users to view satellite images at the touch of a mouse button.

make the weather more dramatic and attract more viewers. In the 1970s, stations started using the chroma keying electronic effect. The announcer stood in front of a wall painted green or blue, and the director merged a slide of the United States from another video camera so that an announcer appeared to be standing before a huge weather map.

The weather segment of a newscast is now the most visually dramatic part of the program. In a three-minute time period, as many as twenty different maps and infographics may be presented in colorful, often mobile, displays. In 1982, John Coleman, the weather personality for ABC's "Good Morning America," initiated the first nationally broadcast 24-hour cable weather service, The Weather Channel. Coincidentally, *USA Today* began publication that same year.

■ Impact of Technology

Allen Neuharth has been in the newspaper business since he was an eleven-year-old paper carrier for the *Minneapolis Tribune*. In 1979, Neuharth sent some of his key staff members to a window-covered (to avoid spies) bungalow a few blocks from his Cocoa Beach, Florida, home to develop the national newspaper. One of the experts in the early days was graphics editor George Rorick, who had been recruited specifically to create the weather map.

After the introduction of *USA Today*, newspapers throughout the country began dropping their drab, black and white satellite photographs and introducing spot color graphic elements, color pictures, and a variety of infographic illustrations. Color, computers, and satellite delivery now are commonplace elements of newspaper technology.

■ ANALYSIS OF THE INFOGRAPHICS IN USA TODAY

Communications experts link the future for newspapers to the World Wide Web (Chapter 16). Hence, *USA Today* is a cheery, easily readable example on paper of what is offered on a portable computer screen. The stories are written in a short, feature-oriented style that could easily fit on a few computer frames. The headlines are easily distinguished from the other elements on the page and are written in a light, casual style. The typography is a mixture of the sans serif and roman typeface families, which creates variety on the page and is eminently readable. Photographs, infographics, and most rules are in color to maximize visual impact. Graphic elements are selected for their eye-catching impact. Consequently, a reader needs to expend only a little more effort than when watching thirty minutes' worth of national news on television.

Although the newspaper has been criticized for its abbreviated writing style, its more important contributions are its use of colorful graphic elements and method of distribution. The latter innovation receives most of the attention from traditional scholars. For example, Michael and Edwin Emery in their widely used textbook *The Press and America* label the publication as "the national satellite newspaper." But just as important was the newspaper's effect on other print and screen media when it showed that informational graphics could be a vital and accepted way to tell stories. Its large-scale weather map, USA Snapshots that feature a pictograph on the first page of every section, and sophisticated use of other types of informational graphics are a tribute to newspaper graphic designers of the past.

Through the use of computer technology, an enormous number of infographics can be created and printed in each day's edition. For example, a content analysis of the editorial content for October 9, 2001, reveals that the 56-page edition contained 194 stories, 85 photographs, and 286 informational graphics—an average of 5.1 infographics per page. The editors of *USA Today* demonstrate their faith in the newspaper's designers by publishing more infographics than stories.

In the same edition, only 5 percent (18) of the infographics were statistical in the form of graphs. All of the others were simple tables (184), diagrams (9), fact boxes (51), illustrations (5), locator maps (18), and one television guide. The problem with such a low statistical infographic percentage is that readers never learn to make complex associations if multivariate data aren't presented.

The weather map infographic receives the most praise (Figure 10.6). It is a tribute to the efficient, competent, and innovative use of computers, which allow such technological marvels to happen daily. We can hardly imagine how page colors first viewed on a computer screen can be transmitted so accurately by satellite to printing presses thousands of miles away.

The map itself takes up approximately 34 percent of the page. It is a bold rendering of the United States that contains a light gray shadow around it for a three-dimensional effect. Separate boxes show Alaska, Hawaii, and Puerto Rico. Logically, cool colors on the map represent lower temperatures than yellow and red high-temperature hues. Tables, a pictograph, and fact boxes constitute about 48 percent of the rest of the weather infographic on the page. An advertisement section first added to the page in February 1986 runs along the bottom of the page to complete the layout.

Color certainly is used on the page not only to show in an instant the high temperature in Denver, but also to attract attention to the page and the newspaper. If business executives notice the newspaper between flights, they may decide to purchase advertising to run along the bottom of the weather page and elsewhere in the paper.

■ *INFORMATIONAL GRAPHICS AND THE SIX PERSPECTIVES*

Statistical designer and Yale University professor Edward Tufte estimates that between 900 billion and 2 trillion informational graphics are published annually worldwide. If television and computer use is included, the number may be half again higher. Television meteorologists stand before colorful

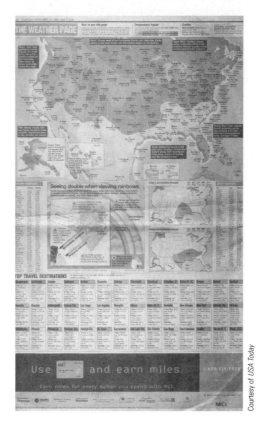

Figure 10.6

The complete USA Today weather page.

Courtesy of USA Today

animated weather maps. Presidential candidates use multiple-colored charts when making campaign infomercials. Corporations regularly use computer-generated infographics for business presentations. Almost every page in magazines, newspapers, corporate annual reports, and textbooks seems to have some type of statistical graphic. The informational graphic helps tell a story that is too tedious for words, yet too simplified for photographs alone.

Personal Perspective

Besides creating a record of a society's major news and trends, the media also provide a place for corporations to advertise their goods and services. But one of the main utilitarian missions of the media is to educate. Reporters attempt to construct stories that answer the six journalistic questions of who, what, when, where, why, and how. The first four satisfy the basic requirements for most news stories, but *why* and *how* are part of the educational function of journalism and require more space or time. Research indicates that a reader or viewer learns and remembers better if the journalistic questions are answered with a combination of words, images, and infographics. In this increasingly visual age, communicators find that images and graphics often help clarify factual accounts that in the past were the domain of word descriptions alone. As Tim Harrower in his workbook *The Newspaper Designer's Handbook* reports, "When we want information, we say show me—don't tell me."

Infographics combine the aesthetic sensitivity of artistic values with the quantitative precision of numerical data in a format that is both understandable and dramatic. A company's growth and decline over several years can be communicated simply with a line chart that replaces several thousand words. It may be impossible for a photographer to capture the scene of a late-breaking news story in some remote part of the world, but a locator map can at least let a reader know where the event has occurred. Infographics combine the intellectual satisfaction of words with the emotional power of visual messages.

Historical Perspective

The first clear-cut use of informational graphics by an advanced civilization took the form of maps. Carved in the Sumerian clay in about 3800 B.C.E., crude maps showed a vast agricultural estate in Mesopotamia. Two thousand years later, the Egyptians used simple maps to denote boundaries between properties. When the Greeks invented the concepts of latitude and longitude for dividing the world into coordinates in about the sixth century B.C.E., their maps became much more accurate. That innovation enabled mariners to explore farther regions of the world with the confidence that they could find their way home. Much later, in the eleventh century, a three-foot-square stone was the medium for a detailed map of the eastern coast of China. The map, called the "Yü Chi Thu" (Map of the Tracks of Yü the Great), was produced with a sophisticated grid system for an accurate representation.

With the spread of printing during the Renaissance, maps and detailed medical illustrations were regularly included with text. Sketch artists often used a camera obscura to render accurate diagrams of the human skeletal system. In his notebooks, Leonardo da Vinci often illustrated his innovative ideas with diagrams. A 1546 edition of Petrus Apianus's *Cosmographia* contained a map that showed many details of the European continent (Figure 10.7).

Informational Graphics Pioneers

Informational graphics might forever have been limited to simple maps or diagrams if not for individuals who had the creative intelligence to understand that graphics could be more than simple drawings. The power of a graphic representation of empirical data lies in its explanation of complex processes by an immediate visual message. William Playfair, Dr. John Snow, and Charles Minard, in particular, had the insight to link numbers with traditional graphic forms to tell complex stories with eloquent simplicity.

Playfair, an English political economist, is considered by many to be the founder of infographics. He was educated by his brother, a mathematician at the University of Edinburgh, and learned drafting while working for an engineering company in England. In his 1786 publication *The Commercial and Political Atlas,* he printed forty-four charts that gave details about the British economic system. But one of his charts was unlike any graphic previously seen (Figure 10.8). Because he had only one year's data for Scottish exports and imports, a time-series line chart was inappropriate. Consequently, Playfair invented a graph that used black bars for exports and ribbed bars for imports. He showed dollar amounts at the top and listed individual countries down the right side. His innovation became the first bar chart, showing that infographics could convey complex messages powerfully and simply. Today, bar charts are one of the most common elements of infographics.

London in the 1850s, like many overly crowded and unsanitary cities, was ravaged by several outbreaks of cholera, which killed thousands of people. Dr. John Snow, a physician concerned about the cause of the dreaded disease, obtained the names and addresses of about 500 of those who had died during an 1854 epidemic. When faced with

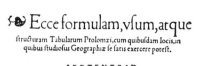

Courtesy of Edward Tufte

all the street numbers written on several sheets of paper, Snow could make little sense of the data and could discern no patterns. But when he plotted each death on a street map of a tiny section of central London, the visual representation of the data clearly showed the deaths clustered around the Broad Street water pump and not any other source (Figure 10.9). Snow ordered the pump handle replaced, and the plague was arrested.

Figure 10.7

Map accuracy improved greatly when locations were superimposed on a grid representing latitude and longitude. In his 1546 edition of Cosmographia, Petrus Apianus plotted the location of various European cities with the help of bodiless hands holding threads.

Figure 10.8

William Playfair is an important figure in the history of informational graphics because he was one of the first to substitute time and money data for the latitude and longitude coordinates of maps. Charts, then, may be thought of as maps that plot economic positions against time rather than geographic locations.

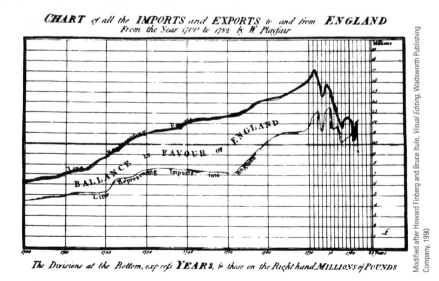

Modified after Howard Finberg and Bruce Itule. *Visual Editing.* Wadsworth Publishing Company, 1990

Figure 10.9

Dr. John Snow identified the Broad Street water pump as a cholera culprit when he combined the addresses of those who had died with a map of central London.

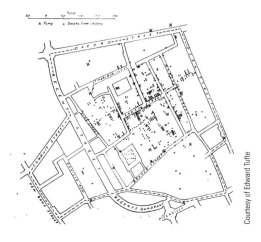

Courtesy of Edward Tufte

As with Snow, French engineer Charles Minard in 1869 combined statistical information and a map to tell a complicated story simply (Figure 10.10). Minard created an infographic of Napoleon's disastrous march to Moscow and retreat during the War of 1812 that has been called "the best statistical graphic ever drawn." Historian E. J. Marey complimented the infographic as "seeming to defy the pen of the historian by its brutal eloquence." Minard told the incredible story of the loss of more than 400,000 soldiers in

one military campaign through an infographic that combined six different series of information. He showed the size and the location of the army and the direction of its movements on a two-dimensional surface, as well as the temperature on various dates. Minard proved that a complex story could be reduced to its simplest elements in a compelling visual format.

Newspaper Infographics

Unfortunately, most newspaper and magazine graphic designers in the nineteenth century didn't have the same enlightened philosophy. Nevertheless, highly skilled visual artists fashioned maps and illustrations from eyewitness accounts and photographs for numerous publications. In the United States, two leaders in the use of illustrations were publications established in 1850: *Frank Leslie's Illustrated Newspaper* and *Harper's Weekly*. With the halftone engraving process for photographs not becoming standard practice for another thirty years, the *Philadelphia Inquirer* and other newspapers used maps mostly to tell

Figure 10.10

Charles Minard eloquently portrays Napoleon's disastrous military advance on Moscow in 1812 in an informational graphic that has been called the best ever produced. The width, shading, and position of the horizontal lines indicate troop strength, direction, and position. This single visual message clearly shows why Napoleon started with 422,000 troops and ended with 10,000.

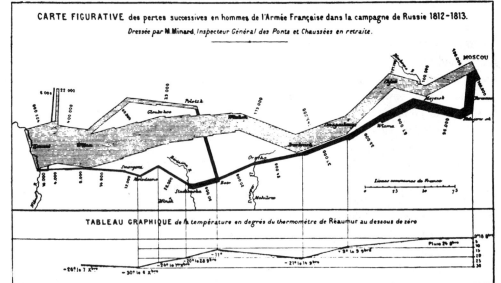

Modified after Howard Finberg and Bruce Itule, Visual Editing, *Wadsworth Publishing Company, 1990*

about important Civil War battles (Figure 10.11). Large, horizontal maps caused front-page designers to rethink the customary rigid, vertical column look of newspapers of the day. Because these horizontal, hand-drawn maps had to extend across more than a single column, designers of front pages let headlines and stories follow that same pattern. Consequently, the use of maps encouraged the advent of a more modern look.

Maps always have been the chief infographic in wartime. During the two world wars, hand-lettered maps and diagrams dominated the pages of newspapers and magazines as readers eagerly sought information about military actions around the world. With Americans unsure about the location of battles during the world wars and later the geography of Korea and Vietnam, maps were the main type of infographic used during those conflicts (Figure 10.12).

Computer technology gradually became affordable and easily manageable allowing newsrooms to produce custom-made illustrations. Television stations or graphics firms under contract made logos, titles, and other graphics for TV shows. The introduction of sophisticated switching software allowed special visual effects. An electronic frame or viewport that included a map or other graphic could easily be included in the same frame as the news anchor. As a result of the new emphasis on graphic design in television, newspaper editors saw a need to give their newspapers a more modern appearance. Graphics editors were hired to oversee both the photography and graphics departments. In 1974, the *Chicago Tribune,* a leader in graphics production since before World War II, became the first newspaper to hire a graphics editor. By 1988, 340 members, or 17 percent, of the Society of Newspaper Designers classified themselves as graphics editors. In addition to the artist, who is responsible for production, the graphics researcher has

become a vital part of the infographic team. The researcher seeks resource material from databases and libraries for use in word and image descriptions.

Newspapers lagged behind television in the use of graphics until the early 1980s. Charts and tables generally were reserved for the business and sports sections until the introduction of *USA Today.* Graphics production got a big boost when personal computers introduced by IBM, Apple, and many other companies made fast machines with large memories commonplace. An operator can now create and print infographics in a matter of minutes instead of days.

Infographics came of age in January 1991, during the Gulf War. Because of the isolated desert battleground action and government press restrictions, journalists had trouble obtaining pictures, both still and moving. Consequently, graphic artists for print and broadcast media produced infographics to tell the story of the war. The difficulty of getting visual messages from the battleground, a greater awareness of infographics generally, and the prevalence of desktop computers led to the

Figure 10.11

Before the halftone printing process, photographs could not be used to illustrate news stories. In one of the bloodiest battles of the Civil War, Antietam, the horror of the fighting could only be described by words and a map.

Modified after Howard Finberg and Bruce Itule, *Visual Editing,* Wadsworth Publishing Company, 1990

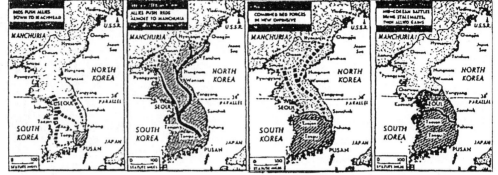

Courtesy of Vis-Com, Inc.

Courtesy of Vis-Com, Inc.

Figure 10.12

Maps have always helped readers understand conflicts in foreign locales. Many battlefield stories were illustrated with maps during the Korean War (right) and the Vietnam War (left). Arrows and shading often are used to show troop movements and areas secured.

Figure 10.13

This line chart instantly shows the reader the rise and fall of the Dow Jones Industrial Average (stock prices) on a particular day. Note the subtle decisions by the infographic designer that make it easy to read: background shading, sans serif typefaces, careful alignment, a grid, and a bold data line.

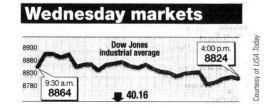

Courtesy of USA Today

explosion of infographic production during the Gulf War.

Computer technology not only makes possible the easy and economical production and distribution of infographics, but it also educates producers and consumers in the ways that data and images can be combined to communicate complicated information quickly and memorably.

Technical Perspective

There are two main types of informational graphic: statistical and nonstatistical. Statistical infographics are visual displays that present empirical, quantitative data. Nonstatistical infographics are visual displays that rely on a visually pleasing arrangement of verbal and visual qualitative information.

Statistical Infographic Elements

The two main types of statistical infographic elements are charts (also called graphs) and data maps. Charts may be line, relational, pie, or pictograph. Data maps combine numeric data on a simple locator map.

Charts Much of the news contains numeric information. The president's budget, the value of the U.S. dollar compared with the values of currency in other countries, the increase or decrease in criminal activity, and election results are examples of stories that are primarily about numbers. Reading a story that simply listed in sentence form all the figures generated by such stories would be tedious and mind numbing. Charts (graphs) were invented to display numerical information concisely and comprehensibly and to show trends in the data that a reader might overlook in a verbal format.

The technical term for a line chart is a rectilinear coordinate chart (Figure 10.13). Other names for it are fever charts (data rise and fall as if on a thermometer) and time-series plots. A line chart contains a rule that connects points plotted on a grid that corresponds to amounts along a horizontal, or x, axis and a vertical, or y, axis. Designers often use line charts to show variations in quantities over a period of time; they are most effective when the quantities change dramatically over time. A significant upsurge or decline in a company's sales, for example, can be easily shown on a line chart. Occasionally, graphic designers will color the area below the line of the chart for a more dramatic effect. The graph then becomes an area chart.

Although it depends on the type of data used, the y-axis for line charts usually should begin at zero. Intervals of time usually are displayed along the x-axis and should be consistent and evenly spaced to avoid visual misrepresentation of the data.

In contrast to line charts, which best show broadly based trends over time, relational charts best show significant changes in two or more specific items during a particular period of time. For example, gold and silver prices for a particular year would be represented best by two bars of different heights, if set on the x-axis, or lengths, if placed on the y-axis. When horizontal boxes present the amounts the chart is called a bar chart. When vertical bars represent the amounts, the chart is called a column chart. Whether the graphic is a bar or column chart depends on the designer's preference.

Pie charts are so named because a circle is used to represent 100 percent of something and the individual items that make up that total are identified by pie slices, or wedges, that are proportional to their shares of the total (Figure 10.14). Thus a pie chart compares amounts individually and with the whole. The only way that pie charts can be used to show complex trends is to use several pie charts, which isn't very effective. Designers usually avoid pie charts because they often have to show too much information or are misleading. A pie chart shouldn't have more than seven slices, and no slice should be smaller than 1 percent of the total; a pie chart with too many or too small slices is difficult to read. Colors of individual slices should contrast, and each slice should be labeled clearly. Finally, all the wedges should be drawn accurately to correspond to the percentages they represent. Use of computer graphics software

By Anne R. Carey and Bob Laird, USA TODAY

Courtesy of USA Today

Figure 10.14

Pie charts are best used when they comprise five or fewer classifications. Note how the infographics designer attempts to add interest to the chart with upright and three-dimensional orientations.

ensures pie-slice accuracy. However, slanting or canting a pie chart for a three-dimensional effect may lead to inaccuracy in pie-slice sizes. Although pie charts are distinctive and immediately attract attention by their round shape, as Edward Tufte points out, "a table should almost always be used over a dumb old pie chart."

A pictograph uses a representative drawing of the items the graph explains in the production of the graph itself. For example, instead of showing the shrinking costs of computer hardware on a line or relational graph, the designer shows the cost differences by using smaller and smaller computer monitors. Pictographs are the most criticized of all graph forms because they often employ cute, contentless drawings to represent numerical information for the sole purpose of attracting the reader's attention. These visual representations often are misleading and wrong. Although pictographs are criticized for insulting the intelligence of readers, they are widely used. For example, *USA Today* features pictographs in the bottom corner of the first page of each of its sections (Figure 10.15).

Data Maps Maps that combine geographic information with numeric data can be the most eloquent type of infographic produced. Data maps can represent hundreds of figures in a visual format that an

Figure 10.15

Pictographs combine the statistical information of a chart with the artistic rendering of a diagram, but often for attention getting, rather than educating, motives as in this example after the attacks of September 11.

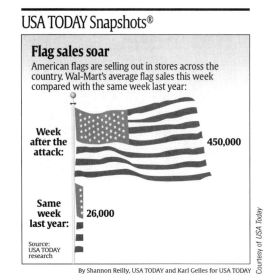

USA TODAY Snapshots®

Flag sales soar

American flags are selling out in stores across the country. Wal-Mart's average flag sales this week compared with the same week last year:

Week after the attack: 450,000

Same week last year: 26,000

Source: USA TODAY research

By Shannon Reilly, USA TODAY and Karl Gelles for USA TODAY

Courtesy of *USA Today*

unsophisticated reader can instantly analyze. Data maps combine the drawing techniques used in diagrams with quantitative data to help tell a complicated story in a simple presentation (Figure 10.16). The *USA Today* weather map with colored strips representing different temperatures is the type of data map most commonly used in the media. The maps produced by Dr. Snow and Charles Minard are classic examples of the use of numbers and simple geographic maps. Investigative reporters have discovered the power of visually combining numeric data and geographic locator maps in telling their stories. For example, cancer death or crime statistics in the form of columns and keyed to specific geographic locations enable readers to notice patterns

Figure 10.16

A data map explains to readers where the second-day targets of the US military campaign against the Taliban in Afghanistan are located as well as areas controlled by the various factions.

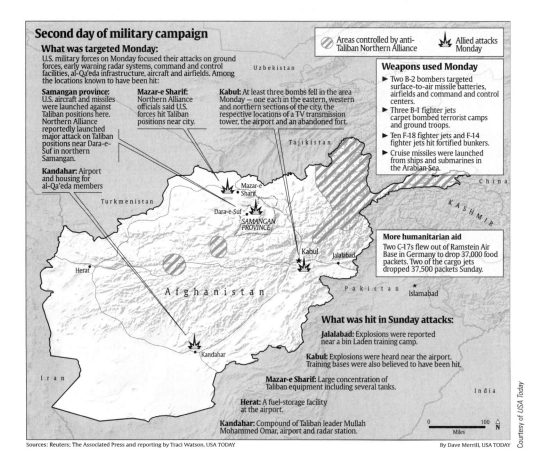

Second day of military campaign

What was targeted Monday:

U.S. military forces on Monday focused their attacks on ground forces, early warning radar systems, command and control facilities, al-Qa'eda infrastructure, aircraft and airfields. Among the locations known to have been hit:

Samangan province: U.S. aircraft and missiles were launched against Taliban positions here. Northern Alliance reportedly launched major attack on Taliban positions near Dara-e-Suf in northern Samangan.

Kandahar: Airport and housing for al-Qa'eda members

Mazar-e Sharif: Northern Alliance officials said U.S. forces hit Taliban positions near city.

Kabul: At least three bombs fell in the area Monday — one each in the eastern, western and northern sections of the city, the respective locations of a TV transmission tower, the airport and an abandoned fort.

◢ Areas controlled by anti-Taliban Northern Alliance
✦ Allied attacks Monday

Weapons used Monday

► Two B-2 bombers targeted surface-to-air missile batteries, airfields and command and control centers.
► Three B-1 fighter jets carpet bombed terrorist camps and ground troops.
► Ten F-18 fighter jets and F-14 fighter jets hit fortified bunkers.
► Cruise missiles were launched from ships and submarines in the Arabian Sea.

More humanitarian aid

Two C-17s flew out of Ramstein Air Base in Germany to drop 37,000 food packets. Two of the cargo jets dropped 37,500 packets Sunday.

What was hit in Sunday attacks:

Jalalabad: Explosions were reported near a bin Laden training camp.

Kabul: Explosions were heard near the airport. Training bases were also believed to have been hit.

Mazar-e Sharif: Large concentration of Taliban equipment including several tanks.

Herat: A fuel-storage facility at the airport.

Kandahar: Compound of Taliban leader Mullah Mohammed Omar, airport and radar station.

Uzbekistan · Tajikistan · China · KASHMIR · Turkmenistan · Mazar-e Sharif · Dara-e-Suf · SAMANGAN PROVINCE · Herat · Kabul · Jalalabad · Afghanistan · Pakistan · Islamabad · Iran · Kandahar · India

0 — 100 Miles ⏃ N

Sources: Reuters; The Associated Press and reporting by Traci Watson, USA TODAY

By Dave Merrill, USA TODAY

Courtesy of *USA Today*

that words alone could not emphasize as well.

Nonstatistical Infographic Elements

Although not as sophisticated as the statistical infographic elements, nonstatistical infographic elements are a vital part of storytelling in this visual age. They comprise fact boxes, tables, nondata maps, diagrams, and miscellaneous formats.

Fact Boxes Fact boxes contain a series of statements that summarize the key points of a story (Figure 10.17). These boxes catch the reader's attention in a graphic and entertaining way. They closely resemble the journalistic sidebar—a short article that elaborates on a specific topic mentioned in a longer story. Fact boxes first appeared in newspapers during World War II. Fighting fronts in Asia and Europe generated a lot of news, and fact boxes were a convenient way to summarize events. When paper had to be rationed because of shortages and the number of newspaper pages reduced, fact boxes sometimes replaced longer stories altogether. A fact box, as the name suggests, simply lists the key points that the accompanying story explains in detail. It serves the same function as a headline or photograph in that it entices the reader to read an entire article. However, fact boxes have been criticized because they may encourage a reader to skip the longer story for the information contained in the fact box alone.

Fact boxes rarely stand alone; they usually are part of a story. However, television and presentation graphic frames often use a variation of the fact box as subject headings for voice-overs by announcers. Fact boxes in print media often are used with photographs, icons, and other infographics.

Tables Tables simply display numbers or words in an orderly format of rows and columns, with enough white space for readability (Figure 10.18). The most familiar types of tables in print media are baseball box scores and stock market results. Although they are the least visually appealing of all

Zen and the Art of Making a Living

Instant Recall (Page 155)

Reviewing highlights from your past may reveal clues to your life's work. Additionally, the questions may help you get a feeling for what it would be like to actually be engaged in your life's work. When giving your answers to the questions below, do not limit yourself to previous work experience. Draw upon your entire life experience.

■ Recall times when you have been most creative. These are times when you created something (an event, a thing, a product, a system).

■ Recall times when you have been most committed. These are times when you were deeply involved, emotionally committed, and determined to persist in spite of all obstacles.

■ Recall times when you were most decisive. These are times when you knew exactly what to do. You knew you were right, and you acted deliberately and confidently, perhaps even in spite of the doubt and objections of others.

■ Recall a time when everyone said you couldn't do it, but you knew you could, and you did it anyway. what was it? How did it feel?

■ Recall times when you have been so absorbed in what you were doing that you hardly noticed the time. What were you doing?

"You will find as you look back upon your life that the moments when you have really lived are the moments when you have done things in a spirit of love."

— Henry Drummond

Courtesy of the Capital Times

Figure 10.17

Fact boxes are studies in the visual organization of textual information. A reverse, sans serif typeface makes this headline stand out. The text is justified on both sides, with equal white space around its edges. The leading is tight, but square bullets instantly identify each fact presented. Finally, the name of the person quoted is set in italics and justified to the right. These visual elements attract readers to a quick synopsis of a longer story.

Figure 10.18

Tables, like fact boxes, simply organize words in a visual format and are found most often in the business and sports sections of a newspaper. Alignment of rows and columns, consistent spacing, and viewer interest in particular items are keys to a successful table. Shown here are stock market quotations (left) and Tennessee State's football record.

Courtesy of USA Today

Lean years at Tennessee State

Tennessee State has had some lean years since its last appearance in the NCAA Division I-AA playoffs in 1986.

Year	Overall Record	OVC Record	Comment
1997	4-7	4-3	tied for fourth in OVC
1996	4-7	3-5	tied for sixth in OVC
1995	2-9	1-7	worst record since 1962 (1-7-1)
1994	5-6	4-4	tied for fourth in OVC
1993	4-7	4-4	three-way tie for fourth in OVC
1992	5-6	5-3	fourth in OVC
1991	3-8	2-5	sixth in OVC
1990	7-4	4-2	third in OVC
1989	5-5-1	3-3	three-way tie for third in OVC
1988	3-7-1	2-4	three-way tie for fourth in OVC
1987	3-7-1		first year in OVC, didn't play league schedule

Source: USA TODAY research

Courtesy of USA Today

graphics, tables are useful in presenting large amounts of information in a logical and ordered way. Headings run horizontally along the top and identify categories of information placed under them in vertical columns enabling the reader to compare numbers or items easily. Tables are considered to be half text and half chart and are best used when many items have to be displayed. If three or fewer numbers or items are presented, text is the best choice. A chart should be used for more than three but not more than twenty items. A table is the best choice for more than twenty items. Try to imagine a complete list of stock market results in text or chart formats! Obviously, the best choice for such a large amount of data is a table with carefully aligned rows and columns that neatly organize the information.

Nondata Maps Research supports the widely held belief that Americans generally lack geographic knowledge. One of the reasons that so many maps are published dur-

ing times of war in the *New York Times,* other newspapers, and magazines is that the American public needs to be educated about foreign locations. But simple maps also may be used to answer an important journalistic question: They show immediately where a news story has taken place. One of the first maps published in a newspaper was in *The Times* of London on April 7, 1806, as part of a story about a murder (Figure 10.19). The simple floor plan of a house printed on the front page revealed, in almost Clue-like fashion, that Richard Patch shot Isaac Blight in the back parlor. It was used for the same reason similar maps are used today: Words are too tedious and photographs are impossible to obtain. Maps enable understanding at a glance.

There are two types of nondata maps: locator and explanatory. Locator maps show a geographic location or a road system in a simplified design that lets the reader or viewer know where something of importance has occurred (Figure 10.20). In large cities, television news programs include a traffic report about which highways are heavily congested and identify each one with a circle on a map. If a major news story happens anywhere in the world, a locator map might be the only visual information available until pictures can be taken at the scene. Explanatory maps not only reveal where a news story has occurred but also tell how a series of events has taken place. Usually designated with numbers, events leading to the arrest of a serial murderer, for example, are plotted on a locator map. Readers not only learn where a news story has broken but also discover the background and time frame of events leading up to it.

With computer technology, mapmaking has become much simpler. Published maps in atlases cannot be directly printed or broadcast without permission from the

Figure 10.19

One of the first infographics ever printed in a newspaper was the floor plan of a house in which a murder had been committed. The Times *of London in 1806 satisfied curious readers with its illustrations.*

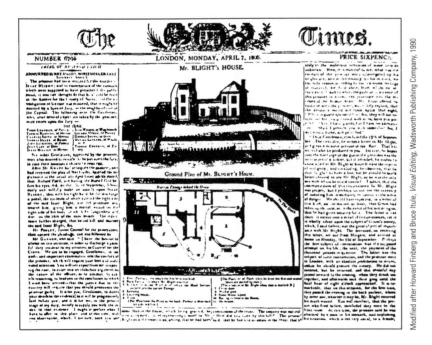

Modified after Howard Finberg and Bruce Ittule, *Visual Editing,* Wadsworth Publishing Company, 1990

mapmaker. However, a map can be traced by a graphic designer, digitized by a flatbed scanner, and stored in the computer's memory. The infographic artist can then include the map in the layout of a story. Companies also sell to media outlets high-quality maps that can be placed on a page or frame by a telephone modem, input directly from a hard drive or CD-ROM disc, or scanned as if it were a traced image. By these methods, maps that used to take several hours to draw can now be produced in a matter of minutes. Computers also make it easy for a designer to add color, labels, and special effects, such as tilting, slanting, and three-dimensional perspective.

But despite their sometimes banal and apolitical perception, maps and mapmaking can be quite controversial. Take a map of the Earth, for example. Because the Earth is round, representing it on a flat surface is difficult. A mapmaker can either represent the shapes of the Earth's land masses or their sizes—but it is almost impossible to represent them both accurately on a flat surface. Over the course of history there have been thousands of different map projections of the earth, but none more controversial than the two most common ones—the Mercator and Peters projections (Figures 10.21 and 10.22).

A Flemish mathematician and cartographer, Gerhard Kremer, in 1569 created the commonly used Mercator projection map. Kremer lived with his wealthy uncle, Gisbert Mercator, and took his name. With the Mercator map, the farther away a country is from the equator the larger it appears. This "view" of the world was convenient for European colonists who were pleased that their countries were in the center of the world and larger than they appeared while the size and importance of developing countries were diminished. Nevertheless, it is still

the dominant worldview in most geography textbooks and classrooms.

In 1974, the German historian and journalist, Arno Peters, introduced his "equal-area" projection map that showed the sizes of the countries accurately, but distorted the shape of them. The Peters projection map inspired controversy from its inception because it represents developing countries in their true proportion. In responding to that controversy, Peters admitted, "Maps are unavoidably political." If you look closely, the television program "The West Wing" features an upside down version of a Peters projection map on a wall of the set that further distorts the socially acceptable view of the world.

Diagrams Some of the most dramatic and artistically rendered infographics involve the use of diagrams. Diagrams can reveal the details of how processes and machines work with line drawings and color (Figure 10.23). Because diagrams are complex, designers often prepare them in advance. A team of graphics researchers and artists works with the graphics editor to find verbal and visual

Figure 10.20

A locator map with different scales reminds users of MSNBC on the World Wide Web (www.msnbc.com) where Kosovo is located.

Figure 10.21 (left)

Called the "Greenland problem," the Mercator map projection enlarges the size of countries the farther they are from the equator. Greenland looks to be the size of Africa when in fact Africa is fourteen times larger. In addition, the size of Europe is larger than in reality giving the continent a status that politicians, military leaders, and business leaders encouraged.

Figure 10.22 (right)

The Peters projection map accurately represents the size, but not the shape, of land masses on the Earth. Nevertheless, it has sparked controversy as it challenged the standard view of the world as shown in the Mercator projection.

resource materials that will ensure accuracy. Because diagrams can be quickly prepared on desktop computers, they have become an everyday part of newspaper and magazine coverage of important stories.

Miscellaneous Formats Infographic artists also are asked to produce a variety of designs that don't fit any of the preceding categories. Again, because of the widespread use of desktop computers, print and screen media regularly present these types of graphics to catch the viewer's attention and help explain a story. Miscellaneous formats include courtroom drawings, television schedules, calendars, icons, logos, flowcharts, time lines, and illustrations.

Courtroom Drawings Sensational courtroom trials generate communitywide and even nationwide interest. Most readers and viewers want to know what the participants in a trial look like and how they acted. Unfortunately, many courts still do not allow still or moving pictures of the proceedings. A sketch artist is a highly specialized individual, usually hired on a **freelance** basis by a media organization, to produce courtroom drawings during a trial. A good artist reveals not only what the principals look like, but also how they feel about being called to testify. To protect the identity of those involved, some judges do not allow sketch artists to reveal identifying facial features. The media must respect the privacy of

the people involved when the court orders them to do so or they may be held in contempt of court.

Television Schedules A common infographic element is the television schedule. The wide-scale use of cable and satellite broadcasting since the 1980s made the task of designing the TV program table much more complicated than when there were only three major networks. A large community may have several competing cable companies that offer different services and as many as fifty separate channels. Color coding and alignment aid in the readability of these complex tables.

Calendars Business meetings and other kinds of events often are shown in a calendar format because it is a graphic design that everyone understands. An artist or draftsperson will draw the background template or shell for the calendar and reuse it each month. New information is written in the days of the calendar.

Icons and Logos In the past thirty years, executives have realized the importance of visual symbols that identify their companies and products. Such symbols, or logos, are important visible links to consumers. Graphic designers such as Saul Bass and Paul Rand have created eye-catching icons and logos for some of the most important businesses in the world (Figures 10.24 and 10.25). Print and screen media infographic artists have extended those ideas to simple line drawings that attract attention to a story, briefly summarize its content, and help anchor a reader or viewer to the page or frame.

Flowcharts   Depending on the type of story, an infographic artist may also be called upon to produce a flowchart that shows a corporation's organizational structure, a series of mechanical or chemical processes, or steps in a decision-making process. Most flowcharts use a specialized symbol system that must be explained to the novice reader in order for the labels and the connections between them to have meaning.

Time Lines   Some stories that detail events over a long period of time benefit from a more graphic representation than a chronological fact box. A time line shows significant events along a horizontal or vertical line on which important dates are indicated. Some of the most effective use of time lines involves a combination of two or more such lines, making relationships between them visually obvious.

Illustrations   Illustrations are the least factual form of graphics. They instantly attract readers' attention and make them want to read the accompanying story (Figure 10.26). Illustrations usually exhibit traditional artistic techniques. Illustrators favor pen, ink, brushes, and paints over computers because they more easily can create pieces that have a unique style. However, recent developments in hardware and software make determination of whether an illustration was created with traditional or innovative tools much more difficult. Pressure-sensitive styluses used with large tablets can now simulate any type of pen, brush, or spray device.

Infographics evolved from simple maps and line charts to complex combinations of visual and textual elements. Many newspapers and magazines seldom use just one type of infographic to tell a story anymore. For a complex story, diagrams and icons might be combined with fact boxes, line and pie charts, and tables. Television producers still hesitate to use many infographics because viewers need time to absorb a complex array of information. World Wide Web services, however, allow viewers the option of repeating frames for better understanding.

Ethical Perspective

Through accident, ignorance, or intent, visual representations of empirical data can easily mislead unsuspecting and trusting readers and viewers. Writers in the field cite two main reasons why errors and visual distortions occur frequently:

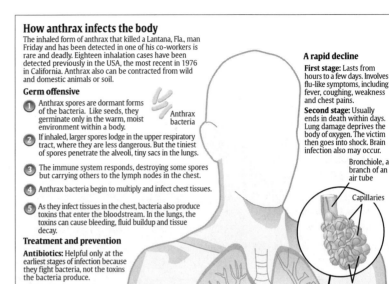

How anthrax infects the body
The inhaled form of anthrax that killed a Lantana, Fla., man Friday and has been detected in one of his co-workers is rare and deadly. Eighteen inhalation cases have been detected previously in the USA, the most recent in 1976 in California. Anthrax also can be contracted from wild and domestic animals or soil.

Germ offensive
1 Anthrax spores are dormant forms of the bacteria. Like seeds, they germinate only in the warm, moist environment within a body.
2 If inhaled, larger spores lodge in the upper respiratory tract, where they are less dangerous. But the tiniest of spores penetrate the alveoli, tiny sacs in the lungs.
3 The immune system responds, destroying some spores but carrying others to the lymph nodes in the chest.
4 Anthrax bacteria begin to multiply and infect chest tissues.
5 As they infect tissues in the chest, bacteria also produce toxins that enter the bloodstream. In the lungs, the toxins can cause bleeding, fluid buildup and tissue decay.

Treatment and prevention
Antibiotics: Helpful only at the earliest stages of infection because they fight bacteria, not the toxins the bacteria produce.
Vaccination: An anthrax vaccine was licensed in 1970 and is reserved for military use. Supplies are limited because of delays getting Food and Drug Administration approval for a new production facility in Lansing, Mich. The military plans to immunize more than 2 million servicemembers. So far, it has been given to about a half-million. Person-to-person spread of anthrax is extremely unlikely.

Anthrax bacteria

A rapid decline
First stage: Lasts from hours to a few days. Involves flu-like symptoms, including fever, coughing, weakness and chest pains.
Second stage: Usually ends in death within days. Lung damage deprives the body of oxygen. The victim then goes into shock. Brain infection also may occur.

Bronchiole, a branch of an air tube

Capillaries

Magnified alveoli

Sources: Centers for Disease Control and Prevention; Monica Schoch-Spana, Johns Hopkins University; Jeff Bender, University of Minnesota; AP

By Adrienne Lewis and Suzy Parker, USA TODAY

Courtesy of *USA Today*; used by permission

Figure 10.23

Diagrams are useful because they can explain complicated information that would be difficult or impossible to describe in any other way. This USA Today *diagram explains how anthrax infects a human body and also includes treatment and prevention information. The infographic was published during heightened security worries after the aerial attacks on September 11.*

Figure 10.24

Icons and logos communicate vital messages visually, as demonstrated by these examples. A well-designed logo not only presents a clear message but can also provide a memory link to the company, service, or function. Top left: Sports pictographs by Time *magazine graphics director Nigel Holmes. Top right: The familiar disabled parking icon, overlooking Hoover Dam.*

Figure 10.25

See color section following page 276.

Modified after Nigel Holmes, *Designing Pictorial Symbols*, Watson-Guptill Publication, 1985

Paul Martin Lester

Figure 10.26

As during the nineteenth century when hand-drawn illustrations were the norm for newspapers, artistically rendered drawings often illustrate an editorial or column that would be difficult for a photographer to capture or set up.

1. Few infographic producers have much experience with statistical information.

2. Many infographic producers believe that if the sole purpose of infographics is to grab the reader's attention, presentation errors and decorative flourishes can be overlooked.

It is the rare staff member of a newspaper, magazine, or TV station who has taken a statistics class. Moreover, infographics production usually isn't offered as a separate university course. Consequently, few individuals are knowledgeable enough about words, numbers, pictures, and computer operations to know when an infographic is inaccurate or misleading.

Edward Tufte is one of the more vocal critics who favors more education for infographic producers. He has been a consultant for the visual display of empirical data for such corporations as CBS, NBC, *Newsweek,* the *New York Times,* the Census Bureau, and IBM. His self-published books *The Visual Display of Quantitative Information* and *Envisioning Information* were instant classics because of the combination of useful information and pleasing graphic design presentation. Tufte travels around the world giving workshops in how best to link graphic design and statistical information. For Tufte, a high-quality infographic should do the following:

Geo Sipp/Creative Freelancers

1. have an important message to communicate

2. convey information in a clear, precise, and efficient manner

3. never insult the intelligence of readers or viewers

4. always tell the truth

Tufte argues for a conservative approach in which the presentation is never more important than the story. "Ideally," he admits, "the design should disappear in favor of the information." Tufte calls infographics loaded with gratuitous decorations or window dressing "chartjunk." Such graphic devices serve merely to entertain rather than educate readers, he maintains.

At the very least, charts should accurately reflect the numbers that they portray. For example, dollar amounts over many years should be adjusted for inflation, and monetary values of different currencies should be translated into one currency value. Because images generally have a greater emotional impact than words, the potential to mislead with visual messages is higher. Inappropriate symbols used to illustrate an infographic can be confusing. A serious subject, for example, demands serious visual representation and not cartoon characters. Such graphic devices may attract attention, but the risk is that the audience will be offended.

Inaccurate charts can be produced inadvertently when the *y*-axis does not have a zero base. Lines in a chart have more dramatic upward and downward swings when the *y*-axis isn't zero based. But because of space limitations, using a zero base for certain graphs—of stock market data, for example—might take up too much space. Often a designer will insert a line break near the bottom of a chart to indicate that numbers have been removed. However, the lines in the chart still should be produced on a scale that begins at zero and not on some

higher number above the break. In the former, the line will be a visually accurate representation of the data. In the latter, the data are condensed and the line is a distortion (Figure 10.27).

Although computers have greatly aided the production of infographics, the technology also makes easy the inclusion of decora-

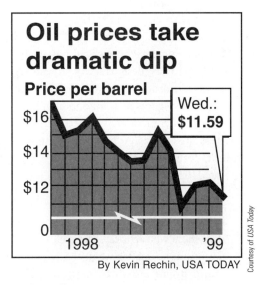

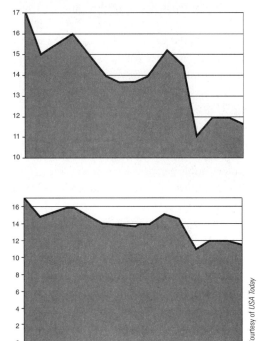

By Kevin Rechin, USA TODAY

Courtesy of USA Today

Figure 10.27

A serious problem with charts can be the misleading visual representation of data. Although omitting part of a scale to save space is acceptable (as indicated by the zigzag line at the bottom of many charts), constructing a chart from a y-axis point other than zero can drastically change the visual message and is not acceptable. As printed in a newspaper and reproduced using the Excel program (center), the price of oil appears dramatic with the zero point set at 10. But with the zero point set at zero, the infographic is more accurate and less visually alarming.

tive devices that distract the reader from the chart's message. Three-dimensional drop shadows, colored backgrounds, icons, and other illustrations may catch the reader's eye but not engage the brain. Tufte notes the trend in television and computer presentations in which the numbers get lost in animated, colorful effects. Weather maps for television or newspapers sometimes are so crowded with cute illustrations that their informational content is lost.

Infographic designers should avoid the temptation to base designs solely on aesthetic or entertainment criteria, a hedonistic approach. Designers miss an opportunity to educate a reader or viewer whenever they rely on decorative tricks. At best, such gimmicks distract from the message and at worst give wrong information. Tufte said it best:

> Consumers of graphics are often more intelligent about the information at hand than those who fabricate the data decoration. And, no matter what, the operating moral premise of information design should be that our readers are alert and caring; they may be busy, eager to get on with it, but they are not stupid. Disrespect for the audience will leak through, damaging communication.

Cultural Perspective

The key to understanding infographics from the cultural perspective is to know the cultural context of sign use and interpretation (Chapter 5).

Austrian statistician Otto Neurath wrote in 1925 that "words divide, pictures unite." As they become more visually literate, people from different cultures may be united in their common understanding of the information conveyed by the pictures contained in informational graphics. Infographic designers need to be concerned that mass audiences can understand their work. Carefully choosing the symbolism for communicating a message is vital in infographic production.

Critical Perspective

Computer technology makes using words and numbers with pictures to produce sophisticated visual messages in the form of informational graphics easier than ever. Computer hardware and software can make up for a lack of artistic talent. Unfortunately, much of the power of the computer is given to the creation of entertaining, decorative illustrations on subjects of little social importance. The computer can be used to make associations and inferences about seemingly incomprehensible data only if an operator has the skill to work comfortably with numbers.

The best infographic designs "draw the viewer into the wonder of the data" and represent the true merging of word and image. The convergence of verbal and graphic reasoning should be a prime concern of educators, students, professionals, and consumers. Mark Monmonier in his book *Maps with the News* makes the point that most individuals view infographics as "a means of analysis, not of communication." A simple locator map, argues Monmonier, is equivalent to third-grade prose. And yet, a graphic is praised as if it were a thing of wonder simply because it can be produced quickly. If words and pictures are united in form and function, the typical locator map suddenly becomes ridiculously rudimentary. Locator maps that show meaningful physical relationships, reveal an event's sequences, and explain complicated patterns within a specific area are intriguing and challenging. Infographics run the risk of becoming an entertainment medium when only entertainers use computers.

■ *FUTURE DIRECTIONS FOR INFORMATIONAL GRAPHICS*

Although infographics will have even greater importance in storytelling in the future, producers of entertainment and education messages understand that images alone do not convey enough information to be fully comprehensible. Words always will be a vital part of communication. When all media—newspapers, magazines, books, movies, television, and computers—become combined through the World Wide Web, viewers will be able to learn as much as they want about each infographic element. Infographic designers will need to know how to work with sound, music, and time sequences with animated graphic presentations (Figure 10.28). Designers need to be prepared to supply the words and pictures that will be needed when readers and viewers are transformed into users.

Figure 10.28

See color section following page 276.

DISCUSSION AND EXERCISE IDEAS

- Try to write a business story containing all the information within a typical stock market report without using an infographic. Comment on the tediousness of this procedure.

- Clip out or videotape an example of an infographic that serves to educate readers about the complexity of a story; find an example in which readers are more confused because of the use of the infographic.

- Find a chart within a newspaper, magazine, or Web site and using a spreadsheet program such as Excel, duplicate it and check to see if it is zero based. If it is not, note and comment on the difference in visual perception of the information between the two charts.

- Lead a discussion as to the future of informational graphics.

INFOTRAC COLLEGE EDITION ASSIGNMENTS

- With "Subject guide" checked, type "News Graphics" in the search area. Click "View" for the "Periodical references" under "Reuters News Graphics Service." Read the article about the news service's informational graphics division. How much research skill do you think it takes to help create an infographic? What do you think is necessary for an informational graphic to be effective in communicating details of a complex story?

- With "Subject guide" checked, type "Edward Tufte" in the search area. Click the first "View" for the "Periodical references." Scroll down and read the article "Why today's graphics fail" and then read the interview of Tufte at the top of the list originally printed in *The Lancet*. What do you think are Edward Tufte's greatest contributions to the field of informational graphics and communications generally? How do you think his personal life influences his professional life?

Go to the Web site for this book at www.wadsworth.com/product/0534562442 to find more Web links on this subject.

CARTOONS

By the end of this chapter you should know:

- The cultural significance and foundation for the popularity of "The Simpsons."
- That cartoons are much more than simply animated motion pictures.
- The historical roots and significant achievements of various types of cartoons.
- The various techniques used to produce and explain cartoons.
- The various ethical concerns associated with cartoon production, presentation, and marketing.
- The reason why cartoons are a complicated visual art form.

Matt Groening (rhymes with "raining") created an unforgettable family for his popular cartoon program on the Fox television network, "The Simpsons" (Figure 11.1). Groening's Homer is a beer-and-bacon-loving family man. As a haphazard safety inspector for a nuclear power plant, he has working-class roots linked to such television characters as Fred Flintstone, who was a brontosaurus operator for the local quarry in the cartoon hit "The Flintstones"; Ralph Kramden, the bus driver in "The Honeymooners"; Archie Bunker in "All in the Family"; Dan Conner in "Roseanne"; and Al Bundy in "Married with Children." Homer's wife, Marge, is a hardworking but dull homemaker—with a blue-colored beehive hairdo. The three children in the Simpson household are Bart, Lisa, and baby Maggie. Ten-year-old Bart (an anagram for Brat) is easily one of the most popular troublemakers on television. Lisa, the troubled, saxophone-playing, intellectual younger sister, is a favorite of all viewers who are sure that, when born, they were switched with another infant in the hospital. Maggie's main personality trait is that the only sound she ever made, other than from constantly sucking on a pacifier, was "Daddy" (with Elizabeth Taylor supplying her voice), around which an entire episode once revolved. The Simpsons live their ordinary lives in the middle American town of Springfield. Not coincidentally, it is the name of the same city where Jim Anderson and his family lived in the television classic "Father Knows Best," with grown-up equivalents of Bart, Lisa, and Maggie. No one would ever say that Homer knows best, however.

In only two months after the first episode "Simpsons Roasting on an Open Fire" was introduced on December 17, 1989, its Nielsen rating placed it among the top fifteen programs in the country—a remarkable feat considering that the independent Fox network reached only 80 percent of the homes with television in the United States at that time. Young viewers who idolize the mischievous antics of their hero Bart and adults who enjoy the **social satire** disguised as brightly colored cartoons love the Simpsons.

"The Simpsons" is a result of three powerful television forces: producer-director James Brooks, writer Sam Simon, and creator Matt Groening. Brooks, three-time Oscar winner for his movie *Terms of Endearment* and nine-time Emmy winner for television hits such as "The Mary Tyler Moore Show" and "Taxi," asked Groening to produce twenty-second animated cartoons for showing between segments of the short-lived Fox comedy series "The Tracey Ullman Show" in 1987. Simon is a respected and creative situation comedy writer who now acts as the show's executive producer. But Groening gives the show its irreverent energy and goofy, if somewhat bent, emotional appeal.

Matt Groening is the son of retired filmmaker and cartoonist Homer Groening (one of the cartoonist's sons also is named Homer). His family resembles his cartoon creation in name only—his mother is named Margaret, and his sisters are Lisa and Maggie. "When I was a kid," Groening says, "my friends and I used to put on puppet shows, make comic books, and I decided that's what I wanted to do." Groening did well in school, although he was frequently sent to the principal's office for uttering wisecracks in class. After briefly attending a local college, Groening moved to Los Angeles to become a writer. One of his first jobs was a low-paying position for a photocopying shop. His southern California experiences, however, gave him a lode of rich material for his first cartoon, "Life in Hell." The satirical comic features the characters Bongo, Akbar, and Jeff. When asked if the latter two characters are lovers or brothers, he answers, "Whatever offends you the most." "Life in Hell" was originally published in the Los Angeles new wave graphics innovator, *WET* magazine. In 1980, the cartoon was sold to the more establishment newspaper, the *Los Angeles Reader*. When his

AP/Wide World Photos

Figure 11.1

Almost all of the characters for "The Simpsons" are displayed on the Web site www.thesimpsons.com. How many of them do you know by their first names?

girlfriend (now wife) Deborah Caplan published a collection of the cartoons in a book in 1984, the cartoon's popularity soared. Groening still draws one "Life in Hell" cartoon a week for many publications.

When Brooks, a fan of Akbar and Jeff, asked Groening to create the animated segments for his Gracie Films company, he had initially thought of using the "Life in Hell" cast. But Groening wisely decided to resurrect the Simpson family, which he had created originally while in high school. He admits that the show is a perverse takeoff of a popular television family when he was a child, the Cleavers of "Leave It to Beaver." "Bart," he confides, "is like what would happen if Eddie Haskell [the "bad boy" influence in the early sitcom] got his own show."

"The Simpsons" first aired in December 1989 as a separate series and won an Emmy Award for that first year. After every episode, conversations in schoolyards, college dormitories, and around coffee tables and water coolers across the country centered on the comical troubles of the Simpson family and the show's large collection of supporting characters.

One of the reasons for the show's success is that it regularly spoofs celebrities such as Johnny Carson, Hugh Hefner, Bette Midler, and others, who supply their own voices for their cartoon equivalents. When the youngest daughter Maggie starts talking, Whoopi Goldberg wants to supply her voice. "The Simpsons" even makes fun of the cartoon medium—the characters often watch an extremely violent cartoon parody that features the adventures of "Itchy and Scratchy" on their cartoon television set. The show is an international success, with German and French versions. Beginning in 1994, syndication of reruns meant an even wider appeal for the program.

Although originally involved in all aspects of the production process, Groening

is now pursuing the international marketing of Simpson products and other television and movie ideas. A season usually has between twenty-one and twenty-five episodes. Each show takes about six months to produce with various people working on several shows at once (incidentally, one of the producers, Conan O'Brien, replaced David Letterman as the host of NBC's "Late Night" show). After a script is written (which involves nine or more writers), actors make a sound track of the characters' voices. About 80 artists at a Los Angeles animation company draw 2,000 individual drawings, which are sent to Brooks, Simon, and Groening for review. After editing, all the material is sent to a South Korean production company where about 100 workers complete the thousands of drawings necessary for a show.

Groening expected criticism of merchandising the characters and of the antisocial content of the program. He believes that one of the reasons for the negative reaction by some critics is "because animation was always seen as a medium for kiddies." Although somewhat uncomfortable about merchandising the program because of his decidedly counterculture roots, Groening admits "I feel like it's a tidal wave I'm surfing on. And to be honest, the whole Simpsons project was a project to see how far I could go in the mainstream. I may be going to hell, but I did embrace all the stuff—the T-shirts, the Bart phone, the chess set, all of it."

An indication of the scope of the cultural influence of the television show starting its thirteenth season in the fall of 2001, the Oxford English Dictionary added Homer's catch phrase "D'oh," which is defined as "expressing frustration at the realization that things have turned out badly or not as planned, or that one has just said or done something foolish." In addition, Fox Home Entertainment released a three-disc DVD boxed set of the first season of "The Simpsons." The discs include commentary by Matt Groening, James L. Brooks, and others, outtakes from an unaired version of an episode, a gallery of early sketches, original scripts with notes by Groening, and the first "Tracey Ullman Show" short.

Not content with the critical and marketing success of "The Simpsons," Groening also produced the popular animated series, "Futurama." With a Manhattan setting in the year 3000 populated by one-eyed space aliens, a gourmet chef robot, and a confused pizza delivery boy somehow transported to the future, the show, just like "The Simpsons," sports plenty of opportunities for social satire and merchandising.

■ ANALYSIS OF "THE SIMPSONS"

Reaction to the barely functional cartoon family is as varied as the life experiences and attitudes of the viewers who watch it. If you are a fan of animated films, the cartoon may be appealing because it reminds you of your childhood. If you grew up in a similar home, you may laugh about like situations involving your family. If you enjoy watching the symbols of popular culture being gently nudged off their pedestals, you will appreciate the humor of the program. But if you think cartoon characters should be reserved for children and their concerns, you probably will be offended at the many adult themes and jokes expressed during the half-hour. If your opinion is that television should always show ideal families, as in the live television shows in the 1950s and 1960s, you will not favor a household in which one of the father's primary concerns is to make sure that he has enough beer to drink with his pork chops.

As one of the most recent examples of the cartoon art form, "The Simpsons" has roots in every type of comic presentation, both single- and multiframed. When the drawings match the faces of media personalities frequently featured in story lines, the history of the caricature is evoked. Former "Tonight Show" host Johnny Carson was a Simpsons character, and the cartoon character expertly mimicked his nervous mannerisms. The rich tradition of the editorial cartoon is featured in situations that comment on political issues. For example, Homer's careless attitude when it comes to working with highly toxic nuclear waste reflects Groening's view about the dangers of the nuclear power industry. Viewers can easily identify the influence of humorous cartoons that ridicule social hypocrisies in the comical situations, dialogue, and graphic style of "The Simpsons." Comic strips that make viewers laugh, think, and feel are popular among both children and adults. The yellow hair of Bart Simpson reminds us of one of the earliest wisecracking cartoon characters published, Richard Outcault's "Yellow Kid."

Finally, comic books and motion pictures are merged into a single medium in which viewers relate to the family members as if they were live actors. But unlike many animated films, the action that occurs is almost always physically possible in the real world. Except for special Halloween episode, no character in "The Simpsons" can fly or dematerialize into another being, and there is little violence on the program. As a result, the number one rated show in the Fox lineup parts company with many Saturday morning cartoon characters.

"The Simpsons" is drawn in a decidedly elementary graphic style. As Groening says, "I've been drawing this way since fifth grade—people with big eyes and overbites." His "Life in Hell" cartoon also is marked by a minimalist style. "The Simpsons" is composed of such simply rendered images for three important reasons: time, money, and intent. Detailed, realistic drawings require an enormous additional output from animators and cost far more. Spending less time on the visual message allows the producers to concentrate more on the writing and acting. Besides, if complete realism were desired, Groening would have advocated a live-action version of the family. But an animated sitcom, the first such successful prime-time program since "The Flintstones," has a built-in "curiosity factor": new viewers will tune in just to see what all the fuss is about from the critics. Besides corresponding to Groening's drawing style since his earliest school days, the characters look ordinary (some might say unattractive) on purpose. The cartoon is deliberately in opposition to the 1950s and 1960s family-oriented situation comedies on television in which, in the words of radio personality Garrison Keillor, "all the women are smart, the men are good looking and the children are above average." In both look and deed, "The Simpsons" celebrates all who are plain and average.

There is nothing ethically wrong with a television program that features police officials as doughnut-eating goofs, teachers and principals as easy targets for a mean-spirited boy, and parents as insensitive egoists. After all, such character types occasionally exist in the real world. Plots that involve the overt manipulations of people by an evil nuclear power plant owner or Marge's nearly consummated love affair with her bowling instructor may reflect unethical behavior in society, but including such story lines in a television show is not unethical. In fact, the height of unethical behavior and cynicism may be that of television producers, worried about bad ratings and losing advertising support, who ignore social problems by excluding them from adult-oriented programs. Critical reactions from viewers would drive "The Simpsons" off the air if it were a

Saturday morning cartoon. But when run in prime time, the dialogue and plots are entirely appropriate.

However, ethicists are justified in finding fault with two aspects of the program. One criticism involves the way the shows are produced; the other is the way the program is marketed. A South Korean animation company completes the thousands of cels necessary for each program. The only reason for this long-distance arrangement is that Asian workers are paid much less than U.S. animators. Even though the South Korean workers are given specialized skills and money that they might not have any other way, the cost of the exploitation is too high. Those in a position to hire others have the moral responsibility of paying a fair and living wage to workers for their efforts. Hedonistic or utilitarian arguments used to support such hiring practices promote racist stereotypes of Asian workers as worthy only of working in highly pressured animation sweatshops.

The other criticism with the series is its blatant self-promotion. At one point, Simpson family T-shirts were being purchased at a rate of 1 million per week. Presently, more than seventy different products are licensed for sale. The Kellogg Company recently introduced a doughnut-flavored cereal with Homer and the rest of the family on the box. Bart is featured in video games created by Nintendo such as "Bartman Meets Radioactive Man," "Bart vs. the Space Mutants," and "Bart vs. the World."

If only a small portion of the profits from merchandise sales were used to hire U.S. animators, more jobs could be created in the country where the show is produced, or at least Asian workers could be paid equitably for their talents.

As a blue-collar, middle-class family, the Simpsons follow in the comedic footsteps of Jackie Gleason in "The Honeymooners."

Upper-class, white-collar baby boomers and their children constitute the primary audience for the program because they enjoy laughing at these cartoon oafs. Although many real-life working-class families do not appreciate most of the cynical jokes that are directed at them, they still watch the show. University of California sociology professor Mike Moore believes that "unlike other [cultural] groups, [blue-collar families are] not on an upward path." Consequently, shows like "The Simpsons" exploit "the working class's inferiority complex. A lot of these people feel that they don't have what it takes to be a perfect family—to get it right or do it right. 'The Simpsons' buys into that pattern."

Besides cultures based on economic and work-related factors, ethnic differences between cartoon characters, as in real life, sometimes are featured. But for the program, multicultural sensitivity is just another punch line. Once again the society's dominant culture has its way with those who diverge from the mainstream. An East Indian manager of a convenience store perpetuates an offensive stereotype, and an African-American doctor (included perhaps only as a cynical nod to the show's early competition—the Bill Cosby character of Dr. Huxtable), are about the only nonwhite characters in the fictionalized midwestern town of Springfield.

The show teaches that rich people are greedy, politicians are corrupt, police officials are stupid, teachers and parents are easily manipulated, and children are devious. At the same time, Homer's love for bowling, beer, and bacon, Marge's simpleminded support of her sexist husband and ungrateful children, Bart's smart-aleck retorts, Lisa's angst and alienation, and Maggie's . . . (no, Maggie is OK) are symbols that transcend this one family. Yet despite their many personality disorders, the Simpson family members manage to support one another and stay together.

"The Simpsons" is an amusing, fun, colorful, and lively half-hour of television that often features stories and characters that entertain as well as educate countless viewers of almost every age and background. University of Wyoming communications professor Ken Smith writes that viewers easily recognize the offensive behaviors exhibited by the characters and know that such activity is unacceptable in the real world. Part of the amusement of the show also comes from identifying all the mass media references and popular culture hypocrisies that the sitcom satirizes. Thus the cartoon is a complicated collection of visual and verbal symbols that are used to tell the story of this Springfield family.

■ CARTOONS AND THE SIX PERSPECTIVES

Personal Perspective

For most of the history of cartoons, researchers have considered them unworthy of serious attention. Few academic programs or private art schools offer courses in the production or theory of cartoon art. Comic strips, comic books, and animated movies are considered by many to be junk for children and unworthy of serious attention. But with the rise in the use of visual messages in all media, this pictorial art form has gained new converts, with serious studies begun by social and artistic scholars. Although often misleadingly simple in their artistic execution, cartoons reveal complex attitudes of certain people at a particular time through the use of complex visual and verbal symbolism. Stories in books, magazines, and newspapers may concentrate on opinions of the elite in a culture, but cartoons are the best indicators of the concerns of average citizens. As John Geipel in his book *The Cartoon* has stated, cartoons "are a potent weapon of ridicule, ideal for deflating the pompous and the overbearing, exposing injustice and deriding hypocrisy." Cartoons tell as much about the audience as they do about the artist.

Historical Perspective

It is perhaps hard to believe, but the elaborately animated characters in motion picture, television, and computer programs all started as crudely rendered line drawings.

Consequently, it is important to know how cartoons developed in order to fully analyze present efforts.

Single-Framed Cartoons

The historical roots of cartoons can be found in simple, unsigned visual messages that poked fun at others. Scrawled on walls by untrained artists (today we call such examples graffiti), these single-framed cartoons reveal an average person's opinion about someone in power that is missing from many mainstream historical documents. There are three types of single-framed cartoons: caricatures, editorial cartoons, and humorous cartoons.

Caricatures   As an artistic and communicative medium, the cartoon began as a caricature. Cave drawings from 20,000 years ago featured not only detailed paintings of animals but also highly stylized likenesses of people. Because these cave dwellers could paint animals accurately, anthropologists believe that they distorted profile portraits because they believed that an accurate picture might bring harm from supernatural forces. The oldest known caricatures clearly intended to ridicule the individuals portrayed were drawn in Egypt. In about 1360 b.c.e., some unknown cartoonist painted an unflattering portrait of Ikh-naton, the unpopular father-in-law of King Tutankhamen. Artists satirized the actions of other unpopular Egyptian leaders by drawing animals performing similar activities. Even Cleopatra is portrayed in a caricature in which she is seen drinking too much wine.

Throughout the world, visual ridicule was appreciated. In India, cartoonists made fun of their Hindu god, Krishna. Greek terra-cotta vases and wall paintings often were decorated with profane parodies of overweight Olympian gods. Greek actors used caricature for more positive reasons. Actors wore highly stylized and distorted tragic and comic masks to make a character's personality clear to the audience. Much later, an anonymous Roman soldier in C.E. 79 scratched an unflattering portrait of a strict commander on the wall of his barracks that was preserved for centuries when the eruption of Mount Vesuvius buried Pompeii. Examples of sexually explicit publicly displayed graffiti on houses of upper-class residents of Pompeii were so shocking when uncovered that an early excavator "covered them with sheets so that his working men might not be debauched by them." Starting in 2002, however, restored erotic art displayed at an ancient spa is now open for public viewing at the site.

Early Romans also ridiculed religious leaders. For example, the Christian Alexamenos is shown in a drawing standing at the crucifixion of Jesus, who has the head of an ass (Figure 11.2). Most Roman caricatures were aimed at socially despised members of the society. Frescoes in private homes and on public walls showed beggars, thieves, slaves, the handicapped, pygmies, and even drunken old women in unflattering poses for comic purposes. Respected members of society—Caesars, generals, and senators—rarely were satirized visually.

During the Middle Ages, grotesque Gothic imagery in the form of macabre wall gargoyles was popular as outside decorations on buildings. Priests considered many of the carvings obscene and obliterated them. In the margins of illustrated religious books, monks sometimes made sacrilegious drawings that were never erased. One of the most famous drawings by Leonardo da Vinci is a study of unflattering portraits made in 1485, which probably were figments of his imagination rather than based on actual observations. He also made the best defense of the combination of pictures and words to describe the traits of a person when he wrote, "And you who wish to represent by words the form of man and all the aspects of his membrification, relinquish that idea. For the more minutely you describe the more you will confine the mind of the reader, and the more you will keep him from the knowledge of the thing described. And so it is necessary to draw and to describe" (Figure 11.3).

Annibale Carracci, his brother Agostino, and his cousin Ludovico—all from Bologna, Italy—reportedly invented modern caricature in about 1590. The term comes from their family name and the Italian verb *caricare*, "to load." The Carraccis "loaded" their naturalistic paintings with exaggerated yet recognizable human faces from their community to entertain their friends.

With the invention and widespread use of the printing press, religious icons carved in wood and stone and crafted as stained glass windows could be converted to drawings and printed by the hundreds as handbills and passed around. For the first time, people could take the time to study these illustrations without feeling inhibited as when standing before the artwork within a church.

Figure 11.2

Dating from about the third century, this anti-Christian graffiti found in a military barracks reads, "Alexamenos worships his god." Note that, as with children's drawings, there is little attempt to create the perception of depth.

Modified after Camden Cobern, *The New Archeological Discoveries*, Funk & Wagnalls Company, 1929

When people spent more time viewing illustrations and cartoons, criticism in the form of caricatures of religious and political leaders soon followed.

Political caricature came of age in the 1600s during the controversial reigns of Louis XIV in France, Queen Anne in England, and the Prince of Orange in the Netherlands. For the first time, artists drew caricatures with obvious political intent, not

Giraudon/Art Resource, NY

Figure 11.3

The notebooks of Leonardo da Vinci contain examples of caricatures of ordinary and famous people of his day. Some of the drawings are quickly composed sketches; others are more carefully rendered.

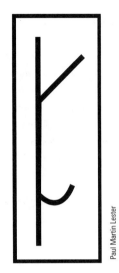

Paul Martin Lester

Figure 11.4
William Hogarth once bragged that, by using only three pen strokes, he could draw a soldier walking into a pub with his rifle and dog.

simply to amuse rich patrons or friends. Surprisingly, almost no political caricatures were drawn during this time in Germany. In Japan, caricature art was for amusement rather than for political purposes. In England caricatures (called *anti-portraits*) were used to make satirical comments about current events and public figures.

The art of the caricature eventually became fused with cartoon representations of public figures as a part of editorial cartoons. However, a single-framed caricature is an important illustrative device. Recent caricature artists include David Levine, Dorothy Ahle, and Al Hirschfeld. Hirschfeld started his long career in 1926 drawing caricatures for Broadway theater stars. His distinctive graphic style sometimes appears on the pages of *The New Yorker* magazine and the *New York Times*.

Editorial Cartoons The founder of the English editorial cartoon is considered to be William Hogarth. Fascinated with drawing since his early childhood, he became an apprentice to an engraver and later started his own print shop at the age of twenty-three. Hogarth established a solid reputation for creating illustrations for coats of arms, crests, bookplates, and advertisements (Figure 11.4). He created ads for companies that were printed on handbills, posters, and handheld fans. Hogarth also, as did other London print shops during the early 1700s, displayed ready-made artwork (called *clip art* today) from which patrons could select drawings to make their party announcements more visually appealing. After Hogarth became enthralled by a set of political cartoons smuggled from France, he started to create his own satirical drawings. In 1731, he published his most famous collection of drawings, *A Harlot's Progress*. Because he was appalled by the living conditions of the poor of his day, he intended his drawings to be

moralistic lessons rather than entertainment. His artistic style and social message brought him immediate success, but he soon became controversial because he didn't respect anyone's rank. Unfortunately, the political and business leaders he ridiculed didn't appreciate the attention. Their influence caused others to question Hogarth's reputation, and his artwork was parodied constantly. Even his name was embarrassingly punned as "Hog-arse." He died in 1764, a financially ruined and broken man. Nevertheless, his consistent style combined with political intent inspired generations of cartoonists.

The last letter Hogarth received while on his deathbed was from Benjamin Franklin, the founder of American political cartooning. Franklin, the seventeenth child of a Boston candle maker, ran away from his crowded home at the age of twelve and eventually started his own print shop in Philadelphia. Franklin's most famous cartoon is a rallying cry for unity. It depicts a divided snake representing the American colonies with the label "JOIN, or DIE." Published on May 9, 1754, in the *Pennsylvania Gazette,* it was the first political cartoon printed in America. Paul Revere, known for his metalwork and revolutionary horse riding, also was a cartoonist. His best-known work is an artistic rendering of the Boston Massacre of 1770 in which British soldiers killed unarmed colonists (Figure 11.5). However, American caricatures and cartoons during this period were poor in quality compared to their English counterparts. Apparently, the early American political leaders were too sacred to ridicule.

In England, at the end of the eighteenth century, one of the first major figures to follow in Hogarth's tradition was James Gillray. He was the leading cartoonist during the reign of King George III, whom he labeled "Farmer George." Gillray bitterly opposed the king's intervention in the affairs of the American colonies. Gillray also was famous for his satirical portraits of Napoleon, whom Gillray and other cartoonists called "Little Boney." The French general reportedly understood the power of the caricature for propaganda purposes and encouraged French artists to support his political policies. Napoleon enjoyed caricatures except those of himself. Gillray was such a famous cartoonist that, in anticipation of his drawings, crowds gathered in front of his publisher's window where his cartoons were displayed. At the top of his form, however, Gillray went insane. In 1811 he tried to kill himself by jumping from a barred window, but his head became caught. Two years later, he died. But his strong graphic style combined with a powerful political message influenced many subsequent cartoonists.

With lithographic printing firmly established by the early 1800s (Chapter 9), cartoons began to appear more often in magazines and newspapers and less often on handbills or posters. For example, caricatures of President Jackson in newspapers during his two terms (1828–1836) were the first printed in America. In the 1830s Joseph Keppler established *Puck*, a humor magazine, first in Germany and later in England. His popular feature called "Puckographs" presented caricatures of famous citizens. In 1841, journalist Henry Mayhew and engraver Ebenezer Landells began another humor magazine, *Punch*—a respected humor magazine that was published for well over 100 years. *Vanity Fair* was started in 1859 in the United States and contained numerous illustrations.

Lithography promoted the work of Honoré Daumier of France because his painterly forms and colors could be accurately reproduced. His bitingly sarcastic political drawings so enraged King Louis Philippe that he had Daumier imprisoned briefly. A onetime

Figure 11.5

Paul Revere not only warned the city of Boston of the coming of the British, he also illustrated stories with cartoons. Here, his simple coffin design and skull-and-crossbones symbolism combine to remind readers of the deaths of four early American patriots.

bookseller and law court messenger, Daumier combined his love for sculpture with drawing to produce works of great three-dimensional depth. His artistic approach to cartooning helped remove the barrier between fine and comic art. During his career he completed more than 4,000 lithographs. One of his most famous shows photographer Gaspard Felix Tournachon, or Nadar, taking the world's first aerial photograph from a hot air balloon. In 1872 Daumier's eyesight started to fail. In six years he was totally blind and desperately needed money. Although the public at that time could not see the value of his work, today his paintings and drawings are valuable collectors' items.

The most famous American editorial cartoonist during this period was Thomas Nast. A native of Landau, Germany, Nast was brought by his mother to America when he was six years old. At the age of fifteen, he was employed as an illustrator for *Frank Leslie's Illustrated Weekly*. In 1862, *Harper's Weekly* hired him as a battlefield artist to cover the Civil War. His drawings improved morale enormously as they were circulated in Union towns, encampments, forts, and ships. General Grant praised Nast as having done "as much as any one man" to preserve the Union. President Lincoln called him "our best recruiting sergeant" because his drawings had great emotional impact.

But Nast is best known for his campaign to bring down the corrupt politician William "Boss" Tweed of Tammany Hall. Tweed and his Democratic cronies stole as much as $200 million from the New York County treasury. Nast drew more than fifty editorial cartoons for *Harper's Weekly* criticizing Tweed. During his fight with Tweed, the magazine's circulation tripled. His cartoons prompted the politician to make the famous statement, "I don't care what they write about me . . . most of the constituents can't read any way—but them damned pictures!" A Tammany banker reportedly offered Nast (who made about $5,000 a year) $100,000 to study art in Europe. After Nast facetiously upped the bribe to half a million dollars, he turned down the offer.

One of his most powerful cartoons appeared in 1872 just before an election. It portrayed a Tammany tiger mauling the symbol of Liberty in the Roman Colosseum, with Tweed as Emperor Nero (Figure 11.6). The cutline read, "What are you going to do about it?" Tweed lost the election but still kept his power. However, an 1876 cartoon led to Tweed's downfall. It showed a good likeness of the politician holding two scruffy children by their collars. It made the point that the Tweed organization was content to catch small-time thieves but let more serious criminals continue their illegal activities. After Tweed fled the country because of a criminal investigation, a police official in Vigo, Spain, recognized him from Nast's cartoon. Tweed was returned to America and put in the Ludlow Street Jail in New York City in 1878.

Nast is responsible for the popular elephant symbol used by the Republican Party (Figure 11.7) and of the popular image of Santa Claus. In 1902, he was appointed U.S. Counsel for Ecuador, a position he was forced to accept after losing all his money in financial speculation. As he predicted before his departure (in a cartoon), he died of yellow fever soon after his arrival.

At the start of the twentieth century, newspaper publishers used cartoons for propaganda purposes, and editors of literary magazines used them as humorous diversions. William Randolph Hearst asked artists

Figure 11.6

As "Emperor" Tweed looks on, the Tammany tiger, a symbol created by cartoonist Thomas Nast to graphically illustrate the corruption in New York, devours Liberty, a symbol of democracy and freedom in the United States.

THE TAMMANY TIGER LOOSE—"What are you going to do about it?"

to draw cartoons of fake Spanish atrocities to whip up support for a war against Spain. In 1904, the humor magazine *Life* employed its most famous cartoonist, Charles Dana Gibson, whose graceful drawings also were used as classy and sophisticated advertisements. In addition, Gibson created popular caricatures of Presidents Woodrow Wilson and Theodore Roosevelt.

During World War I, blatant propaganda for the war effort replaced the earlier creativity of many cartoonists. Typical of this **genre** is James Montgomery Flagg's famous poster for George Creel's governmental agency in which an aggressive Uncle Sam icon points at the viewer and says, "I want you for the U.S. Army. Enlist Now." Influenced by the Dada art movement (Chapter 9), World War II propaganda posters combined cartoons and photomontages. Both totalitarian and democratic governments embraced the medium as a powerful tool of persuasion. Three of the top editorial artists in the United States—Bill Mauldin, Herbert Block, and Paul Conrad—rebelled against the propagandistic use of cartoons.

Sergeant Mauldin drew cartoons for *Stars and Stripes* magazine while a soldier during World War II. His popular characters Willie and Joe boosted morale while letting the readers back home know what the average foot soldier thought. After the war, he worked for the *Chicago Sun-Times*. His most famous cartoon probably is the 1963 drawing of the Lincoln Memorial grieving the death of President Kennedy (Figure 11.8). Mauldin also was known for his devastating attacks against the Ku Klux Klan and other segregationist groups.

Herb Block, professionally known as "Herblock," was the editorial cartoonist for the *Washington Post* and was at his best when taking on the politically powerful. He invented the word *McCarthyism* to describe the Wisconsin senator's Communist witch-

Uncensored Situations, 1966, The Dick Sutphen Studio, Inc.

Figure 11.7
Uncle Sam and the Republican Party elephant walk hand in hand along a boulevard. This nineteenth-century woodcut by an unknown artist symbolically links America and the GOP.

hunt (Figure 11.9). His drawing of the shifty-eyed unshaven Richard Nixon became an unshakable symbol of that political leader from early in his career. Before Nixon's 1968 presidential campaign, a public relations expert advised him to come up with a new image for himself. "I have to erase," he said,

Courtesy of Vis-Com, Inc.

Figure 11.8
After President Kennedy was assassinated, Bill Mauldin drew this famous cartoon of President Lincoln's statue hiding its face in sorrow. At such times words would serve only to diminish a highly emotional visual message.

Figure 11.9

This cartoon is an example of Herbert Block's famous cartoons from the hysterical McCarthy era when many patriotic Americans were accused wrongly of being Communists. Here, Herblock uses symbolism to make his point: The open-mouthed man with "HYSTERIA" written across his pants and a water bucket spilling its contents suggest a rush to douse the flame of Liberty.

"Fire!"

him to tone down his cartoons. In 1969, former mayor Sam Yorty sued the *Times* for $2 million for libel (and lost) because of one of Conrad's cartoons. Ronald Reagan, governor of California before becoming president, complained many times to Chandler that Conrad's cartoons were "ruining his breakfast." In an effort to divert criticism, Chandler moved the cartoon from the editorial to the opinion page, where comments from nonstaffers usually are printed. Conrad's stark visual style and direct messages are an outgrowth of his philosophy about cartoons. He once said, "I figure eight seconds is the absolute maximum time anyone should have" to understand a cartoon's meaning. In 1993 he retired from the paper but still submits cartoons for publication occasionally.

Other contemporary editorial cartoonists of note include Pat Oliphant, Jeff MacNelly, Jack Ohman, and Garry Trudeau. Trudeau's "Doonesbury" comic strip often acts as an editorial cartoon because of the tough political issues he features.

"the Herblock image." Block won three Pulitzer Prizes for his cartoons during his long career. He died in 2001.

Conrad, the angry and insightful liberal voice of the *Los Angeles Times,* graduated from the University of Iowa and worked for the *Denver Post* before starting with the Times in 1964 (Figure 11.10). Conservative publisher Otis Chandler constantly asked

Humorous Cartoons In 1905, Sigmund Freud published a monograph entitled "Wit and Its Relationship to the Unconscious." In

Figure 11.10

Paul Conrad, retired cartoonist for the Los Angeles Times, *uses both a reductionism drawing style and humor to add impact to his messages. Left: In an obvious link to the Rodney King videotape by George Holliday, Conrad symbolizes the poverty program cutbacks by recent Republican administrations. Right: Conrad comically contrasts the different campaign styles of Bill Clinton, George Bush, and Ross Perot.*

VIDEO TAPE OF THE REAGAN – BUSH – QUAYLE ADMINISTRATIONS

the article he made the distinction between humor that is meant to give harmless pleasure and satirical humor that often uses vulgar or grotesque images. For Freud, individuals safely release aggressive impulses when they are allowed to laugh at unthinkable or socially unacceptable situations. The famous psychologist's work was an important development in the history of humorous cartoons because it encouraged artists to include absurd and disturbing imagery in their work.

Humorous cartoons received another boost with the introduction of *The New Yorker* magazine in 1925. Harold Ross, a high school dropout who learned journalism copyediting while employed by the U.S. government's *Stars and Stripes* magazine, had a gift for hiring excellent personnel. One of his first hires was art director Rea Irvin. Irvin not only created the cartoon character for the first cover—the aristocratic, top-hatted "Eustace Tilley"—but established the style for typography and graphic design that continues to this day. Some of the most famous *New Yorker* cartoonists include Charles Addams, of "The Addams Family" fame, Gahan Wilson, and, more recently, George Booth, Roz Ghast, Edward Koren, and Edward Sorel. The magazine is credited with having almost single-handedly developed the art of the humorous cartoon to its highest intellectual potential. Interestingly, cartoons are not called by that name in the magazine—they are called drawings.

But the issue following the World Trade Center twin tower attacks of September 11 was different. The cover, which always features a cartoon, showed a dark illustration of the twin towers titled "Ground Zero" by Art Spiegelman. This contributed to the serious tone of the stories that reflected the solemn mood of the country. The issue contained only one cartoon—a rare editorial cartoon—drawn by George Booth. It showed a sad woman with hands covering her face deciding not to play her violin.

Early in its history *The New Yorker* regularly carried editorial cartoons. One of the leading political cartoonists during the 1920s and 1930s, Reginald Marsh, was called "the pictorial laureate of the sidewalks of New York." His etchings and oil paintings were known for their accurate rendering of the various emotions expressed on the human faces he observed. An enormously popular contemporary humorous cartoonist, whose art is inspired by the bizarre *New Yorker* cartoons of Addams and Wilson, is Gary Larson. "The Far Side" was a syndicated cartoon that people often cut out of newspapers and taped on the office doors of science professors and engineers because Larson frequently poked fun at research methods.

Whether as a caricature, editorial cartoon, or humorous cartoon, the emotional power of images combined with content that critically examines social or political behavior produces memorable cartoons that reflect accurately the culture from which they are produced.

Multiframed Cartoons

Currently, the differences between comic strips, comic books, and animated films are the medium of presentation, the pace at which the drawings are shown, and the amount of effort required of the viewer. In comic strips and comic books, the images are usually printed on cheap newsprint, and the person who turns the page determines the transition from one picture to the next. They require a moderate amount of effort on the part of the reader. With animated films, images can be shown by film, video, or computer media; the pace can be as quick as thirty images per second; and the presentation of animated movies is controlled by a machine that requires little effort from the viewer. As the lines between print, television, and computer technology dissolve, so too will the differences among the three types of multiframed cartoons.

Comic strips, comic books, and animated films all have similar historical roots. Egyptian scholars found papyrus paintings from about 1300 B.C.E. that showed two wrestlers fighting one another in several sequential frames. Many Greek vases decorated with circular drawings of fighting warriors or gymnasts have been found. Turning the vase gives an illusion of movement. Friezes on Greek temples also contained drawings that depicted sequential movement when viewed horizontally. Japanese continuity paintings, called *emakimonos,* simulated motion. These sequential drawings appear to move when the viewer unrolls the long scroll. Completed in 1067, the Bayeux Tapestry is a huge woven wall decoration that depicts actions by characters within separate frames or borders. In the 1500s, inventors created hand-held novelty toys for children that simulated motion. Chinese and Indonesian dancing silhouette toys, called *ombres chinoises,* inspired film animator Lotte Reiniger's early films. The European version was the cruder "flipbook"—a series of small pictures drawn on separate sheets of coarse paper. When the holder thumbed the pages, the images moved. Many of the drawings were adult-oriented and showed women dancing or undressing. Later, the drawings were modified for children's viewing. The toy helped inspire Max Wertheimer to write about the gestalt approach to visual communication (Chapter 5).

But 200 more years passed before artists used the idea of sequenced images to tell stories. In 1744, John Newbery of London published children's illustrated stories as inexpensive pamphlets under the title *Little Pretty Pocket Books:* "Penny Dreadfuls" and "chapbooks," named for the slang word for peddlers who sold them (chapmen), were soon introduced. These cheaply produced works usually were sensational adventure or romantic stories, richly illustrated and sold as serials. By the time people had read an episode, the peddlers were out hawking the next one. Magazine publishers, comic strip and comic book writers, and movie and television producers all adapted the concept of the continuing story. Modern "**soap operas,**" many prime-time television programs, and motion picture sequels (*Jaws, Rocky, Superman,* and others) have chapbook roots.

Comic Strips The German Wilhelm Busch has been called the founder of the modern comic strip because his cartoon, "Max and Moritz," was the first published in a newspaper in 1865 (Figure 11.11). Following Busch's lead, in the 1880s A. B. Frost created sequential drawings for the newspaper, but they were simply commentaries about social mannerisms without plots.

During the last decade of the nineteenth century, William Randolph Hearst and Joseph Pulitzer were locked in a bitter circulation war in New York, and they believed that graphics were important to gaining readership. Although magazines had started using color in the 1870s, not until 1893 did newspapers in New York begin to use color presses.

Publisher James Gordon Bennett's *New York Herald* was the first newspaper to begin a Sunday edition in 1841. The first color Sunday comic strip section was published in Joseph Pulitzer's *Sunday World.* The first color comic strip was Richard Outcault's "Hogan's Alley," first published on May 5, 1895, and it instantly was a smash hit. The cartoon provided social commentary disguised as a collection of orphaned, unkempt children living among the tenement houses in New York City. The central character was a towheaded, unnamed boy in a nightshirt who smoked cigars. A printer in Pulitzer's backshop originally gave the boy in Outcault's cartoon a blue nightshirt. But as he became a central character, yellow was selected to help him stand out in the crowd of children. Soon afterward the strip became known as "The Yellow Kid of Hogan's Alley." The sensational tactics that journalists used to increase circulation were thereafter labeled "yellow journalism."

In a battle between the two giant egos, Hearst and Pulitzer publicly bid for Outcault's services. Hearst's *New York Morning Journal* hired the famous cartoonist, but he later returned to Pulitzer's paper at a higher salary. Hearst was determined and hired Outcault back.

Although Pulitzer lost Outcault, he still retained the rights to the popular strip. He hired George Luks to continue to draw the "Yellow Kid" (Figure 11.12). For all the attention that Outcault received over the comic, he expressed annoyance that he was known only for that one strip. He once wrote, "When I die don't wear yellow crepe, don't let them put a Yellow Kid on my tombstone and don't let the Yellow Kid himself come to my funeral. Make him stay over on the east side, where he belongs." In 1902, Outcault turned his attention to another popular cartoon, "Buster Brown," about the adventures of a mischievous rich kid living in a neighborhood far different from that of the Yellow Kid.

A colorful Sunday comics section proved to be enormously popular with the public. Hearst described his paper's comic strip insert as "eight pages of iridescent polychromous effulgence that makes the rainbow look like a piece of lead pipe."

Many other successful comics were introduced in the highly popular color comics section in Sunday newspapers. Most of the cartoons featured continuing characters, but

Modified after M. Thomas Inge, *Comics as Culture*, University Press of Mississippi, 1990

Figure 11.11

Created by Wilhelm Busch, the childish imps Max and Moritz have found a way to steal chickens from a woman putting sauerkraut on her plate. Instead of horizontal movement of the action as in most comic strips, this cartoon uses a vertical cutaway view of the house.

the story lines weren't in serial form. Winsor McCay drew one of the most artistically rendered cartoons ever to grace the pages of a comics section. His "Little Nemo in Slumberland" was about children who dreamed of flying over cities and exploring buildings and back alleys. But one of the most popular cartoons (begun in 1897) was drawn by a German immigrant artist, Rudolph Dirks, who developed "The Katzenjammer Kids." Inspired by Busch's "Max and Moritz" cartoon, the strip told the often humorous adventures of a group of children living on an island.

Because of the success of the Sunday comics, publishers—led by Hearst—started to run cartoons as a daily feature in their

Figure 11.12

Although Richard Outcault was the original artist for "The Yellow Kid of Hogan's Alley," George Luks continued drawing the character after Outcault went to work for William Randolph Hearst. This drawing by Luks shows the frenetic, three-ring-circus atmosphere of the cartoon. The alley is a noisy, crowded place ruled by children.

Courtesy of Vis-Com, Inc.

Figure 11.13

Influenced by Dada artists, George Herriman inspired cartoon artists such as Chuck Jones and Tex Avery and drew the original violent comic strip "Krazy Kat." In this nighttime desert scene, the little mouse clearly makes a direct hit on his nemesis because of the typographical additions.

Modified after M. Thomas Inge, *Comics as Culture*, University Press of Mississippi, 1990

newspapers. The first daily comic strip was H. C. "Bud" Fisher's "Mutt and Jeff," which first ran in 1907. The cartoon originally ran in the *San Francisco Chronicle;* Hearst purchased it for his *San Francisco Examiner* and ran it as a daily cartoon feature in all his newspapers that same year. Originally the strip was named simply "A. Mutt" and recounted the ups and downs of an unsuccessful racetrack gambler. In 1917, Mutt's partner at the track, Jeff, was added to the

name to acknowledge their **vaudeville** comedy team.

In the years following the introduction of "Mutt and Jeff," many long-lasting and influential cartoons were introduced. The Dada art movement inspired the "Krazy Kat" comic strip by George Herriman. Introduced in 1915, the cartoon described a surreal and often violent world of an alley cat (Figure 11.13). The strip inspired Fred "Tex" Avery, Friz Freleng, and Chuck Jones to produce "Bugs Bunny" and other popular characters in an equally wisecracking, absurd, and often violent style. Following in that "violence resolves conflicts" tradition was a 1929 strip drawn by Elzie Crisler Segar titled "Popeye." Inspired by the character Popeye Vitelli in William Faulkner's novel *Sanctuary,* the main character was rough and headstrong but had a soft place in his heart for his girlfriend, Olive Oyl. A year later, Chic Young introduced one of the most popular and nonviolent comic strips ever. "Blondie" told the story of a housewife, her husband Dagwood Bumstead and his boss, and their family in a strip that eventually had more than 50 million readers in 1,600 newspapers and 50 countries around the world.

An important innovation in the continuing popularity of comic strips—the serial—appeared in the 1920s and 1930s. Harold Gray's "Little Orphan Annie" in 1924 championed the virtues of helping yourself without relying on government aid. Al Capp's "Li'l Abner" in 1934 criticized big business practices at first but gradually became conservative over the years. Such strips with not so subtle political messages were a link between the funnies and the editorial cartoon.

Adventure stories that continued from day to day were enormously popular comic strips, which many newspapers depended on for their survival. In 1929, two important strips that also had lives as motion pictures were introduced. Richard Calkins and Phil Nowlan produced the twenty-fifth-century space traveler "Buck Rogers." Edgar Rice Burroughs's "Tarzan" character was brought to visual life by Harold Foster and later by Burne Hogarth. These adventure cartoons inspired all kinds of western, detective, and superhuman strips. Chester Gould's "Dick Tracy" (1931), Milton Caniff's "Terry and the Pirates" (1934), and later his "Steve Canyon" (1947) continued the adventure strip tradition.

Inspired by the liberal social messages of Walt Kelly's "Pogo," the 1950s and 1960s were a time when cartoonists used satire to poke fun at social hypocrisies. Kelly ridiculed the powerful Senator McCarthy with a character named "Senator Simple J. Malarkey." Mort Walker satirized army life in "Beetle Bailey." From a prehistoric perspective, Johnny Hart gave his views in "B.C." Robert Crumb's irreverently humorous characters, "Fritz the Cat," the "Fabulously Furry Freak Brothers," and "Mr. Natural," poked fun at the hypocrisies Crumb saw in the emerging hippie social movement. These comic strips were published mostly in underground newspapers of the time.

But the most popular cartoon strip of that or any other time was "Peanuts" by Charles Schulz, originally published on October 2, 1950. His tale of a band of small children and a dog in the minimalist artistic tradition became a symbol for America as sure as that of apple pie (Figure 11.14). Appearing in more than 2,000 newspapers worldwide, in books, and on television, the strip has more than 100 million fans. The Apollo 10 astronauts even carried a copy of the cartoon into space. Distributed by the United Features press syndicate, the strip helped make Schultz "the wealthiest contemporary cartoonist in the history of comics." Schultz died on February 13, 2000, but reprints of "Peanuts" continue to grace the

carton section of newspapers around the world.

The National Cartoonists Society gives its Reuben Award for the "Best Cartoonist of the Year." Milton Caniff was the first recipient, and Jack Davis, who from the early 1950s contributed illustrations for *Mad* magazine, was the 2000 winner. Other cartoonists, inspired by such blatantly political strips as "Little Orphan Annie," "Li'l Abner," and "Pogo," disguise social commentary as humorous comic strips—a tradition that has its roots in the "Yellow Kid." Jeff MacNelly's "Shoe," Bill Watterson's "Calvin and Hobbes," and Berke Breathed's "Bloom County" (later renamed "Outland") are contemporary examples. Another brilliant social critic is Jules Feiffer, whose syndicated strip runs in newspapers around the world. Feiffer was particularly active during the 1950s civil rights struggle with his individual comic strip and cartoon book collections. Garry Trudeau's "Doonesbury" often is moved from the comic pages to the editorial or op-ed pages of newspapers because of its controversial content. Begun in 1970 in only 28 newspapers, "Doonesbury" appears in nearly 1,000 papers today. In 1975, Trudeau

"Peanuts" reprinted by permission of United Feature Syndicate, Inc.

Figure 11.14

With its simple backgrounds, typographical variations, and enduring children's characters, "Peanuts" by Charles Schulz often made commentaries about popular culture. "Peanuts" has a direct link to Richard Outcault's "Yellow Kid." However, Charlie Brown, Linus, and Lucy never smoke, and they live in middle-class homes with both parents.

won a Pulitzer Prize for his cartoons about Vietnam, former president Richard Nixon, and the Watergate scandal.

Comic Books   In the 1820s, English printer Jemmy Catnach published cartoon broadsheets that were the forerunner for the modern comic book. Pierce Egan's *Life in London* series, artistically rendered by the illustrator George Cruikshank, told the tale of two characters named Tom and Jerry. He described action entirely through drawings and supplied dialogue, not within **balloons** as is the modern tradition, but under the frames of the pictures. Ten years later, as entertainment for his students, a Swiss schoolmaster, Rodolphe Töppfer, circulated cartoon drawings on more educational subjects. Another 100 years would elapse before comic books became a popular form of visual entertainment.

In the 1930s, newspaper publishers started to promote their comic strip offerings through inexpensively printed giveaway inserts. Publisher Max Gaines expanded the idea, producing *Cheap Little Books* that were reprints of newspaper cartoons (Figure 11.15). With the introduction of the adventure comic strips, Gaines, the father of *Mad* magazine publisher William Gaines, started to seek material not previously printed. The comic book giant, Detective Comics, or DC, began publishing in 1937 with initially limited success. But it was the cartoon created by two high school students from Cleveland, Jerry Siegel and Joe Schuster, that ignited the comic book industry. After several publishers turned down the idea, *Superman* started flying in 1939 when Gaines began Action Comics with the popular superhuman (Figure 11.16). A year later, *Batman* was first published.

The 1950s has been named the "golden age of comic books." C. C. Beck's *Captain Marvel*, Stan Lee's troubled photographer Peter Parker, better known as *Spider-Man*, and William Gaines's Educational Comics, later renamed Entertaining Comics (or simply EC), were started during the decade (Figure 11.17). A collection of horror and science fiction cartoons, EC comic books featured titles such as *Crypt of Terror* and *Weird Science*. Unlike the children-oriented comic books *Superman* and *Captain Marvel*, EC comic books were targeted at adults who enjoyed the social commentary masquerading as children's cartoons. However, the so-called golden age was short-lived. In 1953, psychiatrist Dr. Fredric Wertham published *Seduction of the Innocent*. In his book he linked (without adequate research) the content of comic books to juvenile delinquency. To head off possible government action, the comic book industry established a self-censoring board to regulate comic book content with a Comics Code. Adult comic books, including serious graphic novels, were wiped out. For example, EC could not survive under the strict guidelines for a "seal

Figure 11.15

Originally, comic books were specially prepared publications produced by newspapers as an advertisement for their comic strips. Max Gaines printed 35,000 copies of Famous Funnies *in 1934. The comic book proved to be enormously successful.*

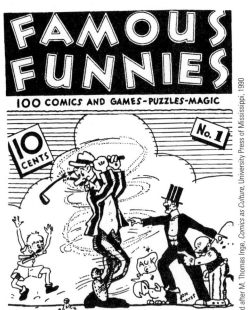

Modified after M. Thomas Inge, *Comics as Culture*, University Press of Mississippi, 1990

of approval" by the board. But in 1954, the gap-toothed, wisecracking character Alfred E. Newman appeared in William Gaines's *Mad* magazine. In a tribute to his father's first foray into comic book publishing, he inserted the word "Cheap" under the price for the magazine. *Mad* is still an enormously popular vehicle for social criticism in the form of irrational humor and visual puns by such artists as Mort Drucker, Jack Davis, and Don Martin.

Inspired by the baseball trading card fad of the 1980s, comic books have become valuable collectors' items. A first-issue *Superman,* for example, can fetch as much as $50,000. Cartoon artists are afforded the celebrity status of rock singers. When Rob Liefield offered to autograph his 1993 comic book called *Youngblood,* more than 5,000 fans lined up to get his valuable signature on their copies of the magazine.

The motion picture and television industries certainly have profited from comic book characters. Many cartoon and comic book titles have been adapted for the screen—"Buck Rogers," "Blondie," "Flash Gordon," "Dick Tracy," "Superman," "Popeye," "Peanuts," "Doonesbury," "The Addams Family," "Brenda Starr," and "Batman." Film directors such as George Lucas (*American Graffiti* and *Star Wars*) and Steven Spielberg (*E.T.: The Extra-Terrestrial* and *Saving Private Ryan*) admit that early in their careers they learned about perspective, framing, and plot techniques by being avid comic book readers. Furthermore, the action-adventure characters brought to the big screen by Sylvester Stallone (*Rocky, Rambo,* and *Judge Dredd*) and Arnold Schwarzenegger (*The Terminator* and *The Last Action Hero*) simply are cartoon characters disguised as humans.

Cartoons also express serious subjects in a nonthreatening way. For example, Art Spiegelman's retelling of the Holocaust in an animal fable called "Maus" won a National

Modified after M. Thomas Inge. *Comics as Culture,* University Press of Mississippi, 1990

Figure 11.16

The first issue of the popular Superman comic book was introduced in June 1938. Interestingly, the illustration for the cover is a departure from the usual characterization of the superhero. Instead of saving lives, this stern Superman appears to be crashing a car into a cliff while three men seem to be running for their lives.

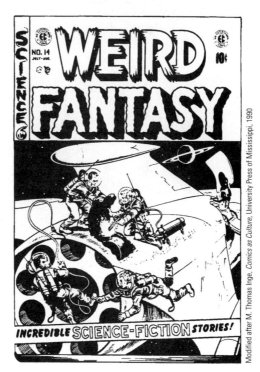

Modified after M. Thomas Inge. *Comics as Culture,* University Press of Mississippi, 1990

Figure 11.17

William Gaines began Entertaining Comics, or simply EC, as a way to interest adults in reading science fiction comic books. This 1952 cover is a typical example of the genre with its mix of typeface styles, font sizes, and action-oriented illustrations.

Book Critics Award in 1987, the first time the award had ever gone to a cartoon. In 1992, Spiegelman received a "Special Award and Citation" from the Pulitzer Prize board.

Animated Films A week before a backshop printer decided to print Outcault's "Yellow Kid," the Lumière brothers in Paris showed their simple movies to a paying audience for the first time. Four months later, in 1896, Thomas Edison demonstrated his Vitascope film machine before a vaudeville audience. The history of animated film, naturally, is tied to the history of the motion picture (Figure 11.18). Moving films are a combination of a camera, film, and a projection device. We discuss their use in motion pictures in Chapter 13 but discuss here the early versions of projection that were invented to animate cartoon drawings.

Projection motion pictures started with Dutch diplomat and poet Christiaan Huygens and Jesuit mathematician Father Athanasius Kircher working independently in the seventeenth century. They invented the *magic lantern,* an early version of a slide

projector (Figure 11.19). The device comprised a box with a lens and a candle in it. The user projected images on glass plates onto a screen by moving them in front of the flame. By 1700, Johannes Zahn had invented a tabletop version in which pictures drawn on a glass wheel simulated movement as they were turned. Entertainers and families throughout Europe used magic lanterns until the Victorian era. A slide could be projected on a screen while live actors performed in front of it. Upper-class Victorians used lanterns for educational and entertainment purposes at home.

Professor Émile Reynaud of France managed to combine several drawings and a projection system similar to the magic lantern's in a device he called the Praxinoscope. In 1882, he opened the first public theater for showing animated films, the Theatre Optique. Reynaud showed thousands of cartoons, many drawn by his assistant Émile Cohl. Unfortunately, the public had become more interested in the live-action short films of the Lumière brothers and others (Chapter 13). Frustrated, in 1910 Reynaud threw all

Figure 11.18

Comic strips are read the same as words—from left to right starting at the top. The cultures of rural and urban gentlemen clash in this comic that resembles a short animated film.

Uncensored Situations, 1966, The Dick Sutphen Studio, Inc.

his equipment in the Seine River and at the end of World War I died in a sanitarium.

Cohl pioneered the frame-by-frame animation technique in which a single frame is photographed and then replaced with another image. He had limited success with his classic 1908 animation *Phantasmagoria,* in which black crayon characters on white paper change shapes. An elephant character, for example, magically transforms into a ballet dancer. Cohl's *Phantasmagoria* was expensive to produce because it contained 2,000 images for the 80-second film. After World War I, Cohl could no longer obtain the funds he needed to make animated films.

In 1902, the first science fiction movie, *A Trip to the Moon,* featured special effects and animated drawings by French magician George Méliès (Figure 11.20). In 1905, Méliès used hand-colored backgrounds with cutout drawings of racecars for the animated film *Paris to Monte Carlo.* He photographed each frame after moving a car slightly in a technique initiated by Émile Cohl.

The founder of the American animated film industry is considered to be the cartoonist Winsor McCay. Born in Michigan in 1871, McCay worked in Chicago as an illustrator of circus posters and later for a Cincinnati newspaper. In 1903, he moved to New York to draw cartoons for the *New York Herald* and the *Evening Telegram,* owned by publisher James Gordon Bennett. In 1906, as part of his "Little Nemo" newspaper cartoon, McCay printed a series of drawings of a trapeze artist inspired from a child's flipbook, and these sequential pictures inspired McCay to make animated movies. His first animated film featured the Little Nemo character. The short movie took four years to complete and included 4,000 hand-colored, 35-mm film frames. In 1912, his next film, *The Story of the Mosquito,* was about a confrontation between a drunken man and an insect. But he is best known for his third

Uncensored Situations, 1966, The Dick Sutphen Studio, Inc.

animated picture. Besides being an able cartoonist and animator, McCay starred in his own comedy act. To make his vaudeville act more interesting, McCay created *Gertie, the Trained Dinosaur* in 1914. Gertie was a charming, crowd-pleasing brontosaurus that happily performed according to McCay's stage instructions.

Animation is enormously expensive and time-consuming. Twenty-four frames per second are needed for convincing movement, so a ten-minute movie needs more than 14,000 drawings. But the process became easier in 1915 when Earl Hurd patented his cel animation technique with the help of his partner John Bray. They used clear plastic sheets for the moving characters, allowing the background to remain unchanged. Consequently, back-

Figure 11.19

This early twentieth-century woodcut is an advertisement for a magic lantern—a device used to project images on a wall.

Figure 11.20

The magic and wonder of George Méliès's animation classic, A Trip to the Moon, *is evident in this scene from the movie. While exploring the surface of the moon, a group of university professors is led by spear-carrying aliens. Note the elaborate foreground and background scenery on this stage set.*

ground artwork could be much more elaborate, the animated characters could be more lifelike, and the time and expense required to produce a film could be drastically reduced. Hurd became rich, as he continued to receive royalties for his invention until the patent ran out in 1940. Today, animation cels are valuable collectors' items.

Always interested in expanding his business interests, William Randolph Hearst established an animation studio in 1916 to make films as a way to promote his newspaper comic strips. The studio produced short cartoons every week of *The Katzenjammer Kids* and *Krazy Kat* that played in movie theaters along with newsreels.

In 1924, Austrian artist Max Fleischer and his brother Dave teamed with radio innovator Lee De Forest to make the first cartoon with sound, *Oh Mabel.* Unfortunately, most theaters showed the silent version because they weren't yet equipped for sound. Fleischer originally worked with John Bray to make films such as *Out of the Inkwell,* featuring the character Koko. He later helped produce cartoons that included the character of the sexually alluring child/woman *Betty Boop* (1930) (created by the artist Myron "Grim" Natwick) and his most famous character, *Popeye* (1933), based on Segar's comic strip. Throughout the Great Depression, the enormously popular *Betty Boop* cartoons kept Fleischer's studio financially secure.

Although Walt Disney usually is credited with making the first feature-length animated movie, the honor actually goes to Berlin-born Lotte Reiniger. In 1926, *The Adventures of Prince Achmed,* about the tales of the Arabian nights, was first shown. Reiniger made more than sixty films during her sixty-two-year career. Her most famous animated works, introduced in 1955, include the cartoon classics *Hansel and Gretel, Jack and the Beanstalk,* and *Thumbelina.*

Walt Disney grew up on a small farm in Missouri and went on to become the undisputed king of American animation. As a soldier during World War I, he tried to sell his cartoons of the front to the humor magazine *Life,* but they were rejected. After the war, he settled in Kansas City, where he worked as an ambulance driver before becoming a commercial artist for the Kansas City Advertising Company and meeting animator Ub Iwerks. Iwerks, Walt, and his brother Roy teamed up to create short cartoons called *Laugh-O-Grams* that they sold to local movie theaters. The three men moved to Hollywood in 1923 and obtained a contract to produce a fifteen-movie series named *Alice in Cartoonland,* which combined a live-action girl with drawn characters. In 1928, the three introduced *Steamboat Willie,* which had a fully synchronized sound track and, perhaps more important, the famous character, Mickey Mouse, originally named Mortimer Mouse. Walt Disney provided the character's high-pitched voice, and Iwerks created the drawings. Mickey Mouse became so popular that Nazi leader Adolf Hitler banned the cartoon from Germany.

In 1929, the trio produced the first of their *Silly Symphonies—The Skeleton Dance.* The *Silly Symphonies* were an expert mix of motion and music, with skeletons dancing to tunes. The 1933 Disney short *The Three Little Pigs* is considered an animation landmark because each of the three central characters had distinctive personalities. After its release, animators tried to give animated characters all the facial expressions common to live actors to promote realism.

By 1945, the Disney studio had employed hundreds of artists and produced several cartoon classics. The first color cartoon, *Flowers and Trees,* won the team an Oscar in 1933. *Snow White* (1937), *Pinocchio* (1939), *Fantasia* (1940), *Dumbo* (1941), and *Bambi* (1942) followed.

Disney introduced the concepts of pre-planned storyboards to organize a film before any cels were drawn and separation of animation artists into several different departments in which workers would complete separate pieces of a long animated project independently. Iwerks invented the multiplane camera that could separate cels from the background to allow realistic, real-time camera movements.

During World War II, the Disney studios made uninspired propagandistic cartoons for the government. After the war, Walt Disney concentrated on live-action nature films, the merchandising of his characters, television programs when the new medium became viable, and theme parks—*Disneyland* in southern California and, later, *Disney World* and *Epcot Center* in central Florida.

Critics originally praised Disney for his animation innovations, but, as the studio became more profitable, they criticized his movies for being too sentimental and pretentious. Because his films were aimed at a large, family-oriented audience, they were necessarily bland and free from controversy. At the other extreme of the animation spectrum was another set of popular animators who were inspired by the absurd violence and cynicism of George Herriman's *Krazy Kat* cartoon. At the center were Fred "Tex" Avery, Friz Freleng, and Chuck Jones, who, at the Warner Brothers studio, created such classic *Looney Tunes* characters as the wisecracking Bugs Bunny, Porky Pig, Daffy Duck, Elmer Fudd, Wile E. Coyote, and the Roadrunner (Figure 11.21). The team made more than 800 films. When Warner Brothers closed in 1963, Jones went to work for MGM. In 1965, Jones won an Oscar for his cartoon *The Dot and the Line.*

Other famous cartoon animators provided many of the most popular characters. Friz Freleng invented the Tweety Pie and Sylvester team and the Pink Panther. Walter

Paul Martin Lester

Figure 11.21

Bugs Bunny greets visitors to the famous Atlanta "Underground."

Lantz created Woody Woodpecker. William Hanna and Joseph Barbera's Mr. Magoo, Huckleberry Hound, and Yogi Bear were successful. Jay Ward produced the popular "Rocky and Bullwinkle" Saturday morning television show with stories that appealed both to children and adults.

Hanna and Barbera also proved that adults, as well as children, would like animated films. In 1960, the team produced the first prime-time television cartoon, "The Flintstones." With the success of that Stone Age family, the production company moved the familiar family situation comedy genre ahead a few centuries to create "The Jetsons." The success of the prehistoric cave and futuristic cloud residents showed studio heads that animated films could attract adult audiences. In 1968, for example, the hit film *Yellow Submarine* featured cartoon characters and music by the Beatles in the pop art classic. Famed animator Ralph Bakshi produced a groundbreaking adult-oriented movie, *Fritz the Cat,* based on the Robert Crumb character (Figure 11.22). Bakshi later directed the 1992 movie *Cool World.*

Because of the success of "The Simpsons," television executives have tried other animated offerings. For example, the success Mike Judge had with his "Beavis and Butthead" led to his creation of another successful animated series for the Fox television network, "King of the Hill."

Beginning in 1989, the Disney studio reasserted itself as the primary producer of mass-audience animated films with the success of *The Little Mermaid, Beauty and the Beast, Aladdin,* and *The Lion King.* Although not a winner, *Beauty and the Beast* was the first movie in the history of animation ever to be nominated for a Best Picture Oscar, in 1992. Disney released *Tarzan* in 1999, *Atlantis: The Lost Empire* in 2001, and *Return to Neverland* in 2002 and plans to release *Finding Nemo* and *The Jungle Book II* in 2003 (Figure 11.23).

John Lasseter of Pixar, whose president is Apple cofounder Steven Jobs (Chapter 15), teamed with Disney and won an Academy Award for the first all-computer-generated short feature, *Tin Toy* (1988) (Figure 11.24). Lasseter also directed *Toy Story* (1995), the first feature-length animated cartoon pro-

duced solely with computer technology, and *A Bug's Life* (1998) and *Toy Story 2* (1999), all-computer productions. Pixar teamed with Disney to produce *Monsters Inc.* in 2001, which featured innovations in computer-generated technology (see Chapter 15). *Monsters* broke the box office record for animated films by reaching the $100 million mark in only nine days. The previous record was eleven days for the movies *The Lion King, Toy Store 2,* and *Shrek.*

Steven Spielberg's DreamWorks motion picture company entered the animation production race with Woody Allen playing the voice of a neurotic insect in *Antz* (1998) and with *The Prince of Egypt* (1998), based on a popular story from the Bible. In 2001, *Shrek* opened with popular success and was awarded the first ever Academy Award in 2002 for a new category, "animated feature." *Tusker* is slated for 2003.

Technical Perspective

Whether cartoons are intended for print or screen media presentations, the cartoonist uses specific devices to convey information to the viewer. The meaning of these graphic conventions often is not obvious—as symbolic codes, they must be learned (Figure 11.25). In order to analyze cartoons, you need to be aware of the various terms used to describe illustrative techniques. For once you know the name of an element, you will notice it more easily.

1. *Frame:* Top and bottom boxes or panels often contain narration and story explanations. In animated films, voice-overs perform the same function.

2. *Setting:* The background illustrations might be highly stylized and simple as in a "Peanuts" cartoon or realistic and elaborate as in the "Spider-Man" comic strip. The degree to which elements of reality

Figure 11.22

In 1972, director Ralph Bakshi introduced his movie Fritz the Cat, *based on the popular 1960s character created by Robert Crumb. In this publicity still, Fritz appears menacing because of his large size, sharp fangs, implied movement, and eye contact with the viewer.*

Getty Images/Hulton Archive

are removed from a cartoon is called *leveling*. Often the artist conveys the seriousness of the cartoon by a high or low degree of leveling.

3. *Characters:* As with the setting, how realistic the characters are drawn often indicates whether the strip is humorous or serious. *Assimilation* is the term used to describe the technique of exaggerating features, usually for a stereotypical effect. Homer Simpson's large belly and Marge's high beehive are examples. As with any pictorial representation of the human face, expressions connote emotional states that may help explain a character's motives.

4. *Motion lines:* Straight lines or little puffs of smoke are used to indicate quick movement by a character. Mort Walker, creator of the popular strip "Beetle Bailey," has given names to various movement lines:

   hites—horizontal movement

   vites—vertical motions

   dites—diagonal movement

   agitrons—wavering or repetitive motions

   briffits—little puffs of smoke or dirt

   waftaroms—odors that float in the frame

   plewds—sweat beads that pop up on a character's forehead that indicate nervousness

5. *Typography:* Unlike in any other art form, a reader is asked to supply a dramatic reading of a character's dialogue by means of typographical variations. By recognizing differences in letter size and thickness, the reader becomes an actor, emphasizing important words either in the mind or out loud.

6. *Balloons:* The way dialogue of characters in comic strips is encircled is an example of a complicated semiotics structure (Fig-

Paul Martin Lester

ure 11.26). The reader must learn to interpret the symbolism of the various balloon types:

unbroken line—normal, unemotional speech

perforated line—a whisper

a spiked outline—loud yelling

little bubbles instead of lines—thoughts by the character

icicles hanging from a balloon—conceited or aloof speech

Uncensored Situations, 1986, The Dick Sutphen Studio, Inc.

Figure 11.23

Posters for the popular Disney animated films, Doug's 1st Movie *and* Tarzan, *were displayed on the outside of the studio's now defunct theme restaurant, Tinseltown in Anaheim.*

Figure 11.24

See color section following page 276.

Figure 11.25

Editorial cartoons often are filled with symbols—some understandable, but many dependent for their meaning on a thorough knowledge of the time in which they were produced. Justice gives up her seat for an unknown corrupt politician in this woodcut.

Figure 11.26

In this nineteenth-century woodcut, warriors are comically polite, as indicated by the dialogue within the balloons.

Uncensored Situations, 1966, The Dick Sutphen Studio, Inc.

tiny words within a large balloon—astonished or ashamed emotional speech

a zigzag line—sound from a telephone, TV set, or computer

the tail of a balloon outside the frame—similar to an off-camera voice

7. *Action sequences:* All the techniques utilized by motion picture directors also are used in comic strips and comic books. Cartoonists use close-ups, perspective, and framing variations, special lighting effects, montage techniques, and panning and quick-cut editing to help move the action from frame to frame. These film techniques once led cartoonist Will Eisner to say, "Comics are movies on paper." Of course, with all the absurd plot lines, killings, explosions, and digital special effects in today's action-adventure movies, we can also say that movies are comic books on film.

Almost all the cartoons intended for the print medium are created with traditional pen and ink materials. Animated films, however, require a variety of special techniques in the creation of moving characters.

Object Animation

Object animation became popular when Willis O'Brien used the technique in his 1925 classic about angry dinosaurs, *The Lost World*. Tooled steel formed the animals' skeletons, which were then covered with foam latex and painted. Animators moved these models slightly and photographed them frame-by-frame. Called stop-motion, the technique also was used in the popular movie *King Kong* in 1933 (Figure 11.27). Assisting O'Brien was Ray Harryhausen, who went on to help make several classic animated monster films. In 1953's *The Beast from 20,000 Fathoms*, an atomic blast awakens a monster that tears up Manhattan. The movie inspired Japanese producers to create films such as *Godzilla* and *Rodan*. Harryhausen also created the effects for *The Valley of Gwangi*, *One Million Years B.C.*, and *Clash of the Titans*.

Another innovator in stop-motion animation in the 1940s was George Pal, who produced a series of short cartoons he called *Puppetoons*. The work of O'Brien, Harryhausen, and Pal inspired special-effects artist Stan Winston to create the dinosaurs in *Jurassic Park* and the creator of the Pillsbury Doughboy, Henry Selick, to direct the 1993 stop-action feature *Tim Burton's Nightmare Before Christmas* for the Walt Disney Company.

Materials

Clay and foam latex are materials commonly used in animation because they give characters depth. In 1953, Art Clockey introduced the popular clay characters Gumby and Pokey in the film *Gumbasia*. Presently, Will Vinton Productions, Inc., is a leader in clay and foam animation techniques. One of the most popular advertisements produced by Vinton and his associates was the one featuring the colorful clay California raisins dancing to the music of "I Heard It Through the

Grapevine." The Raisins generated more than $700 million in merchandizing sales. Vinton's latest projects include M&M candy commercials and the prime-time Fox television show, "The PJs." Nick Park won an Oscar for his short film *Creature Comforts* (1989) in which zoo animals are interviewed about their lives behind bars—a metaphor for all kinds of institutional life. His 1993 work *Wrong Trousers* also won an Academy Award. Clay in the hands of master Park becomes a powerful emotional element in which facial gestures reveal the inner feelings of the characters.

Besides models, clay, and foam, paper is sometimes used as an animation medium. One of the most notable animators in the paper cutout tradition is Terry Gilliam. In 1969, he worked on the British television comedy program "Monty Python." Gilliam, the only American in the comedy ensemble, used cutout photographs and drawings for title and animation segments of the program. Gilliam is now a respected film director credited with *Time Bandits, Brazil,* and *The Fisher King.*

Combined Live Action and Animation

Another common special effect is to combine live action and animated characters in the same scene. This technique is as old as George Méliès's films. More recent examples, using live-action sequences combined with images produced with computer technology, include *Who Framed Roger Rabbit* (1988), *Monkeybone* (2001), and *Osmosis Jones* (2001). Many computer graphics experts predict that dangerous stunts and even humanlike characters speaking dialogue soon will be completely fabricated through digital designs (Chapters 13 and 15).

Ethical Perspective

Critics cite four main ethical issues as problems for cartoons:

Getty Images/Hulton Archive

1. marketing cartoon characters to children
2. using too few multicultural characters
3. introducing political opinions in comic strips
4. showing inappropriate sexual and violent themes

Marketing

Product tie-ins are as old as comic strips. When the "Yellow Kid" was introduced in 1895, the popularity of the strip sparked one of the first mass marketing campaigns in the United States. Illustrations reproduced on buttons, metal cracker boxes, and fans promoted the cartoon character and the newspaper. But the clear-cut winner of the marketing race and the model for other cartoonists and studios is Walt Disney. Disney gave up illustrating his motion pictures himself to organize and manage the lucrative product lines inspired by his company's characters. It seemed that every American child had to have a Mickey Mouse doll. Disney's

Figure 11.27

Willis O'Brien was the special-effects wizard for the classic confrontation between man and beast in King Kong. *Note how the lighting on the back curtain and the platform itself direct the viewer to King Kong's face.*

Aladdin (1992), for example, was the first animated film to gross more than $200 million on North American sales of more than 50 million tickets. But the Disney studio also made an enormous profit on international ticket sales, video rentals, sound track albums, product licensing agreements (from lunch boxes to dolls), and street parades.

At the same time, Saturday morning television programs and motion picture characters frequently appear in advertisements promoting everything from dolls to bicycles. Children are particularly vulnerable to such persuasive commercial techniques, but adults also are easily manipulated.

Stereotypes

As with all mass media, white males have almost exclusively dominated comic strip and cartoon images. When members of another culture are featured, they are almost always represented stereotypically. Some of the newspaper comic strips in the 1920s and 1930s, particularly in the South, used racial stereotypes that are offensive to contemporary readers. During World War II, the U.S. government used cartoon characters to aid its propaganda campaign. Max Fleischer's character Popeye, for example, regularly fought Japanese characters and called his enemy "Japs." That popular racial slur and stereotypical drawings and mannerisms still upset Asian Americans today. Present-day cartoons, whether single- or multiframed, often show few characters from cultures other than the dominant one, which perpetuates negative stereotypes. When cartoons rely on stereotypes for their humor, controversy often ensues. For example, when the prime-time Fox television show "The PJs" was debuted, protests followed. Created by the comedian Eddie Murphy, an African American who also supplied the voice for the main character, the series poked fun at imaginary black residents of a high-rise

housing project (Figure 11.28). Filmmaker Spike Lee was one of the show's most vocal critics. "It is really hateful toward black people, plain and simple," Lee said. "I think it's very demeaning." One of the scenes that Lee objects to shows the characters sitting around a table drinking bottles of malt liquor. However, others noted several beer drinking scenes found on "The Simpsons" that are shown without complaints about perpetuating stereotypes. Perhaps because of the controversy, "The PJs" was canceled.

Political Messages

Many readers object to serious messages disguised as children-oriented comic strips often because they may not agree with the political messages. "Little Orphan Annie" and "Li'l Abner" were criticized for their right-wing messages, whereas "Pogo" and "Doonesbury" offended conservative readers with their liberal perspectives (Figure 11.29). In the 1960s, underground or alternative comic books were intended to shock traditional audiences and establish a counterculture readership. The often humorous comic strip "For Better or for Worse" by Lynn Johnston suddenly became controversial in 1993 when a continuing story line involved a teenage character admitting to family and friends that he was gay. An editor for the Sedalia, Missouri, *Democrat* gave a typical reason why the strip was pulled from the newspaper: "We are a conservative paper in a conservative town. We consider it a family comic strip and felt our readers would not appreciate this striking reference to homosexuality being inserted in it." Apparently there can be no discussion of real-life issues on the comic pages for fear that readers and, more important, advertisers might be offended.

Inappropriate Themes

Although there is no scientific proof for the assertion that violent acts by cartoon characters affect children's behavior, common sense and anecdotal evidence suggest that the hundreds of killings witnessed on Saturday morning television at least promote the idea that conflicts can be resolved, not by thoughtful negotiations and compromise, but by intentional acts of violence. Interactive video games that reward users for their skill at "killing" cartoon opponents have been weakly defended with "they help improve hand-eye coordination," as if such a trait could not be learned any other way. When the Comics Code Authority was established in 1954 after pressure from parental interest groups, many underground comic books in the 1960s, with titles such as *Subvert Comics, Big Ass Comics,* and *Young Lust,* were published to circumvent the attempted censorship.

Many cartoon artists are attempting to communicate serious issues to children without resorting to sensationalism. Maurice Sendak, best known for his 1963 children's book *Where the Wild Things Are,* has a reputation for respecting children's intelligence. His 1993 work, *We Are All in the Dumps with Jack and Guy,* explores the social problems of homelessness, AIDS, and violence on the streets in terms that both children and adults can understand.

First Amendment protection for printed works also applies to printed cartoons. From time to time, however, some members of Congress, under pressure from their constituents, have investigated and criticized the television industry for sensationalizing conflict rather than offering educational programs that seek creative alternatives to violence. Cartoon artists must define for themselves the line that separates hedonistic, entertaining cartoons from utilitarian, educational programs. If the television industry doesn't improve its educational offerings, Congress might impose regulation.

Cultural Perspective

Many times the Sunday comic pages are a child's first introduction to the magical world of reading. Upon seeing the brightly colored funnies, a child is interested immediately. But cartoon strip characters that are amusing to a child no longer provoke the same response in adults. Part of the reason that comic books are not considered a serious art form is that traditionally they have been intended for younger audiences. One of the most common causes of cultural division between people is difference in age. Consequently, the kinds of comic material you read help identify you as belonging to a particular cultural group.

Cartoons are an essential part of any country's culture. The types of cartoon subjects seen in a society reflect the values and beliefs common to the culture at that time. As with many visual messages, cartoons can be studied in terms of society's myths (good versus evil), their various genres (from westerns to soap operas), and their

Figure 11.28

Animator Will Vinton used foam latex to create Thurgood Stubbs, superintendent of the Hilton-Jacobs Projects on the Fox television network show, "The PJs."

Figure 11.29

Perhaps indicative of the growing acceptance of gay and lesbian lifestyles in the United States are the mainstream comic strips that have included homosexual characters.

use of symbolism (both visual and verbal). Large numbers of readers enjoyed the "Yellow Kid" comic strip because the story about a group of lost children, seemingly abandoned by their parents, struck a sympathetic chord with readers, many of whom were immigrants living far away from their families. The threat of world domination by totalitarian regimes beginning in the 1930s inspired comic strips with conservative views or superhuman characters who would fight for the values expressed by the "American way of life," whatever that phrase happened to mean at the moment. Visual symbols expressed in drawings also reflect the culture from which they are produced. Editorial cartoons, much more than any other type of comic, regularly feature symbolic images in the form of religious icons, military designations, and national emblems as a visual shorthand to make the points of the cartoons clear. Consequently, meaning resides in an understanding of these verbal and visual codes.

Critical Perspective

A cartoon, although packaged within a deceptively simple frame, is a complex exercise in semiotics analysis. No other art form, in print or screen media, combines words, pictures, and meaning in such an interwoven way. Like the effects created by motion picture and television images, cartoons form complex intellectual and emotional unions of text and images in a highly personal way. By reciting a cartoon out loud, a reader becomes a character in the unfolding frame-by-frame drama. Cartoons have a powerful, yet not fully understood, effect on those who never outgrow their charm. Pop artists such as Andy Warhol, Roy Lichtenstein, Red Grooms, and Keith Harring knew about the seriousness of the cartoon art that they included in their works. In corporate advertising, government propaganda, and instruc-

tional aids, cartoon art is used because it is a powerful communication medium. To simply label comics as "children's art" and unworthy of serious attention is to deny the impact of all words and pictures that communicate a message when used together. Such an attitude also discounts the enormous effect that cartoons have on all generations of readers and viewers.

Media historians often state that photography and motion pictures taught audiences that stories could be told primarily through pictures. More accurately, however, the honor goes to cartoon artists who taught image-makers the art of visual storytelling. In the conclusion of his book *Comics as Culture*, M. Thomas Inge writes,

> . . . cartoons introduced generations of readers to symbolic ways of addressing the continuing problems of society and the philosophic questions of mankind. . . . [They please] our visual sensibilities by bringing to life the kinds of dramatic conflicts that enable us to work out vicariously our internal frustrations.

Cartoons teach us not only how to combine words and pictures in symbolic ways, but also how to confront the significant issues that all societies face. It is unfortunate that cartoon messages are discounted by a narrow view of their importance (Figure 11.30).

■ FUTURE DIRECTIONS FOR CARTOONS

One of Japan's best-loved newspaper, motion picture, and television cartoonists, Machiko Hasegawa, died in 1993 at the age of seventy-two. Her death might have ended public concern about the artist, except that a grave robber dug up Hasegawa's remains and demanded a ransom for their return. In Japan, comic books (called *manga*) and ani-

Figure 11.30

Cartoons can be used to attract a viewer's attention to a social problem. In a program called "Art Attacks AIDS," Mike McNeilly shows his work on the back of a bus stop bench.

Paul Martin Lester

mations (called *anime*) are read and viewed by many more adults than in other countries. As do many around the world, the thief knew the value of a cartoonist's celebrity status, whether living or dead. In the future, cartoonists—and particularly comic book cartoonists—may attain the celebrity status of movie stars as more and more younger readers buy the brightly colored publications.

Increased attention to cartoon art by academic programs will improve the quality of the art form for editorial and entertainment purposes, breathing new life into caricatures and editorial cartoons. Computer technology will make possible creation of entire movies in which seemingly live-action characters actually are realistic cartoon characters. Comic books about specialized subjects are produced on desktop computers and distributed in comics stores and through the World Wide Web.

Perhaps the luster is off a bit from the shiny cels as several animated cartoon series on television have been canceled recently.

UPN and WB no longer offer cartoon series in prime time. However, the Walt Disney Company released the animated television series, "House of Mouse," "The Legend of Tarzan," and "Lizzie McGuire" in 2001 and "Kim Possible" in 2002. Despite Disney's success, animated movie production is slow. For 2001, production companies in the United States released only seventeen animated motion pictures. Nine animated films were released in 2002 while only five are in production for 2003.

Nevertheless, the World Wide Web increases the number of cartoons, as comic strips, comic books, and animated films become merged into the new medium. As its status improves, the cartoon will even be used to illustrate editorial stories as a form of informational graphics. And finally, the age-old concern that comics corrupt the impressionable minds of those who read them will continue to dominate ethical discussions about the art form with little clear-cut supporting evidence.

DISCUSSION AND EXERCISE IDEAS

- Lead a discussion on "The Simpsons" cartoon show. Why do you think it is so popular? What was its impact on animation generally?

- Describe your favorite cartoon. Why do you like it?

- What do you think is the future of cartoons?

- Write a paper that discusses the ethical concerns with cartoons with particular emphasis on portraying violence.

INFOTRAC COLLEGE EDITION ASSIGNMENTS

- With "Subject guide" checked, type "Postmodern Philosophy Meets Pop Cartoon" in the search area and read the article of the same name by Margaret Hull. In the article, Hull compares the philosophy of Michel Foucault with that of Matt Groening and "The Simpsons." In an interview, Groening, according to Hull, confirmed Foucault's philosophy when he said, "I guess if there is any underlying theme to my work it's that your leaders don't always have your best interests at heart. When people are telling you what to do and how to think, maybe you should take a second look." Do you agree with the comparison that Hull makes between the two? After reading this article, do you have more insight into the notion that cartoons are worthy of serious study?

- With "Subject guide" checked, type "Laughs and gripes about stereotypes" in the search area and read the article of the same name by David Astor that describes editorial cartoonists discussing stereotypes during an Association of American Editorial Cartoonists convention. Create a collection of stereotypes you see in editorial, humorous, and animated cartoons. Why do you think cartoonists use stereotypes? Do you think some cartoon stereotypes are unavoidable?

Go to the Web site for this book at www.wadsworth.com/product/0534562442 to find more Web links on this subject.

PHOTOGRAPHY

By the end of this chapter you should know:

- The historical significance of Dorothea Lange's portrait of Florence Thompson and her children.
- The various types of photographic processes that influenced the history of photography.
- The ethical issues of violence, privacy, and manipulation.
- The importance of still photography and why it will continue to be a factor in storytelling in the future.

Once you see the forlorn face of Florence Thompson, you will never forget her (Figure 12.1). With furrowed forehead, a faraway look, hand cupped to her chin in a gesture of uncertainty, two children shyly hiding their faces in the warmth of her shoulders, and an infant sleeping on her lap, the photograph is more than a simple portrait of a family. The image is reminiscent of the "Madonna and Child" religious icon known to millions because it has been captured on canvas by painters throughout the history of Christianity. But here in black and white is a real-life symbol for all parents struggling to survive and feed their families during the Great Depression and for all uncertain economic times. "The Migrant Mother" is probably the world's most reproduced photograph in the history of photography because it makes people care on a deep, personal level.

But it was a picture that might never have been taken. Dorothea Lange graduated from high school in 1914 and promptly told

Dorothea Lange; Library of Congress

Figure 12.1

Florence Thompson is and forever will be "The Migrant Mother." But is she posing for the photographer or wishing that the photographer would leave?

her shocked parents that she wanted to be a photographer. After studying at Columbia University under Clarence White, she moved to San Francisco, where she enjoyed the Bay Area's bohemian lifestyle. By 1932, she had become an able portrait photographer with a reputation for capturing the personalities of the rich San Francisco matrons of the day.

News reports of the terrible living conditions of rural Americans prompted her to want to document their lives. The country was undergoing the worst drought in its history; dust storms blew away the once-fertile topsoil. The stock market crashed in 1929 and farm prices plummeted, throwing millions of people out of work. People lived from day to day, and thousands of farmers from the Midwest and Great Plains who had lost their land and livelihoods took off in mattress-topped automobiles for the golden West.

Lange obtained a job with the State of California to document agricultural labor conditions. She was teamed with social economist Dr. Paul S. Taylor, whom she later married. After completion of the project, the head of the Resettlement Administration (RA), Rexford Tugwell, reviewed her pictures in Washington and promptly hired her.

The RA, later renamed the Farm Security Administration (FSA), was an agency of the U.S. Department of Agriculture. President Franklin D. Roosevelt created it to help relocate farmers to more fertile farmland, obtain massive subsidies to offset the low prices farmers were getting for their crops, and convince the American public that controversial social programs needed to be passed by the conservative Congress. Thus the FSA was more of a propaganda wing that the government used getting New Deal legislation through Congress than a direct aid to rural residents.

Tugwell hired economics professor Roy Stryker to head the History Section of the FSA because of the types of lectures he gave at Columbia University. Stryker used Lewis Hine's documentary photographs to give a human face to dry statistics during his classes. Although not a photographer, Stryker acted as an editor and teacher. He taught photographers to act as historians, economists, and anthropologists as they looked for images to capture on film. Before someone went out to take pictures of workers in a cotton field, for example, Stryker would lecture the photographer about the economic and social importance of cotton production.

Stryker assembled one of the most accredited teams in the history of social documentation. Besides Lange, famous photographers who worked for Stryker were Walker Evans, Arthur Rothstein, Marion Post Wolcott, John Vachon, Carl Mydans, and Russell Lee.

The FSA still photography and motion picture units were established at a time when photojournalism was just beginning to be recognized. *Life* magazine was started in 1936 and *Look* magazine a year later. Small handheld cameras allowed photographers such as Henri Cartier-Bresson to capture scenes that were difficult to obtain with bulky, large-format cameras.

The FSA photographers produced an exhaustive document of rural and urban life in America during the 1930s and 1940s that has never been equaled. Newspapers and magazines used their pictures because they were free. Their images succeeded in helping pass New Deal legislation and also inspired other photographers to follow in their documentary footsteps. More than 270,000 FSA images are stored in the collection at the Library of Congress, and a copy of each one can be purchased at a nominal price.

But *the* image in the collection—the most revered and reproduced—is Lange's "Migrant Mother."

Tired, hungry, and anxious to get home after a monthlong project taking pictures in central California, Lange drove her car north along the cold and wet Camino Real highway (101) in early March 1936. Along the way she noted a migrant workers' camp of about 2,500 people outside the small town of Nipomo. On the side of the road someone had placed a sign that simply proclaimed, "Pea-Pickers Camp." These sights were all too common, with poor people from all over the country forced to stop for lack of money

and gasoline for their cars and earn a few dollars picking local crops. The Thompson family was forced to move from Oklahoma to California because of the Depression and Dust Bowl. However, when her husband died after an asthma attack, Florence joined thousands of other migrant families finding work where they could.

For thirty minutes, Lange drove toward home and thought about the camp she had passed. Finally, the image of the people she had briefly seen overpowered her desire to get home. She turned her car around and drove back to the camp. Lange retrieved her press camera, a portable version of the **tripod**-bound, large-format camera, and immediately found Florence Thompson sitting in the barely adequate shelter of an open tent surrounded by her three daughters. With the crop destroyed by a freeze, there was no work at the camp. The tires on their Model T Ford had blown, so they could not move on. Thompson's two sons went to town to get the tires fixed, leaving her to care for her daughters. She was pregnant with her sixth child. She would eventually have ten children.

In notes about the brief encounter, Lange later wrote, "Camped on the edge of a pea field where the crop had failed in a freeze. She said that she had been living on frozen vegetables from the surrounding fields and birds that the children had killed." Lange did not ask her name or anything about her past history. She stayed ten minutes and made six exposures (Figure 12.2).

When she returned home, Lange made several prints and gave them to an editor of the *San Francisco News,* where they were published under the headline, "FOOD RUSHED TO STARVING FARM COLONY." Two of Lange's photographs accompanied the story that detailed the situation of the migrant workers and the efforts of relief workers to bring food and cleanup crews to

Dorothea Lange; Library of Congress

Dorothea Lange; Library of Congress

Figure 12.2

Although much richer in content than the famous portrait (notice the breast-feeding baby, the kerosene lamp, and the wedding ring), these images do not have quite the same emotional quality of the close-up image.

the camp. Interestingly, the famous close-up was not published.

But when Roy Stryker saw the "Migrant Mother" photograph, he recognized immediately the historical and social significance of the image. The picture soon became an American classic with a life of its own. Newspapers across the country reproduced it. In 1941, the Museum of Modern Art in New York City exhibited it. When John Steinbeck saw the picture, it inspired him to write *The Grapes of Wrath.* Without question, the picture made Lange famous. But despite her later achievements as a staff photographer for *Life* magazine, her collaboration with Paul Taylor on their book *An American Exodus,* and her documentation of Japanese-American internees during World War II, she is forever linked to it. Frustrated over this fact, she once complained that she was not a "one-picture photographer." In 1965, Lange died at the age of seventy after a long and event-filled life made possible by her photographic skills and her sensitivity to the important moments in everyday life.

But Florence Thompson's life didn't change for the better after the picture was

published. When she first saw it, she didn't like the image and tried to get it suppressed. When that effort failed, she tried to get Lange and the government to pay her for being in the picture. In 1979, forty-four years after the picture was taken, Thompson was still bitter about the fact that the photograph made Dorothea Lange famous but didn't improve her life. In a newspaper article, Thompson, living in a trailer in Modesto, California, complained: "That's my picture hanging all over the world, and I can't get a penny out of it." In 1998, the portrait signed by Lange was sold for $244,500 at Sotheby's auction house in New York to an anonymous collector who promptly sold it to the J. Paul Getty Museum in Los Angeles for an undisclosed sum.

In 1983, Thompson suffered from colon cancer and couldn't pay her medical bills. Family members alerted the local newspaper and a national story was published about her situation. Readers who saw the story and remembered the emotional image were moved to send money to her—more than $15,000—before she died. Many of the letters that contained money noted how the writers' lives had been touched by Lange's close-up portrait of "The Migrant Mother."

■ *ANALYSIS OF*
"THE MIGRANT MOTHER"

A photograph always has many stories to tell: the subjects within the picture's frame, how the photographers made the image, and what happened after the picture was taken and published. But one of the most important stories a photograph, or any visual message, tells is the one the viewer makes up. The way you interpret an image is the story of your life. Even a casual glance at "Migrant Mother" reveals without question an emotionally charged, sad moment in a woman's life.

The image is a reminder of why photography astounded so many people when it was first introduced. It also is a reminder of why this medium (rather than painting) is used to record important and ordinary events in the lives of people around the world. In a sense, Paul Delaroche was correct when he saw one of the first photographs made and said, "From today, painting is dead." A painting of Florence Thompson could never have the same effect as that close-up photograph of a real mother suffering with her children.

With a normal perspective, medium-size lens opening for limited focus, medium shutter speed to avoid camera blur, black and white film to avoid any distractions color might provide, and a 4- by 5-inch negative for maximum resolution, the picture demonstrates the highest quality possible using the gelatin dry plate in combination with a large-format, portable press camera.

Legally and ethically, Dorothea Lange did all that was required. Her job as a visual reporter was to record Thompson's image on film and give prints to a newspaper for publication. But what is strictly legal and what is ethical do not always absolve a person's moral responsibility.

Much of the picture's power comes from its obvious symbolic link to famous "Madonna and Child" religious paintings. But where the Madonna icon is a positive affirmation of future possibilities for her child, the Thompson portrait is an anti-Madonna icon filled with uncertainty about the future for her children.

Lange should have asked Thompson's name. The public learned her name only after newspaper accounts published her complaints about the image. Lange was one year younger than Thompson, and, under different circumstances, they might have had much to say to each other. But Lange was anxious to get home and stayed only ten minutes. Realistically, however, communication between them would have been difficult. They came from different worlds with no common bonds except being at the same place at the same time. The camera became the basis for their relationship, which lasted about as long as the shutter was open.

For Thompson the person, not Thompson the public icon, the image reveals a bone-weary numbness in which she is probably too polite or helpless to refuse the exposure. But she is saying "no" in the photograph the only way she can. She looks off as if wishing this "city girl" would move on and leave her alone. The image forever stereotypes Florence Thompson as a homeless matriarch who can survive only with contributions from the public. Never mind that she has most likely worked hard to feed and clothe her family as best she could, given the country's and her family's economic conditions. That is why she was probably upset that the picture was published.

■ *PHOTOGRAPHY AND THE SIX PERSPECTIVES*

Photography runs the gamut from simple, amateur snapshots to enormously expensive professional enterprises. Artists use images to express their inner emotions, commercial photographers to sell products and ideas, photojournalists to illustrate the lives of those in the news, and scientists to make an unseen world visible. With equipment that ranges from less than ten dollars to several thousand dollars, photographers take and preserve millions of images every year. Since its crude beginnings of looking out from inside a second-floor window of a French country estate in 1827, photography has become the world's most popular medium for creating visual messages in terms of actual users.

Personal Perspective

After learning how to use a pencil and a paintbrush, many children are introduced to a simple point-and-shoot camera, often their first contact with a machine's image-making process. Although their first attempts may be out of focus, blurred, off-center, or incorrectly exposed, they are nevertheless awed by the magic of capturing light onto a postcard-size print. Part of the joy of photography is that high-quality pictures can be taken with relative ease—the machine itself is easy to master.

But there is always a difference between what people remember about a scene and how it photographs. There is often disappointment in an image because it never captures just right the color of the light, the sounds and smells that are still a part of a memory, or feelings about the subjects photographed. Another reason for the negative reaction to a picture is that people in front of a camera seldom act as they would without its presence. For example, family groups with their huddled poses and mandatory smiles often hide relationship problems that are known to the viewer of the picture. Film can record only what it is allowed to expose. Any meaning imposed on a photograph must come from the viewer.

Moments captured by amateur photographers are a combination of space and time that often are prized possessions preserved in ornate frames and leather-bound albums. Pictures give evidence of a trip once taken, a car long since sold, and a baby who is now a grown woman. We use photographs not simply to show others where we have been, what we possess, or whom we have loved, but to remind ourselves of those important events, things, and people in our lives (Figure 12.3).

But perhaps the most significant psychological effect of photography is that a picture constantly reminds us of our own state of mind at a particular moment and place. Throughout our lives we must constantly struggle with the choice between watching and participating. For example, do you passively look at a story about homeless people in your community on television, or do you actively volunteer your time to help alleviate the social problem? Because a photographer almost always is not included in the picture's frame, the decision is made—a photographer watches. Photography, therefore, teaches you to be a keen observer of the environment and of human nature. It also teaches that to simply watch isn't enough. You must also allow yourself to be photographed—to participate.

Historical Perspective

The camera predates the photographic process by at least 1,000 years. Aristotle wrote about the phenomenon of light that allows an upside-down view of the outside world through a pinhole in one wall of a darkened chamber. Alhazen was the first to use the device to watch an eclipse of the sun. Leonardo da Vinci made drawings of the principle in one of his notebooks. In the seventeenth century, Johann Kepler gave the phenomenon the name *camera obscura,* which literally translates as "dark chamber." Later in that century, Robert Boyle constructed a portable model that was most certainly used to mimic accurately the linear perspective of scenes by such famed painters as Carel Fabritius, Jan Vermeer, Samuel van Hoogstraten, and Velázquez. Artists used the camera obscura as a tool to trace rough sketches of natural scenes on paper or canvas, to be filled in with paint later. The camera obscura device led to the idea of using photosensitive materials in place of a canvas.

Throughout the history of photography, nine main photographic processes have preserved the views captured through the camera obscura: the heliograph, the daguerreotype, the calotype, the wet-collodion process, color materials, the gelatin–bromide dry plate, holography, instant photography, and digital photography (Figure 12.4).

Heliography

Joseph Nicéphore Niépce has been called the founder of photography because he produced the first permanent photograph that can still be viewed. Born to rich and well-educated parents in the town of Chalonssur-Saone, France, in 1765, he became interested early in the many scientific and technological discoveries of the day. He could have had a career in the army, but ill health forced him to resign and return to his family's home in 1801 where he devoted the rest of his life to scientific experiments. At the age of 51, Niépce began work that eventually led to the photographic process. He was trying to improve the lithographic

Paul Martin Lester

process for making printing plates that had been recently invented. After trying several substances unsuccessfully, he discovered that bitumen of Judea (a type of asphalt) hardened with exposure to the sun. When the soft, unexposed parts of the picture were washed away, the result was a positive image. Niépce placed his asphalt emulsion on a pewter plate within a crudely constructed camera obscura and produced the world's first photograph—the view outside his home—in 1827 (although some historians say the year was 1826). It was the first and last photograph that Niépce ever made. The image now is a part of the Gernsheim photography collection at the University of Texas. The faint picture is encased within a Plexiglas frame where xenon gas protects it from deterioration.

Niépce named his process **heliography** (Greek for "sun writing"). The process never attracted much public attention for several reasons. The exposure time required was about eight hours, which was much too long for practical applications. The image was extremely grainy in appearance, its content was hard to decipher, and it appeared to be out of focus. The process resulted in a posi-

Figure 12.3

Although instamatic cameras with auto exposure and focus capabilities do not produce professional quality images, they have made photography a fun and popular hobby for millions of people. A tourist (the author's mother) in New York City captures a memory from her hotel window.

Figure 12.4

As this nineteenth-century woodcut shows, before light meters were invented, photographers looked to the sky to gauge the intensity of the sun during an exposure.

Uncensored Situations, 1966, The Dick Sutphen Studio, Inc.

tive image on the plate, so it could not be reproduced. Finally, the public never learned of the procedure until many years after Niépce's death. The Royal Society of London did not allow him to present his findings to that scientific body because he would not agree to reveal details of his invention. Presentation to the Royal Society assured international recognition of scientific and intellectual accomplishments, but members had a firm rule that it would publicize only inventions that were adequately and publicly explained. Nevertheless, the process did attract the attention of Louis Daguerre, a theatrical artist and amateur inventor who used Niépce's basic work to produce the first practical photographic process.

Daguerreotype

Louis Jacques Mandé Daguerre was born in 1789 in Cormeilles, France. His first career was as a tax collector for the govern-

ment. He later became famous in Paris for his **dioramas,** illusionary pictorial effects with painted backdrops and lighting changes. An optician who supplied lenses for Niépce's camera obscura told Daguerre about the heliographs. At the age of sixty-four, in ill health and in serious financial difficulties, Niépce reluctantly signed a contract with Daguerre to share information about the heliographic process. In 1833, Joseph Niépce died before seeing the results from Daguerre's experiments, but his son Isidore maintained the partnership. Daguerre switched from a pewter to a copper plate and used mercury vapor to speed the exposure time. These technical changes resulted in a one-of-a-kind image of extraordinary detail and fine grain. Daguerre modestly named the first practical photographic process the daguerreotype (Greek for "Daguerre's picture").

On January 7, 1839, the French astronomer Arago formally announced Daguerre's invention to the prestigious Academy of Science. Upon seeing the wondrous examples, Oliver Wendell Holmes dubbed the daguerreotype the "mirror with a memory." The French government paid Daguerre and Isidore an annual pension in return for making the process public.

The initial exposure time in bright sunlight was about thirty minutes, or too long for portraits. Soon, however, exposure times were reduced and hundreds of daguerreotype portrait studios sprang up throughout Europe. The precious, positive portraits were an instant hit with the public and often were displayed within elegantly crafted miniature boxes made of papier-mâché, leather, highly finished wood, or plastic, when it was introduced in the 1860s. Samuel F. B. Morse, inventor of the Morse code used in telegraphy, is credited with spreading the daguerreotype craze to America. Morse opened the first photographic studio in New York City and taught many entrepreneurs, including the famous photographer Mathew Brady, the daguerreotype process. A faster chemical process, a larger lens, and a smaller plate size cut exposure time to thirty seconds. England's Sir John Herschel coined the word *photography* for the new light-sensitive process from the Greek words that mean "light writing." Herschel also invented a fixing agent—which is still used in darkrooms today—that made the images permanent. Still lifes, street scenes, family portraits, and exotic locales all became subjects for the daguerreotype photographer.

Calotype

Coincidentally, a different photographic process was announced the same month as the daguerreotype. Sometimes referred to as the **talbotype,** the calotype (Greek for "beautiful picture") was invented by William Henry Fox Talbot. The process is the foundation of modern photography.

Talbot was born in Dorset, England, in 1800. After being educated at Trinity College in Cambridge, he devoted the next fifty years of his life to studying physics, chemistry, mathematics, astronomy, and archaeology. In 1833, while vacationing in Italy, he came to the conclusion that images from a camera obscura could be preserved using light-sensitive paper. After several experiments upon his return home in August 1835, he produced a one-inch-square paper negative of a window of his house. He then produced a positive picture placing another sheet of sensitized paper on top of the negative image after exposure to the sun. The exposure time was about three minutes in bright sunlight. Talbot continued to produce many views of his estate, which were later collected in the first book illustrated with photographs, *The Pencil of Nature,* published in 1844.

When he heard of Daguerre's announcement, Talbot sent an explanation of his process to Michael Faraday, who reported the photographic process to London's Royal Institution on January 25, 1839. Except for the work by the famed Scottish portrait team of David Hill and Robert Adamson, professional uses of the calotype were limited. Because a positive image had to print through the paper fibers of a negative view, Talbot's pictures were never as sharp and finely grained as daguerreotypes. Herschel once told Arago that "compared to the masterful daguerreotype, Talbot produces nothing but mistiness." Nevertheless, the process represents the first instance in which the modern terms *negative* and *positive* were used. Any process that produced a negative image could reproduce any number of positive prints. This concept is the basis for modern photography.

In 1851 the Crystal Palace Exhibition opened in London. This "world's fair" further fueled the photographic craze because of the images exhibited. But this latest round of publicity proved to be short-lived. By the mid-1850s, the daguerreotype and the calotype were replaced forever by the wet-collodion process that combined the sharpness of the daguerreotype with the reproducibility of the calotype.

Wet-Collodion

In March 1851, a man who never made much money from his discovery announced an important photographic process. Frederick Scott Archer published his formula for all to read and use in a popular journal of the day, *The Chemist.* Archer was a British sculptor and part-time calotype photographer. He had grown weary of the poor quality of prints obtained from using paper negatives. He suggested glass as a suitable medium for photographic emulsion. The problem with glass, however, was in making the emulsion adhere to its surface. However, the invention of collodion in 1847 solved that problem.

Comprising a mixture of guncotton or nitrocellulose dissolved in alcohol and ether, collodion was used to protect wounds from infection. When poured on any surface, it forms a tough film. Archer simply mixed collodion with light-sensitive silver nitrate. His wet-collodion process produced glass negatives of amazing detail and subtlety of tone that could be used to make hundreds of positive prints. The exposure time was a remarkable ten seconds. Although the process required that the glass plate be exposed while moist and developed immediately, serious portrait and documentary photographers around the world used the wet-collodion process for the next thirty years. Most of the photographs taken during the Civil War, for example, utilized the wet-collodion process (Figure 12.5).

Although Archer sold some wet-collodion photographs, he never profited from his invention and died impoverished at the age of forty-four. His friends raised some $1,500 to help his wife and three children. Later, the British government added an annual pension of about $450 for his children, or the equivalent of about $8,800 today. They later stated that the motive for such a generous offer was that their father "was the discoverer of a scientific process of great value to the nation, from which the inventor had reaped little or no benefit."

Color Materials

Scottish physicist James Clerk Maxwell, who is better known for his discovery of electromagnetic light energy, is credited with producing the first color slide. In a lecture to the Royal Institution in London in 1861, he admitted that his work was influenced by Thomas Young's discoveries about the eye's photoreceptors.

Maxwell made three separate pictures of a ribbon through three different colored filters. When he projected the three separate pictures with the colored light from each filter and aligned the views, a color slide was the result. Actually, he was lucky that his experiment using a bright tartan ribbon was successful. The photographic film of the day was not sensitive to the color red. The only reason the color could be seen was that the ribbon itself reflected ultraviolet radiation that simulated red. Maxwell later became a professor of experimental physics at the University of Cambridge. He died in 1879. His work in color photography inspired many others toward the reproduction of natural colors.

Because of the impracticality of Maxwell's discovery, attention soon focused on color print materials. In his 1869 book, *Photography in Color,* France's Louis Ducos du Hauron proposed a method for making a color photographic print. Color prints, however, proved to be much more difficult to produce than color slides.

The inventors of the motion picture camera and projector, Auguste and Louis Lumière (see Chapter 13) also invented a contemporary color slide process. In 1903, they started selling their *autochrome* photographic plates to the public. The Lumière brothers mixed red, green, and blue colored potato starch grains randomly throughout a photographic emulsion. Although the film was quite expensive for the day, photographers immediately favored the autochrome plate because of the quality of the images produced. Autochrome plates were available in the United States by 1907, and famous photographic artists such as Edward Steichen and Alfred Stieglitz used them. The manufacture of the autochrome process was discontinued in 1932.

In 1935, two scientists at the Kodak Research Laboratories, Leopold Godowsky,

Alexander Gardner, Library of Congress

Jr., and Leopold Mannes, introduced the popular Kodachrome slide and motion picture film. With its fine grain structure and color constancy, Kodachrome is the industry standard for film used to take pictures for newspaper and magazine publication.

In 1939, the Agfa Company introduced the first modern color print film. For the first time, color negatives could be processed and printed with specially prepared color paper. Three years later, Kodak introduced Kodacolor color print film, which was the basis for all subsequent color negative film products.

Gelatin–Bromide Dry Plate Process

Amateur scientists and photographers fill photographic history with stories of famous inventions. Dr. Richard Maddox of London was one such amateur who helped change the face of photography.

Maddox studied medicine in England and practiced in Constantinople, where he married in 1849. When he returned home, he devoted his time to microphotography. Like many others, he was looking for a substitute for collodion as a photography emulsion. Because ether was used in the process, exposures had to be made while the plate was still moist. Such a procedure was a great inconvenience for the photographer who had to bring a darkroom along whenever taking pictures outside. Maddox also wanted to find a substitute for the ether used in collodion because it affected his already poor health. Experiments had been tried with

Figure 12.5

"Battle-field of Gettysburg Dead Confederate sharp-shooter at foot of Little Round Top." Alexander Gardner, employed by famed photographer Mathew Brady, made this silent study of a young sniper's body.

licorice, sugar, beer, glycerin, and even raspberry syrup as substances for coating a photographic plate. Maddox tried gelatin, an organic material obtained from the bones, skins, and hooves of animals. In the tradition of Frederick Archer, Maddox described his technique of mixing cadmium bromide and silver nitrate in a warmed solution of gelatin in an 1871 edition of *The British Journal of Photography.* The resulting mixture was a light-sensitive emulsion of silver bromide that could be manufactured, stored, and exposed much later by the photographer. The process was called the *gelatin– bromide dry plate process.* Improvements to his process in 1900 reduced exposure times to 1/1,000 of a second, making stop-action photography possible. Maddox's discovery sparked the invention of motion picture film, first demonstrated by Eadweard Muybridge when he exhibited individual frames of a running horse in 1878 and later perfected by the Lumière brothers. Maddox's process also made the amateur photography craze possible when George Eastman of Rochester, New York, invented cameras with gelatin dry plate films in long rolls.

In 1888, Eastman introduced his $25 Kodak camera. *Kodak* simply was an easily pronounced and easily remembered name in any language (Figure 12.6). With the motto "You push the button—we do the rest," the camera came loaded with 100 exposures. After taking all the pictures, a customer mailed the camera back to Rochester, where the round images were printed and the camera was reloaded with film. By 1900, Eastman was selling his cameras for one dollar.

Maddox gave his invention to the world without thought of personal gain. In 1892, photographers from around the world contributed more than $1,000 to help him financially in recognition of his invention. Maddox died in 1902 in relative poverty at the age of eighty-six.

In the years following Maddox's invention, photography steadily improved. Although it had been introduced as early as 1873, not until March 4, 1880, did the New York newspaper the *Daily Graphic* print one of the first examples of a halftone process invented by Stephen Horgan. Photographs could now be published along with words. With improvements in the process by Frederic Ives in 1886, photographs gradually replaced artistic wood or metal engravings (Chapter 9).

Cameras became small enough to fit easily in a person's hand. Oscar Barnack of Germany invented one of the first handheld 35-mm cameras, the Leica, which photographers such as Henri Cartier-Bresson and Robert Frank used to record candid moments of people they saw. Lenses were designed to permit available-light photography. Color and black and white film products were improved to make photography easier and have better quality.

Holography

In 1947, Hungarian scientist Dennis Gabor developed **holography** to improve the quality of views obtained with an electron microscope. The lenses being used with the microscope could not produce a sharply focused picture. Gabor envisioned a process that would not require traditional lenses so that out-of-focus and blurred information in the picture also could be viewed. Consequently, he named his invention from two Greek words, *holos* and *gramma,* or "the whole message." The unique aspect of holographic images is that they reproduce a three-dimensional view of an object photographed on one sheet of film.

Scientists largely ignored Gabor's process for fifteen years until the invention of the laser. As early as 1898, H. G. Wells had written of invaders from Mars with laserlike weapons in his novel *The War of the Worlds*. In 1917, Albert Einstein speculated that radiation from atoms could be stimulated to a higher level of energy. In 1960, Theodore Maiman built and tested the first synthetic ruby laser. Today, laser devices are used for procedures as diverse as reading the bar code prices on goods bought at stores to repairing a damaged retina in a person's eye.

Two U.S. scientists, Emmet Leigh and Juris Upatnieks, were the first to use the light from a laser to develop a process that creates holograms for industrial and scientific purposes. Independent of their efforts, Russian researcher Yuri Denisyuk created a different process that is used for displaying logos on credit cards, jewelry, art presentations, novelty stickers for children, and publications. One of the first mass-produced holographic displays was a picture of an eagle for the March 1984 cover of *National Geographic*. Eleven million holograms were created for the magazine. Many researchers around the world are working on holographic motion picture displays that might make possible regular presentation of three-dimensional television programs and movies. Many believe that holography so far has failed to achieve its full potential as a medium for visual messages.

Instant Photography

Edwin Land was a prolific inventor with more than 500 patents to his name. In 1934, he patented a polarized light filter that helped reduce glare. In 1948, he introduced his most famous invention—a black and white version of the Polaroid fifty-second film camera—and *instant photography*. About fifteen years later he announced a full-color version of the process, calling it Polacolor. The process produced a picture when the backing was peeled away by the photographers after only a sixty-second development time. In 1983, he introduced

the first instant slide film that could be used in a standard 35-mm camera, Polachrome. Today amateur, art, and other professional photographers use the Polaroid instant photography process. Art photographers have learned to manipulate the colors with heat and pressure to produce striking results. Some photographic artists, such as William Wegman, use large-format, 20- by 24-inch cameras to produce fine-quality, one-of-a-kind portraits—a reminder of the past century's daguerreotypes. Commercial photographers regularly use Polaroid materials to check the composition and exposure of a fashion or still-life arrangement before taking pictures with traditional film products.

Digital Photography

In 1984, the Sony company introduced its electronic still video camera, the

Figure 12.6

Frank Church made one of the first snapshots in the history of photography. It shows George Eastman holding his invention—a Kodak camera—that made amateur photography possible.

Mavica—and *digital photography*. Twenty-five color images can be recorded on a two-inch disc and played back through a computer terminal. Since that time, Canon, Nikon, and other companies have introduced their own versions of the computer camera. Innovative newspapers and national news bureaus currently use digital computer technologies, which soon will be common throughout the industry. Whether a subject is photographed with traditional film or by an electronic still video camera where photographers record their pictures on a computer disc, the images can be converted to computerized, digital pictures. The photographers can then make exposure, color balance, and cropping adjustments, just as in a traditional darkroom. The computer images can be sent to an editor anywhere in the world via telephone or satellite links. Once in the newsroom, computer-controlled color separations are automatically made and the pictures are ready for the printing process.

At present, although the new technology saves time, high-quality cameras are expensive and the quality isn't quite as good as that obtained with traditional methods. However, computer equipment and software are rapidly becoming better and more affordable. Many people believe that electronic cameras and computer programs that can easily manipulate images will be common in the next ten years.

The Eastman Kodak Company, which was responsible for the first amateur photography craze in 1880, is now readying another technological breakthrough. It introduced photo compact disc (CD) technology for the amateur photography market. Snapshots taken with traditional film materials can be transferred to a CD, inserted in a player connected to a TV screen, and viewed.

Figure 12.7

A modern 28-mm to 105-mm zoom lens can be set at all three lens types—wide-angle, normal, and telephoto.

Canon USA

Technical Perspective

You should be aware of seven main technical considerations when analyzing an image: lens type, lens opening, shutter speed, film type, camera type, lighting, and print quality.

Lens Type

Lenses come in three variations: wide-angle, normal, and telephoto (Figure 12.7). As their names imply, a wide-angle lens produces an expansive, scene-setting view; a normal lens mimics the angle of view as seen by the human eyes; and a telephoto lens gives a close-up, narrow perspective of a scene. For a 35-mm, single-lens reflex camera, a normal lens has a focal length of 50 mm. Any focal length less than that is considered wide-angle, and any focal length more than that is considered telephoto.

The technical term for the amount of focus within a field of view is *depth of field.* A wide-angle lens will exhibit more depth of field than a telephoto lens, which has a shallow depth of field (Figure 12.8). A photographer must be careful when using a wide-angle lens because the curvature of the lens elements often distorts the sides of the image. A special class of wide-angle lens, the fish-eye lens, is used purposely to distort a scene as a special effect.

Lens Opening

The amount of light exposure hitting the surface of the film is regulated by the size of the lens opening (sometimes called its *aperture*) and the amount of time a camera's shutter stays open. A lens opening also is known as an *f-stop*. Because the f-stop number is based on a fraction, a small aperture has a higher number than a large aperture. For example, an f-stop of 16 is a much smaller lens opening than one of 2. A small lens opening allows less light to enter the camera but gives the picture more depth of field. A large lens opening, necessary during low-light conditions, gives shallow depth of field. A photographer who wants objects in both the foreground and the background to be in focus will use a wide-angle lens with a small aperture opening (Figure 12.9). If the desired effect is for the viewer to concentrate on a single element within a frame, the best choice is to use a telephoto lens with a large lens opening.

Shutter Speed

The amount of time a camera's shutter stays open—its shutter speed—can greatly affect the picture's content. A slow shutter speed will cause blurring of any subject that moves. A faster shutter speed is required to overcome shaking of the camera during exposure (referred to as *camera blur*). An extremely fast shutter speed is necessary to photograph fast-moving subjects without blurring. Sports photographers typically use 1/500 and faster shutter speeds with motor-drive automatic film advancement devices to stop the action (Figure 12.10).

Film Type

Film speed determined by an international standard, "ISO," refers to the amount of light sensitivity in color or black and white films. A low-speed film is considered to be 100 ISO or less; a high-speed film is 400 ISO or above. The higher the ISO number, the more sensitive the film is to light because more light-sensitive crystals are embedded in the film's emulsion. The advantage of using a high ISO film is that the photographer can take pictures in low light. The disadvantage is that the picture appears to look more "grainy" than those shot with low ISO film. A low ISO film gives the best resolution (the least amount of

Paul Martin Lester

Figure 12.8

A telephoto lens isolates singer Mick Jagger from a possibly distracting background.

Paul Martin Lester

Figure 12.9

A wide-angle lens, small aperture opening, and low perspective are techniques used by the photographer to convey a position of power for the man in this portrait taken inside a New Orleans secondhand clothing store. Note that the implied line of hats leads to the reflection of the woman in the mirror.

Figure 12.10

An example of the stopping quality of a camera's shutter is provided by this picture of a young boy seeking relief from the 100 degree heat in Del Rio, Texas. Note how the mesquite tree in the background seems to cradle the boy in space.

Paul Martin Lester

grain) as long as there is enough natural or artificial light.

Color film comes in two types, which are designed for two different lighting sources. *Daylight* color film is balanced for the sun's temperature on a cloudless day between 10:00 A.M. and 2:00 P.M., which is measured at 5,500°K. Because the light from an electronic flash is 6,500°K, the colors recorded on daylight film by sunlight and electronic flash are slightly different. *Tungsten* color film is balanced for indoor lighting in which tungsten-filament lights illuminate the scene. If daylight film is used indoors with tungsten lighting, the picture will have an overall orange cast. If tungsten film is used outdoors, a blue overall color will be the result. Because fluorescent lighting comes in so many variations, no film has been designed specifically for fluorescent lights, although filters can be purchased that correct the color balance slightly. Daylight film used under such lights will have an overall green appearance. Many photographers prefer the slightly orange cast produced with daylight film indoors (as a pleasantly aesthetic value) to the blue or green tones of tungsten film used under nontungsten lighting.

Camera Types

Several different types of cameras are used for various purposes and with varying effects on the picture. Here, we group them as inexpensive, moderately expensive, and high priced.

Inexpensive Cameras Throwaway, instamatic, and instant cameras allow people to take pictures of family members, vacation highlights, and the like but usually without being able to make focusing adjustments. Such cameras usually sell for less than $200.

Moderately Expensive Cameras Single-lens reflex (SLR) cameras that use 35-mm film are today's most popular cameras and usually sell for less than $500 (Figure 12.11). The name refers to a mirror device in the camera that allows the photographer to see and focus on the actual scene that will be recorded by the film. With interchangeable lenses and automatic and manual exposure settings, such cameras produce excellent pictures of subjects ranging from portraits to fast-moving action (Figure 12.12).

Another popular 35-mm camera, which often is used by professional photographers, is the rangefinder. The focusing system relies on two different versions of the scene to be photographed, which the photographer adjusts. When the two scenes merge, the picture is in focus. Many photographers use a rangefinder camera to take sensitive pictures because it is much quieter than a single-lens reflex camera.

High-Priced Cameras This category of camera typically uses film much larger than 35 mm in size. Such cameras and their lenses cost thousands of dollars. Twin-lens reflex cameras have one lens for focusing and another for exposing the film. They use a 120-mm film size, which gives a better quality image than the smaller, 35-mm film size. However, they are seldom used anymore because the popular and handier single-lens reflex 120-mm camera has replaced them generally. These cameras almost always are used for portrait and moderately active fashion photography. As for image quality, the top of the line is the view, or large-format, camera. View cameras typically come in 4-by 5-inch or 8-by 10-inch film formats. Although the cameras must be supported with a tripod, with the image projected upside down on the viewing glass and the picture viewed under a black cloth, the large film size and the perspective adjustment

controls on the camera produce an image of superior quality. View cameras most often are used in studios for advertising and editorial purposes and for architectural photography. A handy, portable version of the 4- by 5-inch view camera, the press camera, was popular with documentary and newspaper photographers from the 1930s until the 1960s (Figure 12.13).

A recent addition to the high-priced camera category is digital cameras for professional photographers. Images can be taken with the cameras and then exhibited and manipulated on a computer; prints can be obtained. Whether a picture is in focus with such a camera isn't as critical as with traditional equipment because more or less focus can be applied to the elements in a picture's frame with the computer's software. Currently, the most popular computer photo retouching software used for publications is Adobe's Photoshop. Sony's Mavica camera can cost as much as $10,000, although amateur versions are priced under $500. Digital photography may get a boost as both Apple Computer and Eastman Kodak have teamed

Courtesy of Nikon, Inc.

Figure 12.11

A modern 35-mm single-lens reflex camera contains a film advance motor-drive mechanism.

Figure 12.12

A newspaper photographer (the author when he was much younger) with two single-lens reflex cameras and motor-drive attachments is about to take a picture of a New Orleans politician.

Courtesy of Bill Haber

Courtesy of George Koshollek, the *Milwaukee Journal*

Figure 12.13

The photographers for the Milwaukee Journal in 1949 pose with their Speed Graphics, 4- by 5-inch press cameras and their bulky flash equipment. Note that there is only one woman and all the men are Anglos.

Figure 12.14

See color section following page 276.

to introduce a professional quality digital camera that costs less than $1,600.

Lighting

Because photography exists due to light, a knowledge of how lighting is used by photographers is essential in the analysis of an image. There are two kinds of lighting: lighting that comes from available sources and lighting that the photographer brings to a location. Natural lighting, most often called available light, is illumination that already exists within a scene. Although its name implies the light from the sun, it can also refer to incandescent bulbs, neon light tubes, or fire from a candle. Lighting equipment that a photographer brings to a photography shoot or that is contained within a studio is called artificial lighting. The most commonly used artificial light for location work is the electronic flash (Figure 12.14). Most photojournalists strive to make their artificial lighting effects look as natural as possible. Experienced photographers avoid harsh shadows on faces and back walls. The use of an electronic flash should never be obvious unless there is a reason for making it so. For example, art photographer Diane Arbus typically included shadows caused by her flash in photographs of unusual people to convey a sense of an ordinary snapshot.

The lighting conditions produced and recorded on film greatly affect the mood of the image. A picture made in low or dim light has a mysterious or a natural quality, a mid-morning shot has a fresh and bright feel, and a picture made at noon with a bright sun gives a healthy appearance. Backlighting gives "life" to a person's hair and separates the person from the background; side lighting often gives a subject a harsh or rugged feel; and silhouettes show an abstract rendering of a subject. The type of lighting used should always match and never distract from the content of the visual message.

Print Quality

Learning how to evaluate the quality of a print in terms of its exposure and contrast is important. But exposure and contrast considerations are different for newspaper, magazine, gallery wall, and screen media reproduction. In addition, the intent of the photographer is vital to an image's aesthetic evaluation. For example, a dark-toned print, although a problem for a printer, may convey a somber mood. Exposure and contrast are closely related. A picture that will reproduce well in a publication must have a full range of tones supplied by proper exposure and contrast.

As a general rule, a picture is considered properly exposed if it shows detail in the shadow areas and in the light areas. Contrast is defined as the difference between the black and white tones of the image. If there are no black or white tones—that is, if all the colors are concentrated around a middle-gray color—the image is said to be low in contrast and will not reproduce well.

Ethical Perspective

Ethical issues are not limited to still photography. The problems associated with making news events public are common to television

Figure 12.15

Photographers in 1911 are shown covering the aftermath of a dynamite explosion in New Jersey in a news picture taken by photojournalist James Hare.

news programs, newspapers, and magazines. Three main ethical issues are associated with mediated images: showing victims of violence, violating the right to privacy, and picture manipulation.

Victims of Violence

After the publication or broadcast of a controversial image that shows, for example, either dead or grieving victims of violence, people often make telephone calls and write letters attacking the photographer as being tasteless and adding to the anguish of those involved. And yet, violence and tragedy are staples of American journalism because readers have always been morbidly attracted to gruesome stories and photographs (Figure 12.15). It is as if viewers want to know that tragic circumstances exist but don't want to face the uncomfortable details.

In 1986, the editors of the *Bakersfield Californian,* an 80,000-circulation newspaper, heard immediately from readers after they ran a controversial photograph on the front page (Figure 12.16). The paper received 500 letters, 400 phone calls, 80 subscription cancellations, and one bomb threat. Most of the reaction centered on the

Figure 12.16

The front page of the Bakersfield Californian *is a study in contrasts. Mickey Mouse and Edward Romero's grieving family share the front page. A reader firestorm of 500 letters to the editor, 400 telephone calls, 80 subscription cancellations, and one bomb threat was the result. Many readers probably were sparked to protest publication of the picture because of its insensitive display near the popular cartoon character.*

golden rule philosophy: Viewers were offended by the picture's strong content. There is no doubt that photographer John Harte's image of the lifeless, five-year-old Edward Romero, halfway zippered in a dark, plastic body bag with family members crying over his body, is a powerful and disturbing picture. Harte applied the categorical imperative; the family scene was a news event that had to be photographed. His editors based their decision to publish the image on utilitarianism—another boy had drowned at the same dangerous location on the Kern River that day. Two months prior to Romero's death, fourteen people had drowned in that stretch of the river. During the month following publication of the picture, only two people drowned in the same area.

Print and broadcast journalists have a duty to report the news as objectively, fairly, and accurately as possible. Editors and producers should be mindful that some images, because of their emotional content, have the potential to upset many people. However, decisions based on ethical philosophies should be guided, never ruled, by viewers.

The Right to Privacy

When victims of violence and their families, through no fault of their own, are suddenly thrust into the harsh light of public scrutiny, they often complain bitterly. Many readers of newspaper and magazine special editions recoiled in horror at the images of people falling from the World Trade Center twin towers (Figure 12.17).

Throughout the history of photography there has been a concern for the privacy rights of those casually enjoying the day without knowing they are secretly being photographed (Figure 12.18). Public officials and celebrities also feel that journalists sometimes cross that "yellow journalism" line in covering their everyday activities. Television actress Roseanne, who frequently advocates her and her family's right to privacy, complained on a national television show that her mother once saw a television camera pointed through the window of her home. Roseanne's mother was forced to lie on the floor to avoid being videotaped.

In 1983, a woman in Florida did more than complain about the loss of her privacy (Figure 12.19). She sued a newspaper for millions of dollars. Hilda Bridges was kidnapped by her estranged husband, Clyde Bridges, and forced to remove all her clothes. He thought that his wife would be unwilling to escape if she were nude. When the police rescued her, photographer Scott Maclay made a picture of Hilda Bridges partially covered by a dish towel running with a police officer. Editors invoked the categorical imperative: The image "best capsulated the dramatic and tragic events." But readers and Bridges complained that the picture caused added grief, the golden rule approach. She argued that the newspaper was simply trying to sell extra copies with a sensational picture

Figure 12.17

The images broadcast from New York City of the World Trade Center during the 2001 aerial attacks from hijacked commercial airliners were almost too unbelievable to be real. Some in the media were criticized for showing images of people desperately searching for help out broken windows or jumping to their deaths.

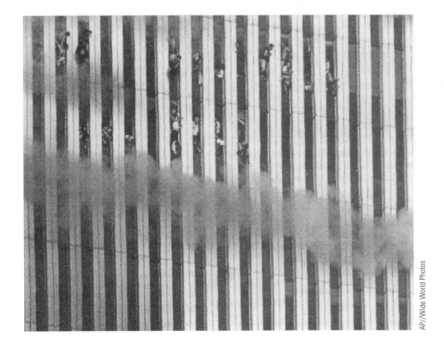

AP//Wide World Photos

on the front page, a hedonistic approach. Bridges won the first court case but was awarded only $10,000. On appeal, that ruling was overturned by a judge who said that the picture "revealed little more . . . than some bathing suits seen on the beaches."

The judicial system in America has recognized that private and public people have different legal rights in terms of privacy. Privacy laws are much stricter in protecting private citizens not involved in a news story than they are for public celebrities who often invite media attention. Although journalists need to be aware of the laws concerning privacy and trespass, ethical behavior should not be guided by what is strictly legal.

Manipulation

To simulate color in daguerreotypes, photo retouchers with brushes and inks added red to cheeks and blue to dresses. Before invention of the halftone process, skillful engravers regularly altered the content of photographs. For example, artists regularly added and subtracted subjects portrayed in photographs for their printed engravings of the Civil War.

More recently, wedding and portrait photographers remove unwanted warts and wrinkles from their subjects. Advertising art directors customarily combine parts of pictures, change colors, and create fantasy images to attract customers. People are well aware of such practices and knowingly suspend belief when looking at portrait and advertising images.

Retouching with a computer is a concern because it alters the original image, which may even be a news image. With traditional retouching methods, the original negative is seldom changed. Because work on a negative would be detectable and difficult, a print is altered. Consequently, if questions about an image arise, the original negative can be consulted. With digital images taken with an

Gernsheim Collection, Harry Ranson Humanities Research Center, University of Texas at Austin

electronic camera, an original can be altered permanently and without detection.

Media critics also express concern about manipulation of documentary images. For a 1982 cover story on Egypt in *National Geographic,* the pyramids of Giza were moved through computer manipulation to accommodate a vertical format. The horseman and

Courtesy of Scott Maclay

Figure 12.18

This 1887 cartoon expresses the opinion of many that photographers often overstep the bounds of decency when taking pictures of the personal and private moments of other people's lives.

Figure 12.19

Scott Maclay of Florida Today *made this picture with a long telephoto lens of the rescue of Hilda Bridges. Bridges later unsuccessfully sued him and his newspaper for invading her privacy.*

tree on the hill on the cover of *A Day in the Life of America* were moved closer together and the moon in the background was enlarged (Figure 12.20). These alterations were made with computer technology to make a horizontal picture fit the cover's vertical format. Rick Smolan, creator of the *Day in the Life* series, for which almost all of the cover images were heavily manipulated, said that "we are very proud of the fact that we were able to use this technology to make covers more dramatic and more impressive."

A picture from a camera that was supposedly found in the wreckage of the World Trade Center was distributed anonymously over the Internet. It showed an unlucky tourist posing on the observation deck seconds before a hijacked airliner hit the building. The initial reaction by many who saw the image on their computers was of shock and sadness (Figure 12.21). But soon after its release, the image was correctly identified as a manipulated fake. Barbara and David Mikkelson on their Web site, "Urban Leg-

ends Reference Pages" (www.snopes2.com), listed a number of incongruities with the image, including: winter clothes were not necessary on September 11, 2001, the wrong type of aircraft was pictured, and the north twin tower is not the one with an observation deck. Later, Peter Guzli, a 25-year-old from Budapest, admitted that he manipulated his tourist snap as a "joke" and sent it to a few friends. One of them distributed it around the world. This case points out the fact that amateurs can easily accomplish picture manipulation. The best defense for such digital tricks is to consider the source. An **email** posting that includes a picture has far less credibility than one displayed on the *New York Times* Web site.

Cultural Perspective

The story of photography, as with any other medium, is never simply about the technical contributions made by scientists and inventors to improve the process. Technological advances allow photographers to communicate the cultural values of the time, but a photographer's style is formed by the culture in which the pictures are made. Studying the images produced within a certain time period is a study of the society from which they come. Throughout the history of photography, various photographic styles have reflected the people and the times.

Photographer as Portraitist

One of the earliest uses of the photographic medium was to capture the faces of people, both famous and ordinary. Eventually, photography became a great equalizer. Because long exposure times and bright sunlight were required for early photography, Victorian portrait subjects appear to be grim, unsmiling people. In reality, they had to keep still in order to get the best picture possible.

Figure 12.20

To make the cover image more eye-catching, editors digitally altered the original horizontal image. The tree and mounted rider were moved closer together and the moon was enlarged with computer technology. Although controversial, the technique no doubt worked—the book was the best-selling photography book in U.S. publication history.

Courtesy of Frans Lanting, *A Day in the Life of America*, © 1986 Frans Lanting

In the nineteenth century, several photographers created a photographic style that reflected the culture of the times. Scottish calotype photographers David Octavius Hill and Robert Adamson made sensitive studies of ordinary people. Julia Margaret Cameron made dynamic, unfocused images of her famous friends: Tennyson, Herschel, Carlyle, Darwin, Browning, and Longfellow. Gaspard Felix Tournachon, or Nadar as he was known, matched his bold shooting style with the strong personalities of the day. Before he photographed the Civil War, Mathew Brady had portrait galleries in New York and Washington. Brady originally took the image of President Lincoln that appears on the five-dollar bill.

From the twentieth century, the portrait tradition continues with August Sander's portraits of everyday workers, Diane Arbus's direct and sensitive portraits of extraordinary subjects, Richard Avedon's large-format images of known and unknown Americans, and Philip-Lorca Di Corcia's "Heads," portraits of random pedestrians at Times Square, New York.

Photographer as Painter

Many painters feared that photography would soon replace their profession. To hedge their bets, some artists became photographers who mimicked the style of allegorical painters to tell a story with photographs in the tradition of paintings of the day. Two photographers who worked in this style during the nineteenth century were Oscar Rejlander and Henry Peach Robinson. Rejlander was a Swede working in Wolverhampton, England, when he perfected the technique of using several negatives to make one picture. Such a procedure was popular among artists-turned-photographers who wanted to make their photographs look like paintings. His most famous allegorical composition, "The Two Ways of Life," involved

the use of thirty separate negatives to produce an image that symbolized the choices that a young man must make (Figure 12.22). Robinson's most famous image, "Fading Away," is a combination print using five separate pictures to show a young woman on her deathbed.

Some photographers tried to imitate painting to gain respect from the fine art world. But others working in the new medium criticized that style because it denied that photography could have its own style distinct and apart from that of the painting of the day. Rejlander himself later criticized the trend toward picture manipulation, and a photographic school known as "straight photography," headed by Edward Weston and Ansel Adams, shunned manipulated work.

Contemporary photographers Vicky Alexander, Richard Prince, and Douglas and Michael Starn use "cut and paste" techniques to produce elaborate artistic renderings from their own or previously published pictures.

Photographer as Landscape Documentarian

Natural scenes have always been a favorite subject of photographers. When the Civil War ended, Timothy O'Sullivan and William Jackson traveled west to explore and photograph scenic views with their awkward wetcollodion technology. In 1873, O'Sullivan made one of his most famous pictures at the

Figure 12.21

The scope of the tragedy in which approximately 3,000 people were killed in the World Trade Center attacks combined with the ordinary look of this snapshot pose give this image initial emotional power. But the picture was quickly and easily disproved as a hoax. Someone used digital software to create the fake.

Oscar Rejlander; George Eastman House

Figure 12.22

One of the first images to be manipulated by a photographer was Oscar Rejlander's "Two Ways of Life." He spliced thirty separate pictures together to form the composite. Gambling, drinking, sexual activity, and vanity are the themes to the young boy's right, and pious behavior, education, philanthropy, and hard work are presented on the other side.

ruins of "White House" at the Canyon de Chelley in Arizona. The power of photography to shape the opinion of others is demonstrated by these views of the land. The images became synonymous with what people thought of as natural and beautiful. Jackson, who lived to be ninety-nine years old, made the first photographs of the Yellowstone area in 1871, which helped convince Congress to set aside the land as the country's first national park because the land was viewed, within the photographs, as naturally beautiful.

Following in the footsteps of the early landscape photographers, Ansel Adams, Wynn Bullock, and Harry Callahan all have made photographs that record exquisitely nature's beauty and sharpen our sense of wonder of it.

Photographer as Artist

Many artists considered photography to be a simple craft, with the camera selecting, composing, and capturing moments.

Another problem artists had with photography was that any number of images could be made from a single negative. Therefore, acceptance of photography as a fine art on the same level with painting was slow in coming. One of the most important figures in elevating the craft to a fine art was the American Alfred Stieglitz. Not only did he exploit photography's unique technological features, he also opened a gallery that exhibited painting and photography on an equal footing and published a critical journal about photography, *Camera Work*. Married to artist Georgia O'Keeffe, he was a strong proponent of modern art photography and inspired many photographers to build that tradition.

Recent photographers who view photography as a way of expressing a deeply personal statement include Neil Chapman, Lucien Clerque, Yasumasa Morimura, and Sandy Skoglund (Figure 12.23). Chapman makes fine-quality palladium prints of subjects that include people, mannequins, and stuffed animals. Clerque creates lush black and white deeply personal nudes. Morimura uses multiple exposures and props to put herself into painterly compositions. Skoglund works hours constructing elaborate sets with painted backgrounds and dreamlike objects that she photographs.

Photographer as Social Documentarian

Because images have the capacity to spark interest and convey emotional messages, many photographers have used the medium to shed light on social problems in the hope of getting the public to act. In 1877, John Thompson teamed with writer Adolphe Smith for a book about London's poor, *Street Life of London.* Newspaper reporter-turned-photographer Jacob Riis used photography to illustrate his writings and lectures on the slums in New York City. In 1890, he published his work in a book, *How the Other Half Lives.* In 1909, Lewis Hine managed to help enact child labor laws with his sensitive portraits of children working in dangerous, backbreaking occupations around the country (Figure 12.24).

Following in their tradition, French photographers Eugene Atget in the 1920s, a social documentarian with a view camera, and Henri Cartier-Bresson in the 1930s, with a small, handheld camera, showed views of ordinary people. Cartier-Bresson captured the "decisive moment"—a term he used to describe the instant when the content and composition of a field of view are at their most revealing.

The FSA photographers documented living conditions of homeless people for the U.S. government during the Great Depression (Figure 12.25). Photographers for *Life* magazine, most notably W. Eugene Smith, produced photographic stories that illustrated the lives of diverse individuals.

Robert Frank, Garry Winogrand, Eugene Richards, and Mary Ellen Mark are maga-

Courtesy of Neil Chapman

Courtesy of Neil Chapman

Figure 12.23

Southern California photographer and educator Neil Chapman has a reputation for making fine-quality prints of unordinary subjects. Although originally a part of two separate exhibits, these two portraits combine into an illustration of Stefan Lorant's "third effect." Discarded objects—whether originally living or inanimate—say much about the culture that produced them.

Figure 12.24

One of the great masters of American documentary photography was Lewis Hine. He helped change child labor laws with his powerful portraits of children working long hours at dangerous jobs. Note the details in the classic Hine picture: the cold harshness of the reflections off the dangerous metal machine where the girl rests her elbow and her tired eyes, slight smile, filthy smock, and shoeless feet.

Lewis Hine; George Eastman House

Figure 12.25

During the Great Depression, the Farm Security Administration of the U.S. government produced numerous classic documents such as this Dust Bowl picture by Arthur Rothstein.

zine and newspaper photojournalists who use a traditional, documentary style of photography. Robert Heincken and Barbara Kruger combine images with text to make critical comments about popular culture.

Critical Perspective

Photography was invented at the height of the Industrial Revolution during which mil-

Arthur Rothstein; Library of Congress

lions of people around the world eventually had more money and free time to spend on taking pictures. Rather than cause the death of painting, photography, with its emphasis on realistic scenes, freed artists to be more expressive. Impressionism and Dadaism, for example, flourished because painters no longer had to render natural scenes exactly on canvas.

Photography educated people about social problems within their own communities and among native peoples around the world. Visual messages inspired immigrants to learn to read the words after the pictures hooked them into buying the newspaper. But photography also was used to mislead and misinform people. Government agencies in both totalitarian and democratic countries used photography to persuade.

Photographs entertain and educate. They provide a historical record that relies on the idea that a camera does not lie (Figure 12.26). Throughout the history of photography, the picture enjoyed far greater credibility than the printed or spoken word. But the picture's credibility is being undermined by computer operators who can alter the content of a digitized news picture as easily as an advertising image.

■ *FUTURE DIRECTIONS FOR PHOTOGRAPHY*

Photography is undergoing exciting and challenging changes. Currently, it is in transition between traditional film and computer technologies. This time in photography's history is not unlike that when the gelatin–bromide dry plate process made the wet-collodion process obsolete. Of the nine major advances in the technology history of photography, only four have significantly changed the way that people think about the medium. The daguerreotype introduced the

Paul Martin Lester

Paul Martin Lester

world to the medium. The wet-collodion process proved that photography could be a high-quality and reproducible method of communicating visual messages to large numbers of people. The gelatin–bromide dry plate process—the most important development—made photography easy for both amateurs and professionals. Finally, digital photography, which combines the medium with television and the computer, promises unlimited possibilities in visual communication.

As electronic digital cameras become common, darkrooms, with their expensive and environmentally hazardous chemicals, no longer will be required (Figure 12.27). As people get used to photographs displayed on an electronic screen, the need for paper prints will fall dramatically. Home entertainment centers of the future are likely to contain collections of images on compact and laser discs that give users the capacity to interact with the images and information on them. With homes linked by cable modems or fiber-optic networks, electronic communication will allow people to instantly send their precious pictures to anyone anywhere in the world and allow electronic newspapers to transmit the latest news stories and images for viewing on teleputers.

Still photography as we currently know it probably will be replaced by digital camcorders that make possible the recording of still and moving images with the same quality. If a viewer wants to see a single frame from a recording, the equipment will simply satisfy that option at the press of a key or utterance of a word or two.

Regardless of how still and moving images are combined and presented, the stilled moment will always be important. A moving image shocks, explains, and entertains, but it is fleeting, quickly replaced by another picture. But a stilled image, one that

Courtesy of Nikon, Inc.

Figure 12.26

News photographs are powerful documents because most viewers still believe that a camera never lies—a naive belief that hasn't been true as long as people have made pictures. Injured firefighters in New Orleans (left) and children throwing stones at British soldiers in Belfast, Northern Ireland (right). If a photographer had used a computer to add more firemen or paid the children to throw stones, would the images have less impact?

Figure 12.27

Nikon's D1X digital camera looks and works much like a traditional film camera but allows direct image transfers to a computer. Compare this camera with the traditional film type in Figure 12.11. Although the two cameras look similar, the digital camera costs about $3,000 more than the Nikon F5 after accessories are purchased for it.

freezes time forever in a powerfully arresting moment, will always have the capacity to rivet a viewer's attention on the subject matter within its frame. There always will be a need for those with the sensitivity and the intellect to produce powerfully emotional still images for educational and entertainment purposes.

DISCUSSION AND EXERCISE IDEAS

- Lead a discussion about Dorothea Lange's portrait of Florence Thompson using the six perspectives.

- Bring in some favorite family snapshots to share in small groups and with the whole class.

- Lead a discussion about the future of photography in this digital age.

- Write a paper that discusses the ethical concerns of showing victims of violence, right to privacy, picture manipulations, pictorial stereotypes, or corporate influences over the newsroom.

INFOTRAC COLLEGE EDITION ASSIGNMENTS

- With "Subject guide" checked, type "Feeding a Vision" in the search area and read the article of the same name by Jack Reznicki. What do you think are the differences between a professional and an amateur photographer?

- With "Subject guide" checked, type "Photojournalism Ethics" in the search area. Read the article "They should not tell a lie" by Deni Elliott and Paul Martin Lester. Do you think it is more harmful for historical pictures to be manipulated than those images seen in a daily newspaper? What is the difference?

Go to the Web site for this book at www.wadsworth.com/product/0534562442 to find more Web links on this subject.

MOTION PICTURES

A film is never really good unless the camera is an eye in the head of a poet.

Orson Welles,

1915–1985

ACTOR, DIRECTOR,

SCREENWRITER, AND

PRODUCER

By the end of this chapter you should know:

- The historical and technical importance of the film *Citizen Kane*.
- Some of the technical considerations that make up a motion picture.
- How the ethical issues of stereotyping and violence within motion pictures are worldwide concerns.

On April 9, 1941, members of the press were treated to an advance showing of a film that many would come to say is the best motion picture ever made. A week after the press showing, *Variety,* the trade magazine for the film industry, ran reviews of fifteen movies. Irene Dunne and Cary Grant were featured in Columbia Pictures' *Penny Serenade.* It was called "an excellent domestic story. Tears and good box office guaranteed." Universal Studios' *Model Wife,* starring Joan Blondell and Dick Powell, was called a "bright domestic comedy." Pre–World War II audiences could try to enjoy indepen-

dent studio Jewel Pictures' *Kidnapping Gorillas,* called "a class D dud."

But the first review in the column, probably placed in that portentous position as a sign of the movie's excellence, was a recent Radio-Keith-Orpheum (RKO) release, *Citizen Kane.* The unknown *Variety* reviewer gushed with excitement over the film and its 25-year-old director: "It happens to be a first-class film of potent importance to the art of motion pictures." First-time film star, writer, producer, and director Orson Welles was called "a workman who is master of the technique and mechanics of the medium . . . [and who] sparkles with originality and

Figure 13.1

Citizen Kane by Orson Welles is an example of master-level performances and technical achievements. Note how the bold use of typography and the printed portrait combine with Welles to reinforce the power of the character.

invention." After the movie's public release, *New York Times* film reviewer Bosley Crowther called *Citizen Kane* "far and away the most surprising and cinematically exciting motion picture to be seen here in many a moon. As a matter of fact, it comes close to being the most sensational film ever made in Hollywood." The highly respected *New Yorker* magazine film critic Pauline Kael, who died in 2001, called the movie the most praised work in the history of cinema (Figure 13.1).

The long-awaited motion picture featured actors from the "Mercury Theater on the Air" radio program that was famous for frightening millions of listeners with its 1938 Halloween broadcast of H. G. Wells's *War of the Worlds*. RKO executives were so impressed with the publicity generated by the controversial program that they offered its director, Welles, a lucrative contract to make pictures for them despite his lack of experience in the medium. But Welles could not have made such a respected film alone; he had a lot of help. Herman Mankiewicz, a Hollywood writer for the previous fifteen years and author of Marx Brothers comedies such as *Monkey Business* and *Horse Feathers,* helped Welles write the screenplay. Welles brought Joseph Cotten, Agnes Moorehead, and several other Mercury radio actors—many making their film debuts—to Hollywood for the picture. Welles also assembled a technical team second to none. Vernon Walker, a photographer for the spectacular movie *King Kong,* coordinated the many special effects in the movie. The film editor, a young RKO staff employee named Robert Wise, would go on to direct *The Day the Earth Stood Still, West Side Story,* and *The Sound of Music.* Mercury Theater colleague Bernard Hermann, who won an Academy Award for his scoring of *All That Money Can Buy,* composed and arranged the music. He became famous for the shrieking violin composition in Alfred Hitchcock's thriller *Psycho* in 1960. Famed cinematographer Gregg Toland, who had just won an Academy Award for his work in *Wuthering Heights,* was in charge of photography. He subsequently photographed such classics as *The Best Years of Our Lives* and *The Grapes of Wrath.*

Despite the excellent work by its cast and production personnel and the over-the-top critical praise, *Citizen Kane* was a financial disaster. Although nominated for several Oscars, the film won only one award—for best screenplay. The best picture award went to John Ford's *How Green Was My Valley,* an ironic winner because it was Ford's

Stagecoach that Welles studied to learn the craft of motion picture production. Within a year RKO had shelved *Citizen Kane* because the studio's executives believed that it would never be a financial success. Although Welles made several movies during his long career, he never again enjoyed the same independence and critical acclaim. Like the motion picture itself—the story of an investigation sparked by the mystery of newspaper tycoon Charles Foster Kane's dying word, "Rosebud"—the story behind the making of *Citizen Kane* partially explains how forces within and outside of Hollywood could squash such a promising career.

◼ ORSON WELLES AND THE MAKING OF CITIZEN KANE

Born on May 6, 1915, Orson Welles was the second son in a troubled, yet creative, family in Kenosha, Wisconsin. His father, Richard, was a frustrated inventor who died early from alcoholism. His mother, Beatrice, was a strong supporter of women's rights, an excellent rifle shot, and a failed professional pianist. His brother Dickie was schizophrenic. The Welleses counted among their friends famous musicians such as Ravel and Stravinsky. From an early age Orson attracted media attention. In newspaper articles he was praised as a "boy genius." At the age of two he could read fluently, at seven he could recite passages from Shakespeare's *King Lear*, and at ten he started producing backyard plays of his own.

During a vacation in Europe when he was eight, his mother died. A few years later, his father died. But his father's love for travel and his mother's independent and artistic influence were firmly entrenched in Welles by that time. His guardian after the deaths of his parents was Dr. Maurice Bernstein, who introduced Welles to magic tricks and puppet

shows. In a tribute to his mentor, Welles included a character in *Citizen Kane* with the same name. Most important, Bernstein gave the young Charles Kane the famous sled named "Rosebud" in the movie (Figure 13.2).

At sixteen, Welles made a walking tour of Ireland, where he ended up at the famous Gate Theater in Dublin and convinced the Irish owners that he was a famous actor for the New York Guild Theater. Welles became the first American actor ever to guest star with the Abbey Players of Dublin. In 1932 he returned to New York but he couldn't find work. So he sailed to Africa and settled in Morocco to write the book *Everybody's Shakespeare*. When he returned to the United States, the prestigious acting troupe led by Katharine Cornell accepted him. At a drama festival he met a teenage actress, Virginia Nicholson, whom he married shortly thereafter. The two had a daughter they named Christopher because they had been hoping for a boy. Five years later, the couple divorced. During this period, Welles also worked in radio. For the NBC broadcast "The March of Time," he supplied the voices for the dictators Mussolini and Hitler. He

Figure 13.2

In the end, the mystery of Kane's last word was relatively simple—the name of the sled young Charles possessed as a child. But the symbolism of the toy is quite complex. While clutching "Rosebud," eight-year-old Kane (Buddy Swan) is introduced to Thatcher (George Coulouris), his future guardian, while his parents (Harry Shannon and Agnes Moorehead) observe.

also played the popular mystery character Lamont Cranston on "The Shadow."

While in New York Welles also became known for his acting abilities and stage productions. In 1936, he directed a famous version of *Macbeth,* set in Haiti, in which he used an all African-American cast. In 1937, he teamed with actor John Houseman, known as the acerbic law professor in *The Paper Chase,* to form the Mercury Theater. The production company staged a popular version of Shakespeare's *Julius Caesar* in 1937 as a modern-day gangster and dictator story. However, lack of funds curtailed the stage productions. In 1938, CBS offered the theater group a contract to produce radio dramas, naming the program "Mercury Theater on the Air."

The radio troupe regularly produced classic works such as *Treasure Island* and *Jane Eyre.* But Welles wanted to stage a science fiction piece for Halloween and selected H. G. Wells's *War of the Worlds.* The night before the broadcast, however, he thought the script too dull and rewrote it in a documentary style similar to the "March of Time" news program. The result was one of the most sensational broadcasts ever produced. Despite numerous reminders that the show was a fictionalized account of a novel, millions of radio listeners were convinced that Martians had invaded Earth. People fled in all directions to escape cities, limbs were broken in fights as people tried to get away, and priests were called to hear final confessions. Numerous people had heart attacks, and, tragically, a woman in Pittsburgh committed suicide rather than face the monsters from Mars.

One of the readers of the "War of the Worlds" controversy was RKO Pictures president George Schaefer. With a promise of complete freedom over production and a three-picture deal worth $100,000 each, Schaefer lured Welles to Hollywood to make movies. To learn the craft, Welles studied many of the films in New York's Museum of Modern Art. He particularly was interested in John Ford's classic 1939 western *Stagecoach,* reportedly watching the film more than forty times.

The early plan was to make a film version of Joseph Conrad's *Heart of Darkness.* But when World War II began in Europe, Schaefer had to cancel the project because filming in Africa wouldn't be possible and the actor chosen for the lead role of Kurtz had been interned in a concentration camp in Austria. Schaefer suggested a more traditional thriller, *The Smiler with a Knife,* but then abandoned that project because stars Carole Lombard and Rosalind Russell refused to work with such a young director. Welles wanted Lucille Ball for the role, but this time Schaefer vetoed the choice because Ball wasn't famous enough. Welles decided to produce a movie that he and screenwriter Herman Mankiewicz had conceived. And here is where, as they say, "the plot thickens."

Mankiewicz's story, originally titled *American,* was an obviously critical biography of newspaper publisher William Randolph Hearst. As a former newspaper reporter, Mankiewicz was familiar with the intricacies of Hearst's financial empire and his personal strengths and failings. As a visitor to Hearst's castle in central California, San Simeon, Mankiewicz had witnessed many of the excesses made possible by the publisher's enormous wealth. Hearst's passion for collecting art objects from around the world, staging elaborate picnics, and supporting his actress protégée Marion Davies all were a part of Mankiewicz's screenplay. Also included in the story were Davies's obsession with jigsaw puzzles and her excessive drinking, characterized by Kane's girlfriend, played by actress Susan Alexander. Although Welles always denied the connection between Hearst and Kane, no one was convinced.

Shooting for *Citizen Kane* began on July 30, 1940, and was completed on October 23 under extremely tight security, which fanned rumors about its connection to Hearst. The film was scheduled to be released on Valentine's Day, 1941. But the opening was delayed after Louella Parsons, Hollywood correspondent for the Hearst newspapers, viewed an early screening. She relayed the message to Schaefer that Hearst would sue the studio if it released the film. However, the Hearst organization quickly dropped the threat as a pointless exercise and tried a different approach. In a one-woman telephone campaign, Parsons put pressure on many Hollywood studio executives by referring to a proposed series of newspaper articles on their use of illegal immigrants. Nicholas Schenck, head of MGM, on behalf of other studio presidents, reportedly offered Schaefer $800,000, the cost of making the movie, if he would destroy it. Luckily, Schaefer considered it an offer he could refuse.

Hearst probably never saw the movie. As a courtesy, Schaefer sent a copy to San Simeon, where Hearst had a movie theater as part of the castle complex. But when the film was eventually returned, the seals that bound the metal film cans hadn't been broken.

Meanwhile, Welles threatened to sue RKO if the film wasn't released. Schaefer took action and invited the press for a sneak preview on April 9. Welles was relaxing in a Palm Springs spa on the advice of his doctor, who was worried that the director was close to a mental breakdown, when he heard that the critics loved the movie. However, the film was still embroiled in controversy.

Because of the threats by Hearst, Schaefer was having trouble finding theaters that would show the movie. For the public openings in New York, Chicago, and Los Angeles, RKO-owned theaters were hastily prepared. New York's Radio City Music Hall refused to run the film after Parsons threatened to run

an uncomplimentary story about John D. Rockefeller in the Hearst-owned *American Weekly*. Rockefeller was part owner of the famous music hall. When Hearst felt that the published attacks on the film gave it too much publicity, the negative stories ceased, but Hearst allowed no advertising about the movie to appear in any of his newspapers. Movie theater chains such as Warner Bros., Loew's, and Paramount counted greatly on advertising and commentary in the Hearst publications about their films. Consequently, they refused to show the movie for fear of retaliation by Hearst. In a last, desperate attempt to have the film shown, Schaefer sent the picture as a package deal with other RKO movies. Nevertheless, most theater owners did not show the movie.

The final blow was the Academy Awards ceremony. Although nominated in several categories and critically acclaimed, *Citizen Kane* came away with a minor award that Welles shared with Mankiewicz for the screenplay. According to *Variety*, many members of the Academy voted in a bloc against Welles because of his reputation as a "genius," the fight with Hearst, and the perception that the movie was a pretentious "art film." In a snub to the Academy Award he shared with Mankiewicz, Welles wrote the screenwriter, "You can kiss my half." Mankiewicz replied, "You wouldn't know your half from a whole in the ground." Tragically, Mankiewicz's promising screenwriting career was cut short by alcoholism.

Even without the Hearst organization's opposition, *Citizen Kane* probably wouldn't have been a financial success. Mass theater audiences of the day were accustomed to seeing lightweight action and comedic films—not a dark, moody psychological drama with an unhappy ending. Film critic André Bazin has written that the motion picture was "decidedly above the mental age of the average American spectator."

Welles continued to fulfill his contractual obligation to RKO with his next film, *The Magnificent Ambersons,* which was released in 1942. The movie never received the critical acclaim of *Kane,* probably because RKO executives appropriated the film while Welles was in South America working on his next picture. About one-third of his movie was changed, including the ending. Afterward, he was locked out of the studio. In 1943, to the surprise of everyone, he married actress Rita Hayworth and made a film with her, *The Lady from Shanghai,* for Columbia Pictures. It turned out to be another financial disaster. After a stormy relationship and a daughter, Rebecca, the two divorced in 1947.

Hollywood branded Welles a troublemaker. Although he achieved success with several Broadway productions and roles in other directors' films, his own pictures, and work on television, the critical praise of *Kane* was never repeated. Late in his life, grossly overweight but still in possession of a Shakespearean voice and able to tell insider Hollywood stories, he made commercials for Eastern Airlines and Paul Masson wines and appeared regularly on Johnny Carson's "The Tonight Show." He died of a heart attack at the age of seventy in his Los Angeles home in 1985. Unlike Kane, no one heard his last word. Welles once said that "Hollywood is a golden suburb for golf addicts, gardeners, men of mediocrity, and satisfied stars. I belong to none of these categories." Indeed. Welles and his *Citizen Kane* are a genre all their own.

Most directors have a permanent place in motion picture history for a body of work that demonstrates their genius. Orson Welles is famous—perhaps infamous—for only one movie, but it is a work of unparalleled brilliance. In public opinion polls sponsored by art councils, film expositions, and television networks, *Citizen Kane* is always at the top of every list of great films. The reason is simple: The movie is a masterpiece.

■ ANALYSIS OF CITIZEN KANE

The opening of the movie is a metaphor for the entire picture. In a series of tracking shots that begin outside the castle gate of the once stately Xanadu estate showing a NO TRESPASSING sign, the camera moves us closer to Kane's bedroom window, which always maintains the same position in various shots. And just when the window is reached, the light suddenly goes off and Kane speaks his last word, the enigmatic "Rosebud" (Figure 13.3). The scene loudly shifts to a newsreel that serves as an obituary for the publishing tycoon. But toward the end of the footage, the documentary stops and the scene shifts to a smoky room filled with journalists who are given the task to discover, through interviews with his associates, why Kane uttered the word "Rosebud." The rest of the film is divided into four sections in which his banker reveals Kane's early life, his business associate tells about the newspaper empire and details of his first marriage, his former best friend analyzes his personality and the reason for his downfall, and his second wife, in an alcoholic haze, gives details about the frustrated and sad old man Kane had become. In the end, none of his associates can solve the mystery of "Rosebud." But the audience learns the secret. The scene of workmen burning some of the objects that have accumulated over the years in the castle shows the name "Rosebud" on a sled given to Kane as a boy. A symbol of lost youth or missed opportunities, or an acknowledgment of Kane's love of objects over people—viewers are left to make sense of the movie's central riddle on their own.

Welles didn't invent any of the film techniques used in the movie. He simply combined many different ideas into one work. Until *Kane,* movies were dominated by snappy dialogue and unusual situations, but the visual messages weren't as important.

Orson Welles combined the most recent technical innovations for producing visual messages with choreographed actions by actors to move the plot along on several levels. Cinematographer Gregg Toland took advantage of new lighting and film stock to perfect a technique called "pan-focus." (The technique is now called **deep focus** so that it won't be confused with *panning,* a camera movement.) A soft-focus shooting style had dominated films previously because low-wattage lamps and slow film meant that lenses had to be set wide open to obtain a shallow depth of field. But with higher-quality lights, faster film, and wide-angle lenses, Toland could have a depth of field that carried from twenty inches to several hundred feet (Figure 13.4). Consequently, Welles was able to exploit this technical advantage in his staging of the actors. Action could take place simultaneously in the foreground and in the background. Bazin has written that the technique gave viewers much more freedom in deciding which part of the screen they wanted to watch. Such deep-focus shots also required that the sets used in the film be enormous. Welles requested that the sets include muslin ceilings so that extreme up-angle perspectives could be used. Few directors ever thought to bother with ceilings for their sets because most shots were at eye level. Also, lighting and recording the actors are more difficult when ceilings are included in a set. Nevertheless, Welles presented a much more realistic visual message with the addition of ceilings. Lighting was high in contrast and usually from behind. The effect dramatically separated the actors from their surroundings. Most previous films had used low contrast and flat lighting techniques.

When asked if he knew that he was making a masterpiece, Welles answered simply, "I never doubted it for a single instant." The trouble with creating a perfect work of art your first time out is: Where do you go from there? Unfortunately, Welles could not

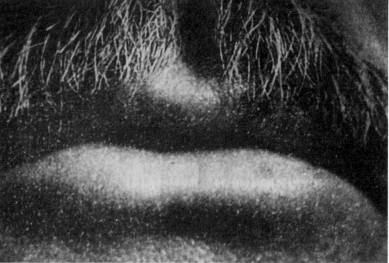

Figure 13.3

The dying word from the lead character in Citizen Kane *was the mysterious "Rosebud." Close-up photography and enhanced audio effects emphasized this important scene in the movie.*

improve upon his initial work because such an effort would have been almost impossible for anyone.

Citizen Kane the movie, Citizen Kane the character, and *Citizen Kane* the critical biography of William Randolph Hearst are facets of a masterpiece that will never be completely understood. As with all brilliant works of art, there are disagreements over its significance, problems with its confusing messages, and questions about its link to actual people. Nevertheless, the reason that the motion picture art form will endure is the hope that someone, someday will produce a work of equal importance.

■ *MOTION PICTURES AND THE SIX PERSPECTIVES*

Personal Perspective

Motion pictures began as simple films of everyday activities, capturing ordinary events to show the capabilities of this new medium. Soon, however, visionaries discovered that motion pictures could be much more than static camera shots of workers leaving a factory. Early in the history of the movies, filmmakers exploited the aesthetic,

Figure 13.4

The "deep-focus" effect created by cinematographer Gregg Toland, as evident in this scene from Citizen Kane, *allowed the viewer more control in selecting which part of a set to watch. Note also that the top of the set is covered—another innovation of the motion picture.*

political, and economic advantages of the film medium. This **triptych** of functions probably explains why so many different terms—motion picture, cinema, documentary, film, and movie—have been used to describe the presentation of single-framed, sequential images that move through a machine so rapidly that they create the illusion of movement on a screen.

Movie theaters are magical places (Figure 13.5). Nowhere else is the screen as large, the sound as clear, the seats as plush, and the popcorn as fresh. People go to the movies because there is nothing else like that feeling when the lights suddenly start to dim, voices quiet to a whisper, and the screen glows from the projector. The huge horizontal frame has the power to take us to another country, another planet, or another person's

point of view. With stars, scenery, and situations, movies are dramatic and riveting. And yet the screen is simply a mirror that reveals all the best and worst qualities of everyone sitting in the theater. That is why the stories and the characters are so familiar.

Historical Perspective

The history of the motion picture can be summed up in one word—adaptation. Innovative studio executives, directors, and inventors worked to make sure that movies would become and remain a popular source of entertainment. Whenever movie sales dipped, the industry created better stories, turned up the publicity about the stars, and developed innovative technology to attract more viewers. When audiences became

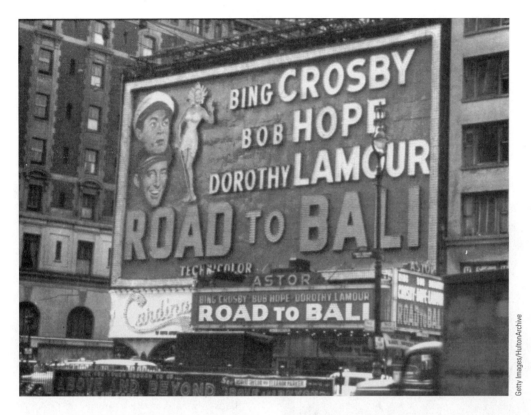

Getty Images/HultonArchive

Figure 13.5

Movie marquees of the 1940s, such as this one for the Astor Theater in New York City, were large and eye-catching to attract attention. Today, newspaper advertisements and television trailers perform the same function.

bored with the documentary, home-movie style of the short films at the turn of the twentieth century, the action-adventure drama was created. When radio became a popular mass medium, movies followed with films that could be both heard and seen. When sales dropped during the Great Depression because so many people couldn't afford a ticket, the studios generated excitement about movies and their stars while at the same time lowering prices and introducing double features. When television threatened to keep moviegoers at home in the 1950s and 1960s, movie screens became larger and wider, films were shot in color, and three-dimensional movies were tried. Today the motion picture industry is adapting to challenges from other entertainment sources by producing "must-see" blockbusters, cutting costs with multiplex theaters, adding improvements in image quality and sound, and diversifying into other entertainment businesses—television, motion simulator amusement park rides, and the World Wide Web.

A Sideshow Amusement

With the invention of Richard Maddox's gelatin–bromide dry plate process in 1871 and George Eastman's roll film innovation in 1888, still photography could be transformed into the motion picture medium (Chapter 12). American inventor Thomas Alva Edison, who had invented the phonograph in 1877, had the idea in the 1880s to etch pictures on his phonograph cylinders so that music could be illustrated with images—an early version of the music video. Some of his early experiments have survived over the years. One of his assistants, William Kennedy Laurie Dickson, however, convinced the inventor to switch to celluloid film produced by the Eastman Company. Dickson reportedly made a motion picture using a machine with the awkward name of Kinetophonograph to demonstrate synchronized motion with sound on celluloid film in 1889, but no record of the movie exists—probably because Edison stood by the phonographic cylinder invention.

In 1891, Edison patented his Kinetograph camera and the Kinetoscope peephole viewer in the United States. His machine contained an eyehole through which a viewer could watch a film strip pulled along

by the machinery. But so little did Edison think of this new invention that he never bothered to pay the $159 patent fee to secure European rights.

In 1891, Edison and Dickson made the first motion picture to be preserved in the collection of the Library of Congress. The short film was a close-up of a slightly self-conscious mechanic pretending to sneeze for the camera in *Fred Ott's Sneeze* (Figure 13.6). Within three years, Edison had established Kinetoscope arcades in which phonographs could be heard on one side and thirty-second movies viewed on the other. Edison sold each viewer to arcade owners for $250 and each film for $10. Customers were charged 25 cents for each viewing. Dickson made the films, which were fifty feet long, with no editing or camera movements. Early movies simply showed dancers, clowns, and other entertainers performing in front of the camera inside a tar paper shack called the "Black Maria" on the grounds of Edison's laboratory in New Jersey.

Because Edison didn't secure patent rights in Europe, an English scientific instruments maker, Robert Paul, bought a Kinetograph and made an important technical improvement. Because Edison was so fond of electricity, his camera was large and not easily moved. Consequently the films produced with the electrified machine had to be staged productions inside a studio. Paul fitted the camera with a hand crank, which allowed more portable setups.

In 1894, the two French brothers Auguste and Louis Lumière purchased one of Paul's Kinetographs. The two were already in the photography business, because their father owned a successful factory in Lyon that made photographic plates. Their variations of the Kinetoscope proved to be the most important technical advance for the medium. The Lumière brothers invented a camera that not only could make films but

Figure 13.6

The first motion picture in the Library of Congress collection is the short Thomas Edison film Fred Ott's Sneeze *of 1891. Ott's sneeze should be viewed column by column starting from the top left.*

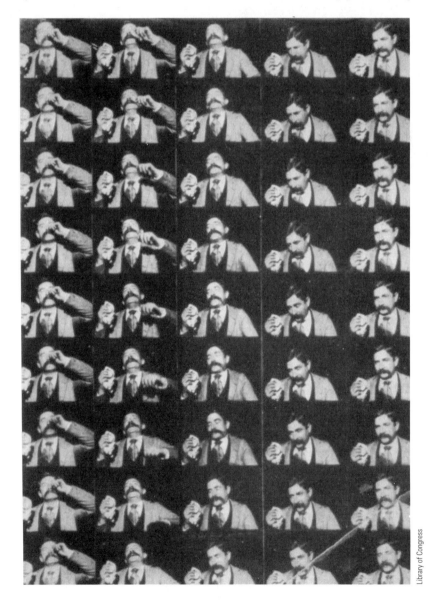

Library of Congress

also could process and project the movies. With Paul's hand-crank variation, the camera easily could be taken anywhere and the films shown to audiences. They made the 35-mm film size the standard for all cameras and projectors. Edison showed his movies at forty frames a second, which resulted in relatively high quality animation but often caused the film to jam in the machine. The Lumières used a film speed of sixteen frames a second, which also became an industry standard until movies with sound required a faster twenty-four frames a second. They named their invention the *Cinématographe,* which soon was shortened to *cinema.*

The Lumières' first films were similar to those created by purchasers of video cameras—glorified home movies. Early in 1895, the two previewed their first effort, *Workers Leaving the Lumière Factory,* with a group of friends and family members (Figure 13.7). After receiving the enthusiastic support of their first audience, the two waited almost a year to announce their invention publicly. They used the time to build a large number of cameras and distribute them around the world. On December 28, 1895, the first public audience for motion pictures was treated to a series of short films in the basement of the Grand Cafe in Paris. Auguste and Louis were not present at this first showing because they were busy preparing for a larger opening in their own movie theater. Their father, Antoine, introduced the silent movie selections that included the factory short, a Lumière baby enjoying a meal, a comedy about a young boy teasing a gardener, and a train arriving into a station. The latter movie produced howls from the audience, who, unaccustomed to the new medium, were afraid that a real train was about to crash through the screen. Shortly thereafter, the Lumières established the first movie theater. It seated 120 people and projected twenty shows a day at half-hour inter-

vals. With an admission price of a single franc, the brothers made about 2,500 francs a day. Filmmakers, with strict instructions not to reveal the secret of the camera, sent films from every part of the world except Antarctica. Soon the Lumières had four movie theaters in Paris.

Edison's short films, usually produced by William Dickson, differed from the Lumière works in a fundamental way. Instead of a documentary approach, where the camera filmed people and situations often without them being aware of its presence, Edison favored heavy-handed staged productions in the fiction genre. Typical was the gruesome *Mary, Queen of Scots,* in which her head was seen to roll off the guillotine. As it turned out, both the Lumières and Edison had it wrong. What the public wanted was the best of both documentary and staged productions—fictionalized films set outside in the open air.

One of the first to realize the aesthetic potential of movies was George Méliès of France (Figure 13.8). The son of wealthy parents, Méliès started his career as a caricaturist, stage designer, magician, and

Figure 13.7

Unlike Edison, Auguste and Louis Lumière thought motion pictures would be viewed in theaters with large audiences and that subjects would be taken outside of a sterile studio. One of the first films by the Lumière brothers is the 1895 film Workers Leaving the Lumière Factory. *With its objective camera approach, the work has a contemporary documentary style.*

Library of Congress

Paul Martin Lester

Figure 13.8

The grave of French director George Méliès, located in Pére Lachaise cemetery, Paris, is adorned with flowers by fans of the man who introduced the field of special effects to the motion picture industry.

actor. At an early Lumière showing, Méliès was intrigued by the new medium. But when he inquired about purchasing a camera, the Lumière brothers, as they did with all requests, politely refused to sell their device. But Méliès purchased a camera from Paul and made his first movie, *A Game of Cards,* in 1896. By 1900 the public had grown bored with documentaries. The Lumière brothers, more inventors than artists, went on to develop the first practical color photographic film—the autochrome (Chapter 12). Méliès stepped in to fill the void left when the Lumière brothers and Edison quit production. Méliès created surreal films inspired by his experiences as a magician and stage performer. By 1907, fiction films outnumbered nonfiction works for the first time.

Méliès is considered to be the founder of movie special effects. Once while he was filming a scene, the camera suddenly jammed, but started up a few moments later. When he processed the film, Méliès discovered that the accident resulted in a "jump cut" in which the actor suddenly disappeared from view. This special trick along with his elaborate sets and animation techniques resulted in charming films that exploited the magical quality of motion pictures. His most famous work is the ten-minute classic *A Trip to the Moon* made in 1902. Roughly based on the Jules Verne stories of *From the Earth to the Moon* and *Around the Moon,* the movie shows a group of professors who take a voyage in a rocket ship that lands in one of the "eyes" of the face on the moon (Chapter 11).

The Action-Adventure Film

One of the early innovators in filmmaking who understood the public's desire to see action movies produced outside a studio was the American Edwin Stratton Porter.

In 1896, he had left the U.S. Navy and went to work for Edison as a mechanic, electrician, and Vitascope operator. He soon left Edison's employ, bought his own camera, made films, rented a theater, and showed his movies under the name of Thomas Edison, Jr. He made his two most famous pictures in 1903—*The Life of an American Fireman* and *The Great Train Robbery.* They showcase his technical achievements in which dramatic exterior chase scenes with innovative angles and panning camera movements are cut with interior, studio views that were dull by comparison, but nevertheless moved the action along. His *Fireman* movie, for example, tells the story of rescue workers outside a burning house and cuts to a frightened woman and child inside. In *Robbery,* he used camera pans and hand-painted some of his prints with red to make gunshots and explosions more dramatic (Figure 13.9).

The First Blockbuster

The rise and fall of David Wark Griffith is a metaphor for the entire silent era. Edwin Porter was making *Rescued from an Eagle's Nest* for Dickson's Biograph Studio in 1907 when he hired Griffith, a young actor, for a lumberjack role. Born in Kentucky, Griffith had been a reporter for a Louisville newspaper and had written and acted for the stage when he was signed as an actor at five dollars a day. Because of the growing popularity of U.S. movies, separate theaters outside of vaudeville houses were built. These nickelodeons, named for the price of a ticket, required the production of many more films. With his stage experience, Griffith soon was offered a director's position.

Griffith is best known for the infamous *The Birth of a Nation.* The movie is a demonstration of the maturity of Griffith's film work, but unfortunately tells a mean-spirited and racist story (Figure 13.10). Originally titled *The Clansman* from the book of the same name by Thomas Dixon, the movie tells of the history of the United

States immediately after the Civil War. When a struggling community is attacked by a ravaging group of African Americans (most were white actors played with heavy black makeup), the people are saved by white-hooded members of the Ku Klux Klan (KKK) who ride into town on horseback. Griffith probably was attracted to the story because he was a southerner and his father had been a Confederate soldier.

Compared to the other Biograph movies, *Birth* was an incredible gamble. Most films of the day cost no more than $100 for the total production. *Birth* cost about $83,000—the most ever invested in a motion picture at that time. It required six weeks of rehearsal, nine weeks to shoot, and the services of thousands of actors and horses. The three-hour movie premiered at Clune's Auditorium in Los Angeles on February 8, 1915, to immediate controversy. The NAACP issued a pamphlet called "Fighting a Vicious Film" and began a boycott of the studio. Many leading politicians and civic leaders were unanimous in their condemnation because of the racist message of the movie. When it was shown in Boston, a race riot followed, but attendance at road show engagements was high. The public probably was drawn to the movie by its controversy, the war theme, the lovers' story, and the dramatic music (supplied by an organist at the theater). Over the years, *The Birth of a Nation* reportedly made some $20 million. Although the KKK had disbanded in 1869, the film also was responsible for the racist extremist group's revival.

Although *Birth* was motion picture's first blockbuster hit and made a fortune for Griffith, he was stung by the adverse commentary about the film. His next movie, *Intolerance,* was an attempt to improve his reputation. Griffith invested all the profits from *Birth* to make the epic that was a complex, eight-hour financial disaster. *Intoler-*

ance told four different stories, from a young man falsely accused of murdering a baby to a historical drama set in ancient Babylon. The critics and the public of his day never appreciated the film. It cost Griffith his financial independence, and he had to ask others for backing. In 1919, Griffith, Charles Chaplin, Douglas Fairbanks, and Mary Pickford formed their own film company, which they named United Artists.

In his later years, Griffith lost much of the creative energy associated with his early films. In the 1930s, he tried to make movies with sound, but his lack of technical experience with audio and studio executives, who viewed him as a quaint, silent-movie dinosaur, prevented him from doing so. For the last seventeen years of his life he lived as a virtual hermit in Los Angeles. He died in 1948 on his way to a Hollywood hospital from a hotel where he had been living alone.

Lasting Legacy of Silent Films

The silent-film period is important because during that time the motion picture industry established itself as a powerful business force, started the careers of

Figure 13.9

The first action-adventure motion picture was the 1903 classic The Great Train Robbery *by Edwin Porter. Unlike the films by Thomas Edison, Porter filmed his movies outside of a stage set. Here, three train robbers make their escape while ducking gunfire.*

Getty Images/Hulton Archive

Figure 13.10

David Griffith glorified the Ku Klux Klan in The Birth of a Nation. *In this publicity still, members of the vigilante organization (and their horses) wear masks to protect their identities. (Present-day Klan members don't wear a spiked-helmet accessory.)*

numerous directors, and began the concept of "stars," which were elevated to a higher status than mere actors. The triad of business dealings, directors, and stars crucial to filmmaking during that time remain vital in today's world of moviemaking.

The Movie Business

Some of the most powerful studio executives had humble beginnings. Adolph Zukor, a Hungarian immigrant, established his first movie theater in 1904. Eight years later he became an independent producer. Porter convinced him to show full-length motion pictures in his theater chain. Zukor's production and theater business was later named Paramount Pictures. Marcus Loew was a successful furrier and owner of a chain of vaudeville houses in 1904. When it became evident that vaudeville would lose out to movie theaters, in 1924 Loew bought the Metro Picture Company and the Goldwyn Picture Company founded by Samuel Goldfish (who had changed his name). When Loew put a theater owner, Louis B. Mayer, in charge of production, their partnership eventually led to the powerful studio

Metro-Goldwyn-Mayer (MGM). During World War I, many European companies were forced to stop commercial production, which allowed Hollywood to take over. By 1915, most American studios had established complexes in the Los Angeles suburb of Universal City, where the weather, environment, and real estate prices were favorable for movie production. Many Europeans who migrated because of the war became successful in the film industry.

Several "poverty row" yet successful studios flourished during this period. Three of the most famous stars in Hollywood—Chaplin, Fairbanks, and Pickford—formed United Artists along with director D. W. Griffith to give them more autonomy over their work. Nevertheless, they found distributing their movies difficult because Paramount owned most of the theaters. In 1925, Gloria Swanson and two years later Samuel Goldwyn joined the group and helped turn United Artists into a major studio. William Fox, an exhibitor and movie distributor in 1912, merged his company with Joseph Schenck and Darryl Zanuck of Twentieth Century. The American Pathé Studio earned its keep with a popular serial, *The Perils of Pauline*, in 1914. The Hearst newspapers also featured cartoon versions of twenty melodramatic films. Theater owners Harry, Albert, Sam, and Jack Warner started making their own films in 1912 under the name Warner Bros.

The proliferation of studios indicated the rise in popularity of motion pictures generally, with the public clamoring for new movies to satisfy their film appetite. The numerous business deals among producers, distributors, and banking groups (J. P. Morgan and John D. Rockefeller) reflected the rising costs of movies.

Directors Although making movies has always been a collaborative effort, the role of the director is the key to a production. A director turns the words of the screenwriter, the talent of the actors, and the expertise of the technical crew into an art form with a unique style.

Several early American film directors became famous. Mack Sennett was an actor under Edison and later worked for Griffith. In 1912, he financed his own production company, the Keystone Film Company of Los Angeles. The studio was famous for its madcap chase scenes involving the Keystone Kops and romantic comedies featuring the sophisticated star Gloria Swanson. Keystone launched the careers of writer-turned-director Frank Capra and comedic actors Harold Lloyd and Charles Chaplin, the most famous silent-film star. But when the silent-film period ended, Sennett's comedies were no longer popular.

Hal Roach was Sennett's biggest competitor in directing comedies. Roach wooed Lloyd away with more money. With his alter ego, whom he called the "Glass Character," Lloyd made more than 100 one-reel comedies that exhibited his acrobatic skills and a sophisticated sense of visual humor. Roach went on to direct Stan Laurel and Oliver Hardy in several comedy classics and the *Our Gang* comedy series.

The most famous silent-film director was Cecil B. DeMille, who often clashed with studio executives over his high budgets. For example, his 1923 *The Ten Commandments* cost more than a million dollars to produce. DeMille had been inspired to become a director after watching Porter's *The Great Train Robbery.* He initially worked for Samuel Goldwyn and moved their production facilities to a barn in Hollywood in 1914 to begin making feature films. DeMille was popular with the public because his movies always contained a hint of sensuality as opposed to Griffith's sentimentality.

In the tradition of the Lumière brothers, the English documentary photographer Robert Flaherty began shooting a Canadian Eskimo's struggle to survive in 1913. In 1922, his documentary classic *Nanook of the North* was released. The film is noted as an early example of documentary filmmaking, but Flaherty often posed Nanook in order to make the movie more dramatic. Modern documentary directors try to be more objective in their presentations.

Erich von Stroheim, a child of Viennese aristocratic parents, arrived in the United States in 1906. He played one of many extras hired by Griffith to portray African Americans in blackface for *The Birth of a Nation.* During the filming of *Intolerance,* he was promoted to assistant director. His most famous work was the 1925 classic *The Merry Widow,* which questioned the social mores of a declining upper class.

In France, Abel Gance expanded the language of film by creating a 1927 masterpiece, *Napoleon.* Gance used three projectors to form a triptych by which he treated the audience to various views of the action-packed scenes.

The silent-film period in Germany was cut short by the interference of Adolf Hitler and the Nazi Party. Robert Wienz's tale of supernatural powers and murder frightened 1919 viewers in his *The Cabinet of Doctor Caligari.* The German expressionist movement inspired the set designs, and the actors walked in "living paintings." F. W. Murnau's *Nosferatu* (1922), the first version of Bram Stoker's *Dracula,* is a film classic for its experimental use of lighting and makeup effects for actor Max Schreck. Probably the most famous German director of this period was Fritz Lang, who produced *Destiny* (1921) and the futuristic *Metropolis* (1926), a film noted for its stunning visual effects (Figure 13.11). Supposedly, the latter was one of Hitler's favorite movies and the Nazi

Figure 13.11

"Metropolis. 1926. Lithograph: 83 × 36½." In this art deco inspired poster by Schulz-Neudamm, architecture and robotic behavior are linked in a dynamic way—as they are in the film by Fritz Lang.

Schulz-Neudamm, *Metropolis* (1926) © 2002 The Museum of Modern Art

leader invited Lang, who was half-Jewish and a liberal, to make films for the Third Reich. Fortunately, Lang and many other German directors escaped from Germany and settled in Hollywood. Unfortunately, director Leni Riefenstahl, inspired by *Metropolis,* committed her talents to the Nazi Party with her 1935 classic propaganda film, *Triumph of the Will.* Nevertheless, her work is every bit as innovative and cinematic as that of the other German directors. Particularly striking is her film about the 1936 Berlin Olympic games, *Olympia* (1938),

which celebrates the human body rather than military might.

By far, one of the most influential directors in the history of silent films was the Russian Sergei Eisenstein. Like Orson Welles, Eisenstein is known primarily for his innovative film technique in one motion picture. The son of a shipbuilder, he studied architecture and engineering before being bitten by the theater bug. He gave up his engineering career when he landed a job with an experimental theater where he designed sets and directed plays. He became interested in filmmaking after watching Griffith's use of montage sequences in *The Birth of a Nation* to tell the story of rich and poor characters. In 1925, he released his classic *The Battleship Potemkin,* which told the story of the 1905 sailors' rebellion in Odessa and the Tsar's brutal reprisal. The movie is probably best known for its famous "steps" scene in which montage and quick editing techniques created dramatic tension (Figure 13.12). Eisenstein was inspired by Dadaism, in which multiple images were employed for maximum graphic effect. With film pieces as short as $\frac{1}{16}$ second, the murder of Russian civilians by the Tsar's troops (an incident that probably was not as severe as shown) is one of the best examples of the art of editing in the history of film. Eisenstein became a teacher of motion picture art and wrote several books about the power of film as a communication medium before his death in 1948.

Stars Some actors and actresses became so popular that people went to the movies to see them rather than their actions. Mary Pickford and Douglas Fairbanks (who were united first in the movies and then in marriage in 1920) and Charles Chaplin were stars of this magnitude. The charisma of these stars boosted their salaries to enormous amounts (and charisma is the reason, even today, why stars are usually paid more than directors). Stars paid a personal price

for their high salaries because they could never escape their on-screen personalities and celebrity status. For example, in only three years the salary of Mary Pickford, the most famous star of the time, jumped from about $25,000 to almost $1 million a year. But the three United Artists' founding members could never escape their typecast roles or find the privacy that ordinary people take for granted. Typified by her movie *Tess of the Storm Country* (1922), Pickford always played an innocent waif. Douglas Fairbanks, a swashbuckling ladies' man, played that role in *Robin Hood* (1922) and *The Thief of Baghdad* (1924). When Pickford hurriedly went to Nevada in 1920 to get a quick divorce and three weeks later married Fairbanks, the public was outraged by the scandal. Fans asked, how could such a sweet, girl-next-door type behave in such an immoral way? A few years later, however, the two divorced.

Charles Chaplin was the most famous screen personality of this or any other day.

He was born in the slums of London and worked hard to achieve his dream of becoming a stage actor. During Chaplin's vaudeville tour of the United States, Mack Sennett spotted him. The director wooed Chaplin from the theater with the promise of $150 a week and a year's guarantee to play in his *Keystone Kop* comedies in 1913. But Chaplin became frustrated, believing that Sennett wasn't using his character, the Little Tramp, enough. In 1915, Chaplin joined the Essanay (S&A) Studio for $1,250 a week. By 1918, Chaplin's character of the sad-eyed hobo with the baggy clothes and dark mustache was so popular that he could command a one-year salary of $1 million. The next year, United Artists was formed, and Chaplin became the first writer, director, and actor in Hollywood. His most famous movies were *The Gold Rush* (1925), with its famous scene in which he eats his own shoe, and *The Great Dictator* (1940), a spoof of Adolf Hitler (Figure 13.13). After criticizing the politics of

Figure 13.12

Adding to the horror of the famous steps scene in the 1925 classic by Russian director Sergei Eisenstein, The Battleship Potemkin, *is the abandoned baby carriage that is left on its own to perilously travel down the steps between dead and dying citizens.*

Getty Images/Hulton Archive

Figure 13.13

In this publicity still for The Great Dictator, *a bewildered Charles Chaplin is arrested by military police while actress Paulette Goddard looks on in fear. Note the many shadows cast by the characters on the floor. Early technical crews for motion pictures weren't adept at eliminating shadows caused by the lights required for a scene.*

the government and losing a paternity suit (in which a blood test revealed he wasn't the father of the child in question), Chaplin left the United States in 1952 and was refused reentry. George Bernard Shaw called Chaplin "the only genius in motion pictures." But when the silent little tramp started talking, the public could not tolerate his opinions.

While Chaplin played a sentimental tramp, his rival comic of the day, Buster Keaton, played an everyday person facing impossible odds. Joseph Francis Keaton was born into an acrobatic vaudeville family in 1895. The famous magician Harry Houdini gave the young performer the nickname "Buster" after seeing him fall down a flight of steps as a toddler. Keaton first performed on stage when he was just one year old. By 1917, he had appeared in three movies directed by Roscoe Arbuckle. His most famous comedy is *The General* (1927), in which he plays a Confederate locomotive operator trying to save his train from Union

soldiers who want to destroy it. Trying to deal with great forces beyond his control that were disrupting his everyday activities—and never changing his pessimistic expression—was a constant theme in Keaton's work (Figure 13.14).

Another reason for Hollywood's dominance over the world's output of motion pictures was that many actors emigrated from Europe. Successful studios knew the public's fascination with these often sensual and mysterious stars. Swedish actress Greta Garbo was discovered when she worked as a hat model for a department store. After she had played in several Swedish productions, MGM Studios brought her to the United States. Rudolpho d'Antonguolla (later changed to Rudolph Valentino) was a playboy and tango dancer in Argentina when he was discovered. Women everywhere adored him, and men admired the rugged adventure tales in which he starred. In *The Sheik* (1923) he established the sultry screen persona that he was never able to shake.

Scandals The new Hollywood sensuality on and off the big screen caused many people to become concerned that movies could have a corrupting influence on the morals of the nation. Sparked by the sensual love scenes on the screen and the personal scandals of a handful of stars, a private censorship board was established to regulate the industry. The actor and director Roscoe "Fatty" Arbuckle was involved in a 1921 scandal. A young actress died during a party at his rented twelfth-floor suite in the St. Francis Hotel in San Francisco, and Arbuckle was charged with rape and murder. Even though he was found not guilty, his reputation was ruined because of vicious attacks in the Hearst newspapers. Mary Pickford's hasty postdivorce marriage and the Arbuckle affair led to the formation in 1922 of the Motion Pictures Producers and

Distributors of America by Will Hays, former Postmaster General in the Harding administration. A Presbyterian elder, Hays and his committee members offered informal advice to movie executives about studio scandals and movie content. More important, the office issued a seal of approval for work that they considered acceptable for mass audiences. Without that approval, a film was doomed to a low-budget status. This early form of censorship led to sanitized and banal works in the 1930s and 1940s that could win easy approval from the Hays office. The office inspired the 1945 group the Motion Picture Association of America, which was created for the same purpose, and the 1970s Motion Picture Rating System.

The Oscar The Academy of Motion Picture Arts and Sciences first presented its Academy Awards on May 16, 1929, partly as a public relations ploy to help dignify the criticized film industry. The treasured, eight-pound, 13½-inch-tall, gold-plated award originally was called "The Statuette." But when an Academy librarian remarked that the standing man looked like her uncle Oscar, the name stuck.

Hollywood Finds Its Voice

The 1930s and 1940s are considered by most motion picture historians to be Hollywood's great age. Technical innovations brought improvements in presentation, studios became powerful arbitrators of careers and content, and the public flocked to films in record numbers.

Sound Beginning with Edison's Kinetophonograph, linking pictures and sounds was considered an inevitable technical development. However, the advent of "talking pictures" was delayed because various inventors produced different sound systems.

Getty Images/Hulton Archive

Figure 13.14

Buster Keaton's universal "everyman" appeal is evident in this publicity still from The Passionate Plumber. *Keaton represented for many the struggle to understand and cope with the problems of ordinary life.*

Another reason for the delay was that theater owners were not convinced of the necessity to fit their movie houses with expensive sound equipment.

Amplified sound that could be heard by large audiences was made possible by Lee De Forest's invention of the audio tube. Based on an earlier idea of Edison's, De Forest created a **vacuum tube** that eventually led to public address systems, radio, stereo equipment, and television. The American Telegraph & Telephone Company (AT&T) bought De Forest's technology and developed it in the company's Western Electric Bell Laboratories subsidiary. General Electric's scientists also were working on sound development. Both Western Electric and General Electric announced their amplification systems at about the same time.

The next step in the process was to combine synchronized dialogue, music, and sound effects during a movie's filming. Two sound systems—the **Vitaphone** (sound on disk) and the Phonofilm (sound on film)—

became available to filmmakers at about the same time. Vitaphone was an adaptation of Edison's phonographic cylinder in which a recording disk was made when the film was shot. To produce sound during a movie, a theater exhibitor had to run the picture and the cylinder with two different machines. Occasionally problems arose (considered humorous by early audiences) when the two didn't match or a haphazard projector technician accidentally played the wrong disk. *Phonofilm,* the technology eventually selected, was a sound-on-film innovation that converted recorded sounds into visual representations that were printed on the film itself. Consequently, no separate machine was required because the visual and the audio components of the movie always matched.

Warner Bros. studios invested heavily in Vitaphone, whereas Fox advocated Phonofilm. On October 5, 1927, Warner debuted Al Jolson's *The Jazz Singer* using the Vitaphone process. Although not the first sound picture—there had been earlier experiments with recorded voices and music—*The Jazz Singer* was the first movie in which sound was used in a feature motion picture to tell a story. The movie is forgettable except as a footnote in the history of sound presentations. It basically is the story of a vaudeville star who returns home to sing for his mother. In blackface makeup Jolson sings the song "Mammie" and speaks the famous line "You ain't heard nothin' yet." Although the film contained only four sequences in which sound was heard, audiences immediately reacted favorably to the innovation. The heyday of the silent movie was quickly coming to an end. Warner's next movie, the first all-talking film, was the following year's *The Lights of New York,* a gangster genre Vitaphone picture. Fox hyped the Phonofilm process by showing Charles Lindbergh's famous departure for Paris in one of its 1927 *Movietone* newsreels.

Although the public demanded talking movies, critics and studio executives were lukewarm to the innovation. Because of technical limitations with early microphones, actors had to speak their lines in static positions. Action-adventure films were practically impossible to make with the limited equipment. Writers criticized the return to indoor stage productions. Many people predicted the eventual end of the movies. In *Singin' in the Rain* (1952), "talkies" are portrayed comically as microphones are hidden in flowers.

Studio heads and movie distributors didn't favor sound because it added to the cost of making a movie: Camera sound equipment and speaker systems for theaters had to be purchased. One reason that Adolph Zukor of Paramount was against sound was that he had recently invested in several new movie theaters. He thought the technology unnecessarily disrupted the industry. Other problems were soon discovered with audio production. Shooting schedules had to be lengthened because of technical difficulties and choreographic problems, and few directors knew how to use sound effectively. Silent movies, because of their emphasis on mime to tell stories, were easily exportable to non-English-speaking audiences around the world. Finally, many famous stars on the studio payrolls had amusing or heavily accented voices that audiences thought comical. Despite the many problems, most people in the industry believed that the switch to sound was a necessary evil. But the best system still had to be chosen. The major movie studio executives met in secret in 1926 and agreed not to use sound techniques until a clear winner was established between the two techniques.

Because of the public's demand, studios borrowed heavily from banks and switched to sound production when the Phonofilm technology was adopted. By 1929, more than 9,000 theaters around the world could show talking pictures. Soon after, camera blimps to muffle their noise and boom microphones were invented to improve the quality of audio and provide outdoor shooting capabilities. Synchronized sound on film helped revive the slumping movie industry.

In the 1970s, Ray Dolby introduced his noise reduction technology. Stanley Kubrick first used the process in the 1971 movie *A Clockwork Orange*. Digital sound offers high-quality audio similar to music CDs or DVDs. Recently there have been several innovations in sound technology for motion pictures. In 1990 Kodak introduced its Cinema Digital Sound for *Dick Tracy*, Dolby Digital was first heard in *Batman Returns* (1992), and in 1993 Digital Theater Systems (DTS) introduced its technology for *Jurassic Park* while Columbia used Sony Dynamic Digital Sound (SDDS) for *The Last Action Hero*.

Color   The tedious method of hand-tinting individual frames of a motion picture was used commercially as early as Porter's *The Great Train Robbery*. The first color film innovations were complicated, time-consuming, and expensive. The first full-length movie filmed and projected in color was *The World, the Flesh and the Devil* (1914). That British production used a short-lived process called Kinemacolor. In 1915, the Technicolor Motion Picture Corporation announced its two-color additive process. Seven years later a modern, subtractive color system was introduced. This three-color process was used in the first movie shot entirely in color, which had the ironic title *The Black Pirate* (1926). The Walt Disney Studio was one of the first to take advantage of color systems, which it used in its animated classics. In the Technicolor process, three strips of film had to be exposed in the

camera at the same time through three different color filters. In 1933, the studio won an Academy Award for its *Flowers and Trees,* an all-color production. Eastman Kodak entered the color film market when it introduced Kodachrome 35-mm slide film for still photography in 1935.

As before with sound, studio executives were hesitant to make color movies because the process could add as much as $200,000 to the cost of a picture, owing to the need for special cameras, skilled technical personnel, and processing. In a brilliant marketing move, the Technicolor Corporation contracted with producer David O. Selznick to convince other movie studios to use its product. To ensure the quality of a Technicolor production, the company insisted on the use of its cameras, processing, printing, and even specially fabricated makeup for the actors. Selznick demonstrated the effectiveness of color in the 1937 musical *A Star Is Born* and the 1939 classic *Gone with the Wind*.

Widescreen   Another technical innovation employed to lure viewers to the theater was widescreen presentations. Early in its history, the Academy of Motion Picture Arts and Sciences selected the 4:3 width-to-length **aspect ratio** as the industry standard for screen presentations in order to avoid costly differences in film stock, cameras, and theaters. The earlier, almost square proportions of the film image had to be changed in the 1930s to allow for the sound track along the side of the film. Eventually, widescreen became the standard presentation format.

In 1952, the first commercial widescreen format—Cinerama—was introduced. Although it was a complicated process that required a movie to be shot with three cameras and shown with four projectors (one reserved for the sound track), the widescreen, expansive look was a great success with the public. The next year CinemaScope (later called Panavision) provided directors with a widescreen process that needed only one camera and projector (Figure 13.15). Some early widescreen hits included *The Robe* (1953), *How the West Was Won* (1962), and *It's a Mad, Mad, Mad, Mad World* (1963). The large, 70-mm filmstock was first introduced in a 1930 production *Happy Days,* but not until the 1970s were its commercial opportunities exploited. Directors had to learn how to fully appreciate the change in composition required when using the widescreen format. Contemporary directors who are particularly good at filling the wide screen are Francis Ford Coppola (*The Godfather* and *Apocalypse Now Redux*) and Martin Scorsese (*Taxi Driver, Raging Bull,* and *Goodfellas*).

The widescreen trend continues today in the form of the IMAX and OMNIMAX presentation formats that require specially built auditoriums. IMAX theater screens are 120 by 85 feet in size. A twenty-minute film can cost as much as $1 million.

Television screens were standardized on the Academy format because no sound track was required. However, widescreen movies shown on the small screen frustrate film buffs when the side cropping ruins compositions. "Pan and scan" techniques are used to select the important parts of a widescreen movie for presentation on the small TV screen. "Letterbox" presentations and widescreen television sets solve this problem (see Chapter 14).

Hooray for Hollywood

From about 1935 until 1950, the intersection of Hollywood and Vine streets was the most famous corner in the world. Young, good-looking men and women, encouraged by stories of highly paid actors discovered in cafés or gas stations, flocked to southern California with the often unfulfilled dream

Figure 13.15

The widescreen CinemaScope technique made its debut at Grauman's Chinese (now Mann's) Theater on Hollywood Boulevard in the 1953 opening of The Robe. *Note that the name of the process is more prominent than the name of the movie.*

Getty Images/Hulton Archive

of becoming a movie star. Hollywood's "golden age" wasn't so much a result of the movies produced as it was a lack of competition—no other site in the world made movies on the scale that Hollywood did.

Moviemaking was an enormously successful enterprise with almost everyone—from studio heads to extras—reaping unheard-of monetary rewards. MGM, for example, produced forty-two movies a year. Today directors rarely make more than one movie a year. John Ford, director of *Stagecoach* (1939), made twenty-six films in one year.

Hollywood studios became known for the type of movie they presented. Columbia Pictures produced family-oriented movies exemplified by the work of Frank Capra's *Mr. Deeds Goes to Town* (1936) and *It's a Wonderful Life* (1946). MGM, with Irving Thalberg responsible for business decisions, also was known for family pictures and stars that included Joan Crawford, Greta Garbo, Clark Gable, and Spencer Tracy. Paramount Pictures was associated with sophisticated comedies and dramas by director Cecil B. DeMille and with stars such as Gloria Swanson, Gary Cooper, and Claudette Colbert. Warner Bros. made fast-moving gangster movies with Edward G. Robinson, James Cagney, and Humphrey Bogart and high-kicking chorus line musicals by Busby Berkley.

Although television was available, World War II delayed the new medium's growth, allowing the motion picture industry to enjoy one last fling as the most popular mass medium for entertainment. But once television became common in people's homes, the movies were forever relegated to second place. Unfortunately, few movies made during the war years (1941–1945) are considered noteworthy. One important exception is Warner Bros.' timeless classic about a lovesick bar owner briefly reunited with a former lover in *Casablanca* (1943). Most

Hollywood producers, directors, and stars were busy making quickly produced and ill-conceived propaganda and training movies for the government.

Immediately following the war and with prosperity promised and optimism high, people felt like going to the movies. Theater attendance soared to record levels that never again were to be achieved. But just when studio executives were feeling confident that the movie industry was on sure financial footing, the government pulled the rug. A 1948 antitrust ruling against Paramount disallowed the vertical economic structure by which studios could own both movie production and distribution. Several film companies were sold or went out of business when production costs skyrocketed and executives didn't have funds from theaters to cover expenses.

Another postwar blow to Hollywood from the government caused more trouble for individuals than for the studios. At the beginning of the Cold War with the Soviet Union, the U.S. House of Representatives formed the House Un-American Activities Committee (HUAC) in October 1947, chaired by J. Parnell Thomas. The committee's responsibility was to identify Communist Party members or sympathizers in the movie industry. Its actions ruined many successful and promising careers. Numerous people in the industry who were called before the committee refused to testify because they were asked to supply names of colleagues they thought might be Communists.

In the 1930s, many people in the entertainment and academic communities had viewed the Communist Party as a viable option to the stagnation of the Republican and Democratic parties. Consequently, many directors, screenwriters, and stars that merely supported causes sponsored by the Communists along with actual party members were tarred with the same "un-American" brush. Receiving the most publicity were those **blacklisted** by the industry, who became known as the "Hollywood Ten." Weak economically (and morally), the studios refused to hire blacklisted personnel. One of the most famous blacklisted writers was Dalton Trumbo, who wrote the screenplays for *Roman Holiday* and *The Brave One* under an assumed name.

In 1951, during the height of the Korean War, the committee reformed—but without Thomas, who was in prison for extortion. The HUAC, with the help of eager witnesses such as Ronald Reagan and tireless members of Congress such as Richard Nixon and Joseph McCarthy, expanded the "Hollywood Ten" to a list of more than 300 people in the movie industry thought to have ties to Communism. Many of those blacklisted were

Figure 13.16

Marlon Brando is The Wild One. *The motion picture is an excellent example of a 1950s political picture, featuring plots centered on alienated and lost youth. Note how the pose, with the lighting effect on his right leg, acts as a phallic symbol, emphasizing the sexual power of Brando's personality.*

Getty Images/Hulton Archive

forced to find work in other countries; some, tragically, killed themselves over the scandal. Actor Kirk Douglas called blacklisting "one of the most shameful stains in American history."

For the most part, media executives went along with blacklisting, except for one powerful reporter. The program "CBS Reports" hosted by Edward R. Murrow exposed McCarthy's unethical tactics of smearing reputations. After the Senate censured McCarthy in 1954, the Communist scare died down. Director Otto Preminger defied the blacklist by hiring Trumbo to write the screenplay for *Exodus* (1960). Soon, other studios began to hire blacklisted people. The anti-Communist crusade was a dark time for Hollywood, a time when political affiliation, not talent, became a reason to hire someone. Always eager to take advantage of the fears sparked by the Cold War, the atomic bomb, and teenage alienation in the 1950s, the studios produced low-budget "Red menace" movies such as *I Married a Communist* (1949), several science fiction movies with subtle links to political issues such as *The Invasion of the Body Snatchers* (1956), movies with atom-bomb-created mutant creatures such as *Them!* (1954), and alienated teenager movies such as *The Wild One* (1954) and *Rebel Without a Cause* (1955) (Figure 13.16).

Hollywood Adapts

When it became obvious that television was not a passing fad, movie studios adapted or lost the battle. The first feature-length three-dimensional motion picture was *The House of Wax* (1953) starring the great horror actor Vincent Price. In the 1950s, three-dimensional movie effects were a fad that culminated in Alfred Hitchcock's 1954 classic *Dial M for Murder*. However, that version of the movie was never released because of

Figure 10.1

Using a software program called Macromedia Flash, graphic artists for USA Today *created this interactive infographic that includes a chronology of events linked to animation of the airliners hitting the towers and their subsequent destruction.*

Figure 10.2

The USA Today *weather map is an excellent example of a visual message that combines high informational and aesthetic qualities. Note that to the left is a shaded box detailing the weather in the Caribbean (due to storms) and in Afghanistan (because of the events following September 11).*

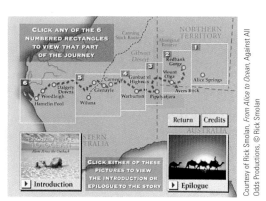

Figure 10.25 (left)

Probably the most recognizable corporate trademark worldwide is the white, stylized script typeface of Coca-Cola on a red circle, shown here in front of the Coca-Cola museum in Atlanta.

Figure 10.28 (right)

Rick Smolan's From Alice to Ocean *interactive multimedia presentation is an innovative way to show animated maps on a computer.*

Figure 11.24

The Pixar computer company won an Academy Award for the first all-computer short subject film, Tin Toy, *in 1988. The use of perspective and lighting gives a realistic rendering to the enduring characters.*

Courtesy of Pixar, Inc.

Courtesy of Pixar, Inc.

Figure 12.14

Photographers often use an electronic flash to help balance different light sources for a setting and isolate the subject in the foreground from the background.

Paul Martin Lester

Figure 13.28

This scene is from Ridley Scott's acclaimed science fiction masterpiece, Blade Runner. *In this shot, Harrison Ford leaps between vehicles while foreground and background graphic elements offer a visual treat for the viewer.*

Getty Images/Hulton Archive

Figure 15.1

In the movie The Abyss, *computer-generated image technology comes of age in the form of a lifelike pseudopod created by a race of underwater creatures sent to investigate the crew of an underwater oil rig.*

Figure 15.2

Two views of the T-1000 cyborg character in the movie Terminator 2. *Note how the use of lights and shadows aids in creating the illusion of depth for the computer-generated image.*

Figure 15.14 (left)

Apple Computer's current trademark is a round, organic, colorful logo that emphasizes the computer's ease of use, enjoyment, and slightly irreverent company philosophy.

Figure 15.21 (right)

Acclaim's Mortal Kombat, *designed for Sega and Nintendo video game machines, has been criticized for its violent scenarios.*

Figure 16.4

In Rick Smolan's From Alice to Ocean *interactive multimedia presentation, a user can sit back and watch the unfolding story of Robyn Davidson's 1,700-mile trek across Australia or use a mouse to chart a personalized course.*

Courtesy of Rick Smolan, *From Alice to Ocean,* Against All Odds Productions, © Rick Smolan

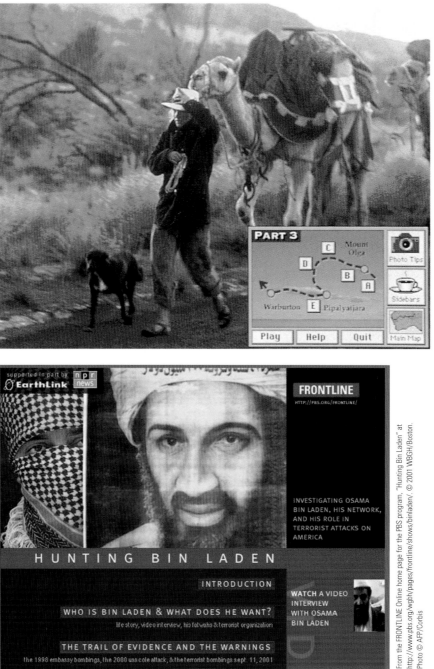

Figure 16.9

The clean, modern appearance of the Web site for the PBS series "Frontline" is an excellent example of a combination of words, images, and interactivity that makes the Web a unique medium.

From the FRONTLINE Online home page for the PBS program, "Hunting Bin Laden" at http://www.pbs.org/wgbh/pages/frontline/shows/binladen/. © 2001 WBGH/Boston. Photo © AFP/Corbis

public reaction against projection limitations, pointless plots, and glasses that made
the viewer look like a geek. Double features
began in the 1930s as a way to convince
money-conscious viewers that they would
get more for their money. With a newsreel, a
cartoon, trailers, and two feature-length
movies, moviegoers stayed in the theater for
several hours while owners made money
from drinks, popcorn, and candy sales. Keno
and bingo-type games of chance were played
and door prizes were raffled between shows
to attract additional viewers. After World
War II, the need for double features and
gambling declined as people returned to the
theaters in great numbers without extra
incentives. Nevertheless, double-feature presentations survived until the 1970s and
spawned a motion picture genre known as
the "B" movie. Cheaply produced, short
motion pictures were needed to fill the bill
with the main feature. One of the early B
movie directors was horror maven William
Castle, who produced B horror classics such
as *The Tingler* and *The House on Haunted
Hill* in 1959. Castle also was known for supplying life insurance policies for audience
members and skeletons and tingling seats in
theaters. Occasionally a B movie achieves
critical success. The 1957 science fiction
thriller *The Incredible Shrinking Man* is an
excellent example.

During the 1950s, drive-in movies prospered throughout the country. Owners of
cheap land away from city lights saw drive-
ins as a way to put the unproductive real
estate to better use. But television killed off
drive-ins too. In 1980 there were 3,561
drive-in movie screens. In 2000 there were
only 717 screens. Despite being a haven for
lovers and parents with children, drive-ins,
with their colorfully painted front screens,
are hard to find. Many are used today as
convenient open spaces for flea markets
(Figure 13.17).

Figure 13.17
Drive-in theaters have been virtually eliminated as places for showing movies. Nevertheless, the screens of many are still in demand as advertisement space for swap meets.

Getty Images/Hulton Archive

Another casualty of the war with television was the large, often enchanting movie
theaters that could hold up to 3,000 people.
With architectural and sculptural curiosities,
moody and mysterious lighting effects, and a
huge screen behind a heavy maroon or blue
curtain, these movie houses were truly magical places that matched the wonder of the
motion pictures themselves. Sid Grauman's
(now Mann's) Chinese Theater on Hollywood Boulevard, with the handprints and
signatures of famous movie stars preserved
in concrete, is one of the last monuments to
the old Hollywood. Also on the famous
boulevard is the renovated El Capitan Theater that offers luxury viewing in the tradition of the past. The trend is against theaters
with large, single screens because owners can
make more money with multiscreen theaters.

Beginning in the 1970s, as downtown areas in most cities became depressed, theater owners created the suburban mall theater, called a multiplex or cineplex, to reduce their overhead. The term *multiplex* is a broadcast word used to describe a communications system in which two or more messages can be transmitted over the same channel. Multiscreen theaters actually are an old idea. Southern California theater owner James Edwards, Sr., built his first multiplex in 1939. Multiplexes today are much more elaborate. Typical is Universal Studios' *City Walk* multiplex movie house in Hollywood, which contains eighteen separate screening rooms. Some cineplexes have as many as twenty-seven separate theaters under one roof. In 2000 there were 6,909 indoor movie theaters in the United States with 36,679 screens, or about five screens per theater. Multiplexes are here to stay.

Movies are enormously expensive to make and market. In 2000, D. W. Griffith's *Birth of a Nation* would have cost about $1.3 million to make. The average cost for making a movie in 2000 was $54.8 million. The studios at 20th Century Fox were sold in 1973 so that the land could be used for new apartments and a shopping mall. A French bank, Credit Lyonnais, owns the production facilities that MGM and United Artists share. The financial institution recently invested more than $1 billion in the hope of reviving the film heritage of MGM, more known now for its Las Vegas hotel than for filmmaking. Warner Bros. merged with the communications giant Time, Inc., which was bought by America Online, and now shares a Burbank studio with Columbia Pictures, which was once owned by Coca-Cola and is now owned by Sony. Disney and Universal Studios are involved in motion pictures, television program production, and popular amusement park attractions.

An estimated 75 percent of all Hollywood production work is now for television. Hence, huge profits are to be made from mergers of movie studios, television networks, and cable companies.

Technical Perspective

Auguste and Louis Lumière and Thomas Edison were inventors, not artists. They were concerned with what the film medium could do rather than what it could show. Méliès, Porter, and Griffith began the investigation of a motion picture's aesthetic possibilities with their creative achievements. Méliès introduced special effects, Porter cut scenes together to tell a story, and Griffith used close-ups to rivet the viewer's attention to the screen.

Eventually, other directors provided visual insights. Alfred Hitchcock used subjective camera and quick-editing techniques to add suspense to his thrillers. Orson Welles used his technical skills to help explain the story. Innovative directors such as Michelangelo Antonioni, Ingmar Bergman, and Federico Fellini never hesitated to make motion pictures with a slow, hypnotic pace. The last scene in Antonioni's *The Passenger* (1975) is an excellent example of a zoom and tracking **shot** in which the rhythm of the visual can be compared to music. Robert Altman, Francis Ford Coppola, and Martin Scorsese, in the tradition of Orson Welles, have mastered the craft of filmmaking. Altman used sound effects and dialogue to make transitions between scenes in *The Player* (1992). Coppola experimented with lighting and montage effects in *One from the Heart* (1982). Scorsese used slow zooms or quick cuts, depending on the mood of the story, in *Goodfellas* (1990) (Figure 13.18).

A motion picture has two major technical components: what you see and what you hear.

Visual Considerations

As with the cartoon and photographic media, movies primarily communicate in a visual format. By studying previous works and by being creative, directors have learned to exploit the visual considerations inherent in static or dynamic shots, film choices, text, and special effects.

The Shot   The basic unit of a movie is the shot, defined as a continuous picture in which there are no cuts. A shot can be as quick as 1/24 second—one frame—or can last the entire length of a picture. Hitchcock's 1948 classic, *Rope,* with Jimmy Stewart, is a stage production that seemingly is portrayed in only one camera shot (cuts were creatively masked). A camera shot can be static or dynamic. In a static shot the camera or the lens does not move. In a dynamic shot the camera and lens are manipulated in several different maneuvers.

A static shot allows the viewer to concentrate on the actors and not be distracted by the camera's movements. With depth of field manipulations (Chapter 12), however, a filmmaker can direct attention to different areas on the screen. In Griffith's *Broken Blossoms,* the foreground and background were expertly separated by the shallow focus of the lens. Conversely, in *Citizen Kane* Orson Welles often used extreme depth of field techniques to link the foreground and background action.

Because a motion picture may be dull if there are no camera movements, good directors constantly cause the camera to flow with the rhythm of a scene. Rack focus adjustments, zooms, pans, trucks, tilts, **dollies,** and tracking shots are the most common types of lens or camera manipulations.

Rack focus involves turning the focus ring on the lens during a shot in order to keep a moving character in focus or make the audience concentrate on another part of

the screen without having to use any other lens or camera manipulations.

Zooms are movements of a special zoom lens that simply increase or decrease the size of the image without changing perspective. When a lens zooms in, the viewer feels more a part of the action. Often tension between characters can be emphasized with a slow, zoom-in movement. The opposite effect is achieved when the lens zooms out. Viewers feel distance between themselves and the action on the screen. Use of the zoom-out technique at the end of a movie is a subtle clue that the film is over.

A pan is a horizontal movement of the camera, to either the left or right, while it sits on a sturdy, motionless tripod. A pivoting ball and socket connection moves the camera. A truck is the same horizontal movement as a pan except that the entire camera and the tripod move. A simple pan usually follows small gestures by actors in a scene, while characters walking or running are best shown with the truck technique. Tilts and dollies are vertical versions of the pan and truck.

Getty Images/Hulton Archive

Figure 13.18

"Ray Liotta, left, as Henry Hill . . . and Robert De Niro as Jimmy Conray . . . listen to fellow mobster Frenchy (Mike Starr) in Warner Bros.' Goodfellas . . ." Director Martin Scorsese is a master of using film lighting and composition to emphasize the importance of a scene.

A tracking shot (sometimes referred to as a crane shot) is a combination of a truck and dolly shot in which the camera sits on a "cherry picker," or crane, and makes longer, sweeping movements, making the audience most aware of the camera but helping set the actors in a scene.

The extent of a camera's movements often marks the difference between the two types of documentary approaches to moviemaking—direct cinema and cinema verité. The minimal use of camera movements often identifies the objective, direct cinema approach, but a camera that is handheld by the operator is an example of the highly subjective technique of cinema verité—viewers get the feeling that they are actually part of the action.

The journalistic techniques of early television news influenced direct cinema. Richard Drew, a former still photographer for *Life* magazine, was asked by NBC to produce a film about Senator John Kennedy in 1960 during his primary campaign for the presidency. Drew's *Primary* influenced many other filmmakers to follow that same objective style. Lawyer-turned-director Frederick Wiseman makes classic documentaries such as *High School* (1969), *Basic Training* (1971), and *Domestic Violence* (2001). Barbara Kopple won an Academy Award for her direct cinema documentary, *Harlan County, USA* (1972). Woody Allen's *Annie Hall* (1977), which received an Oscar for best film, featured a direct cinema approach to the fictionalized autobiography.

Cinema verité, or "truthful camera," originated from the Dada art movement and was influenced by the new wave art movement (Chapter 9). This documentary approach acknowledges the fact that the presence of a camera influences the events and people it records; hence, the viewer often is aware of the camera and filmmaker. For example, Woody Allen's *Husbands and Wives* (1992) and the ABC network television program

"NYPD Blue" use direct cinema interviews of characters with cinema verité highly subjective camera movements. With the steadicam and the Aaton 35-III, bounce-free filming can be done with handheld cameras.

The transitions between individual shots or editing cuts may be static or dynamic. A static edit (sometimes called a direct cut) is simply a quick, sometimes purposefully jarring transition from one scene to another, in which one image instantly replaces another. A deliberate, sometimes frenetic pace can be achieved with quick cuts, particularly if used in succession. The shower scene in Hitchcock's *Psycho* is a classic example often cited by movie historians. Because Hitchcock preferred long, continuous shots, the violently dynamic quick cuts in the shower scene were contrary to his second nature (Figure 13.19). After graphic designer Saul Bass had created the storyboards for the scene and lined up the first shot with the camera, Hitchcock asked Bass to direct the sequence (Chapter 9). Bass created an impressionistic murder image with shocking intensity by using sixty-seven separate editing cuts for the ninety-second scene.

Editing cuts also can involve special effects by which the scene is wiped off the screen and replaced with another. Such obvious manipulations are best employed during major scene transitions as in the movie *Star Wars* (1977). A slow, hypnotizing dissolve out of one scene and into another often connotes a romantic and gentle transition.

A successful editor must be a thorough and well-organized person. Geraldine Peroni edited Robert Altman's 1993 film *Short Cuts*. The movie was a complicated editing project because twenty-two major characters are featured in a dozen different stories. Action between stories and characters shifts back and forth. Altman shot about forty hours' worth of film that Peroni eventually edited down to the motion picture's three hour and nine minute length.

Film Choices Motion pictures can be shot in black and white, color, or a combination of the two. Movies also can be tinted or colorized. Black and white always has been associated with serious, documentary-style subjects, whereas, at first, color was thought to be a distracting attribute better used for fantasies. Today, nearly all movies are shot in color because of public demand. The 1939 classic *The Wizard of Oz* is the best example of the dual use of black and white and color in one motion picture. When Dorothy is in Kansas, black and white filmstock connotes everyday life on the plains. But when she lands in Oz, the fantasy is shown in color.

Black and white filmstock can be as colorful and sensational as color material. Scorsese's *Raging Bull*, the story of boxer Jake LaMotta, is considered one of the best movies made in the 1980s. Shot in black and white, the rich tones lend a documentary atmosphere to the brutal story. Tinting entire frames of a film was a common practice in the early history of motion pictures to add interest to a presentation. The modern equivalent of the practice, however, has caused an uproar among directors. Colorization—using the computer to make a black and white movie a pastel-painted color version—is criticized by those who value the original intent of the director to make the movie in the chosen filmstock. The practice also is criticized as a blatant attempt to attract television viewers who might not watch black and white movies.

Text Text also is a visual component of a movie. Text for opening title sequences and movie credits (Chapter 9), narration, or subtitles that translate the dialogue to another language must be designed for the screen as for any thoughtful typographical presentation. Cutlines also help give deaf moviegoers a more complete experience. In special showings of Universal's *Jurassic Park,* for example, Cinetype, Inc., of Holly-

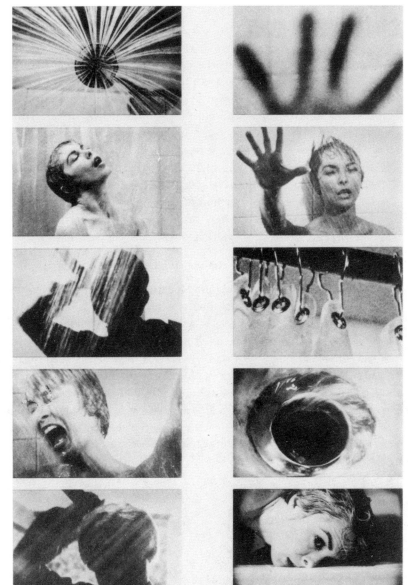

Courtesy of Saul Bass

wood, normally employed to write cutlines for non-English-speaking audiences, produced cutlines that included the sounds the dinosaurs made. The terrifying roar of the Tyrannosaurus rex was written as "ROOOOAAAAARRRR!!!!"

Special Effects Finally, special effects are vital components of a movie's visual message. *The Battleship Potemkin, Woodstock,*

Figure 13.19

One of the most unforgettable moments in motion picture history is the shower sequence with Janet Leigh in Alfred Hitchcock's 1960 Psycho.

and *One from the Heart* use montage effects that show many quick cuts of a scene. Stanley Kubrick's *2001: A Space Odyssey* (1968) expertly engages masks in which multiple images photographed at different times appear as one shot. **Rear projection,** once a common technique to link on-location footage with actors using props in studios, can be seen in *Some Like It Hot* (1959) (Figure 13.20) and comically parodied in *Airplane!* (1980). Currently, the most common method of creating special visual effects is through computer digitization techniques (which we discuss in Chapter 15).

Audio Considerations

James Monaco notes that sound occurs in real time—no such phenomenon as persistence of vision relates to the audible components of a motion picture. Consequently, sound effects often heighten a sense of realism in the minds of the viewer. In fact, research indicates that good sound quality actually can give a viewer the illusion that the picture quality is better. Movie sound

has three components: speech, music, and noise.

Speech Speech is the dialogue spoken by the actors or narration heard as a voice-over. Some of the great movies written by Joseph Mankiewicz, brother of *Citizen Kane* screenwriter Herman Mankiewicz, are classic films with a sophisticated use of language: *All About Eve* (1950) and *The Barefoot Contessa* (1954). More recent examples of all-speech movies are *My Dinner with Andre* (1981), directed by Louis Malle, and *Swimming to Cambodia* (1987), directed by Jonathan Demme.

Automated (or automatic) dialogue replacement (ADR) is a necessary component of moviemaking. Often a passing airplane or some other loud noise drowns out an actor's lines during an on-location shooting session. As a result, the dialogue has to be re-recorded in a studio. Actors also may want to make their lines more dramatic than when read on location. For example, the screaming by the actors heard in *Jurassic Park* actually was recorded in sound studios in New York and Los Angeles. An ADR expert carefully matches the new sound recording with the existing film so that the audience is never aware of the studio re-recording.

Music As emphasized by Bernard Hermann's score in *Kane,* music is a powerful emotional component to a movie. With visual messages speeding past the viewer, any one shot may be lost in a blur. Whether the scene on the screen is exciting or tender, music reinforces an audience's emotions when watching a shot. Musicals such as *West Side Story* (1961), *The Sound of Music* (1965), and *A Funny Thing Happened on the Way to the Forum* (1966) exploit emotional responses when music and words are linked with scenes. Instrumental

Figure 13.20

Joe E. Brown and Jack Lemmon (right) act in the famous final scene for Some Like It Hot. *After Lemmon removes his wig, he confesses, "I'm a man" to Brown, his groom to be. Brown responds, "Well, nobody's perfect." Backscreen projection is often employed by directors to simulate an outdoor view. Here, the actors sit on a stationary boat in a studio while film of the ocean is displayed behind them.*

music helps explain and move the plot. John Williams uses themes for individual characters in movies such as *Star Wars, E.T.: The Extra Terrestrial,* and *Saving Private Ryan.* When a particular character comes on the screen, the musical counterpart is heard.

Noise Noise is any other sound heard in a movie (or the noisy person talking behind you). Sound quality usually is poor when it is recorded during an on-location movie shoot, so special sound effects must be created in the studio and included in the movie on a separate sound track. In a throwback to the days when radio required sound effects for its productions, a sound technician (called a *foley artist*) watches a projected version of a scene and uses sound effects tricks to simulate scene noise. For example, when ruffled, a thick sheet of metal duplicates the sound of thunder; a coconut cut in half and tapped on a table sounds like a horse running. Previously recorded sounds can be purchased in a digital format from companies that supply noise "libraries" at a reduced cost. However, the producer of a major motion picture will spend the money for a foley artist to create custom sounds for the movie and record them on discs. For example, in *Jurassic Park* the breathing of the mighty Tyrannosaurus rex was a complicated mix of live animal sounds—lions, seals, and dolphins for inhales and whales and elephants for exhales. *Park* won the 1993 Oscar for best sound effects.

Ethical Perspective

As with cartoons, television, and computer programs, there are two main ethical concerns about the movie industry: stereotypical portrayals and emphasis on sexual and violent themes.

Stereotypes

Although several groups objected to the characterization of African Americans as sex-crazed beasts in *The Birth of a Nation* (1915), efforts to have the film banned were unsuccessful. However, on screen or on stage white actors in blackface almost always played black characters. When an African American was hired for a role, it was to play the stereotypical maid, butler, or offensive, shuffling character "Steppin' Fetchit"—a name more suitable for a dog than a person. As liberal acts of conscience, King Vidor made *Hallelujah* in 1929 and Elia Kazan directed *Pinky* in 1949, both using all African-American casts. But these films, although motivated by good intentions, were subtly condescending.

Several movies with all African-American casts were produced from the 1920s on, but white audiences seldom saw them. The Black Power movement in the 1960s loudly criticized the movie industry's racism. As a result of lobbying efforts and the improved economic well-being of African Americans, movies in the 1960s included more African-American actors in meaningful roles. Sidney Poitier became the first African-American movie star. Nevertheless, African Americans were still cast in films in which race was an important component of the plot and not selected for roles in which race did not matter. In the 1970s, "blackploitation" movies were produced with almost all African-American casts and marketed to African-American audiences. Gordon Parks, former photographer for *Life* magazine, directed *Shaft* (1971), which was loaded with violent and sexual story lines. Currently, African-American directors such as John Singleton with *Boyz N the Hood* (1991) and Spike Lee with *Malcolm X* (1992) produce thoughtful dramas that try to get beyond the stereotypes (Figure 13.21). However, most films about African Americans still concentrate on

Figure 13.21

"Tre (Cuba Gooding, Jr.) clings to his girlfriend, Brandi (Nia Long), in despair over the seemingly endless violence in South Central Los Angeles in Boyz N the Hood, *a Columbia Pictures release." Director John Singleton, in his first motion picture, created sensitive characters with universal appeal. As evidenced by this publicity still, he also gave women characters much more power than other films of the genre usually do.*

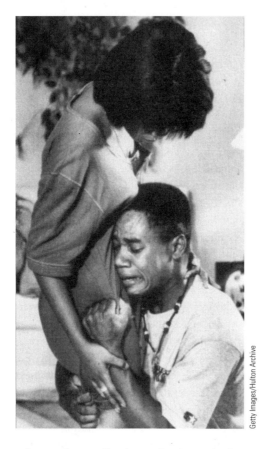

Getty Images/Hulton Archive

crime and sex, reflecting society's continuing stereotypes.

But perhaps there is a glimmer of hope. For the first time in Academy Award history, the best male and female actor awards went to two African Americans—Denzel Washington and Halle Berry for their work in the 2001 motion pictures, *Training Day* and *Monster's Ball.* The last time an African American had won the "Best Actor" award was in 1963—Sidney Poitier for *Lilies of the Field.*

African Americans aren't the only group to feel the sting of stereotyping in motion pictures. Native Americans, although seen in films frequently in the early westerns, almost always were portrayed as murderous savages. Lobbying from Arab groups, upset over the stereotypes in Disney's *Aladdin* (1992), convinced the studio to change offending lyrics

in a song, although many other common Arab stereotypes remain. One controversy involved the use of "terrorist" stereotypes of Arabs in *The Siege* (1998) that has been revived since the aerial attacks on September 11, 2001. Rita Moreno (born Rosita Dolores Alverio in Puerto Rico) lamented the fact that after her Academy Award win in 1961 for her role in *West Side Story,* she was offered only Spanish spitfire-type parts. Asian-American stereotypes in movies are the "dragon lady" and the "kung fu master."

Hollywood promoted 1993 as "The Year of the Woman" in recognition of their achievements in motion pictures (Figure 13.22). Ally Acker presents many notable women directors, producers, writers, and editors in her book *Reel Women.* No other cultural group has enjoyed such a notable and condescending history. In the 1920s, Clara Bow, the "It girl," and Mae West were independent, sexy women who served male fantasies. Hattie McDaniel won the first Academy Award for an African American in her supporting role in *Gone with the Wind.* But the mindless maid stereotype was typical of the era in which African-American women were either asexual domestics or sexual playthings for white men. In the 1940s, probably because of the influence from World War II, women enjoyed a co-equal social position with men—at least in the movies. Strong, independent women such as Katharine Hepburn, Bette Davis, and Joan Crawford filled the screen with their powerful performances. After the war, however, the dumb blonde or easily manipulated character surfaced in the Marilyn Monroe and Doris Day movies. The feminist influence in the 1970s fostered more roles for women that reflected realistic expectations of them. Martin Scorsese's *Alice Doesn't Live Here Anymore* (1975) was praised for its realistic depiction but criticized because Alice couldn't survive without a man's help.

Figure 13.22

Barbra Streisand takes a break from directing a scene in The Prince of Tides, *a Columbia Pictures release." Most publicity pictures for male directors show them behind the camera, directing. Note that in this photograph a woman director is pictured in a more casual moment.*

Getty Images/Hulton Archive

Actress Michelle Pfeiffer at an annual "Women in Film" luncheon summed up the low status of women in which characters sell their bodies for sex in *Indecent Proposal* (1991), *Mad Dog and Glory* (1992), and *Pretty Woman* (1990). Upon accepting an award, Pfeiffer said, "So . . . this is the Year of the Woman. Well, yes, it's actually been a very good year for women. Demi Moore was sold to Robert Redford for $1 million, Uma Thurman went for $40,000 to Mr. De Niro, and just three years ago, Richard Gere bought Julia Roberts for . . . What was it? . . . $3,000? I'd say that was real progress." The "Year of the Woman" was a noble gesture focusing attention on women's contributions to motion pictures, but with few significant roles and directorial positions, the gesture smacks of a hollow public relations campaign.

Sex and Violence

Offering the simplistic argument that the sex and violence seen in motion pictures is responsible for all of the social problems in a society is always politically popular. Undeniably, action-adventure movies, always a popular genre, are filled with sexual and violent activities. In 2000, the Motion Picture Association of America noted that for all the movies produced that year 69 percent were rated "R."

Aerial Attacks Effects

Either because of sensitivity to the issue of violence or out of marketing concerns, several Hollywood pictures have been postponed, rewritten, or digitally altered after the aerial attacks on the World Trade Center towers and the Pentagon in September 2001. *Sidewalks of New York,* a romantic comedy starring Edward Burns and Heather Graham; a Tim Allen comedy, *Big Trouble,* that features a hunt for a black-market nuclear bomb that ends up on an airplane; and *Collateral Damage,* which stars Arnold Schwarzenegger as a firefighter whose wife and children are killed when Colombian terrorists blow up a U.S. consulate, were all postponed. *Men in Black 2* was rewritten because it originally had a finale that was set against the World Trade Center towers. *Nosebleed* was planned to star the martial arts actor Jackie Chan as a window washer for the World Trade Center who becomes aware of a plot to blow the towers up, but the project was canceled. The producers for the film *Serendipity* planned to edit out a still shot of the towers from the movie's title sequence. In perhaps the most controversial edit of all, production personnel for Ben Stiller's *Zoolander* digitally removed the twin towers from all skyline shots because as Stiller admitted, he didn't want the audience to be distracted by the sight of them. However, many who saw the movie reported that the twin towers *not* being in the movie distracted them.

Marketing Violence Overseas

Despite momentary sensitivity among U.S. film producers, violence will continue to be a staple of American films. One of the main reasons that the number of sexual and violent movies is increasing is the economic situation of the major studios. Studio executives need big, blockbuster hits to maintain the economic health of their enterprises. As fewer and fewer Americans go to movies, studios are producing films with sexual and violent themes for foreign distribution where huge amounts of money can be made. In fact, 81 percent of all the movies shown in Europe are from the United States. Executives have learned that action-adventure films are popular throughout the world. Countries with diverse cultures and languages always understand violent themes.

However, few credible studies have linked screen sex and violence with the committing of actual physical acts, although occasionally there is a demonstrable connection. Larry

Gordon directed *The Warriors* (1979), about a tough street gang. Paramount recalled the motion picture from theaters after the first week when three deaths were linked to the movie. Violence also was connected to showings of *Boyz N the Hood* and *New Jack City.*

Gordon explains why some audiences are attracted to violence: "If I tell a joke, you may not get it, but if a bullet goes through the window we all know how to hit the floor, no matter the language." Gordon also directed Bruce Willis in the violence-filled *Die Hard 2*. The movie made more than $500 million, but only one-third of the total was from U.S. sales. Creating sexual and violent movies in order to make money in some foreign country is morally indefensible.

Sometimes, a violent action portrayed in a film gives impressionable people the same idea. After two young men entered their high school in Littleton, Colorado, a suburb of Denver, and terrorized students with automatic weapons and pipe bombs killing thirteen and injuring twenty-four before killing themselves, part of the blame for the violent incident was directed toward a similar scene in *The Basketball Diaries* (1995). Also blamed were violent video games (Chapter 15).

Cultural Perspective

Motion pictures, just like any art form, reflect the **archetypes** and myths that are popular within a particular culture at a particular time. All visual messages, movies included, help shape what we think of our society and ourselves. Hollywood stars give us ideals to strive for, and the mythic stories of good versus evil, social order versus anarchy, and group dependence versus independence strike deep, cultural chords. At least eleven genres, or types, of stories created on film reflect a society's cultural values: comedy, crime, epic, horror, musical, romance, science fiction, social impact, thriller, war, and western. Some of the most famous examples of each genre from past years with recent additions are listed below with their cultural implications.

Comedy: *City Lights* (1931), *Some Like It Hot* (1959), and *Cats & Dogs* (2001)—from sophisticated situations to sophisticated cartoons.

Crime: *Scarface* (1932), *Bonnie and Clyde* (1967), and *15 Minutes* (2001)—from stories with clear good and evil characters to sympathetic psychological profiles of dangerous criminals.

Epic: *Napoleon* (1926), *Dr. Zhivago* (1965), and *Elizabeth* (1998)—an important genre that is always underrepresented in filmmaking.

Horror: *Frankenstein* (1931), *Night of the Living Dead* (1968), and *Hannibal* (2001)—from human-created to inhuman monsters (Figure 13.23).

Musical: *The Wizard of Oz* (1939), *The Sound of Music* (1965), and *Glitter* (2001)—from unrealistic fantasies to hard-edge pop singer promotions.

Romance: *Gone with the Wind* (1939), *Casablanca* (1943), and *You've Got Mail* (1998)—from love in the midst of civil and world war to a couple that meets because of email messages.

Science fiction: *Metropolis* (1926), *2001: A Space Odyssey* (1968), and *Ghosts of Mars* (2001)—from thoughtful commentaries about the future to violent films with little relationship with reality.

Social impact: *The Grapes of Wrath* (1940), *On the Waterfront* (1954), and *Smoke Signals* (1998)—always a strong film genre, but not as popular as in past years.

Getty Images/Hulton Archive

Figure 13.23

One of the greatest horror films of all time is Frankenstein. *Here, the monster, played by Boris Karloff, is bound from neck to feet. Note how the harsh, overhead lighting helps create a scarier look for the monster.*

Thriller: *The Maltese Falcon* (1941), *Psycho* (1960), and *Along Came a Spider* (2001)—from well-written dramas with fine acting to well-acted, yet vacuous crowd pleasers.

War: *All Quiet on the Western Front* (1930), *Apocalypse Now* (1979), and *Captain Corelli's Mandolin* (2001)—the best are critical examinations of why wars are necessary.

Western: *Stagecoach* (1939), *The Wild Bunch* (1969), and *Unforgiven* (1992)—from uncritical dramas to films that question the need for such violent actions.

Because motion pictures are visual media, they tell their mythic stories through visual symbolism. Myths are the stories of our culture, whereas symbols are the way those stories are communicated.

Moviemaking demands a collaborative effort. From directors to drivers, hundreds of people are responsible for the end product. But creative control ultimately rests with the director. Some directors seem to understand

Figure 13.24

*Annie Hall (Diane Keaton)
and Alvie Singer (Woody
Allen) share a friendly
moment in the Academy
Award-winning* Annie Hall.
*Limited depth of field helps
rivet the viewer's attention
on the two characters.*

the link between myth and symbolism better than others.

Woody Allen makes comical and serious films that reveal the social angst involved with love and relationships, as in *Annie Hall* (1977) and *Husbands and Wives* (1992) (Figure 13.24). Robert Altman shows how lives are linked in his movies *M*A*S*H* (1970), *McCabe and Mrs. Miller* (1971), and *Cookie's Fortune* (1999). Michelangelo Antonioni exploits the emotional quality of film with long, hypnotic camera movements in *The Red Desert* (1964), *Blow-Up* (1966), and *The Passenger* (1975). Laslo Benedek presented a symbol of rebellious youth in actor Marlon Brando in *The Wild One* (1953). Ingmar Bergman makes films that reveal metaphysical concerns and difficult relationships such as *The Seventh Seal* (1957), *Cries and Whispers* (1972), and *Scenes from a Marriage* (1974). Bernardo Bertolucci explores the notion of lust without love in *Last Tango in Paris* (1973) and the nobility of the human spirit in the epic drama *The Last Emperor*

(1987). Luis Buñuel showed the power of human desire in the documentary *Land Without Bread* (1932) and *The Discreet Charm of the Bourgeoisie* (1972). James Cameron pioneered the art of using digital effects in such movies as *The Abyss* (1989) and the Oscars' best picture, *Titanic* (1997) (see Chapter 15). Francis Ford Coppola in *One from the Heart* (1982), *The Outsiders* (1983), *Apocalypse Now Redux* (2001), and his Academy Award best pictures, *The Godfather* (1972) and *The Godfather: Part II* (1974), uses color and lighting symbolism in intriguing ways. Roger Corman, a B movie king, created low-budget horror when he combined actor Vincent Price with a series of Edgar Allen Poe stories, including *The Pit and the Pendulum* (1961). Peter Davis's documentary on the Vietnam War, *Hearts and Minds* (1975), used such strong visuals and such a direct, personal approach that many thought it could have shortened the war if released sooner. Federico Fellini mixed poetry and fantasy in outrageous settings in

Getty Images/Hulton Archive

Figure 13.25

Federico Fellini, the Italian master of the surreal, had made eight and one-half motion pictures up until his latest, 8½. In this publicity still, some of the magic and visual stimulation of a Fellini film are evident.

La Dolce Vita (1959), *8½* (1963), and *Amarcord* (1974) (Figure 13.25). Jean-Luc Godard, as in *Breathless* (1959) and *Weekend* (1967), makes movies about thieves and car accidents that comment about social conventions. Alfred Hitchcock was a master of suspense with camera movements and editing techniques that added to the thrill in *The 39 Steps* (1935), *North by Northwest* (1959), and *Psycho* (1960). Stanley Kubrick always made compelling, visually innovative, politically conscious works, including *Spartacus* (1960), *Dr. Strangelove or How I Learned to Stop Worrying and Love the Bomb* (1963), *2001: A Space Odyssey* (1968), and his last that unfortunately was a critical disaster, *Eyes Wide Shut* (1999). Akira Kurosawa in *Rashomon* (1950), *The Seven Samurai* (1954), and *Ran* (1984) has inspired many imitators because of his use of exciting and well-choreographed fights and scenic views (Figure 13.26). Spike Lee proved that he can direct quirky love stories, musicals, and epic motion pictures as well as serious dramas and social criticism in *Malcolm X* (1992), *4 Little Girls* (1997), and *Bamboozled* (2000).

Richard Lester is a master at bringing musicals to the big screen in *A Hard Day's Night* (1964), *Help!* (1965), and *A Funny Thing Happened on the Way to the Forum* (1966). George Lucas uses mythical battles for love and country in his movies, such as *American Graffiti* (1973) and the *Star Wars* franchise: *Star Wars* (1977), *Star Wars: Episode I* (1999), *Star Wars: Episode II* (2002), and *Star Wars: Episode III* planned for 2005. David Lynch has a highly symbolic and unique visual style that works well for motion pictures or television productions, exemplified in such movies as *Dune* (1984), *Blue Velvet* (1986) (Figure 13.27), *Lost Highway* (1997), and *The Straight Story* (1999). Louis Malle made sensitive dramas about ordinary people, as in *Pretty Baby* (1978), *My Dinner with Andre* (1981), and *Damage* (1992). Erroll Morris combines strong visual messages with compelling content to create a new documentary approach, as in *The Thin Blue Line* (1988), *Fast, Cheap & Out of Control* (1997), and *Mr. Death: The Rise and Fall of Fred A. Leuchter, Jr.* (1999). Sam Peckinpah directed gritty realistic and violent films

Figure 13.26

Japanese director Akira Kurosawa made the classic The Seven Samurai *in 1954. The motion picture inspired a number of American productions, including the westerns* The Magnificent Seven *(1960) and* The Outrage *(1964).*

Figure 13.27

Director David Lynch has a reputation for creating unforgettable visual messages in his motion picture and television work. Harsh, direct lighting and a tight composition help add tension to this scene in Blue Velvet.

such as *The Wild Bunch* (1969), *Straw Dogs* (1971), and *The Getaway* (1972). Nicholas Ray in *Rebel Without a Cause* (1955) used the actor James Dean as a symbol of all alienated teenagers of the time. Satyajit Ray made movies that helped people in one culture understand people from other cultures, particularly in *The World of Apu* (1958). Alain Resnais exploits ambiguous actions of people involved in overwhelming tragedies, as in *Night and Fog* (1955) and *Hiroshima, Mon Amour* (1959). Ridley Scott, who once said that "movies are visual novels," always produces works of great visual design, including *Alien* (1979), *Blade Runner* (1982) (Figure 13.28), *Thelma and Louise* (1991), *Gladiator* (2000), and *Hannibal* (2001). Martin Scorsese uses the camera like a spotlight to reveal people at their most honest, as in *Taxi Driver* (1976), *Raging Bull* (1980), *Goodfellas* (1990), and *Dino* (2002). John Singleton tackles important social problems of a community through tender, sensitive visual storytelling, exemplified by *Boyz N the Hood* (1991) and *Poetic Justice* (1993). Steven Spielberg knows how to exploit popular culture icons and at the same time make technically competent and widely successful pictures, such as *Jaws* (1975), *E.T.: The Extra Terrestrial* (1982), and *Jurassic Park* (1993). But Spielberg also knows how to make tender, human dramas with universal appeal, as demonstrated by *The Color Purple* (1985), *Saving Private Ryan* (1998), *A.I.: Artificial Intelligence* (2001), and the critical masterpiece, *Schindler's List* (1993), which won the Oscar for best picture. The acerbic Billy Wilder made what is considered the greatest comedy ever produced, *Some Like It Hot* (1959), and one of the best **film noir** examples in the history of the movies, *Sunset Boulevard* (1950).

Motion pictures are cultural artifacts. Movies affect us emotionally because the powerful visual messages, on a screen as large as a house and with sound quality that is better than being on a set, tell stories that we understand.

Critical Perspective

Movie attendance has been declining slowly since World War II because of the popularity of television. The number of tickets sold annually in the United States immediately after the war averaged about 4 billion. In 2000, the number of tickets sold was about 1.1 billion. However, the movie industry is still profitable because ticket prices have risen, sales of refreshments have exploded, and the number of screens has increased. With multiplex suburban theaters, first-run blockbuster movies with huge marketing budgets are sold out the first few weeks of their runs. But after the attention wanes, theater seats without someone sitting in front of you aren't hard to find.

Today, many forms of entertainment are available to those who can afford them—restaurants, lectures, art museums, music concerts, comedy clubs, shopping malls, traditional theaters, athletic activities, and sporting events. But by far the biggest threat to the existence of motion pictures is in the home, with radio, broadcast television, cable and satellite television, videotapes, DVDs, traditional and video games, World Wide Web presentations, reading, yardwork, talking, and sex all keeping people occupied.

Moviemaking is a business. If anticipated blockbusters bomb embarrassingly at the box office, the studio executives responsible sometimes get the ax. This blockbuster mentality, in which most of the profits for a studio are made during the summer months, forces producers to make films that appeal to large audiences. More often than not,

proven formulas from the past—remakes and sequels—with sexual and violent themes do well at the box office.

In 1969, communications critic Thomas Guback warned of thinking about film simply as a commodity with Hollywood in control of the international market. Such a trend produces films that are dehumanizing and anticulture. He writes, "Because film is an art which portrays man's interpretation of life, it is imperative that contrasting perspectives be given the opportunity to exist and develop. It would be a pity to have but one control over all the printing presses in a nation—or in the world. The same can be said for film production and distribution. Yet this is coming about in the world of the West."

With movies costing millions of dollars and production facilities concentrated in southern California, films that appeal to small, selective audiences are seldom made.

For movies to have lasting cultural significance, directors must be free to make the kind of work that they believe is important without content or time limitations. Unfortunately, the movie industry has sometimes compromised a director's independence because of monetary considerations.

■ *FUTURE DIRECTIONS FOR MOTION PICTURES*

Why do we go to movie theaters? The picture is large, the image is high in resolution, and the sound is excellent. Seeing a well-advertised blockbuster in the first week of its showing is exciting. No commercial breaks interrupt the unfolding of the story. Watching and reacting to the show's images with a large group of people is fun. But every one of those reasons for attending a movie, except the last one, will soon be addressed at home.

High-resolution and large-screen monitors with digital sound connected to cable

Figure 13.28

See color section following page 276.

and satellite operators that provide viewing of first-run movies before they are shown at the local theater will soon be an ordinary part of watching movies. The major studios recently announced a joint venture in which computer users will be able to watch first-run movies after paying a rental fee and downloading them via high-speed Internet connections. The films will erase themselves 24 hours after they are viewed. Motion picture companies are also making commercials and shows for television, selling violent movies to audiences around the world, and diversifying their products as much as possible.

Besides hotel and amusement park operations, studios also have forged alliances with video game and cable companies. In the United States, Nintendo and Sega dominate the video game industry. Video games represent a $6 billion annual market—a figure that about equals the film industry's annual U.S. box office receipts. Movie studios, with their inherent talent for story production and a ready supply of images, are serious contenders for the video game market. For example, Paramount, Columbia, and Universal all produced CD-ROM game versions of their latest movies. And when video game producers team with cable companies, online interactive games will become a popular source of home entertainment that may further erode movie attendance (see Chapter 16).

The film industry is eager to adapt to compelling competitive forces in order to maintain audiences. Communications professor Bruce Austin in his book *Immediate Seating: A Look at Movie Audiences* writes:

> The history of mass communications shows that the introduction of new media forms forces existing media to specialize as a result of the "demassification" of their audiences. For example, the introduction of television killed general-circulation magazines and

prompted the development of special-interest periodicals. Thus we might expect film exhibitors to begin narrowing their range of offerings. A few distinct genres already have their own theaters; perhaps obvious are theaters that show sexually explicit movies exclusively. Other types of specialty theaters may evolve, including an increase in the number of houses that screen only art or classic films, martial arts movies, and so on.

Will people continue to go to movie theaters? Of course they will. The year 2001 was a record year for the industry as more than $8 billion was spent in U.S. box offices with 1.5 billion tickets sold, beating 2000's record of $7.7 billion. The best evidence that many enjoy the shared experience of watching a motion picture with a large audience is the success of blockbuster movies. George Lucas's prequel, *Star Wars: Episode I—The Phantom Menace* broke the one-day opening box office record with $28.5 million in sales in 1999. However, *Harry Potter and the Sorcerer's Stone,* an AOL Time Warner production (see Chapter 16), beat that record in 2001. *Potter* earned $32.9 million in its first day while showing in a record number 3,672 theaters or on about 24 percent of all the screens in North America. *Harry Potter* also reached the $100 million mark in its fifth day of release—tying the record previously set by *The Phantom Menace*. However, *Menace* reached the $200 million mark in 13 days; *Potter* took 15 days to reach that box office milestone. Coincidentally, when *Harry Potter* was playing in theaters, *The Phantom Menace* aired on the Fox television network.

Humans are social animals and simply enjoy the company of one another too much to stay home for long. As the motion picture industry adapts its stories, techniques, and theaters to satisfy audiences, undoubtedly there will always be a market for large, first-run theaters for cinemaphiles, just as there is always a market for staged theater productions. Theater owners also are enticing viewers with restaurant food fare—pizza, tacos, and cappuccino. But many more moviegoers will want something more. Filmmakers, special-effects artists, computer specialists, and amusement park operators have combined to create thrilling adventures that have been described as "jumping in a blender and hitting puree." With chairs that move in sync with the action on the screen—some as large as the ninety-foot IMAX domes—many predict that movies will truly become an equal combination of motion and pictures. For example, Dream Quest Images created *The Batman Adventure* for the Warner Bros. *Movie World* theme park in Queensland, Australia. Special-effects wizard Douglas Trumbull, who designed *Back to the Future—The Ride* for Universal Studios in Florida and Hollywood, has also produced *In Search of the Obelisk* for the Luxor Hotel and Casino in Las Vegas (Figure 13.29). In 1997, Disneyland opened *Honey, I Shrunk the Audience* with state-of-the-art 3-D film techniques and a floor that shakes the audience in sync with the film, and in 2001 tourists in California were able to experience the motion simulation/IMAX ride called *Soarin' Over California* at Disney's "California Experience" theme park in Anaheim.

Will moviegoers want to leave their home television sets to watch television in a movie house? Whatever the means of presentation and whether in the theater or the home, feature-length motion pictures always will be produced, presenting fascinating dilemmas for social scientists and politicians to ponder.

DISCUSSION AND EXERCISE IDEAS

- Lead a discussion on the motion picture *Citizen Kane*. Why do you think it is considered the greatest movie of all time?

- Describe your favorite motion picture.

- Lead a discussion about the future of motion pictures.

- Write a paper that discusses the ethical concerns with motion pictures with particular emphasis on portraying sex and violence.

INFOTRAC COLLEGE EDITION ASSIGNMENTS

- With "Subject guide" checked, type "Citizen Kane" in the search area. Read the article "Founding brothers: Kane, Corleone, and the American dream" by Steve Erickson, which compares the Kane character in *Citizen Kane* with Michael Colleone in *The Godfather*. Both characters pursued, according to the author, the American dream to a tragic end. Are there any other characters in movies you are aware of that focus on the same theme? Comment how through this exercise you appreciate that watching a movie is not merely taking note of acting or aesthetic considerations. Many times motion pictures reflect the most positive and negative aspects of a particular culture.

- With "Subject guide" checked, type "Motion Picture Actors and Actresses" in the search area. Click "View" in "Periodical references." Choose any of more than 4,000 articles to read about a particular actor or actress. Do you think American culture overemphasizes actors and actresses as celebrities? If so, why do you think that is so? What can be done to prevent a concentration on the person rather than the person's work?

Go to the Web site for this book at www.wadsworth.com/product/0534562442 to find more Web links on this subject.

Figure 13.29

Many critics of the movie industry predict that motion simulator rides, such as the Back to the Future attraction at Universal Studios in Florida, are the future for large audience presentations.

TELEVISION AND VIDEO

By the end of this chapter you should know:

- The importance of George Holliday's video in shaping public opinion about the police beatings of Rodney King.
- The pervasive effect television has had on culture worldwide.
- Some of the ethical concerns many have about television and video.
- Some of the future directions that the television medium might take.

Our lives have been irrevocably transformed in ways that make pre-TV America seem like the dark ages.

Meg Greenfield,

1930–1999

JOURNALIST, EDITOR,

AND SOCIAL CRITIC

Their lives could not have been more different. One was a recently released convict whose alcoholic father died at age forty-two; the other was an upper-middle-class son of an oil executive, who had been born in Canada but had lived most of his life in Argentina. One was out of work and angry; the other was a manager of a plumbing company and contented. One was beaten severely by members of the Los Angeles Police Department (LAPD); the other was watching the beating through the viewfinder of his new $1,200 Sony Handycam. One was African American; the other was Anglo. One was Rodney King; the other was George Holliday. By coincidence the two were brought together on a mild, southern California winter night to create what has been called "the most famous home video of all time." Many blame the video for causing the worst rioting in the history of the United States.

■ *THE RODNEY KING INCIDENT*

At the time, Rodney King was twenty-five. He had recently been paroled after serving a two-year prison term for robbing a Korean grocer in 1989 of $200 and hitting him with a tire iron. On March 3, 1991, King and two of his neighborhood friends, Bryant Allen and Freddie Helms, were enjoying the sunny day drinking "eightballs"—high-alcohol-content beer called *Olde English.* By midnight, King had consumed the equivalent of twenty-four 12-ounce beers. Later, his blood-alcohol level would be measured at twice the legal limit. Nevertheless, he was still thirsty, so he and his buddies took off to buy some more beer. With the car radio turned up as high as it would go, King raced through the Los Angeles streets in a white 1988 Hyundai at speeds estimated at up to 100 miles per hour. Quickly, his drug-induced, happy feeling changed to dread as he noticed the flashing lights of a patrol car in his rearview mirror. His friends begged him to pull over, but King's one thought was to try to escape. If he were caught violating his parole, he surely would find himself back in prison. King tried to evade the police for the next eight miles, but even in his alcoholic haze, he knew the chase was lost. Pursued by several police cars, two helicopters, nineteen LAPD officers, seven California Highway Patrol officers, and at least three city officials, King finally stopped his car at about 12:30 A.M. on a gravel lot near the corner of Osborne Street and Foothill Boulevard in the Lake View Terrace community of northern Los Angeles.

Although King slowly got out of his car, his energy level quickly picked up when he saw all the officers present for his arrest. He reportedly smiled and danced for the assembled troop of officers. He waved up at the circling helicopter while its searchlight aimed down on the surreal late-night drama. He threw a kiss and wiggled his rear end at a female officer. When four officers grabbed him from behind to handcuff him, the six-foot-three, 225-pound King simply shrugged them off. When a Taser dart (sometimes called a "stun gun") delivered a 50,000-volt electric shock that renders most victims passive but had no effect on King, the officers mistakenly feared the worst—that King was high on the dangerous drug PCP. The police were further agitated when a second Taser dart fired by Sergeant Stacey Koon also failed to get a reaction from King. At that point, unknown to King or the officers at the scene, George Holliday, on the balcony of his apartment across the street, turned on his video camera.

■ *Making and Airing the Video*

Earlier in the day, Holliday, thirty-one, had taken his camera to record scenes of Arnold Schwarzenegger's blockbuster hit *Terminator 2: Judgment Day* that happened to be filming two blocks from Holliday's apartment. The movie's director, James Cameron, later called the coincidence—that his film was on the same tape as the police beating—"the most amazing irony." By midnight, Holliday was asleep; he awoke to the noise of the helicopter and his neighbors talking. He put his pants on, stepped out on his balcony with his video camera, and began recording the frightening scene below him.

For about ten minutes, Holliday recorded the police officers' attempts to subdue King (Figure 14.1). In the shaky, out-of-focus, grainy, and mostly black and white video (because of the low light level), King leaps off the pavement and runs toward Officer Laurence Powell, who lays King flat with a baton blow to his head. Officers Timothy Wind and Powell then strike King repeatedly with their nightsticks. At one point, Officer

Theodore Briseno tries to stop Powell from hitting King again, but Briseno later steps on King's head. Tired, bloodied, and eventually hog-tied, King slumps on the ground angrily screaming curse words.

Shaken and upset, Holliday called the Foothill Division of the LAPD to report the incident. The officer on the phone did not ask for Holliday's name, nor did Holliday admit that he had videotaped the brutal arrest. Holliday probably knew he would have to give up his tape to the police if he mentioned its existence. The next morning, Holliday called Los Angeles television station KTLA because "I just wanted someone to know about it, and I thought the media would be the way." But to "know about" the beating would cost some money. Holliday sold the video to the station for $500, three times the normal freelance rate. He submitted the tape with the understanding (he thought) that the station would air it, keep it for a few days, and give it back. But KTLA, as an independent station, has an agreement with the Cable News Network (CNN) of Atlanta to give the national network videotapes shot by amateurs that the station considers newsworthy.

CNN aired an excerpt from the Holliday tape, which was seen immediately around the world. President Bush called the police beatings "revolting." Television news and newspaper stories featured analysis and commentary about the actions of the officers. Calls for the resignation of controversial LAPD Chief Daryl Gates were numerous. Charges of police brutality and racism were revived against the LAPD, but with a startling difference—that of clear-cut, irrefutable, visual evidence. The District Attorney's office confiscated the videotape for use in an upcoming state trial against four Anglo officers—Powell, Wind, Briseno, and their supervisor, Koon. Around the world, those who had seen the shocking videotape came to one apparently obvious conclusion: The four officers involved in the beating of Rodney King had overstepped their authority and criminally assaulted him.

Because of television's need to fill the small screen with images, pop artist Andy Warhol once predicted that everyone in America would get at least fifteen minutes of fame. King and Holliday immediately became media celebrities. The two were recognized wherever they traveled. People wanting to shake his hand stopped Holliday on the street. More than 100 requests for interviews by the world's media organizations overwhelmed the young plumber. Friends from Argentina called him to say that they'd seen him on television. He had to change his phone number twice and hire a lawyer to sort out all the business deals offered to him. Once, while walking out of a gasoline station in Van Nuys, Holliday heard someone call his name. He looked up and recognized Rodney King. For the first and only time, the two met. King enthusiastically shook his hand and said, "Hey, man, you saved my life." But that was about all the two could think to say to each other, and they parted.

Paul Martin Lester

Figure 14.1

This high contrast and blurry still image taken from a television monitor shows Los Angeles police officers Wind and Powell standing over the crouched form of Rodney King in front of his automobile.

■ *The Trial and Its Aftermath*

Holliday was the first witness called to testify in the trial of the four police officers, which had been moved to suburban Simi Valley in the hope of getting an unbiased jury. Almost everyone who had viewed the tape thought they knew the eventual verdict. But the defense lawyers persuaded the jurors to come to a different conclusion. With high-quality sound, a stabilized picture, digitally enhanced exposures, and super-slow motion, the jurors saw a much different version of the tape than did television viewers. Slow motion exaggerated even the tiniest movements by King, some lasting less than a second, that were interpreted by the lawyers as aggressive acts. Never mind that such small gestures were probably impossible to notice in "real time." According to the defense, each baton blow was necessary, justified, and within departmental guidelines. The jurors also saw Holliday's tape about fifty times, desensitizing their emotions about its content. Much of the horror experienced during an initial viewing of the video was lost.

On April 29, 1992, the all-Anglo jury acquitted the four LAPD police officers. The surprising verdict sparked one of the bloodiest and costliest chapters in America's history. The civil disturbance that followed claimed more than 50 lives, caused 2,300 injuries, resulted in hundreds of arrests, and cost more than $1 billion in property damage.

During the riots, Holliday started to receive anonymous phone calls blaming him for the disturbances. Holliday admitted that, at first, "I felt it was all my fault—especially when people started getting killed. But I can't blame myself. I'm just the guy who took the video."

The beating of Rodney King, George Holliday's videotape, the trial of the police officers, and the riots in the streets of Los Angeles all contributed to one of the most important stories of the twentieth century. As always, some tried to profit from the tragedy. Rodney King originally sued the city for $56 million—$1 million for each baton blow he suffered. When the city offered him $1.75 million to settle his suit, King's lawyer called it an insult. In the civil suit that followed, King demanded $15 million while city officials offered $800,000. In 1994, a jury awarded King $3.8 million in compensatory damages.

Holliday sued KTLA and all the major television networks for $100 million for showing the tape without his permission. In addition, he wanted $7,500 from individual television stations that aired the tape and $2,500 for any use of the video by a station for the next five years. U.S. District Judge Irving Hill dismissed the suit, saying that the news organizations had a right to air the video because of First Amendment freedoms and the social importance of its content. He argued, "No words could substitute for the public insight gained by looking at the motion picture. . . ." Nevertheless, according to published reports, Holliday received up to $100,000 because of the videotape, but he claims he made less than $10,000. For his promotion of a commercial videotape called "Shoot News and Make Money with Your Camcorder," he received a small royalty. Director Spike Lee paid Holliday to use the video in the opening sequence of his movie *Malcolm X.*

Other individuals involved in the story have made money. Chief Gates and Sgt. Koon both wrote best-selling books. Koon earned $10,000 for an "A Current Affair" interview, and Phil Donahue paid Briseno $25,000 for an appearance.

Because of the state trial's not-guilty verdicts, prosecutors in the federal trial of the four police officers didn't rely as heavily as the state had on the videotape to tell the story of the beating. The federal trial was held in Los Angeles before a multicultural jury. This time, all the officers except Briseno, who tried to stop one of Powell's baton strikes, were found guilty. The Reverend Jesse Jackson remarked that although he was pleased with the verdict, "There are many other police beating victims without the benefit of a Holliday videotape." In August 1993, Judge John Davies sentenced Koon and Powell to less than three years each. Davies concluded that only six of the fifty-six baton blows were illegal and that Rodney King's erratic, alcohol-induced behavior was partly responsible for the officers' behavior.

Rodney King's life since the verdict has been anything but ideal. He has been arrested several times for misdemeanor drug charges, driving with illegally tinted windows, and physically abusing the mother of his teenage daughter. In September 2001 he was arrested for allegedly being under the influence of a psychedelic drug and exposing himself in a public park. In a final irony, George Holliday no longer has the camcorder he used to take the famous footage. When his wife and he divorced, she took the camera. "I'll get another one," he admits. "I like gadgets. But not right now. I can't afford it."

■ ANALYSIS OF THE RODNEY KING VIDEO

Witnessing such a vividly shocking example of government-sponsored violence from any country is rare—especially in the United States with our democratic traditions and rights spelled out in the Constitution, which are supposed to protect citizens from such abuses by government. The visual message is shocking, sickening, and unforgettable. The tape exemplifies the emotional power of images better than any words could possibly explain.

For many viewers of the videotape, the sight of Anglo police officers with wooden clubs brutally beating the slumped form of an African-American man reminded them of the still photographs and newsreel footage supplied by journalists at the height of the civil rights movement in the 1950s. Forty years separate the Rodney King incident and the sight of African Americans struck by high-powered water hoses and attacked by police dogs.

The George Holliday tape is a grainy, low-exposure, out-of-focus, high-contrast, high-perspective, remote location, single camera, poor audio, and shaky version of reality. As such, the picture is an excellent example of the cinema verité approach to documentary filming, in which the camera distorts the content within the camera's frame. Motion picture and television directors try to grab a viewer's attention by using the techniques that Holliday unknowingly applied in his amateur effort.

KTLA paid Holliday $500 for the videotape because the images were unusual, dramatic, and important—a common definition of news for most journalists. The categorical imperative guided the initial reaction to the tape—if an image is newsworthy, the news organization must show it. Utilitarianism came into play in the suspension of the rights to privacy of King and the officers. More important than their rights to privacy was showing their actions to a wider audience.

Unfortunately, however, hedonism was at play more than any of the other ethical philosophies. Undoubtedly, Rodney King should be compensated by the city of Los Angeles for the acts inflicted by its employees—but $56 million seems excessive. Likewise, George Holliday probably should have been paid more than $500 for his video-tape—but is it worth $100 million?

The arrest of Rodney King, the videotape by George Holliday, and the phenomenon of the videotape's notoriety are three separate components of the cultural perspective. Because of few educational and economic opportunities for an African American born into a depressed urban center in the United States, arrests for speeding, driving while intoxicated, and resisting arrest and more serious crimes are far too common. The media's fascination with and reliance on sensational, so-called reality-based video reflect the culture's obsession with the violent. With so many fictionalized stories on television, actual dramatic footage from the scene of a tragedy attracts even more attention from viewers. At the same time, however, the broadcasting of violent home videos supplied by a growing number of eager, camcorder-holding neo-journalists distorts reality.

What is truthful for a single moment is not always the whole truth. The unusual visual content of the Holliday tape perpetuates stereotypes about those arrested and those attempting to make arrests. Most African Americans are never arrested. Most people with a video camera record the actions of their family members, not crimes in progress or arrests. Most police officers are professional, reasonable individuals. But the videotape fits the mentality of a culture that emphasizes short-term goals, quick fixes, and easy solutions to complex social problems.

When King thanked Holliday for saving his life at their coincidental meeting at a gas station, he did not mean the term literally—none of the officers knew of the taping at the scene. King's life was saved (or at least given a second chance) by his celebrity status as a result of the video. His sudden exalted position in society caused the charges to be dropped, gave him wealth he had never had

before, and produced rapt attention from others whenever he spoke. In the middle of the civil disturbance, he helped calm the city's fury with a hastily prepared press conference in which he spoke five memorable words: "Can we all get along?" If there had been no videotape of that dark winter night, he would have been thrown back in jail, without enough money to pay his bail, and no one would have cared what he had to say. Rodney King entered jail that night as a poor, degraded African American. But television transformed him into the equivalent of a rich, respected Anglo. The power of television comes from the power of visual messages to manipulate emotions. The best visual messages are memorable because they are simple. Memorable images, however, do not always reveal the truth—only the truth from a particular point of view (Figure 14.2).

■ *TELEVISION AND VIDEO AND THE SIX PERSPECTIVES*

Personal Perspective

Television is easy to criticize. Former Federal Communications Commission chairman Newton Minow, in a 1961 speech, called the medium "a vast wasteland." Philosopher Bertrand Russell growled that it was nothing more than "chewing gum for the eyes." In some cultures, it is hip to criticize "the boob tube." Mark Miller, in his book *Boxed In,* writes that "a great deal of the time when we are watching TV we know that it is stupid and enjoy the feeling of superiority." Mark Frost, co-creator with David Lynch of the short-lived and critically acclaimed "Twin Peaks" television series, admits that "in this country, television is used primarily as a narcotic to prepare people for the commercial."

Many viewers use a remote control device to flip from one program to another in the sometimes frustrating effort to find something interesting to watch. Called *channel grazing,* the curious habit of discovering a good program without the aid of a television guide evokes the wide-open plains of the Old West—the metaphor of a better life over the next hill or around the bend.

That promise of a better program through the next push of a button is where television gets its power. In the early history of the medium, viewers were content to be intrigued by the low-quality flickering pictures. With few stations and programs, people watched whatever was broadcast. Today, viewers are more fickle, demanding constant entertainment. The reason is simple—television actually is radio with pictures, and radio has roots deep in vaudeville theater. Consequently, television always was meant to be more of an entertainment than an educational medium. The high ideals and educational hopes came later. If you learn something from "The Beverly Hillbillies" or "Masterpiece Theatre," that is only because you the viewer have made entertainment educational (Figure 14.3). Conversely, producers of television shows hope that they make education entertaining. Whether you watch no television or seven hours a day, one conclusion is clear: TV is a medium in which the viewer is charged with the task of making sense of it all. Jack Perkins says that his Arts & Entertainment cable network "shows the entire scope of television, which is, of course, the entire scope of life." Television is life because it reveals much about the lives of those inside and outside the screen. As in the introduction to the 1960s medical drama "Ben Casey," television is "birth, death, man, woman, infinity." Whether conscious of television's effect or blissfully unaware, people eventually succumb to the enticing images that dance across the glowing glass frame.

ONE PICTURE IS WORTH ZERO

Courtesy of Paul Conrad; reprinted by permission, Los Angeles Times Syndicate

Figure 14.2

In a powerful re-creation of the beating of Rodney King, Los Angeles Times *editorial cartoonist Paul Conrad demonstrates his anger at the acquittal in the state trial of the four police officers.*

Television is a uniquely twentieth-century form of entertainment. No other culture during any other time in history has had the opportunity to enjoy the magical tube. If you were born after 1950, chances are that television has been your primary source of in-home, mass communication entertainment and information. Because the images come into familiar and intimate home settings, the characters are more easily recognizable, seem friendlier, and become more a part of your life than characters presented in any other media.

Probably the chief reason why television is so routinely criticized is the queasy feeling that comes from the thought that despite all the great moments presented—all

Figure 14.3

Many critics complained that shows like "The Beverly Hillbillies" were examples of the worst the medium has to offer. Note how the overloaded jalopy is purposely set in this publicity still to contrast with the expensive automobiles on a palm-lined southern California boulevard.

Getty Images/Hulton Archive

the news, drama, comedy, and sports—television never has lived up to its potential. There is always a feeling that television should be something more—something better. But no one is quite sure what that is. The hope is that 500-channel *teleputers*—a combination of telephones, televisions, and computers—will turn passive viewers into active, creative users. Stay tuned.

Historical Perspective

In the 1930s, when Hollywood executives first learned about the new medium of tele-

vision, they laughed at the idea of radio with pictures. In the 1940s they were concerned enough to reduce ticket prices and offer double features. In the 1950s the war was over—television had become the single most popular form of entertainment for Americans. Since the 1960s, the attitude of movie industry executives has been cooperation. The swift rise in the popularity of television reflects fascination with the medium itself, the types of programs offered on the small screen, and the fact that the pictures are delivered into the intimate surroundings of the home.

Television's Roots

The history of television dates from experiments conducted in the nineteenth century. There are two methods for producing televised images: mechanical and electronic scanning. In 1884, German scientist Paul Nipkow advocated the short-lived mechanical scanning technology. Similar to the earlier zoetropes, the machine scanned small pictures on a spinning wheel one line at a time. The American Charles Jenkins in 1923 first demonstrated a mechanical scanning apparatus publicly. He transmitted a photograph of President Harding from Washington to Philadelphia. However, this technology could only reproduce small, poor-quality images. Consequently, electronic scanning became the dominant technology for television. However, the principle behind mechanical scanning later helped develop laser disc technology.

In 1920, the American Allen DuMont invented the cathode-ray tube (CRT) in the form of an oscilloscope, a device that turns electromagnetic waves into visible patterns on a monitor. In 1922, an Idaho high school student, Philo (or Phil, as he preferred) Farnsworth, created a television set using DuMont's CRT. In 1927, Farnsworth transmitted images with his invention. After a lengthy court case, RCA officials worked out a royalty agreement that gave Farnsworth $1 million from 1939 to 1949. Because of the interest in television, GE, RCA, and Westinghouse scientists in 1930 merged their research operations. Russian immigrant Vladimir Zworykin headed the television team. In their laboratory in New Jersey, the scientists invented the iconoscope electronic scanning tube for television. The first transmission was a crude, 60-line reproduction of a small cartoon drawing of the popular character Felix the Cat. Its developers soon improved the iconoscope to a 441-line picture scanner. The success of these experiments led David Sarnoff, president of RCA, to decide in 1932 to invest heavily in this new technology. It was Sarnoff who came up with the word *television*—a combination of hearing and seeing by radio. The New York World's Fair in 1939 first introduced the public to television. Amazed fairgoers could enjoy early vaudeville acts, view the opening festivities of the long-awaited movie *Gone With the Wind* in Atlanta, and see Franklin D. Roosevelt, the first U.S. president to appear on television.

The 1940s

Concerned about competing technologies that would delay the spread of television, the Federal Communications Commission (FCC), a U.S. regulatory body overseeing radio and television, authorized sets to contain a 525-line electron scanner for black and white transmission in 1941. The FCC also allowed twenty-three very high frequency (VHF) channels for television. In a further concern over the dominance of RCA, the FCC told the corporation that it had to sell one of its networks. It sold a network in 1943 to Edward Noble of the Lifesaver Candy Company for $8 million, which eventually became ABC. Allen DuMont also made his own television sets and started his own network. However, World War II temporarily halted the spread of television because of the need for industry to concentrate on the war effort. The vacuum tubes required for the sets often burned out, but because of the war, replacement parts were impossible to find. During the war years, only six stations were broadcasting to about 10,000 sets in the United States. Most of the television sets were in bars, bowling alleys, appliance store windows, and the homes of wealthier families. Early television network executives simply saw the medium as a way to make additional money for their radio productions. No one believed that the small screen would become the cultural phenomenon that it is today.

In the 1940s, television broadcasting was limited to a short time in the evening. Radio employees re-created radio programs, announced some news, and narrated sporting events. After the war, attention once again turned to television. In fact, commercial television broadcasting began in earnest in 1946. NBC, CBS, ABC, and, to a lesser extent, the DuMont Network dominated the market because of the expense of establishing a station and the limited number of stations operating in any one area. A station cost about $1.5 million to construct, and, once built, it had to supply entertaining programs. The FCC authorized seven powerful VHF channels for commercial broadcasting in each market area. Consequently, large media corporations secured a VHF frequency in every large city in America. If some independent station operator wanted to supply programs for a particular market, the economical choice often was—and still is—the lower quality and weaker ultra high frequency (UHF) channels. The major networks were able to dominate the medium because most television sets received only VHF broadcasts.

Owing to concern over spectrum interference between two powerful VHF stations in adjacent areas, in 1948 the FCC imposed a freeze on further station construction until the problem could be solved. Nevertheless, the Rose Bowl parade and football game in Pasadena, coverage of the political conventions, and the popular vaudeville-style variety shows of Milton Berle and Ed Sullivan (Figures 14.4 and 14.5) were broadcast. Movie executives at war with the television medium prohibited their stars or motion pictures from appearing on television. The result was a bias against television acting by film stars (which still exists today) and the advent of television celebrities distinct from those in other forms of entertainment. Nevertheless, some farsighted movie moguls,

particularly after a 1948 antitrust ruling and the activities of the HUAC against the motion picture industry (Chapter 13), became interested in television production. For example, Columbia Pictures was the first studio to open a television production division, called Screen Gems, in 1951. Many others soon followed. Walt Disney agreed to make programs for ABC and later for NBC. Jack Warner's studio produced the popular "Cheyenne" western series, and in 1960 Warner Bros. made more than $40 million on its television productions.

The 1950s

Many writers have dubbed the 1950s "the golden age" of television because of technological and programming innovations. One fact is clear: During the decade, television gained a tremendous number of viewers and became a true mass medium. For example, the "I Love Lucy" show was a landmark production in 1951 for many reasons. Produced by Lucille Ball and Desi Arnaz by their Desilu production company in studios purchased from the failed movie studio RKO, the situation comedy (sitcom) was filmed with three cameras in front of a live audience and was enormously successful. Filmed productions meant that the shows could be shown again and again as reruns for additional profits.

When the FCC lifted its station freeze in 1952, television suddenly became a true mass medium with 108 stations. Fifteen million homes in the United States had television sets. Talk shows, with personable hosts such as Arthur Godfrey and Dave Garroway, dominated the morning and evening hours. "The Tonight Show," the longest running entertainment-oriented talk show, began in 1954. It has been hosted by Steve Allen, Jack Parr, Johnny Carson, and Jay Leno (Figure 14.6). Advertising revenue reached $324 million by 1953. Advertising agencies for particular products "sponsored" or purchased entire programs so that all the commercials would be for those products. Stars for the shows often would pitch products on the air. Today, selling commercials on an individual basis, with advertising rates set according to the Nielsen Company's viewer, is much more profitable.

Because of the high cost of television production, ABC merged with United Paramount Theaters in 1953 and survived. DuMont failed to attain additional funding and went out of business in 1955. In 1956, Hollywood lifted its ban on television. With movie stars and movies on television, the medium became even more popular. Movie theater attendance declined, and radio serial programs became obsolete. Radio became the medium for music and news, ironically Frank Conrad's original idea.

By 1956, 500 broadcast stations in the United States were generating more than $1 billion in advertising sales. Besides movie stars, theater actors were persuaded to perform on television in the mid-1950s. Programs such as "Philco Playhouse," "Studio One," "Kraft Television Theatre," and "Playhouse 90" produced such dramatic shows as "Marty," "The Days of Wine and Roses," and "Requiem for a Heavyweight." However, advertisers complained about the depressing content. Consequently, in the 1960s, shows that had happy endings replaced these "high-culture" productions.

Several attempts were made in the 1950s to censor content and individuals. In 1950, Senator Estes Kefauver led a movement to curtail the violence perceived in television programs. Kefauver's attempts at censorship coincided with another senator's effort to root out alleged Communists in the government and media. Joseph McCarthy of Wisconsin helped publish "Red Channels: The Report of Communist Influence in Radio and Television." The report listed 151

Getty Images/Hulton Archive

Getty Images/Hulton Archive

Figure 14.4

Tuesday night was called Berle night in the early days of television. Milton Berle's variety show, "The Texaco Star Theater" (as if you couldn't guess), was so popular that restaurant and movie theater owners often gave up trying to attract customers away from their television sets. Here, Berle roughs up a young magician on stage for a laugh.

Figure 14.5

Ed Sullivan's talent was that his personality never competed with those of the stars on his show—a glorified vaudeville theater presentation. Here, he poses with actress Gina Lollobrigida.

Getty Images/Hulton Archive

Figure 14.6

The original "Tonight Show" host, Steve Allen, speaks into a microphone on a set that resembles a bank president's office.

suspects, whom the networks blacklisted because of fear of advertiser boycotts (Figure 14.7). In 1952, the FCC, concerned about the content of programs sent into homes, required that 10 percent (later increased to 35 percent) of a day's broadcasting be educational. This regulation marked the beginning of the FCC's shift from frequency allocation to content regulation. However, direct censorship proved to be ineffective. McCarthy was discredited and later censured by the Senate in 1954 after a news broadcast in which Edward R. Murrow, the CBS journalist, revealed McCarthy's unfair smear practices (Figure 14.8).

The 1958 quiz show scandal rocked the television industry. A congressional investigation discovered that contestants had been coached with the correct answers in order to make the programs more dramatic. The networks canceled many quiz shows after Charles Van Doren testified that he had been given the answers for the show "Twenty-One." Quiz shows soon returned to daytime television, but under stiffer regulations (Figure 14.9).

As with the motion picture industry, television also was subjected to political efforts by conservatives to control program content. Since the 1950s, television program content has been regulated by the networks themselves, the government, advertisers, and public pressure groups to varying degrees.

Color, videotape, and cable were introduced in the 1950s, and CBS and RCA proposed two different systems for camera and receiver color. The FCC tried to delay the switch to color, fearing that the transition would be too expensive. Nevertheless, the FCC approved RCA's color technology as the industry standard. Because of the time required for stations to convert and for the public to purchase color television sets, not until the 1960s did color transmission and reception become common. One of the first shows in color was NBC's "Wonderful World of Color." It opened with the network's brightly painted peacock and was hosted by Walt Disney. The show was as much a promotion of color television as it was a commercial for Disney productions. In the late 1950s, videotape technology revolutionized television production. Shows could be scheduled for taping at any time, and mistakes could be corrected easily. Eventually, much of television was pretaped. More important, videotape allowed high-quality reproductions of programs so that huge amounts of money could be made from showing reruns of previously aired shows.

Cable or pay television began as a way to bring television to communities in Pennsylvania that were nestled among mountains that prevented over-the-air reception. The cable company received television signals and then piped them into individual homes through **coaxial cable** links. Customers paid about $10 a month for the service. By 1952, some seventy cable systems across the United States served 14,000 subscribers.

Figure 14.7

*"The focus of attention."
Senator Joseph McCarthy in
1954 answering charges that
a photograph he is holding
was altered to fit his political
agenda (it was). Eventually,
the U.S. Senate censured
him, but not before he ruined
the careers of many people
connected with the motion
picture and television
industries.*

Figure 14.8

*CBS journalists Edward R.
Murrow (left), Charles
Collingwood, and Eric
Sevareid discuss election
returns on a program.*

Getty Images/Hulton Archive

Figure 14.9

Game shows in the 1950s were rocked with scandal when it was learned that some contestants were given correct answers in order to make the shows more exciting. "The $64,000 Question," sponsored by the Revlon makeup company, typified the classic elements of a game show: a hostess wearing an evening gown with nothing much to do but smile, a congenial host (Hal March) with the questions and answers, contestants who appear to be ordinary people, and the "soundproof booth," which often was wheeled to the middle of the set to add drama.

The 1960s

By 1960, more than 90 percent of the homes in the United States had at least one television set. Cable companies flourished, with more than 650,000 subscribers and 640 firms. Besides better reception, viewers with cable could get many more channels and commercial-free sporting events and movies than could viewers of the broadcast networks. However, most programs were dull and formulaic. As a result of the criticism of the pretentious theatrical productions of the 1950s, networks concentrated on action-adventure dramas produced outside of theater studios. "The Defenders" and "East Side, West Side" are examples of New York, on-location productions. One of the most controversial was the Desilu production of "The Untouchables." With its Elliot Ness–inspired stories, car crashes, and flying bullets, the show, according to a Senate subcommittee, was "the most violent program on television." Concerned that Congress might seek censorship through legislation, network

executives moved most of their production facilities to California, where Hollywood was responsible for mass-appeal, inoffensive sitcoms such as "Mr. Ed," "Gilligan's Island," and "The Beverly Hillbillies." Motion picture executives also were scrambling to offset losses from falling theater attendance. The first prime-time movie program, "Saturday Night at the Movies," started in 1961. Home viewers could watch successful second-run motion pictures, if they didn't object to the commercials. By 1968, movies were being broadcast every night of the week. Because the trend rapidly depleted Hollywood's supply of movies, in 1969 ABC started to produce its own made-for-television movies for its program "The Movie of the Week."

Although most entertainment programs were criticized, news and sports during the politically troubled 1960s were experiencing their own golden age. The 1960 John Kennedy and Richard Nixon televised presidential debate for the first time showed political managers the importance of a candidate's image on television (Figure 14.10). Many thought that Nixon's five o'clock shadow and nervous appearance, seen clearly with the small screen's close-ups, caused his narrow defeat. In 1962, AT&T and NASA collaborated to develop and launch the first communications satellite, Telstar I. Live television transmission between Europe and the United States became possible, but only for short periods at a time because of the satellite's movement through space. To correct the problem, NASA launched the first geosynchronous satellite, Early Bird, in 1964 to provide continuous transmission of television signals. It could do so because it traveled at the same speed as the Earth's rotation, 22,300 miles above the equator. The idea for a geosynchronous orbit for satellites initially came from science fiction writer Arthur C. Clarke and is often referred to as "Clarke's Orbit."

Figure 14.10

Journalists scramble on stage to interview Richard Nixon and John Kennedy after their first televised debate. The power of the visual medium was evident, as many who heard the debate on radio thought that Nixon had won, but those watching television were sure that Kennedy was the clear winner.

Getty Images/Hulton Archive

With the advent of instant replay technology for sports programs, ABC became a leading network. New leagues were formed to take advantage of the tremendous profits provided by televised sporting events.

With satellite and videotape technology, news programs could cover many social and political events. Vivid images of assassinations, civil rights marches, political speeches, and the Vietnam War had a tremendous impact on viewers who watched them on their home screens. The effect of bringing the outside world's problems into the home was that the social problems protested in the 1960s could not be ignored. Consequently, African-American actors were selected for dramatic series and as news reporters. Jackie Gleason was one of the first producers to hire an African-American dancer for the chorus line of a variety show. Bill Cosby in "I Spy" and Diahann Carroll in "Julia" portrayed upper-class African-American characters. But when variety shows tried to inject political humor into their prime-time pro-

grams, they were soon canceled. "The Smothers Brothers Comedy Hour" and "Laugh-In" were short-lived casualties of executive censorship.

The 1970s

In the 1970s, the federal government became proactive in regulating television content. Congressional action banned cigarette commercials from television in 1972. (To avoid a similar fate, beer company advertisements never show a person actually drinking.) In 1973, broadcasters were required to provide time for opposing viewpoints. This followed a 1969 Supreme Court ruling in *Red Lion Broadcasting v. FCC.* The Fairness Doctrine is an FCC rule that dates from 1941. It is based on the opinion that minority points of view cannot get a fair hearing because of the limited number of channels. However, a 1987 FCC ruling diluted the doctrine, and the advent of many new technologies for transmitting programs has made it irrelevant. In 1972, cable became competitive with the broadcast networks when Home Box Office (HBO) started to air second-run movies.

In an effort to forestall FCC action against adult-oriented programs, the National Association of Broadcasters (NAB) accepted a code for stations in 1975 that established the "family hour" before 9:00 P.M. Excessive sexual or violent programs were not allowed during that time, when large numbers of children were likely to be watching television. Widely opposed by program producers, the code was repealed after a court battle. Nevertheless, concern over the amount of sexually explicit and violent action programming has resulted in the latest effort to head off direct censorship— a violence rating symbol that identifies a program as excessively gruesome.

During the 1970s, spin-offs, or shows based on characters from previously broadcast programs, proliferated. For example, the popular sitcoms "All in the Family" and "The Mary Tyler Moore Show" resulted in fifteen separate spin-offs and gave independent television production companies—Tandem for "Family" and MTM Productions for "Moore"—as much financial clout as the movie studios.

The 1980s

In the 1980s, Capital Cities Communication bought ABC, General Electric purchased NBC's parent company, RCA, and Westinghouse purchased CBS. Cost-cutting measures at all three networks resulted in fewer highly trained journalists in their news divisions. This move allowed Ted Turner's 24-hour news channel, the Cable News Network (CNN), to become the preeminent source of worldwide news. In 1985, Australian tabloid mogul Rupert Murdoch bought half control of 20th Century Fox. Two years later the Fox Broadcasting Company, a fourth broadcasting network, intro-

duced one night a week of Fox-produced shows to its 105 independent stations. With the success of "The Simpsons" (Chapter 11), its programming, once dominated by reruns, expanded to include several original productions. To protect their investments, television networks, cable companies, and movie studios have formed partnerships. For example, HBO, CBS, and Columbia Pictures formed TriStar Pictures, Inc., to make motion pictures for both the big and small screens.

The 1990s and Beyond

Concern over excessive commercialism during children's shows prompted a 1990 law, the Children's Television Act, that limited stations to 12 minutes of commercials per hour on weekdays and created guidelines for educational programming for kids.

Two news events—the U.S. presidential election of 2000 and the aerial attacks upon the World Trade Center towers in New York City and the Pentagon in Washington, D.C., and the subsequent "War on Terrorism"—contributed greatly to the way news was presented on television. The way both stories were covered demonstrates how a desire for individuals within a news organization to "scoop" the competition sometimes leads to inaccurate reports and unethical practices.

The 2000 presidential election between Vice President Al Gore and George W. Bush was the closest race in the history of the United States. It was finally decided by the results in one state—Florida. Who can forget the coverage concerning confusing "butterfly ballots" in Palm Beach County, Florida, and "pregnant chads" during the recount? In the end, the election was in effect decided by a historic 5–4 vote among members of the U.S. Supreme Court. A desire to get the results out before anyone else produced one of the most embarrassing episodes during election night. The major news outlets—

ABC, the Associated Press, CBS, CNN, Fox News, and NBC—all own the Voter News Service (VNS), a company that conducts voter exit polls in order to project winners in political races. Relying on one news source proved costly for the news media. First, Vice President Al Gore was declared the winner by all the major networks. Then early in the morning, that announcement was recanted. Following that, Bush was announced the winner. Finally, it was reported that the election was too close to call, setting up subsequent weeks of agonizing details about ballot confusions, counting processes, and legal maneuvers by attorneys from the Democrat and Republican sides. This dark episode in the history of election coverage points out the fact that news organizations often want to be the first to proclaim an important announcement, even at the cost of being wrong. In the future it is quite possible that television newscasts will be forced to wait until all the polls are closed before announcing a projected winner.

Given the magnitude of the colossal damage and tremendous loss of life because of the aerial attacks in New York, Washington, D.C., and Pennsylvania, it seems obvious that the national television news organizations would pool their video footage in order to provide anxious viewers around the world with images from the events of September 11, 2001. But such an agreement was not standard procedure. Concerned about the need for the public to get as much information as possible, CBS's "60 Minutes" executive producer Don Hewitt called all the broadcast and cable news organizations and formed an alliance in which "generic video," but not reporters, would be shared equally. Eason Jordan, Chief News Executive for the CNN News Group, said, "This transcends competition. There's just no precedence for the horror of what we saw today, at least in the history of TV news."

Yet less than a month later, CNN executives were forced to explain why they demanded exclusive rights to video of the attack on Kabul, Afghanistan. The Al-Jazeera Satellite Channel, a news outlet based in Qatar, had an agreement with CNN that gave the American cable company a six-hour exclusive right to any video produced by Al-Jazeera. All the other major television news organizations condemned CNN for the arrangement given the scope of the story. Typical of the condemnation was this statement from ABC News, "We felt there was overwhelming national interest in showing the American people those images from Afghanistan, which far outweighed whatever commercial agenda CNN was attempting to pursue." After Jordan was reminded what he had said a month earlier concerning the shared coverage, CNN decided not to enforce the exclusivity agreement for the time being. The nature of the twin towers story caused executives, at least momentarily, to resist their competitive urges.

The 1990s and beyond also saw delivery methods for expanded channel systems that include broadcast, high-powered satellites, telephone, standard and digital cable, and fiber-optic technology. Another innovation that has tremendous effect for television and the motion picture industry is digital versatile discs (DVDs). Because of the huge amount of data that can fit on a DVD, movies can include additional footage, director and actor comments, entire screenplays, and so on. In the fall of 2001 DVD boxed sets of the *Godfather* motion picture trilogy and *Star Wars: Episode I—The Phantom Menace* were introduced that are the finest examples this new technology has to offer.

But whether television is an intellectual wasteland that makes people ignorant, more violent, and more prone to stereotype individuals or a "window on the world" that educates and informs people, broadening their horizons and empowering them as citizens, will always be debated.

Videotape

Before the "I Love Lucy" show, the only way to preserve a copy of a program was in low-quality kinescopes—low-resolution film shot directly from a television screen. Kinescopes were simply used as low-cost, fuzzy, historical records. No one thought of the earning potential of reruns until Desi Arnaz's idea of using film and three cameras (Figure 14.11). But film from three cameras was expensive to produce and tedious to edit. Consequently, the industry started to look for alternatives to kinescopes and film. The invention of videotape technology allowed taped rather than live productions, high-quality syndicated programs, and delayed newscasts for the West Coast. It inspired artistic applications and helped build the billion-dollar home video market for the production and playing of videotape programs. David Sarnoff of RCA predicted in 1953 that viewers at home someday would be able to record television programs and play them endlessly, as they did phonograph records. Three years later, his prophecy began to take shape.

A southern California company, Ampex, more known for its sound equipment, began working in the early 1950s on a videotape system. At the NAB annual convention in Chicago in 1956, Charles Ginsburg demonstrated the new method for recording programs. The convention was set up with closed-circuit television for those not able to get into the auditorium. Ginsburg tapped into the system, recorded a few minutes of the proceedings, and played the tape back for astonished attendees. Within days of the NAB convention Ampex had received about fifty orders for its $74,000 videotape system. CBS was one of its first customers and began rebroadcasting the nightly news program

hosted by Douglas Edwards to its West Coast affiliates at a normal viewing time. Previously, low-quality kinescope reproductions had been the only alternative to unacceptably early airing of the news. Editing the videotape was difficult at first because the tape, like film, had to be spliced together. By 1963, the technology advanced to make editing much easier.

Despite Ampex's lead in videotape technology, American executives didn't foresee the enormous popularity of the medium. As a result, Japanese firms entered the market. In 1965, the Sony Corporation introduced its Portapak—an easily transported videotape camera and recording machine that could fit in a backpack.

When the major networks adopted videotape production for their programs, they almost eliminated the need to broadcast live performances. Shows often were produced before a live studio audience with a "laugh track" supplied by special-effects technicians. When the actors made mistakes, the performance was halted, the action started again, and the tape was easily edited in the control room. Live sports programs, however, could not be edited. But in 1967 the public became aware of the potential for videotape technology to add to their viewing pleasure when TV introduced the instant replay during the Super Bowl football game. In the 1970s, professional electronic news gathering (ENG) videotape trucks were equipped with all the switching and editing equipment found in a station's control room. Large ENG trucks became common sights outside sports stadiums when games were televised. When the technology became linked with satellites and the equipment grew smaller, local news stations could send news teams to cover events anywhere in a city or the world.

To further increase the popularity of home video recording equipment, in the

1980s Sony introduced its Video 8 camera (the palmcorder). It is a small, lightweight camera that uses high-quality 8-mm tape. Although a loser in the videocassette recorder (VCR) industry, Sony is clearly ahead in camera technology. Small, easily operated cameras have led to an explosion in personal visual recordings that have replaced old-fashioned technologies. Hardly anyone anymore has family and friends over to watch pictures with slide or 8-mm movie projectors.

As many people carry and use video and digital cameras, camcorders or palmcorders also allow news organizations to show dramatic video of tragic events shot by amateurs. Reality-based television programs and electronic video monitoring systems are common uses for the equipment. Security systems at homes and businesses record the actions of every passerby; police officers

Getty Images/Hulton Archive

Figure 14.11

Above: In this publicity still for the "I Love Lucy" show, the characters of Ricky and Lucy Ricardo are portrayed as they are forever remembered by countless fans throughout the world. Below: But as evidenced by the expressions on the faces of Desi Arnaz and Lucille Ball between scenes, making a situation comedy is hard work. Note the large film cameras in the foreground. "I Love Lucy" was the first television program to be filmed in front of a live audience.

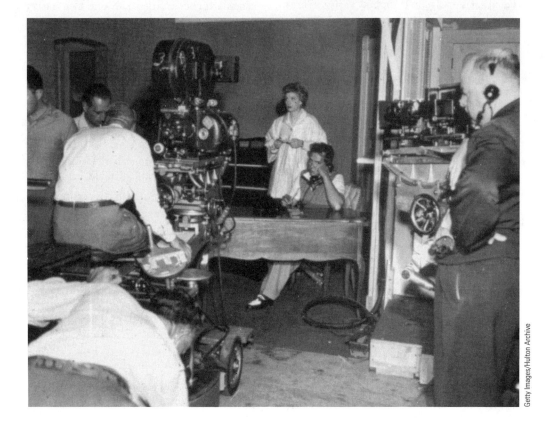

Getty Images/Hulton Archive

have video cameras in their patrol cars to monitor the actions of those detained or arrested; and news teams hide cameras in their clothing to record illegal practices for the visually oriented nightly newscasts. Sometimes gruesome shootings during convenience store robberies captured by video monitoring equipment are aired on newscasts. Made possible by the video revolution, the spread of sensational news is a chief concern of many of television's social critics.

Home users clearly desire the ability to record and watch feature-length movies. Thus in 1979, Hollywood executives started to make their motion pictures available on portable cassettes for purchase by consumers. In 1981, sales for previously released movies totaled $1 million. When videotaped movies became available for overnight rental in the early 1980s, they were instantly and enormously popular. In 1997, the number of video sales and rentals topped $330 million. That led Mel Brooks, the director of *Blazing Saddles* and *Young Frankenstein,* to remark that "pictures never die. They go to heaven. It's called video."

Executives of large movie rental companies, such as Blockbuster Video, are concerned about the advent of pay-per-view motion pictures over cable, telephone, or fiber-optic lines. Many experts predict that the rental and sale of videotaped films will become obsolete when watching electronically transmitted movies at home on teleprompters through the World Wide Web becomes much more convenient.

Technical Perspective

Movie studio executives laughed when they first saw television because they never believed that the small, fuzzy black and white picture, with its poor audio component, would ever be a serious threat to their industry. What the studio heads did not imagine was how resourceful technicians would be in improving the medium. Over the years, cameras, transmission modes, and receivers have been refined continuously.

Cameras

Using the video camera's controls is the same as using a still camera (Chapter 12), and shot considerations are determined the same way as in motion pictures (Chapter 13). The chief difference between a camera used for still or motion picture production and one used for television is that video cameras have a tube or microchip, called a *charge-coupled device* (CCD), that converts the image into an electrical equivalent. When a television operator focuses on a subject with the camera's lens, the picture strikes a layer of photosensitive material consisting of dots, which emit an electrical charge. A dot in a light part of a picture sends a higher charge than one in a darker part of the image. All the electrical charges from the dots strike a target and compose an electrical version of the image in the form of 525 lines (636 or 840 lines for non-U.S. systems). An electron gun in the back of the camera generates a steady stream of electrons that scan the target. In the U.S. system, the electron scanning starts with the odd-numbered lines and repeats the process with the even-numbered lines. The two scans take 1/30 second, or accomplish the scanning at a rate of 30 frames a second (Figure 14.12).

The scanned electrical images are sent through a wire to monitors in the master control area of the station where a director composes the program by switching from one camera's image to another. These images are recorded on videotape to be sent at a later time or are transmitted immediately.

Transmission Modes

Television signals can be sent to a home in many different ways. Air transmission includes broadcast and satellite. Earth connections involve coaxial cable and fiber-optic cable.

Air Transmissions

Broadcast Originally a home required a large roof-mounted antenna to pick up the audio and video signals sent by a television station. The sound signal is sent via FM radio; the pictures can come from either VHF or UHF channels on the electromagnetic spectrum. Both VHF and UHF are known as line-of-sight **carrier waves.** The more powerful VHF stations can usually go around barriers such as buildings, mountains, or large weather systems, but UHF channels are susceptible to interference. The broadcasting of television programs by VHF and UHF stations first introduced television into people's homes. However, such methods are quickly becoming obsolete.

Satellite Since the 1970s, consumers have been able to buy a large and expensive receiving dish pointed in a southern direction that was required to capture television images from a satellite in a geosynchronous orbit around the earth. People living in rural communities where broadcast stations didn't reach and the distance was too far for the local cable company to string wire to their houses first used satellite dishes. But viewers in cities learned that they could receive hundreds of channels from all over the world and many premium cable networks (HBO, Showtime, the Playboy Channel, and others) without having to pay a monthly charge. Direct broadcast satellites (DBSs) are the new generation of reception technology that use digital transmission to send hundreds of channels to 18-inch-diameter, window-mounted dishes with high-quality images and sound. For example, Hughes Electronics Corporation, with its DirecTV service, has three high-power satellites in space that

Courtesy of Hitachi

Figure 14.12

Television broadcast stations will need to convert from analog to digital transmissions when HDTV replaces the current broadcast standard. Consequently, companies such as Hitachi are ready to sell cameras that are capable of transmitting both types of signals.

enable home users to receive more than 185 television channels. There is a problem with satellite transmission, however. As vast as space is, only a limited number of communications satellites can be put in the sky. A satellite must be placed in a "slot" that is 916 miles wide to avoid collision and frequency interference with another satellite (although sometimes more than one satellite occupies a space). Around the earth, therefore, there are 180 slots for satellites. Because company executives naturally want their equipment flying over heavily populated areas, satellite use and slots will become more expensive.

Earth Transmission

Coaxial Cable One of the most common home connections for television is through traditional cable. Coaxial cable comprises two metal cables that are separated by insulation; one cable transmits the sound, and the other transmits the picture. A cable company pays a fee to receive signals from program producers via a large satellite dish. The coaxial cable connects the cable operator's facility to a person's home. Depending on the services desired, a home can receive 50 to 150 channels. If needed, the cable company supplies a converter box that connects to the television set and changes the cable signal so that the receiver can show the images. However, most new TV sets are "cable ready," having a built-in signal converter. With digital compression of the cable signal and a much more sophisticated converter box that decodes compressed digital signals, experts predict that coaxial cable could easily be used to transmit more channels. For example, Comcast Cable offers standard and digital cable as well as high-speed Internet access for a total of 8.4 million customers in the United States.

Fiber-Optic Cable Many experts predict that fiber-optic cable will be the delivery system of choice in the future. The reason is simple—audio and video signals can be sent in both directions via pulses of light within a hairlike glass filament with little static. Because visible light is the carrier wave, the amount of information that can be sent is virtually unlimited. Fiber-optic cable will make advanced educational and entertainment services possible as it replaces current transmission technologies for home communications—coaxial cable and broadcast—with light pathways. Although rewiring the entire country will be extremely expensive, fiber-optic cable has the potential to turn television into a completely different medium—one in which the best features of the book, newspaper, magazine, telephone, movie, radio, television, and computer are combined into a single machine, the teleputer. However, because of the economic downturn in the United States and throughout the world (see Chapter 16), fiber-optic technology will be delayed.

Receivers

Curved screens, lack of sharpness, little contrast, and broadcast reception that often was snowy or distorted hampered early TV viewing. Because of different standards, U.S. television screens are inferior to the European version. For an American set, an average receiver contains 210,000 phosphorescent dots arranged in a pattern of 30 lines

per inch, or 525 lines. The European system has better resolution because the screen has a total of 90 lines per inch, or 625 total lines. But the resolution for both screens is lower than that of an average halftone photograph, which usually is printed at 133 lines per inch.

Essentially, reproduction of the signal for home viewing is the reverse of the process that occurs inside the video camera. In the rear of a CRT an electron gun scans the back of a picture screen in the same manner as the camera tube. Color television is produced when electrons cause the phosphorescent red, green, and blue dots on the screen to glow, corresponding to the brightness of the picture. At thirty frames a second, one frame blends into another (as with motion pictures) to form a continuous image. Ten lines of the 525 that make up a U.S. television set aren't used for the picture. Called the video blanking interval (VBI), this black strip can be used for textual information. For example, cutlines for the hard-of-hearing are sent via the VBI when programs are designated "closed-caption."

When TV sets first were produced, the screen had the same aspect ratio as that of early motion picture theaters—1.33 (sometimes referred to as 4:3), or the **Academy standard.** The almost square format seemed logical until the movie industry introduced widescreen technology (Chapter 13). Details from each side of a widescreen movie are lost because of cropping to fit the television screen. The letterbox format, named after the wide slot in mailboxes, shows the entire side-to-side image but the overall picture is smaller. A new generation of television sets, however, overcomes that problem with screens that are the same ratio as in a theater. Philips, JVC, Sony, Sharp, and Panasonic all produce widescreen receivers so that none of a movie's picture is lost.

High-definition television (HDTV) is a leap in technological development akin to the switch from black and white to color. With digital transmission, pictures are as sharp as high-quality photographs—ten times the picture resolution obtained by **analog** television broadcasts. In addition, the sound is of CD quality. But more important, with digital transmission, television sets can become interactive computers in which users can order shows when they want to view them, watch sporting events from specific cameras on the field, learn more information about a program's topic, order products seen in shows, and so on (Chapters 15 and 16).

In the spring of 2002, 256 television stations in the United States broadcast digitally, but few transmit high-definition signals. It is estimated that consumers have purchased more than 2 million digital television sets, but without a separate decoder box, fewer than 200,000 can receive the high-definition signals. With new digital television sets costing about $10,000 and few programs being shown in the new format, the digital revolution in television will take some time.

Ethical Perspective

If you let water gush into a kitchen sink for hours, keep all the lights on during the day, or leave the doors and windows wide open at your home, chances are that eventually you will be criticized for such careless behavior. But a television set left on, even when no one is watching, is a cultural standard. Over a twenty-year period the average household will have had a television set turned on for almost six years. It is no coincidence that a television set usually sits in the most comfortable room in a home. Although an impersonal appliance, it evokes the same emotional response as a favorite chair, a soft pillow, or an interesting friend. Television characters become comfortable personalities whom we invite into our lives.

Talk show hosts and nightly newscast announcers look right into the camera and talk directly to us. The illusion is maintained when friendly Dan Rather ends a news program with "I'll see you tomorrow." The television set must remain on—no one wants to offend a friend.

Television demands a price for its friendship. The cost is acceptance of the image of the moment as real and representative of society as a whole. Such a belief comes from the cultural notion that education and learning are bitter tasting medicines that end once you are out of school. Such acceptance comes from laziness and peer acceptance. The popular notion is that television is only a form of entertainment, meant to give a laugh or a thrill. Serious, sensitive social issues do not belong on television. Such programming is considered boring, high-minded, and elitist.

Entertainment and education get merged into something called "edutainment." Programs and commercials all have the same interest level and visual style. Fiction and nonfiction in drama and news shows get jumbled together. Small, insignificant issues become important trends because the medium blows them out of proportion. Vital, important concerns get reduced to a small screen—war over dinner. Simple-minded stereotypes about people and generalizations about communities are reinforced. As much as we love television, it is a medium that we love to hate—especially for its reliance on ratings, stereotyping, and sexual and violent themes.

Ratings

Lynn Gross, in her textbook *See/Hear: An Introduction to Broadcasting*, writes that an unnamed television executive once said, "There are only two rules in broadcasting: Keep the ratings as high as possible and don't get in any trouble." The A. C. Nielsen

Company determines a program's rating. The company began as a rating service for radio audiences in 1935 and naturally evolved into television. There are 1,200 Nielsen households scattered throughout the United States that reflect the diversity of television interests. Each home television set is connected to an electronic device—called the *audiometer*—that determines the programs to which the set is tuned during the prime-time hours of 8:00 P.M. to 11:00 P.M. Eastern Standard Time. A high rating is vital for the success of a show because executives with a highly rated show can charge more for its commercial time than with a poorly rated program. A thirty-second commercial aired on a Super Bowl telecast can cost hundreds of thousands of dollars.

The only networks that sell entertainment in the tradition of Hollywood are the premium cable channels that show second-run movies. All other networks, especially the **"big three,"** rely on ratings. A single rating point can amount to millions of dollars in revenue to a network. And with individual programs costing as much as $1 million network executives need not only large audiences but also viewers who are younger, upscale, and likely to buy the advertised products. A show with an audience of 5 to 10 million, although much larger than the circulation of most daily newspapers and subscribers to many magazines, is considered a bomb. A program may be popular, may attract a huge audience, but still may be canceled because its viewers are of the wrong demographic type. In the 1970s, for example, although it was enormously popular, "Gunsmoke" was canceled because it attracted a largely rural audience with little buying power.

An emphasis on ratings relegates high-quality broadcasting to the low-rated Public Broadcasting Service (PBS), which depends on government support and viewer and corporate donations. One reason that British television enjoys a reputation for creating high-quality programs is because its citizens pay an annual license fee for every TV set purchased. Sophisticated dramas such as "Upstairs Downstairs" and "Brideshead Revisited" and comedies such as "Till Death Do Us Part," the inspiration for "All in the Family," are shown on English television without the fear that a poor rating will cause a cancellation. Another problem for local and network programming comes during the rating period known as "sweeps week." Three times a year, for one week in February, May, and November, the Nielsen Company provides a rating for all time periods. Local stations use the sweeps to determine their advertising rates. About 200,000 households keep diaries and are interviewed in order to determine their television viewing habits during these crucial weeks. Because attracting large audiences is important during these times, more often than not, most of the gratuitous sex and violence most critics complain about show up during the sweeps weeks.

Stereotypes

Of the seventy-four prime-time shows in the fall 1998 television schedule, twelve involved all (or almost all) African-American casts. There are generally two schools of thought about multicultural group representation in the media: Some believe that quantity is better than quality, but others believe that the opposite is true. "Amos 'n' Andy" was the first prime-time show to feature an all African-American cast (Figure 14.13). The comedy about the troubles encountered by a group of African Americans played for twenty years on radio by Anglo actors with little controversy. But when the program aired on television in 1950, the NAACP organized a boycott of its sponsor, Blatz Beer, while middle-class African Americans complained that "every black is either a clown or a crook." Seeing the program rather than simply hearing it made racism more obvious. The program featured characters with "baggy pants, foul cigars, pushy wives, misfired schemes and mangled grammar." Anglo audiences in the 1950s enjoyed the wholesome suburban tales of "Father Knows Best," "The Donna Reed Show," and "Leave It to Beaver" (Figures 14.14 and 14.15). At the time, popular African-American musician Lionel Hampton said, "I look upon the new 'Amos 'n' Andy' television show as an opening wedge toward greater opportunities and bigger things for scores of our capable artists." But Sandra Evers-Manley of the NAACP complains that the use of stereotypical characters, no matter how many, is not progress.

Other cultural groups also have their complaints about television portrayals. Italian Americans protested the violent acts committed by members of their culture in "The Untouchables" (Figure 14.16). Likewise, Mexican Americans managed to get the Frito Bandito, a cartoon character used by the Frito-Lay company to sell its corn chips, off the air. Emir, an "Ali Baba" stereotype character in "Major Dad," offended Arab Americans.

Expecting television programs to be completely free from some kind of stereotyping of individuals is unreasonable. Someone, somewhere, is bound to object to a media characterization. But because of the enormous scope and influence of television, producers need to be especially sensitive to characterizations that have the potential to cause harm. The problem is that Anglo producers often are unaware of the concerns of those from other cultures. One way of ensuring sensitivity to cultural awareness is by hiring people from diverse cultures.

Sexual and Violent Themes

A recent study of viewer behavior estimated that an American child who watches three hours of television a day will have seen

Figure 14.13

When two Anglo actors portrayed the "Amos 'n' Andy" characters for many years on radio, hardly a soul complained. When it was brought to television, however, the show was quickly taken off the air because of criticism concerning its stereotypical characters.

Getty Images/Hulton Archive

8,000 murders and some 100,000 other acts of violence by the time the child is twelve years old. No distinction is made between fictional and nonfictional violence. Media images generally, but on television particularly, are blamed for everything from an increase in sexual harassment in schools to drive-by shootings.

Common sense raises the question of whether sweeps week sexy scandals and gruesome made-for-television movies take a toll on the culture. Local news shows take their cues from pseudo news shows such as "Hard Copy" and "A Current Affair" and make their nightly reports visually dramatic and simplistic. One of the traditional definitions for news is a story's intrinsic value in explaining a particular facet of a community. Today the only criterion for newsworthiness seems to be whether there are video images of the tragedy. As a result, Bill Moyers complained that "journalists are supposed to gather, weigh, organize, and evaluate information—not just put on pictures."

The biggest fear that parents express in national polls—greater than drug use,

Figure 14.14

The Anderson family in the 1950s sitcom "Father Knows Best" poses for a publicity still that is an example of social perspective. The husband/father is the obvious center of attention while the wife stands nearby ready to pour him more coffee.

Figure 14.15

Another classic early 1960s sitcom was "Leave It to Beaver." The show was popular among viewers and advertisers because its plots and sets championed middle-class values.

contracting AIDS, and paying for their children's future needs—is of sex and violence in the media. Such fears from constituents have led members of Congress to ponder whether legislation is needed to curb violent content on television. To head off direct censorship, at the start of most television shows, a small icon displays information about the

program's content. Some cynics categorize the warning labels and their impact as equivalent to painting an obviously polluting smokestack in a town bright red. Moreover, when children learn that a program contains violent scenes, they will be attracted to it like moths to a glowing screen. Nevertheless, sensitivity to problems that may be caused by showing violent acts may make television executives carefully consider a program's content. For example, CBS chief Jeff Sagansky has stated that his network will reduce the number of television movies that are based on real-life crime situations. One alternative to direct censorship is the use of a so-called v-chip, with which parents can restrict their children from watching a violently rated show by programming their **set-top boxes.** However, when v-chip decoder boxes went on sale for about $100 each in 1999, few were purchased. Television sets manufactured after July 1, 2000, as required by the 1996 Telecommunications Act, must contain v-chip technology.

Television critic Howard Rosenberg makes the point that, although the medium shows thousands of acts of violence, television also displays just as many acts of kindness. "Television violence," Rosenberg writes, "is too simple a solution for violence in the country. It's human nature to seek easy answers to complex questions. Rather than acknowledge the root causes of violence as being deep and complicated, there's a tendency on the part of many to automatically blame television." Sexual aggression and other violent acts committed by members of a culture are partly a result of societal pressures—the easy availability of guns, few employment and educational opportunities, and family hardships—not simply violent portrayals on the screen.

The best defense against gratuitous sex and violence, as well as stereotyping and an emphasis on ratings, is to make intelligent viewing choices. Parents should monitor the viewing habits of their children and explain scenes that disturb them. Offensive shows should not be watched, and uplifting shows should be supported. Because the content of television programs is a result of the collective will of at least part of the culture, each viewer has an ethical and moral responsibility to ensure that positive values are communicated through the media. At the same time, the strength of a democratic society comes from allowing diverse viewpoints in the media. Sexual and violent acts that are not portrayed for sensational impact can serve as models of inappropriate social behavior. Television is the most powerful and encompassing medium for cultural communication in a modern society. Because it must serve both individuals and entire cultures, television executives have a responsibility to fairly serve all viewers.

Cultural Perspective

Television actually is a mix of four preceding media: the theater, radio, motion pictures, and, perhaps more important, the comic book. From the theater came the familiar stage sets so common in sitcoms. The vaudeville theater also gave the idea of variety acts to the medium. Radio brought its characters, personalities, and storytelling ideas—and the technology to broadcast programs to homes. From motion pictures, television producers learned how to tell their stories in a visual format with the use of multiple cameras and editing techniques. Finally, the comic book gave television its most important concept. Except for made-for-television movies, the basic unit of television isn't an individual program but a continuing series of programs that cast basically the same characters in comfortable surroundings. From week to week and from episode to

Figure 14.16

Complaints about the violence shown on television have their roots in "The Untouchables." Here, Robert Stack incongruously poses with a submachine gun in business attire.

Getty Images/Hulton Archive

episode, viewers may live with television actors and their problems over a period of several years. Consequently, television is more a medium of personalities than stories. The small screen is a poor place for dramatic action and spectacles. But subtle character development reinforced by close-up shots that fill the frame with the face of a friendly actor works well for television (Figure 14.17).

In his book *TV Genres,* Brian Rose lists eighteen different types of programs that have been shown on television since its inauguration: police, detective, western, medical melodramas, science fiction and fantasy, soap opera, made-for-television movies, docudramas, news, documentary reports, sports, game shows, variety shows, talk shows, children's programming, educational and cultural shows, religious programming, and commercials. The Emmy Awards divide program types into ten categories: comedy series, drama series, miniseries, made-for-television movies, variety or

Figure 14.17

Because television programs come into the home, characters often are familiar to viewers. Here, cast members of the popular NBC sitcom "Cheers" share a laugh. Note how the camera's perspective almost puts the viewer at the bar.

Getty Images/Hulton Archive

music series, variety or music specials, children's programs, nonfiction specials, nonfiction series, and animated programs.

Any classification scheme is bound to omit some types. For example, legal melodramas, adult programming, reality-based shows, instructional courses sponsored by local colleges, infomercials, home shopping programming, music videos, and, in the near future, World Wide Web services also are important categories. The reason for the large number of categories for television, compared with motion pictures, is that television is an intimate medium. Television images come right into the homes of viewers, whereas movies are a social experience separate from everyday home life. Consequently, television is able to explore many more commonly held cultural beliefs and values within a much more varied array of formats than motion pictures can.

The most memorable television shows are those that have actors whom viewers want to invite into their homes. And throughout the history of the medium, the

strength of visual messages yielded thousands of memorable moments. Tuesday night was known as Milton Berle Night. Berle, in his 1948 variety show, was a perfect fit for the new medium—he was loud and outrageous. When Lucille Ball was pregnant with Little Ricky, she started a craze for pickles and ice cream after she ate the unpleasant combination in an episode of "I Love Lucy." When her baby was born, 44 million viewers—almost everyone in America who had a television set—watched the episode and contributed to the baby boom in the 1950s. "The Dick Van Dyke Show," produced by Carl Reiner (a former comedy writer for Sid Caesar), was the first sitcom that offered behind-the-scenes views of work and home environments in equal proportions. When television production moved from New York to Hollywood to take advantage of motion picture studio facilities and services, sexy stars started to appear on the screen. Troy Donahue and Tab Hunter chased bad guys and women in their fast cars. Richard Chamberlain as Dr. Kildare, and fellow medical actor Vince Edwards as Ben Casey, were enormously popular teen idols. The comedy team of Tom and Dick Smothers fought CBS censors during their brief tenure to offer political satire for the first time during the Vietnam War. Archie Bunker's overstuffed chair set in the center of the living room gave the bigot a central position for his ludicrous views in "All in the Family." Football fans enjoyed the lively banter among former Dallas Cowboys quarterback Don Meredith, Howard Cosell, and Frank Gifford on ABC's "Monday Night Football" as much as the game. Walter Cronkite's voice choked as he read the news of President Kennedy's death live over the air. Gene Roddenbery, a writer for the western "Have Gun, Will Travel," produced one of the strongest cult followings in the history of television when he, not surprisingly, combined western and science fiction genres in "Star Trek." Jim Bakker and Jimmy Swaggart in their religious programs created memorable images of cynical extravagance. David Letterman, in the tradition of Steve Allen, Jack Parr, and Johnny Carson before him, pokes fun at popular culture and often his guests (Figure 14.18). Alex Trebeck always wears a designer suit and always knows the answers in the game show "Jeopardy!" "Saturday Night Live," the only live-feed regularly broadcast program (except on the West Coast) on television except for sports programming, uses an ensemble cast that concentrates on visual humor in the tradition of the British classic, "Monty Python." And some of the most innovative visual messages can be found on the MTV network that offers twenty-four hours of news and music videos seven days a week. With quick editing and special effects, a popular music visual can mean thousands of additional album sales.

But there are many forgettable moments on television. The following choices were available to a subscriber of AT&T Cable TV

Figure 14.18

In the tradition of Steve Allen and Johnny Carson, David Letterman rules the late-night television time slot with his zany antics and irreverent interviews. Here, Letterman's pose is strikingly similar to that of Steve Allen's, down to a large microphone desk prop.

Getty Images/Hulton Archive

in Missoula, Montana, on October 8, 2001, starting at 8:00 P.M.

Channel	Name	Program
*2	KMMF	"Love Cruise: The Maiden Voyage"
3	SHOWTIME	"Leap Years"
4	HALLMARK	*Reunion*
5	KSPS	"Antiques Roadshow"
*6	KUFM	"Prime Minister"
7	MCAT	"Missoula City Council Meeting"
*9	KTMF	"NFL Football"
*10	KPAX	"Raymond"
*12	KECI	"Dateline"

14	ENCORE	*Working Girl*
15	STARZ	*Bad Girls*
17	HBO	*Anywhere but Here*
*18	WB	"Drew Carey"
20	LIFETIME	*No Ordinary Baby*
22	TBS	*The Green Berets*
23	DISCOVERY	"Wild Discovery"
31	CNN	"CNN Special Report"
33	VH1	"Behind the Music"
34	TNN	"WWF Raw Zone"
35	FAMILY	*Au Pair II*
36	AP	"Dog Show"
37	TNT	*The Craft*
38	ESPN	"Jump Rope"
40	ESPN2	"Drill"
43	PLEX	*The Prince and the Showgirl*
44	CARTOON	"Dexter"
46	TLC	"Medical Mysteries"
48	MTV	"Road Rules"
49	DIS/PAC	"Lizzie"
50	H&G	"Restore America"
51	COMEDY	"The Daily Show"
52	FOXNEWS	"War on Terror"
53	USA	*Clueless*
54	AMC	"Backstory"
55	PAX	"Touched by an Angel"
58	FX	"Buffy the Vampire Slayer"
59	CNBC	"Brian Williams"
60	FOXSP	"Best Damn Sports Show"
61	A&E	"Minute by Minute"

*Broadcast channels

You can find just about anything you want to watch on one of those stations, if you are willing to take the time necessary to watch all of the choices. The list clearly shows that the "big three" networks no longer dominate programming. In fact, only 6 of the 39 channel offerings are broadcast, with 10 channels offering motion pictures.

Further evidence of cable's acceptance by viewers and critics is HBO's 94 Emmy nominations in 2001 for such programs as "The Sopranos" (receiving a record 22 nominations), "Sex and the City," the made-for-television movie *Wit*, and the mini-series "Conspiracy." NBC, ABC, and CBS received 76, 63, and 46 nominations, respectively. After two postponements due to the aerial attacks of September 11, the ceremony started with a patriotic theme that was exemplified by former "CBS News" anchor Walter Cronkite when he said, "Television, the great common denominator, has lifted our vision as never before. And television also reminds us that entertainment can help us heal." In the end, HBO tied NBC for the most Emmy awards won—16—with Fox next at 15. "Sex in the City" became the first cable series ever to win a best comedy or dramatic series award. With cable as a model for future programming, television channels will necessarily become as content-specific as specialized magazines.

Besides cable offerings, the three original networks must also compete with other broadcast networks. Inspired by the tremendous success of the Fox network, Paramount Communications, Inc., and Warner Bros. executives started their own broadcast networks, UPN (United Paramount Network) and WB (Warner Bros. Network). The seventh broadcast network is government-and-viewer-sponsored PBS (Public Broadcasting Service). Although it has a highly educated viewership, its ratings are quite low compared with the other six. NBC, CBS, and

ABC will survive the competition from cable networks by sticking with a concept originated by the early motion picture studios—the star system. The big three can differentiate from all the other channels (even 1,500) by establishing a stable of well-known performers who are cast in familiar situations and dramas.

Critical Perspective

Television caused serious declines in all other mass communications media. But the media that survive are those that can adapt to the challenge offered by television. Many magazines in the 1960s and 1970s, such as *Colliers, Saturday Evening Post, Life,* and *Look,* ended publication because national advertisers preferred television. But many other magazines survived by attracting specialty audiences based on specific interests. In fact, the magazine industry has never been more prolific and popular than it is today. These new readers appeal to advertisers. Newspapers suffered severe declines because of television. Polls show that 50 percent of those under thirty-five years of age prefer to learn about news events from television. But the news shows they are watching are more likely to be produced by MTV or "Entertainment Tonight." Many newspapers have folded, but others have survived because of chain ownership, a more feature-oriented approach, zoned editions, and colorful graphics. Radio quit airing dramatic serials and concentrated on obtaining specialized audiences for specific kinds of music. Motion pictures made their screens larger, their pictures more vivid, and the sound clearer. But, more important, Hollywood swallowed its pride and accepted the power of television. One indication of the strong link between the two media is in the number of motion pictures that began as television programs. The trend started in the

1950s with "Marty." Recently, movies have been made from such television shows as "My Favorite Martian," "The Mod Squad," and "Charlie's Angels." Audiences grow fond of TV characters and want to see them on the large screen, too.

Commercial television emphasizes mainstream political, economic, and cultural views—and champions consumerism. It is no wonder that television can be both addicting and alienating. Wars and other personal tragedies reduced to a small screen image suddenly segue into a commercial. These curious transitions occur because the bottom line for television executives isn't to sell programs to audiences but to sell audiences to advertisers. Until that system of funding changes, few changes will occur in the types of shows the medium offers. But for the first time in its short history, television is getting serious competition from other media, which may fundamentally alter the way television is presented. More people than ever are watching less network offerings, preferring cable programs, videotaped movies, and video games. The reason that cable and alternative video sources are successful is that they rely on the diversity of audience interests—not advertisers' preferences.

In the meantime, a viewer must make intelligent choices to seek alternative, high-quality programs. In letters to networks and in conversations with friends and family, such shows should be supported. Ken Burns, producer of the enormously popular documentaries that air on PBS, said this about television when he received a journalism award from the University of Southern California:

Television is rapidly eroding the strength of our republic from within, substituting a distracting cultural monarchy for the diversity and variety and democracy promised in its conception and unveiling. Television has equipped us as citizens to live in an all-consuming, and thereby forgettable and disposable, present, blissfully unaware of the historical tides and movements that speak not only to this moment, but to our vast future as well.

But television can remind us too, if we let it—as we gradually become a country and a society without letter writing and diary-keeping, more and more dependent on visual signs and language—that it is an important part of the making of history. More and more, we will be connected to the past by the images we have made, and they will become the glue that makes memories.

Television may be "a vast wasteland," but it allows a lot of space for the creation of memorable visual messages if a culture demands such value from it. Viewers need to graze less and learn to settle for more.

■ FUTURE DIRECTIONS FOR TELEVISION AND VIDEO

An old saying states, "What goes around, comes around." Fashion fads are perfect examples—those who held onto their tie-dyed shirts and love beads from the 1960s are pleased to see that those items are back in style. As early as 1938, television was envisioned as a communal visual experience that would be watched in motion picture theaters. It was imagined as a medium that could broadcast current news and, more important, live sporting events to theater audiences. In 1947, RCA and Paramount Pictures teamed to produce the first experimental television screenings in theaters with a projection system invented by RCA researchers. By 1949, more than 100 movie theaters and outdoor sites with specially built receivers aired the World Series from New York City, featuring the New York Yankees versus the Brooklyn Dodgers. But the FCC refused to authorize a separate channel on the spectrum for theater presentations. Consequently, exhibitors could only show programs that could be seen at home. An alternative at that time was to connect theaters with copper wire supplied by AT&T, but such systems were too expensive and home entertainment centers eventually replaced television theaters.

Ironically, television will once again become a social experience when movie theaters are eventually equipped with high-definition, digital, large, liquid crystal displays that exhibit programs via high-speed Internet links from an entertainment provider just as with viewers at home, but with an important interactive difference. The old-fashioned idea of television as a one-way, anesthetizing viewing experience soon will be an anachronism. The days of videotape and DVD presentations may be numbered. Television will be replaced by large, flat-screen, high-resolution digital teleputers in which viewers can watch almost any program or movie made at any time, connect to the World Wide Web to learn more about the presentation, and talk to a friend over the telephone all with the same device (see Chapter 16) (Figure 14.19).

DISCUSSION AND EXERCISE IDEAS

- Lead a discussion on the Rodney King video by George Holliday. Why do you think it had such an impact after the first trial of the police officers?
- Describe your favorite television show.

Paul Martin Lester

- Bring in your home videos to show to the class. Lead a discussion on the importance of video technology for preserving memories.

- Lead a discussion about the future of television.

- Write a paper that discusses the ethical concerns with television and video with particular emphasis on portraying sex and violence.

- Try to go a week without watching television. What did you learn about yourself and society?

INFOTRAC COLLEGE EDITION ASSIGNMENTS

- With "Subject guide" checked, type "Rodney King case symbolizes huge divide between black and white" in the search area and read the article of the same name by Claude Lewis. The author makes the point that there is a difference in perception between African-American and Anglo citizens about the police beating of Rodney King. Do you think that is a fair observation? How has that difference, if there is one, manifested itself in other high-profile cases such as the verdict of O. J. Simpson, for example?

- With "Subject guide" checked, type "Compuvision or teleputer?" in the search area. Read two articles in the list presented to you. First, read Larry Press's 1990 article "Compuvision or teleputer?" Next, read the article published in 2000 "What's Next? Compuphones? Teleputers? Compuvision?" What differences do you find in the two articles? Why do you think teleputers—communication machines combining the features of the telephone, television, and computer—have not gained widespread acceptance?

Go to the Web site for this book at www.wadsworth.com/product/0534562442 to find more Web links on this subject.

Figure 14.19

Many of those living in rural communities are too far away to receive television broadcast signals, or getting a cable connection is too expensive. Consequently, they are forced to buy satellite dishes. This photograph is a study in contrast. A woman outside Bloomington, Indiana, is burning her own trash—an ancient chore—amid two satellite dishes.

COMPUTERS

By the end of this chapter you should know:

- The innovative breakthroughs in computer graphics by writer and director James Cameron.
- The history of graphical **interfaces** for computers and its importance to visual communicators.
- Ethical concerns with computer software programs.
- Where the "fear of computer" mythology comes from.

Two of the most memorable characters in recent motion picture history never complained about long working hours, costume problems, or the quality of the catered lunches. That's because they were never paid, never wore clothes, and never ate anything. Many of the other actors never saw them—not even during filming—until the picture was finished. Both characters played nonhuman beings. One was a gentle, compassionate, and positive living force; the other was a violent, insensitive, and cold-blooded killer. The smiling, rippling water snake, termed "water weenie" by the crew featured in the motion picture *The Abyss* (1989), and the murderous T-1000 liquid-alloy robot in *Terminator 2: Judgment Day* (1991) introduced theater audiences not only to strong visual messages but to images totally fabricated through the use of the computer (Figures 15.1 and 15.2). For the first time in major motion pictures, characters with emotional responses and complex movements were computer-generated images (CGI). Utilizing the morphing technique and directed by James Cameron, both movies won Academy Awards for their special effects.

The success of those computer creatures has led to an explosion of CGI in all manner of media. In the summer of 2001, for example, every major motion picture released contained numerous special effects created on the computer. The success of *Terminator 2* has also led to the regular use of CGI for television commercials. And when Cameron needed to show the last desperate moments of those who lost their lives on an ill-fated ocean liner, he didn't use live stunt men and women. Cameron employed the knowledge he had learned from his previous motion pictures by creating CGI effects that contributed to *Titanic* winning the "Best Picture" Academy Award in 1998.

■ COMPUTER-GENERATED IMAGES

The history of computer-generated images for film goes back to 1963 when a researcher for Bell Laboratories (now Lucent Technologies), Edward Zajac, produced the first computer-generated motion picture—a simulation of a trip around the Earth based on satellite still photographs. By the late 1960s, NASA was producing numerous computer movies of the Earth's surface.

Hollywood caught on several years later. The first major motion picture that included any computer graphic effects was the 1974 science fiction thriller *Futureworld,* directed by *Jurassic Park* and *Rising Sun* novelist Michael Crichton. The movie featured a computer-mapped head of actor Peter Fonda on a monitor. Three years later, George Lucas directed *Star Wars,* which contained a limited amount of computer graphics on video display terminals. Computerized plans for the Death Star were displayed on a large screen during a briefing about battle strategies.

The first movie to feature the extensive use of computer graphics was the Disney box office disappointment *Tron* (1982). About twenty minutes of the film, much of it during the Light Cycle race, was produced on a computer. *Newsweek, Time,* and *Rolling Stone* hailed computer graphics as an important advance in motion picture production. However, the technological benefits were delayed because the public wasn't interested in a story about a video game operator who could go inside his machine. *Star Trek II: The Wrath of Khan* in 1982 also contained a computer-generated shot of the transformation of a barren planet into a Garden of Eden.

In 1984, two movies contained highly praised computer sequences—*2010,* for its stormlike atmosphere of Jupiter, and *The Last Starfighter,* for its spacecraft dogfights. Because of the complexity of images, Cray XMP supercomputers were employed to render each frame of the digital handiwork. *Starfighter* contained about twenty-five minutes of CGI. But again, as in *Tron,* the public wasn't interested in a teenage video game player who saves the universe. That same year, performance artist Laurie Anderson introduced her CGI-laden music video "Sharkey's World."

During the next two years other science fiction and fantasy films contained examples of computer graphics technology. *Young Sherlock Holmes* (1985), Steven Spielberg's fantasy film in which a knight with a sword leaps out of a stained glass window; *The Flight of the Navigator* (1986), which featured a silvery, computer-generated alien spaceship; and Muppet master Jim Henson's rendition of a flying owl through the opening credits of *Labyrinth* (1986) were excellent examples of magical computer graphic effects. However, all made a poor showing at the box office.

If *Tron* had been a blockbuster success, the advent of computer graphics would have occurred a decade sooner. It took a hit

Figure 15.1

See color section following page 276

Figure 15.2

See color section following page 276

movie—*Terminator 2*—that was filled with computer graphic effects and was a highly successful financial enterprise to convince producers to invest in CGI research. But *T2*, as it was named by insiders, couldn't have happened without the vision of James Cameron in his movie *The Abyss*.

Born in Kapuskasing, Ontario, Canada, in 1954, Cameron had an early fascination with science and movies. When his family moved to Brea, California, in 1972, he started making short films. Roger Corman, "King of the 'B' Movies," eventually hired Cameron for his independent studio, New World Pictures, as a production designer and second unit director. Cameron worked on science fiction projects such as *Planet of Horror* and *Battle Beyond the Stars*. The first film that he directed was the forgettable *Piranha II*. Cameron also was a talented writer. He cowrote the script for *Rambo: First Blood Part II* and wrote and directed *The Terminator, Aliens, The Abyss,* and *Terminator 2: Judgment Day*.

The 140-minute *Abyss* (1989) was a moderate box office success about an underwater oil-rig crew led by actors Mary Elizabeth Mastrantonio and Ed Harris. The military recruits the aquanauts to retrieve a nuclear weapon from a damaged submarine. The plot twists when they discover an underwater civilization at the bottom of the ocean.

Computer-generated imaging technology took a breathtaking leap forward in the form of a creature that investigates the human vessel. The shimmering, water-filled pseudopod in The *Abyss* was called by computer innovator Mark Dippé "one of the most significant pieces of computer animation done up until that time." The water entity is an astonishingly realistic water snake that playfully mimics the startled faces of Mastrantonio and Harris. When Mastrantonio pokes a finger into the being's "face," the computer-generated rippling effect adds to the realism

of the moment. Dennis Muren of George Lucas's special-effects company, Industrial Light and Magic (ILM), who worked on the *Star Wars* effects, created the "water weenie," which won him an Academy Award. Although not a box office smash, the $45 million picture generated a lot of excitement because of its realistic and friendly computer creature.

With the knowledge gained from making *The Abyss,* Cameron no longer had to worry about the ability to produce his fantastic mental images on film. Before the sophisticated use of computer graphics, a movie's plot was limited by what was physically possible to create. Motion pictures could produce incredibly lifelike illusions, but there always was a limit. Now there are almost no limits. Cameron wrote the script for *T2* with the confidence that computer artists would be able to turn his storyboards into reality.

In the first *Terminator,* a murderous cyborg played by Arnold ("I'll be back") Schwarzenegger is transported from the future by advanced computers that have taken over control of the world from their human programmers. The robot's mission is to kill a woman who is to give birth to a son who will eventually lead a revolution against the machines. The movie cost about $7 million and made more than $35 million.

In *T2* Linda Hamilton trains her son, portrayed by Edward Furlong, to take a leadership role in the upcoming rebellion. But images of a nuclear war eventually drive her insane, and she is committed to a mental hospital. Meanwhile, in the post-nuclear-war future, her now-grown son sends a reformatted Schwarzenegger robot back to the past. But this time it is programmed to protect the boy and his mother because the evil computers (are you following this?) have sent a new and improved model—the liquid metal, metamorphic cyborg, played in human form by Robert Patrick—to kill the family and anyone else who gets in its way.

The T-1000 chrome robot in *Terminator 2* was one of forty-five special CGI effects used in the blockbuster movie. Some of the most riveting scenes occur in the insane asylum, in which the T-1000 character assumes the shape of a section of linoleum floor, makes his hands turn into deadly swords, has his "face" sliced in two by the force of Schwarzenegger's weapon (but it quickly reconstitutes itself), and changes back and forth between a uniformed police officer, a hospital security guard, and the chrome-colored, metal monster. The over-the-top visual effect, however, is when the cyborg oozes through the bars of a security gate to attack Hamilton, Furlong, and Schwarzenegger. The through-the-bars scene was created by filming Patrick and the bars separately, matching a computer model of the actor's face with the live-action film.

The movie, unlike any other that used CGI, woke up Hollywood executives to the potential of computer graphics. The success of *T2* showed that stories are more important than effects. *Tron* and *The Last Starfighter* failed, not because the computer graphics scenes were poorly rendered, but because their stories weren't compelling. *Titanic* was a great success because the CGI effects enhanced and did not distract from the characters and story. As with other media, visual messages must always stress the message before the visual.

James Cameron continues to be an innovator in the field of computer graphics. His post-*Titanic* activities include writing for a Fox television series, "Dark Angel," and although not directing, Cameron is listed as a contributing writer concentrating on character development for *Terminator 3* set for a 2003 release. "Dark Angel" is about a genetically enhanced girl who works for a messenger service in Seattle after a magnetic bomb

destroys every computer in the world in the year 2019. Cameron will no doubt continue his CGI-inspired story lines that point to the fears many people have about computers having too much control over their lives.

■ *ANALYSIS OF MOTION PICTURE COMPUTER GRAPHICS*

Not too long ago, computer graphics could be identified easily. Colored lights on video displays, fantastic transformations between animals and people, or unrealistic fantasy creatures within equally strange make-believe environments were easily recognizable as being computer-generated. Even the digitized dinosaurs in *Jurassic Park,* as wondrous as they are, cannot be mistaken for clay models, mechanized puppets, or existing animals with a lot of makeup and theatrical body appliances. The audience necessarily suspends reality during a motion picture in order to be entertained. Context therefore may be more important than content for establishing the degree of believability of the visual message.

The next generation of computer graphic effects breaks down the notion (which was never true anyway) that seeing is believing. Pixar filmmaker John Lasseter (see Chapter 11) was executive producer for the 2001 hit, *Monsters, Inc.* The movie featured several innovations in computer animation technology mostly related to how hair and clothing were rendered. The fur of "Sulley," an 800-pound monster, and the clothing of the human girl "Boo" were simulated to a level not previously achieved in cartoon animation. One of the reasons computer cartoons of the past had a plastic, unrealistic look, Lasseter explained, was because "the more organic something is, the harder it is to do." Despite advances in computer power, animators painstakingly re-created each hair of

Sulley's coat—about 3 million of them—and took two years to write the software required for the clothing used in the film in order to achieve a natural and lifelike appearance. Lasseter wants theatergoers to say to themselves, "Oh, we know it's not real, but it sure does look real."

But another 2001 release may have been a preview of the possibilities of computer technology in re-creating humans. Japanese filmmaker and video game producer Hironobu Sakaguchi and his team of animators from Hawai'i produced startlingly realistic characters in *Final Fantasy: The Spirits Within*. One reviewer noted that the movie featured a "photo-realistic presentation that often fools viewers into thinking they could be watching a live film. [For example,] the beautiful character, Dr. Aki Ross: Her shoulder-length ebony hair sways as she turns her head. Her liquid eyes reflect dreamy surroundings. Her supple skin shows pores and slight blemishes. It's quite a technical milestone. Only lip movements and some facial expressions need more work." But like *Tron* and *The Last Starfighter, Final Fantasy* was criticized for its weak plot. After its initial release, it went straight to DVD.

Eventually, determining whether any image—for print or screen media—is a picture that represents a live-action actor or is a completely computer-generated fabrication simply will be impossible. Within the context of entertainment, viewers who want to be thrilled, writers and directors who want to turn their imaginations into screen reality, and producers who want to save money by not having to hire so many actors await such a technical innovation with great anticipation. Agents, actors, stunt personnel, prop people, makeup artists, and even caterers are among those who will not be thrilled by such advances. Others involved with social welfare and criminal activities favor laws against the use of exact simulations of human behavior—particularly with regard to computer-generated children having sex. This issue will be discussed later in this chapter within the ethical perspective.

■ COMPUTERS AND THE SIX PERSPECTIVES

Personal Perspective

Computer technology, with its ability to create, access, and manipulate large **databases** filled with words and numbers, inspired writers to call the twentieth century the "Information Age." In reality, the time during which words dominated images in communication began shortly after Gutenberg's invention. Culminating in the word processing computer, words became more valued than images to tell stories. But with new-generation computers that make possible the inclusion of pictures as easily as words in print and screen media, some writers are beginning to anticipate a new age. For example, Sean Callahan, founding editor of *American Photo* magazine, writes that

> our culture is moving from an Information Age, where communication is based on words and numbers, to a Visual Age, based to a great extent on images and symbols. By allowing us to capture, store and use images in entirely new ways, these emerging technologies are destined to have a wide-ranging impact on personal and business communication.

More accurately, however, the next decade will be known for the way that words and pictures are used together as equal partners in the communication process—an Information Age, Part 2, in which all forms of communication are included through the World Wide Web.

Whatever the period is called, computer technology clearly has grown to such an extent that imagining a world without the machine is difficult. From buying groceries to watching a movie, innovations brought about by the computer affect our lives for better or worse. Portable computers and **bulletin board** services, for example, are powerful tools that help with business deals and classroom note taking. But image credibility, privacy concerns, and access to computer advantages for all in a society are problems that are not easily solved.

Historical Perspective

Charles Babbage of London has been credited with inventing the computer. In fact, he designed a steam-powered, program-controlled calculator. When he finished his first design in 1833, he claimed that it would mechanize the thought process itself. The huge, noisy contraption had pulleys and wheels that were used to make calculations (Figure 15.3). Although theoretically capable of storing 1,000 numbers of 50 decimal places each on punched cards, the Analytical Engine, as it was called, never got much beyond the design stage. Although brilliant in its conception, Babbage's machine was too far advanced for the technology of the day. He died a lonely and bitter man.

Herman Hollerith, an American, had more success with his machine. He invented the first electric calculator, which was used for the enormous task of compiling the decennial U.S. census. The son of German immigrants, Hollerith went to work for the Census Office in 1879. By 1880 the task of collecting the data took months, and analyzing all the information took almost nine years. Hollerith invented an electromechanical system that could count and sort data from punched cards. Holes punched in each card represented demographic information (age, sex, educational level, and so on) for each American. When the cards were placed in the machine, it collated the data so that it could be analyzed more easily. Hollerith's

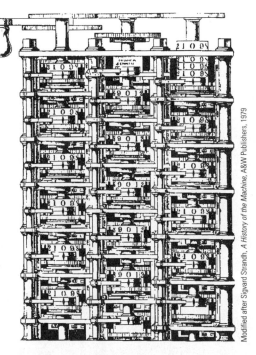

Modified after Sigvard Strandh, *A History of the Machine*, A&W Publishers, 1979

Figure 15.3

Charles Babbage interrupted the construction of his complicated computer (he called it the Analytical Engine) in 1834 after cost overruns and the resignation of his chief instrument maker. Nevertheless, Babbage continued his work and developed a one-program computer that inspired the development of modern computers.

device was first used for the 1890 census (Figure 15.4). Although it was only two years faster than the previous system and cost almost twice as much money, the machine was a great financial success. Orders came from all over the world from banks and other institutions that required quick tabulations. In 1911, Hollerith had too much business to handle alone, so he merged his company with three others to form the Computing-Tabulating-Recording Company (CTR). This business eventually became the International Business Machines Corporation (IBM).

Thomas Watson built IBM into an international leader, and with the help of his son, Thomas Watson, Jr., moved IBM into making computers. The elder Watson started his career as a salesman who hawked everything from sewing machines to pianos (Figure 15.5). At nineteen he grew tired of his hometown and left it for Buffalo, New York, where he eventually got a job with the National Cash Register Company (NCR). Company officials were so impressed by his selling abilities that he was transferred to NCR

In the 1940s and 1950s computers were room-size behemoths that cost millions of dollars and performed haphazardly. Early computers were analog devices—that is, they converted data (words and numbers) into measured electrical impulses. The conversion process occurred in a row of vacuum tubes of the same type used for sound amplification in radios and early television sets. The electrical charge generated by the tubes translated words and numbers into either the **decimal** numerical system or the **binary** numerical system. The former (also known as base 10) required more tubes because, in order to show every possible number, the 10 digits (0 to 9) needed to be separately represented. Thus decimal-based computers were large and slow. The binary numerical system (also called base 2) needed far fewer tubes because it represented all numbers by translating them into 0 and 1 combinations. For example, the numbers 3 through 9 are represented in base 2 as 11, 100, 101, 110, 111, 1000, and 1001. Vacuum tubes can represent 0 and 1 simply by being off or on. Hence the binary system is the simplest, fastest, and most efficient numbering method to use with computers.

In 1946, the first computer based on the binary system was announced to the public. Called the ENIAC (for Electronic Numerator, Integrator, Analyzer, and Computer), it was a top-secret project sponsored by the U.S. military and produced by a team led by John Mauchly at the Moore School of Electrical Engineering at the University of Pennsylvania (Figure 15.6). The machine, given the code name PX, could multiply 333 ten-digit numbers in one second. Its first use was to perform complicated calculations for hydrogen bomb research. But the computer was an expensive and awkward machine that required workers to set hundreds of switches, replace defective vacuum tubes, and make connections through telephone

Figure 15.4

This 1890 issue of Scientific American *magazine introduced readers to Herman Hollerith's electrical tabulating machine. Although it was faster than counting census data by hand, it was still an enormous and tedious job to process the census data.*

Courtesy of International Business Machines, Inc.

headquarters in Dayton, Ohio. His future looked bright until he was jailed for a year and fined $5,000 along with other company officials for violating the Sherman Antitrust Act. After his release from jail, NCR fired him, but CTR soon hired him. He applied an impressive personality and business mind to advance rapidly, and, when the president of CTR died, Watson was named to replace him. In 1924, CTR changed its name to IBM. The company grew tremendously during World War II and became the leading producer of data-processing machines in the world for government and business applications. In 1952, the senior Watson retired and his son succeeded him.

patch cords before they could perform any calculations.

An important innovation for computers, which eventually led to visual computer displays, was the combination of computer and cathode-ray tube (CRT). At Manchester University in England, F. C. Williams and colleagues used CRTs similar to those in radar and television sets to view the inner workings of their Manchester Mark I computer in 1948. The following year Jay Forrester and graduate student Kenneth Olsen, who later established the Digital Equipment Corporation (DEC), began working on the Whirlwind computer at MIT. After the Soviet government exploded an atomic bomb in 1949, U.S. military officials asked Forrester to develop a comprehensive air defense system to warn the military of a nuclear missile attack.

The last room-size, vacuum tube computer of note was the UNIVAC (for UNIVersal Automatic Computer). The UNIVAC computer system was intended for general purposes. In other words, it could be programmed by an operator to perform almost any type of data-sorting task. In 1950, J. Presper Eckert and John Mauchly developed the computer, which Remington Rand bought immediately. The significance of the machine was that it could store instructions in the form of random access memory (RAM). With ten round magnetic tapes, the UNIVAC could reserve 10 million zeros or ones to run the computer's internal operations. No longer did the tedious job of loading hundreds of punched cards have to be performed before each operation. This development led Grace Murray Hopper in 1951 to produce a high-level program to scan a set of computer instructions and carry them out. Hopper's computer language, Pascal, led IBM to write FORTRAN (for FORMula TRANslation) so that anyone could learn to be a computer programmer.

Courtesy of International Business Machines, Inc.

Figure 15.5

Above: A middle-aged Thomas Watson, Sr., sits in his austere office and appears to be too absorbed in a document to notice the photographer. Below: A few years later, his portrait is radically different. Bound volumes of classical books—note the Holy Bible prominently displayed on the shelf to his right—within a wooden bookcase, a globe turned to Africa, a Foreign Affairs *journal, a book entitled* Chinese Art, *the IBM company magazine,* Think, *with the word repeated above, and direct eye contact with the camera combine to convey the image of a person of wealth, worldwide influence, and confidence.*

Later, COBOL (for Common Business-Oriented Language) and BASIC (for Beginner's All-purpose Symbolic Instruction Code) were introduced and further allowed amateurs to get involved in writing computer programs.

Figure 15.6

The 1946 ENIAC machine was linked with telephone patch cords and powered through vacuum tubes. One of the most time-consuming tasks of working with the computer was checking and replacing defective tubes—a duty the two people in this picture are performing.

The general public knew more about the UNIVAC than the other computers of the day because CBS News used it to predict the outcome of the 1952 presidential election. The machine was fed the results from thousands of voting districts in previous elections and from early voting returns on election night. With only 7 percent of the vote in, the machine announced that Dwight Eisenhower would defeat Adlai Stevenson in a landslide of electoral votes—438 to 93. In a reverse of what happened during election night for the 2000 presidential election (see Chapter 14), CBS officials instantly panicked because every political analyst had predicted a close vote. CBS faked the data on television to make it appear that the voting was tight. But the machine had it right: The actual electoral vote result was 442 to 89.

The SAGE (for Semi-Automatic Ground Environment) project became operational in 1955. The important aspect for graphic designers about the Whirlwind computers used by the SAGE system was that they introduced the concept of the individual workstation (Figure 15.7). Fifty monitors could display the radar blips of up to 400 planes at a time. An operator seated in front of a large CRT monitor could aim a light pen at a specific blip on the screen, and the computer would supply information about that plane and its location.

Transistors

One of the most important discoveries in the twentieth century was announced to the public in 1948 with almost no coverage by the media. A team of scientists working for Bell Telephone Laboratories in Murry Hill, New Jersey, invented the **transistor**—a semiconductor with the same function as the vacuum tube but made of silicon, the chief component of sand. As opposed to tubes, silicon transistors didn't get hot, cost pennies to make, and could be as small as a pencil's eraser (Figure 15.8). In 1956 the Nobel Prize in physics was awarded to the three-person team, William Shockley, Walter Braittain, and John Bardeen, who had invented the transistor. One of its first applications was for hearing aid amplifiers in 1953, and the next year transistor radios were introduced. In 1958, Jack Kilby worked for Texas Instruments in Dallas where he linked transistors on an integrated circuit board, allowing complex computer operations to occur in a vastly reduced space and at much faster speeds (Figure 15.9). Kilby received the National Medal of Science in a ceremony at the White House for his important invention in 1970. Room-size computers, commonly referred to as mainframes, were soon replaced with much smaller machines called minicomputers (Figure 15.10).

Minicomputers

In 1963, DEC researchers developed the first minicomputer, the PDP-8. It was still the size of a refrigerator and slower than a mainframe, but it was far less expensive. The DEC computer cost about $18,000, compared to several million dollars for an ENIAC or a UNIVAC.

Minicomputers were too expensive and large to be used by people generally. But in 1975, a cover story in *Popular Electronics* about the Altair 8800 computer launched the personal computer industry. Floridian Edward Roberts began Micro Instrumentation and Telemetry Systems (MITS) in 1974 to make and sell pocket calculators. But he soon fell into debt when many transistor companies flooded the market with cheap calculators. His next project, however, would give him an important place in the history of computing. He decided to sell computer kits to amateurs. He convinced a bank's loan officer to let him borrow $65,000 with the assurance that he would sell 800 kits a year. After the *Popular Electronics* article about the Altair reached newsstands, Roberts immediately received thousands of orders. However, the computer was a simple design that could

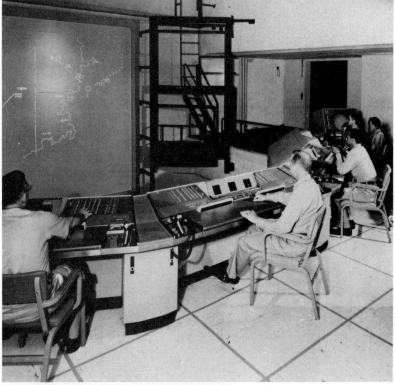

Courtesy of International Business Machines, Inc.

Figure 15.7

The SAGE computer system was designed as an early warning defense system in the event of enemy attack. It was one of the first to use a monitor. Above: Military personnel study a map generated by the computer system. Below: A technician obtains more information about a specific plane with a light pistol.

be used only to play uncomplicated games. To become a more fully functional machine, it needed a built-in (called an *interpreter*) program that would allow the computer to understand BASIC commands. When Harvard student Paul Allen saw the article about the $650 computer at a newsstand, he was intrigued and showed it to his friend, fellow

Courtesy of International Business Machines, Inc.

Figure 15.8

Advances in computer technology reduced machine cost and size and increased machine power and speed. The most important advances were from the vacuum tube (left) to the transistor (center) to the silicon chip (right).

Figure 15.9 (left)

In 1958, Jack Kilby linked numerous transistors on a circuit board to give computers added speed and reliability.

Figure 15.10 (right)

Silicon chip circuit boards as small as sewing needles further reduced size and cost without sacrificing speed or accuracy.

freshman Bill Gates. They called MITS to offer their services in writing a BASIC interpreter. Six weeks later the two had finished. MITS hired Allen, and Gates dropped out of college to become a freelance computer software writer. The two eventually teamed up again to form Microsoft Corporation, America's largest and most successful software company. "Windows" is an enormously popular computer interface program that runs on about 90 percent of all desktop computers in the world.

The Altair also inspired numerous computer clubs around the country to share information and programs that could be used on the simple computer. A Silicon Valley (named for the many silicon semicon-

ductor chip companies established near San Francisco) organization, the Homebrew Computer Club, with about thirty interested members, met for the first time in 1975 near Stanford University. Soon its membership exceeded 500. Present at the first meeting was a young computer genius named Stephen Wozniak. "Woz," as he is known by his friends, built a transistorized calculator when he was thirteen years old. Although he attended colleges in Colorado and California, he dropped out because the courses didn't interest him. Hewlett-Packard (HP) eventually hired him as an engineer in its calculator division in Palo Alto. In 1971, he met Steven Jobs, a sixteen-year-old, long-haired, and somewhat shy individual (Figure 15.11).

Wozniak had fabricated a simple machine that used a BASIC interpreter. Although it was even less sophisticated than the Altair, it could be plugged into a television set to play video games. Jobs immediately searched for buyers and funding for the computer. Jobs sold his Volkswagen bus, borrowed $5,000 from a friend, and formed Apple Computer. In 1975, the two introduced their Apple I computer and sold 175 machines at $500 each (Figure 15.12). While Wozniak worked on a more sophisticated model, Jobs tried to get financial backers. He found a thirty-two-year-old millionaire, Armas C. Markkula, Jr., former marketing manager for Intel, a manufacturer of semiconductor chips used in

Courtesy of International Business Machines, Inc.

Courtesy of International Business Machines, Inc.

IBM computers. Markkula came by Jobs' garage, Apple's manufacturing and business center, and liked what he saw. He invested $91,000 of his own money, arranged a $250,000 line of credit with Bank of America, and found investors who eventually contributed more than half a million dollars. In 1977, the Apple II computer was introduced and became an enormous success. In the first year, sales of the $2,000 computer totaled $775,000. In a brilliant marketing move, Jobs offered the Apple II at a nominal cost to elementary schools throughout the United States. Schoolchildren across the country soon were experiencing computing for the first time on Apple computers. And when those children became adults, they often bought Apple computers for themselves. When Apple's stock went public in 1980, Wozniak was $88 million richer, Markkula $154 million richer, and Jobs $165 million richer by the end of the first day of over-the-counter trading. By 1981, annual sales had reached $335 million, making Apple Computer the fastest growing firm in American history.

Apple versus IBM: A War of Logos and Machines

Although many companies make desktop computers, Apple and IBM used to dominate the industry. Various publications carried stories that pitted the counterculture gurus with their long hair, beards, and sandals against the establishment executives with their white shirts, conservative ties, and blue suits. Jobs parked his motorcycle next to several video games and a grand piano in the lobby of Apple Computer. Uniformed security guards greet visitors to an IBM site. But since the advent of clones that allow users to purchase good-quality computers at a much lower price using Macintosh or IBM operating systems through licensing agreements, today Compaq is ahead of the pack.

Courtesy of Apple Computer, Inc.

But never is the contrast between the two companies as clear as in their two logos. The original Apple logo was a black and white line drawing of Sir Isaac Newton sitting under a tree reading a book (Figure 15.13). Above his head is an apple that has just become detached from the branch. The apple is on its way to inspire Newton to theorize about the law of gravity. Around the picture is the strangely cryptic quotation: "A mind forever voyaging through strange seas of thought—alone." Soon, however, the company changed the logo to a symbol that could be easily condensed into one, simple visual message (Figure 15.14). The rainbow-colored Apple with a bite out of it symbol-

Figure 15.11

Holding the first Apple I circuit board are two Steves—Stephen Wozniak (left) and Steven Jobs. The two are living examples of Stefan Lorant's "third effect." Each one alone probably could never have achieved what the two of them accomplished together.

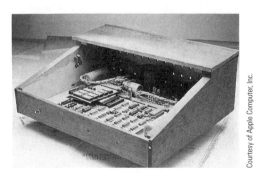
Courtesy of Apple Computer, Inc.

Figure 15.12

An inside view of the original Apple I computer built by Stephen Wozniak in his garage. All that is missing is the monitor and keyboard. Note that the wood-grain paneling never became a computer standard.

Figure 15.13

The original Apple Computer logo was a confusing array of text and graphics—not the kind of symbol that can be easily reduced and remembered by consumers. Nevertheless, the trademark introduced the world to the connection of the computer firm to Sir Isaac Newton and apples.

Figure 15.14

See color section following page 276.

Figure 15.15

Paul Rand's IBM trademark presents bold, capital, square serif letters linked by horizontal white lines. The logo symbolizes the company's powerful position in the industry and its worldwide networking capabilities.

ized two different messages: (1) a computer was the pot of gold awaiting a user at the end of the Apple rainbow, and (2) the Garden of Eden myth made it somewhat sinful to bite into the forbidden fruit. The logo perfectly summarized Apple Computer—bright, innovative, perfectly natural, rewarding, and anti-establishment.

The IBM logo is certainly a contrast in style (Figure 15.15). Designed by Paul Rand and architect Eliot Noyes in 1956, it originally comprised three black capital letters in a square serif typeface. Rand added the blue color and the distinctive horizontal stripes later because, as he writes, "since each letter is different, the parallel lines, which are the same, are the harmonious elements that link the letters together." But for others, the stripes reminded them of a prison uniform. The logo is a no-nonsense, conservative design, and like the Apple logo, visually complements the underlying philosophy of the company.

IBM introduced its first personal computer in 1975, but sold only about 15,000 of the machines, called the 5100. After Apple's success, IBM officials decided to try the personal computer market again. In 1981, it introduced the IBM PC, which was an instant hit. Through the company's worldwide distribution system, it sold more than 800,000 PCs the first year. The letters "PC," standing for "personal computer," became synonymous with IBM desktop computing. Suddenly, IBM was the most popular maker of personal computers in the world and inspired many other companies to create similar machines, called clones.

But IBM executives still were not convinced of the importance of the home computing market. This attitude resulted in decisions that they would later regret. In order to rush the development of the PC, IBM used Intel semiconductor chips and Microsoft software. Consequently, IBM officials could only watch as Intel and Microsoft became enormously successful enterprises, selling licenses for their products to other companies. IBM PCs also appealed more to those who used computers at their companies or for home office applications. Without a mouse and convenient visual interfaces, the PC was used mainly for word processing (letter and report writing) and statistical analysis. Although the IBM machine was an effective business tool, learning its word-based program commands wasn't easy. As a result, many consumers weren't interested in the computers.

In the middle of the 1984 Super Bowl telecast, viewers watched a stunning commercial made by motion picture director Ridley Scott (*Blade Runner, Thelma and Louise,* and *Gladiator*). With an obvious link to George Orwell's novel *1984,* the advertisement presented a "Big Brother" (i.e., IBM) theme in which computer operators all looked alike and worked in drab surroundings. Suddenly a young, athletic woman wearing running clothes and carrying a sledgehammer runs toward the giant screen. When she throws the hammer at the picture of the leader, the screen crashes to reveal behind it the latest revolution in computing—a lower priced version of Apple's Lisa computer, the Macintosh. The Macintosh sold for less than $2,000 and contained a graphic interface that made many of the functions of the computer intuitively simple for the average person. The overworked phrase "user friendly" became a part of the popular culture to describe the Macintosh computer line. With its connection to a high-quality laser printer introduced soon

afterward, everyone from home users to newspaper personnel suddenly had access to a low-cost machine for word processing and graphic design. Desktop or computer-aided publishing was born with the Macintosh computer (Figure 15.16).

In 1998 Apple's low-cost iMac computer was introduced to attract home users, and in 2002 a newly designed iMac was introduced to popular reviews for its futuristic, lamplike look. One critic wrote that the new computer is "the kind of thing that you'd expect to see in an *Architectural Digest* photo shoot of Captain Kirk's bed table." Apple introduced the new designs in an effort to regain its market share lead held during the early years of the Macintosh (Figure 15.17). However, getting back to that level of consumerism is beyond Apple's reach—the company would need to gain more than 40 percent of the market—an improbable likelihood given the current economic situation (see Chapter 16). In addition, an indication of the synergy

Figure 15.16

Below: As a marketing gimmick, IBM used Charles Chaplin's Little Tramp character to promote its new PC, probably to assure potential consumers that the computer was easy to operate. Below right: Meanwhile, Apple Computer introduced its graphic interface computers that included a mouse—the Lisa 2 (left) and the original Macintosh. Many people discovered that they were much easier to operate than the IBM PC. Note that the screen is dark in the IBM photograph and that Apple highlighted its icon-driven screens.

Courtesy of Apple Computer, Inc.

Courtesy of International Business Machines, Inc.

Figure 15.17

With its bold, futuristic design, Apple introduced its newest line of iMac computers and immediately found commercial success as with the original Macintosh computers introduced in 1984.

between Apple and IBM because of competitive pressures from other computer companies is the fact that most of the Power PC processors used in iMac and iBook computers are actually produced by IBM.

Technical Perspective

A computer has five basic components: memory and storage, the central processing unit (CPU), a switching device, peripherals, and software (Figure 15.18).

Memory and Storage

Memory in a computer refers to information that the computer uses to operate itself. Memory can be either volatile (lasting only as long as the computer is turned on) or long-term (retained after the machine is turned off). Storage is the housing of information on recording devices that can be part of or separate from a computer. No computer is capable of storing information indefinitely.

In order to speed its processing time, a computer uses the binary numerical system rather than the decimal system. Conse-

quently, the basic unit of a computer is the binary digit or **bit.** Eight bits combined form a **byte.** A single byte can represent up to 256 bits—from 00000000 to 11111111. A computer software program is simply a large collection of zeros and ones that act like individual off or on switches. An 8-bit byte is required to represent a single number, letter, or symbol. The words kilobyte, megabyte, gigabyte, and terabyte are used to make talking about a large number of bits easier. Although the prefix means "thousand," a kilobyte (called a K) is actually 1,024 bytes. The extra 24 bytes represent the difference between the binary and decimal systems. A single K equals about 171 words. A megabyte (MB) is 1,024 kilobytes, a gigabyte (GB) is 1,024 megabytes, and a terabyte (TB) is 1,024 gigabytes, or more than a trillion bytes. If a megabyte is the equivalent of an average-size book, a terabyte equals about 10,000 books.

There are three types of computer memory: random access memory (RAM), read only memory (ROM), and a new type, flash memory or flash RAM. All types of memory store information on tiny microchips. Random access memory, sometimes called inter-

Figure 15.18

IBM introduced its personal computer in 1981 as a business-oriented machine for the home office. The monitor (with uncharacteristic graphic display) rests on the CPU and is connected to a keyboard and an inexpensive dot-matrix printer.

nal memory, is the more common type. Random access means that the computer can quickly find and display data regardless of the sequence in which it is stored. Unfortunately, that information is lost when the computer is turned off. RAM is used for opening, changing, and saving files. Words and images are stored temporarily in RAM while a user makes changes to text or pictures. When a computing session is finished, the user can save the work in permanent storage. If the work isn't transferred into permanent storage, it is lost as soon as the machine is turned off.

Read only memory refers to information that is permanently stored in the computer by the manufacturer and that gives the computer operating instructions. For the IBM PCs, the **operating system** is Windows, created by Microsoft. For a Macintosh, the operating system is called Mac OS, followed by the latest version number. ROM cannot be altered by the typical user and lasts for the life of the machine. A high-end, desktop publishing computer typically has 512MB of RAM and at least 1MB in its ROM. The higher RAM figure allows a user to work on several different software programs at the same time. For example, a user often will switch from a word processing to a graphics program when creating a complicated document. Because ROM needs only to be large enough to start up a computer and tell it how to communicate with its parts, it can have much less capacity than RAM.

Flash memory is a type of memory that can be erased and reprogrammed. It is used within an operating system for easy updating. It gets its name from the fact that it updates information all at once—or in a "flash." It is used in digital cell phones, digital cameras, notebook computers, and other devices.

Storage refers to a way of creating a permanent space for information that the user wants to save for a long time. Most storage systems are capable of both reading and writing information. After data are placed in storage, they can be accessed any number of times, changed, and saved for as long as the storage mechanism is operational. There are two kinds of storage devices: magnetic and optical. Floppy disks and most hard disks are magnetic computer media, whereas CD-ROM (laser) discs use laser technology for their optical drives.

All floppy disks have an iron-oxide (the chief component of rust) coating layered on a substrate, a flexible backing (which is why the disks are called "floppies") that is similar to recording tape (Figure 15.19). Inside the disk's plastic shell is a round substrate with a hole in the center. A computer's read/write head is mounted on an arm that moves from the center to the outer portion of the disk. As the disk spins quickly, the arm places data on the disk in the form of magnetic charges when writing to the disk or moves throughout the disk to read information previously

Courtesy of International Business Machines, Inc.

Figure 15.19

The original floppy disk (when the disk was still flexible) as introduced by IBM. Note that this publicity photograph uses a female model's hands. Many users of IBM products worked as secretaries in large corporations.

saved. After formatting (also called initializing), a disk is divided into various sectors where data are stored. Floppy disks are 3.5 inches in size. A floppy drive comes in double-sided or high-density formats with varying memory capacities. A double-sided, high-density disk, with its layer of more finely ground iron-oxide flakes, has a storage capacity of 1.44MB. More commonly, however, Zip disks, high-capacity floppies that can hold hundreds of megabytes of information, are used. Hard disks (sometimes called hard drives) are so named because their substrate usually consists of nonfloppy aluminum platters set on top of each other. The number of platters that a hard disk contains determines the amount of storage possible. Computers have internal hard disks that contain from 1GB to 100GB and higher. A typical user will start with a computer with at least 15GB and purchase internal or external hard disks for additional memory capacity.

Because visual messages require many more bytes of information than words, a computer graphics designer must have as much memory available in a computer system as he or she can afford. For example, a low-resolution, black and white picture might use about 400K of memory, a high-resolution black and white image needs about 8MB of disk space, and a high-resolution color picture may take 40MB of disk space. Consequently, many graphics designers use Zip disks. A desktop publisher can easily take them to a **service bureau** to have multipage documents and color images printed. However, more and more visual communicators send work to service bureaus through broadband communication networks and CD-R discs.

When Eastman Kodak's Cinesite was asked to clean the dust from the film of the 56-year-old movie *Snow White,* computer operators scanned the entire animated classic frame by frame so that it could be digitally retouched. As each digital color frame used 40MB, the entire 119,500-frame movie required almost 5TB of memory. The motion picture was stored on about fifty high-density removable gigabyte tapes that look like videotape cassettes. More than *3.5 million* regular 1.4MB high-density disks would be required to record the same amount of information.

The other type of storage medium is the optical disc. A compact disc, read only memory (CD-ROM or laser disc) device is the most common optical disc system. Like an old-fashioned phonograph record, information in the form of words, pictures, and sound can only be played, not recorded, with CD-ROM discs as they are presently offered to the public. In the late 1980s, CD-Recordable (CD-R) discs were introduced at a price of about $20,000. Consumers were introduced to CD-ROM technology in the form of movies and educational programs on 12-inch laser discs. The public recognized that 4-inch computer-digitized music discs were superior in quality to cassette tape and long playing (LP) recordings when Sony and Philips introduced them in 1984. In the late 1990s, DVDs were introduced. One side of a DVD can hold about 8.5 gigabytes of information or 17GB on both sides, which makes them ideal for presenting motion pictures. Many computers have DVD-Video players built in with DVD-RAM.

But the storage technology of choice for today's visual communicator is the CD-R. Not only are they as inexpensive as $60, but, for example, all of the high-end Macintosh computers come with a SuperDrive that allows the user to record and play CD-Rs and DVD-Rs as many times as desired. Consequently, independent film producers and others use the technology to make high-quality DVD movies that can be viewed on television sets.

Central Processing Unit

Although it is housed in a large section of the computer, the central processing unit (CPU) actually is composed of several microchips. The CPU receives information from a user, executes the tasks specified by a software program, and conveys the output to various peripherals. A computer software program may contain millions of lines of instructions that the CPU reads. Some CPUs can read more than one line at a time for quicker processing. Obviously, the faster a CPU can process information, the more the computer will be able to accomplish. There are several different types of computers: supercomputers, mainframes, minicomputers, desktops, and portables. Each kind of computer processes information in the same way, but at vastly different speeds. Since the 1940s, the processing speed of computers has increased, on average, ten times every seven years. The fastest computer in the world used to be the Cray T3E-900, developed by Seymour Cray and his company. Cray founded Control Data in 1957, Cray Research in 1972, and the Cray Computer Company in 1989. His Cray T3E-900 supercomputer could process 1 trillion mathematical calculations per second (or one teraflop) because it used gallium arsenide chips, which are even faster than silicon. It was a great loss to the computer industry when Seymour Cray died in an automobile accident in 1996. An IBM computer developed in 2001 for the National Center for Atmospheric Research to predict global climate changes can compute at a speed of 7 trillion calculations per second while another IBM computer used by the U.S. Department of Defense to simulate nuclear explosions reaches a speed of 12.3 teraflops. But the speed winner goes to a computer the size of four basketball courts recently installed and maintained by the Japanese government in Yokohama. It can perform an incredible 35.6 trillion calculations per second and is used for climate predictions and other functions.

But supercomputers that cost millions of dollars and mainframe machines might not be needed in the future for even the most complex computer operations. In 1986, motion picture special-effects personnel had to use a Cray supercomputer to perform their movie magic. Today much smaller workstations produced by companies such as Silicon Graphics can perform the same duties at much less cost. In 1993, IBM officials announced RISC System 6000. The supercomputer has the power of a Cray machine but at one-tenth the cost. Cray responded to the competition by offering a downsized computer, Superserver 6400, that features a Sun Microsystems Sparc microchip.

The coprocessor made the switch to desktop workstations possible. Coprocessors are companion chips that perform many high-level math and graphic functions faster than the CPU can. When the CPU gets a job that the coprocessor can handle, it simply hands off the task to the coprocessor. That way the CPU is available for other tasks.

A visual communicator needs a computer that holds the fastest CPU that can be afforded. A chip's speed (called clock speed or clock rate) is measured in millions of cycles per second, megahertz (MHz), or billions of cycles per second, gigahertz (GHz). A graphic designer should have a CPU chip with a speed of at least 600MHz. Most of the chips in high-end models satisfy that requirement. Most Macintosh computers contain processors made by Motorola and IBM. Motorola's first-generation 68000 chips were used in the early Macintosh computers. A more recent chip, the PowerPC, was developed by Apple, IBM, and Motorola and can run as much as 866MHz. The

Altivec engine of the Macintosh G4 allows the computer to run multimedia programs up to five times faster than the G3 computers. Most IBM computers use chips manufactured by Intel Corporation. In 1997, Intel introduced the Pentium II processor that had a clock speed of up to 450MHz. The 500MHz Pentium III was introduced in 1999 and was specifically designed for viewing multimedia presentations on the World Wide Web. The recently released Pentium 4 is, of course, faster. In 2000 Advanced Micro Devices Inc. reached the 1GHz milestone with its Athlon processor that can process 1 billion bits of information per second, but so can the Macintosh G4 with the Altivec engine running at 400MHz (Figure 15.20).

The Macintosh G5 of PowerPC 7500 are planned to have a chip speed of an incredible 2GHz and more.

Switching Devices

Switching devices simply are cords that connect the CPU with all other functions of a computer. They can be telephone-type links or complex 64-pin devices called *small computer systems interface* (SCSI, pronounced "scuzzy") connectors. Memory and storage, as well as all the peripheral functions, are connected through switching devices sometimes referred to as a *bus*. A bus can be an internal or external connection. Program instructions and other information are sent through a switching device to the CPU and out to a monitor or printer depending on the need of the user. The Universal Serial Bus (USB), manufactured by Intel, and Firewire, an Apple product, are devices that have revolutionized peripheral connections by making them faster, more versatile, and easier to obtain.

Peripherals

Desktop publishing is the production of printed materials through the aid of a computer, whereas presentation graphics is the production of frames for screen media. Sometime in the near future, publishing and presentation probably will be merged into a form of screen communications. Consequently, a visual communicator will need to be familiar with all the tools that will make the new Information Age happen. Peripherals are the tools at a graphic designer's disposal, of which there are three types: those that send messages to the CPU, those that deliver messages from the CPU, and those that both send data to and receive data from the CPU.

Incoming Peripherals Incoming peripherals include the keyboard, mouse, tablet, voice, and scanner devices. The keyboard is an out-of-date, almost quaint, computer connection that reflects the machine's link with the manual typewriter. The Q-W-E-R-T-Y letter configuration, so named for the first six letters of the top row, initially was designed to be a confusing arrangement of characters that would slow down a typewriter operator to prevent the mechanical arms from jamming in the machine. But with other letter placement schemes (the most popular is called the Dvorak), more than 5,000 words can be typed with the home keys (those in the center of the middle row). With foot pedals, as with a piano, shift and space keys let keyboard operators greatly speed up their words-per-minute production. A computer keyboard doesn't have mechanical arms that jam, so converting from the QWERTY system makes sense. However, old habits are hard to break.

Nevertheless, skill with a typewriter is a dying art. High schools no longer require typewriter courses. The mouse, whether tied to a computer through its "tail," connected through infrared radiation like a television's remote control, or using a radio frequency, reduces the number of keystrokes required.

Figure 15.20

One of the latest computers from Apple is the Macintosh dual 800MHz Power Mac G4. A "SuperDrive" allows a user to record on DVDs for playback in any standard DVD player.

Courtesy of Apple Computer, Inc.

The Microsoft Corporation earns more than $250 million annually on sales of its mice alone. But concern over carpal tunnel injuries and "mouse finger," a form of tendonitis from too much mouse clicking and keyboard typing, has forced researchers to develop stylus, voice, and even "data glove" technologies in which more natural movements of the hand and fingers and use of the voice can effect changes on the computer monitor. On some computers, users make screen selections by pressing a finger on a pressure-sensitive interface. Illustrators often use a pressure-sensitive stylus on a graphics tablet to create art that has all the nuances of hand-drawn creations. With a MessagePad, users have the opportunity to write notes and commands with a stylus on a flat-screen pad, which the computer's CPU can interpret. But the most exciting development that forecasts the end of the keyboard as it is presently known is voice-activated technology. Some programs can already identify more than 30,000 words spoken by the computer user. The next generation of computers will include voice-activated technology. In the future, writers may simply dictate their text into the computer. Applications of voice recognition software (VRS) may include lecture, media interview, and courtroom transcript production. Computer users with physical challenges also have more access with such systems.

A scanner is a device that converts words or images into digital form so that the computer can manipulate and store them. There are two types of scanners: microdensitometers and charge-coupled devices (CCDs). Microdensitometer scanners can be large, flatbed units similar to a photocopying machine, units that digitize a single frame of photographic negative or slide film, or handheld units used for smaller images. A scanner moves a beam of light across a page of text, a picture, or a frame of film and measures the amount of brightness reflected from the surface of the scanned material (or the amount of light transmitted, in the case of film). It then divides the picture into a grid of small rectangles called picture elements or *pixels.* The scanner software assigns a number to each pixel based on a gray or color scale. The number corresponds to shading levels from black to white; 16 levels of gray tones will produce an image of moderate quality, but 264 levels of gray tones obviously are much better. Color images require more memory space because, instead of one number assigned to each pixel, a color scan assigns three numbers—one for the brightness level of each primary color. The physical act of converting a page of text or an image into a series of pixels is called *digitization.* If the digitized material is text, optical character recognition (OCR) software converts it to a format that can be used by a word processing program. If a picture is digitized, image manipulation software can be used to make exposure and content changes. A good quality color flatbed scanner can cost as low as $50. However, scanners such as the Nikon LS-4000 cost much more.

CCD scanners are light-sensitive semiconductor chips that can digitize millions of pixels instantly. Their speed coupled with their high resolution makes them valuable for lightweight video and electronic still cameras. Unfortunately, CCD chips are extremely expensive because they are difficult to make. Sony's Mavica electronic digital camera introduced in 1984 is not a CCD scanner. It captures images with a low-resolution, analog video signal and saves them on a small floppy disk. Conversion software digitizes the image when the disk is placed in a computer. Nikon D1H and D1X and the Canon 1D are CCD digital cameras (see Chapter 12). Unfortunately, their price is high. These cameras used by photojournalists cost between $5,000 and $10,000. But most users will be quite content with a digital camera that sells for around $300.

Currently, the best image scanner possible is used for movie special effects. A frame of 35-mm, fine-grain film contains about 18 million pixels in the form of light-sensitive crystals. The Kodak CCD chip in the DCS 465 divides a picture into 6 million pixels in about two seconds. Kodak's Cinesite company with its high-priced Cineon technology for motion picture scanning uses a high-resolution CCD chip that creates a digital equivalent with more than 4 million pixels in about three minutes. Even though there is a big difference between 4 and 18 million pixels, the resolution of the image has approached the point where the human eye cannot detect the difference between film and digital images. The photoreceptors (or pixels) responsible for color vision in the eye (the cones) number about 7 million. But because many share channels to the brain, the number of pixels that reach the mind is much less (Chapter 3). Consequently, the resolution of a single frame of digitized film with the Cineon process is so good that even under a microscope no difference can be discerned between analog film and digital imagery.

However, a problem with digital images is that their resolution is portrayed as symmetrical, whereas film grain is not. Consequently, when you enlarge a digital image your eyes can spot imperfections much faster. Fortunately, a software program called Genuine Fractals converts the symmetrical pixels into a more filmlike asymmetrical pattern.

Outgoing Peripherals The monitor and printer are two of the most common computer peripherals that send information from the CPU. Monitors can be discussed in terms of their size, color, and resolution. A visual communicator who works with images on a screen for long periods of time shouldn't choose a monitor casually. A graphic designer should try to obtain the largest and most colorful monitor with the best resolution affordable.

The original Macintosh screens were only nine inches in size (as with television monitors, screens are measured diagonally probably to make you think that the frame is larger than it actually is). Viewing an entire page on the little screen was impossible. A designer should have at least a 19-inch monitor, available in either the standard horizontal (landscape) format or a vertical (portrait) format. Many companies now make 19- and 24-inch, two-page displays that show two vertical pages side by side. This feature is extremely useful for designers producing multipage documents, video, or motion pictures. Princeton makes a 17-inch monitor, which pivots for either horizontal or vertical viewing, that is a little cheaper than a two-page display monitor. Most computer screens mimic television's almost square Academy standard for its display. However, more and more monitors, like Apple's 22-inch Cinema display, coincide with a widescreen orientation similar to newer television models.

Color and resolution are closely related. The more colors that can be displayed on a screen at one time, the better is the monitor's picture. High-definition teleputers will display sharp, digital images because of their high resolution. The original Macintosh black and white screen contained only about 175,000 pixels. Modern high-definition monitors display images at a resolution rate twenty-five times higher—much better than an ordinary television screen.

All monitors require a video card that plugs into a computer that controls the output to the screen. The more memory a video card contains, the more colors the screen can display. Some computers come with a built-in video card; for those that don't, a video card can be purchased separately. Because each color is assigned a number in the binary system, a video card with an 8-bit (one byte) memory can display 256 possible colors. But graphic designers and animators often need more colors, requiring 24-bit color video cards. Monitors today display millions of colors on the screen at one time.

Many people think of monitors as passive windows to information sources. But they can be dynamic and do not have to depend on a keyboard or a mouse. Touch-sensitive screens use a programmable clear layer that fits on top of a monitor. A command is activated whenever the screen is touched in a particular location. Touch displays are useful in public places where a keyboard or mouse may be damaged or stolen. Many shopping malls and hotel lobbies have computer kiosks that offer information about various stores or entertainment opportunities in a city. Touch-sensitive controls combined with voice-activated commands also may speed up the editing process, so long as the user's fingers aren't covered with pizza grease.

High-definition television (HDTV) allows monitors to have as much sharpness as film. Even nonprofessional viewers notice the tremendous improvement between traditional monitors and HDTV screens. There are two main ways HDTV can be broadcast into homes: interlaced and progressive scan technologies. Although the human eye can't tell the difference between the two systems, there is an important difference. Interlaced HDTV is not computer friendly, whereas progressive scan systems easily allow the digital transmission of information. Because Japanese scientists, particularly from Sony, had been working on interlaced HDTV technology longer than anyone else, viewers in Japan can use the technology to watch programs on their TV sets. However, com-

puter manufacturers who want to merge the telephone, television, and computer into a teleputer advocate the progressive scan system. Digital HDTV systems took a giant leap forward in 1994 when Japanese government officials announced they favored digital HDTV instead of their outdated analog systems. For home television viewers to take full advantage of database offerings provided by digital electronic highways, television sets will have to be retooled to act more like computers. In 1998 the motion picture *101 Dalmatians* became the first presentation to be aired in the HDTV format to a national American audience. Unfortunately, few had television sets equipped for the innovation. However, sometime around the year 2006 the FCC will order all analog TV transmitters off the air in order to switch to digital transmission.

Another problem with large-screen televisions is their size and weight. For example, Sony's HDTV 38-inch set weighs about 800 pounds. Monitors do not have to be thick boxes that house cathode-ray tubes as do television sets. Liquid crystal display (LCD) technology allows the use of flat-screen monitors that can be used for large, wall-mounted or 15-inch portable computers. JVC and Hughes Communication have developed a 38-*foot* LCD video projection screen that works with any video system. Its clear, bright image may soon revolutionize motion picture theater projection. For several years, portable computers have used LCD technology to make screens that can be carried easily.

There are three types of printers: dot-matrix, inkjet, and laser. A dot-matrix printer is a low-cost alternative that should be avoided because of its poor quality. "What you see is what you get" (or WYSIWYG, pronounced "wizzy-wig") describes printers that faithfully reproduce what is presented on a computer monitor. A graphic designer needs a close approximation between the two. Dot-matrix printers convert screen characters into a pattern of dots that have tiny spaces between them giving a rough appearance. A printer's resolution is measured in dots per inch (dpi). Dot-matrix printers typically have a resolution of only 72 dpi. Relatively inexpensive inkjet and laser printers have resolutions of 300 to 2,400 dpi. Consequently, the quality of the printout is much better. Most graphic designers use a black and white laser printer to check work for mistakes and give a disk to a service bureau to print the file. With professional-quality printers that cost several thousand dollars, such as those manufactured by Linotronic-Hell, dpi resolution as high as 3,386 is possible. Such a dpi is more than 1,000 times better than dot-matrix printers.

Interactive Peripherals Interactive peripherals offer two-way communication between one computer user and another. The information typed on a keyboard or duplicated with a scanner can be sent electronically to another computer user anywhere in the world and returned. Electronic mail (email) is one of the most popular forms of computer activity and is a valuable communications feature (see Chapter 16). Generally, computers may be connected to email through a device known as a modem (short for modulator/demodulator). A modem sends and receives data over telephone lines at varying speeds. A graphic designer should have the fastest modem affordable. Modems are measured in bits per second (bps), sometimes called the **baud rate.** Obviously, a modem that transfers data at 56,000 bps is more desirable than those that run at only 2,400 bps or less.

There are other alternatives for visual communicators working at home. One is a Digital Subscriber Line (DSL), a technology that brings high-**bandwidth** information using ordinary copper telephone lines. Another popular choice is a cable modem through a cable company. With a cable modem, the speed for World Wide Web downloads can be as high as 50 times that of a 56K telephone modem and twice as fast as a DSL 640,000 bps connection. However, some DSL lines are as fast as 1,500,000 bps.

Other types of interactive peripherals include interactive laser discs, image "frame grabbing" devices, special-effects technology, DVDs, and CD-ROMS. Designers for the World Wide Web can create interactive programs for entertainment, education, or a combination of the two for use on another computer (see Chapter 16).

Frame grabbing is the ability to capture a still image from a videotape or digital video and use it in some other program. A newspaper or magazine graphic designer might want to include a single image from a news event on a page layout if a still photograph of the event doesn't exist. CNN and other media outlets offer licensing of their images to newspapers for that purpose.

Television station and independent producers often utilize special-effects devices to make visually stimulating transitions between scenes. Many products, including Charisma X-VTL from Questech, Premiere and After Effects from Adobe, Media Composer from Avid, and Final Cut Pro from Apple, allow sophisticated switching between two or more videotapes with numerous special effects. The final output can be another videotape, a film, or some other computer. More and more, interactive peripherals—in which words, images, and sounds are created for presentation in some other venue—are becoming more important as new communication ideas are developed.

Software

A computer with its memory, CPU, switching devices, and peripherals is good only as a place to stick yellow Post-it Notes without software. Software is a set of instructions that links the user with the computer. One of the chief attributes that separates a computer from many other machines is that the same device can be used for several different purposes. A single computer can be used to write letters or books, draw pictures or make movies, and play or record music for educational or entertainment benefits. What makes the computer so versatile is the programs that run its many functions. Graphic designers, like the computers they work on, also must be versatile. A visual communicator must be comfortable writing and editing words, creating and manipulating still and moving images, working with numerical output, and sorting and finding information in databases. The visual communicator also must have a working knowledge of audio reproduction and be able to put all the elements together in graphic designs for both print and screen presentations. Hence, a full-service visual communicator should be familiar with

1. word processing programs such as *Word*

2. illustration programs such as *FreeHand* or *Adobe Illustrator*

3. picture manipulation software such as *Photoshop*

4. spreadsheet software such as *Excel*

5. page layout programs such as *PageMaker, QuarkXPress,* or *InDesign*

6. presentation programs such as *Power-Point*

7. motion picture software such as *Director, Flash, Premiere, Final Cut Pro,* or *After Effects*

8. World Wide Web editors such as *Front-Page* or *Dreamweaver*

In the past, hardware always has been considered separate from software. Some people knew more about hardware and others concentrated on software. Just as words and images are being united, hardware and software are becoming intricately linked. Probably the ultimate software-hardware fusion is the technology called virtual reality (VR), so named by self-confessed VR guru Jaron Lanier, an early advocate. Also called virtual world and virtual environment, VR challenges the old-fashioned notion that hardware is separate from its software—or even that a user is separate from a computer (see Chapter 16).

Physical Concerns about the Technology

Care should be taken to avoid unnecessary contact with any device that emits electromagnetic radiation. Scientists still aren't sure whether CRT screens produce harmful side effects. Anti-glare filters can block up to 99.9 percent of radiation emitted from monitors, as well as reduce the glare from lights in a room. In an office, users should avoid sitting next to the back of a computer, where radiation tends to accumulate. One of the advantages of LCD screens is their extremely low radiation level.

Ergonomics is the study of human-machine interaction. A computer workstation should be designed ergonomically so that a user has comfortable lighting, desk, and seating arrangements. One of the most serious physical conditions resulting from repeated hand and wrist movements and poorly designed computer workstations is called *carpal tunnel syndrome.* The carpal tunnel is a small passageway between the small bones of the wrist through which tendons, blood vessels, and nerves extend from the lower arm to the hand. Numbness and weakness in the wrist and hand may result if the tunnel becomes swollen from repeated actions. The condition was first noticed in the 1800s and was called the "washer woman disease." Typists, grocery store checkout personnel, and even salmon cannery workers who use their hands in a repetitive motion are susceptible to repetitive strain injuries, of which carpal tunnel syndrome is one form. A computer user should always stop and exercise the wrists if they start to grow numb. Otherwise, the condition can worsen and may even require surgery. Many products have been developed that help alleviate the strain from using a computer— adjustable tables, chairs, and monitors, arm and wrist supports, different keyboard configurations, and footrests. Changing to a **trackball**-style mouse from a traditional finger-click mouse can also help.

Ethical Perspective

As with motion pictures and television, computer games have been accused of displaying scenarios that feature gratuitous sex, violence, and stereotypes. Many critics are concerned that children become obsessed with playing video games at home and thus are slow to learn how to interact socially with other people. As pressing as those issues are, there are also concerns about image manipulation (Chapter 12).

Violent Themes

Atari of Sunnyvale, California, pioneered computer video games with its 1972 tennis-like simulation, *Pong.* The company followed its success with the action-adventure game *Space Invaders* (1978) and the hungry chalk-colored robot *Pac-Man* (1981). But the video game fad quickly faded, and no American company was willing to invest in the video game business. This lack of vision allowed two Japanese companies, Nintendo and Sega, to dominate the genre completely. In the early 1980s, Japanese playing card manufacturer Hiroshi Yamauchi successfully expanded his business into video games with his Nintendo Entertainment System. Yamauchi's son-in-law, Minoru Arakawa, leased a warehouse in Seattle to produce

Donkey Kong and bring the business to the United States. The red-capped *Mario* was named after the warehouse landlord who often complained about late rent payments. Sega was a small company barely managing to compete with giant Nintendo until 1989 when company officials introduced the Genesis, a 16-bit high-quality game system, with an aggressive advertising strategy. With its game character, *Sonic the Hedgehog,* Sega sales exceeded those of Nintendo. Mario and Sonic now are almost as familiar to children around the world as Mickey Mouse.

In 2001, the U.S. stand-alone and online video game industry reached a record $7 billion in total annual sales, just shy of the $7.6 billion made from motion pictures. Responding to the need of consumers for higher-quality products, video game systems have been introduced by many companies. Early computer games ran at a slow 16MHz. Using the fastest processing chips available, the newest game systems are much more lifelike than anything seen previously. That realism pays off. Sony's PlayStation 2 sold more than 4.5 million units the year after it was released in the fall of 2000. In 2001 new game systems from Nintendo (GameCube) and Microsoft (Xbox) were introduced. But the real competition for Nintendo and Sony may come from video game producers who team with cable operators and Web site publishers. These alliances will make possible the provision of interactive games without the need for separate systems attached to television sets and computers (see Chapter 16).

Gaming systems don't mean much without the software they run. And increasingly, that software involves interactive "shooting" games. Software makers such as Konami and Ubi Soft compete with established companies for computer gaming dollars. Social critics raise important concerns about children who become obsessed with video game playing. Users often forsake homework, friends, family, and even meals as they move through the fantasy scenes. Most video games can be criticized because they reward a player for committing some kind of violent act. The object of most video games is to kill as many other video characters as possible with guns, knives, or kicks. Critics point out that the games teach a child, as do violent examples in other media, that conflicts are easily resolved, not through compromise, but through direct, violent action. Critics believe that video game violence has a higher potential for adverse personality disorders among children than motion pictures or television because a child is actually responsible for the killing in the game, rather than being a passive viewer of the action on a screen.

One alarming fact concerning the two young men who killed thirteen people and themselves at a Littleton, Colorado, high school in 1999 was they were obsessed with playing two "first-person shooter" CD-ROM video games, *Doom* and *Quake*. Consequently, Disney banished all violent video games from its theme parks and hotels while the U.S. government investigates marketing of movies, music, and video games in a study on children and media violence.

A CD-ROM game that raised alarms of concern was *Mortal Kombat*. *Kombat* featured decapitations and spinal cord and heart removals (Figure 15.21). Nintendo and Sega both sold versions of *Kombat*, which was produced by Acclaim Entertainment. Sega offered two different versions—one that was toned down and one that was gruesome. Super Nintendo's *Mortal Kombat II* contained only the gruesome version. Nevertheless, in both versions the object is to kill people, many of them women. Despite criticisms about the game, in the first two months of its introduction, more than 3 million copies were sold. The game is no

longer produced. Because of criticism, Sega was the first to introduce a rating system for its games that is similar to that of the motion picture industry. Almost all game manufacturers use the system today to let parents know of the contents.

In the wake of the aerial attacks upon the World Trade Center towers in New York and the Pentagon in Washington, D.C., on September 11, 2001, software creators are looking closely at the content of their video games and how they are marketed. Activision's next *Spider-Man* game had to be edited because its final battle occurred on a building resembling the twin towers. Konami's *Metal Gear Solid 2: Sons of Liberty* for PlayStation 2, which featured a hero up against terrorists all around New York City, removed the twin towers. Producers for Microsoft's popular *Flight Simulator 2002* and the Xbox game *Project Gotham Racing* both edited out images of the World Trade Center. Sensitive to customer feelings about the aerial attacks, Ubi Soft postponed the release of *Tom Clancy's Rogue Spear: Black Thorn,* a realistic counterterrorist game. But one game user reportedly plans to buy *Metal Gear Solid 2* because it allows users "to vividly imagine that they are with the commandos in Afghanistan, taking out the bad guys." It will be left to others to determine if that action is a good or bad feature of the program.

Sexual Themes

In this age of "safe sex," many interactive video and CD-ROM games feature soft pornography, as opposed to hard-core pornographic adult themes. The popularity of these discs shouldn't be surprising— pornographic materials are a cultural phenomenon. For example, in the first years of the videotape rental business, pornographic programs accounted for more than 50 percent of total revenue. Today it is down to 15

Figure 15.21

See color section following page 276.

percent, largely because of the many types of videotapes available. Most of the CD-ROM games involve women characters that are willing to take their clothes off and perform sexual services in response to a mouse-generated command. Digitized video images and audio effects give the illusion of a one-on-one encounter. One of the first sex-oriented "games" was *MacPlaymate,* created by Mike Saenz. As the user clicked a mouse on various parts of the main character's cartoon clothing, Maxie would oblige by undressing. The program also contained a "panic button." If someone came into the room unexpectedly, the user could quickly switch the screen to a simulated spreadsheet program. Saenz produced one of the most popular CD-ROM adult games, *Virtual Valerie 2.* The CD-ROM game is an enhanced animation version of the Maxie line drawing. Promotional material describes the CD as "the ultimate in cyberotica and the embodiment of every red-blooded technophile's deepest desires." ICFX of San Rafael, California, has *Penthouse Interactive*—the user is a *Penthouse* magazine photographer taking pictures of the models. At the end of the shooting session, printouts can be obtained if the computer is hooked up to a printer. Interotica has a program called *NightWatch Interactive III,* in which you are a voyeur in control of a singles' resort security camera system and can spy on all sorts of people who don't know that you're watching them.

Responsible industry executives have established guidelines for adult themes. They state that no underage models, animals, sadistic and masochistic (S&M) practices, or violence toward women are to be featured in these programs. But they are only guidelines with which compliance is voluntary. A bulletin board system ran into trouble with police officials when a group of individuals sent scanned images of underage models performing sexual acts over its telephone network. Computer users may be arrested if they download child pornography to their home systems. In the movie *The Lawnmower Man* the lead character has virtual-reality sex with his girlfriend. The movie was forgettable, but the scene inspired many stories in the media. Some writers have predicted that VR sex between partners thousands of miles from each other but linked through a fiber-optic network may be the "killer app"—jargon among program developers for an application that everyone will want to have.

The name for VR computer sex is **teledildonics.** Mike Saenz defends the use of adult-oriented games as educational. "Just as a flight simulator is used to train pilots before they climb into a real plane," Saenz says, "I think sex simulation could be used to prevent unwanted pregnancies and warn about sexually transmitted diseases." One writer states that, with VR technology, "you may be able to experience love, sexual orgasm and ultimately death, and then remove your Walkman-like headset, have a smoke, take a shower and go to work." What if the games become so popular that no one goes to the trouble of making real babies?

However, a much more serious consequence of the increased realism of humans in computer games and presentations is the issue of where you draw the line between innovative presentations and child pornography. The U.S. Supreme Court heard arguments in the fall of 2001 whether the First Amendment protects producers of computer animated movies that show simulated children—not real actors—having sex. The case comes from a federal appears court decision that rules a 1996 pornography law passed by Congress was unconstitutional. That law, the Child Pornography Act, banned video and digital images of youths under the age of eighteen involved in sexually explicit scenes. Given the advances in computer technology as seen in such movies as *Titanic, Monsters, Inc.,* and *Final Fantasy,* it can be imagined what lengths producers can go in order to achieve sexual realism. In fact, Deputy Solicitor General Paul D. Clement argued before the Court that "computer-generated images can be so lifelike that the government cannot prove that real children were used, so it needs authority to prosecute any sex scene with someone who appears to be a minor, even if the image only seems real." However, in the spring of 2002 the U.S. Supreme Court ruled in a 6–3 vote that the government went too far in banning computer simulations of children having sex. Nevertheless, Attorney General John Ashcroft promised to work with Congress to enact new legislation that would hold up to court challenges.

Image Manipulation

Manipulation of still digital photographs is a valuable tool for photographers who can easily and without chemicals perform all the functions that traditionally were reserved for darkrooms (Figure 15.22). However, critics are concerned that manipulations are going beyond simple cropping or color balance adjustments and altering the content of news editorial pictures (Chapter 12). The ability to alter motion pictures, disks, and videotapes by computer technology also exists.

Journalism manipulation, especially by amateurs with access to inexpensive software, is a serious threat to the integrity of the profession because it distorts the historical record of a culture (see Chapter 12). Bob Greenberg of R/Greenberg Associates, Inc., a computer image manipulation company, has boasted that with the technology at his disposal he could make it look like Rodney King had never even been touched by the LAPD police officers. Of equal concern is the fact that many media organizations are

willing to publish or broadcast questionable images (Figure 15.23).

Computer technology also allows taking parts from one film and combining them with another film. A Coca-Cola commercial featured living musician Elton John singing with several dead entertainers—Louis Armstrong, Humphrey Bogart, and James Cagney while Fred Astaire appeared to dance with a vacuum cleaner in a Dirt Devil commercial and John Wayne popped up in a Coors Light ad.

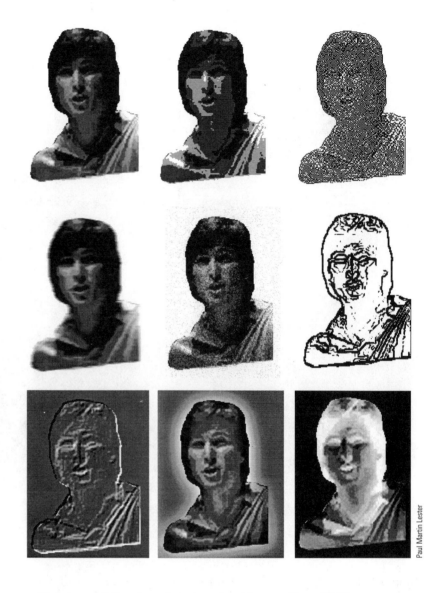

Paul Martin Lester

Figure 15.22

Steven Jobs' image is easily manipulated with the help of the Photoshop software program manufactured by the Adobe Corporation.

Figure 15.23

TV Guide *magazine caused a minor controversy when it was learned that the cover photograph of talk show host Oprah Winfrey actually was a computer-manipulated composite using a publicity still of actress Ann-Margret. Note that the cushion changed into a pile of bills.*

One positive application of computer technology is the preservation of old motion pictures. The reissues of Disney's classic animation movie *Snow White* and MGM's classic *The Wizard of Oz,* released by Warner Bros., are cleaner now than when they were viewed originally in theaters. The movies also are permanently preserved because they are now digital, rather than analog, motion pictures. Early motion picture filmstock used a substrate composed of cellulose nitrate, which shrinks, emits gas, and can ignite spontaneously. Consequently, half of all the films made before 1950 have been lost

through deterioration. After 1950, cellulose acetate (also called safety film) was developed and used. Although it isn't explosive, safety film can fade. The original negatives for movie classics such as *Stagecoach* and *Dr. Strangelove* have been lost to fading. The cable network American Movie Classics (AMC) and the Film Foundation of Hollywood Directors are investing in the transfer of documentaries and newsreel footage to safety film because of their historical value. An example of an ethically positive application of colorization is AMC's restoration of the faded 1935 color classic *Becky Sharp,* the first three-strip Technicolor motion picture, to its original luster. Computer technology can preserve a digital version of a motion picture permanently. However, at present, transferring a movie to a computer format is quite expensive.

Much of the concern over digital still and moving image manipulations is because the *original* often is altered. Once a picture is changed, it is changed forever. Photographic credibility—the idea that seeing is believing—may be a naive, old-fashioned concept.

But *every* image in the mind's eye, every subject before a camera's lens, and every still and moving picture produced in the dark or light is manipulated to begin with. And because more and more people are learning how images are produced, fewer and fewer believe in the inherent truthfulness of a picture anymore. An early signal of how little images are believed was the jury's reaction to the videotape of George Holliday. Viewers saw Rodney King beaten, but the pictures, although dramatic and purportedly the truth, didn't make much difference to the jury.

When a picture's content no longer is credible, context and the words that accompany a photograph will become more crucial to deciding what is true. The credibility of a picture may rest more on a media outlet's reputation and the text used to explain an image than the picture itself in this computer-manipulation age. Computer technology didn't start the decline in the credibility of pictures, but it has hastened it.

Cultural Perspective

The stereotypical image of an individual (usually a male) with mussed hair, glasses held together at the bridge of the nose with white tape, about ten pens and pencils carried in a shirt pocket protector, wrinkled clothing, and a laugh similar to a donkey's

bray is identified in this culture as that of the "computer nerd." This stereotype emerged during the time when research scientists and technicians dominated the computer industry. The general public was all too eager to make fun of these learned, yet socially awkward, individuals because the technology scared most people senseless. No culture ever generated a "printing press nerd" or a "typewriter nerd" because those machines never evoked the irrational fears that computers did.

Science fiction writers helped spread computerphobia. People in their stories often are controlled by giant, impersonal "superbrains." During the 1950s, audiences were frightened by a computerized robot featured in *The Day the Earth Stood Still* that was so powerful it could halt the flow of electricity to every machine on the planet. Fear of nuclear Armageddon, in which people had no control over the powerful machines they had created to protect them, fueled such movies as *Failsafe* and *Dr. Strangelove*. In Arthur C. Clarke's *2001: A Space Odyssey,* the benign, protective, and slightly condescending computer HAL (each letter in the name is one down from the letters IBM) suddenly turns into a psychopathic killer. In both *Terminator* movies and in Universal Studio's *Terminator 2 3D: Battle Across Time* computer-controlled machines can be stopped only if the robot is destroyed—usually through some lucky circumstance. Even real-life serial killers are described in media reports as having the "calculating mind of a computer." With the vision of computers as so forceful that they control every aspect of a person's life, stereotyping the creators and operators of these mighty machines as impotent and unattractive isn't surprising.

The desktop publishing revolution has helped end the nerd stereotype and the negative view of computers. The image of a sterile, serious, and a bit obsessed IBM executive in a white starched shirt has been replaced by the image of a passionate, relaxed, and a bit obsessed Apple user who doesn't own a tie. With easy-to-operate computers and software programs, anyone could learn how to operate the machine. Desktop publishing educated the average user about the difference between a software program and the task of computing. No longer does a computer user need to know how to write the program that makes a computer operate. Similar to the time when George Eastman invented roll film cameras so that anyone could enjoy photography, the diversity of tasks that can be performed relatively easily on a computer makes it a tremendously popular machine.

The mystique of the computer is lessened further when elementary school children can create their own graphic programs and write papers for assignments. With computer chips now essential for the operation of such diverse machines as wristwatches, microwave ovens, and automobiles, computers and their users are admired by the culture that embraces such technology. A computer, especially in the home, is a status symbol—not nerdism. Its owners are considered to be forward thinking, progressive, and mentally sharp. The same terms were spoken about those in the 1940s who had a television set at home. Because almost everyone has a TV set, the new symbol of an upwardly mobile family is the computer in the extra bedroom. Soon, however, the sight of a computer at home will be as ubiquitous as that of a television set.

Critical Perspective

Without question, computers represent a major technological breakthrough on a par with Gutenberg's printing press. The fact that all the media are becoming dependent on computers—"digital convergence"—ensures that the world will never return to a precomputer time. But computers simply are machines that reflect the culture that makes them. As with other means of expression, if a society accepts violence, sexism, and the perpetuation of cultural stereotypes, that type of content will pervade the digital medium. A society always gets the media images it deserves.

Computerphiles advance the simplistic notion that more computer technology can solve all the evils of the world. But capitalistic, free-market democracies have consistently demonstrated that almost any innovation divides people into those who can afford to use it and those who cannot. For example, some schools are better equipped to teach and some restaurants have higher-quality entrées because of the economic status of those who live nearby. Many experts look to teleputers—interactive multimedia, network-connected machines on the World Wide Web—to help solve many of society's problems. As more people are educated through technology, so the argument goes, the world will become a better and more tolerant place.

At present, half of all the messages on worldwide electronic information networks are simple notes that could just as easily be sent by telephone or postcard. If teleputers simply turn out to be low-cost alternatives to telephone and postal services with unfair access, a potentially great societal benefit will be lost.

■ FUTURE DIRECTIONS FOR COMPUTERS

Speculating about the future of computers is always risky. Because of the delay between writing a manuscript, having it published, and your reading these words and images, this book already may be outdated in some respects, which is why a Web site was created for this textbook that gives additional information and updates. One trend is clear: Computers as they are presently known eventually will become as quaint and old-fashioned as manual typewriters. They are turning into workstations, desktops, desksides, multiprocessing units, servers, development tools, high-end processors, information appliances, virtual-reality stations, and, of course, teleputers.

DISCUSSION AND EXERCISE IDEAS

- Lead a discussion on the films of James Cameron—*The Abyss, Terminator 2,* and *Titanic.* What is the lesson of combining computer graphics and interesting story lines?

- Describe your favorite computer graphic effect in motion pictures, on television, or on computers.

- Lead a discussion about the future of computers.

- Write a paper that discusses the ethical concerns with computer interactive programs with particular emphasis on portraying sex and violence.

INFOTRAC COLLEGE EDITION ASSIGNMENTS

- With "Subject guide" checked, type "James Cameron Embarks on Next Voyage" in the search area and read the article of the same name by John Hiscock. In the piece, Cameron says about a planned project set in the international space station, "I want to communicate what a great adventure it is, and it probably should be a non-fiction experience of some kind." Do you think audiences gravitate most toward stories that are based on true stories or fictionalized ones? Do you think computer graphic effects can be just as compelling for both types of presentations?

- With "Subject guide" checked, type "Violence in E-Rated Video Games" in the search area and read the results of a research study by Kimberly M. Thompson and Kevin Haninger published in *The Journal of the American Medical Association* (be sure to take note of the minor correction in the article as well). Do you think there is a connection between violence in video games and violence in real life? What do you think are the causes of violence in society?

Go to the Web site for this book at www.wadsworth.com/product/0534562442 to find more Web links on this subject.

WORLD WIDE WEB

> The World Wide Web is
> the most important
> single outcome of the
> personal computer. It is
> the Gutenberg press that
> is democratizing
> information.
>
> *Bill Atkinson, 1942–*
>
> SOFTWARE DESIGNER AND
>
> NATURE PHOTOGRAPHER

By the end of this chapter you should know:

- The importance of the World Wide Web for commercial, educational, and entertainment purposes.
- The importance of a critical view of media mergers and the Web.
- The historical developments that led to the Web as we know it today.
- Some of the ethical concerns involved with the World Wide Web.

From all accounts, Stephen McConnell Case could sell tea to Juan Valdez, the latest version of Netscape to Bill Gates, or an Arizona Diamondbacks baseball cap to Ted Turner. With steadfast determination, marketing know-how, and a vision of the future that was correct, Steve Case moved from being a traveling pizza topping salesman to being chairman of the largest media corporation in the world—AOL Time Warner, Inc. His story is a remarkable testament to the entrepreneurial spirit and the commercial success of the World Wide Web.

Steve Case is a product of a hardworking, independent-thinking family from Hawai'i. Both of his parents were fourth-generation islanders. His father worked long hours as a corporate lawyer. His mother was a retired teacher content to raise Steve and his two brothers, Dan and Jeff, and sister, Carin. Growing up in the Manoa Valley section of Honolulu, Steve had a strong entrepreneur's spirit. Early on, he shared a limeade stand and a newspaper route with his brother Dan. They later expanded their businesses by selling greeting cards and seed packets door-to-door. He often woke up his brother in the middle of the night with new business ideas. He liked to fool around with technological devices—cameras, rockets, and weather stations. But he also enjoyed time alone in his bedroom, which his family called his "office." He would hatch mail-order business schemes or send off for materials from scientific catalogs. He liked getting mail.

In the mid-1970s he left the island to attend Williams College, a liberal arts school three hours northwest from Boston. He majored in political science because he thought it was "the closest thing to marketing." As in high school, he was an average student doing enough just to get by. He took a computer course, but hated it. In that era of punched cards, he didn't like waiting to see if his programs worked. Despite his childhood fascination with all things scientific, later in life he was more concerned about what things could do rather than how they worked. He once wrote that he learned enough about technology so that he would be "able to understand what might be possible."

But again, his love of marketing and selling just about anything got him noticed. One schoolmate remarked that Steve was "that guy from Hawai'i who was always trying to sell stuff." He set up fruit baskets for sale in the cafeteria and ran a shuttle service to and from the airport. His love for rock and roll led him to be a member of the campus entertainment committee where he tried to bring headline acts—Bruce Springsteen and the Cars—to a nearby hockey rink for concerts. He also sang in two new wave bands. When others complained about his manic approach to marketing, he would simply shrug and keep at it. On weekends he borrowed a car and drove to nearby Smith College where he saw Joanne Barker, whom he had met while she was a visiting student at Williams. Apparently, she was his hardest sale. It took until 1985 before they were married.

Case was also a bit of a loner. He would spend hours in the library reading marketing trade publications. He was particularly enthralled with Alvin Toffler's book *The Third Wave* that envisioned a world connected by machines that communicated with one another. He became captivated by the promise that cable television offered— hundreds of channels and two-way communication. In 1979 he spent the summer selling cable TV subscriptions door-to-door in Oahu. He also became inspired after listening to the outspoken cable TV executive Ted Turner, who founded CNN, give a Rotary Club speech.

About to leave Williams, he applied for several MBA programs, but every one turned him down. He applied for marketing jobs for New York advertising and media companies, including Time Inc.'s Home Box Office. But he didn't even get an interview so he failed to meet the executive who ran HBO, Gerald Levin. Case then applied to work for Procter & Gamble, a company known for training marketing professionals, but he was rejected as well. However, he drove to the home office in Cincinnati and was given another interview. He got the job.

Case was assigned a product called Abound that was a towelette soaked in hair conditioner. While there, he invented an elaborate point-of-sale interactive display to sell the product. Although considered a good idea, it was deemed too expensive to use. He lasted two years with the company—longer than Abound did. He then took a job with a PepsiCo subsidiary, Pizza Hut, out of Wichita, Kansas. His job was to drive around the country in rental cars developing pizza flavors and checking on quality control. Lonely in hotel rooms, he spent his nights playing on his Kaypro CP/M personal computer, logging on to "The Source," one of the first online bulletin boards accessible with a modem, where he emailed others from all over the world. About his first experience with email he said, "It was magical because after thinking about it and reading it and imagining it I was actually doing it."

In 1983, his brother Dan knew he was bored at Pizza Hut and told him to attend an electronics trade show in Las Vegas. There, he talked with the owner of Control Video Corp., a start-up company that supplied Atari video games to personal computers through phone lines, and joined the company. Despite his best efforts, the company went bust because this was years before the video game industry became popular. But with an executive Case formed Quantum Computer Services Inc. in 1985. Quantum provided tools, games, news, and soap opera accounts for those using Commodore computers with a modem.

At that time, the online market was quite small, being dominated by one company— Prodigy. It was an online service funded with $1 billion from Sears, Roebuck and Co. and IBM. To be successful, Quantum had to convince computer manufacturers to use its online service. Case moved to Cupertino, California, to try to convince those at Apple

Computer to use his company for their online service with their Apple II. In another example of his headstrong single-mindedness, Case showed up at Apple headquarters every day for three months until they gave him the account.

■ THE BIRTH OF AMERICA ONLINE

In 1985 the World Wide Web was a decade away, but Case sensed a growing interest among nontechnical users to chat with each other through the Internet. In 1989, Quantum's online service was renamed America Online (AOL)—a self-contained Internet bulletin board service with news, shopping, entertainment, and chat rooms (Figure 16.1). Soon afterward, Case launched a controversial marketing campaign that flooded America's households and businesses with AOL disks that allowed users, with a credit card, to hook up to the Internet through AOL. Even those on American Airlines flights received an AOL disk with their peanuts and a drink.

By 1991, AOL had 130,000 customers and 120 employees. An initial public offering (IPO) the next year raised $66 million. Case, thirty-four, who was largely paid with stock options, was suddenly worth $2 million, named chief executive of the company, and could buy all the pizza he wanted.

However, in the mid-1990s when the Web was starting to become popular there was some concern that the Internet would diminish the need for AOL's online bulletin board. Consequently, AOL developed its own trademark **Web browser** so that customers could not only look through offerings AOL had, but also surf the entire World Wide Web. However, the browser was criticized for its awkward design. It was called, derogatorily, the "Internet on training wheels." In 1998 AOL purchased the first

Figure 16.1

Early in the company's history, modem users saw this version of a logon screen before connecting to the Internet through AOL. The graphics elements in the center designate that an electrical and perhaps spiritual force links the key of knowledge with the AOL logo— where almost unlimited information within the bulletin board awaits.

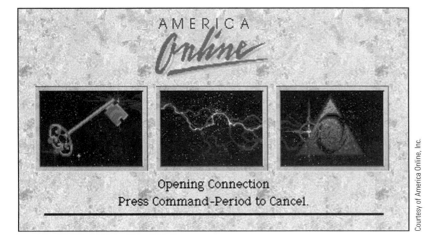

Courtesy of America Online, Inc.

commercial Web browser Netscape and made Marc Andreessen, the inventor of Netscape, the chief technology officer. But in a disagreement over the future of the browser and the company, Andreessen resigned. This was a hard time for Case personally as he divorced his wife. Steve and Joanne Case had three young children. He later married AOL Marketing Vice President Jean Vilanueva and for a time his personal life became a media spectacle.

Despite these professional and personal challenges, AOL (www.aol.com), based outside of Washington, D.C., has more than 30 million customers worldwide and more than 15,000 employees. Case's current net worth is estimated to be about $1.5 billion, or about 150 million Pizza Hut pizzas.

AOL is the largest interactive service in the world enabling users to keep in touch through email, stay informed through news sites, shop at various online stores, find entertainment, take advantage of educational opportunities, manage finances and schedules, and many more services all within the AOL brand. In addition to the AOL service, the company also operates several other supporting concerns:

- *AOL Anywhere:* Allows users to access the Web using pagers, cell phones, and other devices (Figure 16.2).
- *AOL International:* Operates within sixteen countries using eight different languages.
- *AOL@School:* Provides educators and students low-cost links to educational information.
- *CompuServe:* With 3 million users worldwide, offers advanced online features.
- *Digital City:* Provides entertainment and visitor guides to 200 markets in the United States.
- *Digital Marketing Services:* Online marketing and research service.

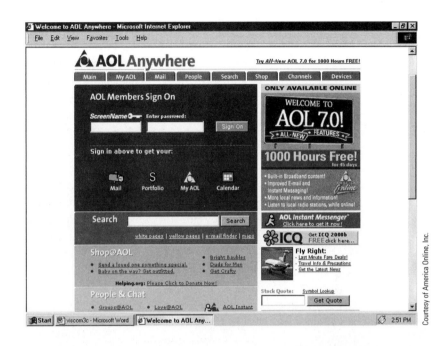

Courtesy of America Online, Inc.

- *ICQ:* With 88 million registered users, allows telephone calls over a computer and other communications services.
- *IPlanet:* An alliance with Sun Microsystems, Inc., that offers an Internet software platform for businesses.
- *MapQuest:* With 10 million users a month, provides mapping and navigation services.
- *Moviefone:* Gives online movie listings, information, and the opportunity to purchase tickets.
- *Netscape:* The first commercial Web browser.
- *AOL Music:* A place to listen to and buy music on the Web.

AOL has been called the "first Blue Chip company of the Internet" and was the first online company to be listed on the Fortune 500. About 50 percent of all U.S. home computer users access the Web through AOL.

Case has donated about $200 million of his personal wealth to various charities. In addition, AOL has established the AOL

Figure 16.2

AOL Anywhere (www.aol.com) indicates graphically that the company wants you to join the club. From a "Sign On" button to links for discount Internet access, the Web site reminds users of its roots to the original concept—a closed network bulletin board.

Foundation, which fosters community, teaching, and learning; PowerUp, which gives young people access to technology; and Helping.org, which helps charitable organizations be successful. In 2000, Case received the Kellogg Award for extraordinary career achievement from his alma mater, Williams College.

At a newspaper industry convention in 1998 he started his speech with a quote from Louis XVI of France. After hearing of the revolt by peasants on July 14, 1789—the storming of the Bastille in Paris—King Louis said, "Why, it's only a revolt." The aide responded, "Sire, it's not a revolt. It's a revolution." Many have called Case's view of the online world by the same name.

■ AOL MERGES WITH TIME WARNER, INC.

Perhaps it was because of his early days watching Saturday morning cartoon shows featuring Bugs Bunny and Daffy Duck, the rock and roll music he loved to listen to, the speech given by the iconoclast Ted Turner, or the fact he never got an interview with HBO chief Gerald Levin, but Case wanted to turn AOL from an online giant into a media giant. And he did so in 2000.

On January 10, the largest corporate merger in the history of the United States was announced. For $183 billion, AOL, the largest online service company in the world, and Time Warner, Inc., the largest media corporation in the world, became one. AOL shareholders now own 55 percent of Time Warner, a company known around the world for such holdings as *Time* magazine, CNN, and Warner Bros. studio.

The merger also made Case the boss of Ted Turner, founder of Turner Broadcasting System (TBS), which includes CNN and the Atlanta Braves. TBS had merged with Time

Warner earlier, but Turner had little impact anymore on day-to-day operations. Case could also get all the interviews he wanted with Gerald Levin, who had moved from HBO to head of Time Warner. Case would be chairman while Levin would be the chief executive officer for the new company.

"This is really an historic moment," Case said at the merger news conference. "This merger will launch the next Internet revolution." At that conference much was said about the difference between Levin and Case. Levin, sixty, wore an open-collar shirt while Case, forty-three, dressed in a suit and tie. It was perhaps a symbolic gesture—the young kid on the block co-opting the older generation.

■ ANALYSIS OF AOL TIME WARNER, INC.

The deal between these media giants was made in extraordinary haste. Levin and Case met at conferences in Paris and Shanghai in September 1999 and became friends. A month later, they started merger talks over the telephone. The two reached a tentative agreement on January 6. Three days later AOL and Time Warner directors and staffers, investment bankers, and lawyers met in a Manhattan law firm and ironed out the details. The merger was announced at a news conference the next day. Almost two years later, however, Levin announced his retirement from the company. Co-chief operating officer Richard Parsons was named to take his place. One of Parson's first tasks will be to oversee a pending bid for AT&T's cable unit that would double AOL Time Warner's cable reach.

It was once assumed that given the tremendous size of the World Wide Web there would be no way that a corporation, no matter how large and global in its reach, could control a user's access to the information that is available. Electronic Frontier Foundation's John Perry Barlow dismissed concerns about media mergers in a speech in 1995. Barlow noted that the large media corporations are "merely rearranging deck chairs on the *Titanic*." The iceberg is the World Wide Web with its 500 million channels. How could any company control access to that many channels? And perhaps that is still true.

But after a hectic pace of corporate mergers and buyouts from the 1980s on, where there used to be fifty firms controlling worldwide media, there are now only nine. Such mergers are possible because the FCC relaxed many of its strict rules concerning media ownership. Included below are the nine corporations with their Web site address, country of origin, and major holdings:

AOL Time Warner, Inc.
www.aoltimewarner.com
USA

In addition to the AOL holdings described above, Turner Broadcasting (CNN, TBS Superstation, TNT, WB, Cartoon Network, Atlanta Braves, Atlanta Hawks), HBO (Cinemax, Comedy Central), Time, Inc. (*Time, Sports Illustrated, People, Entertainment Weekly*), and more than twenty others), Time Warner Trade Publishing (Little Brown and Company, Warner Books), Warner Music Group (Atlantic, Elektra, Rhino), Warner Bros. (Castle Rock, New Line Cinema, Fine Line Features, Looney Tunes, Hanna-Barbera, DC Comics, *Mad* magazine, Time Warner Cable, Six Flags theme parks

AT&T Comcast Corp. (upon approval)
www.att.com
USA

Internet Broadband Service (with Microsoft), Cable Television (Comcast Cable and formerly TCI), and Digital Telephone, AT&T Labs

Bertelsmann Media Worldwide
www.bertelsmann.com
Germany

European television stations and cable channels, BMG (Arista, RCA, Windham Hill), Barnes & Noble, Inc., Random House, Alfred A. Knopf, Doubleday, *Family Circle*

Walt Disney Company
www.disney.com
USA

ABC, ESPN, ABC Family Channel, Disney Channel, Touchstone, Hollywood Pictures, Miramax, Pixar, Walt Disney Internet Group, theme parks worldwide, Anaheim Angels, Mighty Ducks

General Electric
www.ge.com
USA

Besides aircraft engines and appliances, NBC, CNBC, MSNBC (with Microsoft), NBC Internet, Inc.

The News Corporation, Ltd.
www.newscorp.com
Australia

Fox Television, Fox News, FX, more than thirty television stations in the USA, 20th Century Fox, Fox Searchlight Pictures, Sky Global Networks, *TV Guide,* Harper-Collins Publishers, *New York Post,* LA Dodgers

Sony Corporation
www.sony.com
Japan

Sony Electronics, Sony Music Entertainment, Inc., PlayStation, Columbia Pictures, Screen Gems, Sony Pictures

Viacom, Inc.
www.viacom.com
USA

CBS, CBS Enterprises, Paramount Television, MTV, Nickelodeon, VH1, Nick at Nite, TV Land, Showtime, The Movie Channel, FLIX, Black Entertainment Television, UPN, Paramount Pictures, Blockbuster Video, thirty-four television stations in the USA, Infinity Broadcasting, Simon and Schuster

Vivendi Universal
www.vivendi.com
France

Universal Studios, USA Networks, Universal Music Group (A&M, Decca, Motown, Verve), Houghton Mifflin, Canal+ (French pay television service), Seagram, Ltd.

These nine corporations control all the major Hollywood studios, all of the most popular cable television systems and channels, most of the magazines, most of the book publishing companies, most of the recording industry's record labels, most of the amusement parks, radio and television stations, several sports franchises, and of course many World Wide Web sites with **links** between all of their worldwide interests.

■ MEDIA MERGER IN ACTION

When one company owns so many media connections, the interplay between products and services becomes easy to manage. What's more, most customers are not aware of the connection between the products owned by the same company. For example, Moviefone is an AOL company that provides information about motion pictures, stars, entertainment news, and ticket purchasing online. A user can simply type in a title or a zip code to find out where and when a movie is playing. Of course, since the merger, Moviefone is also part of the AOL

Time Warner empire. Its Web site (www.moviefone.com) is an excellent example of the synergy that exists between a Web site and its controlling company's interests. It is also a lesson in why the need for being critical of media mergers and power is so important.

This analysis of the Moviefone Web site took place one day in October 2001. Because of the dynamic nature of the site—for example, advertisements that regularly change—your analysis of the site may be slightly different (Figure 16.3).

The logo at the left is honest—underneath "moviefone" are the words, "A SERVICE OF AMERICA ONLINE." But of course, to be more truthful, Time Warner should be included. At any rate, it's not surprising, then, that the banner ad at the top hawks "1000 HOURS FREE!" of AOL service (for 45 days) using its version 6.0 software. But there are many hidden connections between this Web site and the company.

At the top left is a small logo that is a link to the American Express (AE) Web site. With a click of your mouse you can sign up for one of their cards or various financial and travel services. Besides numerous mutual funds controlled by American Express that include AOL Time Warner stock, American Express's interactive travel service, "Express Reservations," is a service on AOL. In addition, AE and AOL announced a publishing agreement in April 2001. AE will promote the AOL online services in their magazines such as *Food & Wine* and *Travel and Leisure*. If that's not enough of a connection, a member of the board of directors for American Express, Daniel F. Akerson, chairman and chief executive officer of XO Communications, Inc., a communications services provider, is also on the board of directors for AOL Time Warner. Presumably both companies are helped by the decisions he makes. Plus, additional user hits to the American

Express Web site from Moviefone's site help both companies too.

Two of the movies featured at the top right are produced by AOL Time Warner studios—*Lord of the Rings* from New Line Cinema and *Training Day* from Warner Bros. The other two, *Spy Game* and *K-Pax,* are from Universal Studios. Since the "Top Ten" list of movies is user controlled, the motion pictures come from nine different studios. Nevertheless, four companies—AOL Time Warner, Disney, News Corporation, and Viacom—own these nine studios.

The "pop up" advertisement in the center that annoyingly covers part of the Web site entices a user to subscribe to four magazines—*Sports Illustrated, Entertainment Weekly, People,* and *Time*—all owned by AOL Time Warner. The feature at the lower left on actor Denzel Washington and the link to the Six Flag's amusement park's "October Fright Fest!" seem innocent enough, except that Washington is currently starring in *Training Day* from Warner Bros. and Six Flags is owned by AOL Time Warner, which features Warner Bros.' "Looney Tunes" cartoon characters in theme parks around the world.

Media critic, educator, and journalist Ben Bagdikian, in the third edition of *The Media Monopoly* published in 1990, warned of the type of mergers that unite huge, multinational conglomerates like AOL and Time Warner. He wrote:

> The economic and political goals of these corporations are quite uniform, their output quite similar, and their communications power is greater than that of most nations. Once their commercial empires have achieved monopoly-like power, they can control their profit levels and be free to pursue their own political and economic agendas with less restraint.
>
> We know enough to fear governments that possess unaccountable power. And we

Courtesy of America Online, Inc.

know how to prevent creation of private power that possess the same traits, and to do it by business principles that leave each corporation free to publish, broadcast, and record whatever it wishes, and provide the public with real alternatives. But if that freedom exists without true competition in the marketplace of ideas, and if each media corporation is permitted to wipe out all effective rivals and dominate its field, these corporations become as unaccountable as a dictatorial censorship.

In a speech given to the National Press Club in Washington, D.C., in 1998, Steve Case said, "Unlike radio and television, the Internet is not the product of scarcity; and unlike telephony and cable, the Internet is not the natural home of monopolists. And unlike all other media, the Internet is—and should be—whatever its users, not private or public gatekeepers, want it to be." One could assume that he has changed his mind since making that statement.

It is perhaps not surprising that the World Wide Web is being used, not always as a liberating product in the hands of users,

Figure 16.3

The Moviefone Web site home page is a graphic cacophony of words and pictures that mostly entices potential customers to link to products of companies owned by AOL Time Warner, Inc.

but as a commercial entity to enforce branding and market dominance just as with every other media presentation before it. Media and social critic John R. Squillante writes, "The World Wide Web in control by only a few major corporations is like traveling across the U.S. hoping to see unique places along the way, but what you get are homogenized small towns with every shopping mall looking exactly the same. There is only an illusion of choice—and that illusion is being repeated for users of the Web."

■ WORLD WIDE WEB
AND THE SIX PERSPECTIVES

Personal Perspective

Despite the fact that it comes from military officials who needed to find a way to communicate with one another in the event of a nuclear holocaust, is the basis for warnings by (mostly) conservative social critics that it is a plaything for those interested in corrupting young minds with a steady stream of easily accessible child pornography materials, is the subject of a relentless barrage of mass media hyperbole, and is considered either the future of mass media or a colossal waste of time and resources, the World Wide Web has earned its place as a valuable resource for information, entertainment, and blatant commercialism—as all media eventually do.

But the Web is similar and yet unlike any previous media for communications. It has the immediacy of radio and television, the totality of information of print, and the visual and audio qualities of motion pictures, but it is more than all of those media. When the first automobile was introduced, no one predicted the fast cars of today and interstate road systems, pollution, the sub-

urbs, and drive-through liquor stores. And 100 years from now people will no doubt chuckle about how the Web was used way back in the year 2002.

Historical Perspective

In 1945, Dr. Vannevar Bush, Director of Scientific Research and Development for the U.S. government, in an article for *The Atlantic Monthly,* predicted worldwide access to information databases using computers. "Consider a future device for individual use," he wrote, "which is a sort of mechanized private library." He called his machine a **memex.** "A memex is a device," he explained, "in which an individual stores all his books, records, and communications, and which is mechanized so that it may be consulted with exceeding speed and flexibility. It is an enlarged intimate supplement to his memory." It took more than twenty years before his dream became a reality.

After World War II, the Cold War set in. The U.S. military was concerned that in the event of a nuclear war in which major cities were destroyed, communications across the country between military and other governmental personnel would be difficult if not impossible with the mode of telephonic communication at that time. With the help of the RAND Corporation, a governmental think tank, an office of the Defense Department, the Advanced Research Projects Agency (ARPA), created a communications network via computers. It was dubbed the ARPANET. In 1969 the first email message was sent between researchers at UCLA and the Stanford Research Institute.

During the 1970s, powerful mainframe computers were popular at government, business, and university research sites around the world. With all the activity generated by these machines, scientists soon realized that they needed communications links among research centers so that computer operators could transfer data and talk with each other electronically. Consequently, more and more computer users started using the ARPANET for work-related and personal messages.

In 1983, ARPANET had become so popular with university researchers that the network was divided into two—the original ARPANET for university use and MILNET for military use. When satellite links were added to the system, international communication became possible. ARPANET's name was changed to the International Network, or Internet.

Gradually, researchers started to see commercial use for communication technology for the general public. Interactive multimedia (IM) as stand-alone programs and networked interactive multimedia (NIM) in the form of videotex systems, bulletin boards, and the World Wide Web followed.

Interactive Multimedia

Imagine sitting in a coffee shop with a longtime friend who has just returned from a vacation in Ireland. She excitedly starts to tell you the story of her summer, aided by a stack of color photographs. As you quietly sip coffee from a white mug, you are amused by your friend's enthusiastic tale that is filled with magical moments. Her story begins with touchdown at the Limerick airport when the plane's passengers clapped and proceeds to the customs check, a sleepy check-in at a bed-and-breakfast, the train trip to Dublin and adventures there, a music festival near Tralee on the west coast, seeing the Atlantic Ocean for the first time in Donegal, the friends she met and the countless pints of Guinness enjoyed while music seemed to always play in the background, the conversations with beggar children in downtown Galway, the frightening urban violence witnessed in Londonderry and

Belfast in Northern Ireland, hiking the Morne Mountain, the sunrises and sunsets, the country walks through the "forty shades of green," and on and on.

Throughout her recitation, as you finger her precious photos, you interrupt with questions: How much money did you take? How did you know where to go? Were you ever afraid? What camera did you use? How much film did you take? How did you get that photograph? Did you fall in love? Did you hear any great music? Did you discover the heart and soul of Ireland?

After every query, she patiently diverts from her main story and answers your question. When you are satisfied with her response, you nod and she returns to her description. At the end of her tale, you pay the check and thank your friend for a wonderful story by giving her a hug. As she waves good-bye on the busy, downtown sidewalk, you promise yourself that someday you will make that same journey.

Because the give-and-take of two-way conversation is an ancient form of human communication, interactive multimedia should be as effortless and rewarding as talking with an old friend. Consequently, the best IM presentations combine words and images in such a way that they surprise, delight, teach, and satisfy the user.

Although often referred to by writers and producers as if they are the same medium, multimedia and interactive multimedia are quite different. Multimedia without an interactive feature is a book with pictures, photographs with cutlines, a movie, a television program, or listening to a friend explain a snapshot without asking any questions. An interactive multimedia presentation uses words in both text and audio formats, sound as music and noise, and images in animated and live-action still and moving formats, as do many multimedia presentations, but in addition has a design interface that lets a

Figure 16.4

See color section following page 276.

person be either a passive viewer or an inquisitive user. The computer operator can control the order, amount, and type of information presented (Figure 16.4).

Interactive multimedia presentations have three principal applications: government, corporate, and consumer. State and federal governments use CD-ROMs for training employees, storing large database collections, and keeping archives. For example, California government officials have established stand-alone kiosks featuring laser disc technology whereby a resident can renew a driver's license or pay a minor traffic ticket. The Central Intelligence Agency uses IM lessons for foreign language training. And because of their large storage capacity and ease of use, more and more word, number, and image databases are being created on CD formats for simple access to information by government and private researchers. In addition, CD-ROM lessons in 4-inch formats for students of all ages have been created to teach everything from mathematics to multicultural awareness. Although not replacing traditional textbooks yet, the programs offer an added approach to the teaching of a growing number of subjects.

Training, point-of-sale kiosks, interactive brochures, and database collections are some of the uses of laser technology for business. Steelcase, the furniture manufacturer, and American Airlines have training CD-ROMs for their employees. The American Medical Center in Denver provides a kiosk to help cancer patients who cannot read English. General Motors offers in-depth CD-ROM informational sales pitches, and Sony and many other companies give out press releases in the form of CD-ROMs to media representatives.

Children and adults use CD-ROM programs for entertainment, informational, and educational purposes at home. Robert May, president of Ikonic Interactive, an IM pro-

ducer, says, "We're at the birth of a new Hollywood." Interactive multimedia versions of *Cliffhanger, The Addams Family,* and *The Last Action Hero* include scenes from the movies for added realism. Players imagine themselves as characters in the movies and control their own actions. But many film directors, James Cameron included, believe that viewers won't be attracted to these games because many adults just want to sit and be entertained without having to work at it.

Nevertheless, role-playing games and informational CDs are popular. The Voyager Company has an IM version of Shakespeare's *Macbeth* in which the user can select a character to perform. Murder mysteries such as *Voyeur* and *Sherlock Holmes, Consulting Detective,* are popular; users can interview witnesses, examine evidence, and make arrests. The Beatles is a popular topic for adults in their thirties and forties. Compton's *The Compleat Beatles* offers a two-hour documentary, featuring sixty-six songs and facts about the rock-and-roll band in its laser disc. An Apple QuickTime movie version of the Beatles' *A Hard Day's Night* with the sound track included is on a Voyager disc with a complete script that includes a brief history of rock and roll. Microsoft's *Encarta* and Grolier's entire twenty-one-volume encyclopedia are huge databases with moving video, still images, illustrations, and text on disc.

With all their unique features, IM presentations without network connections remain tightly controlled computer programs that merely give the illusion of interactivity. Although entertaining and educational, they are similar to a frustrating conversation with a secretive or uneducated friend who answers your questions with "I can't say" or "I don't know." That inadequacy is why Bill Gates, cofounder of Microsoft, predicted that CD-ROM discs will be a transitional phase in the history of communication. Current IM formats should be considered only a first-generation effort. Someday IM technology will be viewed with the same quaint amusement as Niépce's photograph of his country view, the Lumière brothers' factory film, and Zworykin's first televised image of Felix the Cat.

Videotex Systems

The first commercial use of networked computers was called *videotex* (teletext or viewdata in Europe). Videotex is the name for communications systems that deliver information over the video-blanking interval of a broadcast television signal to a person's home. With a small keypad and a television set-top computer, a home user can control which frames are viewed. Viewers can access hundreds of televised "pages" from which news, shopping, and other kinds of information can be read. In 1974, the British Broadcasting Corporation began Ceefax, and a group of independent stations started Oracle—both teletext systems. British users paid about $200 a year for the service. However, a user at home could download only selected pages, and the system had no interactive feature. In 1979, the British Post Office (known as British Telecom) began the first truly interactive system, Prestel. The Prestel system connected computer databases to the home through telephone or cable lines. Users could receive the latest news, order products from stores advertised on the system, and make hotel and airline reservations.

Other countries soon followed the British model. One of the most successful communications systems in the world is the French government's Minitel system, begun in 1981 by the French Telecom telephone company. It provides low-cost computers to every telephone subscriber in France. The government saves millions of dollars by not having to print telephone directories because users obtain phone numbers through their home computers. Since its adoption, Minitel has created dozens of new businesses and more than 30,000 new jobs and has generated millions of dollars for the French economy.

The first U.S. videotex system wasn't successful. The Knight-Ridder newspaper chain and AT&T teamed up in 1981 to provide a videotex service called Viewtron to users in Coral Gables, Florida, an affluent suburb of Miami. In the initial experiment, users weren't asked to pay for the videotex terminals or the service. But beginning in 1983, home viewers were asked to pay for the computer terminal (which cost about $300) and pay a monthly service charge of about $30. After investing more than $50 million in the electronic information experiment, Knight-Ridder abandoned the project. However, lessons learned from the Viewtron experiment helped commercial bulletin board operators launch successful systems (Figure 16.5).

Bulletin Boards

Concurrent with the growth of the Internet and videotex was another platform for computer-mediated communication—the electronic bulletin board. Bulletin boards (BBs) range from local text-only systems with a handful of users to worldwide networks that have millions of subscribers. BBs are popular because they offer a wide range of services—news, information, shopping, banking, software downloads, chatting, and airline reservations within a stylistically consistent structure. The appeal of a bulletin board is that users get easy access to the Internet within a program that is organized in content and graphic design similar to a magazine. Users don't get lost as easily when searching for information within a bulletin board. Before the advent of the Web, some of the most popular BB systems were America Online, CompuServe, Delphi, Genie, Prodigy, the Source, the WELL, and ZiffNet. But all that has changed.

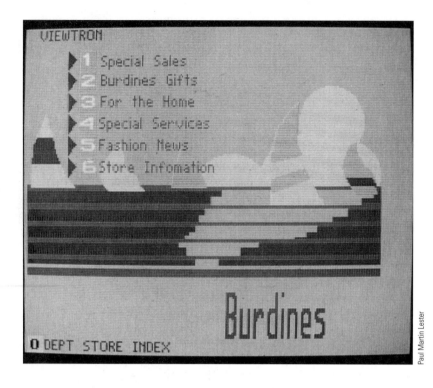

Paul Martin Lester

Figure 16.5

By today's World Wide Web standards, the graphic look of the Viewtron Videotex Service was simple, yet easy for Miami area users to shop online at a Burdines department store.

The World Wide Web

In 1991, Tim Berners-Lee of the European Laboratory for Particle Physics (CERN) in Switzerland developed a computer language that was used to access information on the Internet. The World Wide Web was born, but it still took someone with advanced computer skills to use.

In 1993, interest in the Internet expanded tremendously because of what was called the "killer app" for the Internet, the Mosaic software program developed by Marc Andreesson while a student at the University of Illinois. Mosaic, a Web browser, made accessing and downloading Internet files that contained still and moving pictures with audio as simple as clicking a computer's mouse. Web browsers turned the **ASCII,** text-dominated Internet into a colorful, content-filled excursion. Apart from the program's graphic capabilities, much of the appeal of browsers comes from the fact that they allow a person to create and use a

hypertext link (colored or underlined keywords a user presses with a mouse) within a text file to discover a seemingly inexhaustible amount of information and services.

Microsoft in the Courts

Andreesson quit school to form his own company, Netscape (Figure 16.6), which was purchased by AOL in 1995. When Microsoft's Internet Explorer was introduced soon afterward, the "browser wars" between the two Web giants began. But with most computers around the world using Microsoft Windows operating software with Internet Explorer built in, Microsoft had a tremendous marketing advantage over Netscape.

Consequently, the U.S. Justice Department brought Microsoft to court. In April 2000, U.S. District Judge Thomas Penfield Jackson determined that Microsoft violated the Sherman Antitrust Act. Jackson found, among other rulings, that Microsoft illegally attempted to maintain its monopoly over the Web browser market by tying its browser to its Windows operating system. Two months later, he issued controversial remedies—Microsoft must be broken into two companies, one for operating-system development and the other for software. Microsoft appealed that ruling. In June 2001 a U.S. appeals court ruled that Microsoft acted as an illegal monopoly but set aside Judge Jackson's order that the company should be broken up. Microsoft appealed to the U.S. Supreme Court to throw out the case, but in October 2001 the Court rejected Microsoft's appeal clearing the way for a new judge, Colleen Kollar-Kotelly of the Federal District Court for the District of Columbia, to require settlement talks between the company and the government.

A month later an agreement was reached that was criticized for letting Microsoft off too easy. One critic wrote that the terms were "so favorable that one could hardly characterize them as even a light slap on the wrist." The company doesn't have to admit its guilt, must share some of its code so that competitors can design products for it, must allow computer users to more easily exchange Microsoft's Internet Explorer and other software products of their own choosing, and must submit to a three-person committee that will monitor Microsoft's activities for the next five years. In addition, Microsoft is required to provide $1 billion worth of its own software, refurbished computers, and other resources to more than 12,500 of the nation's poorest schools. Not surprisingly, Apple Computer Inc. chief executive Steven Jobs, whose company claims 47 percent of the educational market, said in a statement, "We're baffled that a settlement imposed against Microsoft for breaking the law should allow, even encourage, them to unfairly make inroads into education—one of the few markets where they don't have a monopoly power."

As of this writing, half of the eighteen U.S. states plus the District of Columbia that joined the federal lawsuit rejected the settlement and will press for tougher sanctions. Regardless of the ultimate outcome, it seems certain that Microsoft will continue to dominate the PC software field (the Windows operating system runs 95 percent of all the personal computers in the world). Coinciding with the agreement, Microsoft introduced its new operating system, Windows XP, for U.S. consumers. Some predict that the software might cause a new round of antitrust litigation. Stay linked (Figure 16.7).

Another Web browser, Opera, was created in 1994 as a research project for the national telephone company in Norway. The software for Opera takes much less space on a hard drive than for Netscape and Internet Explorer. However, it contains all of the popular features as the other browsers and runs much faster and more efficiently. Con-

sequently, it has been called, "The little software that could." You can download a free version of Opera that contains banner ads, or pay a small fee and get a version without ads.

Media Convergence

The concept of a machine some have named the teleputer is that services offered through the existing technologies of the telephone, television, and computer will be combined into one. Consequently, **media convergence** will take place as the media become increasingly interrelated. AT&T probably will be a major participant in teleputer technology and services because of its unique history.

Judge Harold Green split the huge AT&T telephone company into regional "Baby Bells" in 1984 because of fears about monopolization. His ruling banned the newly formed regional communications companies from participating in long-distance services, equipment manufacturing, and information services. AT&T could offer long-distance service but was prevented by

Figure 16.6

The Netscape home page or portal is a useful collection of Netscape services, AOL-type topics, and news items. An interactive polling feature— whether users support the use of ground troops in Afghanistan—gives users a sense of community.

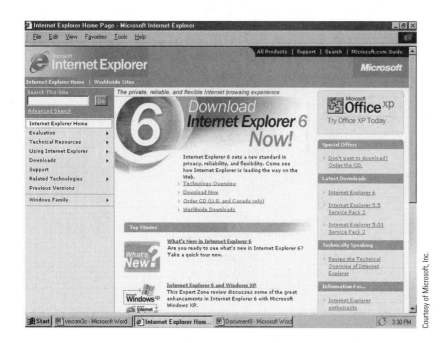

Figure 16.7

Unlike the AOL Netscape home page with its links to current news, services, and entertainment, the main page for Internet Explorer is a site to find out about and order products from Microsoft.

the ruling from entering local telephone markets. More important, AT&T could not offer information services similar to the features offered on the World Wide Web and through bulletin boards, while the Baby Bells, prevented from long-distance markets, could offer information services. AT&T lawyers tried to persuade federal judges and legislators to allow the company to offer information and entertainment services.

In 1996 their lobbying efforts were successful as the U.S. Congress passed the Telecommunications Act. The Act allows all telephone companies to offer information services and allows television, cable, and satellite companies to offer telephone services. Two years later, AT&T made the first major step toward a teleputer future and media convergence when it acquired the global data network of the IBM Corporation for $5 billion in cash. The telephone giant can enter the online communications field. Not coincidentally, AT&T was the first company to air teleputer commercials in its "You Will" campaign (Figure 16.8). In one advertisement, teleputer users are shown selecting a movie and the time they want to

watch it, asking a professor questions during a distance-learning class, and saying goodbye to a child through the teleputer's picturephone feature. In 2000, AT&T had annual revenues of nearly $66 billion. Backed by the research and development capabilities of AT&T Labs, the company runs one of the world's largest, most sophisticated communications network and became the largest cable operator in the United States when it merged with TCI.

The Stock Market Takes a Dive

The 1990s seemed like a never ending opportunity for executives of new Internet companies or "dotcoms" to make millions of dollars without even showing that a profit would be forthcoming anytime in the near future. Practically all a start-up company had to do to make their creators rich would be to find those willing to invest in the product or service, rent office space and equipment, print business cards, and offer the public the chance to buy stock in the company through an IPO. Hundreds of established and new companies used this strategy successfully because so many people wanted to invest in the U.S. stock market. Consequently, the market rose higher than ever before in its history with no end in sight.

But the end did come. On Monday, October 27, 1997, the Dow Jones industrial average fell 554 points; about 7 percent of its value was wiped out. Trading was stopped early to avoid any additional losses—something that has happened only two times before—when President Ronald Reagan was wounded and when President John F. Kennedy was assassinated. It was the worst day in a decade and the twelfth worst drop ever. The Nasdaq market, where most of the technological company stocks are traded, also fell about 7 percent.

But then on Friday, April 14, 2000, the Dow industrials recorded the worst ever drop in its history of 616 points, or 5.6 percent. The Nasdaq market fell an incredible 25 percent for the week. A kind of ripple effect caused stock markets in Asia and Europe to also plunge.

The years since the stock market crash of 1997 and 2000 haven't been kinder to dot-com companies. Dozens of promising companies have folded. A good example is EToys, Inc. which sold toys and other products over the Web. At its IPO, EToys stock quadruped to $81 a share giving the company a value of $8.18 billion. A year later, the stock was worth $6 a share with the company no longer in business. Hundreds of dotcom companies have declared bankruptcy. Computer sales have slumped with all the major hardware and software companies earning far less than a few years ago.

One of the results of this economic downturn is that funds from a booming stock market are no longer available to initiate new communications services. Consequently, the dream of linking every home in America with broadband fiber-optic technology has long ago faded. Another result is that major communications companies have been able to solidify their place in the market by merging with other media giants and buying smaller companies at fire sale prices. The year 2001 was one that saw huge corporate layoffs—affecting more than 1.5 million Americans. The aerial attacks on the World Trade Center and the Pentagon and the war with the Taliban in Afghanistan have caused further economic worries around the world.

Nevertheless, the Web cannot be stopped. When this book's first edition was written in 1993, the Internet had about 15 million users worldwide. Nine years later in the United States alone, there are about 200 million people with Web access either from home or work. And with better communications links and easier-to-use teleputers, television executives, as motion picture producers learned when competing with television

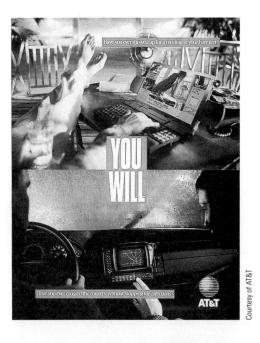

Courtesy of AT&T

Figure 16.8

The "You Will" advertising campaign by AT&T is the first set of commercials that feature the technology, lifestyle, and promise of tele-puters. The World Wide Web—at least envisioned by telephone company officials—has the potential to radically change everyday life.

(see Chapter 13), will adapt their medium to be more like the World Wide Web.

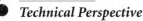 *Technical Perspective*

Early in its history, those who envisioned the communication system known as the World Wide Web realized that there needed to be a set of rules or protocols for those who create Web sites so that Web files could be viewed on any type of Web browser and on any kind of computer. The standard protocol for Web file creation is called **HyperText Markup Language** (HTML). This fairly simple software language assures that your Web browser can request information from a Web server so that you can see all of the words and images on your own computer screen. For any Web site that has been downloaded to your computer, you can view this HTML source code and study how the site was created. Simply click and drag from a menu item on your browser's toolbar. Popular HTML editors—Dreamweaver and FrontPage—make the task of Web site creation much easier than writing software code from scratch.

Figure 16.9

See color section following page 276.

The technical information to create a Web site is beyond the scope of this book; however, you should be aware of how to analyze a Web site to make sure the information contained within it is credible. Two research librarians, Jan Alexander and Marsha Ann Tate at the Wolfgram Memorial Library, Widener University in Chester, Pennsylvania, offer a five-point checklist for Web site credibility:

1. *Authority:* Who is responsible for creating the information?

2. *Accuracy:* Can sources of information be easily checked?

3. *Objectivity:* Is news, advertising, and opinion clearly separated?

4. *Currency:* Is it clear how often the files are updated?

5. *Coverage:* Does it seem as if the subject is adequately discussed?

In an evaluation of a Web site, you should also look at three technical aspects of the site itself:

- Do the files download quickly?

- Are the typographical and visual message choices appropriate for the content?

- Does the site contain useful information without spelling or typographical errors?

World Wide Web sites can use every medium of presentation discussed in Chapters 8–15. One of the best examples of Web design, technology, and credibility is the "Frontline" Web site (www.pbs.org/wgbh/pages/frontline/us/), produced by PBS's affiliate, WGBH in Boston. Since 1983, "Frontline" has been one of the best programs on television to view investigative documentaries. *Newsday* calls the program, "Television's last fully serious bastion of journalism." The Web site is also an excellent example of the synergy between television and the Web (Figure 16.9):

1. *Typography:* The typographical presentations include headlines, text blocks, and cutlines printed in an easy-to-read sans serif typeface. Colored text, boldface, and backgrounds signal special areas and features so that a user can easily find them.

2. *Graphic Design:* The **home page** for the site is divided into eight sections with each one clearly separated from another by colored backgrounds. Words and images are neatly displayed in a gridlike approach that denotes a serious attitude among the producers to the content of the site. Red circles around white arrows graphically cue a user to click the link for more information.

3. *Photography:* The image at the left clearly shows the destruction of one of the twin towers of the World Trade Center while a smaller close-up portrait of Osama bin Laden offers a visual counterpoint. Both images key a user to more information only a mouse click away.

4. *Television and Video:* With software loaded in a user's computer, digitized video reports can be watched.

5. *Computers:* Unlike a motion picture or a television program, users can decide their own path through the Web site. Built-in interactive features allow users to search for specific information and programs and link to other Web sites and databases.

Ethical Perspective

As can be imagined with a medium barely a decade old, there are many ethical issues that are worthy of serious discussion. Because space is limited, four concerns are noted here: free speech versus censorship, privacy concerns, access considerations, and accessibility issues.

Free Speech versus Censorship

Imagine you're a sixth-grade student writing a report about the White House in Washington, D.C. After checking with traditional sources in the library, you decide to use a computer to access the White House's Web site that is available on the school's computer through the World Wide Web. But you have a slight problem—you don't know the exact address (called the **Uniform Resource Locator** or URL) for the site. You decide to take a guess. Within your Web browser's location window you type: "http" (which stands for **hypertext transfer protocol**)"://whitehouse" with the extension (called a domain name) ".com." You use the .com (commercial) suffix because you've noticed that most sites have that extension. You press the "return" key, and your face suddenly turns red from embarrassment. You have landed on a cleverly named Web site that offers pictures and stories that are, to say the least, inappropriate for your age (Figure 16.10). You should have used the ".gov" (government) suffix to view the actual White House's Web site (Figure 16.11). Such innocent (or intentional) downloads to a child's computer cause some educators, social scientists, politicians, and parents great concern as the World Wide Web seems to be a huge, unregulated bookstore in which a child can suddenly wander into a back room where all the pornographic magazines and lewd videos are shelved.

Besides access to nude sites, there is also easy access to hate-speech sites. Using a search engine called HotBot (www.hotbot.com), the phrase "white power" produced more than 500,000 Web sites that contained the term. Among the sites listed are Stormfront (www.stormfront.org) with links to the home page of David Duke (Figure 16.12), a "white racist activist and former Louisiana legislator."

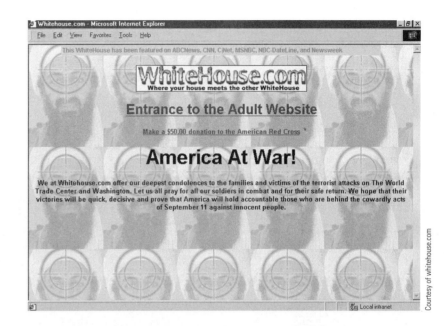

Courtesy of whitehouse.com

Figure 16.10

Whitehouse.com is a pornographic Web site. Note the effort to gain respectability with a tribute to those who died during the aerial attacks on the United States, a link where users can donate money to the American Red Cross, and Osama bin Laden's pictures with superimposed targets.

Because of such Web sites and the easy access to them, there has been a rush to create computer programs that can block sites with controversial content. CyberPatrol (www.cyberpatrol.com), SurfWatch (www.surfwatch.com), and X-Stop (www.xstop.com) are content-filter software programs you can install on your computer that identify words, phrases, or URLs that are known to be controversial.

The trouble with filters is that they can also prevent users from viewing noncontroversial sites. For example, the word "breast" that appears in a Web site about chicken recipes or a government page from Middle-*sex* County in Massachusetts will cause the site to be blocked. X-Stop was criticized because its software blocked such sites as the AIDS Quilt (www.aidsquilt.org) and the Quakers' home page (www.quaker.org).

In 1996, the U.S. Congress passed the Communications Decency Act that attempted to severely penalize those downloading material that is deemed indecent. The U.S. Supreme Court overturned key portions of the Act in 1997 citing First Amendment rights coupled with the almost

Figure 16.11

The actual Web site for the U.S. government's White House has a modern, portal look with sans serif typography and dynamic design.

impossible task of regulating the global network. However, the next year Congress passed the Child Online Protection Act (COPA) making it illegal for Web sites to knowingly present material that is considered "harmful to minors," such as pornography. COPA was blocked in 1999 by the federal district court in Philadelphia, but affirmed by an appeals court in 2000. In the fall of 2001 the U.S. Supreme Court heard arguments based on an appeal from the American Civil Liberties Union among others arguing that the law violates the First Amendment. A decision from the Court is due in the spring of 2002.

Whatever the outcomes from the U.S. Supreme Court, the answer, it seems, is similar to the suggested approach with motion pictures and television—parents need to be responsible for the materials their children watch. But in a public setting—as in a university or library—adults should be given the opportunity to view a wide variety of material available on the World Wide Web.

Privacy Concerns

Because computers connected through electronic networks make communication between individuals and databases easy, millions of users take advantage of services offered by private companies. But computers also can record every message and purchase made through a network. Computers also have long memories. Hence buying products and services over email systems can chip away at a person's right to privacy. When you write a letter to a friend and seal it in an envelope, you are sure that no postal employee will open and read it. But a personal note transmitted over an email network can be intercepted and read by any number of individuals. Moreover, management may monitor employees who work on computers to make sure that they are engaging only in company-approved computer use. Some businesses even require employees to wear a beeperlike device on their clothing. Through sensors in the ceiling, the tiny snap-on computer lets a boss know where employees are at all times. It even reveals how much time is spent in the restroom.

One alarming feature of an interactive television set-top box known as TiVo, which allows users to record up to thirty hours of programming, is that every night the TiVo machine sends the users' viewing records via a built-in modem back to corporate headquarters. If advertisers have access to a person's buying habits, they can amass a detailed computer-based profile on that individual. Marketing firms can use the information to try to sell consumers additional products or services. But the data also can be used to investigate the unique habits, political beliefs, economic situation, and other personal information divulged through networks. Not surprisingly, a lobbying group composed of Microsoft, AOL Time Warner, and Yahoo!, among others, is against any legislation that would restrict such personal prying.

An answer to privacy concerns may lie with digital signature technology (DST). Conducting official business, transmitting government documents, and writing checks in security may be possible with electronic mail services using DST. An electronic signature—actually a series of coded electronic numbers—creates a file with a secret key. Only a reader with another key can read the information. This system may be a step toward a true paperless society in which all transactions can take place electronically. However, government officials are concerned that such a system would make it impossible for them to conduct investigations into criminal activity that takes place through electronic transmissions. Therefore, they are asking that a government agency be given a record of every person's key. Those concerned with privacy fear that government might overstep its authority and pry into personal activities.

Indeed, six weeks after the aerial attacks of September 11, President Bush signed the "USA Patriot Act," which authorized broad new powers for law enforcement agencies. Both houses of Congress overwhelmingly passed the new law. Among the provisions the law permits is wide latitude in checking computer files, including email messages and address books. The FBI can much more easily gain access to private records "to protect against international terrorism." But the American Civil Liberties Union criticized the law because it said the law "gives the federal government "unchecked powers.'"

One software feature of Web browsers that is often criticized by users is the "cookie." A cookie is information that a Web server puts on your hard disk so that it can remember specific details about how you use the Web. This information may include your preferences for using a specific site or data

Courtesy of David Duke

that keeps track of banner ads displayed so you don't see the same ones over and over. Cookies can also be used to customize pages for you so that you can enter sites in a seamless manner. If you ever take an online course, for example, cookies help guide you to login and password files so you can take your class without too much hassle. Some Web users object to the concept of cookies because they are most often used for marketing purposes—depending on the sites you visit, cookies can customize the advertising banners you see to fit your presumed interests. However, you must agree to let cookies be saved on your computer. Nevertheless, protecting your privacy online is your choice. If you don't want business interests to know how you use the Web, don't allow cookies to be stored on your computer. Incidentally, the term "cookie" has nothing to do with the sweet treat but is a well-known computer term that is used when describing any type of data stored through an intermediary process.

Figure 16.12

With its dynamic use of patriotic images and strong iconic symbolism, David Duke's Web site attracts a young, modern audience.

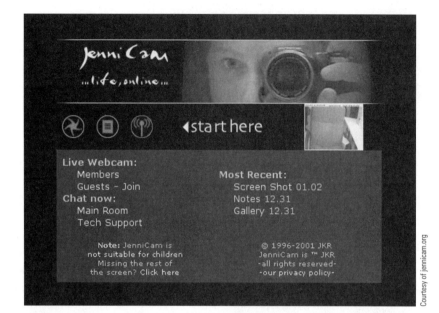

Figure 16.13

"Jennicam life online" is the name of one of the places in which users could get an inside peek into the not so private life of the creator of the site. With its dark background, muted colors, and simple typography, the site beacons users to enter the world of Jennifer Ringley.

But there is another side to the privacy issue—the exploitation of the privacy issue for commercial and hedonistic reasons. For some, privacy is simply not a concept that causes much concern. Television shows such as "Real World," "Big Brother," and "Survivor" attest to the fact that some individuals will do just about anything to become media "stars." The Web is no different. As with television shows that tear down the walls between viewer and performer, the Web is filled with sites that offer free or subscription-only looks into others' private lives. The advent of small digital cameras or "cams" and software that automatically updates pictures with them have caused Web entrepreneurs to turn their lives into cyber peep shows. These sites almost always use the word "cam" in their Web site names and contain sexual and/or scatological content for those eighteen years of age or older—AnaCam, dormcam, upskirtcam, and toiletcam.

In 1996, Jennifer Ringley was a junior at Dickinson College in Carlisle, Pennsylvania, who simply wanted a technological way to easily show her mother and her friends that she was doing well. On a whim she bought an expensive digital camera in her college bookstore and attached it to her computer. What resulted was a social phenomenon that started the whole "cam" craze and made Ringley quite a bit of money when she started to sell subscriptions and advertising on her Web site. On jennicam.org you can see Ringley in various conditions of dress with and without friends and read her journal entries and refrigerator poetry (Figure 16.13). Most of the time, however, there is nothing but an empty room or view out a window. The pictures refresh every fifteen minutes. If you're willing to pay $15 for a three-month subscription, however, you get images that are refreshed every minute plus access to archives of images. More than 5,000 signed up while she claims the site gets over a million hits a week. She admits, "I never really contemplated the ramifications of it and told myself I'd give it a week. After that week, I decided to give it another. I'm still here." The issues of privacy and voyeurism are still here as well.

Access Considerations

A "wired America," in which all individuals can obtain information and educational benefits from computer databases, will work only if prices of computer equipment and access to networks are lowered. Many experts advocate a telephone model for computers in which the price for the computer and services is low enough that most families can afford them. Public libraries also offer computers and database access for those without the economic means to purchase home systems. The Internet is a good model for database access. Besides the tremendous amount of information available, the cost of the service is about fifty cents an hour. Private BB systems charge from $10 to $100 an hour for specialized services. More than likely, future networks will consist of multitiered services similar to the television medium—low-cost, low-value basic services as in broadcast channels and high-cost, highly informative premium databases similar to cable movie channels. Such a system at least would guarantee access to everyone and would be a familiar and accepted payment system.

But even if everyone is given the opportunity to participate in this new Information Age, many people won't want or be able to do so. Besides costing a lot of money, taking advantage of all the services offered with a teleputer network takes a lot of motivation—something that passive television viewers might not favor. An AT&T survey of potential teleputer system users revealed that almost all of them wanted simple-to-operate remote control devices that they could use to select movies whenever they want to see them. Most respondents said that they wouldn't bother with many of the other databases and services that might be offered.

Consequently, the explosion in verbal and visual services available to teleputer users will require a commitment from the educational system. Besides reading, writing, and arithmetic, students from an early age must also be taught visual literacy, how to use computers, and more important, *why* using teleputers for more than watching television and movies is important. However, without careful long-term planning by government, corporate, and educational interests, many individuals will not bother.

Accessibility Issues   President George W. Bush's father signed the Americans with Disabilities Act (ADA) into law in 1990. At the time the elder Bush said that the ADA let disabled people "pass through once-closed doors into a bright new era of equality, independence and freedom." But "doors" that have been shut for many disabled people for some time are the portal openings that lead to the World Wide Web. Part of the language of the ADA established a clear and comprehensive prohibition of discrimination on the basis of disability. One of the findings of the ADA stated:

> Individuals with disabilities continually encounter various forms of discrimination, including outright intentional exclusion, the discriminatory effects of architectural, transportation, and communication barriers, overprotective rules and policies, failure to make modifications to existing facilities and practices, exclusionary qualification standards and criteria, segregation, and relegation to lesser services, programs, activities, benefits, jobs, or other opportunities.

To understand the concern, here's an exercise you can try at home in front of your computer. Next time you want to find some news or information, buy a present for a loved one, or take a course online through the World Wide Web, try doing it with your eyes closed. What you will discover rather quickly is that many Web sites are not designed to accommodate those with disabilities. Without sight, for example, you won't be able to tell pictures from words or be able to click a button for another link. Now, imagine you need to use the Web for your job or to get a promotion but you can't because the door is closed.

Just as architectural and transportation barriers can thwart an individual from participating freely and equally, barriers to the World Wide Web can be just as prohibiting. There are about 30 million Americans with physical disabilities. Poor design techniques make Web sites as inaccessible to those with physical disabilities as a curb on a sidewalk or a bus without a wheelchair lift.

When the needs of disabled people are not considered in Web site design, there is a significant and important percentage of the

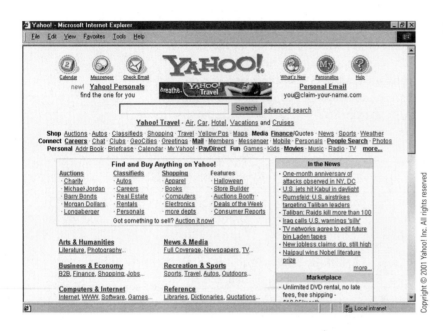

Rank	Name	Type	URL
1	AOL Time Warner	Portal	www.aol.com
2	Yahoo!	Portal	www.yahoo.com (Figure 16.14)
3	MSN	Portal	www.msn.com
4	Microsoft	Product Support	www.microsoft.com
5	Google	Search	www.google.com
6	eBay	Auctions	www.ebay.com
7	Lycos Network	Portal	www.lycos.com/sitemap.asp
8	Primedia	Publisher	www.primedia.com
9	Amazon	Bookstore	www.amazon.com
10	Walt Disney Internet Group	Portal	www.go.com

Figure 16.14

One of the first and most successful database collections on the World Wide Web is Yahoo! created by two Stanford University students, David Filo and Jerry Yang. Like other portals, Yahoo! offers links to news, information, and services.

population that is being left out of the benefits that can be found from the information superhighway. It is the right thing to design Web sites that give those with physical disabilities equal access.

Fortunately, once a visual communicator is sensitive to the issue of designing Web sites that are accessible to those with vision, hearing, and/or mobility challenges, there are several Web sites that can help. One of the best is named after an English law enforcement officer, Bobby (www.cast.org/bobby). With Bobby, after you type in a Web site's URL, follow the directions for altering the HTML code to make the Web site accessible.

Cultural Perspective

At the Nielsen/NetRatings Web site (www.nielsen-netratings.com), a marketing and polling company that also comprises Nielsen Media Research, the leading television audience measurement company in the United States, the most popular Web sites according to the number of user accesses are listed. The top ten sites for the week of March 3, 2002, were:

Note that six of the sites are **portals**—sites that have news, information, and links from airline tickets to the yellow pages. All ten are commercial (.com) sites. There should be no doubt that the World Wide Web has moved far away from its educational roots.

Web browsers offer a user the chance to create your own most popular list. A "bookmarks" or "favorites" list can be created to personalize a user's Web experience. Whenever you find a site that you want to remember, simply add it to your **bookmark** list so that you don't have to type in the URL. For example, some of the author's bookmarked URLs include:

Function	URL
Find a person	www.whowhere.com
Find a university	www.mit.edu/people/cdemello/univ.html
Translate a language	world.altavista.com/
Convert currency	www.oanda.com/convert/classic
Check the news	www.latimes.com
Check the weather	www.usatoday.com/weather/basemaps/wcity1.htm
Find a map	www.mapquest.com
Book a flight/hotel	www.travelocity.com

Listen to the radio   www.kcrw.org/online/
Buy a concert ticket   www.ticketmaster.com
Buy a book or CD   www.amazon.com
Find a program   www.download.com
Movie information   us.imdb.com/search
Find a menu   www.mymenus.com

In his science fiction novels, William Gibson uses the word *cyberspace* to describe the ethereal world of the electronic highway where unusual and unlimited communication links are available. Space on the electronic highway comprises not asphalt or concrete, but electricity and light. Writer John Perry Barlow describes cyberspace as having

A lot in common with the 19th Century West. It is . . . vast, unmapped, culturally and legally ambiguous, verbally terse, hard to get around in, and up for grabs. . . . To enter it, one forsakes both body and place and becomes a thing of words alone. . . . It is, of course, a perfect breeding ground for outlaws and new ideas. . . .

The World Wide Web is an almost unimaginable resource too huge to be easily understood or used effectively, but by creating a list of sites that you find useful, you make the Web your own. This activity is how the culture of electronic communication is created and also how it prospers.

Critical Perspective

In the wake of the worst domestic attacks upon America in its history on September 11, 2001, the Pew Research Center's "Pew Internet & American Life Project" (www.pewinternet.org) published results of a telephone poll conducted between September 12 and 13 with 1,226 adults, 18 and older. In a report titled, "How Americans Used the Internet After the Terrorist Attacks," findings included that the World Wide Web was not the primary source of information after the attacks—television and personal telephone calls were preferred, but the Internet "was a helpful supplement to TV and the telephone with many finding it useful for expressing their sorrows and anger at the assault." Users most often used the Internet and the Web to send an email message to a friend to make sure all was fine, to look up news and information from a portal site, and to attend virtual chat room meetings to give sympathy or vent anger. It seems fairly clear that this medium of technology has become a staple of most people's media diet.

Technological innovations once again have brought human civilization to a great crossroads. Do we use the new tools of communication to perpetuate the same old themes of violence as a way to resolve conflicts, sexual objectification as a positive value, and stereotypes that promote the dominant culture's way of life? Or do we use the technology to learn from one another in the hope of creating a world in which ideas are valued more than physical attributes? Will the World Wide Web be used to easily search through the most titillating stories and pictures found on a Web site called "Rotten Dot Com" (Figure 16.15) or will the Web be used to take one of hundreds of college courses offered online from the California Virtual University (www.california.edu) (Figure 16.16)? In either event, we live in an extremely exciting and challenging time in the history of communication—both in interpersonal relationships and the mass media.

■ FUTURE DIRECTIONS FOR THE WORLD WIDE WEB

The Knight-Ridder newspaper chain, the same company that was part of the videotex experiment in Florida in the 1980s, introduced one of the first online newspapers in

Figure 16.15 (top left)

There should be no mistake about the content within the pages of rotten.com. Users are warned of the site's content by the skeleton image, the red on white typography, and the text, "An archive of disturbing illustration." From autopsy and execution photographs to strange and eerie stories from around the world, rotten dot com is not the place to spend a few pleasant, relaxing moments.

Figure 16.16 (top right)

Every state in the United States sponsors some sort of long-distance educational opportunities via the World Wide Web. The matter-of-fact graphics and typography indicate the serious nature of taking courses online—and lend a sense of credibility to that form of higher education.

Figure 16.17 (bottom right)

One of the first newspapers in the United States to offer an Internet version was the San Jose Mercury News. Like so many popular sites, the World Wide Web version is now a portal, or entry into news, services, and shopping.

the world, the *San Jose Mercury News'* Mercury Center (Figure 16.17). The newspaper was first introduced on America Online in 1993. In 1997, the newspaper chain introduced its Real Cities network (www.real-cities.com) with forty newspaper sites containing news, information, and entertainment options from selected communities around the United States. A typical site is the Charlotte Observer Online (www.charlotte.com) with features you would find in a printed newspaper plus 24-hour updates, online shopping, chat rooms, and interactive features such as being able to add your personal events to an online calendar (Figure 16.18).

At the present time almost all of the 1,600 newspapers in the United States and most around the world have a version of their paper on the World Wide Web. In the future most people will receive their news through online rather than printed sources. Newspapers, in order to survive, will combine with computer, telephone, and television companies to provide the equipment and programming that make the teleputer revolution a reality. Typical of this media convergence is the Web site of ABC affiliate WFAA in Dallas, Texas (www.wfaa.com) (Figure 16.19). The television station offers all the information and entertainment services that a newspaper Web site contains, but with one important difference—with a video software program, RealPlayer (www.realplayer.com),

that can be downloaded to your computer free, Web users can watch a live video feed of local and national news programs (Figure 16.20).

In the future there will be little difference between World Wide Web portals, newspapers, and television stations.

Another prediction by many in the field of communications is the widespread, everyday use of virtual-reality (VR) technology. Recall that VR refers to numerous three-dimensional formats—from projected screens that the user can control with arm movements to elaborate setups in which a person wears a helmet and a bodysuit—with which the user enjoys the illusion of being a character within a computerized scenario (Figure 16.21).

Ivan Sutherland at MIT originally developed the technology in the early 1960s for flight simulators to train commercial and military pilots. In research labs, NASA later developed the technology to control robots

Charlotte.com

WFAA.com/Belco Interactive

Courtesy of RealPlayer.com

Courtesy of Virtual Realities and Dynovisor, Inc.

working on space stations. A lightweight helmet that displays a low-power LCD image for each eye (for a stereoscopic view) and body gear (gloves and a suit) maintain the illusion of being "virtually" within a computer environment. Virtual reality has been described as "jumping into your television." In the cyberspace computer world, VR can be a realistic view of a city in which the user has the feeling of flight or the illusion of being inside a complicated organic molecule. When the head is turned, the image also turns; when a computer object is grabbed and squeezed, the bodysuit simulates its weight. Virtual-reality motion simulator rides are a common feature of amusement parks around the world.

Imagine a future in which teleputers are combined with much more sophisticated virtual reality. There will be little need to physically visit some other person when the illusion of VR communication is real

enough. Work in your office or attend any lecture or conference as a VR participant from the comfort of your home. Be an actor in a Broadway play or sit on a couch with the cast of "Friends" with users playing other roles while in their homes anywhere else in the world. Tour an Egyptian bazaar or your local grocery store to buy food for your dinner. Fly like a bird around your city or walk the streets of nineteenth-century New Orleans. Editing with VR will mean that a user can actually step inside a page and move words around. A picture can be easily manipulated when a user is reduced to the size of an individual pixel and can move pixels around like building blocks.

Such applications may seem far-fetched (and admittedly they are), but imagine what it must have felt like to see a photograph, a motion picture, or a television program when each medium was first invented. No one in awe of the early reproduction of images could anticipate where visual communication would lead a hundred years later.

But the future is now for teleputers. Whether by DSL, Internet cable, or high-bandwidth fiber-optic connections, several teleputers can operate at the same time in the office, kitchen, den, and bedroom. The user of each machine decides the task to be performed—whether for desktop publishing, to talk with a friend across town or in another country, to watch the previous night's episode of "Friends" that was missed, to select from which camera's perspective to watch a sporting event, to buy groceries, to take a college course, to listen to the radio or CD player, to read a multimedia book, to choose a movie from thousands of choices, or many other services.

Portable teleputers are already available. A wireless network technology known as Wi-Fi, short for wireless fidelity, allows laptop users to read their email and surf the Web on city street, in coffee shops, in airports, in hotels, and in many homes and offices. It is estimated that there are more than 10,000 wireless networks across the United States, each with about a 300-foot radius. As long as the network is unsecured, any user within range and with a small radio transmitter plugged into a computer can piggyback on the network without having to plug into a wall. However, cable and telephone company executives that set up the networks would argue that such use is illegal. Nevertheless, wireless providers such as Wayport offer hotel and airport access at a nominal monthly fee while many Starbucks coffee shops allow users to pay for the convenience of high-speed Web access for about the price of a grande latte with a shot of espresso.

In the future, information highways will be as valuable and necessary for communication as backwoods trails, shipping lanes, telegraph wires, railroad lines, roadways, and airline flight paths are. The challenge for government agencies, corporate executives, creative producers, educators, and concerned citizens is to ensure that everyone can ride the highways as easily as those made of asphalt.

The author's great-grandmother lived to be 100 years old. She once admitted that she laughed when she first heard about automobiles. When the author asked why she thought cars were so funny, she replied simply, "Because how could everyone have their own train?" People always tend to evaluate and anticipate technology based on our previous experiences. But the future of mass communication may have little to do with our understanding of the past or present. The best plan for anticipating the future is to keep an open mind so that you will be prepared, to paraphrase Aldous Huxley, for the brave new (visual) world. We can only hope that it is a world in which everyone is, can be, and wants to be invited to participate.

DISCUSSION AND EXERCISE IDEAS

- Describe how you personally use the World Wide Web.
- Describe your favorite Web site.
- Make a Web site that features one of your hobbies or interests.
- Lead a discussion about the future of all other media given the quick growth of the World Wide Web.

InfoTrac College Edition Assignments

- With "Subject guide" checked, type "America Online," Scroll down to "America Online-Time Warner." Click to "View" the Newspaper reference and read the short article "Internet Service Providers, American Civil Liberties Union, Consumer Advocates Come Out Against America Online And Time Warner Merger." Why do you think the American Civil Liberties Union, consumer advocates, and other groups were opposed to the merger of these two media giants? What safeguards can you think of that might have allayed their fears? At the present time, do you think the merger is as threatening as it was once believed? Why or why not?

- With "Subject guide" checked, type "Equal access to all." Read the article "Equal access to all: New federal accessibility guidelines for electronic information technology may open new roads to the online learning superhighway" by Joel Schettler. Why do you think it is an important issue to make Web pages available for those with disabilities? If you have your own Web page, go to www.cast.org/bobby and see if it is accessible to those with disabilities. If not, follow the directions on the site to make your site in compliance with the standards set forth by the Americans with Disabilities Act.

Go to the Web site for this book at www.wadsworth.com/product/0534562442 to find more Web links on this subject.

THE MORE YOU KNOW, THE MORE YOU SEE

The light that slants

upon our western doors

at evening,

The twilight over

stagnant pools

at batflight,

Moon light and star

light, owl and

moth light,

Glow-worm glowlight

on a grassblade.

O Light Invisible, we

worship Thee!

T. S. (Thomas Stearns)

Eliot, 1888–1965

POET, EDITOR,

AND NOBEL PRIZE WINNER

By the end of this chapter you should know:

- Aldous Huxley's philosophy for understanding the way we see.
- The importance in combining words and images in equally respectful ways.
- The powerful emotional quality of pictures from national disasters.
- The various meanings of the word *light* and how they can apply to the study and production of visual communication.

The theme for *Visual Communication: Images with Messages* is taken from *The Art of Seeing* by Aldous Huxley, a book he wrote in the hope that others would learn to see more clearly (Figure 17.1). To Huxley, the eyes of a police officer on the lookout for criminal activity or a youngster playing a video game would be basically the same. There is no such thing as superhuman eyesight, but a police officer knows more about apprehending a criminal in the real world than does a teenager, who is better able to hunt down bad guys on a computer moni-

tor. If the situations were reversed, the officer and the youth would be lost in unfamiliar environments.

Huxley understood, as do many researchers in the field of visual communication, that seeing is a complex process that involves the mind as well as the eyes of the viewer. Consequently, clear seeing is a combination of how much you know and how you feel at any particular moment. The mental state of the viewer is a vital link in the visual communication process. As Huxley notes:

The most characteristic fact about the functioning of the total organism, or of any part of the organism, is that it is not constant, but highly variable. Sometimes we feel well, sometimes we feel poorly; sometimes our digestion is good, sometimes it is bad; sometimes we can face the most trying situations with calm and poise, sometimes the most trifling mishap will leave us irritable and nervous. This non-uniformity of functioning is the penalty we pay for being living and self-conscious organisms, unremittingly involved in the process of adapting ourselves to changing conditions.

The functioning of the organs of vision—the sensing eye, the transmitting nervous system, and the mind that selects and perceives—is no less variable than the functioning of the organism as a whole, or of any other part of the organism.

Because the retina is the only part of the human body where brain cells are exposed to the outside world, vision (unlike hearing, smelling, tasting, or feeling) has much to do with how you feel about what you see.

But this book isn't concerned only with seeing. Visual communication requires a two-way path between the producer and receiver of a message. Consequently, the focus of this work has more to do with remembering than seeing. If you learn to analyze visual messages in terms of your personal reaction, their historical context, how they are made, the ethical responsibilities of the producer, and their impact on society, you will be able to create and use memorable pictures.

More often than not, images that are remembered are the ones that combine aesthetically pleasing design elements with content that matters. However, works that combine both beauty and meaning are enormously difficult to produce. Because emotional and intellectual attributes are cul-

Figure 17.1

Aldous Huxley's facial gesture indicates a person who later in his life learned to combine his natural curiosity about the world with improving his eyesight.

turally bound, the two seldom agree. Abstract art is a clear example of visual works that depend on the mental state of the viewer for their appreciation.

■ PICTURES—LEARNED BEFORE WORDS

Before we are four years old, most of us have learned "The Alphabet Song." Sung to the same tune as "Twinkle, Twinkle Little Star," it is unlike any other song because no pictures came to mind when we sang it. With "Twinkle," we could look up into the night's sky and imagine a little star among the billions shining just for us. But a song about the letters of the alphabet doesn't have any visual equivalents. However, we soon began to match concrete nouns with images for each letter in the song. Children's books helped solve the mystery. "A is for apple." Each letter of the alphabet became a picture that corresponded to a complex set of direct and mediated images. We no longer had to think of an actual red, juicy apple. We simply saw the letter "A" and knew that it stood for that fruit.

Before we learned to read and write, we didn't know the difference between a line drawing and a letter. When we first wrote an "A," it was simply another drawing. It was a picture, different from a face or a house, but still just another image drawn with a colored crayon on white paper. Soon we learned that combinations of these letter-pictures mean more complicated things. When the individual drawings "A-P-P-L-E" are combined, they form another picture, which, we learned, stood for the name of the fruit. Now the letter-pictures became word-pictures that could spark other images in our minds of the thing they stood for. We further learned that these word-pictures could be combined with other word-pictures to form sentence-pictures. But we still couldn't differentiate between words and pictures—they remained one and the same.

Soon afterward, however, we were taught to distinguish words from pictures—to not think of them in the same way. We were taught that, although we could gain meaning from each, reading words was valued more than reading pictures. We were taught that pictures play a separate and subservient role to the words. And although we learned how to make pictures with our colored pencils and our watercolor paints, we received much more instruction on how to form, with our large lead pencils, the lines and curves that made letters and words. We usually had one class where we made pictures—art. The other classes were devoted to writing or reading stories, whether in a grammar or in a geography class. We were taught to read stories but we're never taught how to read images.

In the Disney classic *Beauty and the Beast*, the macho Gaston satirizes Belle's reading habits. "How can you read this?" he asks. "There are no pictures." She answers with a condescending, "Well, some people use their imagination." And yet, when the viewer of the animated movie is shown a close-up of a page in her book, she points to a picture of a castle that illustrates the story.

■ LIVING IN A PICTURE-FILLED WORLD

There are strong indications that the status of images is improving. We live in a blitz of mediated images. Pictures fill our newspapers, magazines, books, clothing, billboards, TV screens, and computer monitors as never before in the history of mass communications. We are becoming a visually mediated society. For many, understanding of the world is being accomplished, not by reading words, but by reading images. Philosopher Hanno Hardt warns that television is replacing words in print as the important factor in social communication. Shortly, predicts Hardt, words will be reserved only for bureaucratic transactions by means of business forms and in books that only a few individuals will read. Reading is losing to watching because viewing requires less mental processing.

Critics blame everything from the rise in the crime rate to the deterioration of educational institutions on the concurrent rise in the number of mediated images that we see daily. Rebellious youths cling to visual symbols because words are associated with old ways of communicating and old ways of establishing social order. Words are repressive, but pictures are fascinating, are easily understood within a particular culture, and can be used for propaganda purposes. One of the first acts in 1917 by the new Russian government was to transform churches into motion picture theaters in order to show propaganda films. All leaders understand that to control a country, they must also control the pictures. Leaders of the Taliban government in Afghanistan, for example, did not allow their citizens to watch any television programs.

More than thirty years ago, a headline alarmed many parents around the country: Why Johnny Can't Read. Educators who worry about the thinking and writing capabilities of their students still ask the question. Often, the answer is simplistic: too many pictures and not enough words. But there are other answers. Maybe little is written that people—particularly young people—want to read. Maybe people now believe that there is no point in reading when many jobs require no reading. Maybe parents don't read and don't encourage their children to do so. Or maybe individuals are reading, but what they read is not understood by those from other cultures.

Visual messages, with their own rules of syntax, are being read, but this language means nothing to those who can read only words. Wall space and signs in many cities often are coated with multicolored spray-painted messages (Figure 17.2). Termed folk art, vandalism, graffiti, or tagging, depending on the viewer, these visual messages actually are a complex written form of communication. Graffiti may mark the border of a gang's territory, plea for understanding and hope for the future, express grief for a killed loved one, vent anger toward an enemy, demonstrate playfulness and humor as part of a national fad, be acts of criminal vandalism, or simply signify the writer's existence. As with any symbolic communicative system, if you do not know the language, you will have trouble deciphering the message.

Look at the most common medium for visual expression—television. Programs can be watched from direct broadcast, from cable and fiber optics, from satellites, from VCRs, from DVDs, and from the World Wide Web. On some TV sets you can watch more than one program at a time. In a television commercial for Kodak's Photo CD technology in which still images can be viewed on the screen by a laser disc player, the announcer asserts that "pictures have never been so powerful." When television sets and computers are linked into teleputers, viewers will be able to alter the content and technical considerations of programs to suit their individual interests. The combination will indeed be a powerful medium for pictures.

Computers make the production and distribution of images available at incredible speed. More than any other technological innovation, computers are responsible for the explosion in images. In 1988, 50 percent of U.S. households had a computer with about half hooked to the Internet. Today,

Figure 17.2

Vandalism, folk art, or communication, graffiti is a controversial visual message because of its antisocial connotations. Nevertheless, spray-painted symbols on buildings, street signs, or drainage culverts offer a unique look at a pictorial language that has roots to the ancient Sumerians.

Paul Martin Lester

most of the words and pictures created in the world are computer mediated. Within ten years, teleputers—the ultimate fusion of telephone, television, and computer technologies in which viewers become active users of the medium—will be inexpensive and accessible.

Educational psychologist Jerome Bruner of New York University cites studies showing that people remember only 10 percent of what they hear and 30 percent of what they read but about 80 percent of what they see and do. When people, whether at home, in school, or on the job, learn to use computers for word and picture processing, they switch from passive watching to active using. When that happens, the barrier between the two symbolic structures falls, and words and pictures become one powerful and memorable mode of communication. Although the social, religious, and educational effects that a visual culture may have on society are unclear, the use of images may foster a return of the word's importance. Or rather, a communication medium in which words and pictures have equal status may be a result of the recent explosion in pictures.

■ *VISUAL MESSAGES ARE DEEPLY PERSONAL*

You, a family member, or a friend probably will never forget where you were when you learned that:

- President Kennedy was assassinated in 1963.

- The space shuttle *Challenger* exploded in 1986.

- The Murrah federal building in Oklahoma City was destroyed by a bomb in 1995.

- The World Trade Center's twin towers were attacked and destroyed in 2001.

These were moments of incredible historical significance, and yet deeply personal. These were personal moments because reporters and visual journalists made us feel those stories. These were moments destined to be forever a part of our visual memory. And soon, after hearing of each tragic news event from a teacher, a friend, or Bob Edwards on NPR's "Morning Edition," we all quickly found a television set because we wanted to see, we *needed* to see, pictures.

The moments from those events we most remember are the ones that communicated our enduring humanity—the saluting John F. Kennedy, Jr., during his father's funeral, children in a classroom crying over the death of their teacher, Christa McAuliffe, Chris Fields gently carrying Baylee Almon after the Oklahoma City bombing, and a photograph of three firefighters erecting an American flag amid the rubble of the World Trade Center twin towers (Figure 17.3).

The most recent example on the list of memorable news events will no doubt have the most effect upon people for generations to come. Seeing a commercial airliner slam into a building, the telephoto shot from across the river of the twin towers bellowing smoke, the incredibly destructive power of buildings collapsing in a hail of concrete, steel, dust, and death, and the ash-filled post-apocalyptic scene of smashed cars, steel girders, and dust-covered rescue workers are images that make the front pages of newspapers and Web sites around the world.

Pictures. Moments. Emotions. But fortunately, it will forever be the tiny moments, and not the most tragic ones, we will remember from this story—a doctor borrowing a suck of air from a firefighter's air nozzle, a man and his mother hugging after being lost then reunited, and the mental images evoked by Steven E. Frischling, a photojournalist for Corbis Sygma out of Amherst, Massachusetts:

AP/Wide World Photos

This scene is the most horrific thing I have ever seen in my life, just totally inconceivable. The destruction, the loss of life, finding out shooters were injured, and a firefighter and a medic I knew killed (or believed to be dead). The entire drive down I had no idea how bad it could be, and the entire drive back just wondering how it could have been that bad.

Covered in ash and having yet to sleep or bathe I stopped by my daughter's day care to see her, and since it was nap time just to kiss her and look at her. I am so grateful that the destruction was not "here," but it still happened in my "home," and I am just devastated physically (burns on the back of my neck) and emotionally.

I do not think I will be sleeping for a while, I think the sounds and the smell will linger very much longer for me as I block the images from my mind.

Be grateful for what you have and remember the sun will rise tomorrow.

The job of a visual journalist is to sometimes record and present horrific scenes in print, on television, in motion pictures, and on the World Wide Web. But we as consumers of their visual messages should know that the greater the tragedy, the greater is our capacity to find humanity within the tiniest moments visual journalists capture with their machines, their eyes, and their hearts.

©2001 Thomas E. Franklin, staff photographer, *The Record* (Bergen County, N.J.)/CORBIS

It is your choice of which images you want to make and which ones you want to remember.

■ *LIGHT—THE LINK*

Regardless of whether a presentation is meant for print or screen media, words and pictures have a better chance of being remembered if they are used together. That union is possible because of light. In fact, light links all the information presented in this book.

> Light, with its color component, creates and shapes our visual world.

> The eye, retina, and brain receive and process raw light data so that they can be interpreted.

> The visual cues of color, form, depth, and movement quickly sort light into helpful or harmful classifications.

Figure 17.3

Photojournalist Tom Franklin, thirty-five, had just returned from an assignment in the Dominican Republic when he drove as close as he could to the World Trade Center site. Throughout the day he made pictures of the destruction and happened upon the three firefighters— Dan McWilliams, George Johnson, and Billy Eisengrein—erecting an American flag that reminded him of the famous flag raising over Iwo Jima (left) photographed by Joe Rosenthal during World War II. About the image Franklin said, "It told of more than just death and destruction. It said something to me about the strength of the American people and of these firemen having to battle the unimaginable." Copies of the picture were left behind by U.S. Army Rangers and special forces operatives during a raid in Afghanistan, in October 2001.

Gestalt, constructivist, semiotics, and cognitive approaches help explain why some light messages are remembered longer than others.

Techniques used in advertising, public relations, and journalism help explain how light can so effectively attract and persuade.

Light without reason or compassion produces pictorial stereotypes that mislead and harm.

Light in the form of typography, graphic design, informational graphics, cartoons, photography, motion pictures, television and video, computers, and the World Wide Web makes us sad, angry, happy, tense, calm, smart, dumb, loving, cynical, or bored—but by all means, it always makes us something.

Light.

The light of day, the light of reason, and the light of compassion make us who we have been, who we are, and who we will become.

Huxley probably would disagree with too literal a reading of "the more you know, the more you see." Seeing certainly is a major component in visual communication, but it isn't the only way to know.

Get invited to a photographic darkroom. But you'd better hurry because they won't be around much longer. Ask the photographer to turn out all the lights—the fluorescent, the incandescent, and the phosphorescent. Stand or sit quietly in the dark chamber for a few moments. Study the blank, enveloping absence of photons. You will soon hear the sound of running water, smell the chemicals, taste the stale air, and feel the temperature.

Knowing how and why sensations are produced increases your repertoire of observations. And the more observations you collect, the more you learn about the world, people, and yourself.

The more you know, the more you hear.

The more you know, the more you smell.

The more you know, the more you taste.

The more you know, the more you feel.

The more you know, the more you see.

The more you know, the more you are you.

Your generation of communicators has the tools necessary to activate all the senses with words, pictures, and sounds. When you do, memorable messages—the only ones that challenge and enrich a person's life—will be the result.

DISCUSSION AND EXERCISE IDEAS

- Find a copy of Aldous Huxley's book, *The Art of Seeing,* and complete some of the exercises within it. Are you able to see more clearly?

- Ride along with someone from the police department or a social services organization who understands the meaning of wall graffiti and murals in your community. What new insights have you developed as to the complexity of this visual style of writing?

- Sit quietly in a place that exhibits light falling on a surface or through a window and contemplate all of the different meanings for the word *light.*

INFOTRAC COLLEGE EDITION ASSIGNMENTS

*   With "Subject guide" checked, type "The art of seeing." Scroll down to Mike Stensvold's article "The art of seeing." In the article Stensvold quotes photographer Bob Llewellyn in Derek Doeffinger's book *The Art of Seeing,* "Every photograph you make is a self-portrait." Do you think every visual message you see and remember is a self-portrait? What do you think that means?

*   With "Subject guide" checked, type "graffiti." Under the "Graffiti" category, click to "View" the "Periodical references." Scroll down to read "The writing's on the wall, and we want it off" by Janet Ward. Return to the "Periodical references" page, scroll to the bottom, and click "Next Page." Scroll down to read "Village Voice" by Carlo McCormick. Why do you think people have such opposing views of graffiti? Are there any social benefits to the art form or do you think it is simply a form of vandalism? Why?

*   With "Subject guide" checked, type "Dial 9/11 for Absurdity and Nobility; Hold the Profundity" and read the column by Tish Durkin. In the piece written a few days after the attacks, Durkin tries to make sense of her world as she observed it. Now that some time has passed, how do you think you have changed since the initial attacks?

COMMUNICATION CAFE Go to the Web site for this book at www.wadsworth.com/product/0534562442 to find more Web links on this subject.

G L O S S A R Y

—

... *words, words, words.*

—

Note: The chapter containing the first instance of the word or phrase below is in parentheses.

abolitionists: those who were for the abolition of slavery in the United States (7).

Academy standard: the 4:3 aspect ratio approved for early motion pictures (before sound) and television screens (before widescreen teleputers) (14).

advertorials; infomercials: paid announcements in print or screen media designed as an entertainment or educational presentation (6).

aesthetic qualities: relating to the often fleeting and evolving concept of beauty (8).

alley: the white space in print media between columns of text (8).

analog: numerical data represented by measurable quantities, such as lengths or electrical signals (14).

anime: term for Japanese-inspired animated cartoons (11).

archetypes: original models that inspire other things or ideas (13).

artifact: object produced by human effort (4).

ASCII text: most common format for text files in computers and on the Internet, based on a seven-bit binary number (16).

aspect ratio: the look or appearance of a screen or frame (13).

attitudes: feelings about a person, situation, or idea (6).

balloon: enclosed area in a comic strip (usually) for a character's dialogue (11).

bandwidth: the number of frequencies allowed for a given signal (15).

banner headlines: large newspaper text lines that run across several columns (8).

baud rate: the speed of a modem measured in bits per second (15).

belief: conviction of truth or reality (6).

"big three" networks: the original set of broadcast companies: ABC, CBS, and NBC (14).

binary: any system composed of two different parts (15).

binocular vision: using both eyes at the same time (4).

bit: a single unit of information in a binary system (15).

blacklisted: denied employment (usually) or suspected of disloyalty to a company or country (13).

bookmark: a URL saved on a Web browser so the user can return to a Web site without having to retype its address (16).

brightness: amount of luminance of a light source in the area where a visual message is viewed (4).

bulletin board: any display intended for public viewing—from file cards stuck with thumbtacks on a corkboard to computer-mediated systems (15).

byte: a series of binary numbers acting as a unit (15).

caption; cutline: text presented above or below a picture that contains information about the image (8).

carrier waves: electromagnetic frequencies that can be used to transmit text, sounds, and images (14).

chroma: hue, the common expression of an individual color (4).

coaxial cable: a transmission line comprising a wire (usually) surrounded by another wire that is insulated (14).

codes: systems of signs for textual or visual messages (5).

communication: the exchange of messages between a sender and a receiver in which the message is understood by the receiver (3).

comparative method: way to describe individual colors through comparisons with known objects (4).

consumerism: the consumption of goods and services (9).

credibility: believable and deserving of respect and confidence (6).

cultural norms: standard and acceptable sets of customs of a particular society at a particular time (7).

database: a full-text and/or image-based system containing an enormous amount of information that can (usually) be accessed through digital communications networks (15).

decimal: number system having ten different parts (15).

decisive moment: Henri Cartier-Bresson's concept of the instant when form and content are one (6).

deep focus: film technique used by Orson Welles that maximizes sharpness in a scene (13).

demotic script: writing used in ancient Egypt for everyday uses, unlike hieroglyphics, which was for special occasions (8).

dioramas: theatrical presentations that offer works in a naturalistic setting (12).

discrimination: to act in a prejudiced or biased way toward people (usually) having apparent, but not essential, differences (3).

dissonance: unpleasant combination of words, sounds, and/or images (5).

dollies: low, wheeled platforms for cameras (13).

dominant culture: societal group with superior power or authority (7).

email: the exchange of computer-generated messages using the Internet (12).

ergonomics: field of study for designing objects that are easy to use by humans (15).

ethos: a particular culture's system of values (6).

film noir: a style of movie production that uses stark visuals, hip characters, and mysterious plots (13).

font: a set of letters for a particular typeface family that includes all its sizes and attributes (8).

fovea field: region of the retina where sharp focus and color vision originate (3).

freelance: to sell work or services to clients but not have permanent employment status (10).

genre: a particular type of written or visual work (11).

habituation: unconscious patterned or repeated behavior (5).

heliography: name of the first photographic process, Greek for "sun writing," invented by Joseph Niépce (12).

hippocampus: that part of the brain where long-term, memorable images are permanently stored (3).

holography: photographic process using laser light beams to record images in three-dimensional depth (12).

home page: usually the first page that is presented from a Web site (16).

hypertext: mouse-clickable words that are formatted with HTML to enable a user to connect to another file (16).

HyperText Markup Language (HTML): a set of computer commands that translate presentation elements for viewing on the World Wide Web (16).

HyperText Transfer Protocol (http): the method by which a Web browser communicates with a Web server (16).

interface: where two or more systems have common boundaries (15).

Internet: a worldwide system of computer networks that allows a user to communicate with other users and computers (6).

iris: muscle in the center of the eye that causes the pupil to change its size and gives color to the eye (3).

legibility: the degree to which text or images are capable of being read or seen (8).

link: a connection to another World Wide Web file through hypertext or an HTML programmed image or other presentation element (16).

lithographic process: a printing method that allows artwork and type to be printed at the same time (8).

logo: a distinctively identifying symbol for a company, publication, or screen presentation (5).

logos: part of persuasive communication in which an argument makes logical sense (6).

macula lutea: tiny yellow pit in the center of the retina that protects the photosensitive cells in the fovea field (3).

mass communication: media techniques and devices that reach a large number of people (6).

media: plural of *medium* (1).

media convergence: the combination of traditional mass communications presentation elements and network computer technology (16).

mediated images: visual messages that are reproduced by means of print or screen presentations (1).

medium: format for communicating messages (1).

memex: Dr. Vannevar Bush's 1945 imagined device that predicted the Internet and World Wide Web (16).

metonymic codes: a semiotics term that describes assumptions made by the viewer (5).

mnemonics: any procedure that aids the memory (5).

montage: an artistic composition of several different parts (9).

myths: stories in words or pictures that people in a culture understand because they express deep and commonly held emotions (7).

Nobel Prize: annual international award used to promote science, literature, and peace (2).

objective method: way to describe individual colors through known standards of measurement (4).

occipital lobe: part of the brain's cortex where visual processing first takes place (3).

operating system: a software program that supports the running of a computer (15).

opinion: a view or judgment not supported by facts or absolute knowledge (6).

pathos: any element that causes the viewer to feel for a subject on an emotional level (6).

perceive: the last stage in the visual process in which the viewer makes sense of what is seen (1).

peripheral field: outside region of the retina with photosensitive cells that detect movement and objects in dim light (3).

perspective: an element of an image that gives the illusion of distance and depth (4).

pictographs: images that stand for objects, plants, or animals (8).

pointillism: a painting technique in which an image is composed of small dots that blend together as the viewer moves away from the picture (4).

popular culture: widespread, prevalent, and current trends or fads (9).

portal: sometimes called a gateway, a major starting site for mainly commercial Web site users (16).

prejudice: bias for or against a person or idea without knowing all the facts (3).

print media: any presentation that uses paper or a paperlike substrate (1).

racism: discrimination based on the belief that some races are better than others (7).

rear projection: film technique in which a picture appears on a screen behind actors (13).

salience: the degree to which a subject is important or prominent (5).

sarcophagus: any stone coffin, usually Egyptian (8).

scale: the relative size of a graphic representation in relation to the actual object (4).

screen media: motion picture, television, and computer messages (1).

scribe: a person employed as a copyist of manuscripts (8).

search engine: a software application that allows a user to find information on the World Wide Web through keyword input (6).

select: the second stage in the visual process in which a specific part of a visual array is isolated (1).

semiotics: the study of the meaning of signs in aural, verbal, or visual presentations (5).

sense: the first stage in the visual process in which light enters the eyes (1).

service bureau: printing firm that can output high-quality reproductions (15).

set-top boxes: devices that enable television sets to connect with the Web (14).

shot: a single photographic image or continuous take in motion pictures (13).

sign: a symbol that stands for an object, idea, or quantity (5).

situation comedies (sitcoms): television genre that features characters in familiar settings, whether animated or live-action (9).

soap operas: a television genre that features long-running, continual story lines (11).

social satire: caustic verbal or visual wit that critically attacks a person, group, thing, or situation (11).

stereotype: a highly opinionated, biased, and simplistic view (4).

stylus: any pointed device used for writing (8).

subjective method: way to describe individual colors through the emotional response received by the color (4).

substrate: the final layer in which all others rest or fall (8).

surreal: any presentation that surprises the viewer through grotesque or fantastic elements (9).

symbol: any aural, verbal, or visual element that represents some other, nonliteral meaning for the viewer (4).

symmetry: any arrangement of graphic elements that is balanced and harmonious (8).

tablet: any flat pad or panel used for the production of a presentation (8).

talbotype: alternative term for the calotype named after its inventor, William Talbot (12).

tarot cards: a set of twenty-two fortune-telling cards that uses symbolic illustrations to depict various human traits (5).

teledildonics: possible term for virtual-reality sex simulation presentations (15).

teleputer: possible term that will be used to describe a machine that combines the functions of a telephone, television, and computer (9).

textur: patterned after the style of calligraphic scribes, the typeface used within the pages of Gutenberg's Bible (8).

trackball mouse: a type of handheld clicking device for computers that gives some relief for carpal tunnel injuries (15).

transistor: a semiconductor device used for the sending and amplification of an electrical signal (15).

tripod: a three-legged device for making a camera steady during exposure (12).

triptych: any presentation consisting of three pages or screens (13).

typeface: any specific style of printing font (8).

Uniform Resource Locator (URL): the address for a Web site (16).

vacuum tube: a sealed glass or metal tube once commonly used in electronic devices (13).

value: amount of shading or tinting of a color (4).

vaudeville: any stage show that consists of a variety of entertainment genres—songs, animal acts, and comedy sketches (11).

virtual reality: term used to describe a technology that simulates an actual, living experience for the user (9).

visual communication: any optically stimulating message that is understood by the viewer (1).

visual cortex: area in the back of the brain where sight-related nerve cells are located (3).

visual journalist: a professional in the mass communication field who works with words, images, and graphic designs for print and/or screen media (10).

visual message: any direct, mediated, or mental picture (1).

Vitaphone: adaptation of Thomas Edison's phonographic cylinder in which a recording disk plays during a motion picture to simulate sound (13).

vitreous humor: clear, jellylike substance that fills the main cavity of the eyeball (3).

Web browser: an application such as Mosaic, Netscape, and Internet Explorer that allows access to the World Wide Web (16).

Web site: a collection of HTML files that present information to a World Wide Web user (3).

World Wide Web: a collection of network-accessible information through computer technology on a global scale (6).

BIBLIOGRAPHY

■ Chapter 1: To Sense. To Select. To Perceive.

Barry, Anne Marie. (1997). *Visual Intelligence: Perception, Image, and Manipulation in Visual Communication.* New York: State University of New York Press.

Berger, Arthur Asa. (1998). *Seeing Is Believing: An Introduction to Visual Communication.* Mountain View, Calif.: Mayfield Publishing Company.

Elkins, James. (1999). *The Domain of Images.* Ithaca, N.Y.: Cornell University Press.

Harris, Christopher R., & Lester, Paul Martin. (2001). *Visual Journalism: A Guide for New Media Professionals.* Needham Heights, Mass.: Allyn & Bacon.

Helfand, Jessica. (2001). *Screen: Essays on Graphic Design, New Media, and Visual Culture.* Princeton, N.J.: Architectural Press.

Hoffman, Donald. (2000). *Visual Intelligence: How We Create What We See.* New York: W. W. Norton and Company.

Huxley, Aldous. (2000a). *Brave New World Revisited.* New York: Harperperennial Library.

———. (2000b). *Complete Essays by Aldous Huxley,* Robert S. Baker (ed.). Chicago: Ivan R. Dee, Publisher.

———. (1942). *The Art of Seeing.* New York: Harper.

Huxley, Laura Archera. (2000). *This Timeless Moment: A Personal View of Aldous Huxley.* Berkeley, Calif.: Celestial Arts.

Kress, Gunther, & Van Leeuwen, Theo. (1996). *Reading Images: The Grammar of Visual Design.* New York: Routledge.

Messaris, Paul. (1994). *Visual Literacy: Image, Mind, and Reality.* Boulder, Colo.: Westview Press.

Mirzoeff, Nicholas. (1999). *Introduction to Visual Culture.* New York: Routledge.

O'Gorman, Francis. (1999). *John Ruskin.* London: Sutton Publishing.

Stephens, Mitchell. (1998). *The Rise of the Image the Fall of the Word.* New York: Oxford University Press.

Williams, Rick. (Autumn, 2000). "Omniphasic Visual-Media Literacy in the Classroom Part III," *Journal of Visual Literacy.*

———. (Spring, 2000). "Visual Literacy and Intuitive Visual Persuasion Part II," *Journal of Visual Literacy.*

———. (Autumn 1999). "Beyond Visual Literacy: Omniphasism, a Theory of Cognitive Balance Part I," *Journal of Visual Literacy,* pp. 159–178.

Worth, Sol. (1981). *Studying Visual Communication.* Philadelphia: University of Pennsylvania Press.

Zettl, Herb. (1998). *Sight, Sound, Motion: Applied Media Aesthetics, 3rd Edition.* Belmont, Calif.: Wadsworth.

■ Chapter 2: Light

Baierlein, Ralph. (2001). *Newton to Einstein: The Trail of Light.* New York: Dimensions.

Bova, Ben. (1988). *The Beauty of Light.* New York: John Wiley & Sons.

Crick, Francis. (1994). *The Astonishing Hypothesis: The Scientific Search for the Soul.* New York: Macmillan.

Davis, Keith. (1990). *Clarence John Laughlin: Visionary Photographer.* Albuquerque, N.M.: University of New Mexico Press.

Fleisher, Paul. (2001). *Waves: Principles of Light, Electricity, and Magnetism.* New York: Lerner Publications Company.

Park, David. (1997). *The Fire Within the Eye.* Princeton, N.J.: Princeton University Press.

■ *Chapter 3: The Eye, the Retina, and the Brain*

Ackerman, Diane. (1990). *A Natural History of the Senses.* New York: Random House.

Begley, Sharon, et al. (April 20, 1992). "Mapping the Brain," *Newsweek,* pp. 66–70.

Bianki, V. L. (1988). *The Right and Left Hemispheres of the Animal Brain.* New York: Gordon and Breach Science Publishers.

Blakeslee, Thomas. (1980). *The Right Brain: A New Understanding of the Unconscious Mind and Its Creative Powers.* Garden City, N.Y.: Anchor Press.

Cassel, Gary. (2001). *The Eye Book: A Complete Guide to Eye Disorders and Health.* Baltimore: Johns Hopkins University Press.

Edelman, Gerald. (ed.). (2000). *The Brain.* New York: Transaction Publishers.

Farndon, John. (2000). *The Big Book of the Brain: All About the Body's Control Center.* New York: Peter Bedrick Books.

Gaarder, Kenneth R. (1975). *Eye Movements, Vision and Behavior: A Hierarchical Visual Information Processing Model.* New York: John Wiley & Sons.

Gluck, Mark, & Myers, Catherine. (2000). *Gateway to Memory.* Cambridge. Mass.: MIT Press.

Glynn, Ian. (2000). *An Anatomy of Thought: The Origin and Machinery of Mind.* New York: Oxford University Press.

Goldstein, E. Bruce. (1989). *Sensation and Perception.* Belmont, Calif.: Wadsworth.

Hubel, David H. (1988). *Eye, Brain, and Vision.* New York: Scientific American Library.

Jaynes, Julian. (1990). *Origin of Consciousness in the Breakdown of the Bicameral Mind.* Boston: Houghton Mifflin Company.

Kabrisky, Matthew. (1966). *A Proposed Model for Visual Information: Processing in the Human Brain.* Urbana: University of Illinois Press.

Kalat, James W. (1992). *Biological Psychology.* Belmont, Calif.: Wadsworth.

Land, Michael, & Nilsson, Eric. (2002). *Animal Eyes.* New York: Oxford University Press.

Mueller, Conrad G., & Rudolph, Mae. (1972). *Light and Vision.* New York: Time-Life Books.

Pinker, Steven. (1997). *How the Mind Works.* New York: W. H. Norton & Company.

Price, Ira, & Comac, Linda. (2000). *Coping with Macular Degeneration: A Guide for Patients and Families to Understanding and Living with Degenerative Vision Disorder.* New York: Avery Penguin Putnam.

Quackenbush, Thomas. (ed.). (2001). *Better Eyesight: The Complete Magazines of William H. Bates.* Berkeley, Calif.: North Atlantic Books.

Roth, Gerhard. (ed.). (2000). *Brain Evolution and Cognition.* New York: Wiley-Liss.

Russell, Peter. (1979). *The Brain Book.* New York: Hawthorn Books.

Ryan, Stephen. (2000). *Retina.* St. Louis: Mosby-Year Book.

Sacks, Oliver. (1997). *The Island of the Colorblind.* New York: Alfred A. Knopf.

Weale, R. A. (1982). *Focus on Vision.* Cambridge, Mass.: Harvard University Press.

Whalley, Lawrence. (2001). *The Aging Brain.* New York: Columbia University Press.

■ *Chapter 4: What the Brain Sees: Color, Form, Depth, and Movement*

Birren, Faber. (1961). *Color Psychology and Color Therapy.* Secaucus, N.J.: The Citadel Press.

Boyle, Cailin. (2001). *Color Harmony for the Web: A Guidebook to Create Color Combinations for Web Site Design.* Gloucester, Mass.: Rockport Publishers.

Cabarga, Leslie. (2001). *Designers Guide to Global Color Combinations: 750 Color Formulas in CMYK and RGB from Around the World.* Berkeley, Calif.: North Light Books.

Conover, Theodore E. (1985). *Graphic Communications Today.* St. Paul, Minn.: West.

Dondis, Donis A. (1973). *A Primer of Visual Literacy.* Cambridge, Mass.: The MIT Press.

Eiseman, Leatrice. (2000). *Pantone Guide to Communicating with Color.* New York: Hand Book Press.

Finke, Gail. (2001). *Graphics: The Power of White in Graphic Design.* Gloucester, Mass.: Rockport Publishers.

Holtzschue, Linda. (2001). *Understanding Color: An Introduction for Designers, 2nd Edition.* John Wiley & Sons.

Margolin, Victor. (ed.). (1989). *Design Discourse: History, Theory, Criticism.* Chicago: The University of Chicago Press.

Morgan, John, & Welton, Peter. (1992). *See What I Mean?* London: Edward Arnold.

Pring, Roger. (2000). *www.color.* Toronto: Watson-Guptill Publications.

Rossotti, Hazel. (1983). *Colour.* Princeton, N.J.: Princeton University Press.

Stoops, Jack, & Samuelson, Jerry. (1983). *Design Dialogue.* Worcester, Mass.: Davis Publications, Inc.

Stroebel, Leslie, Todd, Hollis, & Zakia, Richard. (1980). *Visual Concepts for Photographers.* New York: Focal Press.

Thiel, Philip. (1981). *Visual Awareness and Design.* Seattle: University of Washington Press.

■ *Chapter 5: The Sensual and Perceptual Theories of Visual Communication*

Altschul, Charles. "The Center for Creative Imaging and the Influence of Technology on Creativity," in Charles Altschul (ed.). (1992). *Ethics, Copyright, and the Bottom Line.* Camden, Me.: Center for Creative Imaging, pp. 59–61.

Arnheim, Rudolf. (1974). *Art and Visual Perception.* Berkeley: University of California Press.

Aunger, Robert. (ed.). (2001). *Darwinizing Culture: The Status of Memetics as a Science.* New York: Oxford University Press.

Barthes, Roland. (1981). *Camera Lucida.* New York: Hill and Wang.

———. (1977). *Image, Music, Text.* New York: Hill and Wang.

Berger, John. (1977). *Ways of Seeing.* London: Penguin Books.

Berger, John, & Mohr, Jean. (1982). *Another Way of Telling.* New York: Pantheon Books.

Biederman, Irving. (1987). "Recognition-by-Components: A Theory of Human Image Understanding." *Psychological Review,* Vol. 94, no. 2, pp. 115–147.

Bloomer, Carolyn M. (1990). *Principles of Visual Perception.* New York: Design Press.

Bruce, Vicki, & Green, Patrick. (1985). *Visual Perception: Physiology, Psychology and Ecology.* London: Lawrence Erlbaum Associates.

Bryson, Norman, & Holly, Michael. (eds.). (1991). *Visual Theory: Painting & Interpretation.* New York: HarperCollins.

Burnett, Ron. (1995). *Cultures of Vision: Images, Media, and the Imaginary.* Bloomington: Indiana University Press.

Davies, Duncan, Bathurst, Diana, & Bathurst, Robin. (1990). *The Telling Image: The Changing Balance Between Pictures and Words in a Technological Age.* Oxford: Clarendon Press.

Deely, John. (1990). *Basics of Semiotics.* Bloomington: Indiana University Press.

Fineman, Mark. (1981). *The Inquisitive Eye.* New York: Oxford University Press.

Fiske, Susan T., & Taylor, Shelley E. (1984). *Social Cognition.* Menlo Park, Calif.: Addison-Wesley.

Floch, Jean-Marie. (2001). *Visual Identities.* New York: Continuum.

Foss, Sonja K. (1992). "Visual Imagery as Communication." *Text and Performance Quarterly,* Vol. 12, pp. 85–96.

Friedhoff, Richard Mark, & Benzon, William. (1988). *The Second Computer Revolution: Visualization.* New York: W. H. Freeman.

Gardner, Howard. (1982). *Art, Mind, and Brain: A Cognitive Approach to Creativity.* New York: Basic Books.

Ghiselin, Brewster. (1952). *The Creative Process.* New York: The New American Library.

Gregory, R. L. (1970). *The Intelligent Eye.* New York: McGraw-Hill.

Hardt, Hanno. (April, 1991). "Words and Images in the Age of Technology." *Media Development,* Vol. 38, pp. 3–5.

Hatcher, Evelyn P. (1974). *Visual Metaphors: A Methodological Study in Visual Communication.* Albuquerque: University of New Mexico Press.

Hicks, Wilson. (1973). *Words and Pictures.* New York: Arno Press.

Hochberg, Julian. "Attention, Organization, and Consciousness," in David Mostofsky (ed.). (1970). *Attention: Contemporary Theory and Analysis.* New York: Appleton-Century-Crofts.

Hoffman, Howard S. (1989). *Vision & the Art of Drawing.* Englewood Cliffs, N.J.: Prentice Hall.

Hoistad, Gunnar. (April, 1991). "How Vulnerable Are Children to Electronic Images?" *Media Development,* Vol. 38, pp. 9–11.

Holmes, Nigel. (1985). *Designing Pictorial Symbols.* New York: Watson-Guptill.

Hunter, Jefferson. (1987). *Image and Word: The Interaction of Twentieth-Century Photographs and Texts.* Cambridge, Mass.: Harvard University Press.

Hyerle, David. (2000). *A Field Guide to Using Visual Tools.* Alexandria, Va.: Association for Supervision & Curriculum Development.

Kassim, Husain. (2000). *Aristotle and Aristotelianism in Medieval Muslim, Jewish, and Christian Philosophy.* San Francisco: Austin & Winfield Publications.

Kepes, Gyorgy. (ed.). (1966). *Sign, Image, Symbol.* New York: George Braziller.

Kling, J. W. & Riggs, Lorrin A. (eds.). (1971). *Experimental Psychology.* New York: Holt, Rinehart and Winston.

Koole, Wim. (April, 1991). "Imagination Depends on Images." *Media Development,* Vol. 38, pp. 16–17.

Landau, Barbara. (ed.). (2000). *Perception, Cognition, and Language.* Cambridge: MIT Press.

Langer, Susanne K. (1960). *Philosophy in a New Key.* Cambridge, Mass.: Harvard University Press.

———. (1953). *Feeling and Form: A Theory of Art.* New York: Charles Scribner's Sons.

Lawson, Bryan. (2001). *Language of Space.* New York: Architectural Press.

Lodge, David. (1984). *Small World.* New York: Warner Books.

Marin, Louis, & Porter, Catherine. (2001). *On Representation.* Stanford: Stanford University Press.

McCafferty, James D. (1990). *Human and Machine Vision: Computing Perceptual Organization.* Chichester, England: Ellis Horwood Limited.

Natali, Carlo. (2001). *The Wisdom of Aristotle.* New York: State University of New York Press.

Paivio, Allan. (1971). *Imagery and Verbal Processes.* New York: Holt, Rinehart and Winston.

Parker, D. M., & Deregowski, J. B. (1990). *Perception and Artistic Style.* Amsterdam: North–Holland.

Perecman, Ellen. (ed.). (1983). *Cognitive Processing in the Right Hemisphere.* Orlando, Fla.: Academic Press, Inc.

Phelan, John M. (April, 1991). "Image Industry Erodes Political Space." *Media Development,* Vol. 38, pp. 6–8.

Richards, Stan. (1974). *Hobo Signs.* New York: Barlenmir House.

Ritchin, Fred. "An Image-Based Society," in Charles Altschul (ed.). (1992). *Ethics, Copyright, and the Bottom Line.* Camden, Me.: Center for Creative Imaging, pp. 19–35.

Saint-Martin, Fernande. (1990). *Semiotics of Visual Language.* Bloomington: Indiana University Press.

Schapiro, Meyer. (1996). *Words, Script, and Pictures: Semiotics of Visual Language.* New York: George Braziller.

Sculley, John. "Computers, Communications and Content," in Charles Altschul (ed.). (1992). *Ethics, Copyright, and the Bottom Line.* Camden, Me.: Center for Creative Imaging, pp. 15–21.

Sebeok, Thomas A. (1991). *Semiotics in the United States.* Bloomington: Indiana University Press.

Shepard, Roger N. (1990). *Mind Sights: Original Visual Illusions, Ambiguities, and Other Anomalies.* New York: W. H. Freeman.

Sontag, Susan. (1978). *On Photography.* New York: Farrar, Straus and Giroux.

Ullman, Shimon. (2000). *High-Level Vision.* Cambridge: MIT Press.

Wade, Nicholas. (1990). *Visual Allusions: Pictures of Perception.* London: Lawrence Erlbaum Associates.

Walker, John A., & Chaplin, Sarah. (1998). *Visual Culture: An Introduction.* Manchester, England: Manchester University Press.

Yazdani, Masoud. (ed.). (2001). *Iconic Communication.* New York: Intellect.

Zakia, Richard. (2001). *Perception and Imaging.* Oxford: Butterworth-Heinemann.

■ *Chapter 6: Visual Persuasion in Advertising, Public Relations, and Journalism*

Allen, Dianne. (July 17, 1992). "Benetton Not Sorry About AIDS Ad." *The Toronto Star,* p. G4.

Bateson, Mary. (1994). *Peripheral Visions: Learning Along the Way.* New York: HarperCollins.

Campbell, Joseph, & Moyers, Bill. (1988). *The Power of Myth.* New York: Doubleday.

Cimons, Marlene. (December 23, 1992). "Food Labels May Be More Honest, But Are the Ads?" *Los Angeles Times,* p. A5.

Curry, Cheryl. (April 26, 1992). "The Man Who Died in an Ad for Benetton." *The Toronto Star,* p. D1.

Fox, Stephen. (1984). *The Mirror Makers.* New York: William Morrow.

Frare, Therese. (November, 1990). "The End." *Life,* pp. 8–9.

Hawthorn, Jeremy. (ed.). (1987). *Propaganda, Persuasion and Polemic.* London: Edward Arnold.

Horovitz, Bruce. (March 22, 1992). "'Shock Ads': New Rage That Spawns Rage." *Los Angeles Times,* p. D1.

Jaubert, Alain. (1986). *Making People Disappear.* Washington, D.C.: Pergamon-Brassey.

Kerwin, Ann Marie. (January 16, 1993). "Advertiser Pressure on Newspapers Is Common: Survey." *Editor & Publisher,* pp. 28–29, 39.

Knightley, Phillip. (1975). *The First Casualty.* New York: Harcourt Brace Jovanovich.

Lambeth, Edmund. (1992). *Committed Journalism.* Bloomington: Indiana University Press.

Lippmann, Walter. (1961). *Public Opinion.* New York: Macmillan.

Marchand, Roland. (1985). *Advertising the American Dream.* Berkeley: University of California Press.

Messaris, Paul. (1996). *Visual Persuasion: The Role of Images in Advertising.* Beverly Hills, Calif.: Sage Publications.

Moeller, Susan. (1989). *Shooting War: Photography and the American Experience of Combat.* New York: Basic Books.

O'Neill, Michael. (1986). *Terrorist Spectaculars: Should TV Coverage Be Curbed?* New York: Priority Press.

Petty, Richard, & Cacioppo, John. (1981). *Attitudes and Persuasion: Classic and Contemporary Approaches.* Dubuque, Ia.: Wm. C. Brown.

Pincus, David, & DeBonis, Nicholas. (1994). *Top Dog.* New York: McGraw-Hill, Inc.

Pratkanis, Anthony, & Aronson, Elliot. (2001). *Age of Propaganda: The Everyday Use and Abuse of Persuasion.* New York: W. H. Freeman & Co.

Rosenberg, Howard. (February 15, 1993). "A Tabloid Pattern of Behavior at NBC." *Los Angeles Times,* pp. F1, F12.

Schiller, Dan. (1981). *Objectivity and the News.* Philadelphia: University of Pennsylvania Press.

Schudson, Michael. (1978). *Discovering the News: A Social History of American Newspapers.* New York: Basic Books.

Schwartz, Dona. (1991). "To Tell the Truth: Codes of Objectivity in Photojournalism." Paper presented at the 74th annual convention of the AEJMC, August 7–10, 1991. Boston, Massachusetts.

Tuchman, Gaye. (1978). *Making News.* New York: The Free Press.

Tumulty, Karen. (March 2, 1993). "Clinton Bashes Lobbyists, But They Like It Just Fine." *Los Angeles Times,* p. A5.

Veneto, Ponzano. (February 17, 1993). "The True Colors of Luciano Benetton." *The Washington Post,* p. B1.

Vestergaard, Torben, & Schrøder, Kim. (1985). *The Language of Advertising.* Oxford: Basil Blackwell Publisher.

Wilcox, Dennis, Ault, Phillip, & Agee, Warren. (1992). *Public Relations: Strategies and Tactics.* New York: HarperCollins.

Willis, Jim. (1991). *The Shadow World: Life Between the News Media and Reality.* New York: Praeger Publishers.

Wisan, Joseph. (1965). *The Cuban Crisis as Reflected in the New York Press (1895–1898).* New York: Octagon Books.

Wood, Richard. (ed.). (1990). *Film and Propaganda in America.* New York: Greenwood Press.

■ *Chapter 7: Images That Injure: Pictorial Stereotypes in the Media*

Berelson, Bernard, & Salter, Patricia J. "Majority and Minority Americans: An Analysis of Magazine Fiction," in Stanley Cohen and Jock Young (eds.). (1973). *The Manufacture of News.* Beverly Hills, Calif.: Sage Publications, pp. 107–126.

Billings, Dwight. (ed.). (2001). *Back Talk from Appalachia: Confronting Stereotypes.* Lexington: University of Kentucky Press.

Black, Jay, Steele, Bob, & Barney, Ralph. (1993). *Doing Ethics in Journalism: A Handbook with Case Studies.* Greencastle, Ind.: The Sigma Delta Chi Foundation and the Society of Professional Journalists.

Bolton, Richard. (ed.). (1992). *The Contest of Meaning: Critical Histories of Photography.* Cambridge, Mass.: The MIT Press.

Brookhiser, Richard. (March 1, 1993). "The Melting Pot Is Still Simmering." *Time,* p. 72.

Buck, Genevieve. (August 26, 1992). "And You Thought Thought-Provoking Art Could Only Be Found in Museums." *Chicago Tribune,* p. 16.

Christians, Clifford. "Reporting and the Oppressed," in Deni Elliott (ed.). (1986). *Responsible Journalism.* Beverly Hills, Calif.: Sage Publications, pp. 109–130.

———, Rotzoll, Kim, & Fackler, Mark. (1983). *Media Ethics: Cases and Moral Reasoning.* New York: Longman.

Cobern, Camden. (1929). *The New Archeological Discoveries.* New York: Funk & Wagnalls.

Crookall, David, & Saunders, Danny. (eds.). (1989). *Communication and Simulation: From Two Fields to One Theme.* Clevedon, England: Multilingual Matters Ltd.

D'Agostino, Peter, & Muntadas, Antonio. (eds.). (1982). *The Unnecessary Image.* New York: Tanam Press.

Dennis, Everette, & Merrill, John. (1991). *Media Debates Issues in Mass Communication.* New York: Longman.

Dickson, Thomas. (Winter, 1993). "Sensitizing Students to Racism in the News," *Journalism Educator,* pp. 28–33.

Emery, Michael, & Emery, Edwin. (1988). *The Press and America.* Englewood Cliffs, N.J.: Prentice Hall.

Goffman, Irving. (1979). *Gender Advertisements.* New York: Harper & Row.

Goldberg, Vicki. (February 28, 1993). "Still Photos Trace the Moving Image of Blacks." *The New York Times,* p. H23.

———. (May 3, 1992). "Images of Catastrophe as Corporate Ballyhoo." *The New York Times,* p. 33.

———. (1991). *The Power of Photography.* New York: Abbeville Press.

Gross, Larry. (1988). "The Ethics of (Mis)representation," in Larry Gross, John Stuart Katz, & Jay Ruby (eds.). *Image Ethics* (New York: Oxford University Press, 1988), pp. 188–202.

Hall, Jane, & Lippman, John. (February 26, 1993). "Logging Story Leaves NBC Red-Faced Again." *Los Angeles Times,* pp. D1–D2.

———. (February 15, 1993). "NBC News: A Question of Standards." *Los Angeles Times,* pp. F1, F15.

Harrison, Randall. (1981). *The Cartoon: Communication to the Quick.* Beverly Hills, Calif.: Sage Publications.

Kitch, Carolyn. (2001). *The Girl on the Magazine Cover: The Origins of Visual Stereotypes in American Mass Media.* Chapel Hill, N.C.: University of North Carolina Press.

Kovel, Joel. (1984). *White Racism.* New York: Columbia University Press.

Lester, Paul Martin. "Girls Can Be Doctors and Boys Can Be Nurses: Surfing for Solutions to Gender Stereotyping," in Meta Carstarphen & Susan Zavoina (eds.). (2000). *Sexual Rhetoric: Media Perspectives on Sexuality, Gender and Identity.* Westport: Praeger Publishers, pp. 283–292.

———. "Images and Stereotypes," in Elliott Cohen & Deni Elliott (eds.). (1997). *Contemporary Ethical Issues: Journalism.* (1997). Santa Barbara, Calif.: ABC-CLIO, Inc., pp. 69–72.

———. "Photojournalism Ethics: Timeless Issues," in Michael Emery & Ted Smythe (eds.). *Customized Readings in Mass Communication.* Dubuque, Ia.: W. C. Brown Publishers.

———. (Summer, 1994). "African American Photo Coverage in Four U.S. Newspapers, 1937–1990." *Journalism Quarterly.*

———. (1991). *Photojournalism: An Ethical Approach.* Hillsdale, N.J.: Lawrence Erlbaum Associates.

———. (ed.). (1990). *The Ethics of Photojournalism.* Durham, N.C.: NPPA.

Lester, Paul Martin, & Ross, Susan D. (eds.). (2003). *Images That Injure: Pictorial Stereotypes in the Media, 2nd Edition.* Westport, Conn.: Praeger Publishers.

Lester, Paul Martin, & Smith, Ron. (Spring, 1990). "African American Photo Coverage in *Life, Newsweek* and *Time,* 1937–1988," *Journalism Quarterly,* pp. 128–136.

Moog, Carol. (1990). "Are They Selling Her Lips?" *Advertising and Identity.* New York: William Morrow.

Pearce, Frank, "How to Be Immoral and Ill, Pathetic and Dangerous, All at the Same Time: Mass Media and the Homosexual," in Stanley Cohen & Jock Young (eds.). (1973). *The Manufacture of News.* Beverly Hills, Calif.: Sage Publications, pp. 284–301.

Prida, Dolores, & Ribner, Susan. "A Feminist View of the 100 Books About Puerto Ricans," in J. Stinton (ed.). (1976). *Racism and Sexism in Children's Books.* New York: Council on Interracial Books for Children, pp. 42–48.

Riccio, Barry. (1994). *Walter Lippmann–Odyssey of a Liberal.* New York: Transaction Publications.

Rickards, Maurice. (1979). *Posters of Protest and Revolution.* New York: Walker and Company.

Ritchin, Fred. (1990). *In Our Own Image: The Coming Revolution in Photography.* New York: Aperture Foundation.

Scott, Jeffery. (2000). *Resistance to Multiculturalism: Issues and Interventions.* New York: Brunner/Mazel.

Smith, Ron F., & Goodwin, H. Eugene. (1999). *Groping for Ethics in Journalism, 4th Edition.* Ames: Iowa State University Press.

Stangor, Charles. (ed.). (2000). *Stereotypes and Prejudice: Essential Readings.* New York: Psychology Press.

■ *Chapter 8: Typography*

Butler, Pierce. (1949). *The Origin of Printing in Europe.* Chicago: The University of Chicago Press.

Carter, Rob. (2002). *Typographic Design: Form and Communication, 3rd Edition.* New York: John Wiley & Sons.

———. (1989). *American Typography Today.* New York: Van Nostrand Reinhold.

Chappell, Warren. (2000). *A Short History of the Printed Word.* London: Hartley & Marks.

Clunas, Craig. (1998). *Pictures and Visuality in Early Modern China.* Princeton, N.J.: Princeton University Press.

Davies, Duncan, Bathurst, Diana, & Bathurst, Robin. (1990). *The Telling Image: The Changing Balance Between Pictures and Words in a Technological Age.* Oxford: Clarendon Press.

Eisenstein, Elizabeth. (1979). *The Printing Press as an Agent of Change, Volume II.* Cambridge, England: Cambridge University Press.

Fuhrmann, Otto. (1937). *The 500th Anniversary of the Invention of Printing.* New York: Philip C. Duschnes.

Gutjahr, Paul C. (ed.). (2001). *Illuminating Letters: Typography and Literary Interpretation.* Amherst, Mass.: University of Massachusetts Press.

Harper, Laurel. (ed.). (March/April, 1992). "Typography Today," in *How.*

Jean, Georges. (1992). *Writing the Story of Alphabets and Scripts.* New York: Harry N. Abrams.

McLuhan, Marshall. (1966). *The Gutenberg Galaxy.* Toronto: University of Toronto Press.

Muller, Lars. (ed.). (2000). *Helvetica: Homage to a Typeface.* Princeton, N.J.: Lars Muller Publishers.

Pollard, Michael, & Sproule, Anna. (2001). *Johann Gutenberg: Master of Modern Printing.* New York: Blackbirch Marketing.

Thorpe, James. (1975). *The Gutenberg Bible.* San Marino, Calif.: The Huntington Library.

Type Directors Club. (2001). *Typography 21: The Annual of the Type Directors Club.* New York: Watson-Guptill Publications.

Van Loon, Hendrik. (1937). *Observations on the Mystery of Print.* New York: Book Manufacturers' Institute.

Weingart, Wolfgang. (2000). *Wolfgang Weingart: Typography.* Princeton, N.J.: Lars Muller Publishers.

Ziegler, Kathleen. (ed.). (2001). *The Designer's Guide to Web Type: Your Connection to the Best Fonts Online.* Cincinnati: Writers Digest Books.

■ *Chapter 9: Graphic Design*

Art Directors Club of Europe. (ed.). (2001). *The Best of European Design and Advertising.* London: Neues Publishing Company.

Barnard, Malcolm. (1999). *Art, Design and Visual Culture.* New York: St. Martin's Press.

Barnhurst, Kevin. (1994). *Seeing the Newspaper.* New York: St. Martin's Press.

———. (December, 1991). "News as Art," *Journalism Monographs.*

Bettley, James. (ed.). (2001). *The Art of the Book: From Medieval Manuscript to Graphic Novel.* Victoria & Albert Museum.

Bivins, Thomas, & Ryan, William. (1991). *How to Produce Creative Publications.* Lincolnwood, Ill.: NTC Business Books.

Conover, Theodore. (1985). *Graphic Communications Today.* St. Paul, Minn.: West.

Denton, Craig. (1992). *Graphics for Visual Communication.* Dubuque, IA.: Wm. C. Brown.

Friedman, Milton, et al. (1989). *Graphic Design in America.* New York: Harry N. Abrams.

Garcia, Mario, & Stark, Pegie. (1991). *Eyes on the News.* St. Petersburg, Fla.: The Poynter Institute for Media Studies.

Heller, Steven. (1998). *The Education of a Graphic Designer.* New York: Allworth Press.

———, & Chwast, Seymour. (1988). *Graphic Styles.* New York: Harry N. Abrams.

Klanten, Robert. (ed.). (2000). *72 dpi.* Copenhagen: Die Gestalten Verlag.

Kosslyn, Stephen, & Chabris, Christopher. (1993). *Elements of Graph Design.* New York: W. H. Freeman.

Margolin, Victor. (ed.). (1989). *Design Discourse: History, Theory, Criticism.* Chicago: The University of Chicago Press.

Meggs, Philip. (1983). *A History of Graphic Design.* New York: Van Nostrand Reinhold.

Moen, Daryl R. (2000). *Newspaper Layout & Design: A Team Approach.* Ames: Iowa State University Press.

Nelson, Roy. (1991). *Publication Design.* Dubuque, Ia.: Wm. C. Brown.

Society of News Design. (2000). *The Best of Newspaper Design.* Rockport Publishers.

Swanson, Gunnar. (ed.). (2000). *Graphic Design and Reading: Explorations of an Uneasy Relationship.* New York: Allworth Press.

■ *Chapter 10: Informational Graphics*

Finberg, Howard, & Itule, Bruce. (1990). *Visual Editing.* Belmont, Calif.: Wadsworth.

Holmes, Nigel. (1985). *Designing Pictorial Symbols.* New York: Watson-Guptill Publications.

Meyer, Eric K. (1997). *Designing Infographics.* Indianapolis: Hayden Books.

Monmonier, Mark. (1989). *Maps with the News.* Chicago: The University of Chicago Press.

Paulos, John Allen. (1995). *A Mathematician Reads the Newspaper.* New York: Anchor Books.

Prichard, Peter. (1987). *The Making of McPaper.* Kansas City: Andrews, McMeel & Parker.

Tufte, Edward. (1997). *Visual Explanations: Images and Quantities, Evidence and Narrative.* Cheshire, Conn.: Graphics Press.

———. (1990). *Envisioning Information.* Cheshire, Conn.: Graphics Press.

———. (1983). *The Visual Display of Quantitative Information.* Cheshire, Conn.: Graphics Press.

■ *Chapter 11: Cartoons*

Berryman, Clifford. (June 7, 1926). "Development of the Cartoon," *The University of Missouri Bulletin.*

Bongco, Mila, & Philipzig, Jan. (2000). *Reading Comics: Language, Culture, and the Concept of the Superhero in Comic Books.* New York: Garland Publishing.

Cartwright, Nancy. (2000). *My Life as a Ten Year Old Boy.* New York: Hyperion.

Geipel, John. (1972). *The Cartoon.* South Brunswick, N.J.: A. S. Barnes and Company.

Groening, Matt. (2001). *Simpsons Comics Royale.* New York: Harperperennial Library.

Hahn, Don. (2000). *Animation Magic: A Behind-the-Scenes Look at How an Animated Film Is Made.* New York: Disney Press.

Inge, M. Thomas. (1990). *Comics as Culture.* Jackson: University Press of Mississippi.

Irwin, William. (ed.). (2001). *The Simpsons and Philosophy: The D'oh! of Homer.* Ashland, Ohio: Open Court Publishing Company.

Lent, John A. (ed.). (2001). *Animation in Asia and the Pacific.* Bloomington: Indiana University Press.

Lucie-Smith, Edward. (1981). *The Art of Caricature.* Ithaca, N.Y.: Cornell University Press.

Magnussen, Anne, & Christiansen, Hans-Christian. (eds.). (2000). *Comics & Culture: Analytical and Theoretical Approaches to Comics.* Copenhagen: Museum Tusculanum.

Mankoff, Robert. (ed.). (2000). *The New Yorker Book of Literary Cartoons.* New York: Pocket Books.

Pustz, Matthew J. (2000). *Comic Book Culture: Fanboys and True Believers.* Jackson: University Press of Mississippi.

Reaves, Wendy. (1990). *Oliphant's Presidents.* Kansas City: Andrews and McMeel.

Schulz, Charles M. (2001). *A Boy Named Charlie Brown.* New York: Metro Books.

Webb, Graham. (2000). *The Animated Film Encyclopedia: A Complete Guide to American Shorts, Features, and Sequences, 1900–1979.* Jefferson, N.C.: McFarland & Company.

Wells, Paul. (2002). *Animation: Genre and Authorship.* London: Wallflower Press.

■ *Chapter 12: Photography*

Berger, John. (1977). *Ways of Seeing.* London: Penguin Books.

Bernard, Bruce. (1980). *Photodiscovery.* New York: Harry N. Abrams.

Coe, Brian. (1977). *The Birth of Photography.* New York: Taplinger Publishing.

Eder, Josef. (1972). *History of Photography.* New York: Dover Publications.

Edom, Clifton. (1980). *Photojournalism: Principles and Practices.* Dubuque, Ia.: Wm. C. Brown.

Evans, Harold. (1978). *Pictures on a Page.* New York: Holt, Rinehart and Winston.

Flukinger, Roy, Schaaf, Larry, & Meacham, Standish. (1977). *Paul Martin: Victorian Photographer.* Austin: University of Texas Press.

Ford, Colin. (ed.). (1976). *An Early Victorian Album.* New York: Alfred A. Knopf.

Fulton, Marianne. (1988). *Eyes of Time: Photojournalism in America.* New York: New York Graphic Society.

Goldberg, Vicki. (1991). *The Power of Photography.* New York: Abbeville Press.

Grazda, Edward. (2000). *Afghanistan Diary: 1992–2000.* New York: Power House Cultural Entertainment.

Hunter, Jefferson. (1987). *Image and Word: The Interaction of Twentieth-Century Photographs and Texts.* Cambridge, Mass.: Harvard University Press.

Kobre, Kenneth. (2000). *Photojournalism: The Professionals' Approach, 4th Edition.* New York: Focal Press.

———, & Brill, Betsy. (2000). *Photography, 7th Edition.* Prentice Hall.

Kozloff, Max. (1987). *The Privileged Eye: Essays on Photography.* Albuquerque: University of New Mexico Press.

Larson, Gale. (ed.). (2001). *The Annual Bernard Shaw Studies.* Philadelphia: University of Pennsylvania Press.

Lewis, Greg. (1991). *Photojournalism: Content and Technique.* Dubuque, Ia.: Wm. C. Brown.

Lyons, Nathan. (ed.). (1966). *Photographers on Photography.* Englewood Cliffs, N.J.: Prentice Hall.

Meltzer, Milton, & Lange, Dorothea. (2000). *Dorothea Lange: A Photographer's Life.* Syracuse, N.Y.: Syracuse University Press.

Newton, Julianne H. (2001). *The Burden of Visual Truth: The Role of Photojournalism in Mediating Reality.* Hillsdale, N.J.: Lawrence Erlbaum.

O'Neal, Hank. (1976). *A Vision Shared.* New York: St. Martin's Press.

Ohrn, Karin. (1980). *Dorothea Lange and the Documentary Tradition.* Baton Rouge: Louisiana State University Press.

Oliphant, Dave, & Zigal, Thomas. (eds.). (1982). *Perspectives on Photography.* Austin, Tex.: Humanities Research Center.

Perlmutter, David D. (1998). *Photojournalism and Foreign Policy: Icons of Outrage in International Crises.* Westport, Conn.: Praeger Publishers.

Pollack, Peter. (1977). *The Picture History of Photography.* New York: Harry N. Abrams.

Ritchin, Fred. (1990). *In Our Own Image.* New York: Aperture Foundation.

Rosen, Marvin, & DeVries, David. (1993). *Photography.* Belmont, Calif.: Wadsworth.

Rothstein, Arthur. (1965). *Photojournalism.* New York: American Photographic Book Publishing.

Szarkowski, John. (1980). *The Photographer's Eye.* New York: The Museum of Modern Art.

Venezia, Mike. (2001). *Dorothea Lange.* New York: Children's Press.

Welling, William. (1978). *Photography in America: The Formative Years 1839–1900.* New York: Thomas Y. Crowell.

Winston, Brian. (1997). *Technologies of Seeing: Photography, Cinematography and Television.* London: British Film Institute.

■ Chapter 13: Motion Pictures

Austin, Bruce. (1989). *Immediate Seating: A Look at Movie Audiences.* Belmont, Calif.: Wadsworth.

Barnouw, Erik. (1974). *Documentary: A History of the Non-Fiction Film.* London: Oxford University Press.

Bazin, Andre. (1972). *Orson Welles: A Critical View.* New York: Harper & Row.

Beaver, Frank. (2000). *100 Years of American Film.* New York: Macmillan Library Reference.

Carringer, Robert. (1985). *The Making of* Citizen Kane. Berkeley: University of California Press.

Cowie, Peter. (1965). *The Cinema of Orson Welles.* London: A. Zwemmer.

Eke, Maureen N. (ed.). (2000). *African Images.* New York: Africa World Press.

Fell, John. (1979). *A History of Films.* New York: Holt, Rinehart and Winston.

Guback, Thomas. (1969). *The International Film Industry.* Bloomington: Indiana University Press.

Hammond, Paul. (1974). *Marvelous Méliès.* New York: St. Martin's Press.

Mast, Gerald. (1981). *A Short History of the Movies.* Indianapolis, Ind.: Bobbs-Merrill.

Mitry, Jean. (2000). *The Aesthetics and Psychology of the Cinema.* Bloomington: Indiana University Press.

Monaco, James. (1977). *How to Read a Film.* New York: Oxford University Press.

Stempel, Tom. (2001). *American Audiences on Movies and Moviegoing.* Lexington: University Press of Kentucky.

Winkler, Martin M. (ed.). (2001). *Classical Myth and Culture in the Cinema.* New York: Oxford University Press.

Wyver, John. (1989). *The Moving Image.* Oxford: Basil Blackwell.

■ *Chapter 14: Television and Video*

Abramson, Albert. (1987). *The History of Television, 1880 to 1941.* Jefferson, N.C.: McFarland & Company.

Adir, Karin. (1988). *The Great Clowns of American Television.* Jefferson, N.C.: McFarland & Company.

Allen, Steve. (2001). *Vulgarians at the Gate: Trash TV and Raunch Radio.* New York: Prometheus Books.

Barad, Judy, & Robertson, Ed. (2000). *The Ethics of Star Trek.* New York: HarperCollins.

Bianculli, David. (2000). *Teleliteracy: Taking Television Seriously.* Princeton, N.J.: Princeton University Press.

Bogle, Donald. (2001). *Primetime Blues: African Americans on Network Television.* New York: Farrar Straus & Giroux.

Greenfield, Meg, & Graham, Katherine. (2001). *Washington.* New York: G. K. Hill Publishers.

Gross, Lynn. (1979). *See/Hear: An Introduction to Broadcasting.* Dubuque, Ia.: Wm. C. Brown.

Javna, John. (1985). *Cult TV.* New York: St. Martin's Press.

Kerbel, Matthew R. (2000). *If It Bleeds, It Leads: An Anatomy of Television News.* Boulder, Colo.: Westview Press.

O'Connor, John. (ed.). (1985). *American History, American Television.* New York: Frederick Unger.

Rose, Brian. (ed.). (1985). *TV Genres.* Westport, Conn.: Greenwood Press.

Spigel, Lynn. (1992). *Make Room for TV.* Chicago: The University of Chicago Press.

Sterling, Christopher, & Kittross, John. (1978). *Stay Tuned: A Concise History of American Broadcasting.* Belmont, Calif.: Wadsworth.

Valenti, Miguel. (ed.). (2000). *More Than a Movie: Ethical Decision Making in the Entertainment Industry.* Boulder, Colo.: Westview Press.

Wilk, Max. (1976). *The Golden Age of Television.* New York: Delacorte Press.

Yoakam, Richard, & Cremer, Charles. (1989). *ENG: Television News and the New Technology.* Carbondale: Southern Illinois University Press.

■ *Chapter 15: Computers*

Augarten, Stan. (1984). *Bit by Bit: An Illustrated History of Computers.* New York: Ticknor & Fields.

Baird, Robert M. (ed.). (2000). *Cyberethics: Social & Moral Issues in the Computer Age.* New York: Prometheus Books.

Clarke, Arthur C., & Lewis, C. S. (2002). *Arthur C. Clarke & C. S. Lewis: A Correspondence.* New York: Anamnesis Press.

Freiberger, Paul, & Swaine, Michael. (1984). *Fire in the Valley: The Making of the Personal Computer.* Berkeley, Calif.: Osborne/McGraw-Hill.

Friedhoff, Richard Mark, & Benzon, William. (1988). *The Second Computer Revolution: Visualization.* New York: W. H. Freeman.

Johnson, Deborah G. (2000). *Computer Ethics, 3rd Edition.* New York: Prentice Hall College Division.

Langford, Duncan. (ed.). (2000). *Internet Ethics.* New York: Palgrave.

Papert, Seymour. (1993). *Mindstorms.* New York: Basic Books.

Shurkin, Joel. (1984). *Engines of the Mind: A History of the Computer.* New York: W. W. Norton.

Chapter 16: World Wide Web

Bagdikian, Ben H. (2000). *The Media Monopoly: With a New Preface on the Internet and Telecommunications Cartels, 6th Edition.* Boston: Beacon Press.

Barnouw, Erik. (1998). *Conglomerates and the Media.* New York: New Press.

Beekman, George. (1990). *Hypercard in a Hurry: Hypercard 1.0.* New York: International Society for Teaching in Education.

Berners-Lee, Tim. (2000). *Weaving the Web: The Original Design and Ultimate Destiny of the World Wide Web.* New York: Harperbusiness.

Cailliau, Robert, & Gillies, James. (2000). *How the Web Was Born: The Story of the World Wide Web.* New York: Oxford University Press.

Halperin, Ian. (2001). *Best CEOs: How the Wild, Wild Web Was Won.* New York: Ogo Books.

Shane, Ed, & Fishman, Donald. (2000). *Disconnected America: The Consequences of Mass Media in a Narcissistic World.* Armonk, N.Y.: M. E. Sharpe.

Stauffer, David. (2001). *Big Shots, Business the AOL Way: Secrets of the World's Number 1 Webmaster.* New York: Capstone Publications.

Stewart, Melissa. (2001). *Tim Berners-Lee: Inventor of the World Wide Web.* New York: Ferguson Publishing.

Swisher, Kara. (1999). *AOL.com.* New York: Times Books.

Thornally, George. (1999). *AOL by George! The Inside Story of America Online.* New York: Urly Media.

Weaver, David. (1983). *Videotex Journalism.* Hillsdale, N.J.: Lawrence Erlbaum Associates.

Wolinsky, Art. (2000). *The History of the Internet and the World Wide Web.* New York: Enslow Publishers, Inc.

■ *Chapter 17: The More You Know, The More You See*

Bova, Ben. (2001). *The Story of Light.* Naperville, Ill: Sourcebooks, Inc.

Harris, Bill. (2001). *The World Trade Center: A Tribute.* New York: Running Press.

Moody, A. David. (ed.). (1994). *The Cambridge Companion to T. S. Eliot.* Cambridge, Mass.: Cambridge University Press.

Shields, Charles J. (2001). *World Trade Center Bombing.* New York: Chelsea House Publications.

I N D E X